Routledge History of Philosophy
Volume IV

The philosophy discussed in this volume covers a period of three hundred and fifty years, from the middle of the fourteenth century to the early years of the eighteenth century: the birth of modern philosophy. The chief topics are Renaissance philosophy and seventeenth-century rationalism – in particular Descartes, Spinoza and Leibniz. The volume does not deal with these movements exclusively, but places them within a wider intellectual context. It considers the scholastic thought with which Renaissance philosophy interacted; it also considers the thought of seventeenth-century philosophers such as Bacon, Hobbes and Gassendi, who were not rationalists but whose thought elicited responses from the rationalists. It considers, too, the important topic of the rise of modern science in the sixteenth and seventeenth centuries, and its relations to the philosophy of the period.

This volume provides a broad, scholarly introduction to this period for students of philosophy and related disciplines, as well as some original interpretations of these authors. It includes a glossary of technical terms and a chronological table of philosophical, scientific and other cultural events.

G. H. R. Parkinson is Emeritus Professor of Philosophy, University of Reading. His numerous books include works on Spinoza, Leibniz, Wittgenstein and Lukács; he is also the General Editor of *An Encyclopaedia of Philosophy* (Routledge, 1988).

Routledge History of Philosophy
General editors – G. H. R. Parkinson and S. G. Shanker

The *Routledge History of Philosophy* provides a chronological survey of the history of Western philosophy, from its beginnings in the sixth century BC to the present time. It discusses all major philosophical developments in depth. Most space is allocated to those individuals who, by common consent, are regarded as great philosophers. But lesser figures have not been neglected, and together the ten volumes of the History include basic and critical information about every significant philosopher of the past and present. These philosophers are clearly situated within the cultural and, in particular, the scientific context of their time.

The History is intended not only for the specialist, but also for the student and the general reader. Each chapter is by an acknowledged authority in the field. The chapters are written in an accessible style and a glossary of technical terms is provided in each volume.

R

Routledge History of Philosophy
Volume IV

The Renaissance and Seventeenth-century Rationalism

EDITED BY

G. H. R. Parkinson

London and New York

First published 1993
by Routledge
11 New Fetter Lane, London EC4P 4EE

Simultaneously published in the USA and Canada
by Routledge
29 West 35th Street, New York, NY 10001

© 1993 G. H. R. Parkinson and individual contributors
Set in 10½/12 pt Garamond by Intype, London
Printed and bound in Great Britain by T J Press (Padstow) Ltd, Cornwall

British Library Cataloguing in Publication Data
Routledge History of Philosophy. – Vol. 4:
Renaissance and Seventeenth-century
Rationalism
I. Parkinson, G. H. R.
190.9

Library of Congress Cataloging in Publication Data
The Renaissance and seventeenth-century rationalism/edited by G.H.R.
Parkinson.
p. cm. – (Routledge history of philosophy; v. 4)
Includes bibliographical references and indexes.
Contents: The philosophy of the Italian Renaissance / Jill Kraye – Renaissance
philosophy outside Italy / Stuart Brown – Science and mathematics from the
Renaissance to Descartes / George Molland – Francis Bacon and man's two-faced
kingdom / Antonio Pérez-Ramos – Descartes, methodology / Stephen Gaukroger
– Descartes, metaphysics and philosophy of mind / John Cottingham –
Seventeenth century materialism / T. Sorell – Spinoza, metaphysics and
knowledge / G. H. R. Parkinson – The moral and political philosophy of
Spinoza / Hans W. Blom – Occasionalism / Daisie Radner – Leibniz / Nicholas
Jolley.
1. Philosophy, Renaissance. 2. Philosophy, Modern–17th century.
I. Parkinson, G. H. R. (George Henry Radcliffe) II. Title:
Renaissance and 17th century rationalism. III. Series.
B770.R38 1993
190'.9'031–dc20
92–37350

ISBN 0-415-05378-1

Contents

General editors' preface   vii
Notes on contributors   x
Chronology   xiii

Introduction
    G. H. R. Parkinson   1

1 The philosophy of the Italian Renaissance
    Jill Kraye   16

2 Renaissance philosophy outside Italy
    Stuart Brown   70

3 Science and mathematics from the Renaissance to Descartes
    George Molland   104

4 Francis Bacon and man's two-faced kingdom
    Antonio Pérez-Ramos   140

5 Descartes: methodology
    Stephen Gaukroger   167

6 Descartes: metaphysics and the philosophy of mind
    John Cottingham   201

7 Seventeenth-century materialism: Gassendi and Hobbes
    T. Sorell   235

8 Spinoza: metaphysics and knowledge
    G. H. R. Parkinson   273

CONTENTS

9   The moral and political philosophy of Spinoza
    Hans W. Blom   313

10 Occasionalism
    Daisie Radner   349

11 Leibniz: truth, knowledge and metaphysics
    Nicholas Jolley   384

    Glossary   424
    Index of names   436
    Index of subjects   440

General editors' preface

The history of philosophy, as its name implies, represents a union of two very different disciplines, each of which imposes severe constraints upon the other. As an exercise in the history of ideas, it demands that one acquire a 'period eye': a thorough understanding of how the thinkers whom it studies viewed the problems which they sought to resolve, the conceptual frameworks in which they addressed these issues, their assumptions and objectives, their blind spots and miscues. But as an exercise in philosophy, we are engaged in much more than simply a descriptive task. There is a crucial critical aspect to our efforts: we are looking for the cogency as much as the development of an argument, for its bearing on questions which continue to preoccupy us as much as the impact which it may have had on the evolution of philosophical thought.

The history of philosophy thus requires a delicate balancing act from its practitioners. We read these writings with the full benefit of historical hindsight. We can see why the minor contributions remained minor and where the grand systems broke down: sometimes as a result of internal pressures, sometimes because of a failure to overcome an insuperable obstacle, sometimes because of a dramatic technological or sociological change and, quite often, because of nothing more than a shift in intellectual fashion or interests. Yet, because of our continuing philosophical concern with many of the same problems, we cannot afford to look dispassionately at these works. We want to know what lessons are to be learnt from the inconsequential or the glorious failures; many times we want to plead for a contemporary relevance in the overlooked theory or to reconsider whether the 'glorious failure' was indeed such or simply ahead of its time: perhaps even ahead of its author.

We find ourselves, therefore, much like the mythical 'radical translator' who has so fascinated modern philosophers, trying to understand an author's ideas in his and his culture's eyes, and at the same time, in our own. It can be a formidable task. Many times we fail in the historical undertaking because our philosophical interests are so strong, or lose sight of the latter because we are so enthralled by the former. But the nature of philosophy is such that we are compelled to master both techniques. For learning about the history of philosophy is not just a challenging and engaging pastime: it is an essential element in learning about the nature of philosophy – in grasping how philosophy is intimately connected with and yet distinct from both history and science.

The *Routledge History of Philosophy* provides a chronological survey of the history of Western philosophy, from its beginnings up to the present time. Its aim is to discuss all major philosophical developments in depth, and with this in mind, most space has been allocated to those individuals who, by common consent, are regarded as great philosophers. But lesser figures have not been neglected, and it is hoped that the reader will be able to find, in the ten volumes of the History, at least basic information about any significant philosopher of the past or present.

Philosophical thinking does not occur in isolation from other human activities, and this History tries to situate philosophers within the cultural, and in particular the scientific, context of their time. Some philosophers, indeed, would regard philosophy as merely ancillary to the natural sciences; but even if this view is rejected, it can hardly be denied that the sciences have had a great influence on what is now regarded as philosophy, and it is important that this influence should be set forth clearly. Not that these volumes are intended to provide a mere record of the factors that influenced philosophical thinking; philosophy is a discipline with its own standards of argument, and the presentation of the ways in which these arguments have developed is the main concern of this History.

In speaking of 'what is now regarded as philosophy', we may have given the impression that there now exists a single view of what philosophy is. This is certainly not the case; on the contrary, there exist serious differences of opinion, among those who call themselves philosophers, about the nature of their subject. These differences are reflected in the existence at the present time of two main schools of thought, usually described as 'analytic' and 'continental' philosophy. It is not our intention, as general editors of this History, to take sides in this dispute. Our attitude is one of tolerance, and our hope is that these volumes will contribute to an understanding of how philosophers have reached the positions which they now occupy.

One final comment. Philosophy has long been a highly technical subject, with its own specialized vocabulary. This History is intended not only for the specialist but also for the general reader. To this end, we have tried to ensure that each chapter is written in an accessible style; and since technicalities are unavoidable, a glossary of technical terms is provided in each volume. In this way these volumes will, we hope, contribute to a wider understanding of a subject which is of the highest importance to all thinking people.

G. H. R. Parkinson
S. G. Shanker

Notes on contributors

G. H. R. Parkinson is Professor Emeritus of Philosophy at the University of Reading. His publications include *Spinoza's Theory of Knowledge* (1954), *Logic and Reality in Leibniz's Metaphysics* (1965) *Georg Lukács* (1977) and (as editor) *Leibniz: Logical Papers* (1966), *The Theory of Meaning* (1968), *Leibniz: Philosophical Writings* (1973) and *The Routledge Encyclopaedia of Philosophy* (1988).

Jill Kraye is Lecturer in the History of Philosophy at the Warburg Institute, University of London. She is Associate Editor of *The Cambridge History of Renaissance Philosophy* (1988) and editor of *The Cambridge Companion to Renaissance Humanism* (forthcoming).

Stuart Brown is Professor of Philosophy and Dean of the Faculty of Arts at the Open University. He has edited several volumes of philosophical papers, including *Reason and Religion* (1977), *Philosophical Disputes in the Social Sciences* (1979), *Philosophers of the Enlightenment* (1979), *Objectivity and Cultural Divergence* (1984) and *Nicolas Malebranche: His Philosophical Critics and Successors* (1991), and he is the author of *Leibniz* (1984) in the 'Philosophers in Perspective' series.

George Molland is Honorary Senior Lecturer in the Department of History at the University of Aberdeen; he is the author of several articles on medieval and early modern science and mathematics.

Antonio Pérez-Ramos teaches philosophy at the University of Murcia. He is the author of *Francis Bacon's Idea of Science and the Maker's Knowledge Tradition* (1988).

Stephen Gaukroger is Reader in Philosophy at the University of Sydney. He is author of *Explanatory Structures: Concepts of Explanation in Early Physics and Philosophy* (1978) and *Cartesian Logic: An Essay on Descartes' Conception of Inference* (1989); editor of *Descartes:*

Philosophy, Mathematics and Physics (1980) and *The Uses of Antiquity: The Scientific Revolution and the Classical Tradition* (1991); and translator of Arnauld, *On True and False Ideas* (1990).

J. G. Cottingham is Professor of Philosophy at the University of Reading. His books include *Rationalism* (1984), *Descartes* (1986), *The Rationalists* (Opus Books, 1988) and *A Descartes Dictionary* (1992). He is co-translator of *The Philosophical Writings of Descartes* (3 vols, 1985, 1991), editor of *The Cambridge Companion to Descartes* (1992) and editor of the journal *Ratio*.

T. Sorell is Reader in Philosophy at the University of Essex. He is the author of *Hobbes* (1988), *Descartes* ('Past Masters' series 1987) and *Scientism* (1991) and is the editor of *The Rise of Modern Philosophy* (1993).

Hans W. Blom teaches in the Philosophy Department at the Erasmus University, Rotterdam. He edited a book on the brothers de la Court, is the co-author of a bibliography of Dutch seventeenth-century political theory and is the author of several articles on seventeenth-century political philosophy.

Daisie Radner is Professor of Philosophy at the State University of New York at Buffalo; she is the author of *Malebranche* (1978).

Nicholas Jolley is Professor of Philosophy at the University of California, San Diego. He is the author of *Leibniz and Locke* (1984) and *The Light of the Soul: Theories of Ideas in Leibniz, Malebranche and Descartes* (1990). He is also the editor of *The Cambridge Companion to Leibniz* (forthcoming).

Chronology

Unless otherwise specified, the dates assigned to books or articles are the dates of publication, and the dates assigned to musical or stage works are those of first performance. The titles of works not written in English have been translated, unless they are better known in their original form.

	Politics and Religion	The Arts
1304		
1337		Giotto d.
1370		
1374		
1401		
1405		
1407		
1413	Jan Hus, *De Ecclesia*, proposes church reform	c. 1413–16 Limburg brothers, *Les très riches Heures du Duc de Berry*
1415	Hus burnt Battle of Agincourt	
1433		
1434	Cosimo de' Medici in power in Florence	Jan van Eyck, *Arnolfini Wedding Portrait*
1438	1438–45 Council of Florence tries to unify East and West churches	
1440		c. 1440 Josquin des Pres, Flemish composer, b.
1444		
1445		Botticelli b.
1452		Leonardo da Vinci b.
1453	Hundred Years' War ends Constantinople falls to Sultan Mehmet II 1453–5 'Gutenberg Bible' printed in Mainz	
1454		
1457		
1462		
1463		
1464	Cosimo de' Medici d.	
1466		
1468		
1469	Lorenzo de' Medici in power in Florence Machiavelli b.	
1472		
1475		Michelangelo b.
1479	Spanish Inquisition established	
1482	Savonarola, preacher and reformer, active in Florence	
1483	Luther b.	Raphael b.

Science and Technology	Philosophy	
	Petrarch b.	1304
		1337
	Leonardo Bruni b.	1370
	Petrarch d.	1374
	Nicholas of Cusa b.	1401
	Bruni's Latin version of Plato's *Phaedo*	1405
	Lorenzo Valla b.	1407
		1413
		1415
	Ficino b.	1433
		1434
		1438
	Nicholas of Cusa, *De docta ignorantia* c. 1440 Lorenzo Valla, *De libero arbitrio* written	1440
	Bruni d.	1444
		1445
		1452
		1453
	Angelo Poliziano b.	1454
	Lorenzo Valla d.	1457
	Pomponazzi b.	1462
	Giovanni Pico della Mirandola b.	1463
	Nicholas of Cusa d.	1464
	c. 1466 Erasmus b.	1466
	Cajetan b.	1468
	Gianfrancesco Pico della Mirandola b. c. 1469 Agostino Nifo b. 1469-74 Ficino, *Theologia Platonica de immortalitate animae* written	1469
	1472-4 Latin version of Aristotle (Venice)	1472
		1475
		1479
		1482
	1483/6 Francisco de Vitoria b.	1483

	Politics and Religion	The Arts
1484		
1485		Malory, *Morte d'Arthur* c. 1485 Titian b.
1486		
1489		
1491		
1492	Conquest of Granada: Muslims expelled from Spain Jews expelled from Spain Columbus's voyage to West Indies Lorenzo de' Medici d.	
1493		
1494		Rabelais b.
1495		
1496		
1497		
1498	Savonarola executed	
1499	Amerigo Vespucci explores coast of Venezuela	
1501		
1508		Palladio b. 1508–12 Michelangelo paints ceiling of Sistine chapel
1509	Calvin b.	
1510		Botticelli d.
1511	Erasmus, *In Praise of Folly*, attacks church corruption	
1513	Machiavelli writes *The Prince* 5th Lateran Council restricts freedom of philosophers	
1515		
1516	Erasmus, edition of the Greek New Testament	
1517	Luther posts his ninety-five theses at Wittenberg	
1519		Leonardo da Vinci d.
1520		Raphael d.

Science and Technology	Philosophy	
	Ficino, Latin version of Plato Mario Nizolio b.	1484
		1485
	Agrippa von Nettesheim b.	1486
	Ficino, *De vita libri tres*	1489
	Giovanni Pico, *De ente et uno*	1491
	Latin version of Plotinus	1492
Paracelsus, Swiss alchemist, b.	Valla, *De libero arbitrio* printed	1493
	Giovanni Pico d. Poliziano d.	1494
	Aldine edition of Greek text of Aristotle	1495
Regiomontanus, *Epitome of Ptolemy's Almagest*		1496
	Latin version of Epictetus Melanchthon b.	1497
		1498
	Ficino d.	1499
Cardano b.		1501
		1508
	Telesio b.	1509
		1510
		1511
	Aldine edition of Plato	1513
	Ramus b.	1515
	Pomponazzi, *Tractatus de Immortalitate Animae*	1516
		1517
		1519
	Gianfrancesco Pico, *Examen Vanitatis Doctrinae Gentium*	1520

	Politics and Religion	The Arts
1592		
1593		Marlowe d.
1594		
1596		
1597		Bacon, *Essays* (1st edn)
1598	Edict of Nantes: guarantees given to French Protestants	
1599		Globe Theatre opened, London Velasquez b.
1600		
1601	Jesuit Matteo Ricci goes to Peking	
1603		
1604		
1605		Cervantes, *Don Quixote*, Part I
1606		Rembrandt b.
1608		Milton b.
1609	Truce between Spain and the United Provinces; Dutch achieve *de facto* independence	
1610		Monteverdi, *Vespers*
1611	'King James Bible' published	Shakespeare, *The Tempest*
1612	Bœhme, *Aurora*	
1614		El Greco d.
1615		Cervantes, *Don Quixote*, Part II
1616		Shakespeare d. Cervantes d.
1617		
1618	Beginning of Thirty Years' War 1618–19 Synod of Dort strengthens position of Calvinists in Holland	
1619		
1620	*Mayflower* sails to America	
1621		
1622		Molière b.

Science and Technology	Philosophy	
	Gassendi b. Montaigne d.	1592
	Charron, *Les trois véritez*	1593
	Du Vair, *De la constance et consolation ès calamités publiques*	1594
Kepler, *Mysterium cosmographicum*	Descartes b.	1596
	Suarez, *Disputationes metaphysicae*	1597
		1598
	Fonseca d.	1599
Gilbert, *De magnete*	Bruno burnt at Rome Molina d.	1600
	Charron, *De la sagesse*	1601
	Charron d.	1603
	Lipsius, *Manuductio ad Stoicam philosophiam*	1604
	Bacon, *The Advancement of Learning*	1605
	Lipsius d.	1606
Hans Lippershey applies for a patent for his telescope		1608
Galileo constructs his first telescope Kepler, *Astronomia nova*		1609
Galileo, *Sidereus nuncius*		1610
		1611
	Arnauld b. Suarez, *Tractatus de Legibus ac Deo legislatore*	1612
		1614
		1615
Inquisition pronounces in favour of the Ptolemaic system		1616
	Suarez d.	1617
		1618
Kepler, *Harmonices mundi*		1619
	Bacon, *Novum Organum*	1620
	Greek text of Sextus Empiricus published Du Vair d.	1621
	Johannes Clauberg b.	1622

	Politics and Religion	The Arts
1554		
1555	Peace of Augsburg recognizes the coexistence of Catholics and Lutherans in Germany	
1556		
1558		
1559	*Index Librorum Prohibitorum* promulgated	
1560		
1561		
1562		
1564	Calvin d.	Shakespeare b. Marlowe b. Michelangelo d.
1565		
1567		Monteverdi b.
1568	Revolt of the Netherlands from Spain	
1569		
1571		
1572	St Bartholomew's Day massacre of French Protestants in Paris	John Donne b.
1575	Bœhme b.	
1576		Titian d.
1578		
1579	Union of Utrecht: Northern provinces of Netherlands unite	
1580		Palladio d.
1581		
1584		
1586		El Greco, *Burial of Count Orgaz*
1588	Defeat of Spanish Armada	
1589		
1591		

Science and Technology	Philosophy	
	Petrarch, *Opera Omnia* published	1554
	Ramus, *Dialectique*	1555
Agricola, *De re metallica*	Guillaume du Vair b.	1556
	Molina, *Concordia*	1558
		1559
	Melanchthon d. Latin translation of Proclus	1560
	Francis Bacon b.	1561
	Latin version of Sextus Empiricus, *Outlines of Pyrrhonism*	1562
Galileo b.		1564
	Telesio, *De rerum natura*	1565
	Nizolio d.	1567
	Campanella b.	1568
	Latin version of Sextus Empiricus, *Adversus mathematicos*	1569
Kepler b.		1571
Latin version of Euclid	Ramus killed in St Bartholomew's Day massacre	1572
		1575
Cardano d.		1576
	Estienne (Stephanus), edition of Plato	1578
		1579
	Greek text of Plotinus published Montaigne, *Essais*, I–II	1580
	Sanches, *Quod nihil scitur*	1581
	Bruno, *De la causa* Bruno, *De l'infinito universo e mondi* Lipsius, *De constantia in publicis malis*	1584
Stevin, *Elements of the Art of Weighing* (On the principles of statics)		1586
	Hobbes b. Telesio d. Molina, *Concordia liberi arbitrii cum gratiae donis*	1588
Latin version of Pappus	Lipsius, *Six Books on Politics* Zabarella d.	1589
	Campanella, *Philosophia sensibus demonstrata*	1591

	Politics and Religion	The Arts
1592		
1593		Marlowe d.
1594		
1596		
1597		Bacon, *Essays* (1st edn)
1598	Edict of Nantes: guarantees given to French Protestants	
1599		Globe Theatre opened, London Velasquez b.
1600		
1601	Jesuit Matteo Ricci goes to Peking	
1603		
1604		
1605		Cervantes, *Don Quixote*, Part I
1606		Rembrandt b.
1608		Milton b.
1609	Truce between Spain and the United Provinces; Dutch achieve *de facto* independence	
1610		Monteverdi, *Vespers*
1611	'King James Bible' published	Shakespeare, *The Tempest*
1612	Böhme, *Aurora*	
1614		El Greco d.
1615		Cervantes, *Don Quixote*, Part II
1616		Shakespeare d. Cervantes d.
1617		
1618	Beginning of Thirty Years' War 1618–19 Synod of Dort strengthens position of Calvinists in Holland	
1619		
1620	*Mayflower* sails to America	
1621		
1622		Molière b.

Science and Technology	Philosophy	
	Gassendi b. Montaigne d.	1592
	Charron, *Les trois véritez*	1593
	Du Vair, *De la constance et consolation ès calamités publiques*	1594
Kepler, *Mysterium cosmographicum*	Descartes b.	1596
	Suarez, *Disputationes metaphysicae*	1597
		1598
	Fonseca d.	1599
Gilbert, *De magnete*	Bruno burnt at Rome Molina d.	1600
	Charron, *De la sagesse*	1601
	Charron d.	1603
	Lipsius, *Manuductio ad Stoicam philosophiam*	1604
	Bacon, *The Advancement of Learning*	1605
	Lipsius d.	1606
Hans Lippershey applies for a patent for his telescope		1608
Galileo constructs his first telescope Kepler, *Astronomia nova*		1609
Galileo, *Sidereus nuncius*		1610
		1611
	Arnauld b. Suarez, *Tractatus de Legibus ac Deo legislatore*	1612
		1614
		1615
Inquisition pronounces in favour of the Ptolemaic system		1616
	Suarez d.	1617
		1618
Kepler, *Harmonices mundi*		1619
	Bacon, *Novum Organum*	1620
	Greek text of Sextus Empiricus published Du Vair d.	1621
	Johannes Clauberg b.	1622

	Politics and Religion	The Arts
1623		First Folio edition of Shakespeare William Byrd d.
1624	Richelieu chief minister of Louis XIII Bœhme d.	
1626		
1627		
1628		Bunyan b.
1630		
1631		John Donne d.
1632		Rembrandt, *Dr. Tulp's anatomy lesson* Vermeer b.
1633		Donne, *Poems*
1635		
1637		
1638		Milton, *Lycidas*
1639		Racine b.
1640		
1641		
1642	Richelieu d., succeeded by Mazarin English Civil War begins	Rembrandt, *Night Watch*
1643	Accession of Louis XIV	Monteverdi d.
1644		Milton, *Areopagitica*
1646		
1648	Peace of Westphalia ends Thirty Years' War. Dutch independence formally recognized	
1649	Execution of Charles I of England	
1650		
1651	The Netherlands: Republican statesman Jan de Witt in power English Civil War ends	
1655		
1656		Velasquez, *Las Meninas*
1658		
1660		Velasquez d.

Science and Technology	Philosophy	
	Bacon, *De Augmentis Scientiarum* Sanches d.	1623
	Gassendi, *Exercitationes paradoxicae* Geulincx b.	1624
	Cordemoy b. Bacon d.	1626
Robert Boyle b.	Bacon, *New Atlantis*	1627
Harvey, *Concerning the Motion of the Heart and Blood*	c. 1628 Descartes's *Regulae ad directionem ingenii* written	1628
Kepler d.		1630
		1631
Galileo, *Dialogue on the Two Chief World Systems*	Spinoza b. Locke b. La Forge b.	1632
Galileo condemned by the Inquisition for upholding the Copernican system		1633
Académie Française founded		1635
Descartes, *Geometry, Optics, Meteorology*	Descartes, *Discourse on Method*	1637
Galileo, *Discourses on Two New Sciences*	Malebranche b.	1638
	Campanella d.	1639
	Hobbes, *The Elements of Law*	1640
	Descartes, *Meditations*	1641
Galileo d. Newton b.	Hobbes, *De Cive*	1642
		1643
	Descartes, *Principles of Philosophy*	1644
Mathematical works of Vieta published in Latin	Leibniz b.	1646
		1648
	Gassendi, *Animadversiones in decimum librum Diogenis Laertii*	1649
	Descartes d.	1650
	Hobbes, *Leviathan*	1651
	Hobbes, *De Corpore* Gassendi d.	1655
	Spinoza excommunicated	1656
	Gassendi, *Syntagma philosophicum*	1658
		1660

	Politics and Religion	The Arts
1661	Mazarin d. Louis XIV governs France	
1662		
1664		
1665		
1666		Molière, *Le misanthrope*
1667		Milton, *Paradise Lost*
1669		Rembrandt d.
1670		Molière, *Le bourgeois gentilhomme*
1671		
1672	France invades Netherlands; Jan de Witt murdered	
1673		Molière d.
1674		Milton d.
1675		Vermeer d.
1677		Racine, *Phèdre*
1678		Bunyan, *The Pilgrim's Progress*, Part I
1679		
1683		
1684		Bunyan, *The Pilgrim's Progress*, Part II
1685	Louis XIV revokes Edict of Nantes; emigration of French Protestants begins	Bach b. Handel b.
1686		
1687		
1688		Bunyan d.
1690		
1691		
1692		
1694		Voltaire b.

Science and Technology	Philosophy	
Boyle, *The Sceptical Chemist*		1661
Royal Society founded	Arnauld and Nicole, *Port Royal Logic*	1662
	Clauberg, *De corporis et animae in homine conjunctione*	1664
Newton discovers differential and integral calculus Hooke, *Micrographia*	Geulincx, *Disputatio ethica de virtute* La Forge, *Traitté de l'esprit de l'homme* Clauberg d.	1665
Académie Royale des Sciences founded	Cordemoy, *Discernement du corps et de l'âme* La Forge d.	1666
		1667
	Geulincx d.	1669
	Spinoza, *Tractatus Theologico-Politicus*	1670
	Third Earl of Shaftesbury b.	1671
		1672
		1673
	1674–5 Malebranche, *Recherche de la vérité*	1674
Leibniz's independent discovery of the differential and integral calculus		1675
	Spinoza d. Spinoza, *Ethics* Malebranche, *Conversations chrétiennes*	1677
Huygens, *Treatise on Light* written		1678
	Hobbes d.	1679
	Malebranche, *Méditations chrétiennes et métaphysiques*	1683
	Cordemoy d.	1684
	Berkeley b.	1685
	Leibniz writes his *Discourse on Metaphysics*	1686
Newton, *Principia*		1687
	Malebranche, *Entretiens sur la métaphysique et la religion*	1688
Huygens, *Treatise on Light* published	Locke, *Essay concerning Human Understanding* Locke, *Two Treatises of Civil Government*	1690
Boyle d.	Geulincx, *Metaphysica vera*	1691
	Joseph Butler b.	1692
	Hutcheson b. Arnauld d.	1694

	Politics and Religion	The Arts
1695	Locke, *The Reasonableness of Christianity*	
1697		
1699		Racine d.
1700		
1703		
1704		Swift, *The Battle of the Books*
1709		Samuel Johnson b.
1710		
1711		Pope, *Essay on Criticism* Handel, *Rinaldo*
1712		
1713		
1714		
1715	Louis XIV d.	
1716		

Science and Technology	Philosophy	
	Leibniz, *New System*	1695
	Bayle, *Dictionnaire*	1697
		1699
Berlin Academy of Sciences founded		1700
	1703–5 Leibniz's *New Essays on the Human Understanding* written	1703
Newton, *Optics*	Locke d.	1704
	Berkeley, *New Theory of Vision*	1709
	Leibniz, *Theodicy* Berkeley, *The Principles of Human Knowledge*	1710
	Shaftesbury, *Characteristics* Hume b.	1711
	Rousseau b.	1712
	Berkeley, *Dialogues between Hylas and Philonous* Shaftesbury d.	1713
	Leibniz's *Monadology* written	1714
	Malebranche d.	1715
	Leibniz d.	1716

Introduction
G. H. R. Parkinson

The philosophy that is discussed in this volume covers a period of some three hundred and fifty years, from roughly the middle of the fourteenth century to the early years of the eighteenth. What is offered, however, is not a comprehensive history of the philosophy of this period. Topics such as the later stages of scholasticism, and the beginnings of British empiricism in the seventeenth century, are not discussed here, but are reserved for other volumes in this series. The substance of the volume is the history of certain important philosophical movements that occurred during this period: namely, Renaissance philosophy and seventeenth-century rationalism. But the volume does not deal with these movements exclusively. If one is to understand Renaissance philosophy, one must also examine the scholastic thought against which it reacted and with which it frequently interacted. Similarly, if one is to understand the seventeenth-century rationalists, one must also understand some of their contemporaries who were not rationalists – men such as Bacon, Gassendi and Hobbes. They therefore find a place here, as do Renaissance scholastics such as Pomponazzi and Cremonini.

The division of the history of philosophy into a number of movements is a procedure that has often been followed, but it has its critics. In recent years, historians of philosophy have emphasized what one might call the individuality, the 'thisness' of philosophers, and have argued that to try to force this or that individual into pre-set categories can lead to distortions. There is indeed a danger of such distortions; on the other hand, it seems fair to say that during certain epochs certain philosophical questions came to the forefront, and that philosophers provided answers which (although different) had some kinship, so that it is possible to speak of a 'movement' in such cases. Such, at any rate, is the assumption made in this volume; whether the assumption is a fruitful one, the volume itself will show.

The term 'Renaissance philosophy' is a controversial one, as indeed is the term 'seventeenth-century rationalism'. It has been argued that the very notion of the Renaissance is a myth,[1] and one may wonder how it can be useful to speak of the philosophy of a myth. But it is important not to exaggerate. Scholars are in general agreement that there was in Western Europe, between roughly 1350 and the first decades of the seventeenth century,[2] a cultural movement which may usefully be called 'the Renaissance', and that a philosophy or group of philosophies formed a part of this movement. What is at issue, when people talk of the myth of the Renaissance, is the making of certain inflated claims on behalf of this movement.

In explaining what is meant here by 'Renaissance philosophy', I will begin by stating a commonplace. This is, that the area covered by the term 'philosophy' has shrunk in the course of the centuries; that, for example, what was once called 'natural philosophy' is now called 'physics', and an important part of what was once called 'mental philosophy' is now called 'psychology'. In the Renaissance, the term 'philosophy' had a very wide sense indeed, covering not only physics and psychology, but also such subjects as rhetoric, poetics and history, and even magic and astrology.[3] However, the term also covered what would now be called 'philosophy'; scholars speak of Renaissance logic and metaphysics, Renaissance theory of knowledge, and Renaissance moral and political philosophy. It is Renaissance philosophy in this sense that will be the concern of the present volume.

I have already implied a distinction between Renaissance philosophy and scholasticism – a movement which, incidentally, continued to exist up to the seventeenth century. This indicates that when 'Renaissance philosophy' is spoken of here the term is not taken to mean every philosophy which existed during the period of the Renaissance. Rather, it means a philosophy which was distinctively Renaissance in character. At this stage, it is necessary to try to be a little clearer about the term 'Renaissance'. I have spoken of the period which the Renaissance is generally agreed to have covered; there is also general agreement that the movement began in Italy and spread to the rest of Western Europe. It was a movement in which (to quote one eminent specialist in the field) 'there was a revival of interest in the literature, styles and forms of classical antiquity'.[4] But this definition generates a problem. I have distinguished Renaissance philosophy from scholasticism; but it is well known that the scholastics, too, derived much inspiration from classical philosophy. The question is, then, what distinguishes Renaissance philosophy from scholasticism. Here, one must first consider what the term 'scholasticism' means. As a philosophical movement, scholasticism reached its peak during the Middle Ages, and for some people the terms 'scholasticism' and 'medieval Christian philosophy' are interchangeable.[5] There is a more precise sense of the term, however. In this sense, scholasticism begins in cathedral schools in the eleventh century, and reaches its peak in the universities of Paris and Oxford during a period that lasted from the early thirteenth to the middle of the fourteenth century. As a guide to the nature of scholasticism, taken in this sense, it is helpful to follow the account given by Dom David Knowles in his book *The Evolution of Medieval Thought*.[6] Knowles argues that scholasticism was distinguished by its goal, form and technique. Its goal was to provide a preparation for theology and to explain and defend Christian doctrines. In its form, it depended heavily on ancient philosophy, and in particular on Aristotle. Its technique was, *par excellence*, the method of *quaestio*, *disputatio* and *sententia*: the posing of a problem which was such that authorities differed about the correct answer, arguments concerning the problem, and a solution.[7]

Although Renaissance philosophy did not follow the method of *quaestio*, *disputatio* and *sententia*, it might be argued that it resembled scholasticism in respect of the fact that it was a book-centred philosophy, deriving its inspiration from the writings of the ancients. It would be granted that Renaissance scholars rediscovered many classical texts, with the result that their knowledge of ancient philosophy was much wider than that which the medievals had. But it may be said that this would not of itself justify one in regarding the Renaissance as a separate movement; it might simply be a movement that did more effectively what the scholastics had tried to do. In order to answer this point, it is necessary to examine more closely the relation between Renaissance writers and classical texts. More specifically, one has to consider that aspect of the culture of the Renaissance which is called 'humanism'. The abstract noun 'humanism', like the term 'the Renaissance', is a nineteenth-century coinage; however, the term 'humanist' is much older. It originated in Italy in the late fifteenth century and was used to refer to a teacher or student of the *studia humanitatis* – the humanities – a term which was used to mean the study of classical texts concerning, in the main, five subjects: grammar, rhetoric, poetics, moral philosophy and history.[8] The deeper knowledge of classical Latin and Greek that the humanists acquired led them to scorn both the scholastics' translations of the classics and their barbarous misuse of the Latin language.[9] Instead of using the cumbrous Latin of the scholastics, the humanists wanted to write about philosophical topics in elegant Latin of the kind that Cicero might have written.

I have said that the philosophy that most concerned the humanists was moral philosophy: that is, a branch of philosophy that concerns human beings and their relations with each other. This concentration of interest upon human beings was emphasized by the Swiss scholar Jakob Burckhardt in his influential book *The Civilisation of the Renais-*

sance in Italy (1860). Burckhardt saw the Renaissance as an epoch in which man for the first time became a genuine individual; an epoch in which the modern age began. Modern critics are sceptical of Burckhardt's claim, arguing that although the writers and artists of the Renaissance distanced themselves from the Middle Ages, they were in fact more medieval than they realized. When such scholars speak of 'the myth of the Renaissance' it is above all Burckhardt's picture of the Renaissance that they have in mind.[10]

What, then, was the importance of the Renaissance in the history of Western philosophy? Some scholars point to the way in which late Renaissance philosophy questioned 'all authorities, even the classics'; they also see it as leading to seventeenth-century attempts to establish the unity and coherence of knowledge.[11] To this it may be replied that the philosophers of the Middle Ages were by no means uncritical in their response to the classical philosophers, and that the establishment of the unity of knowledge was surely the aim of the authors of the great medieval *Summae*. That must be granted; but if one is concerned, not with what was new, but rather with what is important about Renaissance philosophy, then what has been said may stand. There is at least one further respect in which the Renaissance did differ from the Middle Ages – though here we are concerned with the Renaissance in general rather than with Renaissance philosophy in particular, and with the sociology of philosophy rather than with philosophy as such. It was during the Renaissance that there began what one may term the laicization of the European culture of the Christian era.[12] Some of the humanists were in holy orders – one may mention Petrarch and Erasmus – but most were not. From the time of the Renaissance onwards, a clerk (in the sense of a scholar) no longer had to be a cleric. In this way, the first moves were made towards loosening the hold that Christian institutions had upon philosophy.

I must emphasize that by the laicization of European culture I do not mean what has been called 'the secularisation of the European mind';[13] that is, the decline in the importance that religious ideas, and more specifically Christian ideas, have had for European thinkers. It is plausible to argue that the two were connected; but they were different from each other. To speak of laicization in this context is to speak of the people who were the bearers of culture, and it is to say that they ceased to be predominantly clerical; it is not to say anything about the content of what such people believed. In fact, what were regarded as Christian concepts and Christian truths continued to be dominant in Renaissance philosophy, just as they had been dominant in the Middle Ages. Humanists might disagree over the answer to the question whether Plato or Aristotle was more compatible with Christianity; but that a sound philosophy should be so compatible was

4

not in dispute. Even the arguments of the ancient sceptics, whose writings became widely available in the sixteenth century, were made to serve religious purposes.[14]

From the Renaissance we move to the beginnings of what may be regarded as modern (as opposed to ancient, medieval or Renaissance) philosophy. For the majority of contemporary philosophers, the first modern philosopher was Descartes. There are two main reasons for this view. One of the main features of the European philosophy of the eighteenth and nineteenth centuries was the role played in it by one form or other of philosophical idealism, and it is argued that one can trace this idealism back to Descartes's view that the human mind is known before any physical object is known. But even those philosophers for whom idealism is no longer a live issue find that Descartes is relevant to their concerns. When Gilbert Ryle published his influential book *The Concept of Mind* shortly after the end of the Second World War,[15] he presented Descartes as the source of philosophical views about the human mind which were profoundly wrong. However, if one's concerns include science and its philosophy, then there is a case for regarding as the first modern philosopher someone who was born thirty-five years before Descartes. This was Francis Bacon.

Born in 1561, Bacon is sometimes discussed in books on Renaissance philosophy,[16] but it is better to regard him as a modern in whom some traces of the Renaissance remained. Certainly, he agreed with the Renaissance philosophers in his scorn for the scholastics; he agreed, too, with some Renaissance writers in his view that magic was not to be rejected entirely, and his views about the nature of knowledge have a Renaissance ancestry.[17] But he was as dismissive of Renaissance authors as he was of the scholastics, saying of them that their concern was primarily with words.[18] He saw himself as a revolutionary, the provider of a new logic – a 'Novum Organum' – which was to supercede the old 'Organon' of Aristotle. Aristotle's logic had already been attacked by humanist logicians, of whom the most influential in the sixteenth and seventeenth centuries was Ramus (Pierre de la Ramée, 1515–72).[19] But the aims of Bacon and Ramus were quite different. Ramus was concerned with thinking in general, and his aim was to replace the Aristotelian syllogism by a less formal logic, which would correspond more closely to the way in which people actually think.[20] Bacon, on the other hand, was concerned chiefly with scientific thinking.

It has been said of Bacon that he made 'the first serious attempt to formulate and justify the procedure of natural scientists'.[21] For many, this attempt is to be found in Bacon's discussions of induction – that is, of that type of argument in which one reaches universal conclusions from particular instances. His 'Novum Organum', his 'New Instrument', was to be a systematic way of reaching such conclusions. Tables of observations were to be drawn up, and universal laws were to be derived from these by the application of certain rules.[22] Such laws, Bacon thought, were not wholly satisfactory, in that they told us nothing about the fundamental structure of reality; none the less, they were *known*, in that they provided us with rules for the manipulation of nature.[23] This introduces Bacon's distinctive view about the nature of knowledge: namely, that to know is to make. As mentioned earlier, the view has Renaissance antecedents, but Bacon applies it to what we now regard as the beginnings of modern science. It is his emphasis on the fact that the inquirer should not just observe, but should also intervene in nature, that has led him to be called, not the first philosopher of induction, but the first philosopher of experimental science.[24]

Whatever its merits, Bacon's philosophy of science also had serious deficiencies; it is widely recognized that Bacon has no grasp of the importance that mathematics has for the sciences.[25] This cannot be said of the philosophers whose ideas are the concern of over half of this volume: namely, the seventeenth-century rationalists. As mentioned earlier,[26] the term has generated some controversy. It is used to pick out a number of seventeenth-century philosophers, the chief of whom were Descartes, Spinoza and Leibniz, though Malebranche and the Flemish philosopher Geulincx are also included. Now, it must be admitted that none of these ever called himself a rationalist, nor can they be said to have constituted a school, in the sense of a group of people who saw themselves as separated from others by virtue of their adherence to certain shared principles. They seem, indeed, to have been more conscious of their disagreements with each other than with the respects in which they agreed; so, for example, Spinoza criticized Descartes, Malebranche criticized Spinoza, and Leibniz criticized Descartes, Spinoza and Malebranche. Again, those who regard these philosophers as a group often contrast them with the 'British empiricists', namely Locke, Berkeley and Hume. Yet Locke's use of the important term 'idea' owed something to Descartes, and Malebranche influenced both Berkeley and Hume. Despite all this, the philosophers who are commonly called the seventeenth-century rationalists did have a number of basic views in common. All agreed that it is possible to get to know the nature of reality simply by means of *a priori* reasoning; that is, that we can get to know by means of the reason, without any appeal to the senses, truths about reality that are *necessary* truths. It is these points of resemblance, above all, that the term 'rationalist' picks out. In this sense, rationalism is not peculiar to the seventeenth century; the 'dialectic' that is described in Plato's *Republic* (510–11, 532–4) is a rationalist theory. Nor did rationalism come to an end after the death of Leibniz. It continued to exist, not just in the writings of Leibniz's follower Christian Wolff, but also in the form of the 'objective idealism' of Hegel, and perhaps even after that.[27] Our concern, however, is with its seventeenth-century manifestations.

The time-span of the movement is well enough indicated by the name given to it. Its first public manifestation was in Descartes's *Discourse on Method*, published in 1637; it ended in 1716, the year in which Leibniz – still philosophically active – died. Though not as widespread as the Renaissance, it was by no means confined to one country. Descartes worked in France and the Netherlands; Malebranche worked in France; Geulincx and Spinoza worked in the Low Countries, and Leibniz worked mainly in Germany (though one should not overlook a very productive period which he spent in Paris between 1672 and 1676). Seventeenth-century rationalism also spanned the religions. Descartes and Malebranche were Roman Catholics (Malebranche, indeed, was a priest); Geulincx was initially a Catholic but became a convert to Protestantism after being persecuted for Cartesian views; Spinoza was an excommunicated Jew, with friends among some of the smaller Protestant sects.

Like Bacon, the rationalists saw themselves as making a new start. Most of them were contemptuous of Aristotle and the scholastics;[28] indeed, they rejected everything that passed for received wisdom in their time, as long as it did not meet the demands of rational scrutiny. This is very clearly expressed in Descartes's resolve, stated in the first part of his *Meditations*,[29] 'to demolish everything completely and start again right from the foundations'. But no one philosophizes in an intellectual vacuum, and it is important to note that the rise of rationalism in the seventeenth century occurred at the same time as, and was closely associated with, the rise of what one now calls 'modern science'. The new science is discussed at length in Chapter 3 of this volume; here it must be sufficient to say that the old and largely Aristotelian science stressed the qualitative aspect of nature, and was primarily concerned to classify, whereas the new science stressed the quantitative aspect of things, offering explanations that were mathematical in character. Of the seventeenth-century rationalists, some played an important part in the new science. Descartes was philosopher, mathematician and scientist; so, too, was Leibniz. Spinoza and Malebranche, for their part, made no serious contribution to science or mathematics, but were well informed about them. The question is how the seventeenth-century rationalists saw philosophy as related to the natural sciences.[30] For present-day philosophers of science, the sciences stand in no need of justification by philosophy, the business of the philosopher being exclusively one of analysis: the clarification of the nature of scientific propositions and of the methods of science. But it is clear that this was not Descartes's attitude; his search for foundations included a search for the foundations of science,[31] and it is generally held that this is true of the other seventeenth-century rationalists.[32]

For the seventeenth-century rationalists, the foundations that they sought could be discovered only by *a priori* reasoning. Perhaps the clearest arguments for this thesis are provided by Descartes's account of systematic doubt in the *Meditations*, from which it emerges that he regards as known only those propositions whose truth cannot be doubted, and also takes the view that such propositions cannot be empirical. There would be general agreement that there is such knowledge of the truths of logic and of mathematics; but Descartes argued that these truths are only hypothetical, stating that *if*, for example, there is such a figure as a triangle, then its interior angles must equal two right angles.[33] What distinguishes the rationalists is their view that there are existential propositions whose truth can be known *a priori*. Mathematics, although concerned only with hypothetical truths, provided them with methods of procedure.[34] Roughly speaking, what the rationalists tried to do was first of all to obtain *a priori* knowledge of certain basic truths about what exists, and then to derive further truths from these by means of pure reasoning.

As is well known, Descartes stated that the existential truth that he knew first of all was the proposition that he existed as a thinking being, a proposition that he could not doubt as long as he was actually thinking. But it is evident (and it did not escape Descartes's notice) that the truth of this proposition was in a way far from fundamental, in that Descartes's existence depended on that of many other beings. Ultimately, the rationalists argued, it depended on the existence of a supreme being. In a sense, therefore, the fundamental item of knowledge is the knowledge that there must exist such a supreme being, or, as the rationalists said, a 'most perfect' or a 'necessary' being. Belief in the existence of such a being was not peculiar to the rationalists, but their arguments for its existence were distinctive. These arguments had to be *a priori*, and the rationalists based them on the concept of God. One argument offered by Descartes was that this concept was such that only a God could have implanted it in us. Alternatively, Descartes argued that the concept was such that one could not, without self-contradiction, deny that God existed. This was the celebrated 'ontological argument', whose soundness was accepted by Spinoza and Leibniz also.[35]

Given a knowledge of the existence and nature of the supreme being, the task of the rationalist was, as it were, to build on this foundation by deriving the consequences which followed. But there were important differences between the ways in which the seventeenth-century rationalists saw this being. For all of them except Spinoza, the supreme being was a personal deity, creator of the universe, and choosing freely to create it. Spinoza argued that such a concept was incoherent, and that a consistent account of the necessary being must present it as an impersonal being, within which particular things exist, and which cannot rationally be regarded as exercising free will. This was clearly opposed to orthodox Christian doctrine; however, one should not exaggerate Spinoza's role in ending the predominance of Christian ideas in philosophy.[36] His philosophy, at first bitterly attacked, was later largely forgotten until its revival by the German romantics towards the end of the eighteenth century. A more important factor in the loosening of the ties between Christianity and philosophy was the rise in the seventeenth and eighteenth centuries of deism; that is, of belief in a creative deity, unaccompanied by any belief in a divine revelation. With this, rationalism had little to do.[37]

Today, there is widespread agreement that the seventeenth-century rationalists failed to provide an *a priori* proof of the existence of God, however that God was conceived by them. It would also be agreed that they failed to find, by pure reason, necessary connections between the nature of God and the laws of science.[38] But these failures do not deprive their philosophy of all value. For them, science was not merely something that had to be justified; it was also something that posed problems, and their attempts to solve these problems are still found interesting.

The question whether human beings can strictly speaking be called free had long exercised philosophers. Before the seventeenth century, the problem took a theological form. Philosophers, such as Boethius in the sixth century AD and Lorenzo Valla in the fifteenth, asked how human freedom could be consistent with the foreknowledge and providence of God. These problems continued to be discussed in the seventeenth century, but in that era there was a new problem of freedom. For the new science, all physical events were determined by necessary laws; so the question arose how there could be any human freedom, given that we are (even if only in part) physical objects. Spinoza and Leibniz offered solutions which took the form of what are now called 'compatibilist' theories, arguing, in very different ways, that freedom and determinism can be reconciled.[39]

Science posed another problem for the seventeenth-century rationalist. One of Descartes's best known theses is his view that mind and body are 'really distinct', that is, that each can exist without the other. Behind this, there lay a view about scientific explanation: namely, that bodies are to be understood solely in terms of physical concepts, and minds solely in terms of mental concepts.[40] To explain physical events, therefore, we do not need to postulate the intervention of incorporeal agents (such as, for example, the planetary intelligences). But this raised the philosophical problem of how mind and body could influence each

9

other, and could also constitute one human being. Descartes's solution was notoriously unsatisfactory, and other rationalists took up the problem. Spinoza offered a classical version of the double-aspect theory of mind-matter relations; Malebranche, Geulincx and Leibniz offered various versions of a theory which denied that any created thing strictly speaking acts on any other, and asserted that the apparent interaction was really a divinely produced order that existed between the states of created things – that is, finite minds and bodies.

When Descartes's rationalist successors tried to solve the problem about mind-matter relations that he had bequeathed to them, there were already other solutions in the field. These took the form of saying that there really was no problem, in that mind and matter did not form different kinds of existence. The philosophers who offered these solutions were Gassendi and Hobbes, who were among the contributors to the 'Objections' which were published together with Descartes's *Meditations* in 1641. Neither was a rationalist, but both influenced some of Descartes's rationalist successors,[41] and for this reason their philosophy finds a place in this volume.

Both Gassendi and Hobbes offered materialist theories, though Gassendi was not an out-and-out materialist. A Catholic priest, he resembled the philosophers of the Renaissance in a certain respect, in that he found inspiration in the writings of the ancients. In his case, the inspiration came from the writings of Epicurus; but Gassendi's version of atomism was tailored to fit Christian requirements. In particular, Gassendi shrank from giving a totally materialist account of the human mind, saying that, although the non-rational soul could be explained in materialist terms, such an account could not be given of the rational, immortal soul. In explaining the rational soul and its relation to the human body, Gassendi fell back on the ideas of the scholastics, viewing the soul as the substantial form of the body.

Such Aristotelian ideas were rejected firmly by Hobbes, who offered a materialism of a more radical sort. He was, as his biographer Aubrey put it, 'in love with geometry',[42] and this love was manifested in a theory of method which has undertones of rationalism. Science, Hobbes asserted, is 'the knowledge of consequences, and dependence of one fact on another';[43] what we must do, therefore, is define our terms correctly and argue deductively from them.[44] Like the rationalists, too, Hobbes offered a far-reaching metaphysical system, within the context of which he placed a theory of man and society. But there were also important differences between Hobbes and the rationalists. Although rationalism is not obviously inconsistent with materialism, none of the seventeenth-century rationalists was a materialist; but Hobbes was. A more important difference lies in the field of the theory of knowledge, Hobbes arguing (contrary to the rationalists) that the ultimate source of all our knowledge of what exists is provided by the senses.[45]

The philosophy of Hobbes was found deeply offensive by seventeenth-century divines, who accused him of atheism. If they were right, then we must add the name of Hobbes to the list of those philosophers who began to weaken the links between Christianity and philosophy. But it is not certain that they were right; the subject is one on which scholars still disagree.[46] What is certain is that Hobbes's political philosophy, with its sombre view that a life that satisfies the demands of reason can be lived only under conditions of absolute rule, still fascinates philosophers.[47]

∾ NOTES ∾

1 The arguments for this view have been clearly set out by Peter Burke in his book *The Renaissance* (London, Macmillan, 1987), pp. 1–5. Burke himself does not accept these arguments, saying (p. 5) that the term 'the Renaissance' is 'an organising concept which still has its uses'.

2 See, for example, C. B. Schmitt and Q. Skinner (eds) *The Cambridge History of Renaissance Philosophy* (Cambridge, Cambridge University Press, 1988: abbreviated, CHRP), p. 5.

3 CHRP, Introduction, p. 3.

4 C. B. Schmitt, in R. Sorabji (ed.) *Philoponus and the Rejection of Aristotelian Science* (London, Duckworth, 1988), p. 210.

5 See, for example, the entries for 'scholasticism' and 'medieval philosophy' in J. O. Urmson and J. Rée (eds), *The Concise Encyclopaedia of Western Philosophy and Philosophers* (London, Unwin Hyman, 1989).

6 London, Longman, 2nd edn, 1988, pp. 76–82. Dom David's account applies to what one might call the golden age of scholasticism, up to the middle of the fourteenth century; on the new scholasticism of the late sixteenth century, see Stuart Brown in Chapter 2 of this volume, pp. 76, 81–3.

7 cf. R. W. Southern, *Grosseteste* (Oxford, Clarendon, 1986), p. 32.

8 See, for example, P. O. Kristeller, 'Humanism', in CHRP, pp. 113–37. One should stress the phrase 'in the main'; humanism, like the Renaissance, has a long history, and in the late fifteenth and sixteenth centuries humanists became involved in a range of subjects from logic and science that do not fall within a simple five-part scheme. On this, see the chapters on humanism and science and humanism and philosophy in Jill Kraye (ed.) *The Cambridge Companion to Renaissance Humanism* (Cambridge, Cambridge University Press, forthcoming). See also Anthony Grafton, 'Humanism, Magic and Science', in A. Goodman and A. Mackay (eds) *The Impact of Humanism on Western Europe* (London, Longman, 1990), pp. 99–117.

9 See especially some remarks of the fifteenth-century Florentine chancellor Leonardo Bruni, quoted by B. P. Copenhaver, CHRP, p. 106.

10 cf. Burke, op. cit.

11 Cesare Vasoli, 'The Renaissance Concept of Philosophy', CHRP, p. 73.

12 See especially J. Stephens, *The Italian Renaissance* (London, Longman, 1990), pp. xvi, 54, 137, 149.

13 The phrase comes from Owen Chadwick, *The Secularisation of the European Mind in the Nineteenth Century* (Cambridge, Cambridge University Press, 1975).

14 A Latin translation of Diogenes Laertius' *Life of Pyrrho* was available in the late 1420s; but it was above all the printing of Latin versions of Sextus Empiricus in 1562 and 1569 which stimulated interest in the ancient sceptics. See CHRP, pp. 679–80, and Richard Popkin, *The History of Scepticism from Erasmus to Spinoza* (Berkeley, Calif., University of California Press, 1979), p. 19.

  Superficially, the sceptical thesis that one must suspend judgement about everything might seem incompatible with Christian claims to knowledge. In the sixteenth century, however, Catholics employed sceptical arguments against Protestants, arguing that sceptical doubts about the worth of reason meant that it was unsafe to base religion on such a foundation. Religious beliefs must be based on faith, and more specifically on the faith of a community which had endured through the centuries – the Catholic Church. See Popkin, op. cit., pp. 55, 58, 70–3, 78–82, 90, 94–5.

15 London, Hutchinson, 1949.

16 E.g. B. P. Copenhaver, 'Astrology and Magic', CHRP, pp. 296–300.

17 Bacon and the scholastics: *The Advancement of Learning*, Book I, ch. 4 (Everyman's Library Edition, London, Dent, 1973), p. 26. Bacon and magic: Copenhaver, op. cit. Bacon and knowledge: A. Pérez-Ramos, Chapter 4 of this volume, pp. 145–7.

18 Theirs, said Bacon, was a 'delicate learning', as opposed to the 'fantastical learning' of the scholastics, and they 'began to hunt more after words than matter': *The Advancement of Learning*, Book 1, ch. 4, p. 24.

19 Bacon knew of Ramus's work, and gave it his (highly qualified) approval (Bacon, op. cit., Book II, ch. 17, p. 144). On Ramus's logic, see for example Lisa Jardine, 'Humanistic Logic', CHRP, pp. 184–6, and William and Martha Kneale, *The Development of Logic* (Oxford, Clarendon, revised edn, 1984), pp. 301–6.

20 CHRP, pp. 185, 673.

21 W. Kneale, *Probability and Induction* (Oxford, Clarendon, 1949), p. 48.

22 In this connection, Bacon is praised for having seen the importance of the negative instance – that is, of eliminative induction as opposed to induction by simple enumeration. See Bacon, *Novum Organum*, I, secs 46, 105, and Anthony Quinton, *Francis Bacon* (Oxford, Oxford University Press, 1980), p. 56.

23 cf. A. Pérez-Ramos, Chapter 4 of this volume, p. 151.

24 Ian Hacking, *Representing and Intervening: Introductory Topics in the Philosophy of Natural Science* (Cambridge, Cambridge University Press, 1983), p. 246.

25 See, for example, Quinton, op. cit., p. 47.

26 See p. 2 above.

27 For an interesting survey of rationalism as a whole, see J. Cottingham, *Rationalism* (London, Paladin, 1984).

28 Leibniz is an exception: cf. N. Jolley, Chapter 11 of this volume, p. 384.

29 J. Cottingham, R. Stoothoff and D. Murdoch (eds), *The Philosophical Works of Descartes* (Cambridge, Cambridge University Press, 3 vols, 1985, 1991: abbreviated, CSM), ii, p. 12; cf. *Discourse on Method*, CSM i, pp. 111–19.

30 The term, incidentally, is to be found in Spinoza, who speaks of believers in miracles as hostile to natural scientists – 'iis, qui scientias naturales colunt'. *Tractatus Theologico-Politicus*, ch. 6; Spinoza, *Opera*, ed. C. Gebhardt (Heidelberg, Winter, 4 vols, 1924–6), vol. 3, p. 81.

31 cf. to Mersenne, 11 October 1638 (CSM iii, p. 124), where Descartes criticizes Galileo on the grounds that 'his building lacks a foundation'. (See also G. Molland, Chapter 3 of this volume, p. 129.)

32 This view has been challenged, where Spinoza is concerned, by Alan Donagan (*Spinoza*, Brighton, Harvester, 1988, esp. p. 68). Donagan argues that Spinoza did not so much try to justify the principles of the new physics as generalize from them. It has also been argued by Stuart Brown that Leibniz was a foundationalist only during his early years, but later took the view that the philosopher should seek out and explore fruitful hypotheses (Stuart Brown, *Leibniz*, Brighton, Harvester, 1984). I have discussed this thesis in my paper, 'Leibniz's Philosophical Aims: Foundation-laying or Problem-solving?', in A. Heinekamp, W. Lenzen and M. Schneider (eds) *Mathesis Rationis: Festschrift für Heinrich Schepers* (Münster, Nodus, 1990), pp. 67–78.

33 *Meditations* V, CSM ii, 45. Compare Leibniz, *Nouveaux Essais*, IV.11.14, on the 'eternal truths' of mathematics.

34 There were two such methods, traditionally known as 'analysis' and 'synthesis'. These are discussed in this volume in Chapter 3 (pp. 107–9), Chapter 5 (pp. 183–6) and Chapter 8 (pp. 279–80).

35 Though Leibniz added the qualification that it must first be shown that the concept of God – i.e. of a most perfect or necessary being – is self-consistent. See, for example, Leibniz, *Discourse on Metaphysics*, sec. 23.

36 cf. p. 4 above.

37 The main sources of deism were Lord Herbert of Cherbury, *De Veritate* (1624), and Locke, *The Reasonableness of Christianity* (1695). However, they were not the sole sources; as Professor Stuart Brown has pointed out to me, there is reason to believe that the seventeenth-century rationalists had some influence on deistic thought. Deism has a long history, and the term meant different things to different people. (Samuel Clarke, in his *Demonstration of the Being and Attributes of God* (1704–6), recognized no fewer than four types of deism.) What matters here is that many deists believed in a creative deity whose wisdom and power are such as to make it irrational to suppose that he should intervene in the workings of the universe, once he has created it. This position is close to that taken by seventeenth-century rationalists. Pascal declared that he 'could not forgive' Descartes for reducing God's role in the workings of the universe almost to nothing (*Pensées*, Brunschvicg ed., No. 77), and a similar position is implied by what other seventeenth-century rationalists said about miracles. For Spinoza, it was impossible that any miracles should occur; for Leibniz and Malebranche, God's miraculous intervention in the universe was a possibility, but such interventions were very few. See, for example, G. H. R. Parkinson, 'Spinoza on Miracles and Natural Law', *Revue internationale de philosophie* 31 (1977) 145–57, and *Logic and Reality in Leibniz's Metaphysics* (Oxford, Claren-

don, 1965), pp. 102, 155–6; Daisie Radner, *Malebranche* (Assen, Van Gorcum, 1978), p. 32.

38 Descartes tried to derive universal laws of science from the immutability of God. Spinoza seems to have thought that no scientific laws other than those that actually hold are strictly speaking thinkable, though in his attempt to establish such laws he was compelled to appeal to experience. (See Chapter 8, pp. 289, 298, on Spinoza's 'postulates'. See also Chapter 3, pp. 131–2, for Descartes's views about hypotheses and experience.) Leibniz rejected both these approaches, and argued that scientific laws have to be seen in relation to the wise and good purposes of God.

39 Spinoza argued that human beings have no free will, since everything in the mind is determined by a cause, and that by another, and so on to infinity (*Ethics*, Pt II, Proposition 48). His way of reconciling determinism and freedom was to say that freedom consists, not in an absence of determination, but in self-determination. Such self-determination occurs when the reason controls the passions, which are in a way outside us. This view – which amounts to saying that to be free is to be master of oneself – is a form of what Isaiah Berlin has called the concept of 'positive freedom' (Berlin, 'Two Concepts of Liberty', *Four Essays on Liberty* (Oxford, Oxford University Press, 1969), pp. 118–72). Leibniz, for his part, discussed both the theological forms of the problem of freedom and the problems posed by the thesis that every event is caused. He accepted this thesis, but argued (contrary to Spinoza) that there is freedom of the will. In essence, his argument was that human actions are indeed necessary, but that they are only *hypothetically* necessary. That is, given that X is, at the moment, my strongest motive, then I must act in accordance with this motive. But I still could have acted otherwise – that is, my will is free – in that my acting in some other way is always *logically* possible.

On Spinoza's views about determinism see (besides Chapter 8, pp. 294–5, and Chapter 9, pp. 323–6) Jonathan Bennett, *A Study of Spinoza's 'Ethics'* (Cambridge, Cambridge University Press, 1984), pp. 315–29; R. J. Delahunty, *Spinoza* (London, Routledge, 1985), pp. 35–48, 155–65; G. H. R. Parkinson, 'Spinoza on the Power and Freedom of Man', in E. Freeman and M. Mandelbaum (eds) *Spinoza: Essays in Interpretation* (La Salle, Ill., Open Court, 1975), pp. 7–33. A general survey of Leibniz's views about human freedom is provided by G. H. R. Parkinson, *Leibniz on Human Freedom* (Wiesbaden, Steiner, 1970). See also, for example, A. Burms and H. de Dijn, 'Freedom and Logical Contingency in Leibniz', *Studia Leibnitiana* 11 (1979) 124–33; Lois Frankel, 'Being Able to do Otherwise: Leibniz on Freedom and Contingency', *Studia Leibnitiana* 16 (1984) 45–59; Pauline Phemister, 'Leibniz, Free Will and Rationality', *Studia Leibnitiana* 23 (1991) 25–39.

40 In Descartes's terminology, I can have a 'clear and distinct idea' of a mind as a being which is thinking and non-extended, but I have a clear and distinct idea of a body in so far as this is non-thinking and extended. See *Meditations* VI, CSM ii, p. 54, and *Replies to First Objections*, CSM ii, p. 86.

41 Gassendi's atomism influenced the young Leibniz (see especially K. Moll, *Der junge Leibniz* (Stuttgart, Frommann-Holzboog, 1982), vol 2, who was also influenced by Hobbes (see, for example, J. W. N. Watkins, *Hobbes' System of Ideas* (London, Hutchinson, 2nd edn, 1973), pp. 87–94). Whether Spinoza

borrowed from Hobbes is a matter of controversy, but he certainly defined his
position by reference to Hobbes. See, for example, A. G. Wernham, *Benedict
de Spinoza: The Political Works* (Oxford, Clarendon, 1958), pp. 11–36.

42 John Aubrey, *Brief Lives and Other Selected Writings*, ed. Anthony Powell
(London, Cresset Press, 1949), p. 242.

43 *Leviathan* (Oxford, Blackwell, 1946), ch. 5, p. 29.

44 ibid.

45 ibid., ch. 7, p. 40.

46 For a recent discussion of this issue, see Arrigo Pacchi, 'Hobbes and the
Problem of God', in G. A. J. Rogers and Alan Ryan (eds) *Perspectives on
Thomas Hobbes* (Oxford, Clarendon, 1988), pp. 171–88.

47 I am very grateful to Dr Jill Kraye and Professor Stuart Brown for their helpful
comments on an earlier draft of this introduction.

CHAPTER 1

The philosophy of the Italian Renaissance

Jill Kraye

Two movements exerted a profound influence on the philosophy of the Italian Renaissance: scholasticism and humanism, both of which began to take root in northern Italy around 1300. Differing from one another in terms of methods and aims as greatly as the scientific- and humanities-based cultures of our own times, scholasticism and humanism each fostered a distinctive approach to philosophy.

The centres of scholasticism were the universities, where philosophy teaching was based on the Aristotelian corpus, in particular the works of logic and natural philosophy. In Italian universities the study of philosophy was propaedeutic to medicine rather than, as in Oxford and Paris, theology. This encouraged an atmosphere in which philosophy could operate as an autonomous discipline, guided solely by rational criteria. Scholastic philosophers consistently defended their right to explain natural phenomena according to the laws of nature without recourse to theological arguments.[1] But although theological faculties were absent in the universities, religious authorities had enough power within society at large to challenge thinkers whose single-minded pursuit of natural explanations was perceived to move beyond the territory of philosophy and into the sacred domain of faith. Aristotelian philosophers who dared, for instance, to argue that the soul was material and hence mortal were quickly forced to recant by the ecclesiastical authorities.[2]

On the equally sensitive subject of the eternity of the world, most scholastics limited themselves to pointing out the opposition between the Peripatetic hypothesis that the world was eternal and the 'truth of the orthodox faith' that it was created *ex nihilo* by God.[3] In such cases where religious and philosophical doctrines were in conflict, Aristotelians maintained that Christian dogma, based on faith and revelation, was superior to explanations founded on mere reason. The scholastic doctrine of the 'double truth' did not present a choice between equally valid alternatives, but rather took for granted the subordination of the relative truth of philosophy to the absolute truth of theology. Philosophers had no desire to challenge this hierarchy. Their primary concern was instead to maintain the separation of the two realms, thus protecting their right to use rational, and *only* rational, arguments in philosophical contexts. Just as it was necessary, they asserted, when discussing matters of faith, to leave behind one's philosophical mentality, so when discussing philosophy, one had to set aside one's Christian faith.[4]

Scholastics read Aristotle in late medieval Latin translations, which were unclassical in style and terminology. This type of Latin continued to be one of the hallmarks of scholastic treatises produced during the Renaissance. Another was their rigidly logical format: works were divided and subdivided into propositions or questions; arguments for and against were laid out; a solution was reached; possible objections were raised and appropriate responses supplied. This structure had the advantage of covering issues from all possible angles and ensuring that the opinions of a wide variety of ancient and medieval thinkers were aired, even if Aristotle's were the most frequently endorsed.

In the judgement of Petrarch (Francesco Petrarca, 1304–74), the founder of Italian humanism, such treatises were barbaric, tediously pedantic, arid and incomprehensible.[5] His own style was diametrically opposed to that of the scholastics. He modelled his Latin prose on that of the best classical authors, avoiding terms and expressions which were unknown in antiquity. He also eschewed the methodical rigour and systematic presentation found in scholastic treatises, favouring instead a loose – almost at times rambling – structure and adopting genres such as the letter, dialogue and invective which had been used by the Roman authors he most admired.

Deeply interested in the state of his own soul, Petrarch ridiculed the scholastics for devoting so much of their energies to natural, rather than moral, philosophy: 'What is the use,' he asked, 'of knowing the nature of quadrupeds, fowls, fishes, and serpents and not knowing or even neglecting man's nature . . . ?' The secrets of nature were 'mysteries of God', which Christians should accept with 'humble faith' rather than attempt to seize 'in haughty arrogance'.[6] As for scholastic logicians, Petrarch had nothing but contempt for what he regarded as their empty loquacity and their addiction to disputation for its own sake: 'They get the greatest pleasure out of strife and set out not to find the truth but to quarrel.'[7] He especially disliked the *logica modernorum*, a highly technical and semantically orientated form of dialectic associated with William of Ockham and his followers, which had come over to Italy from England in the mid-fourteenth century. Petrarch believed that it reduced all speculation to problems of formal terminology, thereby deflecting philosophers from more important matters and turning theologians into mere dialecticians.[8]

Another aspect of scholasticism attacked by Petrarch was the dominance of Aristotelianism. While there was much of value in Aristotle's philosophy, there was also a great deal that from a Christian point of view was harmful, in particular his failure to give a firm endorsement to the immortality of the soul and his belief in the eternity of the world. Aristotle was not alone among pagans in holding these erroneous views, but he presented the greatest danger, Petrarch believed, because he had the most authority and the greatest number of followers. And while the pagan Aristotle could not be blamed for holding these errors, his present-day acolytes had no excuse.[9]

Despite their adulation of Aristotle, the scholastics failed, in Petrarch's opinion, to understand his thought. They disdained eloquence, treating it as 'an obstacle and a disgrace to philosophy', whereas Aristotle had believed that it was 'a mighty adornment'.[10] He blamed the inelegant style which characterized Latin versions of Aristotle not on the author's inattention to style but on the ignorance of his medieval translators – a censure which was to be frequently repeated by later humanists.[11] Yet aside from the ethical treatises, Petrarch's acquaintance with Aristotle's writings was neither wide nor deep.

If Petrarch was ill-informed about 'the Philosopher', he was positively ignorant about 'the Commentator', Averroes, probably never having read anything at all by him. This did not stop him from criticizing the Arabic interpreter even more strongly than he had done the Greek philosopher.[12] In sharp contrast to the scholastics, who considered Arabic learning to be an important part of their intellectual legacy, Petrarch and his humanist successors restricted their philosophical interests almost exclusively to the Greco-Roman past. Among the doctrines traditionally associated with Averroism was the double truth,[13] which theologians such as Thomas Aquinas rejected, maintaining that there was only one truth, the truth of faith, and that any philosophical proposition which contradicted it was necessarily false. Petrarch shared this point of view, arguing that since 'knowledge of the true faith' was 'the highest, most certain, and ultimately most beatifying of all knowledge', those who temporarily set it aside, wishing 'to appear as philosophers rather than as Christians', were in reality 'seeking the truth after having rejected the truth'.[14] According to him, scholastics were forced into this position not by an inevitable conflict between philosophy and religion, but rather by their support for one particular philosophy, Aristotelianism, which on certain crucial issues – the eternity of the world and the immortality of the soul – denied the fundamental truths of Christianity. The solution was therefore not to abandon philosophy *per se*, but to adopt a different sort of philosophy, one which avoided these theological errors.

That philosophy, for Petrarch, was Platonism. Plato, who offered convincing rational arguments in support of both the immortality of the soul and the creation of the world, had risen higher 'in divine matters' than other pagans. Because Plato 'came nearer than all the others' to Christian truth, he, and not his student Aristotle, deserved to be called 'the prince of philosophy'. By promoting Plato as a more theologically correct, and hence more profound, philosopher than Aristotle, Petrarch was able to mount yet another challenge to the scholastic philosophy of his day.[15] But for all his advocacy of Plato, Petrarch's knowledge of his works – like that of all Western scholars in this period – was very limited. Of the four dialogues then available in Latin, he made extensive use only of the *Timaeus*, in which Plato was believed to describe the creation of the world.[16] He owned a manuscript containing many more of the works in Greek; but to his great regret, he never managed to learn the language.[17] The bulk of Petrarch's understanding of Platonism was therefore gained from secondary sources: Cicero, Macrobius, Apuleius, but above all Augustine. It was primarily on Augustine's authority that Petrarch came to believe to strongly in the essential compatibility of Platonism with Christianity and to regard Plato as a Christian by anticipation.[18] Petrarch's Platonism amounted to little more than a propaganda campaign, but it was an effective one, which paved the way for the more philologically and philosophically ambitious efforts of fifteenth-century scholars.

THE NEW ARISTOTELIANISM

Petrarch's antipathy towards Aristotle was far less influential among his followers, many of whom helped to create a new style of Aristotelianism. The key figure in this movement was the humanist Leonardo Bruni (1370–1444), a papal secretary and later chancellor of Florence, who became the most important translator of Aristotle in the early fifteenth century.[19] It was not that he made new texts available, since virtually all of Aristotle had been translated into Latin by the end of the thirteenth century. Rather, he pioneered a novel method of translation. Medieval translators had attempted to find a Latin equivalent for each Greek word and to reproduce as far as possible the exact order of the original. Bruni, who had been trained by the Byzantine scholar Manuel

Chrysoloras (c. 1350–1414), regarded such word-for-word renderings as worthless since they distorted the meaning of the Greek. From Chrysoloras he learned to translate not individual words but units of meaning – phrases and even sentences.[20] From Cicero, on the other hand, Bruni learned to follow the word order and syntactic structure of the target language (Latin) rather than that of the source language (Greek); this meant adopting the prose style of the best classical Latin authors, above all Cicero himself.[21]

A 'classical' Aristotle who wrote in Ciceronian Latin was a direct challenge to the scholastic culture of the universities, where a very different sort of Latin Aristotle had been the mainstay of the curriculum for centuries. By retranslating Aristotle in this way Bruni was tampering with the fundamental terminology used by scholastics and deliberately calling into question all interpretations based on the medieval versions. Following up a line of attack opened by Petrarch, Bruni maintained that it was impossible for the self-professed Aristotelian philosophers 'to grasp anything rightly . . . since those books which they say are Aristotle's have suffered such a great transformation that were anyone to bring them to Aristotle himself, he would not recognize them as his own'.[22] Yet for all his criticisms of these translations, Bruni himself relied on them quite heavily, using his knowledge of Greek to correct their worst mistakes, but for the most part simply polishing their rough-hewn Latin.[23]

For Bruni and his fellow humanists these stylistic changes were by no means superficial. Misled by Cicero's praise of Aristotle's writings, they believed that they were restoring his lost eloquence. They saw this as a significant contribution to their larger programme of replacing the rebarbative treatises of the scholastics with a classically inspired and rhetorically persuasive form of philosophizing.[24] Hardline scholastics responded to the humanist rewriting of Aristotle by complaining that wisdom and philosophy had not been joined to eloquence and rhetoric but rather subordinated to them. Although willing to concede that Bruni's translations were more readable than the medieval versions, they thought that his lacked the scientific precision necessary in a philosophical work. Cicero might be an appropriate model to follow in oratory but not in philosophy, where subtle distinctions had to be made on the basis of careful reasoning.[25]

Bruni's desire to remove Aristotle from the scholastic camp and claim him for the humanist cause was a reflection of his high regard for the philosopher. In his *Vita Aristotelis*, he ranked him higher than his teacher Plato, reversing Petrarch's evaluation. The grounds for this judgement were Aristotle's greater consistency and clarity as well as his caution and moderation, which led him to 'support normal usages and ways of life', in contrast to Plato, who expressed 'opinions utterly abhorrent to our customs', such as the belief that 'all wives should be held in common'. Although he extolled Aristotle's methodical presentation of material in all his teachings, whether 'logic, natural science or ethics', Bruni's interest was in practice limited to moral and political philosophy, as his three Aristotelian translations – the *Nicomachean Ethics*, *Oeconomics* and *Politics* – clearly show.[26] In his *Isagogicon moralis disciplinae*, he contrasted 'the science of morals', whose study brought 'the greatest and most excellent of all things: happiness', with natural philosophy, a discipline 'of no practical use', unless, he added, in words reminiscent of Petrarch, 'you think yourself better instructed in the Good Life for having learned all about ice, snow and the colours of the rainbow'. Also reminiscent of Petrarch was Bruni's belief that Ockhamist logic, 'that barbarism which dwells across the ocean', had reduced contemporary dialectics to 'absurdity and frivolity'.[27]

The narrow range of Bruni's philosophical interests was typical of Italian humanists in the first half of the fifteenth century. The next wave of Aristotle translators, however, were Greek émigrés, who took a much broader view of Aristotelian philosophy. Johannes Argyropulos (c. 1410–87), a Byzantine scholar who taught in Florence, began by lecturing on the *Nicomachean Ethics* and *Politics*, but soon moved on to the *Physics, De anima, Meteorology* and *Metaphysics*.[28] He was able to bring to his teaching and translating of Aristotle an impressive blend of linguistic and philosophical competence, having received his early training in his native Constantinople and later studying at the University of Padua. Argyropulos was concerned to present the entire range of the Aristotelian corpus, which he regarded as the culmination of the Greek philosophical tradition. He did not shy away from logic, producing a compendium on the subject, based primarily on the Aristotelian *Organon* (most of which he himself translated into Latin) but also drawing on Byzantine commentaries and on standard Western authorities such as Boethius and Peter of Spain.[29] Natural philosophy, another subject shunned by humanists like Petrarch and Bruni, was embraced with enthusiasm by Argyropulos, who began his course on the *Physics* by exclaiming: 'How great is the nobility of this science, how great its perfection, its strength and power, and how great also is its beauty!'[30]

In his lectures on *De anima*, delivered in 1460, Argyropulos tackled the same problems which had exercised scholastic commentators since the thirteenth century: whether there was only one immortal intellect for all mankind, which directed the body's operations in the way that a sailor steered his ship, as Averroes maintained; or whether the soul was instead the substantial form of each individual person, giving the body existence (*esse*); and if so, whether it died with the body, as Alexander of Aphrodisias – according to Averroes – believed, or continued to exist after death, as Christian tradition asserted. Argyropulos rejected both the opinion of Alexander of Aphrodisias that the soul was mortal and the Averroist doctrine of the unity of the intellect, which many believed to be the authentic position of Aristotle. Challenging the double-truth doctrine, which dictated that reason should be kept separate from faith, Argyropulos asserted that there were philosophical as well as religious arguments in favour of the Christian dogma of the immortality of individual souls.[31] On other issues, however, Argyropulos had no qualms about relying on Averroes, whose works he had studied while at Padua.[32] And in his lectures on the *Nicomachean Ethics*, he made use of Albertus Magnus, Walter Burley and other medieval commentators. These lectures were assiduously taken down by his devoted student, Donato Acciaiuoli (1429–78), who later reworked them in the form of a commentary, which, despite his humanist credentials, had a great deal in common, in terminology, organization and content, with scholastic treatises.[33] Humanism and scholasticism were still moving down their separate paths, but in the second half of the fifteenth century those paths were occasionally beginning to cross.

A large number of Aristotle's works, mostly in the field of natural philosophy, were translated by another Greek émigré, George of Trebizond (1395/6–1472/3), as part of a plan, devised and financed by the humanist pope Nicholas V, to produce a new version of the entire corpus.[34] Like Bruni and most other fifteenth-century Aristotle translators, George made use of the medieval versions; but unlike them, he went out of his way to acknowledge and praise them. His own translations resembled the medieval ones in that he tried as far as possible to produce word-for-word versions, avoiding, however, their readiness to violate the rules of Latin syntax and usage. George had a sophisticated understanding of Aristotle's style and was aware that he had not attempted, or had not been able, to write eloquently when dealing with technical subjects. It was therefore misguided to impose elegance where it was lacking in the original.[35]

George's comments were directed not at Bruni but at his fellow Greek, Theodore Gaza (c. 1400–75). Gaza was the protégé of Cardinal Bessarion (c. 1403–72), a distinguished Byzantine theologian and philosopher who had transferred his allegiance to the Roman Catholic church. Bessarion's political and intellectual clout (he himself had translated the *Metaphysics*) helped to convince Nicholas V that he should commission Gaza to make new Latin versions of some of the Aristotelian texts translated by George.[36] George's loss of papal favour and patronage was no doubt caused by his notoriously difficult behaviour,[37] as well as his failure on occasion to live up to his own high standards of translation. There was a theoretical difference between his position and that of Gaza, however. Gaza's primary concern was to ensure the elegance and Latinity of his translations even when this entailed imprecision and inconsistency. George, by contrast, took the view that in rendering philosophical works exactitude and fidelity to the author's words were all-important; judged by this criterion, the medieval translators, for all the inadequacies of their Latin style, had been more successful than Gaza.[38]

George believed moreover that Gaza's version, or rather 'perversion', of Aristotle would undermine scholasticism, which relied on the long-established terminology of the medieval translations. For George, a Greek convert to Roman Catholicism, a humanist admirer of medieval thinkers such as Albertus Magnus and Thomas Aquinas, and a deeply paranoid personality, the classical Latin which Gaza put in Aristotle's mouth was part of a conspiracy to destroy Christian theology by removing the scholastic Aristotelianism which underpinned it.[39] And that, he believed, was only the beginning. The hidden agenda of Gaza and his patron Bessarion included the replacement of Aristotelianism by another ancient philosophical system, one which (as we shall see) George thought was destined to pave the way for a return to paganism.

George's merits as a translator of Aristotle found at least one admirer. Angelo Poliziano (1454–94), the most learned Italian humanist of his day, recognized that Gaza's much-praised translation of the zoological works borrowed heavily from the earlier version by George, whom Gaza had ungenerously referred to as a 'brothel keeper'.[40] The fact that Poliziano, a teacher of Greek and Latin literature at the Florentine *studio*, was sufficiently concerned with Aristotelian natural philosophy to study these translations is an indication of the widening philosophical interests of late fifteenth-century Italian humanists. In 1490 Poliziano lectured on the *Nicomachean Ethics*, a treatise which was within the typical humanist ambit of moral philosophy; but during the next four years he worked his way through the entire *Organon*. Though keenly interested in Aristotle's logic, Poliziano – like Petrarch and Bruni – held no brief for the British logicians who dominated the scholastic curriculum. He wanted to apply humanist philological methods to Greek philosophical texts in order to reform subjects such as logic and natural philosophy, corrupted by centuries of scholastic ignorance.[41]

The professional philosophers whose ability to understand Aristotle Poliziano called into question and whose preserve he invaded, responded, not surprisingly, by accusing him of teaching technical subjects which he knew nothing about. These vampires (*lamiae*), as Poliziano called them in his 1492 inaugural lecture on the *Prior Analytics*, had taken to ridiculing him as a would-be philosopher. He in turn replied that he had never claimed to be a philosopher, but rather a philologist (*grammaticus*), a scholar who used his knowledge of classical languages and culture to interpret ancient texts, be they literary, legal or philosophical.[42]

Another philologist who brought his talents to bear on philosophical and scientific works was Poliziano's great friend, the Venetian humanist Ermolao Barbaro (1454–93).[43] In 1474–6 Barbaro lectured at Padua on the *Nicomachean Ethics* and *Politics*, using the medieval Latin versions – no doubt because of university requirements – but correcting them against the Greek.[44] His experiences in the citadel of traditional scholastic Aristotelianism convinced him of the need to promote the new, humanist approach to philosophy. This involved an ambitious plan to retranslate all of Aristotle, although owing to his early death he completed only a version of the *Rhetoric* and a humanistic reworking of the *Liber sex principiorum*, a twelfth-century Latin treatise on the categories which had become a regular part of the Aristotelian logical corpus. The latter work allowed him to prove that even the most technical philosophical subjects could be rendered with elegance. Barbaro also wrote a brief treatise which demonstrated that the English calculatory tradition, a highly technical form of logico-mathematical physics developed in fourteenth-century Oxford, could be treated in classical Latin. His overall goal was to reunite eloquence and philosophy, which he believed had been artificially sundered, to the detriment of both, by generations of scholastics.[45]

Giovanni Pico della Mirandola (1463–94), although on good terms with both Barbaro and Poliziano, did not share their humanist disdain for the 'dull, rude, uncultured' scholastics. Pico, who had spent 'six years on those barbarians', denied that their lack of eloquence detracted from the quality of their philosophical thought. In his view it was rhetoric and oratory which were the greatest obstacles to philosophy, for they were nothing but 'sheer mendacity, sheer imposture, sheer trickery', while philosophy was 'concerned with knowing the truth and demonstrating it to others'. A philosopher's style should therefore be not 'delightful, adorned and graceful' but 'useful, grave, something to be respected'. Orators who sought the roar of the crowd's approval had to be well spoken, but not philosophers, who wanted only the silent respect of the discerning few.[46] Pico's disparagement of eloquence is itself so eloquent that irony is almost certainly in play. But the argument he presented was a serious one, which highlighted a long-standing difference between the scholastic and humanist styles of philosophy.

There were substantive as well as stylistic differences between humanist and scholastic Aristotelianism. While Averroes still reigned supreme as 'the Commentator' in the universities, humanists like Barbaro, echoing – from a more informed position – Petrarch's hostility, were determined to replace this Arabic influence with ancient Greek expositors more acceptable to their classical tastes.[47] A few works by the ancient Greek commentators on Aristotle had been translated into Latin in the Middle Ages, and some of their views, especially those of Alexander of Aphrodisias, were known through reports given by Averroes; but the vast bulk of the material was unavailable to Western readers.[48] To help remedy this situation, Barbaro in 1481 published a Latin translation of the paraphrases of Themistius; and in 1495 Girolamo Donato, a Venetian humanist who belonged to Barbaro's circle, published a translation of Alexander of Aphrodisias's commentary on *De anima*. These versions were soon to have a significant impact on philosophical discussions in Padua.[49]

While Barbaro and Donato were producing their Latin translations of Aristotle and his ancient commentators, other humanists also working in Venice were directing their efforts towards editing the Greek texts of these works. Their supreme achievement was the Greek Aristotle published between 1495 and 1498 by Aldus Manutius (*c.* 1452–1515).[50] This multi-volume deluxe edition was primarily the fruit of humanist philology, but important contributions came from the scholastic side as well: Francesco Cavalli (d. 1540), a physician who taught at Padua, worked out the proper arrangement of the treatises on natural philosophy and convinced Aldus to substitute Theophrastus's botanical works for *De plantis*, a work he recognized to be pseudo-Aristotelian.[51] Aldus also had ambitious plans to publish Greek editions of the Aristotelian commentators, but the project did not get off the ground until early in the next century.[52]

The rest of the thriving Venetian publishing industry, with an eye to profit rather than to intellectual lustre, focused its energies on producing Latin editions of Aristotle, still, and for some time to come, the staple diet of the philosophical curriculum. One such work, published in 1483–4 and containing the commentaries of Averroes as well as the medieval translations of Aristotle, was edited by Nicoletto Vernia (d. 1499), the leading professor of natural philosophy at the University of Padua. For much of his career Vernia was a typical scholastic, who regarded Averroes and Albertus Magnus as the greatest of Aristotelian commentators. Insisting on the double-truth distinction between theological and rational discourse, Vernia maintained that although the belief in the soul as the substantial form of individual human beings was true according to faith, it was nevertheless completely foreign to Aristotle, whose thought should not be interpreted as if he had been a Christian. Averroes, not Thomas Aquinas, had correctly understood Aristotle, recognizing that according to Peripatetic principles (e.g. the indivisibility of separate substances) there was only one intellective soul for all mankind.[53]

Vernia's stance had to be altered when, in 1489, the bishop of

Padua banned any further discussion of the Averroist doctrine of the unity of the intellect. Just as earlier scholastics had been forced to recant views which were unacceptable to the Church, Vernia abandoned his Averroist beliefs. In the 1490s he completely rethought his position on the controversial problem of the soul, making considerable use of the newly Latinized works of Themistius and Alexander of Aphrodisias. No longer accepting Averroes as a reliable guide to Aristotelian psychology, Vernia turned to the Greek commentators, who he believed (wrongly in the case of Alexander) provided evidence that Aristotle, like Plato, had argued for the immortality of individual souls. Christian doctrine was therefore not simply an article of faith but could be demonstrated on purely rational grounds.[54]

This standpoint had already gained philosophical respectability earlier in the century through the influence of Paul of Venice (1369–1429), the most famous scholastic of his time. Although Paul never ceased to regard the Averroist unity of the intellect as the correct interpretation of Aristotle's *De anima*, he did not think that this in itself made the position a demonstrable doctrine, for a number of objections to it could be raised, objections based on reason as well as faith. Although Paul and Vernia came to their conclusions by different routes, they both maintained that there were rational as well as theological arguments in favour of Christian dogma.[55] The barrier separating the realms of philosophy and theology, used by generations of scholastics to defend the autonomy of their discipline, was starting to crumble.

THE REVIVAL OF PLATONISM

Interest in Plato had been stirred among Italian humanists by Petrarch's portrayal of his philosophy as a theologically acceptable alternative to Aristotelianism, one whose closeness to Christianity, moreover, had been endorsed by no less an authority than Augustine. But until the end of the fourteenth century little first-hand knowledge of the dialogues was possible since so few Latin versions existed: the *Timaeus* was widely accessible in the fragmentary fourth-century version of Chalcidius; the *Phaedo* and *Meno* had been translated in the twelfth century by Henricus Aristippus; and part of the *Parmenides* was embedded in William of Moerbeke's thirteenth-century translation of Proclus's commentary.[56]

Although the *Phaedo* was already available in medieval Latin, Bruni chose to produce a new humanist version in 1405. This allowed him, as with his Aristotle translations, to demonstrate the stylistic superiority of the humanist approach to philosophy. But there was another reason for this choice. The theme of the *Phaedo*, the personal immortality of individual human souls, was a minefield for Aristotelians. As such it was an ideal means to emphasize the superiority, from a Christian point of view, of Platonism. In his dedication of the translation to Innocent VII, Bruni told the pope that, although Christian doctrine on the afterlife did not require any confirmation from classical philosophy, it would none the less 'bring no small increase to the true faith' if people were made to see 'that the most subtle and wise of pagan philosophers held the same beliefs about the soul as we hold' and about many other matters as well.[57] These other matters included, as Bruni specified in the dedication of his *Gorgias* translation to John XXIII (1410), God's creation of the world: the doctrine which, along with immortality, had determined Petrarch's preference for Platonism over Aristotelianism.[58]

As he translated more of the dialogues, however, Bruni became increasingly disillusioned with their ethical and political doctrines. In his partial translations of the *Phaedrus* (1424) and the *Symposium* (1435), he resorted to extensive bowdlerization in order to remove any hint of homosexuality; and he refused to translate the *Republic* because it contained so many repellent notions, among them the community of wives and property, one of those 'abhorrent' opinions which led him to transfer his philosophical loyalties to the less wayward Aristotle.[59]

Bruni's intense dislike of the *Republic* was not shared by his teacher Chrysoloras, who appears to have had no scruples about divulging its contents to the Latin reading public. He had produced in 1402 a literal version of the text – the best he could do with his limited knowledge of Latin – which was then revised and polished by one of his Milanese students, Uberto Decembrio (c. 1370–1427). Unfortunately this collaboration resulted in the worst of both worlds: a crude mixture of word-for-word translation and inaccurate paraphrase, which garbled the technical terminology and utterly failed to convey the complexity and sophistication of Plato's doctrines.[60] Thirty-five years later Uberto's son Pier Candido (1399–1477) decided to make a new translation, one which would ensure that the *Republic*, a byword for eloquence among Greeks, would not appear lacklustre in Latin. He was also anxious to prove that Aristotle's account of Plato's work in *Politics* II.1 was misleading – that, for instance, the common ownership of wives and goods was not meant to be universal but rather was restricted to the class of guardians. In line with other humanists, Pier Candido emphasized the points of contact between Platonism and Christianity, identifying in his marginal notes to the translation the Form of Good in Book VI with God, and drawing attention to Plato's proofs of immortality in Book X. Aspects of the dialogue which he found offensive – the equality of the sexes and homosexuality – were treated as ironic or were deliberately mistranslated or, when all else failed, simply left out.[61]

Since none of these humanists had the philosophical training to come to grips with the elaborate conceptual apparatus of Platonism, they were unable to go beyond an appreciation of Plato's style, his (carefully censored) moral thought and his agreement with Christianity. Similarly, humanist educators taught their students to read the dialogues in Greek but were not in a position to provide a philosophical framework that would allow them to interpret what they read in its Platonic context. Instead, they encouraged their pupils to use the works as a quarry for wise sayings and pithy maxims, which they could then insert in their thematically organized commonplace books for future use.[62] The sheer difficulty of Plato's teachings on metaphysics and epistemology forced humanists to rely on more straightforward second-hand accounts even when they had access to the original works. Thus an accomplished Greek scholar such as Francesco Filelfo (1398–1481), who had translated Aristotle (*Rhetorica ad Alexandrum*) as well as Plato (the *Euthyphro* and some of the *Letters*), did not turn to the dialogues when writing his treatise on Platonic ideas but relied on the more accessible treatments of the subject in Cicero, Augustine and certain Middle Platonic sources.[63]

As in the case of Aristotle, it was the Byzantine émigrés who brought a new depth to the study of Plato. Since Platonism was part of their educational background, they were more capable of dealing with the entire range of Plato's philosophy, speculative doctrines as well as practical ethics and politics. Argyropulos allowed a small Platonic element to seep into his university courses on Aristotle and gave at least one private lecture on the *Meno*.[64] Even Aristotle's staunchest defender, George of Trebizond, had gone through a Platonic phase in his youth and was later commissioned by Nicholas of Cusa to make a complete Latin version of the *Parmenides*, only a portion of which was available in the medieval translation. George, who needed the money, agreed with reluctance, and in 1459 produced a reasonably accurate rendering of the text.[65]

Eight years earlier George had made a far less successful translation of the *Laws* and *Epinomis*, this time at the behest of Nicholas V – another offer he could not afford to refuse, although his slipshod and distorted version may have been an attempt to subvert the dialogue's potential influence. After falling out with the pope,[66] George transferred the dedication to the Venetian Republic, suggesting in the new preface that the city's founders must have read the *Laws* – Greek, he pointed out, was spoken in Italy during the early Middle Ages – because their government perfectly exemplified the mixed constitution described by Plato in Book III (692–3): the Grand Council representing democracy, the Council of Ten aristocracy and the doge monarchy. George's real opinion of the dialogue and its author is not to be found in the flattering words he addressed to the Venetians but rather in some marginal notes which he wrote in his own copy of the translation: 'What shallowness!' 'Look at his arrogance!' 'The man should be stoned!'[67]

These harsh remarks were inspired by George's increasing fear that Platonism would not only replace Aristotelianism as the dominant philosophy of the West but would also be the springboard for a world-wide return to paganism. He blamed Cardinal Bessarion and his accomplice Gaza for promoting Platonism, but the *éminence grise* of this ruinous movement was, he believed, Bessarion's teacher, Georgios Gemistos Plethon (*c.* 1360–1454).[68] During the Council of Florence (1439), a last-ditch attempt to reunify the Eastern and Western churches in the face of the approaching Turkish menace, Plethon, a member of the Greek delegation, had written a brief treatise, *De differentiis Aristotelis et Platonis*, which compared the doctrines of the two philosophers to Aristotle's great disadvantage. The work was addressed to Westerners, both the minority who were already convinced of Plato's supremacy and the majority who, taken in by the extravagant claims of Averroes, gave their preference to Aristotle.[69] Plethon, who for many years had taught Platonic philosophy at Mistra in the Peloponnese, discussed a wide range of topics – metaphysics, epistemology, cosmology, psychology, ethics – in each case demonstrating the superiority of Plato's views to those of his student Aristotle.

One of the aims of Plethon's treatise was to suggest that Aristotelian philosophy was unfit to serve as a mainstay of Christian theology and that Platonism would more suitably fill that role. Pouncing on the two issues where Aristotelianism's claims to support Christianity were weakest, the creation of the world and the immortality of the soul, Plethon pointed out, first, that Aristotle 'never calls God the creator of anything whatever, but only the motive force of the universe'; and, second, that Aristotle's position on the afterlife of the soul was at best ambiguous, since he asserted the eternity of the human mind in *De anima* (408^b19–20) and the *Metaphysics* (1070^a 26–7), but never applied this belief to his moral philosophy and even suggested in the *Ethics* (1115^a26–7) that 'nothing whatever that is good lies in store for man after the end of his present life', a premise which had led Alexander of Aphrodisias to the 'deplorable conclusion' that 'the human soul is mortal'.[70]

Plethon's views do not seem on the face of it very far from those of Petrarch and other humanist supporters of Plato. But the difference between them was in fact considerable. While the Italians genuinely wanted to use Platonic philosophy to buttress Christianity, Plethon envisaged it as the foundation on which to rebuild the polytheistic paganism of ancient Greece. Convinced that the Turks were soon to destroy both the Eastern and Western churches, Plethon saw the only hope for the disintegrating Byzantine Empire in the replacement of Christianity by a revitalized paganism, solidly grounded in Platonic metaphysics. He therefore composed – but did not dare to publish – *The Laws*, modelled on the Platonic dialogue of the same name, in which he presented a concrete programme for the revival of the beliefs and moral values of the pre-Christian past.[71] Plethon's paganism contained Stoic as well as Platonic elements: he regarded absolute determinism as a necessary concomitant to the divine providence of Zeus, who had fixed the entire future in the best possible form. Free will, therefore, consisted of voluntary subjection to the absolute good which Zeus had decreed.[72] In *De differentiis* Plethon had revealed nothing of his revolutionary plans, pretending for the benefit of his Italian readers to be sincerely concerned about the conflicts between Aristotelian philosophy and Christian theology. But his long-term goal seems to have been to destroy confidence in Aristotelianism so that it could be supplanted by Platonism, which would then sever its ties with Christianity and renew its former alliance with paganism.

De differentiis, written in Greek and requiring a level of philosophical understanding far beyond the competence of most Italian humanists, made little impact on its intended audience. It did cause quite a stir among the Byzantines, however, many of whom rushed to Aristotle's defence.[73] Writing in Latin and therefore attracting a wider public, George of Trebizond produced the *Comparatio Platonis et Aristotelis* (1458), in which he unstintingly praised Aristotle while heaping abuse on Plato and his present-day followers. George claimed to have had a conversation with Plethon during the Council of Florence in which the latter predicted that the whole world would soon be unified under one religion: neither Christianity nor Islam, but a religion which would 'differ little from paganism'.[74] This proved to him that Plethon was the mastermind behind a Platonic conspiracy to overthrow Christianity. As it turns out, George, who had probably heard rumours about Plethon's *Laws*, was not far from the truth, although he was certainly wrong to assume that Bessarion and his circle were involved in (or even knew anything of) the plot.

In the first book of the *Comparatio* George argued that Aristotle's knowledge of all intellectual disciplines was superior to Plato's. In the second, he showed that although Platonism appeared to be close to Christianity, in reality its doctrines, above all Plato's belief in the preexistence of souls and in the creation of the universe from pre-existent matter, were inimical to religion. Aristotle, on the other hand, was in complete agreement with Christianity since he believed in the personal immortality of the soul, creation *ex nihilo*, divine providence, free will and even had some inkling of the Trinity. These extravagant claims went far beyond what Thomas Aquinas, the father of Christian Aristotelianism, had maintained, for Thomas had always insisted on a firm demarcation between the proofs of philosophy, which could be borrowed from the pagans, and the truths of religion, which were accessible only through revelation.[75] In the third and final book George, drawing on the *Symposium*, *Phaedrus* and the *Laws* (in his own misleading translation), disclosed the sexual depravity and moral corruption of Plato and his disciples, among whom he numbered Epicurus and Mohammed. According to George, Mohammed had been a second Plato, Plethon an even more pernicious third and worse might be in store: a fourth Plato, the most dangerous of all, could soon arise – presumably a reference to Cardinal Bessarion, who was a strong candidate for the papacy, a position which would give him the power to destroy Christianity from the inside.[76]

George knew, however, that this nightmare would not come to pass, for he had been granted an apocalyptic vision which allowed him to predict (just as his arch-enemy Plethon had) the defeat of Western as well as Eastern Christendom by the Turks. This Islamic triumph would not, he knew, be the prelude to the re-emergence of a Plethon-style paganism: the sultan Mehmed II was destined to be converted to Christianity by none other than George himself, who would convince him to turn his might against the true enemies of the Church, Bessarion and his band of paganizing Platonists. Unfortunately, when George travelled to Constantinople, twelve years after its fall to the Turks, in order to play his pivotal role in world history, he failed to gain even an audience with the sultan. On his return to Rome he was imprisoned on suspicion of apostasy, a prophet without honour in his own country.[77]

While George's bizarre drama was unfolding, scholars from the Greek community in Italy were busy composing responses to his *Comparatio*. By 1459 Bessarion, the chief spokesman for Christian Platonism and – as he probably suspected – the main target of George's attack, had drafted a reply, which he sent to Gaza for comments. Gaza, although identified by George as one of the Platonic conspirators, thought of himself as an Aristotelian and had earlier written two tracts against Plethon, one refuting his concept of substance and the other answering his uncompromising determinism. In the second work Gaza attempted, following a long-established Byzantine tradition, to reconcile the views of Plato and Aristotle, demonstrating that the Stoic-inspired determinism postulated by Plethon had been rejected by both philosophers.[78]

In the comments which he sent to Bessarion, Gaza set out his

Aristotelian critique of the hyper-Aristotelianism of George's *Comparatio*. Such a corrective was necessary, he said, because George lacked 'all understanding of Aristotle's language and subject matter'. Similar charges had been levelled against Gaza himself by George in his blast against Gaza's 'perversion' of Aristotle; it was now time to settle old scores.[79] Gaza focused on the two issues which were at the centre of the debate about the relationship between classical philosophy and Christianity: the doctrines of creation and immortality. On the first, he showed that Aristotle had not, as George claimed, believed in creation *ex nihilo* but had maintained that the world was eternal, as indeed had Plato, although with far less clarity than Aristotle. The problem of immortality was more complex. Gaza admitted that the Averroist doctrine of the unity of the intellect was difficult to refute on philosophical grounds but pointed out that Aristotle had never explicitly endorsed it; on the other hand, he had never given any indication that he supported the notion of personal immortality. Given, however, that the expectation of just rewards and punishments in the afterlife is essential for the maintenance of public and private morality, Gaza argued that we should adopt Plato's belief in immortality, even though it is not capable of rational demonstration.[80]

A decade later Bessarion published his own refutation of the *Comparatio*, which appeared in a Latin translation so as to reach the same large readership as George's work. The aim of Bessarion's treatise, *In calumniatorem Platonis*, was to defend Plato against the calumnies which threatened to destroy his reputation among Christians and also to damage the reputation of his calumniator by revealing the shoddy scholarship on which his work was based. Following up Gaza's claim that George censured Platonic doctrines which he could no more understand 'than some rustic fresh from tilling the fields', Bessarion gave a practical demonstration of George's ignorance and incompetence by pointing out over two hundred errors, philosophical as well as linguistic, in his translation of the *Laws*.[81] But while Bessarion wanted to lower George's standing, he had no desire to harm that of Aristotle, whom he respected as a philosopher and whose *Metaphysics* he had translated. Like Gaza, he accepted the Byzantine position that there were no fundamental differences between the two philosophers, although Bessarion tended to follow the ancient Greek commentators in ranking Plato, the supreme metaphysician, higher than Aristotle, the supreme natural philosopher and logician.[82]

What Bessarion could not accept was George's insistence that Aristotle was closer than Plato to Christianity. Both philosophers, Bessarion asserted, were polytheistic pagans who held many beliefs which were entirely foreign to true religion. He therefore had no intention of turning Plato into a Christian, as George had done with

Aristotle. Nevertheless, he maintained that if one was looking for philosophical confirmation of Christian dogmas, there was far more in Plato's works than in those of Aristotle. Although Plato had not fully understood doctrines such as the Trinity, he had received enough illumination from the light of nature to allow him to gain a shadowy knowledge of the mysteries of faith, a knowledge which, however imperfect, could play a valuable role in leading men towards the ultimate truths of the Bible.[83] Bessarion's ability to find intimations and anticipations of Christianity in Plato's dialogues was greatly aided by his familiarity with the hermeneutical techniques of the ancient Neoplatonists, especially Plotinus and Proclus. He learned from them how to go beyond the often embarrassing literal sense of Plato's words: his accounts of metempsychosis, for example, or his frank references to homosexual love, which the Italian humanists had deliberately mistranslated or excised. The Neoplatonists taught Bessarion to look for the deeper meaning of such passages by reading them in terms of allegory, myth and symbol – devices which Plato had used to hide his profoundest doctrines from the gaze of the vulgar.[84] These tools of analysis, combined with his understanding of Platonic metaphysics, also gained from the Neoplatonists, permitted Bessarion to discredit George's slanders of Plato and, far more importantly, to lay the philosophical and theological foundation for a systematic Christian Neoplatonism.

The philosopher who was to construct that system, Marsilio Ficino (1433–99), had just completed the first draft of his Latin translation of all thirty-six Platonic dialogues when Bessarion's *In calumniatorem Platonis* was completed in 1469. Like many others, Ficino wrote to the cardinal to congratulate him on his treatise, from which he clearly learned a great deal.[85] Adopting Bessarion's figurative method of reading the dialogues, Ficino insisted that Plato's doctrine of the transmigration of souls should be interpreted in a moral key, as an allegorical representation of what happened to those who behaved like animals. Similarly, passages describing Socrates's sexual passion for his young disciples were, in Ficino's view, marvellous allegories, 'just like the Song of Solomon'.[86]

Although Ficino relied on the work of the earlier humanist translators of Plato, especially Bruni, he did not share their stylistic concerns. He simply wanted to make his translations as accurate and clear as possible, which meant employing an unadorned Latin and not avoiding useful philosophical terms just because they were unclassical or non-Ciceronian. The fact that Ficino's version remained the standard Latin translation of Plato until the nineteenth century is sufficient testimony of his success.[87] He also made advances in the analysis of Platonic works. Instead of mining the dialogues for isolated nuggets of ethical wisdom, as the humanists had taught their students to do, he offered complex and coherent analyses of themes – metaphysical and epistemological as well as moral – which ran through the entire corpus.

Humanists quickly began to take account of Ficino's work, which inspired new interpretations of classical literature. Cristoforo Landino (1425–98) used Ficino's philosophical ideas in his exegesis of Vergil's *Aeneid*, which he saw as a Platonic allegory of the soul's journey from sensuality and hedonism, symbolized by Troy, to a life of divine contemplation, represented by Italy.[88] Ficino was himself influenced by humanists, sharing many of their prejudices about contemporary scholastics, whom he referred to as 'lovers of ostentation' (*philopompi*) rather than 'lovers of wisdom' (*philosophi*). Like Bruni and Poliziano, Ficino accused so-called Aristotelians of not understanding the texts they professed to expound, reading them as they did in barbarous medieval translations. He also displayed a humanistic distaste for the logical nitpicking to which scholastics were addicted, leaving them little time, he felt, for more serious philosophical endeavour.[89]

Not that Ficino was a stranger to scholastic Aristotelianism. His early university training in logic, natural philosophy and medicine gave him a thorough grounding in Aristotle, Averroes and Avicenna, not to mention more recent writers such as Paul of Venice. Although he soon turned against most of the ideas and doctrines associated with this tradition, it left a lasting impact on his terminology and method of argument: there is a definite scholastic feel about the presentation of most of his treatises.[90] *De vita libri tres* (1489), Ficino's most popular work, contains many scholastic elements. Book II, on methods of prolonging life, borrows liberally from the thirteenth-century English Franciscan Roger Bacon; Book III deals with medical astrology, as transmitted to the medieval West by Arabic thinkers, and also develops a theory of magic based on the doctrine of substantial form elaborated by Thomas Aquinas and other scholastics.[91] Even in his Platonic commentaries scholastic ideas often make an appearance: his defence of the superiority of the intellect to the will in the *Philebus* is taken verbatim from Thomas.[92]

Although significant, this scholastic strain in Ficino's work was overshadowed by ancient Neoplatonism. The philosopher whom he most revered after Plato was Plotinus, the founder of Neoplatonism, whose *Enneads* he translated and commented upon. He also translated works by Proclus, Iamblichus, Porphyry and Synesius, all of whom helped to shape his understanding of the Platonic corpus.[93] By promoting Neoplatonic interpretations, already ventilated to a certain extent by Bessarion, Ficino altered the Western perception of Plato, transforming him from a wise moral philosopher into a profound metaphysician.

It was Plotinus who first systematized Platonic ontology, dividing reality into a series of hierarchical levels of being or hypostases, extending from the highest, the transcendent One, which was above being, to the lowest, matter, which was below it. This metaphysical scheme was taken over, with various modifications, by the later Neoplatonists, who used it, as Plotinus had done, to explain the deepest layers of meaning in the dialogues. Proclus, for instance, saw the *Parmenides* as a metaphysical work dealing with the nature of the One and in particular its ontological priority to being. According to the Neoplatonists, being was co-terminous not with the One but with the second hypostasis, Mind, for it was in Mind that the Platonic Ideas, the primary components of reality, were located. Ficino adopted this view of the *Parmenides*, treating it as a masterpiece of Platonic theology, in which essential truths about the One – God in Ficino's Christian version of the scheme – were revealed.[94]

This interpretation of the dialogue, however, was challenged by other members of the intellectual circle of Medicean Florence. Giovanni Pico, in his *De ente et uno* (1491), recounts how Poliziano asked him to defend the Aristotelian position that being and one are convertible against the Neoplatonic claim that the One is beyond being. To discredit the main evidence for the Neoplatonic stand, Pico went back to the Middle Platonic account of the *Parmenides*, which portrayed it not as a dogmatic exposition of unknowable truths about the ineffable One, but rather as 'a sort of dialectical exercise' in which nothing was definitively asserted or denied. He also criticized the Neoplatonists for misreading the *Sophist*, in which – according to Pico – Plato actually maintained that one and being were equal.[95] Ficino, of course, sided with Plotinus and Proclus against Poliziano and Pico. His commentary on the *Sophist* is likewise deeply indebted to the Neoplatonic view of the dialogue as a metaphysical discussion of Mind, with special emphasis on the various relationships between the Platonic Ideas.[96]

Although Ficino used such Neoplatonic insights to give Renaissance Platonism greater depth and coherence, he never lost sight of the primary motivation which had led his contemporaries to admire this philosophy: its compatibility with Christianity. This was in fact the mainspring of his own commitment to Platonism. At the end of 1473 Ficino became a priest, and in the following year he produced an apologetic work, *De christiana religione*, which attempted to convince the Jews to abandon their obstinate rejection of the true faith. This interest in religious polemics in no way conflicted with his enthusiastic promotion of Platonism. He believed that scholastic Aristotelianism, with its doctrine of the double truth, had given rise to an artificial rift between reason and faith, which were in reality natural allies. By maintaining, as scholastics had traditionally done, that philosophy was of no use to religion and vice versa, the former had become a tool of impiety, while the latter had been entrusted to ignorant and unworthy men. To show those who had separated philosophical studies from Christianity the error of their ways it was necessary to reunite piety and wisdom, creating a learned religion and a pious philosophy.[97]

The answer to this dilemma lay for Ficino, as it had for Petrarch, in Platonism. Plato had been both a theologian and a philosopher, many of whose doctrines were in harmony with the Judaeo-Christian tradition. The Church Fathers had recognized this when they repeated Numenius's description of him as a 'Greek-speaking Moses' and speculated that he had learned of the Bible on his travels in Egypt.[98] Plato was also believed to be the last in a long line of 'ancient theologians', which included Hermes Trismegistus, an Egyptian priest and near-contemporary of Moses. The Hermetic corpus – like the other documents comprising the ancient theology, a Greek forgery from the early Christian era – was translated by Ficino, who thought that it contained a gentile revelation analogous to that granted to the Jews. This quasi-Mosaic wisdom, which had been transmitted to Plato via Orpheus, Pythagoras and other venerable figures, helped to account for the similarity between Platonic doctrines and those of the Old Testament.[99] But Plato had not only followed the Mosaic law, he had foretold the Christian one.[100] All this made Platonism an ideal gateway to Christianity, especially for those intellectuals who so admired pagan antiquity that they could not be convinced by arguments based on faith alone.[101] Aristotelianism, *pace* Thomas Aquinas and George of Trebizond, had been unequal to this formidable task, for on those two crucial issues – the immortality of the soul and the creation of the world – it had failed to provide solid philosophical support for Christian dogma. One had therefore to turn instead to Platonism.

Early humanists like Bruni had looked primarily to the *Phaedo* for Plato's demonstration of immortality. So too did Ficino, but he found further proof in the *Phaedrus* (245C–246A), where Plato puts forward the thesis that the soul, as the self-moving principle of motion, moves and hence lives perpetually.[102] The centrality of this issue for Ficino's synthesis of Platonism and Christianity can be seen in his major philosophical treatise, *Theologia platonica de animorum immortalitate*, 'The Platonic Theology of the Immortality of Souls'. Maintaining that in order to accomplish the goal of our existence as human beings, which is the eternal contemplation of God, our souls must be immortal, he produced fifteen different philosophical arguments which established conclusively, on the basis of reason rather than Christian dogma, that the soul survives the body.[103] Ficino's primary philosophical authorities were Plato and the Neoplatonists, but he believed that Aristotle too had supported the doctrine of immortality, although in a vague and confused manner. Ficino had been persuaded by Themistius and other ancient Greek commentators on Aristotle, as well as by

Bessarion, that the two philosophers were in essential agreement in most areas.[104] Aristotle's ambiguous presentation of this doctrine, how-ever, had given rise to two erroneous interpretations, both 'wholly destructive of religion': Alexander of Aphrodisias's belief that the soul was mortal and Averroes's contention that there was only one rational soul for all mankind.[105] The best way to combat these pernicious opinions was to go back to the pristine Platonic source from which Aristotle's muddled teachings derived.

No such reconciliation of Plato and Aristotle was possible on the issue of creation, since Aristotle had declared the world to be eternal, while Plato had produced in his *Timaeus* a Greek counterpart to the Book of Genesis. Yet although Plato's description of creation was in agreement with the Mosaic account, Ficino questioned its congruence with Christian theology.[106] Recognizing that Plato, as a pagan living long before Christ, was necessarily denied access to mysteries such as the Trinity, Ficino was careful to keep sight of the fact that Plato was not a Christian and that he himself was one.[107]

The revival of Platonism which Petrarch had wished for in the mid-fourteenth century was brought to completion by Ficino at the end of the fifteenth. All the dialogues were now available in reliable Latin translations, as were the major works of the Neoplatonists. A systematic framework of interpretation, closely linked to Christianity but clearly distinguishable from it, had also been established. Platonism had been put on an entirely new and much surer footing. But despite the efforts of its adherents, it had not displaced Aristotelianism, which would continue to be at the centre of Italian Renaissance philosophy for another century.

❧ THE ARISTOTELIAN MAINSTREAM ❧

During the fifteenth century the traditional separation of reason and faith had begun to break down as philosophical arguments were increas-ingly used to confirm religious doctrines, above all the immortality of the soul. Ficino, as we have seen, had employed Platonism as a source of rational support for the Christian belief that individual souls were immortal. Even scholastics like Paul of Venice and Nicoletto Vernia had taken the view – in Vernia's case under pressure from the Church – that personal immortality was demonstrable in philosophical terms. The culmination of this trend was the Fifth Lateran Council's decree of 1513, which compelled professors of philosophy to present philo-sophical demonstrations of the Christian position on immortality. The decree meant that it would no longer be permissible to have recourse to the double-truth doctrine in order to discuss the issue on strictly philosophical grounds, independent of theological criteria.

This deliberate attempt by the Council to restrict philosophy's claims to operate autonomously within its own intellectual sphere was soon challenged by Pietro Pomponazzi (1462–1525), a student of Vernia who succeeded him as the leading natural philosopher at Padua, before transferring in 1512 to Bologna. Throughout his career Pomponazzi lectured and wrote on Aristotelian texts in the time-honoured scholastic fashion: addressing the standard questions, reviewing the opinions of previous commentators and employing the philosophical terminology established during the Middle Ages. Though he was in no sense a humanist himself, he was nevertheless influenced, like Vernia, by the humanist approach to Aristotelianism, particularly by the new avail-ability of the Greek commentators on Aristotle, whom he regarded not as replacements for medieval authorities but rather as further reserves in the arsenal of Aristotelian interpretations on which philosophers could freely draw.[108]

In his early Paduan lectures on *De anima*, Pomponazzi rejected Alexander of Aphrodisias's materialist and mortalist view of the soul. According to Aristotle (I.1), the crucial question in relation to immor-tality was whether the soul needed the body for all its operations. Pomponazzi accepted the answer given by Thomas Aquinas, who admitted that the body was necessary as the soul's object but not as its subject, thereby preserving the soul's immateriality and immortality. Alexander's belief that the soul was the material form of the body had the additional failing of being unable to account for the intellect's capacity to understand immaterial universals. The Averroist thesis, which in these years Pomponazzi regarded as the authentic interpre-tation of Aristotle, was able to explain the comprehension of universals, but at the unacceptable cost of severing the essential unity of body and soul, since the single immortal intellect for all mankind merely guided the activities of individual bodies rather than serving as their substantial form. Pomponazzi never questioned the truth of the Christian belief in personal immortality, but he remained undecided for many years as to the correct position on purely philosophical grounds.[109]

The breakthrough came during a series of lectures on *De caelo* which he gave at Bologna in 1515–16. In discussing the eternity of the world (I.10), Aristotle establishes an indissoluble link between gener-ation and corruption. Pomponazzi realized that, following this prin-ciple, if the soul was immortal it did not have a beginning in time; and if it did have a beginning, it was not immortal. Following Duns Scotus, Pomponazzi now recognized that since Aristotle believed the soul to be generated, he could not have regarded it as immortal.[110] Conse-quently, it was Alexander, not Averroes, who offered the most accurate interpretation of Aristotle and the most satisfactory answer, in terms of philosophy, to the question of immortality. More importantly, since neither this answer nor the Averroist one bolstered the Christian position, as the Lateran decree demanded, it was essential to defy the Council's pronouncement, reasserting philosophy's right to treat philosophical issues philosophically, without theological constraints.

This is precisely what Pomponazzi did in *De immortalitate animae* (1516), which is an attempt to resolve the problem of immortality, remaining entirely within natural limits and leaving all religious considerations aside. Pomponazzi now maintained, against Thomas, that the body was necessary for all the soul's operations, because thought, for Aristotle, always requires the images provided by the imagination from the raw material of sense data. Therefore, based solely on philosophical premises and Aristotelian principles, the probable conclusion was that the soul was essentially mortal, although immortal in the limited sense of participating in the immaterial realm through the comprehension of universals.[111] Despite this, Pomponazzi claimed that his belief in the absolute truth of the Christian doctrine of personal immortality remained unshaken, 'since the canonical Scripture, which must be preferred to any human reasoning and experience whatever, as it was given by God, sanctions this position'. In 'neutral problems' such as immortality and the eternity of the world, natural reasoning could not go beyond probabilities; certainty in such matters lay only with God.[112] Nevertheless Pomponazzi's treatise made the point that, however provisional their conclusions, philosophers must be allowed to pursue them without external interference – wherever they might lead.

Since the thirteenth century theologians had looked to Aristotle for philosophical support of the Christian doctrine on the soul. Pomponazzi was effectively ruling out this role. The theologians were quick to fight back, publicly burning the treatise, lobbying the pope to compel Pomponazzi to retract the work and writing, along with philosophers who shared their perspective, a stream of attacks on him. Pomponazzi responded to this onslaught by restating his position that immortality was not rationally demonstrable since it was contrary to natural principles. As an article of faith, it could – and should – only be founded on supernatural revelation.[113] The theologians, for their part, continued to insist that it was possible to demonstrate immortality. But Pomponazzi forced them to shift their ground. No longer did they argue in terms of natural philosophy; instead, discussions of the soul were transferred to the discipline of metaphysics, where theological considerations were allowed to hold sway. Aristotelian natural philosophy, abandoned by the theologians, was left to the natural philosophers, who were much freer to interpret Aristotle as they chose and to develop an autonomous science of nature.[114]

Pomponazzi himself contributed to the development of this science in his *De naturalium effectuum causis sive de incantationibus*, in which he demonstrated that events normally regarded as miraculous could be explained in natural terms. Dismissing the supernatural agency of angels and demons, he argued that the celestial spheres, governed by the Intelligences, were responsible for most so-called miracles.[115] Scholastic natural philosophy, combining Aristotle with Arabic astrology, regarded the stars as secondary causes by means of which God controlled the sublunary realm.[116] The heavens, though mediators of divine action, were part of nature, operating according to constant, regular and predictable laws, which could be studied scientifically. So Pomponazzi's emphasis on astrological causation transformed miracles into natural phenomena, accessible to reason. He did not, however, apply this scientific explanation to all miracles: those in the New Testament were exempted on the grounds that they, unlike other wondrous occurrences, violated the natural order and could therefore only have been brought about by direct divine intervention.[117] As with the immortality of the soul, he conceded that in religious matters the probable hypotheses provided by scientific enquiry were overruled by the absolute truths of Christian revelation. But in the domain of nature, from which he had excluded theological and supernatural explanations, rational criteria constituted the sole authority.

Alongside the scholastic Aristotelianism of Pomponazzi, the humanist variety continued to thrive, even moving into the universities. Pomponazzi's Paduan colleague Niccolò Leonico Tomeo (1456–1531) was the first professor to lecture on the Greek text of Aristotle. As a Venetian of Greek parentage, Leonico Tomeo inherited the mantle of Byzantine scholars such as Gaza and Argyropulos along with that of Italian humanists like Poliziano and Barbaro. He brought, like his predecessors, an increased accuracy and enhanced elegance to an ever wider range of Aristotelian texts. His finely tuned philological skills – good enough to win the admiration of Erasmus – were deployed in translations of the *Parva naturalia, Mechanics* and other scientific works. In his prefaces all the standard humanist complaints about contemporary scholastics were repeated: their inability to understand Aristotle, their barbaric language and their futile search for answers to pointless questions. And in his learned scholia ample space was given to the Greek commentators, whose method of exposition he tried to imitate.[118]

For humanists like Leonico Tomeo the Greek commentators represented a purer and more authentic exegesis of Aristotle than could be found in the scholastic tradition. By the middle of the sixteenth century virtually all the ancient commentaries on Aristotle were in print, both in the original and in Latin translation. Access to these works affected the way that Aristotle was read in a number of ways. Alexander of Aphrodisias's doubts about the second book of the *Metaphysics* set off a long-lived debate (continued in the twentieth century by Werner Jaeger) about its authenticity and correct placement within the corpus. While Alexander's views on the soul decisively influenced Pomponazzi, many in the Averroist camp preferred Simplicius's exposition of *De anima*, which they believed could be used in support of the unity of the intellect. Simplicius, along with Themistius, also provided evidence for the essential harmony of Aristotle and Plato. And Philoponus, by arguing for the existence of a void in nature, gave ammunition to those – Galileo among them – who were challenging the fundamental principles of Aristotelian physics.[119]

The philhellenic bent of humanist Aristotelianism provoked a backlash among scholastic philosophers, who feared that Arabic and medieval expositors were becoming unfashionable as the Greek commentators gained in popularity. In order to remain competitive, they produced up-to-date editions of approved authors such as Thomas Aquinas, replacing the accompanying medieval translations of Aristotle with modern ones, making editorial improvements to the text and providing indexes, cross-references and other scholarly tools.[120] The most elaborate of such enterprises was the eleven-volume Giuntine edition of Aristotle and Averroes (1550–2). Its editors were happy to borrow what they could from the humanists. They adopted the Aristotle translations of Bruni, Bessarion, George of Trebizond and Leonico Tomeo; and they applied philological techniques to Averroes, collating different texts, revising them to enhance readability and including versions recently translated from Hebrew intermediaries. But this edition was designed to strike at the heart of the humanist assumption that the Greeks had a monopoly on philosophical achievement. 'Our age', wrote the publisher Tommaso Giunta, 'worships only the Greeks', while the writings of the Arabs are treated as 'nothing other than dregs and useless dirt'. Giunta and his editorial team set out to counter this prejudice by presenting Averroes as the only Aristotelian commentator worthy of the name and as a substantial philosopher in his own right, one who had developed and refined the material he found in Aristotle.[121]

Progressive Aristotelians in the second half of the sixteenth century took advantage of both the Arabic and Greek traditions. Jacopo Zabarella (1533–89), a professor of logic and natural philosophy at Padua, developed an extremely influential theory of method by drawing in equal measure on Averroes and Simplicius. Certain knowledge, he concluded, could be attained through a demonstrative regression, proceeding first from effect to cause (*resolutio*), and then working back from cause to effect (*compositio*).[122] Zabarella regarded induction, which dealt only with the effects known to the senses, as an inferior form of 'resolutive' or *a posteriori* demonstration, but he recognized that it was essential for disciplines like natural philosophy.[123] Zabarella was himself a great believer in observation, often calling on his experience of meteorological phenomena or his acquaintance with contemporary technological processes to corroborate Aristotelian theories.[124] The best Peripatetic science in this period showed a similar empirical basis: Andrea Cesalpino (1519 – 1603), who revised the Aristotelian taxonomy of plants, made extensive use of the botanical garden at Pisa and even took into account specimens recently brought back from the New World.[125]

Yet even the most advanced Aristotelians did not progress from empiricism to experimentalism. They remained content to observe nature passively in order to confirm established doctrines rather than trying to devise methods of active intervention or validation. They saw their task not as searching out new approaches to the study of nature but as explaining and at best extending the Aristotelian framework within which they operated. This also meant leaving aside matters on which Aristotle had not made explicit pronouncements, such as the immortality of the soul – a problem which Zabarella referred to the theologians.[126]

Territorial disputes between philosophy and theology were not, however, at an end. Zabarella's successor Cesare Cremonini (1550–1631) was attacked by the Inquisition for discussing from a Peripatetic viewpoint the eternity of the world and the absence of divine providence in the sublunary realm. Reiterating the traditional Paduan commitment to a naturalistic exposition of Aristotle, Cremonini replied: 'I have acted as an interpreter of Aristotle, following only his thought.'[127] This statement was a strong reaffirmation of the autonomy of philosophy.[128] But in the context of the early seventeenth century, it also signified that Aristotelian natural science was a spent force, reduced to sterile and pedantic exegesis of set texts. Cremonini, the most eminent (and highly paid) Aristotelian of his day, was a completely bookish philosopher, lacking the interest in direct observation displayed by the previous generation but sharing their unwillingness to question the doctrinal foundation of Aristotelian philosophy. He is best remembered – appropriately, if perhaps apocryphally – as the man who refused to look in Galileo's telescope, preferring to learn about the heavens from the pages of Aristotle's *De caelo*.[129]

❧ ALTERNATIVE PHILOSOPHICAL ❧ CURRENTS

Flowing around the edges of the Aristotelian mainstream were a number of alternative philosophical currents. Not all of them were hostile to Aristotelianism – though most were – but each challenged the prevailing Peripatetic orthodoxy by putting forward a new model of philosophical enquiry.

Complaints about the impenetrable jargon of scholastic logic were commonplace among humanists, but few critics were as incisive as Lorenzo Valla (1407–57). Believing that the limits of allowable discourse were fixed by the usage of the best classical authors, Valla banned virtually the entire logical and metaphysical vocabulary of scholasticism. Not satisfied with assaulting medieval and Renaissance Aristotelianism, he attacked Aristotle himself, rejecting his basic terminology (e.g. potentiality and actuality) and reducing his ten categories to only three (substance, quality and action). Even more radical was Valla's refusal to consider logic as an independent discipline, treating it instead as a part of rhetoric, on the grounds that the logician's repertoire was limited to the syllogism, while the orator could draw on the full range of argumentative strategies, both necessary and probable, both demonstrative and persuasive. Moreover, orators, who needed to be understood by their audiences, respected the common manner of speech of learned men (by which Valla meant good classical Latin), whereas logicians created their own language, which was meaningless to non-specialists. This subordination of logic to rhetoric entailed a drastic lowering of Aristotle's authority and a concomitant rise in the prestige of Cicero and Quintilian.[130]

Valla's programme did not find another champion until the mid-sixteenth century.[131] Mario Nizolio (1488–1567), a fanatical Ciceronian, who compiled a Latin lexicon devoted entirely to words used by his hero, was indignant when some of his contemporaries questioned Cicero's competence in philosophical matters. In reply to these 'Cicero-bashers' (*Ciceromastiges*) Nizolio wrote a series of works, culminating in the treatise *De veris principiis et vera ratione philosophandi contra pseudophilosophos* (1553). The 'pseudo-philosophers' of the title were Aristotelian logicians and metaphysicians, whose false, obscure and useless disciplines he wanted to replace with a 'true method of philosophizing', one which combined Ciceronian rhetoric, Latin grammar and philological expertise. Nizolio cited Valla's attacks on Aristotelianism with approval and shared his humanist contempt for scholastic terminology as well as his desire to demote logic to a mere subdivision of rhetoric. But Valla had not gone far enough, merely cutting off the foliage and branches of Aristotelian philosophy while leaving its trunk and roots intact.[132] To eradicate it completely Nizolio employed a thorough-going nominalism, dismissing Platonic ideas as harmless poetic fictions, but arguing forcefully against the reality of Aristotelian universals, which he regarded as the pillars of scholastic logic and metaphysics. Through philological and philosophical analysis, he demonstrated that universals were simply collective names given to concrete particulars belonging to the same class.[133] The treatise, which had little impact in the sixteenth century, was reissued in 1670 by Leibniz, who was interested in Nizolio's nominalism and in his attempt to produce a linguistic reform of logic. Leibniz, however, pointed out a number of errors committed by Nizolio, not least his failure to appreciate Aristotle's real merits.[134]

He also criticized Nizolio's claim that there were serious doubts about the authenticity of the works attributed to Aristotle. This line of attack had appealed to Nizolio because it made Aristotelians appear foolish as well as servile by suggesting that the *ipse* of their revered *ipse dixit* was not the genuine Aristotle.[135] The evidence for his assertion was borrowed, with acknowledgement, from Gianfrancesco Pico della Mirandola (1469–1533), a follower of Savonarola, who had learned from him to distrust all human learning and to rely solely on the divine philosophy of the Scriptures. In his *Examen vanitatis doctrinae gentium et veritatis Christianae disciplinae* (1520), Gianfrancesco set out to prove the futility of pagan doctrine and the truth of Christianity. The first half of the work employs arguments from the ancient Greek sceptic Sextus Empiricus – virtually unknown in the West – to discredit secular knowledge by showing that on every conceivable issue scholars have disagreed with one another and adhered to incompatible views. The second half targets Aristotle, by far the most influential pagan thinker and therefore the most important to subvert. Displaying immense erudition about the Aristotelian tradition, particularly the Greek commentators, Gianfrancesco revealed that all facets of Peripatetic philosophy lacked certitude: the works assigned to Aristotle were doubtfully authentic; his sense-based epistemology could not produce reliable data; his doctrines, often presented with deliberate obscurity, had been disputed by opponents and followers alike and had been criticized by Christian theologians; even Aristotle himself was uncertain about some of them.[136] Aristotelian philosophy, the pinnacle of human wisdom, was therefore shown to be constructed on the shakiest of foundations. Christian dogma, by contrast, was built on the bedrock of divine authority and therefore could not be undermined by the sceptical critique. Or so he believed, unaware that scepticism, which he had revived as an ally of Christianity, would eventually become a powerful weapon in the hands of its enemies.[137]

By stressing the dissension among competing philosophical

schools and their fundamental irreconcilability with each other and with Christianity, Gianfrancesco was intentionally deviating from the path set out by his famous uncle Giovanni Pico.[138] Giovanni, the literal and metaphorical 'prince of concord' – he was the hereditary ruler of Concordia and Mirandola – devoted his brief life to demonstrating that, although different philosophical and religious systems appeared to be in conflict, their disagreements were primarily a matter of words, which disguised an underlying unity. The centrepiece of his project was an attempt to reconcile the philosophies of Plato and Aristotle, partially realized in his *De ente et uno*, a treatise which managed to antagonize both Platonists and Aristotelians.[139] Another part of his synthesis involved bridging the gap between the humanist and scholastic approaches to Aristotle. Differing from his friends Poliziano and Barbaro, Pico's interest in the Greek commentators did not prevent him from paying equal attention to scholastic thinkers such as Thomas Aquinas and Duns Scotus – whom, characteristically, he wanted to reconcile – nor from studying the works of Averroes and commissioning translations of those extant only in Hebrew.[140] With help from Jewish scholars, he also acquired enough knowledge of Cabbala, a mystical theology purporting to derive from Moses, to apply its hermeneutic techniques to the first verses of Genesis.[141]

Pico believed that each of these traditions – Greek, Latin, Arabic and Hebrew – despite apparent discrepancies, was an incomplete manifestation of a single truth, whose fullest revelation was to be found in Christianity.[142] The real objective of his syncretism was the confirmation of Christian dogma,[143] although he scrupulously denied that profound mysteries such as the Trinity had any true parallels outside the Church.[144] For Ficino it was Platonism, supplemented by the ancient theology, which provided the philosophical justification of religious beliefs.[145] Pico had a much grander design: to prove that every genuine form of wisdom was a witness to some aspect of the ultimate truth embodied in Christianity.[146] Since there was no room in this scheme for a double truth, doctrines which conflicted with the demands of faith (the attribution of miracles to the power of the stars, the eternity of the world and the mortality of the soul) were excluded as the products of false philosophy and pseudo-science.[147]

Pico's Christian syncretism exerted a formative influence on Francesco Giorgi (1460–1540), a Franciscan theologian, whose *De harmonia mundi* (1525) used the metaphor of musical harmony to express the universal concord of ideas.[148] Giorgi found prefigurations of Christianity wherever he looked and was far less discriminating than Pico in registering the differences between Christian and non-Christian doctrines. He also departed from Pico in his hostility to Aristotelianism, especially the Averroist variety, favouring a more Ficinian synthesis in which Neoplatonic philosophers were combined with Hermes Trismegistus, Zoroaster and other putative ancient theologians.[149] To this mixture he added an interest in the Christian application of Cabbala, which was more enthusiastic – though less informed – than Pico's.[150]

Pico's concordism was also the inspiration behind *De perenni philosophia* (1540), in which Agostino Steuco (1497/8–1548) presented a learned account of the 'perennial philosophy', a divinely revealed wisdom known to mankind since earliest times. Steuco was an Augustinian biblical scholar, bishop and prefect of the Vatican Library,[151] with a solid knowledge of Hebrew and Aramaic along with Greek and Latin. Using the Old Testament – but not Cabbala, which he scorned – and the (spurious) works of ancient theologians, he showed that Jews, Chaldeans, Egyptians and other early peoples had transmitted to the Greeks a body of doctrines which, beneath a diversity of forms, contained the same truths. These included the existence of a triune God, the creation of the world and the immortality of the human soul.[152] Christianity's advent had not brought new truths, as Pico believed, but had simply renewed the knowledge of old ones, which had been corrupted in transmission. Even though Steuco shared Giorgi's predilection for Neoplatonic authors, he did not exclude Aristotle from the perennial philosophy. His Aristotle, however, was the author of *De mundo* and other misattributed works, containing hints – amplified by Steuco – of belief in divine providence and immortality, though not, alas, in creation.[153] Despite (or more likely because of) having studied in Bologna during Pomponazzi's final years there, he distanced himself from scholastic Aristotelianism and strongly opposed the notion that philosophical truth was independent of theology. For Steuco, reason and revelation, which both flowed from God, necessarily led to the same conclusions.[154]

Ficino's Christianized Neoplatonism, although a key element in the syncretism of thinkers like Giorgi and Steuco, did not gain much support as an independent philosophical system. The only aspect which excited general interest was the theory of love elaborated by Ficino in his *Symposium* commentary, a theory which became so popular that it dominated the public perception of Platonism throughout the sixteenth century and beyond.[155] Even Francesco da Diacceto (1466–1522), Ficino's Florentine successor, concentrated on the issues of love and beauty, investing them, however, with a metaphysical and theological significance absent in the stylized, literary treatments that proliferated throughout Italy. Beauty, for Diacceto as for Ficino, was a divine emanation, which inspired the human soul with a celestial love that fuelled its spiritual ascent and guided it to an ecstatic union with the One.[156] As a philosophy professor at the University of Pisa, Diacceto was constrained to lecture on Aristotle; but he took every opportunity to defend Plato against Aristotle's attacks and attempted to establish a concord of the two philosophers which, in deliberate contrast to Pico's, squeezed Aristotle into a Platonic mould.[157]

Not until 1576 did Platonism enter the curriculum at Pisa. Even then it was merely an ancillary subject assigned to a professor whose main job was to lecture on Aristotle.[158] Professorships specifically devoted to Platonism were established in the universities of Ferrara (1578) and Rome (1592), but both were essentially *ad hominem* chairs created for Francesco Patrizi da Cherso (1529–97). An encounter with Ficino's *Theologia platonica* had converted Patrizi, then studying medicine at Padua, into a fervent Platonist, committed to overthrowing the Aristotelian monopoly of the universities.[159] The first stage in this crusade was the demolition of Aristotelianism. Combining superb humanist erudition with unflagging polemical energy, he accused Aristotle of both plagiarizing and misrepresenting earlier philosophers; questioned – like Nizolio and Gianfrancesco Pico – the authenticity of the Aristotelian corpus; and challenged the philosophical competence of ancient, medieval and Renaissance Peripatetics.[160] His most damning charge against Aristotelianism, however, was the same as that made by Petrarch two centuries earlier: its fundamental incompatibility with Christianity. Addressing Pope Gregory XIV, Patrizi pointed out the absurdity of teaching a philosophy so manifestly detrimental to religion in universities throughout Europe and of using its impious tenets as the philosophical foundation of Christian theology. In its place he wanted to substitute the pious philosophy set out in his *Nova de universis philosophia* (1591), which was entirely consonant with Catholicism and which was capable of providing such strong rational proofs of dogmatic beliefs that not only Jews and Muslims but even Lutherans would be won over.[161]

What Patrizi offered the Pope was a Ficinian amalgam of Platonism, Neoplatonism and Christianity, with particular emphasis given to the ancient theology. By the late sixteenth century the genuineness of texts like the Hermetic corpus was beginning to be doubted. But Patrizi, who had read his Steuco, clung to a belief in them as documents of a primitive, divinely inspired wisdom, which had prefigured Christianity and formed the core of Platonism before being crushed by the weight of Aristotelian rationalism.[162] In only one treatise had Aristotle incorporated material from this ancient tradition: the *Theology* (actually a ninth-century Arabic reworking of Plotinus's *Enneads* that had come to be attributed to Aristotle) which, according to Patrizi, was a record of his notes on Plato's lectures concerning Egyptian religion. For Patrizi, as for Steuco, it was pseudonymous works such as this, containing uncharacteristic affirmations of divine providence and immortality, which represented the acceptable face of Aristotelianism.[163] The

Theology was therefore included, along with the works of Hermes, Zoroaster, Plato and the Neoplatonists, in the new canon of godly philosophy which Patrizi hoped would replace the ungodly Aristotelian one.[164] The Roman Inquisitors, evidently unconvinced by Patrizi's claims, placed the *Nova philosophia* on the Index – a fate which had earlier befallen Giorgi's *De harmonia mundi*.[165] These authors, attempting to protect Christianity from the impieties of Aristotelianism, discovered that the Church was not prepared to abandon its long alliance with Peripatetic philosophy.

Patrizi's 'new philosophy', aiming to be as comprehensive as the Aristotelian system it was designed to supplant, was basically Neoplatonic. The cosmos consisted of a hierarchical series of nine levels of being, all emanating ultimately from the One. Patrizi's One was not, like Aristotle's Unmoved Mover, the final cause of motion, but rather the efficient cause of light, which he regarded as one of the four fundamental principles of the physical world, the others being heat, space and fluid or flux (*fluor*).[166] In substituting these building-blocks for those of Aristotle (fire, air, water and earth), Patrizi was working along similar lines to another anti-Aristotelian philosopher, Bernardino Telesio (1509–88). In his *De rerum natura iuxta propria principia* (1565–86), a treatise which Patrizi knew well, Telesio too postulated heat as one of the principles of nature, although the other elements in his tripartite scheme were cold and matter.[167] Telesio's philosophy was also presented as an alternative to Aristotelianism – and also ended up on the Index. But he rejected Platonic as well as Aristotelian metaphysics, grounding his system on an extreme form of empiricism, which maintained that nature could only be understood through sensation and observation – a manifesto which would earn him the qualified praise of Francis Bacon.[168]

Coming from very different directions, Telesio and Patrizi both attacked many of the same weaknesses in the Peripatetic structure, especially Aristotle's concept of space or place as an attribute of body and his denial of the existence of a void in nature. Telesio, appealing to the evidence of the senses, argued that space could indeed exist without bodies and that empty space was therefore possible.[169] Patrizi, building on statements in Plato's *Timaeus* (49A, 52B), regarded space as prior to all bodies, an empty receptacle which, although incorporeal, was an extended, dimensional entity.[170] These views of Patrizi were taken up in the seventeenth century by Pierre Gassendi, whose atomist physics required precisely this sort of vacuist conception of space.[171] Patrizi also maintained, against Aristotle, that there was an infinite stretch of empty space beyond the outermost sphere of the heavens. Below the heavens, however, his cosmos was the traditional Ptolemaic-

Aristotelian one: finite and closed, with the earth – despite Copernicus – at its centre.[172]

A more radical cosmology was proposed by Giordano Bruno (1548–1600), who not merely accepted Copernican heliocentrism but expanded it by making our solar system only one of an infinite number of worlds which existed within an infinite universe.[173] Bruno did not come to these conclusions on the basis of mathematics, for which he had little respect or talent.[174] Nor did he approve of the scholarly method of Patrizi, which he described as 'soiling pages with the excrement of pedantry'. And while Telesio had 'fought an honourable battle' against Aristotle, his empirical epistemology was unable to grasp essential notions like infinity, which were imperceptible to the senses.[175] Bruno looked instead to the cosmological poetry of Lucretius, the metaphysical theories of the Neoplatonists and, above all, the theological speculations of Nicholas of Cusa.[176] For Bruno, the infinity of the universe was a reflection of the infinity of its divine creator, although God's infinity was simple and indivisible, while that of the universe consisted of a multiplicity of finite constituent parts. He furthermore maintained that the universe, as the image of God, partook in His eternity, thus giving an entirely new slant to the standard Peripatetic doctrine. In like manner, Bruno – a renegade Dominican monk, thoroughly trained in Peripatetic philosophy – retained much of the accepted metaphysical terminology while dramatically transforming its significance. He still talked of form and matter, actuality and potentiality, but he treated them (as Spinoza would later treat Cartesian thought and extension) as aspects of a single, universal substance, whose accidents were the particular objects which we perceive.[177]

When put on trial by the Inquisition in the 1590s, Bruno stated that he pursued philosophical ideas 'according to the light of nature', without regard to any principles prescribed by faith.[178] This was as clear a statement of the autonomy of philosophy as any made by the scholastic Aristotelians that he despised. Unlike them, however, he did not believe in a double truth. There was only one truth for Bruno; but it was not the single truth of faith upheld by non-Aristotelian thinkers from Petrarch to Patrizi. While they were aiming for a pious philosophy, Bruno sought a philosophical piety: a rationalistic and naturalistic religion, patterned on that of ancient Egypt, as portrayed in the Hermetic corpus; a religion which left behind Christian superstitions, such as transubstantiation and the virgin birth, and adopted in their place beliefs and values that reflected the cosmological, physical and metaphysical principles which he had uncovered.[179] Bruno was not simply defending the rights of reason, he was usurping those of faith; and it was this, far more than his espousal of Copernicanism or the

49

infinite universe, which led the Church to burn him at the stake on 17 February 1600.[180]

Some of Bruno's ideas had a limited influence after his execution, but his philosophy never gained a wide following.[181] Nor did that of other sixteenth-century opponents of Aristotelianism, although individual doctrines gained the approval of later thinkers. The critiques of Peripatetic philosophy formulated in the late Italian Renaissance undoubtedly helped to weaken it, but it was the scientific and epistemological revolutions of the seventeenth century which delivered the death blow.

❧ NOTES ❧

1 Pietro d'Abano (c. 1250–1316) noted that this outlook had been endorsed by Albertus Magnus: Pietro d'Abano [1.29], diff. IX, propter 3; see also Paschetto [1.40].

2 E.g. Blasius of Parma (Biagio Pelacani, c. 1365–1416): see Blasius of Parma [1.22], I.8, and also Federici Vescovini [1.33].

3 Pietro d'Abano [1.29], diff. IX, propter 3; Blasius of Parma [1.22], 58. See Aristotle, De caelo I.10 and Physics VIII.

4 Blasius of Parma [1.22], 71; see also Federici Vescovini [1.33], 395–402; Nardi [1.14], 47–8, 55–8, 71–3.

5 Petrarch [1.25], 21; see also Foster [1.34]; Mann [1.39]; Kristeller [1.11], ch. 1.

6 Petrarch [1.30], 58–9, 76; see also Garin [1.6], 149–50.

7 Petrarch [1.31], vol. 1, 37 (I.7); see also Petrarch [1.27], 52 (Secretum I); Petrarch [1.28], 75.

8 Petrarch [1.25], vol. 3, 213 (XVI.14); Petrarch [1.32], 245–8 (Seniles V.2); see also Garin [1.6], 150–2; Gilbert [1.36], 210–16; Vasoli [1.19], 9–15.

9 Petrarch [1.24], 40, 62, 65; see also Kamp [1.37].

10 Petrarch [1.30], 53; see also Petrarch [1.26], 65 (II.31); Petrarch [1.24], 61.

11 Petrarch [1.26], 65 (II.31); Petrarch [1.24], 67.

12 Petrarch [1.30], 142–3 (Seniles XII.2 and XV.6); Petrarch [1.32], 247 (Seniles V.2); see also Kamp [1.37], 37–9; Kristeller [1.10], vol. 1, 210; Garin [1.6], 147–9.

13 See, for example, Kuksewicz [1.23], 127–46.

14 Petrarch [1.30], 93, 95, 117.

15 Petrarch [1.26], 27–9 (I.25); Petrarch [1.30], 58, 72, 75; Petrarch [1.25], vol. 1, 93 (II.9), vol. 3, 255 (XVII.8); see also Gerosa [1.35]; Kamp [1.37]; Garin [1.6], 269, 277.

16 Petrarch [1.24], 58, 94. On the availability of Plato in Latin see p. 26 below.

17 Petrarch [1.24], 76. On the Greek manuscript see Kristeller [1.12], 57, 153–4.

18 Petrarch [1.24], 66, 78–9; Petrarch [1.26], 31 (I.25); Petrarch [1.28], 662–4; Augustine, De civitate Dei VIII.9–10 and XXII.7, De vera religione III.3, Confessions III.iv.7; see also Foster [1.34], 170; Gerosa [1.35], 246, 252–3.

19 On Bruni see *Dizionario* [1.4], vol. 14, 618–33; Bruni [1.56], 21–42. Aside from Aristotle, Bruni translated works by Plato, Demosthenes, Aeschines, Xenophon and Plutarch.

20 Bertalot [1.57], vol. 2, 132–3; Bruni [1.46], vol. 1, 17 (I.8); see also Cammelli [1.63], vol. 1; Schmitt and Skinner [1.17], 86–7; Schmitt [1.16], 68; Gerl [1.65], 125–6.

21 Bruni [1.46], vol. 2, 88, 216 (VII.4; X.24); Bruni [1.56], 208, 210, 213; Bruni [1.47], 77, 84–6.

22 Bruni [1.56], 68–9 (*Dialogi*); see also Gilbert [1.36], 209; Vasoli [1.19], 26.

23 Garin [1.64], 62–8.

24 Petrarch [1.24], 67; Bruni [1.56], 82, 91, 226, 229; Bruni [1.47], 48, 77; see also Seigel [1.18], ch. 4. Cicero's praise (*Academica* II.xxxviii.119, *De finibus* I.v.14; *Topica* I.3) was based on Aristotle's lost exoteric works, not on the so-called school treatises we now have.

25 See Alonso de Cartagena's *Liber* in Birkenmajer [1.59], 168, 173, 175; Bruni [1.56], 201–6; see also Garin [1.64], 63–4; Schmitt and Skinner [1.17], 79, 90.

26 Bruni [1.56], 45. For the prefaces to his Aristotle translations, see Bruni [1.47], 70–81, 120–1.

27 Bruni [1.56], 59–60, 268; see also Garin [1.6], 151–2; Vasoli [1.19], 23–7; Gilbert [1.36], 205–13.

28 Cammelli [1.63], vol. II; *Dizionario* [1.4], vol. 4, 129–31; Field [1.92], ch. 5; for his inaugural lectures, see Müllner [1.51], 3–56.

29 Argyropulos [1.42]. He translated Aristotle's *Categories*, *De interpretatione*, *Prior* and *Posterior Analytics*, as well as Porphyry's *Isagoge*: see Cammelli [1.63], vol. 2, 183–4; Garin [1.64], 83–5.

30 Müllner [1.51], 43. He translated the *Physics*, *De caelo* and *De anima*: Cammelli [1.63], vol. 2, 183; Garin [1.64], 84–5.

31 Müllner [1.51], 51–2: he describes Alexander's opinion as 'quite false and totally abhorrent', and Averroes's as 'extremely dangerous'; in support of the Christian position, he produced 'some rational arguments based on natural philosophy', as well as those based on 'faith'; see also Garin [1.5], 102–5.

32 Argyropulos [1.43].

33 Acciaiuoli [1.41]; see also Bianchi [1.58]; Field [1.92], ch. 8. He wrote a similar commentary on the *Politics*.

34 George translated the *Physics*, *De anima*, *De generatione et corruptione*, *De caelo*, the zoological works and the *Rhetoric*, as well as the Pseudo-Aristotelian *Problems*: Garin [1.64], 75–81; see also Monfasani [1.103].

35 George of Trebizond [1.49], 142–3, 191, 268; see also Monfasani [1.103], 26, 42, 76–7; Minio-Paluello [1.67], 264–5; Schmitt and Skinner [1.17], 77, 88.

36 George of Trebizond [1.49], 106–7. Gaza retranslated the zoological works and the *Problems*, as well as translating Latin works, such as Cicero's *De senectute*, into Greek; on Gaza see Monfasani in Hankins *et al.* [1.8], 189–219, esp. 207–19; on Bessarion see Mohler [1.102], vol. 1; Garin [1.64], 74–5.

37 In 1452 he was imprisoned for brawling with another humanist in the chancery of the papal Curia: Monfasani [1.103], 109–11.

38 George of Trebizond [1.49], 107, 132–3; George of Trebizond in Mohler [1.102], vol. 3, 277–342 (*Adversus Theodorum Gazam in perversionem Problematum Aristotelis*); see also Monfasani [1.103], 152–4.

39 George of Trebizond in Mohler [1.102], vol. 3, 319 (*Adversus Theodorum Gazam*); George of Trebizond [1.49], 142; see also Monfasani [1.103], 155–6; Garin [1.6], 288–9. He also treated scholastic logicians with respect and drew on their works in his *Isagoge dialectica*.

40 Poliziano [1.53], 303 (*Miscellanea* I.90); see also Garin [1.64], 78–80; *Dizionario* [1.4], vol. 2, 691–702.

41 Poliziano [1.53], 310 (*Miscellanea* I, Coronis), 529–30 (*Praelectio de dialectica*), 502 (*Praefatio in Suetonii expositionem*); see also Klibansky [1.97], 316; Branca [1.61], 13. The *Praelectio de dialectica*, a by-product of Poliziano's teaching, became a standard introduction to Aristotelian logic: Schmitt [1.16], 61.

42 Poliziano [1.54], xiv–xxiii, 18; Poliziano [1.53], 179 (*Epistolae* XII); see also Wolters [1.69].

43 *Dizionario* [1.4], vol. 4, 96–9; Branca [1.60]; Branca [1.61], 13–15. Aside from his Aristotelian work, Barbaro also produced philological commentaries on Pliny's *Natural History* (*Castigationes Plinianae*) and on Dioscorides.

44 Barbaro [1.44] is based on his lectures; see also Kristeller [1.10], vol. 1, 337–53.

45 Barbaro [1.45], vol. 1, 16–17, 92, 104–5 (*Epp.* XII, LXXII, LXXXI), vol. 2, 108 (*Oratio ad discipulos*); see also Garin [1.64], 87–9; Dionisotti in *Medioevo* [1.13], vol. 1, 217–53; Branca [1.62], 131–3.

46 Pico [1.166]; see also Kristeller [1.182], 56–8; Valcke [1.197], 191; Roulier [1.193], 85–6; Branca [1.60], 227–8.

47 Barbaro *Epistolae*, vol. 1, 77–8 (*Ep.* LXI); see also Branca [1.62], 132.

48 See Kretzmann *et al.* [1.38], 74–8; Kristeller [1.10], vol. 1, 341–2 n. 13.

49 Branca [1.62], 131, 166–7; Nardi [1.14], 366–8.

50 Manutius [1.50], vol. 1, 5–7, 13–18, 22–3; see also Minio-Paluello [1.67], 489–93.

51 Cavalli [1.48], a 2^v; Manutius [1.50], vol. 1, 14; see also Schmitt in Poppi [1.68], 287–314.

52 Manutius [1.50], vol. 1, 7, 17; see also p. 40 below.

53 Minio-Paluello [1.67], 489, 496; Mahoney [1.66]; Mahoney in Poppi [1.68], 135–202.

54 Vernia [1.55], 89^v; see also Mahoney [1.126], 169–70; Mahoney in Poppi [1.68], 156; Mahoney [1.66], 149–63; Schmitt and Skinner [1.17], 493–4; Di Napoli [1.3], 181–93. Vernia corresponded with Barbaro: see Barbaro [1.44], vol. 1, 79–80 (*Ep.* LXII).

55 Paul of Venice [1.52], z7^r–8^r; see also Kuksewicz in Olivieri [1.15], vol. 2, 297–324; Schmitt and Skinner [1.17], 490.

56 Klibansky [1.96].

57 Bruni [1.47], 4; translation in Hankins [1.95], vol. 1, p. 50; Bruni [1.46], vol. 1, 15–16 (I.8); see also Garin in *Medioevo* [1.13], vol. 1, 339–74, esp. 361–3; Di Napoli [1.3], 125.

58 Bertalot [1.57], vol. 2, 269.

59 Bruni [1.46], vol. 2, 148 (IX.4); Hankins [1.95], vol. 1, 58–81. For Bruni's second version of the *Crito* (1424–7) see Plato [1.82]; he also translated the *Apology* (1424): see Garin in *Medioevo* [1.13], vol. 1, 365; for his knowledge of the *Cratylus* see Bruni [1.46], vol. 1, 11–12 (I.6).

60 Bruni [1.46], vol. 2, 148 (IX.4), described the translation as very inept; see

also Garin in *Medioevo* [1.13], vol. 1, 341–4; Hankins in Hankins *et al.* [1.8], 149–88, esp. 149–60.

61 Hankins [1.95], vol. 1, 105–54, vol. 2, 548–75; Garin in *Medioevo* [1.13], vol. 1, 347–57. A third version of the *Republic* was undertaken by the Sicilian humanist Antonio Cassarino (d. 1447): Hankins [1.95], vol. 1, 154–60.

62 Hankins in Hankins *et al.* [1.8], 166–76.

63 Kraye [1.98]; Hankins [1.95], vol. 2, 515–23.

64 See, for example, his lectures on the *Ethics* in Müllner [1.51], 15, 20, 22–3; see also Garin [1.5], 119–20; Field [1.92], 107–26.

65 George of Trebizond [1.49], 304; Klibansky [1.97], 289–94; Monfasani [1.103], 18–19, 167; Garin in *Medioevo* [1.13], 372–3.

66 See p. 22 above.

67 George of Trebizond [1.49], 198–202 (Preface), 746–7 (marginal notes); see also Monfasani [1.103], 102–3, 171–2 and appendix 10 (for the original Preface to Nicholas V); Hankins [1.95], vol. 2, appendix 11.

68 Woodhouse [1.105]; Mohler [1.102], vol. 1, 335–40.

69 Plethon [1.84], 321, trans. in Plethon [1.87], 192; see also Woodhouse [1.105], ch. 10.

70 Plethon [1.84], 321–2, 327–8, trans. in Plethon [1.87], 192–3, 198–9; Monfasani [1.103], 157, 205–6.

71 Plethon [1.83], Woodhouse [1.105], ch. 17; Webb [1.104]; Hankins [1.95], vol. 1, 193–208.

72 Plethon [1.83], 64–79 (II.6); Woodhouse [1.105], 332–4. This portion of the treatise circulated independently in the West under the title *De fato* and was translated into Latin for Nicholas of Cusa: Kristeller [1.100].

73 Woodhouse [1.105], chs 13 and 15.

74 George of Trebizond [1.80], V vi^v; see also Monfasani [1.103], 39.

75 George of Trebizond [1.80], D ii^r–Niii^r; see also Hankins [1.95], vol. 2, appendix 14; Monfasani [1.103], 157; Labowsky [1.101], 175–6.

76 George of Trebizond [1.80], T v^r–X ii^v; Monfasani [1.103], 159; Garin [1.6], 290–2.

77 Monfasani [1.103], 179–94; for his earlier spell in jail see note 37 above.

78 Gaza [1.79]; for his *Adversus Plethonem de substantia* see Mohler [1.102], vol. 3, 153–8.

79 Labowsky [1.101], 180, 194; see also p. 23. Argyropulos also wrote a refutation of the *Comparatio*, which is now lost: Monfasani [1.103], 212, 228.

80 Labowsky [1.101], 180–4, 194–7.

81 Labowsky [1.101], 180, 194. Bessarion's critique of George's translation occurs in Book V, which is not printed in the edition of Bessarion's treatise in Mohler [1.102], vol. 2; see Hankins [1.95], vol. 1, 191; Garin [1.6], 287.

82 Bessarion in Mohler [1.102], vol. 2, 72–3 (I.7), 90–3 (II.4), 154–5 (II.9), 410–13 (III.28); see also Hankins [1.95], vol. 1, 246–7; Monfasani [1.103], 219–20.

83 Bessarion in Mohler [1.102], vol. 2, 3 (I.1), 102–3, 109 (II.5), 282–95 (III.15).

84 Bessarion in Mohler [1.102], vol. 2, 161–3 (II.8), 443–59 (IV.2), 467 (IV.2); see also Hankins [1.95], vol. 1, 255–9, vol. 2, appendix 13.

85 Ficino's letter is published in Mohler [1.102], vol. 3, 544–5, as are the letters of Argyropulos (545–6) and Filelfo (599–600). On Ficino see Kristeller [1.99];

Kristeller [1.11], ch. 4; Kristeller in Garfagnini [1.93], vol. 1, 15–196; Copenhaver and Schmitt [1.2], 143–63.

86 Ficino [1.70], vol. 2, 1304, 1427, 1438, 1484; see also Hankins [1.95], vol. 1, 312–14, 345, 358, 361.

87 Hankins [1.95], vol. 1, 310–12, vol. 2, appendix 18A.

88 Landino [1.81], Books III and IV; see also Field [1.92], ch. 9.

89 Ficino [1.72], 176–7 (I.100); Ficino [1.70], vol. 2, 1300–3 (*In Euthydemum epitome*).

90 Kristeller [1.10], vol. 1, 35–97. The major exception is his exposition of the *Symposium* (Ficino [1.73], trans. in Ficino [1.85], where he adopted a dialogue format and gave more than usual care to literary elegance. It was also the one commentary which Ficino himself translated into Italian.

91 Ficino [1.78]; see also Copenhaver [1.91]. Ficino's attitude towards astrology fluctuated considerably: see, for example, his attack on judicial astrology: Ficino [1.71], vol. 2, 11–76 (*Disputatio contra iudicium astrologorum*); see also the articles by Walker and Kaske in Garfagnini [1.93], vol. 2, 341–9, 371–81.

92 Ficino [1.75], 35–48, 368–83 (I.37); he later moved to a more voluntarist position: see Ficino [1.72], 201–10 (I.115), trans. in Ficino [1.86], vol. 1, 171–8.

93 For his Plotinus commentary, first published in 1492, see Ficino [1.70], vol. 2, 1537–1800; see also Wolters [1.69]; Gentile [1.94], 70–104.

94 Ficino [1.70], 1154 (*In Parmenidem*): see also Allen [1.88].

95 Pico [1.155], 386–9 (Prooemium), 390–6 (cap. II), trans. in Pico [1.165], 37–8, 38–41; see also Allen in Garfagnini [1.93], vol. 2, 417–55; Schmitt and Skinner [1.17], 582–4; Klibansky [1.97], 318–25; Garin [1.175], 75–82; Valcke [1.197], 221–3; Roulier [1.193], 96–7.

96 Ficino [1.77], esp. chs 32–5.

97 Ficino [1.74], vol. 1, 36 (prohemium); Ficino [1.70], vol. 1, 1–2 (*De christiana religione*), 853–4, 871; see also Vasoli [1.20], 19–73.

98 Ficino [1.70], vol. 1, 774, 866, 956. For an earlier use of this argument see Bruni [1.47], 4, 136; Bertalot [1.57], vol. 2, 269. For Numenius, see Eusebius, *Praeparatio evangelica* II.10.14 and Clement of Alexandria, *Stromateis* I.22.150.

99 Ficino [1.70], vol. 1, 156, 268, 386, 854, 871, vol. 2, 1537, 1836; see also Walker [1.21]; Allen in Henry and Hutton [1.9], 38–47; Schmitt [1.195], 507–11; Gentile [1.94], 57–70.

100 See his letter to Prenninger in Klibansky [1.96], 45; Ficino [1.70], vol. 1, 899 (*Ep.* IX).

101 Ficino [1.74], vol. 1, 36 (I.1), vol. 2, 283 (XIV.10); Ficino [1.70], vol. 1, 855 (*Ep.* VII).

102 Ficino [1.70], vol. 2, 1390–5 (*In Phaedonem epitome*); Ficino [1.76], chs 5–6; see also Allen [1.89], ch. 3.

103 Ficino [1.74], vol. 1, 174–222 (V); see also Kristeller [1.99], ch. 15; Di Napoli [1.3], ch. 3.

104 Ficino [1.70], vol. II, 1801 (*Expositio in interpretationem Prisciani Lydi super Theophrastum*).

105 Ficino [1.70], vol. 1, 872 (*Ep.* VIII), vol. 2, 1537 (*In Plotinum*).

106 Ficino [1.70], vol. 2, 1442, 1449, 1463 (*In Timaeum commentarium*); see also Allen in Hankins et al. [1.8], 399–439.

107 Ficino [1.70], vol. 1, 956, vol. 2, 1533 (*Argumentum in sextam epistolam*

Platonis); see also Allen [1.90]; but see Pico's criticism of Ficino in note 144 below.

108 Kristeller in Olivieri [1.15], vol. 2, 1077–99, esp. 1080–4; Kristeller [1.11], ch. 5.

109 Pomponazzi [1.114]; Pomponazzi [1.115]; see also Nardi [1.127], ch. 4; Di Napoli [1.3], 229–34.

110 Nardi [1.127], 197–9; Di Napoli [1.3], 235–8; Olivieri [1.128], 69–76.

111 Pomponazzi [1.112], 36–7, 82–137; see also Aristotle, *De anima* I.1, III.7; Di Napoli [1.3], 245–64; Olivieri [1.128], 76–84.

112 Pomponazzi [1.119], 302, 377; Pomponazzi [1.112], 82, 232; see also Pine [1.129], 109–12.

113 Pomponazzi [1.110], 52–75 (*Apologia*), 81–108 (*Defensorium*); see also Di Napoli [1.3], 265–75; Schmitt and Skinner [1.17], 504–7.

114 Schmitt and Skinner [1.17], 602–5; Lohr [1.125].

115 Pomponazzi [1.111], 198; see also Pine [1.129], 235–53; Schmitt and Skinner [1.17], 273. The treatise, written *c.* 1520, was published posthumously in 1556; it was the only work by Pomponazzi to be put on the Index.

116 The astrological determinism postulated by Pomponazzi in *De incantationibus* was reiterated in Books I and II of his *De fato* (Pomponazzi [1.113], in which he attempts to refute Alexander of Aphrodisias's defence of contingency.

117 Pomponazzi [1.111], 315; see also Pine [1.129], 256–8; Kristeller in Olivieri [1.15], vol. 2, 1093–6.

118 De Bellis [1.122]; Branca [1.60], 225.

119 Schmitt [1.134]; Kraye [1.124]; Cranz [1.120]; Nardi [1.14], 365–442; Mahoney [1.126]; Schmitt [1.135].

120 Cranz [1.121].

121 Aristotle [1.106], vol. 1, AA II 2^v–3^r; see also Schmitt [1.132]; Minio-Paluello [1.67], 498–500.

122 Zabarella [1.117], 178–9 (*De methodis* III.18); see also Gilbert [1.7], ch. 7; Poppi [1.130], ch. 6.

123 Zabarella [1.117], 180–1 (*De methodis* III.19); see also Schmitt and Skinner [1.17], 689–93.

124 Zabarella [1.118], 69, 541–56, 1056, 1067, 1069; see also Schmitt [1.131]; Poppi [1.130], ch. 7.

125 Cesalpino [1.108]; his treatise on minerals and metals, *De metallicis* (1596), also makes use of observational material.

126 Zabarella [1.118], 1004 (*De speciebus intelligibilibus* 8); see also Schmitt and Skinner [1.17], 530–4.

127 Cremonini [1.109], † 3^r; see also Schmitt [1.133], 15; Schmitt [1.16], 101–12, 33, 138; *Dizionario* [1.4], vol. 30, 618–22.

128 Another late Aristotelian, Francesco Buonamici (1533–1603), one of Galileo's teachers at the University of Pisa, was equally insistent on the separation of philosophy and religion: Buonamici [1.107], 810; see also Helbing [1.123], 65.

129 Viviani [1.116], 610; see also Schmitt [1.133], 14; Kessler in Henry and Hutton [1.9], 137–47, esp. 141; Lohr [1.125], 99.

130 Valla [1.159], vol. 1, 1–8 (I, proemium), 128–9 (I.16), 148 (I.17), 175–6 (II, proemium), 277–8 (III, proemium); see also Camporeale [1.171]; Seigel [1.18], ch. 5; Vasoli [1.19], 28–77; Monfasani [1.185], 181–5; Copenhaver and Schmitt

[1.2], 209–27; Kristeller [1.11], ch. 2. For Valla's critique of Aristotelian moral philosophy see Schmitt and Skinner [1.17], 335, 340–1.

131 His *Repastinatio* had only limited manuscript diffusion and was not printed until 1496–1500.

132 Nizolio [1.146], vol. 1, 21–31 (I.1), 34–5 (I.2), vol. 2, 52, 62 (III.5), 92 (III.8), 140 (IV.2); see also Monfasani [1.185], 192; Vasoli [1.19], 606–13.

133 Nizolio [1.146], vol. 1, 29 (I.1), 52 (I.4), 59–68 (I.6), 89–96 (I.8), 112 (I.10); see also Rossi [1.192]; Wesseler [1.202].

134 Leibniz [1.144], 398–476.

135 Leibniz [1.144], 429–30; Nizolio [1.146], vol. 2, 165–77 (IV.6).

136 Pico [1.151], 1011–1264 (IV–VI); see also Schmitt [1.194]; Siraisi in Henry and Hutton [1.9], 214–29, esp. 217–21.

137 Pico [1.151], 853 (II.20), 913 (II.37), 1007 (III.14), 1029 (IV.3); see also Popkin [1.189], ch. 11.

138 Pico [1.151], 738 (I.2), 1026 (IV.2); see also Schmitt [1.194], 47–8, 62.

139 Pico [1.155], 385–441 (*De ente*), trans. in Pico [1.165], 24–5, 37–62; see also p. 35 above. For his announcement of the project in 1486 see Pico [1.154], 54: 'There is no natural or divine enquiry in which Aristotle and Plato, for all their apparent verbal disagreement, do not in reality agree.' For an earlier attempt to establish a concord of Plato and Aristotle see Bessarion in Mohler [1.102], vol. 2, 411–13 (III.28).

140 Pico [1.154], 34–5 (for his Averroist theses), 54 (for the concord of Thomas and Duns Scotus); Pico [1.155], 144–6 (*Oratio*); see also Nardi [1.14], 127–46.

141 Pico [1.155], 167–383 (*Heptaplus*), trans. in Pico [1.165], 65–174; see also Wirszubski [1.204].

142 See his letter to Aldus Manutius (11 February 1490) in Pico [1.152], 359: 'Philosophy seeks the truth, theology finds it and religion possesses it'.

143 See, for example, Pico [1.154], 83–90, where he puts forward Cabbalistic theses that 'confirm Christianity'; see also Pico [1.155], 160–1 (*Oratio*), 246–8 (*Heptaplus*, III, proemium); Pico [1.152], 124 (*Apologia*).

144 Pico [1.155], 466–7 (*Commento* 1.5); he also pointed out important differences between the Christian and Platonic accounts of the angelic intelligence and criticized Ficino for attributing to the Platonists the Christian doctrine of God's direct creation of individual souls: ibid., 464–6 (I.3–4).

145 On the ancient theology see p. 36. Pico shared Ficino's interests: see Pico [1.154], 41–50, for theses taken from Neoplatonists and ancient theologians.

146 Roulier [1.193], ch. 2; Valcke [1.197]; Garin [1.175], 73–89; Kristeller [1.182]; Schmitt [1.195], 511–13.

147 Pico [1.153], vol. 1, 126–37 (II.5), vol. 2, 474 (XI.2). Like Vernia, with whom he studied in Padua 1480–2, Pico brought Alexander of Aphrodisias into his Christian synthesis by denying his mortalist view of the soul: Pico [1.154], 40; see also Di Napoli [1.3], 172; Nardi [1.14], 369; on Vernia, see p. 25.

148 Giorgi [1.143], esp. D ii^r–E vi^v (I.ii.1–13); see also Schmitt [1.195], 513–14.

149 For his anti-Aristotelianism see Giorgi [1.143], B vii^v–viii^r (I.i.13), c vii^v (III.ii.7); see also Vasoli [1.198]; Vasoli [1.20], 233–56.

150 Giorgi [1.143], D vi^v–vii^r, for a list of Cabbalistic books (not necessarily read) which he compiled; and A vii^r (I.i.5) for a parallel between Cabbala and Aristotle's ten categories; see also Wirszubski [1.203].

151 During the late 1520s, Steuco was in charge of the library of Cardinal Domen-
ico Grimani, who had purchased Pico's books: see Kibre [1.178], 18–20;
Crociata [1.172], 16–17.

152 Steuco [1.156], 1–122 (I–II), 279–411 (VII), 490–560 (IX); see also Schmitt
[1.195], 515–24.

153 Steuco [1.156], 166–207 (IV), 364 (VII.15), 537 (IX.22); like Vernia and Pico,
Steuco believed that Alexander of Aphrodisias, as well as Aristotle, supported
the immortality of the soul; see also Kraye [1.181], 344–5.

154 Steuco [1.156], 539–43 (IX.25); see also Vasoli [1.200]; Muccillo [1.187]; Crociata [1.172], ch. 1.

155 Ficino [1.173], trans. in Ficino [1.85]; see also Nelson [1.188]; Kristeller [1.12],
59, 61–2.

156 Diacceto [1.139]; Diacceto [1.141]; see also Kristeller [1.10], vol. 1, ch. 15.

157 Diacceto [1.140], 19, 216, 246, 263, 345; he defended Ficino and the Neoplatonists against Pico by arguing, on the basis of the *Parmenides*, that the One is
superior to being: ibid., 14; see also p. 35.

158 According to Francesco de' Vieri, one of the holders of the chair, his philosophical colleagues objected to Plato being taught in universities because of
the lack of order and method in the Dialogues and their use of probable,
rather than demonstrative, arguments: Vieri [1.160], 97; see also Kristeller
[1.10], vol. 1, 292.

159 See his autobiographical letter of 1597: Patrizi [1.150], 47; see also Muccillo
in Garfagnini [1.93], vol. 2, 615–79. The only subject on which he departed
from Ficino was love, all manifestations of which, even that between man and
God, he believed to be motivated by self-interest: Patrizi [1.149]; see also
Vasoli [1.201]; Antonaci [1.167]; Kristeller [1.11], ch. 7; Copenhaver and
Schmitt [1.2], ch. 3.4.

160 Patrizi [1.147]; see also Muccillo [1.186].

161 Patrizi [1.148], a 2ʳ–3ᵛ.

162 Purnell [1.190]; Vasoli [1.199]; Muccillo in Garfagnini [1.93], vol. 2, 636, 650,
660, 665.

163 Like Steuco, he regarded *De mundo* as authentic (Patrizi [1.147], 44ʳ–45ᵛ) but
he did not place it on the exalted level of the *Theology*.

164 See the appendix to Patrizi [1.148] for his editions of the *Theology*, the
Hermetic corpus and *Chaldaean Oracles* (attributed, by Gemistos Plethon, to
Zoroaster). Patrizi also had high regard for Proclus's *Elements of Theology*,
which he translated, together with the *Elements of Physics*, in 1583.

165 Kraye [1.180], 270–3, 282–4; Vasoli [1.198], 229 n. 249. Steuco's *Cosmopoeia*,
a commentary on Genesis, was also placed on the Index, though for different
reasons: Muccillo [1.187], 51 n. 21, 59 n. 37.

166 Patrizi [1.148], 1ʳ–3ʳ (*Panaugia* I), 74ʳ–79ᵛ (*Pancosmia* IV–VI); see also Brickmann [1.170].

167 Telesio [1.157]. For Patrizi's constructive criticisms of Telesio's work, see
Fiorentino [1.174], vol. 2, 375–91; for Telesio's reply, see Telesio [1.158],
453–95; see also Kristeller [1.11], ch. 6; Copenhaver and Schmitt [1.2], ch. 5.3.

168 Bacon referred to Telesio as 'the first of the moderns', but criticized him
because, like his Peripatetic opponents, he devised theories before having

recourse to experimentation: Bacon [1.136], 107, 114; see also Giachetti Assenza [1.176].

169 Telesio [1.157], vol. 1, 188–97 (I.25).

170 Patrizi [1.148], 61ʳ–73ᵛ (*Pancosmia* I–III).

171 Gassendi [1.142], 246 (I.iii.3); see also Henry [1.177], 566–8.

172 Patrizi [1.148], 63ᵛ–64ʳ (*Pancosmia* I); see also Henry [1.177], 564–5; Brickmann [1.170], 62.

173 Bruno [1.137], vol. 1.1, 191–398 (*De immenso et innumerabilibus*); Bruno [1.138], 343–537 (*De l'infinito, universo e mondi*), trans. in Bruno [1.163]; see also Michel [1.184], chs 6 and 8; Koyré [1.179], 39–55; Kristeller [1.11], ch. 8; Copenhaver and Schmitt [1.2], ch. 5.2.

174 See, for example, his criticism of Copernicus for being 'more interested in mathematics than in nature': Bruno [1.138], 28 (*La cena de le ceneri*); Bruno [1.137], 380–9 (*De immenso* III.9).

175 Bruno [1.138], 260–1 (*De la causa, principio e uno*).

176 See Lucretius, *De rerum natura* II.1048–89, and Nicholas of Cusa [1.145], 57–75 (II.1–4), for discussions of the infinite universe and plurality of worlds. For the influence of Plotinus on Bruno see Kristeller [1.11], 131, 135; his most Neoplatonic work, *De gli eroici furori* (Bruno [1.138], 925–1178, trans. in Bruno [1.161], transforms Platonic love into a heroic but doomed struggle to comprehend God's infinity.

177 Bruno [1.138], 225–53 (*De la causa* II), trans. in Bruno [1.164], 108–23; see also Blum [1.169], ch. 3; Deregibus [1.173]; Kristeller [1.183], 4.

178 See the trial document published in Spampanato [1.196], 708.

179 See, for example, Bruno [1.138], 547–831 (*Spaccio de la bestia trionfante*), trans. in Bruno [1.162]; see also Badaloni [1.168].

180 For a summary of the charges against Bruno see *Dizionario* [1.4], vol. 14, 663–4.

181 Ricci [1.191].

❧ BIBLIOGRAPHY ❧

Italian Renaissance philosophy

Collection of texts

1.1 *The Renaissance Philosophy of Man*, trans. E. Cassirer *et al.*, Chicago, Ill., University of Chicago Press, 1948.

General works

1.2 Copenhaver, B. C. and Schmitt, C. B. *A History of Western Philosophy*, vol. 3, *Renaissance Philosophy*, Oxford, Oxford University Press, 1992.

1.3 Di Napoli, G. *L'immortalità dell'anima nel Rinascimento*, Turin, Società editrice internazionale, 1963.

1.4   *Dizionario biografico degli Italiani*, Rome, Istituto della Enciclopedia Italiana, 1960-.
1.5   Garin, E. *La cultura filosofica del Rinascimento italiano*, Florence, Sansoni, 1961.
1.6   Garin, E. *L'età nuova*, Naples, Morano, 1969.
1.7   Gilbert, N. W. *Renaissance Concepts of Method*, New York, Columbia University Press, 1960.
1.8   Hankins, J. et al. (eds) *Supplementum Festivum: Studies in Honor of Paul Oskar Kristeller*, Binghamton, N.Y., Center for Medieval and Early Renaissance Studies, 1987.
1.9   Henry, J. and Hutton, S. (eds) *New Perspectives on Renaissance Thought*, London, Duckworth, 1990.
1.10 Kristeller, P. O. *Studies in Renaissance Thought and Letters*, Rome, Storia e Letteratura, 2 vols, 1956-85.
1.11 Kristeller, P. O. *Eight Philosophers of the Italian Renaissance*, Stanford, Calif., Stanford University Press, 1964.
1.12 Kristeller, P. O. *Renaissance Thought and Its Sources*, New York, Columbia University Press, 1979.
1.13 *Medioevo e Rinascimento: Studi in onore di Bruno Nardi*, Florence, Sansoni, 2 vols, 1955.
1.14 Nardi, B. *Saggi sull'aristotelismo padovano dal secolo XIV al XVI*, Florence, Sansoni, 1958.
1.15 Olivieri, L. (ed.) *Aristotelismo veneto e scienza moderna*, Padua, Antenore, 2 vols, 1983.
1.16 Schmitt, C. B. *Aristotle and the Renaissance*, Cambridge, Mass., Harvard University Press, 1983.
1.17 Schmitt, C. B. and Skinner, Q. (eds) *The Cambridge History of Renaissance Philosophy*, Cambridge, Cambridge University Press, 1988.
1.18 Seigel, J. E. *Rhetoric and Philosophy in Renaissance Humanism*, Princeton, N. J., Princeton University Press, 1968.
1.19 Vasoli, C. *La dialettica e la retorica dell'Umanesimo*, Milan, Feltrinelli, 1968.
1.20 Vasoli, C. *Filosofia e religione nella cultura del Rinascimento*, Naples, Guida, 1988.
1.21 Walker, D. P. *The Ancient Theology: Studies in Christian Platonism from the Fifteenth to the Eighteenth Century*, London, Duckworth, 1972.

Scholasticism and humanism in the early Renaissance

Original language and bilingual editions

1.22 Blasius of Parma, *Le Quaestiones de anima*, ed. G. Federici Vescovini, Florence, Olschki, 1974.
1.23 Kuksewicz, Z. (ed.) *Averroïsme au XIVe siècle: édition des textes*, Wroclaw, Ossolineum, 1965.
1.24 Petrarch, *Le Traité 'De sui ipsius et multorum ignorantia'*, ed. L. M. Capelli, Paris, Honoré Champion, 1906.
1.25 Petrarch, *Le familiari*, ed. F. Rossi, Florence, Sansoni, 4 vols, 1933-42.

1.26 Petrarch, *Rerum memorandarum libri*, ed. G. Billanovich, Florence, Sansoni, 1943.
1.27 Petrarch, *Prose*, ed. and trans. G. Martellotti *et al.*, Milan, Ricciardi, 1955 (Latin and Italian).
1.28 Petrarch, *Invective contra medicum*, ed. and trans. P. G. Ricci, Rome, Storia e Letteratura, 1978 (Latin and Italian).
1.29 Pietro d'Abano, *Conciliator differentiarum philosophorum et praecipue medicorum*, Venice, Apud Iuntas, 1565; facsimile reprint, E. Riondato and L. Olivieri (eds), Padua, Antenore, 1985.

English translations

1.30 Petrarch, *On His Own Ignorance and That of Many Others*, in *The Renaissance Philosophy of Man*, trans. E. Cassirer *et al.*, Chicago, Ill., University of Chicago Press, 1948, 47–133.
1.31 Petrarch, *Rerum familiarum libri I-XXIV*, trans. A. S. Bernardo, Albany, N.Y., and Baltimore, Md., SUNY and Johns Hopkins University Presses, 3 vols, 1975–85.
1.32 Petrarch, *Letters*, trans. M. Bishop, Bloomington, Ind., Indiana University Press, 1966.

Secondary literature

1.33 Federici Vescovini, G. *Astrologia e scienza: La crisi dell'aristotelismo sul cadere del Trecento e Biagio Pelacani da Parma*, Florence, Vallecchi, 1979.
1.34 Foster, K. *Petrarch, Poet and Humanist*, Edinburgh, Edinburgh University Press, 1984.
1.35 Gerosa, P. P. *Umanesimo cristiano del Petrarca*, Turin, Bottega d'Erasmo, 1966.
1.36 Gilbert, N. W. 'The Early Italian Humanists and Disputation', in A. Molho and J. Tedeschi (eds) *Renaissance Studies in Honor of Hans Baron*, Florence, Sansoni, 1971, 201–26.
1.37 Kamp, A. *Petrarcas philosophisches Programm*, Frankfurt am Main, Peter Lang, 1989.
1.38 Kretzmann, N. *et al. The Cambridge History of Later Medieval Philosophy*, Cambridge, Cambridge University Press, 1982.
1.39 Mann, N. *Petrarch*, Oxford, Oxford University Press, 1984.
1.40 Paschetto, E. *Pietro d'Abano medico e filosofo*, Florence, Vallecchi, 1984.

The new Aristotelianism
Original language and bilingual editions

1.41 Acciaiuoli, Donato *Expositio Ethicorum Aristotelis*, Florence, Apud S. Jacobum de Ripoli, 1478.
1.42 Argyropulos, Johannes, *Compendium de regulis et formis ratiocinandi*, ed. C. Vasoli, *Rinascimento* 15 (1964) 285–339.

1.43 Argyropulos, Johannes, 'On the Agent Intellect: An Edition of Ms. Magliabechi V 42 (ff. 224–228^v)', ed. V. Brown, in J. R. O'Donnell (ed.) *Essays in Honour of Anton Charles Pegis*, Toronto, Pontifical Institute of Mediaeval Studies, 1974, 160–75.

1.44 Barbaro, Ermolao, *Compendium Ethicorum librorum*, Venice, Cominus de Tridino, 1544.

1.45 Barbaro, Ermolao, *Epistolae, orationes et carmina*, ed. V. Branca, Florence, Bibliopolis, 2 vols, 1942.

1.46 Bruni, Leonardo, *Epistolarum libri VIII*, ed. L. Mehus, Florence, Bernardus Paperinius, 2 vols, 1741.

1.47 Bruni, Leonardo, *Humanistisch-politische Schriften*, ed. H. Baron, Leipzig, Teubner, 1928.

1.48 Cavalli, Francesco, *De numero et ordine partium ac librorum physicae doctrinae*, Venice [Matteo Capcasa, c, 1499].

1.49 George of Trebizond, *Collectanea Trapezuntiana: Texts, Documents and Bibliographies of George of Trebizond*, ed. J. Monfasani, Binghamton, N.Y., Center for Medieval and Early Renaissance Studies, 1984.

1.50 Manutius, Aldus, *Aldo Manuzio editore*, ed. and trans. G. Orlandi, Milan, Edizioni il Polifilo, 2 vols, 1975 (Latin and Italian).

1.51 Müllner, K. (ed.) *Reden und Briefe italienischer Humanisten*, Vienna, Hölder, 1899; reprinted, B. Gerl (ed.), Munich, Fink, 1970.

1.52 Paul of Venice, *Scriptum super librum Aristotelis De anima*, Venice, Filippo di Pietro, 1481.

1.53 Poliziano, Angelo, *Opera*, Basel, Nicolaus Episcopius, 1553.

1.54 Poliziano, Angelo, *Lamia: Praelectio in Priora Aristotelis Analytica*, ed. A. Wesseling, Leiden, Brill, 1986.

1.55 Vernia, Nicoletto, *Contra perversam Averrois opinionem de unitate intellectus*, in Albert of Saxony, *Acutissime questiones super libros De physica auscultatione*, Venice, Heredes O. Scoti, 1516, 83^r–91^r.

English translations

1.56 Bruni, Leonardo, *The Humanism of Leonardo Bruni: Selected Texts*, trans. G. Griffiths *et al.*, Binghamton, N.Y., Center for Medieval and Early Renaissance Studies, 1987.

Secondary literature

1.57 Bertalot, L. *Studien zum italienischen und deutschen Humanismus*, Rome, Storia e Letteratura, 2 vols, 1975.

1.58 Bianchi, L. 'Un commento "umanistico" ad Aristotele: L'"Expositio super libros Ethicorum" di Donato Acciaiuoli', *Rinascimento* 30 (1990) 29–55.

1.59 Birkenmajer, A. 'Der Streit des Alonso von Cartagena mit Leonardo Bruni Aretino', in his *Vermischte Untersuchungen zur Geschichte der mittelalterlichen Philosophie*, Münster i. W., Aschendorffsche Verlagsbuchandlung, 1922, 129–210.

1.60 Branca, V. 'Ermolao Barbaro and Late Quattrocento Venetian Humanism', in J. Hale (ed.) *Renaissance Venice*, London, Faber, 1973, 218–43.

1.61 Branca, V. *Poliziano e l'umanesimo della parola*, Turin, Einaudi, 1983.

1.62 Branca, V. 'L'umanesimo veneziano alla fine del Quattrocento: Ermolao Barbaro e il suo circolo', in *Storia della cultura veneta*, Vicenza, Neri Pozza, vol. 3.1, 1980, 123–75.

1.63 Cammelli, G. *I dotti bizantini e le origini dell'umanesimo*, Florence, Vallecchi, 3 vols, 1941–54.

1.64 Garin, E. 'Le traduzioni umanistiche di Aristotele nel secolo XV', *Atti e memorie dell'Accademia fiorentina di scienze morali La Colombaria* 16 (1947–50) 55–104.

1.65 Gerl, H.-B. *Philosophie und Philologie: Leonardo Brunis Übertragung der nikomachischen Ethik in ihren philosophischen Prämissen*, Munich, Fink, 1981.

1.66 Mahoney, E. P. 'Nicoletto Vernia on the Soul and Immortality', in E. P. Mahoney (ed.) *Philosophy and Humanism: Renaissance Essays in Honor of Paul Oskar Kristeller*, Leiden, Brill, 1976, 144–63.

1.67 Minio-Paluello, L. *Opuscula: The Latin Aristotle*, Amsterdam, A. M. Hakkert, 1972.

1.68 Poppi, A. (ed.) *Scienza e filosofia all'Università di Padova nel Quattrocento*, Padua, Lint, 1983.

1.69 Wolters, A. 'Poliziano as a Translator of Plotinus', *Renaissance Quarterly* 40 (1987) 452–64.

The revival of Platonism

Original language and bilingual editions

1.70 Ficino, Marsilio, *Opera omnia*, Basel, Officina Henricpetrina, 2 vols, 1576; reprinted, Turin, Bottega d'Erasmo, 1962.

1.71 Ficino, Marsilio, *Supplementum Ficinianum*, ed. P. O. Kristeller, Florence, Olschki, 2 vols, 1937.

1.72 Ficino, Marsilio, *Lettere*, ed. S. Gentile, Florence, Olschki, vol. 1, 1990.

1.73 Ficino, Marsilio, *Commentaire sur le Banquet de Platon*, ed. and trans. R. Marcel, Paris, Les Belles Lettres, 1956 (Latin and French).

1.74 Ficino, Marsilio, *Théologie platonicienne de l'immortalité des âmes*, ed. and trans. R. Marcel, Paris, Les Belles Lettres, 3 vols, 1964–70 (Latin and French).

1.75 Ficino, Marsilio, *The Philebus Commentary*, ed. and trans. M. J. B. Allen, Berkeley, Calif., University of California Press, 1975 (Latin and English).

1.76 Ficino, Marsilio, *Marsilio Ficino and the Phaedran Charioteer*, ed. and trans. M. J. B. Allen, Berkeley, Calif., University of California Press, 1981 (Latin and English).

1.77 Ficino, Marsilio, *Icastes: Marsilio Ficino's Interpretation of Plato's Sophist*, ed. and trans. M. J. B. Allen, Berkeley, Calif., University of California Press, 1989 (Latin and English).

1.78 Ficino, Marsilio, *Three Books on Life*, ed. and trans. C. V. Kaske and J. R. Clark, Binghamton, N.Y., Center for Medieval and Early Renaissance Studies, 1989 (Latin and English).

1.79 Gaza, Theodore, *De fato*, ed. and trans. J. W. Taylor, Toronto, University of Toronto Library, 1925 (Greek and English).

1.80 George of Trebizond, *Comparationes phylosophorum Aristotelis et Platonis*, Venice, Iacobus Penitus, 1523; reprinted, Frankfurt am Main, Minerva, 1965.

1.81 Landino, Cristoforo, *Disputationes Camaldulenses*, ed. P. Lohe, Florence, Sansoni, 1980.

1.82 Plato, *Il Critone di Leonardo Bruni e di Rinuccio Aretino*, ed. E. Berti and A. Carosini, Florence, Olschki, 1983.

1.83 Plethon, Georgios Gemistos, *Traité des lois*, ed. C. Alexandre, trans. A. Pellissier, Paris, Firmin-Didot, 1858; reprinted, Amsterdam, A. M. Hakkert, 1966 (Greek and French).

1.84 Plethon, Georgios Gemistos, 'Le "De differentiis" de Pléthon d'après l'autographe de la Marcienne', ed. B. Lagarde, *Byzantion* 43 (1973) 312–43.

English translations

1.85 Ficino, Marsilio, *Commentary on Plato's Symposium on Love*, trans. S. Jayne, Dallas, Tex., Spring Publications, 1985.

1.86 Ficino, Marsilio, *The Letters*, London, Shepheard-Walwyn, 4 vols, 1975–88.

1.87 Plethon, Georgios Gemistos, *De differentiis*, in C. M. Woodhouse, *Gemistus Plethon: The Last of the Hellenes*, Oxford, Clarendon, 1986, ch. 11.

Secondary literature

1.88 Allen, M. J. B. 'Ficino's Theory of the Five Substances and the Neoplatonists' *Parmenides*', *Journal of Medieval and Renaissance Studies* 12 (1982) 19–44.

1.89 Allen, M. J. B. *The Platonism of Marsilio Ficino*, Berkeley, Calif., University of California Press, 1984.

1.90 Allen, M. J. B. 'Marsilio Ficino on Plato, the Neoplatonists and the Christian Doctrine of the Trinity', *Renaissance Quarterly* 37 (1984) 555–84.

1.91 Copenhaver, B. P. 'Scholastic Philosophy and Renaissance Magic in the *De vita* of Marsilio Ficino', *Renaissance Quarterly* 37 (1984) 523–54.

1.92 Field, A. *The Origins of the Platonic Academy of Florence*, Princeton, N. J., Princeton University Press, 1988.

1.93 Garfagnini, G. C. (ed.) *Marsilio Ficino e il ritorno di Platone: Studi e documenti*, Florence, Olschki, 2 vols, 1986.

1.94 Gentile, S. 'Sulle prime traduzioni dal greco di Marsilio Ficino', *Rinascimento* 30 (1990) 57–104.

1.95 Hankins, J. *Plato in the Italian Renaissance*, Leiden, Brill, 2 vols, 1990.

1.96 Klibansky, R. *The Continuity of the Platonic Tradition during the Middle Ages*, London, Warburg Institute, 1939; reprinted, Munich, Kraus, 1981.

1.97 Klibansky, R. 'Plato's *Parmenides* in the Middle Ages and the Renaissance', *Mediaeval and Renaissance Studies* 1 (1943) 281–330; reprinted, Munich, Kraus, 1981.

1.98 Kraye, J. 'Francesco Filelfo's Lost Letter *De ideis*', *Journal of the Warburg and Courtauld Institutes* 42 (1979) 236–49.

1.99 Kristeller, P. O. *The Philosophy of Marsilio Ficino*, Gloucester, Mass., Peter Smith, 1964.

1.100 Kristeller, P. O. 'A Latin Translation of Gemistos Plethon's *De fato* by Johannes Sophianos Dedicated to Nicholas of Cusa', in *Nicolò Cusano agli inizi del mondo moderno*, Florence, Sansoni, 1970, 175–93.

1.101 Labowsky, L. 'An Unknown Treatise by Theodorus Gaza', *Mediaeval and Renaissance Studies* 6 (1968) 173–93.

1.102 Mohler, L. *Kardinal Bessarion als Theologe, Humanist und Staatsmann*, Paderborn, Ferdinand Schöningh, 3 vols, 1923–42.

1.103 Monfasani, J. *George of Trebizond: A Biography and a Study of his Rhetoric and Logic*, Leiden, Brill, 1976.

1.104 Webb, R. 'The *Nomoi* of Gemistos Plethon in the Light of Plato's *Laws*', *Journal of the Warburg and Courtauld Institutes* 52 (1989) 214–19.

1.105 Woodhouse, C. M. *Gemistus Plethon: The Last of the Hellenes*, Oxford, Clarendon, 1986.

The Aristotelian mainstream

Original language and bilingual editions

1.106 Aristotle, *Omnia quae extant opera*, Averroes (comment.), Venice, Giunti, 11 vols, 1550–2.

1.107 Buonamici, Francesco, *De motu libri X*, Florence, Bartolomeo Sermartelli, 1591.

1.108 Cesalpino, Andrea, *De plantis libri XVI*, Florence, Georgius Marescottus, 1583.

1.109 Cremonini, Cesare, *Disputatio de coelo in tres partes divisa*, Venice, T. Balionus, 1613.

1.110 Pomponazzi, Pietro, *Tractatus acutissimi, utillimi et mere peripatetici*, Venice, Octavianus Scouts, 1525.

1.111 Pomponazzi, Pietro, *De naturalium effectuum causis sive de incantationibus*, in *Opera*, Basel, Heinrich Petri, 1567; reprinted Hildesheim and New York, Olms, 1970.

1.112 Pomponazzi, Pietro, *Tractatus de immortalitate animae*, ed. G. Morra, Bologna, Nanni & Fiammenghi, 1954 (Latin and Italian).

1.113 Pomponazzi, Pietro, *Libri quinque de fato, de libero arbitrio et de praedestinatione*, ed. R. Lemay, Lugano, Thesaurus Mundi, 1957.

1.114 Pomponazzi, Pietro, 'Two Unpublished Questions on the Soul', ed. P. O. Kristeller, *Medievalia et Humanistica* 9 (1955) 76–101.

1.115 Pomponazzi, Pietro, 'Utrum anima sit mortalis vel immortalis', ed. W. van Dooren, *Nouvelles de la république des lettres* (1989) 71–135.

1.116 Viviani, V. *Vita di Galileo*, in G. Galileo, *Le opere*, ed. A. Favaro, Florence, G. Barbèra, vol. 19, 597–632.

1.117 Zabarella, Jacopo, *Opera logica*, Venice, Paulus Meietus, 1578; reprinted, C. Vasoli (ed.), Bologna, Clueb, 1985.

1.118 Zabarella, Jacopo, *De rebus naturalibus libri XXX*, Frankfurt, Lazarus Zetznerus, 1607; reprinted, Frankfurt, Minerva, 1966.

English translations

1.119 Pomponazzi, Pietro, *On the Immortality of the Soul*, in *The Renaissance Philosophy of Man*, trans. E. Cassirer *et al.*, Chicago, Ill., University of Chicago Press, 1948, 280–381.

Secondary literature

1.120 Cranz, F. E. 'The Prefaces to the Greek Editions and Latin Translations of Alexander of Aphrodisias, 1450–1575', *American Philosophical Society: Proceedings* 102 (1958) 510–46.

1.121 Cranz, F. E. 'The Publishing History of the Aristotle Commentaries of Thomas Aquinas', *Traditio* 34 (1978) 157–92.

1.122 De Bellis, D. 'Niccolò Leonico Tomeo interprete di Aristotele naturalista', *Physis* 17 (1975) 71–93.

1.123 Helbing, M. O. *La filosofia di Francesco Buonamici, professore di Galileo*, Pisa, Nistri-Lischi, 1989.

1.124 Kraye, J. 'Alexander of Aphrodisias, Gianfrancesco Beati and the Problem of *Metaphysics* α', in J. Monfasani and R. Musto (eds) *Renaissance Society and Culture: Essays in Honour of Eugene F. Rice, Jr.*, New York, Italica, 1991, 137–60.

1.125 Lohr, C. H. 'The Sixteenth-Century Transformation of the Aristotelian Natural Philosophy', in E. Kessler *et al.* (eds) *Aristotelismus und Renaissance*, Wiesbaden, Harrasowitz, 1988, 89–99.

1.126 Mahoney, E. P. 'The Greek Commentators Themistius and Simplicius – and their Influence on Renaissance Aristotelianism', in D. J. O'Meara (ed.) *Neoplatonism and Christian Thought*, Norfolk, Va., International Society for Neoplatonic Studies, 1982, 169–77, 264–82.

1.127 Nardi, B. *Studi su Pietro Pomponazzi*, Florence, Le Monnier, 1965.

1.128 Olivieri, L. 'Filosofia e teologia in Pietro Pomponazzi tra Padova e Bologna', in *Sapere e/è potere: discipline, dispute e professioni nell'università medievale e moderna . . . Atti del 4° convegno, Bologna . . . 1989*, Bologna, Comune di Bologna, vol. 2, 1990, 65–84.

1.129 Pine, M. L. *Pietro Pomponazzi: Radical Philosopher of the Renaissance*, Padua, Antenore, 1986.

1.130 Poppi, A. *La dottrina della scienza in Giacomo Zabarella*, Padua, Antenore, 1972.

1.131 Schmitt, C. B. 'Experience and Experiment: A Comparison of Zabarella's Views with Galileo's in *De motu*', *Studies in the Renaissance* 16 (1969) 80–138.

1.132 Schmitt, C. B. 'Renaissance Averroism studied through the Venetian Editions of Aristotle-Averroes (with particular reference to the Giunta edition of 1550–2)', in *L'Averroismo in Italia*, Rome, Accademia nazionale dei Lincei, 1979, 121–42.

1.133 Schmitt, C. B. *Cesare Cremonini, un aristotelico al tempo di Galilei*, Venice, Centro tedesco di studi veneziani, 1980.

1.134 Schmitt, C. B. 'Alberto Pio and the Aristotelian Studies of His Time', in

Società, politica e cultura a Carpi ai tempi di Alberto III Pio, Padua, Antenore, 1981, 43–64.

1.135 Schmitt, C. B. 'Philoponus' Commentary on Aristotle's *Physics* in the Sixteenth Century', in R. Sorabji (ed.) *Philoponus and the Rejection of Aristotelian Science*, London, Duckworth, 1987, 210–30.

Alternative philosophical currents

Original language and bilingual editions

1.136 Bacon, Francis, *De principibus atque originibus*, in F. Bacon, *The Works*, ed. J. Spedding *et al.*, London, Longman, vol. 3, 1857, 63–118.

1.137 Bruno, Giordano, *Opera latine conscripta*, ed. F. Fiorentino *et al.*, Naples and Florence, Morano and Le Monnier, 3 vols, 1879–91.

1.138 Bruno, Giordano, *Dialoghi italiani*, 3rd edn, ed. G. Gentile and G. Aquilecchia, Florence, Sansoni, 1958.

1.139 Francesco da Diacceto, *I tre libri d'amore*, Venice, G. Giolito, 1561.

1.140 Francesco da Diacceto, *Opera omnia*, Basel, H. Petri and P. Perna, 1563.

1.141 Francesco da Diacceto, *De pulchro libri III, accedunt opuscula inedita et dispersa necnon testimonia quaedam ad eundem pertinentia*, ed. S. Matton, Pisa, Scuola normale superiore di Pisa, 1986.

1.142 Gassendi, Pierre, *Syntagma philosophicum*, in P. Gassendi, *Opera omnia*, Lyons, L. Anisson, vol. 1, 1658; reprinted, Stuttgart-Bad Cannstatt, Friedrich Frommann, 1964.

1.143 Giorgi, Francesco, *De harmonia mundi totius cantica tria*, Venice, Bernardinus de Vitalibus, 1525.

1.144 Leibniz, Gottfried Wilhelm, *Philosophische Schriften: 1663–1672, Sämtliche Schriften und Briefe VI.2*, Berlin, Akademie Verlag, 1966.

1.145 Nicholas of Cusa, *De docta ignorantia*, ed. E. Hoffmann and R. Klibansky, Leipzig, F. Meiner, 1932.

1.146 Nizolio, Mario, *De veris principiis et vera ratione philosophandi contra pseudophilosophos libri IV*, ed. Q. Breen, Rome, Fratelli Boca, 2 vols, 1956.

1.147 Patrizi, Francesco, *Discussionum peripateticarum tomi IV*, Basel, P. Perna, 1581.

1.148 Patrizi, Francesco, *Nova de universis philosophia*, Ferrara, Benedictus Mammarellus, 1591.

1.149 Patrizi, Francesco, *L'amorosa filosofia*, ed. J. C. Nelson, Florence, Le Monnier, 1963.

1.150 Patrizi, Francesco, *Lettere ed opuscoli inediti*, ed. D. Aguzzi Barbagli, Florence, Istituto nazionale di studi sul Rinascimento, 1975.

1.151 Gianfrancesco Pico della Mirandola, *Opera omnia*, Basel, Heinrich Petri, 1573; reprinted, Hildesheim, Olms, 1969.

1.152 Giovanni Pico della Mirandola, *Opera omnia*, Basel, Heinrich Petri, 1557; reprinted, C. Vasoli (ed.), Hildesheim, Olms, 1969.

1.153 Giovanni Pico della Mirandola, *Disputationes adversus astrologiam divinatricem*, ed. and trans. E. Garin, Florence, Vallecchi, 2 vols, 1946–52 (Latin and Italian).

1.154 Giovanni Pico della Mirandola, *Conclusiones sive theses DCCC Romae anno 1486 publice disputandae, sed non admissae*, ed. B. Kieszkowski, Geneva, Droz, 1973.

1.155 Giovanni Pico della Mirandola, *De hominis dignitate; Heptaplus; De ente et uno; e scritti vari*, ed. and trans. E. Garin, Florence, Vallecchi, 1942 (Latin and Italian).

1.156 Steuco, Agostino, *De perenni philosophia libri X*, Leiden, S. Gryphius, 1540; reprinted, C. B. Schmitt (ed.), New York and London, Johnson, 1972.

1.157 Telesio, Bernardino, *De rerum natura iuxta propria principia*, ed. and trans. L. de Franco, Cosenza and Florence, Casa del Libro and La Nuova Italia, 3 vols, 1965–76 (Latin and Italian).

1.158 Telesio, Bernardino, *Varii de naturalibus rebus libelli*, ed. and trans. L. de Franco, Florence, La Nuova Italia, 1981.

1.159 Valla, Lorenzo, *Repastinatio dialectice et philosophie*, ed. G. Zippel, Padua, Antenore, 2 vols, 1982.

1.160 de' Vieri, Francesco, *Vere conclusioni di Platone conformi alla dottrina christiana et a quella d'Aristotile*, Florence, G. Marescotti, 1590.

English translations

1.161 Bruno, Giordano, *The Heroic Frenzies*, trans. P. E. Memmo, Jr, Chapel Hill, N.C., University of North Carolina Press, 1964.

1.162 Bruno, Giordano, *The Expulsion of the Triumphant Beast*, trans. A. D. Imerti, New Brunswick, N.J., Rutgers University Press, 1964.

1.163 Bruno, Giordano, *On the Infinite Universe and Worlds*, in D. Singer, *Giordano Bruno: His Life and Thought*, London, Constable, 1950, 225–378.

1.164 Bruno, Giordano, *Concerning the Cause, Principle and One*, in S. Greenberg, *The Infinite in Giordano Bruno*, New York, King's Crown Press, 1950, 76–173.

1.165 Giovanni Pico della Mirandola, *On the Dignity of Man; On Being and the One; Heptaplus*, trans. C. G. Wellis, *et al.*, Indianapolis, Ind., and New York, Bobbs Merrill, 1965.

1.166 Giovanni Pico della Mirandola, 'On the Conflict of Philosophy and Rhetoric', ed. Q. Breen, *Journal of the History of Ideas* 13 (1952) 384–412.

Secondary literature

1.167 Antonaci, A. *Ricerche sul neoplatonismo del Rinascimento: Francesco Patrizi da Cherso*, Galatina, Editrice Salentina, vol. 1, 1984.

1.168 Badaloni, N. *Giordano Bruno: tra cosmologia ed etica*, Bari and Rome, De Donato, 1988.

1.169 Blum, P. R. *Aristoteles bei Giordano Bruno: Studien zur philosophischen Rezeption*, Munich, Fink, 1980.

1.170 Brickman, B. *An Introduction to Francesco Patrizi's Nova de universis philosophia*, PhD dissertation, Columbia University, New York, 1941.

1.171 Camporeale, S. *Lorenzo Valla: umanesimo e teologia*, Florence, Istituto nazionale di studi sul Rinascimento, 1972.

1.172 Crociata, M. *Umanesimo e teologia in Agostino Steuco. Neoplatonismo e* teologia della creazione nel 'De perenni philosophia', Rome, Città Nuova, 1987.

1.173 Deregibus, A. *Bruno e Spinoza*, Turin, Giappichelli, 2 vols, 1981.

1.174 Fiorentino, F. *Bernardino Telesio ossia studi storici su l'idea della natura nel risorgimento italiano*, Florence, Le Monnier, 2 vols, 1872–4.

1.175 Garin, E. *Giovanni Pico della Mirandola: Vita e dottrina*, Florence, Le Monnier, 1937.

1.176 Giachetti Assenza, V. 'Bernardino Telesio: il migliore dei moderni. I riferimenti a Telesio negli scritti di Francesco Bacone', *Rivista critica di storia della filosofia* 35 (1980) 41–78.

1.177 Henry, J. 'Francesco Patrizi da Cherso's Concept of Space and Its Later Influence', *Annals of Science* 36 (1979) 549–73.

1.178 Kibre, P. *The Library of Pico della Mirandola*, New York, Columbia University Press, 1936.

1.179 Koyré, A. *From the Closed World to the Infinite Universe*, Baltimore, Md., Johns Hopkins University Press, 1957.

1.180 Kraye, J. 'The Pseudo-Aristotelian *Theology* in Sixteenth- and Seventeenth-Century Europe', in *Pseudo-Aristotle in the Middle Ages*, ed. J. Kraye et al., London, Warburg Institute, 1986, 265–86.

1.181 Kraye, J. 'Aristotle's God and the Authenticity of *De mundo*: An Early Modern Controversy', *Journal of the History of Philosophy* 29 (1990) 339–58.

1.182 Kristeller, P. O. 'Giovanni Pico della Mirandola and His Sources', in *L'opera e il pensiero di Giovanni Pico della Mirandola nella storia dell'umanesimo. Convegno internazionale (Mirandola . . . 1963)*, Florence, Istituto nazionale di studi sul Rinascimento, vol. 1, 1965, 35–142.

1.183 Kristeller, P. O. 'Stoic and Neoplatonic Sources of Spinoza's *Ethics*', *History of European Ideas* 5 (1984) 1–15.

1.184 Michel, P. H. *The Cosmology of Giordano Bruno*, Paris, London and Ithaca, N.Y., Hermann, Methuen and Cornell University Press, 1973.

1.185 Monfasani, J. 'Lorenzo Valla and Rudolph Agricola', *Journal of the History of Ideas* 28 (1990) 181–200.

1.186 Muccillo, M. 'La vita e le opere di Aristotele nelle " Discussiones peripateticae" di Francesco Patrizi da Cherso', *Rinascimento* 21 (1981) 53–119.

1.187 Muccillo, M. 'La "prisca theologia" nel *De perenni philosophia* di Agostino Steuco', *Rinascimento* 28 (1988) 41–112.

1.188 Nelson, J. C. *Renaissance Theory of Love: The Context of Giordano Bruno's 'Eroici furori'*, New York, Columbia University Press, 1958.

1.189 Popkin, R. H. *The History of Scepticism from Erasmus to Spinoza*, Berkeley, Calif., University of California Press, 1979.

1.190 Purnell, F. 'Francesco Patrizi and the Critics of Hermes Trismegistus', *Journal of Medieval and Renaissance Studies* 6 (1976) 155–78.

1.191 Ricci, S. *La fortuna del pensiero di Giordano Bruno 1600–1750*, Florence, Le Lettere, 1990.

1.192 Rossi, P. 'La celebrazione della retorica e la polemica antimetafisica nel "De principiis" di Mario Nizolio', in *La crisi dell'uso dogmatico della ragione*, ed. A. Banfi, Rome and Milan, Fratelli Boca, 1953.

1.193 Roulier, F. *Jean Pic de la Mirandole (1463–1494), humaniste, philosophe, théologien*, Geneva, Slatkine, 1989.
1.194 Schmitt, C. B. *Gianfrancesco Pico della Mirandola (1469–1533) and his Critique of Aristotle*, The Hague, Nijhoff, 1967.
1.195 Schmitt, C. B. 'Perennial Philosophy from Agostino Steuco to Leibniz', *Journal of the History of Ideas* 27 (1966) 505–32.
1.196 Spampanato, V. *Vita di Giordano Bruno con documenti editi e inediti*, Messina, G. Principato, 1921.
1.197 Valcke, L. 'Entre raison et foi: Le néoplatonisme de Pic de la Mirandole', *Recherches de théologie ancienne et médiévale* 54 (1987) 186–237.
1.198 Vasoli, C. 'Intorno a Francesco Giorgio Veneto e all' "armonia del mondo" ', in C. Vasoli, *Profezia e ragione. Studi sulla cultura del Cinquecento e del Seicento*, Naples, Morano, 1974, 129–403.
1.199 Vasoli, C. 'Francesco Patrizi e la tradizione ermetica', *Nuova rivista storica* 64 (1980) 25–40.
1.200 Vasoli, C. 'A proposito di Agostino Steuco e della "Perennis Philosophia" ', *Atti e memorie della Accademia Petrarca di lettere, arti e scienze* 46 (1983–4) 263–92.
1.201 Vasoli, C. *Francesco Patrizi da Cherso*, Rome, Bulzoni, 1989.
1.202 Wesseler, M. *Die Einheit von Wort und Sache: Der Entwurf einer rhetorischen Philosophie bei Marius Nizolius*, Munich, Fink, 1974.
1.203 Wirszubski, C. 'Francesco Giorgio's Commentary on Giovanni Pico's Kabbalistic Theses', *Journal of the Warburg and Courtauld Institutes* 37 (1974) 145–56.
1.204 Wirszubski, C. *Pico della Mirandola's Encounter with Jewish Mysticism*, Cambridge, Mass., Harvard University Press, 1989.

CHAPTER 2

Renaissance philosophy outside Italy

Stuart Brown

Italy might justly be described as the home of Renaissance philosophy. Many of the important cultural developments of the period originated in Italy and only gradually spread north and west to other countries. But each of the other major centres[1] of West European cultural activity – the German States, France, the Iberian Peninsula, England and the Low Countries – provided a distinct context for philosophical activity. Their very different political and religious histories had a more or less direct effect on the kind of philosophy that flourished in each country or region. Each, in its own way, added to what it inherited from Italy and developed what it received from elsewhere in Europe. In different ways and to varying extents, they prepared for or anticipated the transition to modern philosophy. In one way or another, Renaissance philosophy and philosophies continued to develop and flourish somewhere in Europe throughout the seventeenth century. They provided an often neglected part of the context for modern philosophy, both in some ways being continuous with it and in other ways shaping some of the responses to it. There are a number of philosophers, indeed, such as Gassendi and Leibniz,[2] who can fruitfully be represented as Renaissance as well as early modern philosophers.

A distinguishing mark of Renaissance philosophers was their deference to the thought of the ancients. Their arguments often consisted in citing the support of some ancient authority or the consensus of a number of ancient authorities for the view they wished to advance. The tendency of modern philosophers, by contrast, was to rely on appeals to reason and experience rather than on citing authorities to advance their arguments. Some, of course, did both and the decision whether to call them modern or Renaissance philosophers might depend on whether their arguments turned more on one kind of appeal than the other.

Renaissance philosophy needs also to be distinguished from the earlier style of scholastic philosophy. And Renaissance philosophy, at least originally, was in part a reaction against the philosophy of the academic and ecclesiastical world. A reliance on authority was also a feature of scholastic philosophy, though it is in some ways more difficult to locate. The scholastics relied on a tradition of interpreting Aristotle in which appeals to reason, tradition and the word of 'the philosopher' were confused. Some Renaissance philosophers turned their backs on the Aristotelian tradition and, as we shall see, all the ancient philosophical systems were revived at one time or another during the Renaissance. But, quite characteristically, Renaissance philosophers had a high regard for Aristotle and accused the scholastics of perverting Aristotle's meaning.[3]

Nor did scholastic philosophy remain the same in the Renaissance period. On the contrary, the criticisms from the humanists were often taken to heart and new developments outside were often reflected in changes within the scholastic tradition. Thus the Renaissance did not merely bring back neglected traditions of philosophy but also revitalized the scholastic tradition itself.

It is convenient for the historian of philosophy to label periods by the style of philosophy that predominates or is most significantly new in them. Any period of philosophy, however, is always a period of transition and includes both individuals and movements that are difficult to place. Such qualifications are particularly needed when writing about the significant movements in European philosophy over a period of two centuries or more. For while the sixteenth is the main century for Renaissance philosophy outside Italy, we need to acknowledge some figures who flourished earlier. We also need to recognize its continuing vitality well into the period of modern philosophy and even in the eighteenth century.[4]

For ease of exposition the leading philosophical figures will be grouped under distinct strands within Renaissance philosophy. The strands are often interwoven, however, and, whilst some individuals belong straightforwardly within one strand, other more complex philosophers can be related to two or more. There are even those, such as Nicholas of Cusa, who should arguably be assigned to the late medieval period and others, such as Agrippa, whom some would represent as early modern philosophers. The value of such debates lies less perhaps in the prospect of their receiving a definitive resolution than in the light thrown on the individual philosophers discussed by the possibility of seeing them from quite different perspectives.

CUSANUS (NICHOLAS OF CUSA) AND RELIGIOUS NEOPLATONISM

Nicholas Kryfts or Krebs was born (in 1401) in the German town of Kues or Cusa, hence his Latin name of Cusanus. He became a priest and eventually a bishop, playing an important role in the debates concerning the authority of the Pope and the Church Councils and in negotiations towards a reunion of the communions of Rome and Constantinople. He wrote many theological works and, by the time he died in Italy in 1464, he was a cardinal. His philosophical writings reflect his concern with the nature and knowledge of God. But he was a man of great learning who wrote treatises on science and mathematics. He was influenced by the Italian humanists, learning Greek and amassing a considerable library of manuscripts. Together with his younger contemporary, Ficino, he played an important part in the Renaissance revival of Platonism.

Cusanus and his contemporaries did not make the distinction now recognized between Plato and the school of Neoplatonism begun by Plotinus. By the end of the seventeenth century Leibniz had begun to make distinctions between the true Plato and the distortions of and accretions to his thought to be found in the writings of his successors.[5] But such distinctions were not made by the religious Neoplatonists of the Renaissance. They inherited a tradition in which Plato had been presented in a Christianized form. Important as a background source for Cusanus are the writings of Pseudo-Dionysius – the writings falsely attributed to St Paul's first Athenian convert Dionysius the Areopagite. These writings had influenced Meister Eckhart (c. 1260–1327) and the medieval Rhineland school of mysticism to which Cusanus was indebted. He was also indebted to Proclus and commissioned a translation of his *Platonic Theology*.

Typically of the religious Neoplatonists Cusanus took God's creation of the world to imply that the world reflected God's infinite nature. The world, for him, is a 'contraction' of God and each finite thing is in turn a 'contraction' of the larger universe. It follows that all things, including contradictory opposites, coincide in a harmonious unity. If that is so then the principle of contradiction is not a necessary condition of truth and human reason is not equal to grasping the true nature of the world. Cusanus accordingly taught what he called 'learned ignorance', partly in opposition to the Aristotelians and their insistence on the principle of contradiction. He also taught the 'negative theology' of Pseudo-Dionysius, that God transcends all positive knowledge we can have of Him.

Cusanus's Platonic tendency to mysticism and scepticism in religious matters did not prevent him from having definite opinions in cosmology. If, for example, the universe is a mirror of God then it should, he thought, be conceived as having no determined boundary. The view that everything in the universe is a microcosm of the whole also committed him to rejecting the Aristotelian orthodoxy that the heavenly bodies were made of a different substance from the earth. Cusanus departed in these and in a number of other respects from the established cosmology of Ptolemy and Aristotle.

The case of Cusanus illustrates how Neoplatonism helped to liberate some from the (as it happens, false) assumptions of Aristotelian science and thus contributed to the development of what, with the benefit of hindsight, we would judge to be a truer view of the world. The influence of Neoplatonism on how people thought about the world was not, however, invariably helpful in this way. The view that man is a microcosm of the universe (the macrocosm) played a central part in the thought of Paracelsus and the very influential tradition of occult philosophy during the Renaissance. That view, to which we shall return,[6] led to a number of false beliefs, for instance about what in nature could be used to cure what diseases in humankind.

Cusanus was himself part of a tradition of philosophy in Germany which was to continue throughout the Renaissance period and beyond. That, no doubt, is why he appears to anticipate later German philosophy as much as he does. Cusanus held, for instance, a number of characteristically Leibnizian doctrines such as that each thing in the world is a reflection not only of God but of all other things.[7] Moreover, his doctrine of the coincidence of opposites in God seems like Schelling's theory of the Absolute as the point at which all contrasts and distinctions disappear. But Cusanus, though perhaps the major Renaissance Neoplatonist outside Italy, was neither the first nor the last in the German tradition of Neoplatonism and religious mysticism. Nor were these doctrines peculiar to him. The thought that God's nature is reflected in every created thing is a natural consequence of the characteristically Neoplatonist doctrine of emanation, according to which the world comes about by a kind of overflowing of the divinity. Nor was Cusanus the only German philosopher of the period to hold that in God all contrasts and differences disappear.

One philosopher in the German tradition to hold both of these views was Jakob Boehme (1575–1624), a self-educated artisan. Boehme's ideas were the result of much reading and reflect the work of the occult philosopher and doctor Paracelsus (see pp. 77–8) as well as the mystic Valentin Weigel (1493–1541). But he included highly idiosyncratic elements of his own. For instance he identified God the Father with the Will, the Son with the Heart and the Holy Spirit with the 'moving life' that emanated from these, giving rise to the spiritual world. In Boehme, as in other Neoplatonists, the material world results by a

process of degeneration. His stress on religious intuition put him outside philosophy, as it put him outside religious orthodoxy. He was
immensely influential, however, not only in his own time (some of his
followers formed themselves into a religious sect) but also, much later,
when his work was rediscovered by German Romantics such as Schelling.

Another strand of religious Neoplatonism that became assimilated
into the German tradition was that of the Christian Cabbala. 'Cabbala'
is a Hebrew word (variously transliterated) which means 'tradition'
and became attached to an occult tradition for interpreting the Bible
which legend had it Moses passed down through a succession of Jewish
leaders. Some of the earlier Italian Renaissance philosophers, such as
Giovanni Pico della Mirandola and Francesco Giorgi, had taken a
Christian interest in the Cabbala.[8] This interest was pursued in Germany by the humanist Johannes Reuchlin (1455–1522)[9] and culminated
in the late seventeenth century in a project to put together in Latin
translation the Hebrew writings known as the Zohar with other expository material. This project involved the collaboration of two older
contemporaries and friends of Leibniz, Christian Knorr von Rosenroth
(1636–89) and Francis Mercury van Helmont (1618–99). Knorr was
responsible for the main work of editing and seeing through the publication of *Kabbala Denudata* (1677–84). But amongst van Helmont's
contributions was a short *Cabbalistical Dialogue* in which he sought
to expound Cabbalism and defend it from some of the criticisms levelled against it by one of its former admirers, the distinguished Cambridge Platonist Henry More (1614–87).[10]

Van Helmont's exposition of Cabbalism gives central place to a
recognizably Neoplatonic paradox: how could the base material world
have resulted from a God who is pure Spirit? How, to put it in what
for a Neoplatonist is just another way, can what is passive and inert
be caused by a being whose nature contains nothing of that kind but
who is 'pure activity'? Van Helmont's resolution of the paradox is
through a theory that, in the first place, is a theory of emanation,
according to which God immediately produces from Himself things of
a purely spiritual nature. These spirits do, however, degenerate and
become dull, clinging together to form matter. The individual spirit, in
this reduced state, is 'now a natural *Monade* or *single Being*, and a
very *Atome*'.[11] In common with the other Neoplatonists of the late
seventeenth century – Leibniz, arguably, included – van Helmont produced a monadology that sought to combine a Neoplatonic metaphysics
with contemporary scientific speculation about the nature of matter.

Religious Neoplatonism had some influence in the Iberian Peninsula in the early sixteenth century, for instance on the thought of the
Portuguese Jewish philosopher Leon Hebreo (or Abarbanel) (*c.* 1460–

c. 1523), who wrote a dialogue on love. In France the common Neoplatonic view of Plato's writing as *prisca theologia*, as part of a wisdom shared by Moses and other ancient writers, was taken up by Symphorien Champier and the brothers de la Boderie in the mid-sixteenth century.[12] But Platonism's reputation for containing the seeds of many heresies was not forgotten. And in the reaffirmation of orthodoxy during the Catholic reformation and after the Council of Trent (1545–63) Aristotle was encouraged and Platonism actively discouraged.[13] None the less religious Neoplatonism continued to be influential, at least in liberal Protestant circles in Germany and Britain, right into the eighteenth century.[14]

❧ ERASMUS AND CHRISTIAN HUMANISM ❧

Christian humanism was not so much a philosophical system but a set of attitudes which could be held by people who were sympathetic to any or none of the philosophies of the ancient world. The Christian humanists characteristically opposed metaphysical dogma with a sceptical outlook, preferring to rely on faith than to defend the Christian religion by scholastic proofs, and they stressed a simple undogmatic Christianity rather than doctrinal correctness.[15] They also gave a place to ordinary human pleasures in opposition to the monastic virtues and helped to prepare the way for a revival of Epicureanism.[16] The humanists were very influential in opposing the then academic (scholastic) philosophy and theology during the Renaissance period. They were inclined to defend certain philosophical positions, such as belief in free will, but to do so in a non-theoretical way. Humanism was characteristically a lay movement and naturally encouraged a tendency to address more applied and topical questions.

The doyen of Christian humanism was undoubtedly the great Dutch scholar Desiderius Erasmus (1466–1536). He was a pioneer in applying the critical methods of the humanists to the text of the Bible as well as in advocating its translation into the languages of the people. Erasmus wrote a sceptical work (*In Praise of Folly*) which, if not itself rigorously philosophical, helped to establish the role of Christian sceptic that others adopted in the late sixteenth and the seventeenth century. Like Martin Luther (1483–1546), Erasmus was hostile to scholasticism. More tolerant and less dogmatic than Luther and not in the least schismatic, he remained a moderate and conservative but liberal and sceptical Catholic to the end of his life. The two men engaged in a debate about free will, Luther denying that men were able to achieve salvation of their own accord. Erasmus for his part defended the availability of divine grace and human freedom to accept or refuse it.[17]

Amongst the Christian humanists in England, also distinguished followers of Erasmus, were Thomas More (1478–1535) and John Colet (c. 1467–1519). More's *Utopia* shows some debt to Plato's *Republic*, for instance in its communistic rather than individualistic ideal of human living. Yet his utopians are given to a life of pleasure and the work is Epicurean rather than Stoic or Platonic in its view of the highest good. At the same time the higher pleasures of reading literature are important to them. More's work had a considerable influence on English literature, for instance on Bacon's *New Atlantis*. Colet was an educational reformer who was strongly influenced by the Italian Neoplatonist Ficino.[18]

Erasmus also enjoyed a very considerable following in Spain where the *erasmitas* were influential both at court and in the universities until the mid-sixteenth century. One of the most outstanding Spanish Christian humanists was Juan Luis Vives (1492–1540). Vives was a keen opponent of Aristotelianism and was sceptical about the attainment of knowledge as understood in Aristotelian terms. His thought anticipates the 'mitigated scepticism' of many of the early modern philosophers. He advocated a form of inductive method and a more limited view of what could be achieved in science.[19] His views influenced another sceptical Spanish philosopher, Sanches. Vives was not only a theoretician but also a social reformer who criticized the Church for failing to do enough for the poor and who advocated a system of poor relief.

After the Council of Trent and the revival of orthodox belief and piety in Catholic Spain, the *erasmitas* lost their positions of importance. But their influence was strongly felt in the writings of the new scholastics who emerged in their place. The new scholastics adopted a less formal style of writing than in earlier scholasticism and often their philosophical writings were reflections on problems of practical life. The humanist concern with practical problems was shared by many of the Spanish Jesuits, notwithstanding their commitment to doctrinal orthodoxy and their involvement in doctrinal controversies.

This concern was shown by Juan de Mariana (1536–1624), who risked trouble with his Order and with the Spanish authorities through his pronouncements on the problem of poverty. Mariana also created trouble for himself by a book he wrote that offered guidance on the rights and duties of kings.[20] This book became notorious by appearing to sanction regicide in certain circumstances. Its author went so far as to refer to the assassin of Henry III as 'the eternal glory of France', words which his Order required him to delete from later editions. Such lapses of discretion were perhaps a hazard for a work which adopted the relaxed and personal style of the humanists and which developed its arguments through discussions of particular cases. At the same time Mariana wrote within the intellectual framework for discussing political philosophy provided by Aristotle and Aquinas. His book was thus very traditional and very topical and provocative at the same time. When Henry IV was also assassinated part of the blame fell on Mariana's book, copies of which were publicly burned in Paris. He himself spent some time in prison, but no charges were brought against him in Spain.

It is not certain how much Mariana would have acknowledged a humanist influence on his practical concerns and on his style of writing. But one figure who represented himself as a Christian humanist and who sought the support of Erasmus was the German 'occult philosopher' Heinrich Cornelius Agrippa von Nettesheim (1486–1535). Agrippa wrote a highly iconoclastic book to expose the 'uncertainty' and 'vanity' of the arts and sciences. He wrote the book, as he explained in the preface he wrote for the reader, 'because I see that so many men, puffed up with human knowledge and learning, not only condemn and despise the words of the Sacred Scriptures, but also prosecute and deride it with the same contempt . . .'. To the extent that he sought to encourage scepticism about human learning and institutions and a return to a simple biblical Christianity, Agrippa was similar to Erasmus. But he was more radical though perhaps even less consistently sceptical. He sought to demolish the edifice of received wisdom in order to remove the barriers to the discovery of truth that were placed in people's way by deference to established authorities. Thus he could exclaim: 'how impious a piece of tyranny it is, to capture the minds of students for prefixed authors, and to deprive them of the liberty of searching after and following the truth. . . .'[21] This suggests that Agrippa was by no means content to accept an Erasmian fideism. On the contrary, he seems to have believed that there was a method of attaining truth that was not vulnerable to the sceptic's attack.[22] He remained a Catholic but he was by no means disposed to accept the authority of the Church. Erasmus, by contrast, whilst acknowledging the fallibility and imperfection of the Church and its institutions, taught that in matters of faith they provided the best guide available.

❧ PARACELSUS AND THE TRADITION OF ❧ OCCULT PHILOSOPHY

It is perhaps artificial to distinguish religious Neoplatonism from its manifestations in what has become known as 'occult philosophy'. The former is concerned with the relation of humankind to God and only in a metaphysical way with the material world. The latter is more concerned with the relation of humankind to the world and with possible ways of manipulating the world for human benefit. There is no reason why these concerns should not be shared by the same people, as to some extent they were. They might, moreover, be given almost equal emphasis, as they were in the case of the Christian Cabbalist F. M. van Helmont, who in his own day was celebrated throughout much of Europe as a physician whose alternative medicine brought some spectacular cures where other doctors had failed. None the less there is some justification for the distinction between religious Neoplatonism and the occult philosophy. If the theoretical claims of the former brought charges of heresy, the practical bent of the occult philosophers led them to attach importance to experience.

One of the most influential figures in the Renaissance tradition of occult philosophy was Theophrastus Bombastus von Hohenheim (c. 1493–1541), who styled himself and is generally known as Paracelsus. Paracelsus was a self-taught Swiss physician who, like Agrippa and perhaps partly under his influence, set himself against all established scientific authority. 'My proofs', he insisted, 'derive from experience and my own reasoning, and not from reference to authorities.'[23] In some ways Paracelsus and Agrippa belong in the modern period. But their empiricism was unrigorous and their rejection of past assumptions and traditional authorities was not thoroughgoing. Both accepted the Neoplatonic view of humankind as a microcosm of the universe. Paracelsus based his medicine on this assumption. There are, for him, all sorts of correspondences between what we discover in man and what we discover in nature. These correspondences are evidence of hidden causal relations which the occult philosopher can learn to trigger and so manipulate the course of nature in a magical way. The discovery of such correspondences is a matter of what Agrippa termed 'long experience'. But the occult philosophers lacked a rigorous methodology for identifying them reliably. The kidney bean may look like a kidney but, contrary to what Paracelsians supposed, such beans have no special powers to cure kidney disorders.

Paracelsus, like other practitioners of an alternative medicine, had an erratic career as a physician, but he was credited with some spectacular cures. He did introduce some specific treatments of value, such as the use of laudanum as a pain-killer. Moreover some of his ideas would have been of great benefit had they been adopted. On his account all disease is natural and this led him to reject the view that mental disorders are due to inhabitation by demons. At the same time he was overly optimistic in his belief that nature had a cure for every disease.

Amongst the Paracelsians were some, including Boehme and the younger van Helmont, who have here been categorized as religious Neoplatonists. Mention should be made, however, of John Baptiste van Helmont (1577–1644) – who, though less of a philosopher than his son, is an important figure in the history of chemistry and is credited with the discovery of gases.[24] The Paracelsians were influential through much of the seventeenth century, when they were represented in England by Robert Fludd (1574–1637) and others.[25] But they and many of the religious Neoplatonists were opposed by, and some later opposed themselves to, the mechanical philosophy. Gassendi wrote a book attacking Fludd, and the moderns, especially the rationalists, tended to dismiss the occult philosophers and Neoplatonists generally precisely because they rejected such 'hidden' or unintelligible factors in the explanations for phenomena.[26]

➤➤ ARISTOTELIANISM AND ITS OPPONENTS ➤➤

During the medieval period, Aristotle's authority was undisputed and he was usually referred to simply as 'the philosopher'. But, though Aristotle remained by far the single most important philosopher during the Renaissance, this monopoly came to an end. Some of the Italian Renaissance humanists like Lorenzo Valla (see Chapter 1) associated Aristotle with the scholasticism they rejected. Others, however, such as Ermolao Barbaro (1454–93), sought to revive what they regarded as the true Aristotle, studied in the Greek, as against the distorted Aristotelian doctrines taught by the scholastics. Some, like Ficino, turned to other traditions, particularly the Platonic. Others, like Giovanni Pico della Mirandola, sought to reconcile Aristotle with those other traditions. These were just some of the responses available also to those outside Italy.

Martin Luther seems to have taken the extreme view of Valla and largely opposed himself to all philosophy, taking the view that Christianity had been corrupted by the Greek philosophical influence. Such a view could hardly be sustained in the long run in view of the central role that philosophy played both in the articulation of theological doctrine and in the educational curriculum. Not surprisingly, therefore, one of Luther's closest associates, Philipp Melanchthon (1497–1560), went back to an eclectic Aristotelianism. Melanchthon played a key role in the consolidation of Lutheranism in Germany, partly through his published works such as the *Loci communes*. Though this was a basically theological work, Melanchthon adopted a broadly Aristotelian framework. At the same time he was willing to interpret Aristotle in a modern way (for instance, as a nominalist) and, where the defence of religion might be advantaged by it, he did not refrain from incorporating notions that are quite foreign to Aristotelianism, such as the doctrine of innate principles.

Within the German university context a kind of Renaissance Aristotelianism became possible which embraced the humanist critique of the scholastics but insisted that they had distorted Aristotle's meaning. This had been the position of the so-called 'father of German humanism', Roelof Huysman (1444–85), known by his Latin name of Rodolphus Agricola. It was to become a common humanist position – one held, for instance, by the French humanist Jacques Lefèvre d'Étaples (c. 1460–1536), who sought to reform Aristotelianism via more accurate texts.[27]

The thought that the scholastics had debased Aristotle and departed from his true teachings invited, within the Protestant context, a comparison with the religious Reformation and its return to the correct text and true teachings of the Bible. There could be reformers (reformatores) in philosophy who would call for a return to the true Aristotle – the thought being that Aristotle was right after all and not to be condemned on account of the errors and obscurities of the scholastics.[28] In reality, however, the distinction between such a pure Aristotelianism and scholasticism was virtually impossible to sustain. In the short run, at least, the tacit and unthinking influence of traditional interpretations of Aristotle, like traditional interpretations of the Bible, was likely to be greater than new interpretations based on a humanist treatment of the Greek texts. Moreover the virtual equivalence of Aristotelianism with rationality disposed many to credit Aristotle with any view that had the authority of reason. Aristotelian and scholastic philosophy were inevitably confused and the assignation of individuals to one category rather than another is often highly problematic. Some of the new scholastics (see pp. 81–3) seem to have played an important part in ensuring that Aristotle's texts continued to receive attention. Indeed it is a remarkable fact that the publication of Aristotle's texts reached a high point in the mid-sixteenth century when the Catholic Reformation was at its peak.[29] The return to Aristotle in philosophy may have seemed like a return to good order in intellectual life. That, at any rate, seems to have been the thinking of Ignatius of Loyola, whose quasi-military teaching order, the Society of Jesus (founded in 1534), was committed to the restoration of papal authority, to Aquinas in theology and to Aristotle in philosophy.

If it is difficult to treat scholastics and Aristotelians as a separate class, there is no difficulty about separating the anti-Aristotelians from either of them. One of the most prominent and influential opponents of Aristotle was the French convert to Calvinism, Pierre de la Ramée (1515–72), usually known by his Latin name of Ramus. Ramus's criticisms fastened on the artificiality of Aristotelian logic which, in common with other humanists, he claimed was useless for discovering new truth. What was needed was a 'natural logic' that reflected human thought processes. What was needed was an art of discovery and an art of judgement. Ramus's writings were much more influential than they were original. In particular they helped to focus the preoccupation with method characteristic of such early modern philosophers as Descartes and Leibniz.[30]

☙ SUAREZ AND THE NEW SCHOLASTICISM ☙

I suggested in discussing Christian humanism (pp. 75–7) that part of what was new about the new scholasticism of the late sixteenth century was its reflection of humanistic values. This is already evident in the writings of the Dominican Francisco de Vitoria (c. 1492–1546), who had been acquainted during his time in Paris with Erasmus, Vives and some of the other leading humanists. Vitoria was appointed in 1526 to the most important theological chair at Salamanca and it is partly through this appointment that he was to exercise such a formative influence on the new scholasticism that flourished in Spain in the late sixteenth century.

Vitoria is best remembered for his pioneering work in international law.[31] He gave lectures at the university on current issues and the notes of some of these were published as *relectiones* on particular topics. In his *De Indis* (1532) he considered and defended the rights of the American Indians against the Spanish colonizers. In the same year he also produced a study of the rights and wrongs of war, his *De Jure Belli*, in which he argued for proportionality in the use of force as well as for the rights of non-combatants. Although Vitoria accepted there could be a 'just war', he rejected religious grounds as a 'just cause'. Thus the Spanish had no right, on his arguments, to make war on the American Indians or to dispossess them of their property merely because they were heathens. Vitoria was arguing within a framework of natural law that derived from Aristotle and Aquinas. But his concern with applied questions, which led to his being consulted by Charles V on matters of state, shows the influence of humanism.

As well as lecturing on such topics as the just war, Vitoria also lectured on theology. Here he broke with a centuries-old tradition by lecturing on Aquinas's *Summa Theologica* instead of the *Sentences* of Peter Lombard. This had already been done by another Dominican in Italy, Thomas de Vio, commonly known as Cajetan (1468–1534). But Vitoria pioneered the change in Spain. In doing so he prepared the way for even greater changes from traditional styles of presentation. These were initiated by his pupil, Francisco Suarez (1548–1617), perhaps the most important systematic philosopher of the period.[32] The traditional scholastic mode of presentation was the commentary. Suarez's most important work, his *Disputationes metaphysicae* (1597), was the first systematic and independent treatise on metaphysics. It dealt with a wide range of topics, from the nature of metaphysics to the existence of God, from universals to our knowledge of singulars, causality, freedom, individuality and many others. Although, as a Jesuit, Suarez was committed to Aquinas in theology, he departed from St Thomas in treating philosophy as independent of theology. His Latin was easy to read by comparison with the usual run of scholastic writings. Moreover some of his thought, for instance his nominalism, already reflected a critical approach to traditional scholasticism, and some accommodation to the 'modern way' of William of Occam and his followers. These are among reasons why he may have been so influential. But the pervasive influence of Suarez on seventeenth-century philosophy was not due entirely to the virtues of his own writings – remarkable though they were. Suarez was the major philosopher of the Society of Jesus and the Jesuits played a key role in the best educational institutions of Catholic Europe. Suarez's metaphysics also found its way into textbooks and was widely taught in Protestant universities. In these diverse ways his *Disputations* became an important part of the background to Descartes[33] in a Catholic context and to Leibniz in his Protestant German context.[34]

Suarez was also very influential as a political philosopher. The Dutch theorist Huig de Groot (1583–1645), known by his Latin name of Grotius, was indebted to Suarez and the Thomist tradition of natural law.[35] Grotius, who is regarded as the first theorist of natural rights, found in this tradition an answer to the relativism of Montaigne. Suarez himself drew rather conservative conclusions. Although he held the view that government derives its authority from the consent of the people, Suarez held that the community corporately invested its authority in the monarch in such a way that it could not be taken back. Unlike the more radical Jesuit Mariana,[36] Suarez thought it was almost never right to kill a tyrant, unless he was threatening to destroy the community. Again Suarez distinguished the *ius gentium* from natural law by making the former depend on customary practices of states rather than on what was true for all states. Since slavery conformed to the *ius gentium*, Suarez did not condemn it.

Suarez's work had great influence within the Jesuit order. Some took to writing systematic treatises on philosophy. The Spaniard Roderigo de Arriaga (1592–1667) wrote a systematic introduction to philosophy called *Cursus philosophicus* (1632) which was widely read and cited throughout the century. Others engaged in applied philosophy. One of Suarez's pupils, the Flemish Jesuit Leonard Lessius (1554–1623) wrote a book largely devoted to what nowadays would be called 'business ethics'.[37] Lessius, who taught theology in Louvain, travelled regularly to Antwerp to learn at first hand about business practices in what was then one of Europe's major financial centres. His *De jure et justitia* drew on the thought of Aquinas but sought to answer contemporary moral problems, including the fraught problem of usury. Lessius was the first Catholic theologian to defend the view that lending money with interest was not wrong in itself.

Throughout the late Renaissance period Jesuit philosophers were to be found at the frontiers of the subject. That is not to say that they did not engage in debates relating to traditional philosophical topics. One frequent topic of Renaissance philosophy was free will, and the traditional problem of how this could be reconciled with God's fore-knowledge and preordination was addressed by, amongst others, Luis de Molina (1535–1600).[38] Molina, as also Suarez, held that God knows through what he called the 'middle science' (*scientia media*) what any individual would do (freely) if given sufficient grace to do it. In extending sufficient grace and so preordaining a right action God does not detract from the freedom of the individual. Such freedom is quite consistent, Molina argued, with the fact that nothing happens but God knows it will happen and ordains that it will happen.

Others of the Society of Jesus worked and wrote commentaries on the texts of Aristotle. One who influenced Suarez himself was 'the Portuguese Aristotle', Peter da Fonseca (1528–99). Fonseca's own books – one of which went into fifty-three editions between 1564 and 1625 – were by themselves highly influential in restoring Aristotelianism.[39] Moreover, as a teacher at the University of Coimbra, he was able to instigate the work of a team of Jesuit scholars to produce a set of texts and commentaries on Aristotle's major works. The Coimbra commentaries (1592–1606) were often reprinted and widely used throughout the seventeenth century.

❧ JUSTUS LIPSIUS AND THE REVIVAL OF ❧ STOICISM

Stoicism was one of the great systems of ancient Greek philosophy and one that was adopted by some of the greatest writers of the Roman world, such as Seneca and Cicero. The Stoics believed that events in the material world were profoundly and necessarily interconnected. They believed that there was an underlying cause of these events but did not identify this first cause with a providence. Wise men do not allow themselves to be dependent on the way the world goes but seek to achieve tranquillity through recognizing the interconnection of things.

The Renaissance revival of Stoicism is due, in particular, to the Flemish humanist Joest Lips (1547–1606), usually known by his Latin name, Justus Lipsius. Lipsius's first Neostoic work was his *De con-*

stantia (1584),[40] a dialogue set during the revolt of the Low Countries against Spanish rule. The work commends the virtue of steadfastness (*constantia*) – of being unmoved by changes in external circumstances. Lipsius's main accounts of Stoicism were his *Physiologia Stoicorum* and *Manuductio ad stoicam philosophiam*, both published in 1604. He also produced an edition of the texts of Seneca.

Stoicism was introduced into Germany by Kaspar Schoppe (1576–1649), known by his Latin name of Scioppius, and seems to have become well established in the Low Countries.[41] It was also influential in France,[42] thanks partly to Guillaume Du Vair (1556–1621). Du Vair wrote several works in French, including his *De la philosophie morale des Stoïques*, which he wrote as a preface to his French translation of Epictetus's *Enchiridion* in 1594. Like Lipsius, he advocated a Christianized Stoicism. Both were translated into English in the late sixteenth century – Du Vair's *Moral Philosophie of the Stoicks* being favoured with two translations.[43]

Stoicism was highly influential at the beginning of the seventeenth century, when it was taken to be entirely compatible with Christianity.[44] During the century, however, this compatibility came to be questioned and its influence declined.[45] Epicureanism, on the other hand, seems to have become regarded more favourably.[46] For long misrepresented and dismissed as a debased philosophy, it was revived in a Christianized form by Pierre Gassendi, who published three books on Epicurus in 1647–9. Gassendi was able to do this by presenting Epicurean atomism as a hypothesis and combining it with scepticism as to whether humans are capable of arriving at definitive knowledge of the world.[47]

Stoicism and Epicureanism, together with Platonism and Aristotelianism, comprised what were seen as the four great 'dogmatic' philosophical systems of the ancient world. As we have seen, each of them was revived and defended in the late Renaissance period. The embarrassment of choice was no doubt one factor promoting a more persistent revival, that of scepticism, which opposed itself to the claims of such dogmatic systems. Yet some, like Gassendi, found it possible in practice to combine scepticism with a suitably tempered allegiance to any of the ancient 'schools', except Aristotelianism. Montaigne began as a Stoic before rejecting that system for the scepticism of his later period. But his associate and disciple Pierre Charron (1541–1603) combined his scepticism with a Stoic moral philosophy.[48]

❧ MONTAIGNE AND THE REVIVAL OF ❧ ANCIENT SCEPTICISM

We have already seen that the Christian humanists, in their reaction against academic philosophy and theology, tended to adopt a highly sceptical view of human aspirations to knowledge apart from revelation. In the case of Agrippa this scepticism was argued for in a comprehensive and systematic way by a critical and highly iconoclastic treatment of the pretensions of all the known arts and sciences. Agrippa alluded to the ancient Greek sceptics but made little use of their arguments. Renaissance philosophers often argued by seeking to establish a consensus amongst ancient authorities. Agrippa turned this mode of argument on its head and sought to argue, on the contrary, that on every major point the ancient authorities contradicted one another.

During the Renaissance period some of the important sources for classical scepticism were rediscovered, including Cicero's *Academica*, Diogenes Laertius's *Life of Pyrrho* and the collected writings of Sextus Empiricus.[49] These arguments were frequently taken up in a Christian humanist way – in the first place, to discredit the claims of Aristotelian and scholastic philosophy and, more positively, to underline the 'fideist' claim that humans could not achieve knowledge by their own resources and should rely instead on faith and divine revelation. The Christian Pyrrhonist, François de La Mothe le Vayer (1588–1672), wrote as if the entire purpose of scepticism was to reduce people to a total suspense of judgement (called the *Epoché*). In that state of mind they had abandoned the arrogance of the scholastics (referred to abusively as 'the Pedants') for the humility of those able to receive the fruits of faith: 'O precious Epoché! O sure and agreeable mental retreat! O inescapable antidote against the presumption of knowledge of the Pedants!'[50]

There is little doubt that La Mothe le Vayer was sincere in his profession of a religious motivation. It was so usual, however, to plead such a motivation that it became something of a convention adopted later by many of the best-known sceptics of the modern period such as Pierre Bayle and David Hume. Just because it was a way of making scepticism publicly acceptable and a way of avoiding the charge of subversion, it was a motive that might readily be professed insincerely, either because it was not the motive at all or because it was not as important a motive as was made out. For this reason the interpretation of the writings of Renaissance sceptics such as Agrippa, Michel de Montaigne (1533–92) and Pierre Bayle (1647–1706) has been fraught with difficulty and controversy.[51]

Agrippa sought to present himself, as we have seen, as an Erasmian sceptic whose purpose was to make people turn back to a simple biblical Christianity. But, as the author of *De occulta philosophia*, he was represented in the late sixteenth century as a Faust figure, who had made a pact with the devil in order to obtain a knowledge of the magical arts. This evil reputation should probably be regarded as an almost total fabrication, as a propaganda coup by the monks to whom Agrippa was so bitterly opposed. At the same time it is notable that one form of magic – a natural or empirical magic – was exempted from the otherwise complete scepticism of Agrippa's *De vanitate*. This makes him appear as a Faust figure in a more positive way, as someone who rejected established knowledge as of no value to human beings and who sought rather to unlock the secrets of nature so as to use natural powers for human benefit. But it may be wrong to expect a simple consistent interpretation of the thought of such figures as Agrippa. The existence of tensions and inconsistencies in their thought may more fruitfully be seen as a reflection of what has been identified as the deepening 'sceptical crisis'[52] of Renaissance and early modern philosophy.

Montaigne's *Apologie de Raimond Sebond* (1580) used the arguments of the ancient sceptics in order to cast doubt on the reliability of the senses, to show how human judgements are made fallible by all sorts of social and cultural factors. Montaigne advocated the Pyrrhonian suspension of judgement and urged that people should live in accordance with nature and custom. He professed Christian fideism but at least part of his purpose in using sceptical arguments seems to have been to oppose bigotry and promote greater tolerance. He seems to have been a conservative, suggesting that people, having been led to a due sense of the limitations of human faculties, should accept the guidance of established authority, be it civil or ecclesiastical.

Another direction in which scepticism might be pursued was to the conclusion that only God, strictly speaking, was capable of knowledge, if knowledge be understood in the Aristotelian sense of giving necessary reasons or causes for phenomena. Human beings could not hope to achieve such knowledge. This is the conclusion, for instance, of the arguments put forward by the Portuguese physician and philosopher Francisco Sanches (c. 1550–1623) in his *Quod Nihil Scitur*.[53] One corollary Sanches drew was the fideistic one, that the Christian religion cannot be defended by philosophy and depends wholly on faith. But he also, and quite consistently, proposed an experimental method that would lead to a true 'understanding of natural phenomena'. Sanches thus anticipated one kind of response to scepticism in modern philosophy (for instance in Gassendi and Locke) which was to accept the impossibility of knowledge but to seek a reliable substitute through methods which would at least give results that were highly probable.

The arguments of the sceptics provided an important part of the intellectual context in which Descartes (see Chapters 5 and 6) developed his philosophical thought. Descartes sought to meet the sceptics on their own ground. Yet it is not known that any sceptic thought he had been refuted by Descartes's arguments. On the contrary, the sceptics, notably Simon Foucher (1644–97), were amongst his keenest critics. Foucher presented himself, in Renaissance style, as an apologist for the sceptics of the ancient Platonic Academy. His characteristic mode of attack was to identify the underlying assumptions of the metaphysical dogmatists (Descartes and Malebranche particularly) and then complain that these had not been demonstrated.[54] He did believe that certain truths (e.g. the existence of God) could be demonstrated but denied Descartes's demonstration of the existence of the material world. Foucher was an early critic of the distinction between primary and secondary qualities. He played an important role in showing how Cartesianism tended towards idealism.[55] Indirectly, through Bayle and Berkeley, Foucher's scepticism is linked with that of David Hume.[56]

❧ CONCLUDING REMARKS ❧

It is convenient to distinguish Renaissance from early modern philosophy. But, in some respects, modern philosophy continued tendencies that already existed beforehand. Humanism took philosophy out of the schoolroom and the cloister and made it, to a degree unprecedented in the history of Christendom, a layperson's subject. Whereas previously Latin had been the language for philosophy as for academic discourse generally, the development of printing and a wider lay readership made translation into vernacular languages an increasingly common practice. This in turn led, particularly in France, to the practice of writing philosophical works in the vernacular. Amongst late-sixteenth-century philosophers, Montaigne, Du Vair and Charron all wrote in French.

Another modern tendency already apparent in the late sixteenth century was to treat philosophy as a subject independent of theology. This showed itself even in the new scholasticism, a movement which originated amongst clergy. It is a curious feature of the Catholic reformation that it promoted a more secular view of philosophy. Grotius put it famously, if controversially, in his suggestion that the obligations of natural law hold even 'if we concede that there is no God'. In this respect his view of natural law was no different from that of the Jesuit Suarez, to whom he acknowledged a considerable debt. It seems clear that one reason why Suarez and other Jesuits gave so much time to political theory was that they wished to see a radical separation between the authority of a monarch and the authority of the Church. Whereas the authority of a monarch was secular and derived ultimately from the consent of the people, the Church and papal authority was directly ordained by God.

The respect in which Renaissance philosophy is most obviously different from that of modern philosophy is in its willingness to use arguments that rely upon appeal to traditional authorities. Renaissance philosophers believed, or affected to believe, that they were reviving the thought of the ancients. For some this meant believing in an ancient wisdom that had been lost and needed to be recovered. But ancient authorities could be found to disagree with one another. This consideration left a choice between becoming a partisan of a particular ancient 'sect' or becoming a sceptic.

One might, of course, combine a moderate scepticism with the qualified adoption of one of the ancient systems.[57] To do this consistently, however, it would be necessary to find a basis for accepting what the ancient authors had said which did not consist simply in the fact that they had said it. To do that was to begin to be a modern philosopher. To the extent that this is what Gassendi did in his defence of Epicureanism, he is properly regarded as a modern philosopher.

Some of the early modern philosophers have, like Gassendi, a Renaissance face and indeed philosophy could still be presented in a Renaissance style right through the seventeenth and even in the eighteenth century.[58] But, if moderns could sometimes behave like Renaissance philosophers, it is also true that some Renaissance philosophers were in some respects early moderns. For instance, many of the most sceptical and iconoclastic figures, such as Agrippa, Vives, Sanches and Ramus sought independent methods of making discoveries and verifying them. Methodology was already becoming a preoccupation of late Renaissance philosophy, as it was for the early moderns. The two periods of philosophy are to that extent continuous. For this reason the sixteenth century may as aptly be represented as a period of transition as a period of revival or 'renaissance'.

❧ NOTES ❧

1 These countries and regions were home to most of the major Renaissance philosophers outside Italy. Mention should also be made of Switzerland, which was the native country of Paracelsus. Renaissance philosophy was not, of course, confined to these countries. But other parts of Europe are largely neglected in the literature. For accounts of humanism in Croatia, Hungary and the Czech Lands, see Rabil [2.96], Part III.

2 See, for instance, Brown [2.171]. See also Heinekamp [2.176].

3 See pp. 79–81.

4 See note 14 below.

5 See note 26 below.

6 See pp. 77–9.

7 In his *Discourse on Metaphysics*, sec. IX, for instance, Leibniz put forward a number of paradoxical propositions, beliefs made more credible by his theory of substance, including that no two substances are exactly alike and that each substance is a mirror of God and of the entire universe. These doctrines are all anticipated in *De docta ignorantia*, but it is unlikely that Leibniz owed any of them directly to Cusanus. Indeed he wrote as if the first of them was a refinement by him of a doctrine of Aquinas.

8 See Chapter 1, pp. 45–6, for a more detailed account of the interest in the Cabbala in the Italian Renaissance.

9 See Reuchlin [2.56], particularly the introduction by G. Lloyd Jones.

10 Henry More is discussed in vol. 5, Chapter 1, as is another Neoplatonist, Ann Conway. For a discussion of the connection between these two philosophers, F. M. van Helmont and Leibniz, see Brown [2.170].

11 Van Helmont, [2.62], 13.

12 On the influence of Champier, see Copenhaver [2.115]. On the 'ancient theology' in sixteenth-century France, see Walker [2.108], ch. 3.

13 For the encouragement of Aristotle's philosophy, see note 29 below. The fate of Bruno discussed at the end of the previous chapter is symptomatic of the reaction against Neoplatonism in Catholic orthodoxy. For an account of the reaction against the occult philosophy, see also Yates [2.109].

14 Thus Berkeley, in his late work *Siris* (1744), sought to argue that 'the *Pythagoreans* and Platonists had a notion of the true System of the World' (sec. 266) and explicitly acknowledged key Neoplatonic figures such as Plotinus, Proclus and Iamblichus.

15 Some of those discussed as sceptics on pp. 85–7, such as Montaigne, may also be classed as Christian humanists. Erasmus, Vives and perhaps Agrippa can also be discussed under both heads.

16 See pp. 83–4. See also Allen [2.75] and Jungkuntz [2.93].

17 There is a version of this debate edited and translated by E. W. Winter as *Erasmus-Luther: Discourse on Free Will*, New York, 1961.

18 See Miles [2.137].

19 See Limbrick [2.162], 30ff.

20 See Mariana [2.54]. See also Talmadge [2.148].

21 Agrippa [2.46], from the preface 'To the Reader'.

22 Agrippa also (see pp. 77 and 85–6) had positive commitments to the occult philosophy, in particular to natural magic. Whether his overall position is a consistent one has puzzled those who have studied his work. See Bowen [2.127], Nauert [2.128] and Zambelli [2.129].

23 Quoted from Paracelsus [2.42], 55.

24 See Redgrove and Redgrove [2.166].

25 See Debus [2.111].

26 The Paracelsians invoked an 'Archeus' or 'world soul' as a kind of universal cause and the Neoplatonists generally sought to defend a vitalistic view of the world in opposition to the mechanical philosophy. Leibniz frequently criticized them for doing this (e.g. L. E. Loemker (ed.) *Gottfried Wilhelm Leibniz: Philosophical Papers and Letters* (Dordrecht, Reidel, 2nd edn, 1969), p. 409; P.

Remnant and J. Bennett (eds) *G. W. Leibniz: New Essays on Human Under-standing* (Cambridge, Cambridge University Press, 1981), p. 72). That is partly why he distinguished the Renaissance Neoplatonists from and contrasted them unfavourably with Plato. Thus he criticized Ficino for launching into extravagant thoughts and abandoning what was more simple and solid. 'Ficino speaks everywhere of ideas, soul of the world, mystical numbers, and similar things, instead of pursuing the exact definitions Plato tries to give of notions' (C. I. Gerhardt (ed.) *Die Philosophischen Schriften von G. W. Leibniz* (Berlin, 1875–90), vol. i, p. 380).

27 Lefèvre d'Étaples was not exclusively interested in Aristotle. He was also influenced by Neoplatonism and edited Neoplatonic works.

28 Leibniz cast himself as such a reformer of philosophy, as a reviver of the true Aristotle against the distortions of the scholastics in a letter to his former teacher, Jacob Thomasius, in 1669. He interpreted Aristotle as a nominalist and argued that modern philosophy was consistent with Aristotle's physics. (See Loemker, op. cit., pp. 93ff.)

29 C. B. Schmitt [2.100] has cited the (probably incomplete, but none the less significant) statistical information, which shows the number of Aristotle editions dipping to fifty-one in the 1520s and rising to 219 in the 1550s. The first two sessions of the Council of Trent were held in 1545–7 and 1551–3. The conjecture that this revival of Aristotle owes a good deal to the Catholic Reformation is my own.

30 Leibniz was less dismissive of scholastic logic than was Descartes. But he contrasted the 'true logic' with 'what we have previously honoured by that name' and offered a Ramist redefinition of the subject as 'the art of using the understanding not only to judge proposed truth but also to discover hidden truth' (Loemker, op. cit., p. 463).

31 See Scott [2.167]. See also Hamilton [2.124].

32 See Mora [2.164].

33 Descartes studied at the Jesuit College of La Flèche and is reputed to have carried a copy of the *Disputations* around with him on his travels. On Descartes's debt to Suarez, see Cronin [2.173] and Wells [2.186].

34 See Lewalter [2.177] and Wundt [2.187]. Suarez's followers in Germany included Leibniz's teacher, Jacob Thomasius. Leibniz himself claimed that, as a young man, he could read Suarez like a novel. There is a direct influence of Suarezian nominalism on Leibniz's early dissertation on the principle of individuation. Though his thought developed along quite different lines, Leibniz included Suarez amongst the 'deeper scholastics' and not amongst those whom, as a modern, he frequently abused.

35 See Grotius [2.52]. See also Tuck [2.144].

36 See pp. 76–7 for a brief account of Mariana.

37 Lessius [2.27]. See Chamberlain [2.146].

38 See Molina [2.33]. See also Pegis [2.151].

39 See Ferreira Gomez [2.142].

40 This work was translated into English in 1595 and has been reprinted. See Lipsius [2.53].

41 Lipsius is further discussed in connection with Spinoza in Chapter 9, pp. 316–17. See also Kristeller [2.178].

42 Chesneau [2.114] gives an account of the history of Neostoicism in early-seventeenth-century France.

43 The new Stoicism seems to have been well received in England. There were two English translations of Du Vair's treatise and one of Lipsius's *De constantia* at the end of the sixteenth century.

44 The assumption that it was an inherently Christian philosophy was not confined to lay people. One of the adherents of Stoicism in England was the Anglican Bishop, Joseph Hall.

45 Stoicism was attacked as a naturalistic and unChristian philosophy by the Jansenists, especially by Blaise Pascal. In a paper attacking the 'two sects of naturalists in fashion today', Leibniz placed Hobbes within the Epicurean tradition and Spinoza within the tradition of Stoicism. He criticized Spinoza and the Stoics for their fatalism and for seeking to make a virtue of enforced 'patience'. (See G. W. *Leibniz: Discourse on Metaphysics and Related Writings*, ed. and trans. R. N. D. Martin and S. Brown (Manchester, Manchester University Press, 1988), pp. 104f.)

46 See Jungkuntz [2.93].

47 Gassendi's philosophy is discussed more fully in Chapter 7.

48 See Charron [2.16].

49 See Schmitt [2.98] and Schmitt [2.101].

50 Quoted from Popkin [2.95], 93. The original is from La Mothe le Vayer's 'Petit Traitté Sceptique sur cette façon de parler', La Mothe le Vayer [2.5], IX, 280.

51 Few modern commentators and probably few of his contemporaries have supposed that Hume's fideistic conclusion to his sceptical essay 'Of Miracles' is anything other than ironic. But many of the Renaissance sceptics seem to have been perfectly sincere in their fideism, even as late as Bayle, whom Elizabeth Labrousse [2.131] has suggested should be so interpreted.

52 The phrase is that of Richard Popkin, whose pioneering book [2.182] on the history of scepticism in the early modern period remains one of the most original and perceptive treatments of this topic.

53 This work was written in 1576 and published in 1581. It is available in a modern English translation [2.57] with a good introduction.

54 For an account of late seventeenth-century philosophy that gives some prominence to Foucher, see R. A. Watson, *The Breakdown of Cartesian Metaphysics* (Atlantic Highlands, N.J., Humanities Press, 1987).

55 Foucher seems to have been responsible for Leibniz's perception of Descartes as a Renaissance philosopher, whose most important contribution had been to restore the study of Plato and to add to it the doubts (concerning the senses) of the Platonic Academy. (See, for instance, Loemker, op. cit., p. 469.)

56 Hume's scepticism is treated in the next volume of this series, vol. 5, Chapter 6.

57 See pp. 83–4.

58 When Leibniz wrote his *Specimen of Dynamics*, he presented it as a restoration of Aristotelianism:

> Just as our age has already saved from scorn Democritus' corpuscles, Plato's ideas, and the Stoic's tranquillity in light of the most perfect

interconnection of things, so now we shall make intelligible the teachings of the Peripatetics concerning forms or entelechies . . .
(G. W. Leibniz, *Philosophical Essays*, ed. and trans. R. Ariew and D. Garber (Indianapolis, Ind., Hackett, 1989), p. 118)

Leibniz was himself in many ways a late Renaissance philosopher. But in the early 1690s he was still willing to present himself as a post-modern or neo-Renaissance philosopher, arguing in a modern way without appeals to ancient authority but none the less claiming that, properly understood, his conclusions were not really entirely novel but important confirmation of truths taught by a 'philosophy accepted for so many centuries'. Berkeley's late defence of the Neoplatonists should perhaps also be understood as such a development. See note 14.

❧ BIBLIOGRAPHY ❧

Original language editions

Complete and selected works

2.1 Agrippa von Nettesheim, Henricus Cornelius, *Opera*, Lyons, 1600; reprinted, R. H. Popkin (ed.), Hildesheim, Olms, 1976

2.2 Conimbricenses, *Commentarii Collegii Conimbricensis . . . in universam dialecticam Aristotelis*, Cologne, 1607; reprinted, Hildesheim, Olms, 1976.

2.3 Cusanus, Nicolaus, *Opera omnia*, Leipzig, Felix Meiner, 1932.

2.4 Erasmus, Desiderius, *Opera omnia*, ed. J. Leclerc, 10 vols, Leiden, 1703–6; reprinted, Hildesheim, Olms, 1961–2.

2.5 La Mothe le Vayer, François de, *Oevres*, 15 vols, Paris, 1669.

2.6 Lipsius, Justus, *Opera omnia*, Basle, 1675.

2.7 Montaigne, Michel de, *Oevres complètes*, ed. A. Thibaudet and M. Rat, Paris, Gallimard, 1976.

2.8 Paracelsus, Theophrastus, *Sämtliche Werke*, ed. K. Sudhoff and E. Matthiessen, 14 vols, Munich, 1923–33; reprinted, Hildesheim, Olms.

2.9 Suarez, Francisco, *Opera omnia*, ed. M. Andre and C. Berton, 28 vols, Paris, 1856–78.

Separate works

2.10 Agrippa, Henricus Cornelius, *De incertitudine et vanitate scientiarum atque artium declamatio*, Antwerp, 1530.

2.11 Agrippa, Henricus Cornelius, *De occulta philosophia libri tres*, Cologne, 1533.

2.12 Arriaga, Rodrigo de, *Cursus philosophicus*, Antwerp, 1632.

2.13 Bayle, Pierre, *Dictionaire historique et critique*, 1692–1702, Amsterdam, 5th edn, 1740.

2.14 Berkeley, George, *Siris*, first published as *A Chain of Philosophical Reflexions and Inquiries concerning the Virtues of Tar-Water, and diverse other*

       Subjects connected together and arising from one another, Dublin and London, 1744.

2.15 Boehme, Jakob, *Aurora, oder die Morgenrote im Aufgang*, 1612.

2.16 Charron, Pierre, *De la sagesse*, ed. A. Duval, 3 vols, Paris, 1824; reprinted, Geneva, Slatkine Reprints, 1968.

2.17 Du Vair, Guillaume, *De la sainte philosophie. Philosophie morale des Stoïques*, ed. G. Michaut, Paris, Vrin, 1945.

2.18 Ebreo, Leone, *Dialoghi d'amore*, Rome, 1535.

2.19 Fludd, Robert, *Philosophia Moysaica . . .* , Gouda, 1638.

2.20 Fonseca, Pedro da, *Commentarii in libros metaphysicorum*, Lisbon, 1577–89; reprinted, Hildesheim, Olms, 1964.

2.21 Foucher, Simon, *Dissertation sur la recherche de la vérité, contenant l'apologie des academiciens . . .* , Paris, Estienne Michallet, 1687.

2.22 Gassendi, Pierre, *Exercitationes Paradoxicae Adversus Aristoteleos*, Paris, 1624.

2.23 Gassendi, Pierre, *Epistolica exercitatio, in qua praecipua principia philosophiae Roberto Fluddi . . . reteguntur*, Paris, 1630.

2.24 Grotius, Hugo, *De iure belli ac pacis libri tres*, Paris, 1625.

2.25 Knorr von Rosenroth, Christian (ed.), *Kabbala Denudata Seu Doctrina Hebraeorum Transcendentalis et Metaphysica*, Sulzbach, vol. 1, 1677, vol. 2, 1684; reprinted, Hildesheim, Olms, 1974.

2.26 La Mothe le Vayer, François de (under pseudonym of Oratius Tubero), *Cinque Dialogues, faits à l'imitation des anciens*, Mons, 1671.

2.27 Lessius, Leonard, *De Jure et Justitia*, Louvain, 1605.

2.28 Lipsius, Justus, *Manuductionis ad Stoicam philosophiam libri tres*, Antwerp, 1604.

2.29 Lipsius, Justus, *Physiologia Stoicorum*, Antwerp, 1604.

2.30 Mariana, Juan de, *De Rege et Regis Institutione*, Toledo, 1599.

2.31 Melanchthon, Philipp, *Compendiaria dialectes ratio*, Wittenberg, 1520.

2.32 Montaigne, Michel de, 'Apologie de Raymond Sebond' (1576), in *Les Essays de Michel de Montaigne*, ed. P. Villey, Paris, Alcan, 1922.

2.33 Molina, Luis de, *Liberi Arbitrii cum Gratiae Donis, Divina Praescientia, Providentia, Praedestinatione et Reprobatione Concordia*, Lisbon, 1588.

2.34 Ramus, Petrus, *Dialecticae institutiones. Aristotelicae animadversiones*, Paris, 1543; reprinted, Stuttgart-Bad Cannstatt, Friedrich Frommann, 1964.

2.35 Sanches, Francisco, *Quod Nihil Scitur*, 1581.

2.36 Suarez, Francisco, *Metaphysicarum disputationum, in quibus et universa naturalis theologia ordinate traditur, et quaestiones ad omnes duodecim Aristotelis libros pertinentes*, Maguntiae, 1697; reprint of Paris, 1866, edition by Olms, Hildesheim, 1965.

2.37 Suarez, Francisco, *Tractatus de legibus ac Deo Legislatore*, Conimbriae, D. Gomes de Loureyo, 1612.

2.38 Vitoria, Francisco de, *Relectiones de Indis et De Iure Bello*, Salamanca, 1557.

2.39 Vives, Juan Luis, *Adversus Pseudodialecticos*, Selestadii, 1520; critical edition by C. Fantazzi, Leiden, Brill, 1979.

English translations

Complete and selected works

2.40 Erasmus, *Collected Works*, Toronto, University of Toronto Press, 1974-.

2.41 Montaigne, Michel, *The Complete Essays of Montaigne*, trans. D. M. Frame, Stanford, Calif., Stanford University Press, 1958.

2.42 Paracelsus, *Selected Writings*, ed. J. Jacobi, trans. N. Guterman, London, Routledge & Kegan Paul, 1951.

2.43 Paracelsus, *Hermetical and Alchemical Writings*, trans. A. E. Waite, 2 vols, New Hyde Park, N.Y., University Books, 1966.

2.44 Suarez, Francisco, *Selections from Three Works* (incl. *On the Laws*), trans. G. L. Williams, Classics of International Law Series, Oxford, Oxford University Press, 1944.

2.45 Vitoria, Francisco de, *Political Writings*, ed. A. Pagden, trans. L. Lawrance, Cambridge, Cambridge University Press, 1991.

Separate works

2.46 Agrippa von Nettesheim, Henricus Cornelius, *Of the Vanitie and Uncertaintie of Artes and Sciences*, trans. James Sandford, London, Henry Wykes, 1569; reprinted, C. M. Dunn (ed.), Northridge, Calif., California State University Press, 1974.

2.47 Bayle, Pierre, *Historical and Critical Dictionary* (Selections), ed. and trans. R. H. Popkin, Indianapolis, 1965; reprinted, Indianapolis, Ind., Hackett, 1991.

2.48 Cusanus, *Nicholas of Cusa on Learned Ignorance: A Translation and Appraisal of* De Docta Ignorantia, ed. and trans. J. Hopkins, Minneapolis, Minn., Arthur J. Banning Press, 1981.

2.49 Du Vair, Guillaume, trans. T. James, London, 1598; in R. Kirk (ed.), *The Moral Philosophie of the Stoicks*, New Brunswick, N.J., Rutgers University Press, 1951.

2.50 Erasmus, Desiderius, *In Praise of Folly and Letter to Dorp*, trans. C. H. Miller, Princeton, N.J., Princeton University Press, 1979.

2.51 Fludd, Robert, *Mosaicall Philosophy, grounded upon the essentiall truth or eternal sapience. Written first in Latin, and afterwards thus rendred into English*, London, 1659.

2.52 Grotius, Hugo, *De iure belli ac pacis libri tres*, trans. F. W. Kelsey and others, Oxford, Clarendon, 1925.

2.53 Lipsius, Justus, *Two Books of Constancie*, trans. J. Stradling, London, 1595; reprinted, R. Kirk (ed.), New Brunswick, N.J., Rutgers University Press, 1939.

2.54 Mariana, Juan de, *The King and the Education of the King*, trans. G. A. Moore, Maryland, The Country Dollar Press, 1948.

2.55 Melanchthon, *The Loci Communes of Philipp Melanchthon*, trans. C. L. Hill, Boston, Meador, 1944.

2.56 Reuchlin, Johann, *De arte cabalistica. On the Art of the Kabbalah*, trans. M. and S. Goodman, New York, Abaris Books, 1983.

2.57 Sanches, Francisco, *That Nothing is Known (Quod Nihil Scitur)*, ed. E. Limbrick and D. F. S. Thomson, Cambridge, Cambridge University Press, 1988.

2.58 Suarez, Francisco, *Francis Suarez: On the Various Kinds of Distinction, Disputationes metaphysicae, disputatio VII*, ed. and trans. C. Vollet, Milwaukee, Wisc., Marquette University Press, 1947.

2.59 Suarez, Francisco, *Suarez on Individuation. Metaphysical Disputation V: Individual Unity and Its Principle*, ed. and trans. J. J. E. Gracia, Milwaukee, Wisc., Marquette University Press, 1982.

2.60 Suarez, Francisco, *Francis Suarez: On Formal and Universal Unity*, ed. and trans. J. F. Ross, Milwaukee, Wisc., Marquette University Press, 1964.

2.61 Suarez, Francisco, *The Metaphysics of Good and Evil according to Suarez: Metaphysical Disputations X & XI*, ed. and trans. J. Gracia, Munich, Philosophia, 1989.

2.62 van Helmont, Francis Mercury, *A Cabbalistic Dialogue in Answer to the Opinion of a Learned Doctor in Philosophy and Theology that the World was made out of Nothing, as it is contained in the second part of the Cabbala Denudata & appears in the Lib. Sohar*, London, 1682.

2.63 Vitoria, Francisco de, *De Indis et de iure belli relectiones*, trans. J. Pawley, Classics of International Law Series, Washington, D. C., Carnegie Institution, 1917.

2.64 Vives, Juan Luis, *Against the Pseudodialecticians. A Humanist Attack on Medieval Logic*, ed. and trans. R. Guerlac, Dordrecht, Reidel, 1979.

Bibliographies and concordances

Bibliographies

2.65 Cranz, F. E. and Schmitt, C. B. *A Bibliography of Aristotle Editions, 1501–1600*, Baden-Baden, V. Koerner, 1971; 2nd edn, 1984.

2.66 Kleinen, H. and Danzer, R. 'Cusanus-Bibliographie, 1920–1961', *Mitteilungen und Forschungenbeiträge der Cusanus-Gesellschaft* I (1961) 95–126.

2.67 McCormick, J. F. *A Suarezian Bibliography*, Chicago, Ill., Loyola University Press, 1937.

2.68 Margolin, Jean Claude, *Douze années de bibliographie érasmienne, 1950–1961*, Paris, Vrin, 1963.

2.69 Noreña, C. G. *A Vives Bibliography*, Studies in Renaissance Literature, vol. 5, Lewiston, Edwin Mellon Press, 1990.

2.70 Schmitt, C. B. *A Critical Survey and Bibliography of Studies on Renaissance Aristotelianism, 1958–1969*, Padua, Antenore, 1971.

2.71 Smith, G. 'A Suarez Bibliography', in G. Smith (ed.) *Jesuit Thinkers of the Renaissance*, Milwaukee, Wisc., Marquette University Press, 1939, 227–38.

Concordances

2.72 Bolchazy, L. J. (ed.) *A Concordance to the Utopia of St. Thomas More and A Frequency Word List*, Hildesheim, Olms, 1978.

2.73 Wedick, H. E. and Schweitzer, F. (eds) *Dictionary of the Renaissance*, New York, Philosophical Library, 1967.

2.74 Zellinger, E. *Cusanus-Konkordanz*, Munich, Huber, 1960.

Background and influences on Renaissance philosophy outside Italy

2.75 Allen, D. C. 'The Rehabilitation of Epicurus and his Theory of Pleasure in the Early Renaissance', *Studies in Philology* 41 (1944) 1–15.

2.76 Burnyeat, M. (ed.) *The Sceptical Tradition*, Berkeley, Calif., University of California Press, 1983.

2.77 Gibson, M. (ed.) *Boethius: His Life, Thought and Influence*, Oxford, Blackwell, 1981.

2.78 Gandillac, M. de, 'Neoplatonism and Christian Thought in the Fifteenth Century (Nicholas of Cusa and Marsilio Ficino)', in D. J. O'Meara (ed.) *Neoplatonism and Christian Thought*, Norfolk, Va., International Society for Neoplatonic Studies, 143–68.

2.79 Hillgarth, J. N. *Ramon Lull and Lullism in Fourteenth-Century France*, Oxford, Clarendon, 1971.

2.80 Klibansky, R. *The Continuity of the Platonic Tradition during the Middle Ages. Plato's Parmenides in the Middle Ages and the Renaissance*, Munich, Kraus International Publications, 1981.

2.81 Kristeller, P. O. *Renaissance Thought and its Sources*, ed. M. Mooney, New York, Columbia University Press, 1979.

2.82 Lovejoy, A. O. *The Great Chain of Being*, Cambridge, Mass., Harvard University Press, 1936.

2.83 Schmitt, C. *Aristotle and the Renaissance*, The Martin Classical Lectures 27, Cambridge, Mass., Harvard University Press, 1983.

2.84 Wallis, R. T. *Neoplatonism*, London, Duckworth, 1972.

General surveys of Renaissance philosophical movements and aspects of Renaissance philosophy

2.85 Blau, J. L. *The Christian Interpretation of the Cabala in the Renaissance*, New York, Columbia University Press, 1944.

2.86 Cassirer, E. *The Individual and the Cosmos in Renaissance Philosophy*, trans. M. Domandi, New York, Harper & Row, and Oxford, Blackwell, 1963.

2.87 Conger, G. P. *Theories of Macrocosms and Microcosms in the History of Philosophy*, New York, Russell & Russell, 1922.

2.88 Copleston, F. *A History of Philosophy*, vol. 3, *Late Medieval and Renaissance Philosophy, Part II, The Revival of Platonism to Suarez*, Maryland, The Newman Press, 1953.

2.89 Coudert, A. 'Some Theories of a Natural Language from the Renaissance to the Seventeenth Century', *Studia Leibnitiana (Sonderheft)* 7 (1978) 56–114.

2.90 Giacon, C. *La Seconda Scolastica*, Milan, Fratelli Bocca, 3 vols, 1944–50.

2.91 Gilbert, N. W. *Renaissance Concepts of Method*, New York, Columbia University Press, 1960.

2.92 Henry, J. and Hutton, S. (eds) *New Perspectives on Renaissance Thought*, London, Duckworth, 1990.

2.93 Jungkuntz, R. P. 'Christian Approval of Epicureanism', *Church History* 31 (1962) 279–93.

2.94 Oestreich, G. *Neostoicism and the Early Modern State*, Cambridge, Cambridge University Press, 1982.

2.95 Popkin, R. H. *The History of Scepticism from Erasmus to Spinoza*, Berkeley and Los Angeles, Calif., University of California Press, 1979.

2.96 Rabil, A., Jr (ed.) *Renaissance Humanism. Foundations, Forms and Legacy*, vol. 2, *Humanism Beyond Italy*, Philadelphia, Penn., University of Pennsylvania Press, 1988.

2.97 Rice, E. F. *The Renaissance Idea of Wisdom*, Cambridge, Mass., Harvard University Press, 1958.

2.98 Schmitt, C. B. 'Towards a Reassessment of Renaissance Aristotelianism', *History of Science* 11 (1973) 159–93; reprinted in Schmitt, C. B. *Studies in Renaissance Philosophy and Science*, London, Variorum Reprints, 1981.

2.99 Schmitt, C. B. *Cicero Scepticus: A Study of the Influence of the 'Academica' in the Renaissance*, The Hague, Nijhoff, 1972.

2.100 Schmitt, C. B. *Studies in Renaissance Philosophy and Science*, London, Variorum Reprints, 1981.

2.101 Schmitt, C. B. 'The Rediscovery of Ancient Skepticism in Modern Times', in M. F. Burnyeat (ed.) *The Skeptical Tradition*, Berkeley and Los Angeles, Calif., University of California Press, 1983, 225–31.

2.102 Schmitt, C. B. and Skinner, Q. (eds) *The Cambridge History of Renaissance Philosophy*, Cambridge, Cambridge University Press, 1988.

2.103 Secret, F. *Les Kabbalistes chrétiens de la Renaissance*, Paris, Dunod, 1964.

2.104 Skinner, Q. *The Foundations of Modern Political Thought*, 2 vols, Cambridge, Cambridge University Press, 1978.

2.105 Smith, G. (ed.) *Jesuit Thinkers of the Renaissance*, Milwaukee, Wisc., Marquette University Press, 1939.

2.106 Sommervogel, C. (ed.) *Bibliothèque de la Companie de Jesus*, Brussels, Schepens, and Paris, Picard, 11 vols, 1890–1932.

2.107 Vedrine, H. *Les philosophies de la Renaissance*, Paris, Presses Universitaires de France, 1967.

2.108 Walker, D. P. *The Ancient Theology: Studies in Christian Platonism from the Fifteenth to the Eighteenth Century*, London, Duckworth, 1972.

2.109 Yates, F. A. *The Occult Philosophy in the Elizabethan Age*, London, Routledge, 1979.

Works on Renaissance philosophy in different countries

England

2.110 Cassirer, E. *The Platonic Renaissance in England*, trans. J. P. Pettegrove, London, Nelson, 1953.

2.111 Debus, A. G. *The English Paracelsians*, London, Oldbourne, 1965.

2.112 Schmitt, C. B. *John Case and Aristotelianism in Renaissance England*, Kingston and Montreal, McGill-Queen's University Press, 1983.

2.113 Schoeck, R. J. 'Humanism in England', in A. Rabil, Jr (ed.) *Renaissance Humanism. Foundations, Forms and Legacy*, vol. 2, *Humanism Beyond Italy*, Philadelphia, Penn., University of Pennsylvania Press, 1988, 5–38.

France

2.114 Chesneau, C. 'Le stoïcisme en France dans la première moitié du XVII siècle: les origines 1575–1616', *Etudes franciscaines* 2 (1951) 389–410.

2.115 Copenhaver, B. P. *Symphorien Champier and the Reception of the Occultist Tradition in Renaissance France*, The Hague, Nijhoff, 1977.

2.116 Rice, E. F. 'Humanism in France', in A. Rabil, Jr (ed.) *Renaissance Humanism. Foundations, Forms and Legacy*, vol. 2, *Humanism Beyond Italy*, Philadelphia, Penn., University of Pennsylvania Press, 1988, 109–22.

Germany

2.117 Beck, L. W. *Early German Philosophy. Kant and His Predecessors*, Cambridge, Mass., Harvard University Press, 1969.

2.118 Brann, N. L. 'Humanism in Germany', in A. Rabil, Jr (ed.) *Renaissance Humanism. Foundations, Forms and Legacy*, vol. 2, *Humanism Beyond Italy*, Philadelphia, Penn., University of Pennsylvania Press, 1988, 123–55.

2.119 Petersen, P. *Geschichte der Aristotelischen Philosophie im Protestantischen Deutschland*, Leipzig, Meiner, 1921.

2.120 Spitz, L. W. *The Religious Renaissance of the German Humanists*, Cambridge, Mass., Harvard University Press, 1963.

Low countries

2.121 Dibon, P. *La Philosophie néerlandaise au siècle d'or*, Amsterdam, Elsevier, 1954.

2.122 Ijsewijn, J. 'Humanism in the Low Countries', in A. Rabil, Jr (ed.) *Renaissance Humanism. Foundations, Forms and Legacy*, vol. 2, *Humanism Beyond Italy*, Philadelphia, Penn., University of Pennsylvania Press, 1988, 156–215.

Spain

2.123 Di Camillo, O. 'Humanism in Spain', in A. Rabil, Jr (ed.) *Renaissance Humanism. Foundations, Forms and Legacy*, vol. 2, *Humanism Beyond Italy*, Philadelphia, Penn., University of Pennsylvania Press, 1988, 55–108.

2.124 Hamilton, B. *Political Thought in Sixteenth-Century Spain: A Study of the Political Ideas of Vitoria, De Soto, Suarez and Molina*, Oxford, Clarendon, 1963.

2.125 Noreña, C. G. *Studies in Spanish Renaissance Thought*, The Hague, Nijhoff, 1975.

2.126 Pagden, A. R. D. 'The Diffusion of Aristotle's Moral Philosophy in Spain', *Traditio* 31 (1975) 287–313.

Writings on individual philosophers

Agrippa

2.127 Bowen, B. C. 'Cornelius Agrippa's *De vanitate*: Polemic or Paradox?', *Bibliothèque d'humanisme et Renaissance* 34 (1972) 249–65.

2.128 Nauert, C. G. *Agrippa and the Crisis of Renaissance Thought*, Urbana, Ill., University of Illinois Press, 1979.

2.129 Zambelli, P. 'Magic and Radical Reformation in Agrippa of Nettesheim', *Journal of the Warburg and Courtauld Institutes* 39 (1976) 69–103.

Bayle

2.130 Brush, C. B. *Montaigne and Bayle, Variations on the Theme of Skepticism*, International Archives of the History of Ideas, vol. 14, The Hague, Nijhoff, 1966.

2.131 Labrousse, E. *Pierre Bayle*, Past Masters Series, Oxford, Oxford University Press, 1991.

Boehme

2.132 Koyré, A. *La Philosophie de Jacob Boehme*, Paris, Vrin, 1929.

2.133 Penny, H. E. *Introduction to the Study of Jacob Böhme's Writings*, New York, 1901.

Charron

2.134 Horowitz, M. C. 'Pierre Charron's View of the Source of Wisdom', *Journal of the History of Philosophy* 9 (1971) 443–57.

2.135 Soman, A. 'Pierre Charron: a Revaluation', *Bibliothèque d'humanisme et Renaissance* 32 (1970) 57–79.

2.136 Soman, A. 'Methodology in the History of Ideas: the Case of Pierre Charron', *Journal of the History of Philosophy* 12 (1974) 495–501.

Colet

2.137 Miles, L. *John Colet and the Platonic Tradition*, La Salle, Ill., Open Court, 1961.

Cusanus

2.138 Bett, H. *Nicholas of Cusa*, London, Methuen, 1932; reprinted, Cambridge, Mass., Harvard University Press, 1969.

2.139 Watts, P. M. *Nicolaus Cusanus: A Fifteenth Century Vision of Man*, Leiden, Brill, 1982.

Erasmus

2.140 DeMolen, R. (ed.) *Essays on the Works of Erasmus*, New Haven, Conn., Yale University Press, 1978.

2.141 McConica, J. *Erasmus*, Past Masters Series, Oxford, Oxford University Press, 1991.

Fonseca

2.142 Ferreira Gomes, J. 'Pedro da Fonseca, Sixteenth Century Portuguese Philosopher', *International Philosophical Quarterly* 6 (1966) 632–44.

Grotius

2.143 Knight, W. S. M. *The Life and Works of Hugo Grotius*, London, Sweet & Maxwell, 1931.

2.144 Tuck, R. *Natural Rights Theories*, Cambridge, Cambridge University Press, 1979.

La Mothe le Vayer

2.145 Grenier, J. 'Le Sceptique masqué: La Mothe le Vayer', *Table Ronde* 22 (1949) 1504–13.

Lessius

2.146 Chamberlain, C. H. 'Leonard Lessius', in G. Smith (ed.) *Jesuit Thinkers of the Renaissance*, Milwaukee, Wisc., Marquette University Press, 1939, 133–56.

Lipsius

2.147 Saunders, J. L. *Justus Lipsius: The Philosophy of Renaissance Stoicism*, New York, Liberal Arts Press, 1955.

Mariana

2.148 Talmadge, G. K. 'Juan de Mariana', in G. Smith (ed.) *Jesuit Thinkers of the Renaissance*, Milwaukee, Wisc., Marquette University Press, 1939, 157–92.

Melanchthon

2.149 Hildebrandt, F. *Melanchthon, Alien or Ally?*, Cambridge, Cambridge University Press, 1946.
2.150 Stern, L. *Philipp Melanchthon: Humanist, Reformer, Praeceptor Germaniae*, Halle, Festgabe des Melanchthon-Komitees der Deutschen Demokratischen Republik, 1960.

Molina

2.151 Pegis, A. C. 'Molina and Human Liberty', in G. Smith (ed.) *Jesuit Thinkers of the Renaissance*, Milwaukee, Wisc., Marquette University Press, 1939, 75–132.

Montaigne

2.152 Burke, P. *Montaigne*, Past Masters Series, Oxford, Oxford University Press, 1981.
2.153 Frame, D. M. *Montaigne: A Biography*, New York, Harcourt, Brace & World, 1965; reprinted, San Francisco, Calif., North Point Press, 1984.
2.154 Limbrick, E. 'Was Montaigne really a Pyrrhonian?', *Bibliothèque d'humanisme et Renaissance* 39 (1977) 67–80.
2.155 Schiffman, Z. S. 'Montaigne and the Rise of Skepticism in Early Modern Europe: a Reappraisal', *Journal of the History of Ideas* 45 (1984) 499–516.

More (Thomas)

2.156 Kenny, A. *Thomas More*, Past Masters Series, Oxford, Oxford University Press, 1983.
2.157 Skinner, Q. 'More's *Utopia*', *Past and Present* 38 (1967) 153–68.

Paracelsus

2.158 Pachter, H. M. *Paracelsus*, New York, Schumann, 1951.
2.159 Stillman, J. M. *Paracelsus*, Chicago, Ill., Open Court, 1920.

Ramus

2.160 Ong, W. J. *Ramus, Method, and the Decay of Dialogue*, Cambridge, Mass., Harvard University Press, 1958.

Reuchlin

2.161 Spitz, L. W. 'Reuchlin's Philosophy: Pythagoras and Cabala for Christ', *Archiv für Reformationsgeschichte* 47 (1956) 1–20; revised as 'Reuchlin: Pythagoras Reborn', in L. W. Spitz, *The Religious Renaissance of the German Humanists*, Cambridge, Mass., Harvard University Press, 1963, ch. IV.

Sanches

2.162 Limbrick, E. 'Introduction' to *Francisco Sanches: That Nothing is Known (Quod Nihil Scitur)*, Cambridge, Cambridge University Press, 1988.

Suarez

2.163 Fichter, J. H. *Man of Spain: Francis Suarez*, New York, Macmillan, 1940.
2.164 Mora, J. F. 'Suarez and Modern Philosophy', *Journal of the History of Ideas* 14 (1953) 528–47.

Van Helmont (F. M.)

2.165 Brown, S. 'F.M. van Helmont: his Philosophical Connections and the Reception of his later Cabbalistic Philosophy (1677–1699)', in M. A. Stewart (ed.) *Studies in Seventeenth Century Philosophy*, Oxford, Oxford University Press, forthcoming.

Van Helmont (J. B.)

2.166 Redgrove, H. S. and Redgrove, J. M. L. *J. B. Van Helmont, Alchemist, Physician, Philosopher*, London, W. Rider, 1922.

Vitoria

2.167 Scott, J. B. *The Spanish Origin of International Law*, vol. 1, *Francisco de Vitoria and His Law of Nations*, Washington, D.C., Carnegie Endowment for International Peace, and Oxford, Clarendon, 1934.

Vives

2.168 Noreña, C. G. *Juan Luis Vives*, The Hague, Nijhoff, 1970.

The Renaissance background to modern philosophy

2.169 Berre, Henri, *Du Scepticisme de Gassendi*, trans. B. Rochot, Paris, Michel, 1960.
2.170 Brown, S. 'Leibniz and More's Cabbalistic Circle', in Sarah Hutton and R.

Crocker (eds) *Henry More (1614–1687): Tercentenary Studies*, Dordrecht, Kluwer, 1989, 77–95.

2.171 Brown, S. 'Leibniz: Modern, Scholastic or Renaissance Philosopher?', in T. Sorell (ed.) *The Rise of Modern Philosophy*, Oxford, Oxford University Press, 1993, 213–30.

2.172 Brush, C. B. *Montaigne and Bayle: Variations on the Theme of Skepticism*, The Hague, Nijhoff, 1966.

2.173 Cronin, T. J. 'Objective Being in Descartes and in Suarez', *Analecta Gregoriana*, Rome, Gregorian University Press, 1966.

2.174 Dear, P. R. 'Marin Mersenne and the Probabilistic Roots of "Mitigated Scepticism" ', *Journal of the History of Philosophy* 22 (1984) 173–205.

2.175 Gouhier, H. *Les Premières pensées de Descartes. Contribution à l'histoire de l'anti-Renaissance*, Paris, Vrin, 1958.

2.176 Heinekamp, A. (ed.) *Leibniz et la Renaissance*, Wiesbaden, Steiner, 1983.

2.177 Lewalter, E. *Spanische-jesuitische und deutsche-lutherische Metaphysik des 17. Jahrhunderts*, Hamburg, 1935; reprinted, Darmstadt, Wissenschaftliche Buchgesellschaft, 1967.

2.178 Kristeller, P. O. 'Stoic and Neostoic Sources of Spinoza's *Ethics*', *History of European Ideas* 5 (1984) 1–15.

2.179 Meier, M. *Descartes und die Renaissance*, Munster, 1914.

2.180 Mesnard, P. 'Comment Leibniz se trouve place dans le sillage de Suarez', *Archives de philosophie* 18 (1949) 7–32.

2.181 Politella, J. 'Platonism, Aristotelianism, and Cabalism in the Philosophy of Leibniz', PhD dissertation, University of Philadelphia, 1938.

2.182 Popkin, R. H. *The History of Scepticism from Erasmus to Spinoza*, Berkeley and Los Angeles, Calif., University of California Press, 1979.

2.183 Popkin, R. H. and Schmitt, C. B. (eds) *Scepticism from the Renaissance to the Enlightenment*, Wiesbaden, Harrassowitz, 1987.

2.184 Ross, G. M. 'Leibniz and Renaissance Neoplatonism', in A. Heinekamp (ed.) *Leibniz et la Renaissance*, Wiesbaden, Steiner, 1983.

2.185 Schmitt, C. B. 'Perennial Philosophy: From Agostino Steuco to Leibniz', *Journal of the History of Ideas* 27 (1966) 505–32.

2.186 Wells, N. J. 'Objective Being. Descartes and His Sources', *Modern Schoolman* 45 (1967) 49–61.

2.187 Wundt, M. *Die deutsche Schulmetaphysik des 17. Jahrhunderts*, Tubingen, Mohr, 1939.

CHAPTER 3

Science and mathematics from the Renaissance to Descartes

George Molland

❧❀❧

Early in the nineteenth century John Playfair wrote for the *Encyclopae-dia Britannica* a long article entitled 'Dissertation; exhibiting a General View of the Progress of Mathematics and Physical Science, since the Revival of Letters in Europe'.[1] Ever since the Renaissance's invention of its own self, there has been a persistent belief that, during a general rebirth of learning, the natural and mathematical sciences made advances that effectively eclipsed what William Whewell later called the 'Stationary Period of Science'.[2] No wonder that this myth triggered a 'revolt of the medievalists',[3] who in this century have done much to redress the balance in favour of their own period. But like all myths this one contains truth as well as falsehood, and this chapter will dwell more on the former than the latter, and so concentrate on areas of innovation. But the revolt still reminds us that innovation was not the norm: for most people (both educated and uneducated) the traditional wisdom, together with its non-trivial modifications, was a more import-ant former of consciousness than any radical new developments, and Aristotelian natural philosophy remained firmly ensconced in the uni-versities until well into the second half of the seventeenth century, retaining in many cases a strong vitality of its own.

Besides its bias in favour of innovation, this chapter will exhibit other, perhaps more insidious, forms of selectivity. It will neglect almost completely many important areas, especially in the life sciences, in order to give prominence both in coverage and mode of treatment to those areas that may be 'philosophically' more illuminating. (The inverted commas are intended to emphasize that, for this period, to distinguish rigidly between philosophy and science would be grossly anachronistic, and add even more to the historiographical distortion introduced by the policy of selectivity.) The chapter will comprise just three sections, dealing respectively with general ideas of advancement; a new picture of the heavens; a new mechanics embedded in a new view of nature.

❧ TECHNOLOGY/PROGRESS/METHOD ❧

It will be useful in the manner of Alexandre Koyré to distinguish technics from technology[4] and so allow ourselves to retain an older meaning of the English 'technology' – as 'the scientific study of the practical or industrial arts'.[5] It is now commonplace to refer to the great abundance of technical activity and of technical advances in the Latin Middle Ages, but it is more problematic how far the latter were recognized as constituting a progressive movement. Many, and particularly those emphasizing the effects of Christian doctrine and monastic discipline, have seen a conscious thrust in the direction of improvement, but the evidence is sparse, especially compared with that to be found in the Renaissance and later periods. Then, a frequently met symbolic triad to emphasize the technical superiority of the moderns over the ancients was that constituted by printing, gunpowder and the magnetic compass, although ironically all of these can in one form or another be traced back to China, in whose civilizations few symptoms of a general idea of progress have been located.[6] We should add the example of clocks. In China, and also in the Muslim countries, there had been a penchant for producing very elaborate water-driven clocks. Around 1300, mechanical clocks appeared in Europe, and very soon cathedrals and cities were vying with each other to produce ever more ornate devices, which, by their very public display, had a better chance than the other three of infecting the populace with the ideal of progress. Interestingly enough, Giovanni Dondi, the fourteenth-century constructor of a particularly impressive astronomical clock, was at pains to disparage modern achievements in comparison with those of the ancients.[7] But Giovanni was a university man, associated with the nascent humanism, and particularly that represented by Petrarch. His show of modesty may not have been shared by his less learned contemporaries: it certainly was not by their successors, and very soon humanists also were singing to the same tune.[8]

In a seminal article published almost half a century ago Edgar Zilsel[9] saw the effective genesis of the ideal of scientific progress as located among the 'superior artisans' of the sixteenth century, and with qualifications this thesis has proved remarkably resilient. One necessary modification was to bring contemporary scholars who systematically examined the crafts more centrally into the picture, and, together with this, I think that we should emphasize more than has sometimes been done a somewhat speculative aspect of the indisputably important role of printing. This is in shifting the image of knowledge. In the Middle Ages, knowledge was viewed as predominantly an individual affair, a *habitus* ingrained into a person's mind by education. In acquiring such a *habitus* the individual progressed, but there was no very potent image of a general increase of knowledge. With the advent of printing, books multiplied in overall physical volume far more than ever before, and it is plausible to envisage with this the image of a concomitant (although not proportional) increase in their *contents*, so that the sum total of knowledge itself appeared to have increased. To put it in contemporary terms, we have progress in Sir Karl Popper's 'Third World' of objective knowledge, conceived as existing independently of the knowing subject.[10]

But, whatever the causative influences, the idea of technical progress certainly became prominent in the sixteenth century, and was associated with a search for more strictly scientific progress. This was due partly to superior artisans, such as Leonardo da Vinci, looking at the theoretical bases of their arts as a source for improvement, and partly to scholars publishing surveys of craft techniques, for example the *De re metallica* of Georg Bauer (Georgius Agricola) in which the author gave a systematic account of current mining and metallurgical practices. Many such techniques had remained unchanged since Antiquity, and were simply passed from master to apprentice by word of mouth. Bringing them out into the cold light of print could suggest modes of improvement, and later became formalized in the injunction to produce histories of trades – what can be, and sometimes were, called 'technologies'. These and many other factors provoked a strong urge towards improvement, and a conviction that systematic intellectual activity was at least as important as trial and error or reliance upon tradition. And this applied not only to the more banausic areas of technics, but also to more rarefied and seemingly 'impractical' fields.

But a desire for progress is one thing: achieving it is another. And here we meet more and more frequently with the term 'method' and its relations. The search for this had roots in several fields, mathematical, philosophical, medical, magical . . . . We consider briefly the first two. The mathematical revival of the sixteenth century is characterized particularly by the greater availability of important ancient works, through both the production of new translations and the dissemination of these in print. This gave rise to two reflections. First, it became evident that many significant works were (probably irretrievably) lost, but second, sufficient evidence was often available about their contents for plausible attempts at reconstruction to be made. This did not directly imply method, but it did make for mathematical progress, for restoration was to be achieved not by philology alone but by trying to do mathematics in the Greek spirit. As an attempt at exact replication this failed, but it did produce new mathematics, and so we have a kind of surreptitious progress in which efforts at reviving the old produced developments that were radically new.

Others were more open in their endeavours, and indeed accused the ancients of being clandestine. From Antiquity onwards it had been realized that some of the most impressive results of Greek geometry resembled a beautiful building from which all trace of scaffolding and other accessories had been removed. Hence Plutarch on Archimedes:

> It is not possible to find in geometry more difficult and weighty questions treated in simpler and purer terms. Some attribute this to the natural endowments of the man, others think it was the result of exceeding labour that everything done by him appeared to have been done without labour and with ease. For although by his own efforts no one could discover the proof, yet as soon as he learns it, he takes credit that he could have discovered it: so smooth and rapid is the path by which he leads to the conclusion.[11]

The paradox suggested that the ancients had knowledge of a particularly fruitful way of *discovering* new mathematical truths. As Descartes put it, 'We perceive sufficiently that the ancient Geometricians made use of a certain analysis which they extended to the resolution of all problems, though they grudged the secret to posterity.'[12] Such suspicions were partially vindicated at the beginning of this century (although without evidence of a grudge) by the discovery of a lost work by Archimedes, known as the *Method (Ephodos)*, in which the author showed how to use theoretical mechanics and considerations of indivisibles in order to discover new theorems about equating areas and volumes between different plane and solid figures. These theorems were then open to proof by more rigorous geometrical methods, particularly the *reductiones ad absurdum* involved in the so-called method of exhaustion, in which inequalities of the relevant areas and volumes were shown to lead to contradictions.

There were a few brief and vague ancient references to Archimedes' 'method', but rather more to the procedures of 'analysis and synthesis', whose exact interpretation have caused much scholarly perplexity. In a famous passage Pappus wrote:

> Analysis is the path from what one is seeking, as if it were established, by way of its consequences, to something that is established by synthesis. That is to say, in analysis we assume what is sought as if it has been achieved, and look for the thing from which it follows, and again what comes before that, until by regressing in this way we come upon some one of the things

that are already known, or that occupy the rank of a first principle. We call this kind of method 'analysis', as if to say *anapalin lysis* (reduction backward). In synthesis, by reversal, we assume what was obtained last in the analysis to have been achieved already, and, setting now in natural order, as precedents, what before were following, and fitting them to each other, we attain the end of the construction of what was sought. This is what we call 'synthesis'.[13]

Pappus went on to distinguish theorematic (*zetetikos*) and problematic (*poristikos*) analysis. The general thrust of the passages is clear. In theorematic analysis we work backwards towards the first principles from which a theorem follows, and in problematic analysis our goal is the solution of a problem, say the finding of a figure whose area or other features will meet certain conditions, while in synthesis we in some sense prove our results. But when we descend towards the logical niceties a host of difficulties appear,[14] and these may themselves have made the subject a particularly suitable candidate for seventeenth-century transformation.

An especially important figure in this process was François Viète, who drew on both the Diophantine 'arithmetical' tradition and more general algebraic traditions, as well as those deriving from primarily geometrical works. Viète's most striking innovation in assuming a problem solved was to name the 'unknown' quantity or quantities with letters of the alphabet, as well as those that were 'known', and then to operate on both in the same way. This produced formulae that looked far more like equations in the modern sense than anything that had gone before, and this trend is even more accentuated in the work of Descartes, where we often have no more than minor and accidental features of notation to remind us that we are not in the twentieth century. All this may be seen as reflecting a general psychological trend in mathematics to focus more on written symbols than on what they are meant to symbolize.

It is this movement that has made it seem plausible to speak of Descartes as the founder of 'analytical geometry', meaning thereby a geometry in which curves may be substituted by the equations representing them. But this ignores the extent to which Descartes still demanded explicitly geometrical constructions for solving what we would regard as purely algebraical problems. Nevertheless it does draw attention to how geometry and algebra could seem to proceed in tandem. This trend was to continue into the work of Newton, and can be seen as leading towards an eventual reduction of the former to the latter. With hindsight it is possible to see ripening other fruits of mathematical method, such as those associated with the infinitesimal calculus, but until well past the time of Descartes these are decidedly muted in comparison with the algebraic results.

As may be expected, philosophers were more explicit than mathematicians in their discussions of method, although one head was often capable of wearing two hats, as in the case of Descartes. In the Aristotelian tradition we frequently meet with the methods of analysis and synthesis in the Latinate guise of resolution and composition. As in mathematics, the terms are a little slippery, but resolution was basically a form of argument from effects to causes, whereas composition was demonstration of effects from their causes. The development of these ideas by medieval and Renaissance commentators on Aristotle (and also on Galen's methodological writings) have led some scholars, for instance John Hermann Randall, Alistair C. Crombie and William A. Wallace, to place strong, and perhaps extravagant, emphasis on the positive role of Aristotelianism in furthering the emergence of modern science.

One thinker who would not have been convinced by this was Francis Bacon. Although Bacon had a grudging respect for aspects of Aristotle's own thought, he saw medieval scholasticism as the embodiment of sterility and futile contentiousness. He therefore sought a more fruitful way of eliciting knowledge from nature, of a kind that would eventually prove useful in practice. In this he displayed some affinities with the magical and alchemical traditions, but their secrecy and apparent obscurantism were antithetical to his programme for which he sought more public, methodical and 'democratic' procedures. In this a central role was played by his idea of induction, the careful collection and tabulation of facts (although in practice often derived from none-too-reliable reports), and then the cautious ascent to higher levels of generalization, with only a very wary use of hypotheses, strictly controlled by the use of experiments. Although usefulness was the remote aim, this could not properly be achieved without first seeking the truths of nature: as opposed to what he saw as the alchemists' habits, luciferous experiments must always precede lucriferous ones.

Francis Bacon very soon became a hero of science, and especially of British science, but it remains controversial how much substantive as opposed to rhetorical influence he exerted upon its development. One would be very hard pushed to find anyone successfully following the Baconian method to the letter, and some notable writers denigrated his scientific importance. For instance, it is reported that William Harvey, the discoverer of the circulation of the blood, 'esteemed [Bacon] much for his witt and style, but would not allow him to be a great Philosopher. Said he to me, "He writes philosophy like a Lord Chancellor," speaking in derision.'[15] And in the more mathematical sciences, with which the remainder of this chapter will be mainly concerned, it is less easy to make out a case for his influence than in the biological and descriptive sciences. This is largely due to his generally acknowledged blind spot as regards the potential of mathematics in forwarding the development of science.

❧ THE ASTRONOMICAL REVOLUTION ❧

Developments in cosmology must play a leading, if not the dominating, role in any consideration of the science of this period. It all started very quietly. The first really public event occurred in the year 1543, but it was not accompanied with the stir appropriate to what many used to regard as the inaugural date of the Scientific Revolution (the other symbolic event being the publication of Vesalius's *De humani corporis fabrica*). The title of Copernicus's book of that year, *De revolutionibus orbium caelestium*, incorporated what can now, but not then, be regarded as a pun on the word 'revolution', and also a point of disputed translation concerning the word *orbis*. The book had been a long time in the making, but probably not for the devious reasons sometimes proposed: it simply took a long time to prepare and write. The initial conception had come some thirty years earlier, if not before, by which time Copernicus had completed a good scholastic education at the flourishing university of Cracow, together with a tour around the universities of Renaissance Italy, before settling into a canonry at the Cathedral of Frauenberg (Frombork).

In about 1514 he completed and circulated in manuscript a short work, now usually known as the *Commentariolus*, outlining a heliocentric system of the world, with the Earth rotating daily on its axis and as a planet orbiting the now stationary Sun once a year. His reasons for the change have been a matter of controversy. Here I shall not undertake the delicate, and possibly tedious, task of assaying the various hypotheses, but present what appears a likely story, and one which seems both in accord with the majority scholarly view and with Copernicus's explicit statements as to why he proceeded as he did.

The conventional astronomical wisdom at Copernicus's time derived from Ptolemy's *Almagest*, which provided sophisticated mathematical models for showing where at any particular time a planet (the list included the Sun and Moon) would appear from the vantage point of a stationary Earth against the background of the fixed stars; or, more precisely, in a co-ordinate system determined by the great circles of the ecliptic (the path of the Sun through the sky) and the celestial equator. The devices worked by combining circular motions. Usually we have a deferent circle whose centre is at some distance from the Earth, and an epicycle, a smaller circle whose centre moves around the circumference of the deferent, while the planet is imagined to move about the circumference of the epicycle. Speeds are regulated in terms of an equant point, situated at the same distance from the centre of the deferent as the Earth but on the opposite side, so that the centre of the epicycle moves with uniform angular velocity about this point. The models for Mercury and the Moon were more complicated than this description may suggest, and that for the Sun simpler, but all incorporated sufficient flexibility in choice of parameters to make them good predictive devices. At least, they were good enough for Copernicus, but the status of the equant point was another matter.

> [The theories] were not sufficient unless there were imagined also certain equant circles, by which it will appear that the star is moved with ever uniform speed neither in its deferent orb nor about its proper centre, on which account a theory of this kind seems neither sufficiently absolute nor sufficiently pleasing to the mind.[16]

This famous passage has led some to speak of Copernicus's Pythagorean obsession with uniform circular motion, with the implied suggestion that this was beyond the bounds of rationality. But in fact Aristotle is a better target. In Copernicus's time, as it had been from Antiquity onwards, astronomy was regarded as a branch of mathematics, what Aristotle had referred to as one of its more physical branches; in the later Middle Ages these were often called middle sciences, as lying between mathematics and physics. Whatever Ptolemy may have thought, it was not generally seen as a hallmark of mathematics to look at causes: that was the province of the physicist. For Aristotle the heavens were made of the fifth element or aether, to which it was natural to move eternally with a uniform rotation. In his more detailed astronomical picture, for which he borrowed from the mathematicians (astronomers) of his time, Aristotle had some fifty-five spheres, centred on the Earth, of which nine carried planets. Any deviation from uniformity of motion would need an interfering cause, which could not seem plausible in the perfection of Aristotle's celestial realm. Copernicus did not maintain the Aristotelian distinction between celestial and elementary regions, but he did demand a cause for deviation from uniformity, and none seemed available: hence, if for no other reason, farewell the equant.

Here we must emphasize that Copernicus, although more mutedly than Kepler, was much concerned with causes, and also, in the context of an often bitter recent controversy, that he almost certainly ascribed a fair degree of reality to the orbs (be they spheres, circles, orbits, hoops or whatever) to which the planets were conceived as attached or along which they moved. A causal and harmonious structure for the universe was also theologically supported, for a good Creator God would surely have proceeded according to a rational plan. This attitude clearly lay behind Copernicus's criticism of astronomers in the Ptolemaic tradition for producing fine parts which could by no means be fitted together in a tidy fashion.

> It was with them exactly as if someone had taken from different places, in no way mutually corresponding, hands, feet, head and other members, all excellently depicted but not in relation to a single body, so that a monster was composed from them rather than a man.[17]

Copernicus's own system as portrayed in the famous diagram included in Chapter 10 of Book I of the *De revolutionibus* (with an accompanying panegyric on the Sun) appears admirably simple and rational, but important cracks lie very near to the surface. In the first place the system was obviously physical nonsense. If the Earth is really moving with such huge speed, we should surely experience it by such phenomena as constant high winds and stones that refused to fall at the bottom of the towers from which they are dropped; also its whole body should fly apart, like the materials on a potter's wheel that is spun too fast. Copernicus was not blind to such objections, and answered them in summary fashion, but in terms which we may find easier to accept than did his own contemporaries. And after all, was it worth destroying important foundations of the well-tried edifice of Aristotelian physics at the behest of a mere astronomer? All this relates to Book I of the *De revolutionibus*, understandably the only part that is read by more than a few specialists in mathematical astronomy. But the later five books destroy most of the simplicity of this book in order to make the system work, that is, to 'save the phenomena', or provide a relatively good predictive device for planetary positions, for in doing this Copernicus, although rejecting the equant point, retained most of the techniques of earlier astronomy for explaining the planetary movements by combinations of circular motions, and in so doing produced a system that was arguably as complicated as Ptolemy's. This was not arrant conservatism but a natural use of procedures with which he had been brought up, and which if rejected would almost certainly have prevented him from doing any work worthy of serious astronomical recognition.

With these points made, the result is not surprising. The book did not fall on dead ground, but neither did it win unconditional acclaim. Among the general public it was seen to propose a pleasing or unpleasing paradox, perhaps interesting for idle conversation, but only to be taken seriously by eccentrics or fanatics. For instance, even before the book was published, Luther remarked that,

Whoever wants to be clever must agree with nothing that others esteem. He must do something of his own. This is what that fellow does who wishes to turn the whole of astronomy upside down. Even in those things that are thrown into disorder I believe the Holy Scriptures, for Joshua commanded the Sun to stand still, and not the Earth.[18]

Among professional astronomers the work was greatly admired, but for its astronomy, not its physics. A characteristic posture was to adopt what Robert S. Westman[19] has called the Wittenberg interpretation of the theory: to take a connoisseur's delight in Copernicus's mathematical techniques and employ them about the astronomer's proper business, such as the construction of tables, but to reject as utterly mistaken the idea of a moving Earth. Paradoxically this instrumentalist outlook received support from Copernicus's own volume, for Andreas Osiander, the Lutheran pastor who saw it through the press, inserted an anonymous preface, possibly to ward off theological criticisms, which gave a low truth status to astronomical theories.

It is proper to an astronomer to bring together the history of the celestial motions by careful and skilful observation, and then to think up and invent such causes for them, or hypotheses (since he can by no reasoning attain the true causes), by which being assumed their motions can be correctly calculated from the principles of geometry for the future as well as for the past. The present author has eminently excelled in both these tasks, for it is not necessary that the hypotheses be true nor indeed probable, but this one thing suffices, that they exhibit an account (*calculus*) consistent with the observations.[20]

And some careless readers of the work were misled into thinking that this was Copernicus's own view.

Instrumentalism has rarely been a satisfactory psychological stance for working scientists, and so it is not surprising that soon schemes were brought forward that gave a more realist slant to the Wittenberg interpretation. The most famous of these, and one which he guarded jealously as his very own intellectual property, was by the great Danish astronomer Tycho Brahe. In this the Moon and the Sun orbited the stationary Earth, while the other planets circled the Sun and accompanied it on its annual journey about the Earth. This had all the astronomical advantages of the Copernican system and none of what were perceived as its physical disadvantages. It also had no need to accommodate the fact that no parallax (apparent relative motion among the fixed stars) had been observed, which would have been expected if the Earth were moving. Tycho laid particular emphasis on this difficulty for Copernicanism, and calculated that, if the Earth were moving, then even a star that had only a moderate apparent size would have to be so far away that it would in fact be as big as the whole of the Earth's orbit. Not surprisingly, when Copernicanism came under ecclesiastical fire, the Tychonic compromise emerged as the favourite system of the Jesuits, who were themselves strong pioneers of scientific advance.

But Tycho's theorizing was of less scientific importance than his practice. He was unusual among men of science in being of aristocratic birth, and this made substantial patronage easier to obtain. The King of Denmark granted him the island of Hveen (situated between Copenhagen and Elsinore), on which he built a magnificent observatory called Uraniborg. Up to that time it could only have been rivalled by Islamic or Mongol observatories, such as those at Maragha and Samarkand. Not only was the hardware, so to speak, superb, but Tycho had it manned by a group of able assistants whom he at least tried to rule with a rod of iron. The result was an incomparably accurate collection of observations of stellar positions, which historically was to play a far more significant role than his famous demonstrations that the New Star (to us a supernova) of 1572 and the comet of 1577 were supralunary, and hence symptoms of change in supposedly immutable regions, and that the latter would have to be passing through the solid spheres of Aristotelian cosmology. Nevertheless these made important dents in the old world picture, although ironically Galileo denied the validity of his arguments with regard to the comet.

There is a waggish yet revealing quip that Tycho's most important discovery of all was that of a person, namely Johann Kepler. Kepler was born into a Lutheran family, and was himself heading for the Lutheran ministry when he entered the University of Tübingen in 1587.[21] However, his course was deflected by a growing interest in astronomy, fostered by one of his teachers, Michael Maestlin, who happened to be one of the few convinced Copernicans of the era, and in 1594 with Maestlin's encouragement Kepler accepted the post of District Mathematician at Graz. His duties involved some elementary mathematical teaching and the drawing up of astrological prognostications, but he also pursued his own theoretical interests in astronomy, and in 1596 published a small book entitled *Mysterium Cosmographicum*. It could be tempting to pass this book over as merely 'quaint' were it not for Kepler's much later claim that,

> Just as if it had been literally dictated to me, an oracle fallen
> from heaven, all the principal chapters of the published booklet
> were immediately recognised as most true by the discerning
> (which is the wont of God's manifest works), and have these
> twenty-five years carried before me more than a single torch in

accomplishing the design (initiated by the most celebrated astronomer Tycho Brahe of the Danish nobility) of the restoration of astronomy, and, moreover, almost anything of the books of astronomy that I have produced since that time could be referred to one or other of the chapters set forth in this booklet, of which it would contain either an illustration or a completion.[22]

And an attentive reading shows that much of this was indeed the case.

In the book Kepler reveals himself as one who would out-Copernicize Copernicus in his belief in the physical reality of a heliocentric system, and this attitude is reinforced by a commitment to asking *why*, and answering it in terms of both geometrical and physical causes. An important example is the question of why there are six and only six (primary) planets, Mercury, Venus, Earth, Mars, Jupiter, Saturn. (This question is quite rational, if it is assumed that the world was created much as it is now some finite time ago.) Georg Joachim Rheticus, Copernicus's first champion, had answered it arithmetologically by saying that six was a perfect number. This had a precise meaning, for 6's factors 1, 2, 3, when added together, produce 6 itself, a property shared by relatively few numbers, the next example being 28. Kepler would have none of this *mystica numerorum*, and firmly believed in geometry's priority to arithmetic, so that it, rather than arithmetic as Boethius had held, provided God with the archetype for the creation of the world.

Kepler found the required linkage with geometry in the remarkable fact that there are five and only five regular solids. He then discovered even more remarkably, and we would say coincidentally, that these solids and the spherical shells enclosing the planetary orbits could be fitted together in a sort of Chinese box arrangement, so that, if an octahedron was circumscribed about the sphere of Mercury, it was almost exactly inscribed in the sphere of Venus, and so on, giving the order, Mercury, octahedron, Venus, icosahedron, Earth, dodecahedron, Mars, tetrahedron, Jupiter, cube, Saturn. This idea understandably so excited Kepler that he planned a model for presentation to the Duke of Württemberg. Another preoccupation was with what moved the planets, for Kepler remained in the tradition in which each motion demanded an efficient cause. His answer was that there was a single 'moving soul' (later to be depersonalized to 'force') located in the Sun. This had the natural consequence that the planetary orbits lay in planes passing through the Sun, which in turn virtually removed the messy problem of latitudes (the deviations of the planetary paths from the plane of the ecliptic) from mathematical astronomy.

Kepler circulated copies of his book to other astronomers, including Tycho Brahe, who, perhaps surprisingly, was favourably impressed, although complaining that Kepler had too great a tendency to argue *a priori* rather than in the *a posteriori* fashion more appropriate to astronomy. He invited Kepler to visit him, but this did not come to fruition until, after a series of disputes, Tycho moved from Denmark and came under the patronage of the Emperor Rudolf II, who granted him a castle near Prague for his observatory. Kepler went to see him there and soon became a member of his team. The relationship between the rumbustious and domineering Tycho and the quieter but determinedly independent Kepler was not an easy one, but it did not last too long, for Tycho died in 1601 and was succeeded by Kepler in his post as Imperial Mathematician.

On joining Tycho, Kepler was set to work on Mars, whose movements had been proving particularly recalcitrant to mathematical treatment. We may count this a fortunate choice, for, to speak with hindsight, its orbit is the most elliptical of the then known planets. But it was one of Kepler's important innovations to seek for the actual orbit of the planet rather than for the combination of uniform circular motions that would give rise to the observed appearances. However, he was traditional in at first seeking for a circular orbit and reintroducing an equant point, although not necessarily at the same distance as the Sun from the centre of the orbit. In this manner he formed a developed theory, which he later called his 'vicarious hypothesis'; it became especially famous for a crucial deviation of eight minutes of arc from observational evidence, which would previously have been undetectable.

> Since the divine goodness has given to us in Tycho Brahe a most careful observer, from whose observations the error of 8 minutes in the Ptolemaic account (*calculus*) is argued in Mars, it is fitting that with grateful mind we should recognise and cultivate this gift of God. . . . For if I had treated these 8 minutes of longitude as negligible, I should already have sufficiently corrected the hypothesis. . . . But because they could not be neglected, these eight minutes alone have led the way to reforming the whole of astronomy, and have been made the matter for a great part of this work.[23]

With the vicarious hypothesis rejected, Kepler embarked on a bewildering variety of sophisticated procedures. One strategy was to place the Earth more on a par with the other planets; for it provided the moving platform from which we observed, but hitherto its orbit had lacked an equant point. To this end Kepler found it useful to imagine that he was on Mars and observing the Earth from there. Another strategy was that of quantifying the causes of the planetary motions. A force emanating from the Sun, and inversely proportional to the distance from the Sun, was conceived as pushing the planets around. This eventually led to what we know as Kepler's second law of planetary motion, that the radius vector from the Sun to a planet sweeps out equal areas in equal times. But this force did not explain a planet's varying distance from the Sun. For this purpose a quasi-magnetic push-pull force was introduced with allusion to William Gilbert's *De magnete* which had been published in 1600. This caused a libration of the planet on an epicycle's diameter directed towards the Sun. With this theoretical apparatus Kepler proceeded to seek the actual path of Mars. For this he experimented with a variety of egg-shaped orbits. Readers of *Gulliver's Travels* will remember that eggs have big ends and little ends, but Kepler did use ellipses as calculating devices, and eventually came with a start to a realization that the orbit itself was an ellipse, with the Sun at one focus (the 'first law').

> O, how ridiculous of me! As if the libration in the diameter could not be a way to the ellipse. I have become thoroughly convinced that the ellipse stands together with the libration, as will be evident in the next chapter, where at the same time it will be demonstrated that no figure remains for the orbit of the planet other than a perfectly elliptical one.[24]

Kepler's first two laws (which were soon generalized to the other planets) were published, with a detailed account of his procedures, in 1609 in his *Astronomia Nova*, whose full title is particularly evocative: *New Astronomy, Reasoned from the Causes, or Celestial Physics, Delivered Up by Considerations of the Motions of the Star Mars, From the Observations of the Great Tycho Brahe*.[25] What we call the third law linked together the various planets in stating that the square of the periodic time of a planet was proportional to the cube of its mean distance from the Sun. It appeared in print in Kepler's *Harmonice Mundi* of 1619. As the title indicates, the principal aim of this work was in a very literal way the search for musical harmonies in the heavens, and it is illustrated with scales appropriate to the various planets. This has misleadingly encouraged the anachronistic, and now thankfully outdated, attitude that Kepler can properly be split into two distinct halves, the mystical and the scientific.

Another consequence of this attitude was to cause some unnecessary puzzlement about the subsequent fate of Kepler's laws. To a superficial modern eye, it can seem that Kepler had now definitively established the facts about planetary motion (in a commodious description) which only awaited a Newton in order to explain them, and indeed the Kepler–Newton motif played a marked role in later scientific rhetoric, as with Ampère and Maxwell. But this interpretation raises the question of why Kepler's 'laws' seem to have been so neglected between their formulation and the time of Newton. Certainly Kepler's writings are not easy to penetrate, and the laws themselves are not so clearly sign-posted as a modern reader may expect. Also Kepler's second law in particular was not easy to calculate with, and some astronomers, such as Seth Ward and Ismael Boulliau, found it easier to combine the ellipse with an equant point at the focus not occupied by the Sun. In general it seems that knowledgeable astronomers were well aware of the laws but did not accept them with quite the alacrity that we might think appropriate, so that even Newton could comment that, 'Kepler knew ye Orb to be not circular but oval & guest it to be Elliptical'.[26] The situation has been much clarified in important articles by Curtis Wilson. The validity of Kepler's laws did not rest solely on obser-vational evidence, with the quasi-animist forces (his 'mystical' side) being mere psychological scaffolding that could be cleared away once the building was erected. These laws depended on theoretical support as well, for the former was insufficient by itself. But Kepler's theory, his system of forces, was very much of his own making, and did not transfer easily to other workers, especially in an age in which both conservatives and more mechanistically minded radicals were wary of any suspicion of unmediated action at a distance, and when the latter were moving towards a new type of inertial physics in which the continuance of a motion did not demand a continually acting force to explain it. Thus, before Newton, it was quite rational to regard Kepler as having provided an ingenious and useful, but only approximate, account of the planetary motions. When Newton showed how his inverse square law could be derived from Kepler's second and third laws, and then the first law deduced from this, the 'laws' were back in business with new theoretical support, but, despite the use of dis-tance-related forces, this was very different from that provided by Kepler. It nevertheless fitted well with a new general system of mech-anics, and gave good licence for Kepler's laws to be named as such.

But this was for the future. For the time being popular educated and less educated interest in the new astronomy was to centre on a more accessible figure. One of the people to whom Kepler sent a copy of his *Mysterium Cosmographicum* was Galileo Galilei. This was natural, for Galileo, then in his early thirties, was the occupant of the Chair of Mathematics at one of the foremost scientific centres in Europe, the University of Padua. Galileo replied immediately, saying how much he was looking forward to perusing it, since he had been of Copernicus's opinion for many years. But, remarkably, this docu-ment itself is one of the few pieces of evidence for Galileo's own opinion until some thirteen years later, and the change depended upon a new observational instrument.

It is probably better to think in terms of the emergence of the telescope rather than its invention, but we may take 1608 as a symbolic year, when the Dutchman Hans Lippershey presented a spyglass to Prince Maurice, and also applied for a patent, thereby indicating the passage of the device from the realm of fairground attraction for producing illusions to that of something potentially useful. Whoever should be given the prime credit for the invention, the news spread rapidly, and reached Italy by the following year. Galileo seized on it avidly and constructed glasses for himself, but in his reports probably exaggerated the extent to which he had employed optical theory. Then, like Thomas Harriot in England at almost exactly the same time, he turned his telescope to the skies, but unlike Harriot he quickly published his findings, in a booklet of 1610 entitled *Sidereus Nuncius*.

This caused a sensation, not only because of the new facts themselves, but on account of their possible implications for rival cosmological systems. We isolate three discoveries. The first concerns the Moon. The Man in the Moon was, so to speak, an old friend, and scholastic discussions had frequently touched on the reason for this feature always pointing towards us. The telescope revealed to Galileo that the man was far more pock-marked than hitherto thought, and by observing the changing configuration of the spots he was able plausibly to infer the existence of shadows caused by mountains and chasms on the Moon's surface. This made the Moon more like the Earth, and was a great help in breaking down the gulf separating the perfect celestial regions from the imperfect elementary ones, and as such offered indirect support to heliocentric cosmology.

As regards the fixed stars, Galileo observed far more of them than had been done previously, and plausibly argued that the Milky Way was composed of stars too numerous to separate from one another with the naked eye. But a more important discovery concerned their magnification, for they were not increased in apparent size as much as would be expected from observation of nearer objects. Galileo therefore concluded that much of the observed size was to be attributed not to the body of the star itself, but to twinkle, or, as he called it, adventitious light, and he later confirmed this with experiments using naked eye observations. This had the important implication that the stars could be a vast distance away without needing to be of the enormous size that Tycho thought would have been necessary to explain the absence of observed parallax on the hypothesis of a moving Earth.

But for Galileo the most exciting discovery related to Jupiter. He recounts how in early 1610 he observed three small but bright stars near it, which changed their relative positions without straying far from the planet itself. He was later to add a fourth, and reasonably concluded that all four were satellites of Jupiter, 'four PLANETS never seen from the creation of the world up to our own time'.[27] With a piece of calculated flattery he named them the Medicean stars, after Cosimo de' Medici, the Grand Duke of Tuscany. This paid off, for soon Galileo procured appointment as Chief Mathematician and Philosopher to the Grand Duke, with the phrase 'and Philosopher' being added at his own insistence to emphasize that his interests were not merely mathematical but intimately concerned with the structure of the physical universe. And Galileo was quick to show how his discovery could support (but again only indirectly) the Copernican system of the world.

> Here we have a fine and elegant argument for quieting the doubts of those who, while accepting with tranquil mind the revolutions of the planets about the Sun in the Copernican system, are mightily disturbed to have the Moon alone revolve about the Earth and accompany it on an annual rotation about the Sun. Some have believed that this structure of the universe should be rejected as impossible. But now we have not just one planet rotating about another while both run through a great orbit about the Sun; our own eyes show us four stars which wander around Jupiter as does the Moon around the Earth, while all together trace out a grand revolution about the Sun in the space of twelve years.[28]

The initial reaction to Galileo's book, including that from the Jesuit College in Rome, was favourable, although for some this meant attempts to incorporate the new evidence within a traditional cosmological framework. There were a few who were reported to have refused (probably half jokingly) to look through the telescope on the grounds that they would not trust what they saw there; this was not *completely* unreasonable, given the previous reputation of optical devices for making things appear as they were not, and also given the difficulty of properly manipulating the instrument to show what was in fact there. Meanwhile Galileo continued observing, and also frequently allowed his disputatious temperament to lead him into behaviour which in retrospect we can see as unfortunately tactless. One of his preoccupations was with sunspots, about which he carried on an adversarious correspondence through an intermediary (Mark Welser) with the Jesuit Christopher Scheiner, writing under the pseudonym of Apelles; although Welser informed him that Apelles did not read Italian Galileo persisted in writing in that language rather than the mutually accessible Latin, and the result of Galileo's side of the exchange was published in 1613 as *Istoria e Dimostrazioni intorno alle Macchie Solari.*

Besides a rather fruitless dispute about priority, the authors disagreed about the nature of sunspots, with Galileo favouring the view that they were like clouds around the Sun, thus emphasizing the theme of mutability of the heavens. But other matters were discussed, the most important of which was undoubtedly the phases of Venus. It is a notable consequence of Ptolemaic theory that the two inner planets, Mercury and Venus, never deviate far from the Sun in celestial longitude – hence the position of Venus as both morning and evening star. Also, it was almost universally held that they were nearer to us than the Sun. There accordingly arose the question of how they received the light to make them visible, for on the common assumption that this came from the Sun they would be almost entirely illuminated from behind, and at most we should see a small sliver. One opinion had it that they were possessed of their own light and another that they were translucent, but basically the problem remained unresolved, or, to use T. S. Kuhn's phraseology, was an anomaly within the Ptolemaic paradigm. On the Copernican hypothesis the predictions were different, for, if these planets were orbiting the Sun, they should display phases in the manner of the Moon. And this is what Galileo observed in the case of Venus, and triumphantly reported in the *Letters on Sunspots*.

> These things leave no room for doubt about the orbit of Venus. With absolute necessity we shall conclude, in agreement with the theories of the Pythagoreans and of Copernicus, that Venus revolves about the Sun just as do all the other planets.[29]

So far so good, but what Galileo fails to mention, and what remained a thorn in his flesh, was that these observations were also perfectly compatible with the Tychonic system of the world, which, as mentioned above, soon became a favourite with Jesuit astronomers.

Until the 1610s the Copernican system had aroused little religious discussion, apart from a few casual references to scriptural passages that seemed to contradict it, such as the command to the Sun to stand still over Gibeon in order to lengthen the day, so that Joshua could have time to finish a battle. With the new popularity that Galileo had brought to the issue, the religious implications became of major concern, and opposition to the system was probably egged on by mere conservatism masquerading as high principle. Galileo was himself drawn into the controversy, and wrote a long letter on the relation of Copernicanism to the Scriptures. This closely reasoned piece made relatively liberal use of the principle of accommodation in biblical interpretation. The Bible was addressed to ignorant people, and appealed to the common understanding of the time; it was not intended as a textbook in astronomy. In the epigram of one Cardinal Baronius, which Galileo gleefully quoted, 'The intention of the Holy Ghost is to teach us how one goes to heaven, not how heaven goes.'[30] A tougher line, although also closely reasoned and susceptible of its own nuances of interpretation, was taken by Cardinal Bellarmine in a letter to Paolo Foscarini, a priest who had espoused Copernicanism.

> The Council [of Trent] prohibits interpreting Scripture against the common consensus of the Holy Fathers; and if Your Paternity wants to read not only the Holy Fathers, but also the modern commentaries on Genesis, the Psalms, Ecclesiastes, and Joshua, you will find all agreeing in the literal interpretation that the Sun is in the heavens and turns around the Earth with great speed, and that the Earth is very far from heaven and sits motionless at the center of the world.[31]

In 1616 the matter had become sufficiently serious for Rome to take a hand, and the Theologians to the Inquisition, after what may seem indecently hasty deliberations, reported that the proposition that 'The Sun is the centre of the world and completely devoid of local motion' was 'foolish and absurd in philosophy, and formally heretical', and that the proposition that 'The Earth is not the centre of the world nor motionless, but it moves as a whole and also with diurnal motion' should receive 'the same judgement in philosophy and that in regard to theological truth it is at least erroneous in faith'.[32] What precisely happened next as regards Galileo himself is debatable, but at the least he was at the Pope's behest officially informed of the judgement and acquiesced therein. And so the matter rested for several years. Galileo did not exactly refrain from controversy, and in fact carried on a bitter dispute centring on the nature of comets but taking in many aspects of what constituted proper scientific procedure with the Jesuit Horatio Grassi, but he kept quiet on the question of the motion of the Earth.

In 1623 there was a change of Pope, and Maffeo Barberini, an old friend and supporter of Galileo's, ascended to the Throne of St Peter with the title of Urban VIII. Galileo visited Rome and was granted several audiences, from which he seems to have come away with the impression that he could say what he liked about the Copernican system provided that he treated it as hypothetical and did not bring in scriptural arguments (which should be left to the theologians). He then set to work on one of his most important books, which, after a little sharp practice in getting it past the censor, was published in 1632 as *Dialogo . . . sopra i Due Massimi Sistemi Del Mondo Tolemaico, E Copernicano*. This was in the form of a dialogue lasting for four days between three friends, Salviati, Sagredo and Simplicio. Salviati can usually be taken as acting as spokesman for Galileo, Sagredo as an intelligent layman and Simplicio as the Aristotelian, but not one that is too stupid, for after all there is no honour in winning arguments over fools. The burden of the first three days is basically to show that everything would appear to happen the same whether or not the Earth was moving, and if the book had stopped there (and the Preface had been strongly modified), there would probably have been no trouble. But Galileo was not content with showing that the Copernican system was possible: he wanted to show that it actually was the case. As Salviati says early in the Fourth Day, 'Up to this point the indications of [the Earth's] mobility have been taken from celestial phenomena, seeing that nothing which takes place on the Earth has been powerful enough to establish the one position any more than the other.' He then continued,

> Among all sublunary things it is only in the element of water (as something which is very vast and is not joined and linked with the terrestrial globe as are all its solid parts, but is rather, because of its fluidity, free and separate and a law unto itself) that we may recognise some trace or indication of the Earth's behaviour in regard to motion and rest.[33]

This provided the cue for Salviati to expound, but not in highly developed form, Galileo's notorious doctrine of the tides. This, which attributed the tides to a 'sloshing around' of the seas caused by the Earth's twofold motion of translation and rotation, was based on a phoney argument, even on Galileo's own terms, and Galileo should have known it, but apparently genuinely did not.

But historically its main importance is that Galileo thought that he had found a particularly weighty argument for establishing the Copernican system. To be sure, it could not be regarded as utterly conclusive, but the statement to that effect was put at the end of the Day in the mouth of Simplicio, who had been regularly losing all the arguments.

> As to the discourses we have held, and especially this last one concerning the reasons for the ebbing and flowing of the ocean, I am really not entirely convinced; but from such feeble ideas of the matter as I have formed, I admit that your thoughts seem to me more ingenious than many others I have heard. I do not therefore consider them true and conclusive; indeed, keeping always before my mind's eye a most solid doctrine that I once heard from a most eminent and learned person, and before which one must fall silent, I know that if asked whether God in His infinite wisdom could have conferred upon the watery element its observed reciprocating motion using some other means than moving its containing vessels, both of you would reply that He could have, and that He would have known how to do this in many ways which are unthinkable to our minds. From this I forthwith conclude that, this being so, it

would be excessive boldness for anyone to restrict the Divine power and wisdom to some particular fancy of his own.

The reference to the Pope was unmistakable, and the offence was heavily compounded by Salviati's ironic comment.

> An admirable and angelic doctrine, and well in accord with another one, also Divine, which, while it grants to us the right to argue about the constitution of the universe (perhaps in order that the working of the human mind shall not be curtailed or made lazy) adds that we cannot discover the work of His hands. Let us, then, exercise these activities permitted to us and ordained by God, that we may recognize and thereby so much the more admire His greatness, however much less fit we may find ourselves to penetrate the profound depths of His infinite wisdom.[34]

There has been much discussion as to exactly why Galileo himself was condemned, but it seems clear that this thinly veiled insult to the Pope together with his open flaunting (in all but the letter) of the injunction to treat the Copernican system as no more than hypothetical would in themselves have provided ample reason. In any case he was called before the Inquisition in the following year, made to recant, and spent the rest of his life under house arrest.

As we shall see, this did not prevent Galileo from preparing and having published another book of outstanding importance, but he naturally refrained from making any statements about the motion of the Earth. And for a while the events of 1632–3 did put a damper on discussions of the Copernican system, especially in Catholic countries. Descartes, for instance, had finished his *Le Monde* at about this time, but suppressed it because

> I learned that people to whom I defer and whose authority over my own actions can hardly be less than is that of my own reason over my own thoughts, had disapproved an opinion on physics published a little before by someone else.[35]

But in general the condemnation probably had less lasting effect on the development than did natural inertia, and in both England and Scotland it was well into the second half of the seventeenth century before Aristotelian cosmology was displaced from university teaching. In the eighteenth century the end of the old cosmology was symbolized by the curt note inserted by the minimite friars Le Seur and Jacquier in their standard edition of Newton's *Principia*. At the beginning of Book III, they wrote:

> In this Third Book Newton assumes the hypothesis of the

motion of the Earth. The author's propositions could only be explicated by our making the same hypothesis. Hence we are driven to don an alien persona. For the rest we promise to obey the decrees borne against the motion of the Earth by the high pontiffs.[36]

And they then proceeded to elucidate the work with no further mention of the matter.

❧ MOTION AND MECHANICAL ❧ PHILOSOPHY

The new cosmology necessitated a new theory of motion, for, as had been obvious from the time of Copernicus and even before, Aristotelian 'mechanics' could not accommodate a moving Earth. Some have even seen cosmological reform as providing the prime motivation for reform in mechanics, but the old system also had many strains of its own. Aristotle made a sharp distinction between the celestial and sublunary regions. The former, which we have already considered in summary fashion, was the province of the fifth element and of universal circular motions, but the latter was far more chaotic; as also was Aristotle's account of it, seeing that his usual technique was to start from the situation in front of him and try to impose some semblance of order on it, rather than develop a new science axiomatically from first principles.

All bodies were composed of a mixture of the four elements, earth, water, air and fire, and their basic behaviour was dominated by the doctrines of natural places and natural motions. The natural place of earth was at the centre of the universe and that of fire at the periphery of the elementary regions, with the other two elements being in between. All bodies aspired towards their natural places, so that a heavy, or predominantly earthy, body would tend to move downwards and a predominantly fiery one upwards. These motions were conceived mainly in terms of their final causes, and less attention was paid to the question of their efficient causes. This was not the case with violent motions, in which a body was moving against its own nature. If I am lifting a heavy body, I am clearly the efficient cause of its motion, but if I throw it upwards the situation is more difficult, since there is no obvious mover once it has parted company with my hand. Aristotle proved himself a model of consistency. The projectile has nothing in contact with itself except the air surrounding it: therefore the air must be the mover, and in the process of throwing it I must have communicated a power of continuing the motion to the air, which would then, besides moving the projectile, pass the power on to the succeeding parts of itself. Despite the internal coherence of this scheme, it understandably drew much criticism from different cultural areas, and we find many thought experiments, such as those concerning the efficacy of shooting arrows by means of flapping the air behind them. Along with other Italians, the young Galileo saw these considerations as providing a fine stick with which to beat Aristotle. Like many of their predecessors these 'radicals' replaced the power communicated to the air with an internal moving force communicated to the projectile itself, which in the later Western Middle Ages was often known as 'impetus'.

But Galileo was different in that he came to realize that, even though he was giving anti-Aristotelian answers, he was still asking Aristotelian questions, and this led to his imposing a self-denying ordinance whereby he did not consider causes in his discussions of motion. This new attitude took root from around the beginning of the century, and received its most mature public expression in what is arguably his greatest work, the *Discorsi e dimostrazioni matematiche, intorno à due nuove scienze* of 1638, another dialogue between the three friends Salviati, Sagredo and Simplicio, but this time steering well clear of the dangerous question of the motion of the Earth.

Galileo's strategy in considering local motions (that is, motions according to place rather than to quality or quantity) was to split them into two components, horizontal and vertical. In an amusing exchange in the *Dialogo*, the unwary Simplicio is trapped by Salviati into admitting that a perfectly shaped ball rolling on a perfectly smooth horizontal surface would continue its motion indefinitely and with uniform speed. The context is the question of the behaviour of stones let drop from the mast of a moving ship (relevant of course to arguments about Copernicus). The Aristotelian Simplicio had demanded experiment, but Salviati was adamant that without experiment he could demonstrate that they would fall at the bottom of the mast and not be left behind by the motion of the ship. For this purpose he made use of an ingenious thought experiment with inclined planes. Passages like this led Alexandre Koyré and others to lay great stress on what they saw as Galileo's Platonic streak, and heated controversy continues concerning the importance of experiment in Galileo's work as regards both the context of discovery and the context of justification, but no serious scholar would now go to Koyré's extremes in denigrating its role.

Although Salviati demonstrated to his companions' satisfaction the uniform speed of unimpeded horizontal motion, a complication remained, for such a motion is in fact in a circle about the centre of the Earth. In the *Dialogo* Galileo made some play with this to illustrate the circle's superiority over the straight line, but in the *Discorsi* he quickly approximates this with a straight line, and in doing so appeals to Archimedes (a particular hero of his), who in his *On Floating Bodies* had said that verticals could be treated as parallel even though in fact they all pointed towards the Earth's centre.

Vertical motion needed two considerations. In Day 1 of the *Discorsi* Salviati argued that in a vacuum all bodies, whatever their density, would fall with the same speed. A vacuum was unrealizable in practice, and so his main strategy employed thought experiments concerning ever rarer media, but he does cite somewhat exaggeratedly some actual experimentation with pendulums: we certainly do not need to consider here objects dropped from the Leaning Tower of Pisa. His more famous, and much discussed, argument about falling bodies occurs in Day 3, and concerns the acceleration of falling bodies. That they do accelerate had been known from time immemorial, but since at least the time of Aristotle most discussion had centred on why they did so. Salviati would have none of this.

> The present does not seem to me to be an opportune time to enter into an investigation of the cause of the acceleration of natural motion, concerning which various philosophers have produced various opinions, some reducing it to approach to the centre, others to there remaining successively less parts of the medium to be divided, others to a certain extrusion of the ambient medium which, in being rejoined at the rear of the mobile, is continually pressing and pushing it; which fantasies and others like them it would be appropriate to examine and resolve but with little gain. For now, it suffices our Author that we understand that he wishes to investigate and demonstrate to us some properties of a motion accelerated (whatever be the cause of its acceleration) in such a way that. . . . [37]

The structure of Day 3 is that Salviati reads aloud a Latin treatise by Galileo, which the friends concurrently discuss in Italian.

The form of Galileo's Latin text is mathematical. After a brief introduction, there follow (without interruption for comment) one definition, four axioms and six theorems concerning uniform motion. We then move on to accelerated motion, for which 'it is appropriate to search for and explicate a definition that above all agrees with what nature employs'.[38] The basic criterion of choice was simplicity.

> When therefore I observe a stone falling from rest from on high to acquire successively new increments of speed, why should I not believe these increments to be made in the simplest way and that most accessible to everyone? And, if we consider attentively, we shall find no addition and no increment simpler than that which is applied always in the same way. . . . And so it seems in no way discordant with right reason if we accept that

intensification of speed is made according to extension of time, from which the definition of the motion that will be our concern can be put thus: I call an equably or uniformly accelerated motion one which proceeding from rest adds to itself equal moments of swiftness in equal times.[39]

An obvious point, and one that is made by Sagredo, is that it might be clearer to say that speed increased proportionally with distance rather than with time. Salviati reports that Galileo himself had once held this view, but that it was in fact impossible, and indeed we may say that, if falling bodies did behave in this way, they could not start naturally from rest but would remain suspended as it were by sky-hooks until given a push.

Galileo adds to the definition a principle that will allow him to draw into his discussion of falling bodies the behaviour of balls rolled down inclined planes. 'I accept that the degrees of speed acquired by the same mobile on different inclinations of planes are equal when the elevations of the planes are equal.' After Salviati has adduced some experimental evidence from pendulums for this, he proceeds to quote Galileo's first two theorems on accelerated motion. The first states that

The time in which a space is traversed by a mobile in uniformly accelerated transference from rest is equal to the time in which the same space would be traversed by the same mobile carried with a uniform motion whose degree of speed was half of the last and highest degree of speed of the former uniformly accelerated motion.[40]

The medieval version of this theorem is now usually referred to as the Merton rule, after its probable origins in Merton College, Oxford, in the first half of the fourteenth century. There has been much discussion of the possibility of medieval influence on Galileo in this regard, but it seems ill-advised to look for anything more specific than the import-ant step of (implicitly or explicitly) representing the intensities of speeds by segments of straight lines.

The second theorem and its corollary descend from speeds, or their intensities, to distances. The theorem shows that in a uniformly accelerated motion the distances traversed are as the squares of the times, and the corollary that the successive distances traversed in equal times, starting from rest, are as the successive odd numbers 1, 3, 5, 7, ... We are now reaching directly measurable quantities, and so the stage is set for Simplicio to ask for experimental evidence to show whether this is in fact the mode of acceleration employed by nature in the case of falling bodies. Salviati willingly complies.

As a true man of science [*scienziato*] you make a very reasonable demand, and one that is customary and appropriate in the sciences which apply mathematical demonstrations to physical conclusions, as is seen with perspectivists, with astronomers, with mechanicians, with musicians, and others who confirm with sensory experiences their principles, which are the foundations of the whole succeeding structure.[41]

The experiments involved rolling well-prepared bronze balls down different lengths of an extremely smooth channel arranged at different inclinations to the horizontal, and measuring the times of their descents by water running out of a hole in a pail of water. One's initial impression may be that the set-up smacks of Heath Robinson (or Rube Goldberg), but repetitions of the experiments in recent years have shown that they can be surprisingly accurate, and so we may say that they did indeed give Galileo strong support for his 'law' of falling bodies.

The burden of the Fourth Day of the *Discorsi* is to combine the horizontal and the vertical, and so produce a general description of the behaviour of unimpeded 'natural' motion. The result is the famous parabolic path for projectiles. This was admirable mathematically but less satisfactory empirically for, as gunners and others were quick to point out, the maximum horizontal trajectory was not to be achieved by firing at an elevation of 45°, nor did actual cannon balls follow a neat mathematical parabola.[42] All this goes to show the extent to which, despite his practical rhetoric, such as that provided by setting the *Discorsi* in the Arsenal at Venice, the success of Galileo's mechanics depended on his focusing on ideal situations and ignoring many of the messy complexities of the actual physical world.

The extent of Galileo's reliance upon mathematics, sometimes to the neglect of exact correspondence with empirical facts, may have worried a good Baconian, but to his younger contemporary René Descartes the principal fault lay in a different direction. Writing to Marin Mersenne in 1638, shortly after the publication of the *Discorsi*, he gave the opinion that, although Galileo 'philosophized much better than most, yet he has only sought the reasons of certain particular effects without considering the first causes of nature, and so has built without foundation'.[43] This was to be seen as contrasting with Descartes himself, whose science of mechanics depended intimately upon both his method and metaphysics, and whose *Discours de la Méthode*, together with the *Diotrique*, *Météores* and *Géométrie*, had been published in the preceding year. And before that Descartes had almost completed his *Le Monde*, a major work on natural philosophy, which, as noted above, he then suppressed because of Galileo's condemnation in 1633.

After Descartes had in a familiar manner proved to his own satisfaction the existence of himself, of God, and of an external physical world, he was in a position to consider more exactly the nature of the last of these. And a very austere picture it was that he had of it. As he put it in the *Principia Philosophiae* (published in 1644), if we attend to the intellect, rather than the senses,

> We shall easily admit that it is the same extension that constitutes the nature of body and the nature of space, nor do these two differ from each other more than the nature of the genus or species differs from the nature of the individual. If while attending to the idea which we have of a body, for example a stone, we reject from it all that we recognize as not required for the nature of body, let us certainly first reject hardness, for if a stone is liquefied or divided into the minutest particles of dust, it will lose this, but will not on that account cease to be body; let us also reject colour, for we often see stones so transparent as there were no colour in them; let us reject heaviness, for although fire is so light, we do not the less think it to be body; and then finally let us reject cold and heat, and all other qualities, because either they are not considered to be in the stone, or, if they are changed, the stone is not on that account thought to have lost the nature of body. We shall then be aware that nothing plainly remains in the idea of it other than that it is something extended in length, breadth and depth, and the same is contained in the idea of space, not only full of bodies, but also that which is called a vacuum.[44]

In this way the physical universe is reduced to characterless matter swirling around in the famous Cartesian vortices, and by its actions on our sense organs producing our perceptions of all the different qualities.

Descartes's physical universe has certain similarities with that of the ancient atomists, but there were important differences. In the first place, matter for Descartes was not composed of indivisible atoms moving in void, but constituted a continuous plenum without empty spaces, although for most scientific purposes one could focus on the three different sorts of particles that were separated out, in a manner similar to relatively self-subsistent eddies, by the vortical motion. These were in a way a replacement for the Aristotelian elements. The first comprised extremely subtle and mobile matter, the second small spherical globules, and the third larger particles which were less apt for motion.

> And from these three we show that all the bodies of this visible world are composed, the Sun and the fixed stars from the first,

the heavens from the second, and the Earth together with the planets and the comets from the third.[45]

In this way one is relieved from the almost impossible task of thinking all the time starkly in terms of the motions of fundamentally undifferentiated continuous matter.

A perhaps more important difference from ancient atomism was that the motions of matter were by no means random, and Descartes's system was also more effectively rule-governed than those of Empedocles, with his guiding principles of Love and Strife, and of Anaxagoras with that of Mind. Descartes believed that any system of matter created by God would obey certain laws of motion that followed from God's unchangeableness. The first is that every body would remain always in the same state unless this was changed by the action of external forces, and Descartes was adamant that there be included in this (contrary to the Aristotelian tradition) a body's state of motion. The second[46] is that the motion of any part of matter always tends to be in a straight line, and this when added to the first gives a fair approximation to Newton's first law of motion, the principle of rectilinear inertia, which may rightly be regarded as the foundation stone of classical mechanics. The third law is rather more complicated: it concerns the collisions of bodies, and asserts *inter alia* that in these the amount of motion is conserved. From it Descartes deduces some hideously incorrect laws of impact, which older fashioned histories of mechanics used often to crow over, but this was to neglect the fact that, as regards historical influence, the form of Descartes's discussion was far more important than its exact content.

Descartes's first two laws in particular led to some novel questions about forces. For instance, the acceleration of falling bodies implied the existence of a force to bring about this change from its preferred state of uniform rectilinear motion, and similarly did the deviation of the planetary orbits from this state. Armed with hindsight, the reader will recall how important these questions were for Newton on his journey towards the principle of universal gravitation, but this serves to show up important differences between the two men. Whereas Newton asked typically how big the forces were (at least as a preliminary to deeper explanation), Descartes sought for their causes, and in both cases specified these elaborately, but still vaguely, in terms of what we may call differential pressures from the vortices.

Compared with Newton on this and other issues, Descartes appears a qualitative rather than a quantitative scientist, and this ties in with another important methodological difference. Newton, at least rhetorically within the context of justification, was a strong inductivist.

In experimental philosophy we are to look upon propositions

inferred by general induction from phenomena as accurately or very nearly true, notwithstanding any contrary hypotheses that may be imagined, till such time as other phenomena occur, by which they may either be made more accurate, or liable to exceptions.[47]

For Descartes and his followers, however, hypotheses played a crucial role. The general structure of matter and the general laws of motion could be reached purely by deduction, but this process could not proceed unaided to unique explanations of particular phenomena.

When I wished to descend to [effects] that were more particular, so many different ones were presented to me that I did not think it possible for the human mind to distinguish the forms or species of bodies that were on Earth from an infinity of others which could have been there if it had been the will of God to put them there, nor consequently to relate them to our use without coming to the causes by means of the effects and employing several particular experiences. Following this, in passing my mind again over all the objects which were ever presented to my sense, I indeed dare to say that I have not remarked there anything that I could not explain suitably enough by the principles that I have found. But I must also admit that Nature's power is so ample and so vast and that my principles are so simple and so general that I hardly remark any particular effect without immediately recognising that it can be deduced in many different fashions, and that my greatest difficulty is usually in finding upon which of these fashions it does depend. And for this I know no other expedient than to seek once again some experiences which are such that their outcome will not be the same if it is in one of the fashions that one must explain it as it will be if it is in the other.[48]

In this way Descartes gives a reasonably clear, if not unproblematic, expression of what is often referred to as a hypothetico-deductive methodology, of a kind which was employed by many notable scientists of the later seventeenth century.

Descartes was not alone in producing a mechanical philosophy – one need only think of the work of Pierre Gassendi and of Thomas Hobbes – but it was his system together with later developments and modifications that was most generally influential. And when Aristotelian natural philosophy began at last to be displaced from the universities it was usually replaced by a version of Cartesianism, although this enjoyed a relatively short reign before succumbing to the incursions of Newtonianism. We may thus conveniently regard Descartes's work as representing the culmination of the first phase of the Scientific Revolution.

❧ NOTES ❧

1 *The Works of John Playfair, Esq. . . . with a Memoir of the Author* (Edinburgh, Archibald Constable, 1822), vol. 2. This was being completed at the time of his death in 1819; cf. vol. 1, pp. lxi–lxii, vol. 2, pp. 3–4. For helpful comments on an earlier draft of this chapter I am very grateful to Steven J. Livesey and Jamil Ragep.

2 W. Whewell, *History of the Inductive Sciences, from the Earliest to the Present Time* (London, Parker, 3 vols, 3rd edn, 1857), vol. 1, p. 181.

3 cf. Ferguson [3.10], ch. 11.

4 cf. A. Koyré, *Etudes d'Histoire de la Pensée Philosophique* (Paris, Armand Colin, 1961), pp. 279–309.

5 *Oxford English Dictionary*, s.v.

6 But cf. J. Needham, *The Grand Titration: Science and Society in East and West* (London, Allen & Unwin, 1969), pp. 276–85.

7 cf. N. W. Gilbert, 'A Letter of Giovanni Dondi dall'Orologia to Fra'Guglielmo Centueri; A Fourteenth-Century Episode in the Quarrel of the Ancients and the Moderns', *Viator* 8 (1977) 299–346.

8 See for example A. Keller, 'A Renaissance Humanist Looks at "New" Inventions: The Article "Horologium" in Giovanni Tortelli's *De Orthographia*', *Technology and Culture* 11 (1970) 345–65.

9 Zilsel [3.56].

10 cf. K. R. Popper, *Objective Knowledge: An Evolutionary Approach* (Oxford, Clarendon, 1972), ch. 3; Molland [3.51].

11 I. B. Thomas, *Selections Illustrating the History of Greek Mathematics* (London, Heinemann, 1939), vol. 2, p. 31.

12 Descartes [3.36], vol. 10, p. 373.

13 Pappus of Alexandria, *Book 7 of the Collection*, ed. A. Jones (New York, Springer, 1986), p. 82.

14 See, for instance, R. Robinson, 'Analysis in Greek Geometry', in R. Robinson, *Essays in Greek Philosophy* (Oxford, Clarendon, 1969), pp. 1–15; M. S. Mahoney, 'Another Look at Greek Geometrical Analysis', *Archive for History of Exact Sciences* 5 (1968–9) 318–48; J. Hintikka and U. Remes, *The Method of Analysis: Its Geometrical Origin and General Significance* (Dordrecht, Reidel, 1974).

15 *Aubrey's Brief Lives*, ed. O. L. Dick (London, Secker & Warburg, 1949), p. 130.

16 L. Prowe, *Nicolaus Coppernicus* (Berlin, Weidmannsche Buchhandlung, 1883–4), vol. 2, p. 185.

17 Copernicus [3.33], sig. iii.v.

18 *Luther's Works, Volume 54: Table Talk*, ed. and trans. Theodore G. Tappert (Philadelphia, Penn., Fortress Press, 1967), p. 359.

19 Westman [3.72].

20 Copernicus [3.33], sig. i.v.

21 This is the date of his matriculation; he did not actually move to Tübingen until 1589. See the article on him by Owen Gingerich in the *Dictionary of Scientific Biography*.

22 Kepler [3.46], vol. 8, p. 9; Kepler [3.47], 38–9.

23 Kepler [3.46], vol. 3, p. 178.

24 Kepler [3.46], vol. 3, p. 366.

25 *Astronomia Nova ΑΙΤΙΟΛΟΓΗΤΟΣ, seu Physica Coelestis, tradita comment-ariis De Motibus Stellae Martis, Ex Observationibus G. V. Tychonis Brahe.*

26 *The Correspondence of Isaac Newton*, ed. H. W. Turnbull *et al.* (Cambridge, Cambridge University Press, 1959–77), vol. 2, p. 436.

27 Galileo [3.43], 50–1.

28 Galileo [3.43], 57.

29 Galileo [3.43], 93–4.

30 Galileo [3.43], 186.

31 Finocchiaro [3.65], 67–8.

32 Finocchiaro [3.65], 146.

33 Galileo [3.44], 416–17.

34 Galileo [3.44], 464.

35 Descartes [3.36], vol. 6, p. 60.

36 Isaac Newton, *Philosophiae Naturalis Principia Mathematica. . . . Perpetuis Commentariis illustrata, communi studio pp. Thomae Le Seur & Francisci Jacqu-ier Ex Gallicana Minimorum Familia, Matheseos Professorum* (Geneva, Barrillot, 1739–42), vol. 3.

37 Galileo [3.40], vol. 8, p. 202. In producing my own translations from the *Discorsi*, I have made use of those by Stillman Drake in Galileo [3.45], whose volume includes the page numbers from the *Edizione Nazionale*.

38 Galileo [3.40], vol. 8, p. 197.

39 Galileo [3.40], vol. 8, p. 198.

40 Galileo [3.40], vol. 8, p. 208.

41 Galileo [3.40], vol. 8, p. 212.

42 cf. A. R. Hall, *Ballistics in the Seventeenth Century: A Study in the Relations of Science and War with reference particularly to England* (Cambridge, Cambridge University Press, 1952), and M. Segre, 'Torricelli's Correspondence on Ballis-tics', *Annals of Science* 40 (1983) 489–99.

43 Descartes [3.36], vol. 2, p. 380.

44 *Principia Philosophiae* II. 11, in Descartes [3.36], vol. 8–1, p. 46.

45 *Principia Philosophiae* III. 52, in Descartes [3.36], vol. 8–1, p. 105.

46 The numbering is from the *Principia Philosophiae* (II. 37–40); it was different in *Le Monde*, where the laws are deduced rather more vividly from God's creation of an imaginary world.

47 *Sir Isaac Newton's Mathematical Principles of Natural Philosophy and his System of the World*, trans. Andrew Motte, revised by Florian Cajori (Berkeley, Calif., University of California Press, 1934), p. 400.

48 Descartes [3.36], vol. 6, pp. 64–5.

❧ BIBLIOGRAPHY ❧

General and background works

3.1 Boas, M. *The Scientific Renaissance, 1450–1630*, London, Collins, 1962.

3.2 Burtt, E. A. *The Metaphysical Foundations of Modern Physical Science*, London, Routledge & Kegan Paul, 2nd edn, 1932.

3.3 Butterfield, H. *The Origins of Modern Science*, London, Bell, 1949.

3.4 Cohen, I. B. *The Birth of a New Physics*, Garden City, N.Y., Anchor Books, 1960.

3.5 Crombie, A. C. *Augustine to Galileo*, London, Falcon Educational Books, 1952.

3.6 Dear, P. *Mersenne and the Learning of the Schools*, Ithaca, N.Y., Cornell University Press, 1988.

3.7 Debus, A. G. *Man and Nature in the Renaissance*, Cambridge, Cambridge University Press, 1978.

3.8 Duhem, P. *Medieval Cosmology: Theories of Infinity, Place, Time, Void, and the Plurality of Worlds*, ed. and trans. R. Ariew, Chicago, Ill., University of Chicago Press, 1985.

3.9 Eisenstein, E. *The Printing Press as an Agent of Change: Communications and Cultural Transformations in Early-Modern Europe*, Cambridge, Cambridge University Press, 1979.

3.10 Ferguson, W. K. *The Renaissance in Historical Thought*, Cambridge, Mass., Riverside Press, 1948.

3.11 Funkenstein, A. *Theology and the Scientific Imagination from the Middle Ages to the Seventeenth Century*, Princeton, N.J., Princeton University Press, 1986.

3.12 Gillispie, C. C. *The Edge of Objectivity*, Princeton, N.J., Princeton University Press, 1960.

3.13 Grant, E. *Much Ado About Nothing: Theories of Space and Vacuum from the Middle Ages to the Scientific Revolution*, Cambridge, Cambridge University Press, 1981.

3.14 Grant, E. and Murdoch, J. E. (eds) *Mathematics and Its Applications to Science and Natural Philosophy in the Middle Ages: Essays in Honor of Marshall Clagett*, Cambridge, Cambridge University Press, 1987.

3.15 Hall, A. R. *The Revolution in Science*, London, Longman, 1983.

3.16 Heilbron, J. L. *Elements of Early Modern Physics*, Berkeley, Calif., University of California Press, 1982.

3.17 Hooykaas, R. *Religion and the Rise of Modern Science*, Edinburgh, Scottish Academic Press, 1972.

3.18 Lindberg, D. C. (ed.) *Science in the Middle Ages*, Chicago, Ill., University of Chicago Press, 1978.

3.19 Lindberg, D. C. and Westman, R. S. (eds) *Reappraisals of the Scientific Revolution*, Cambridge, Cambridge University Press, 1990.

3.20 Olson, R. *Science Deified and Science Defied: The Historical Significance of Science in Western Culture from the Bronze Age to the Beginning of the Modern Era*, Berkeley, Calif., University of California Press, 1982.

3.21 Schmitt, C. B. *Studies in Renaissance Philosophy and Science*, London, Variorum Reprints, 1981.

3.22 Schmitt, C. B. *Aristotle and the Renaissance*, Cambridge, Mass., Harvard University Press for Oberlin College, 1983.

3.23 Strong, E. W. *Procedures and Metaphysics: A Study in the Philosophy of Mathematical-Physical Science in the Sixteenth and Seventeenth Centuries*, Berkeley, Calif., University of California Press, 1936.

3.24 Webster, C. (ed.) *The Intellectual Revolution of the Seventeenth Century*, London, Routledge & Kegan Paul, 1974.

3.25 Westfall, R. S. *The Construction of Modern Science*, New York, Wiley, 1971.

3.26 Wightman, W. P. D. *Science and the Renaissance*, vol. I, *An Introduction to the Study of the Emergence of the Sciences in the Sixteenth Century*, Edinburgh, Oliver & Boyd, 1962.

3.27 Wightman, W. P. D. *Science in a Renaissance Society*, London, Hutchinson, 1972.

3.28 Yates, F. A. *The Rosicrucian Enlightenment*, London, Routledge & Kegan Paul, 1972.

Major authors

3.29 Anderson F. H. (ed.) *Francis Bacon, The New Organon and Related Writings*, Indianapolis, Ind., Bobbs-Merrill, 1960.

3.30 Robertson, J. M. (ed.) *The Philosophical Works of Francis Bacon*, London, Routledge, 1905.

3.31 Spedding, J., Ellis, R. L. and Heath, D. D. (eds) *The Works of Francis Bacon*, London, 1857–62.

3.32 Dreyer, J. L. E. (ed.) *Tychonis Brahe Dani Opera Omnia*, Copenhagen, In Libraria Gyldendaliana, 1913–29.

3.33 *Nicolai Copernici Torinensis De Revolutionibus Orbium Coelestium, Libri VI*, Nürnberg, Joh. Petreius, 1543.

3.34 Czartoryski, P. (ed.) *Nicholas Copernicus, Minor Works*, trans. E. Rosen, London, Macmillan, 1985.

3.35 *Three Copernican Treatises*, trans. E. Rosen, New York, Octagon, 3rd edn, 1971.

3.36 Adam, C. and Tannery, P. (eds) *Oeuvres de Descartes*, Paris, Léopold Cerf, 1897–1913.

3.37 *René Descartes, Discourse on Method, Optics, Geometry, and Meteorology*, trans. P. J. Olscamp, Indianapolis, Ind., Bobbs-Merrill, 1965.

3.38 *René Descartes, Principles of Philosophy*, trans. V. R. Miller and R. P. Miller, Dordrecht, Reidel, 1983.

3.39 *The Geometry of René Descartes*, trans. D. E. Smith and M. L. Latham, New York, Dover, 1954; includes a facsimile of the original 1637 edition.

3.40 *Le Opere di Galileo Galilei: Nuova Ristampa della Edizione Nazionale*, Florence, G. Barbèra, 1968.

3.41 *Galileo Galilei, On motion and On mechanics*, trans. I. E. Drabkin and S. Drake, Madison, Wisc., University of Wisconsin Press, 1960.

3.42 Galileo Galilei, *Sidereus Nuncius or the Sidereal Messenger*, trans. A. Van Helden, Chicago, Ill., University of Chicago Press, 1989.

3.43 *Discoveries and Opinions of Galileo, Including The Starry Messenger (1610), Letters on Sunspots (1613), Letter to the Grand Duchess Christina (1615), and Excerpts from the Assayer (1623)*, trans. S. Drake, Garden City, N.Y., Doubleday, 1957.

3.44 *Galileo Galilei Dialogue Concerning the Two Chief World Systems – Ptolemaic & Copernican*, trans. S. Drake, Berkeley, Calif., University of California Press, 1953.

3.45 *Galileo Galilei, Two New Sciences, Including Centers of Gravity & Force of Percussion*, trans. S. Drake, Madison, Wisc., University of Wisconsin Press, 1974.

3.46 von Dyck, W. and Caspar, M. (eds) *Johannes Kepler, Gesammelte Werke*, Munich, C. H. Beck, 1938-.

3.47 *Johannes Kepler, Mysterium Cosmographicum: The Secret of the Universe*, trans. A. M. Duncan, interpretation and commentary E. J. Aiton, New York, Abaris, 1981.

Progress and method

3.48 Bury, J. B. *The Idea of Progress: An Inquiry into its Origin and Growth*, London, Macmillan, 1920.

3.49 Crombie, A. C. *Robert Grosseteste and the Origins of Experimental Science 1100–1700*, Oxford, Clarendon, 1953.

3.50 Gilbert, N. W. *Renaissance Concepts of Method*, New York, Columbia University Press, 1960.

3.51 Molland, A. G. 'Medieval Ideas of Scientific Progress', *Journal of the History of Ideas* 39 (1978) 561–77.

3.52 Randall, J. H. *The School of Padua and the Emergence of Modern Science*, Padua, Antenore, 1961.

3.53 Rossi, P. *Francis Bacon: From Magic to Science*, trans. S. Rabinovitch, London, Routledge & Kegan Paul, 1968.

3.54 Rossi, P. *Philosophy, Technology and the Arts in the Early Modern Era*, trans. S. Attanasio, New York, Harper & Row, 1970.

3.55 Wallace, W. A. *Causality and Scientific Explanation*, Ann Arbor, Mich., University of Michigan Press, 2 vols, 1972–4.

3.56 Zilsel, E. 'The Genesis of the Concept of Scientific Progress', *Journal of the History of Ideas* 6 (1945) 325–49.

Mathematics

3.57 Bos, H. J. M. 'On the Representation of Curves in Descartes' Géométrie', *Archive for History of Exact Sciences* 24 (1981) 295–338.

3.58 Boyer, C. B. *A History of Mathematics*, New York, Wiley, 1968.

3.59 Klein, J. *Greek Mathematical Thought and the Origins of Algebra*, trans. E. Brann, Cambridge, Mass., MIT Press, 1968.

3.60 Lachterman, D. R. *The Ethics of Geometry: A Genealogy of Modernity*, London, Routledge, 1989.
3.61 Molland, A. G. 'Shifting the Foundations: Descartes's Transformation of Ancient Geometry', *Historia Mathematica* 3 (1976) 21–49.
3.62 Rashed, R. (ed.) *Mathématiques et Philosophie de l'Antiquité à l'Age Classique*, Paris, Editions du CNRS, 1991.

Astronomical revolution

3.63 Dreyer, J. L. E. *A History of Astronomy from Thales to Kepler*, New York, Dover, 2nd edn, 1953.
3.64 Field, J. V. *Kepler's Geometrical Cosmology*, London, Athlone Press, 1988.
3.65 Finocchiaro, M. A. *The Galileo Affair: A Documentary History*, Berkeley, Calif., University of California Press, 1989.
3.66 Jardine, N. *The Birth of History and Philosophy of Science. Kepler's A Defence of Tycho against Ursus with Essays on its Provenance and Significance*, Cambridge, Cambridge University Press, 1984.
3.67 Kuhn, T. S. *The Copernican Revolution*, Cambridge, Mass., Harvard University Press, 1957.
3.68 Redondi, P. *Galileo: Heretic*, trans. R. Rosenthal, Princeton, N.J., Princeton University Press, 1987.
3.69 Schofield, C. J. *Tychonic and Semi-Tychonic World Systems*, New York, Arno Press, 1981.
3.70 Swerdlow, N. W. and Neugebauer, O. *Mathematical Astronomy in Copernicus's De Revolutionibus*, New York, Springer, 1984.
3.71 Van Helden, A. *The Invention of the Telescope*, Philadelphia, Penn., American Philosophical Society, 1977.
3.72 Westman, R. S. 'The Melanchthon Circle, Rheticus, and the Wittenberg Interpretation of the Copernican Theory', *Isis* 66 (1975) 165–93.
3.73 Westman, R. S. (ed.) *The Copernican Achievement*, Berkeley, Calif., University of California Press, 1975.
3.74 Wilson, C. *Astronomy from Kepler to Newton: Historical Studies*, London, Variorum Reprints, 1989.

Mechanics and mechanical philosophy

3.75 Clagett, M. *The Science of Mechanics in the Middle Ages*, Madison, Wisc., University of Wisconsin Press, 1959.
3.76 Clarke, D. M. *Descartes' Philosophy of Science*, Manchester, Manchester University Press, 1982.
3.77 Dijksterhuis, E. J. *The Mechanization of the World Picture*, Oxford, Clarendon, 1961.
3.78 Drake, S. and Drabkin, I. E. *Mechanics in Sixteenth-Century Italy: Selections from Tartaglia, Benedetti, Guido Ubaldo, and Galileo*, Madison, Wisc., University of Wisconsin Press, 1969.

3.79 Gaukroger, S. (ed.) *Descartes: Philosophy, Mathematics and Physics*, Brighton, Harvester, 1980.

3.80 Grosholz, E. R. *Cartesian Method and the Problem of Reduction*, Oxford, Clarendon, 1991.

3.81 Hutchison, K. 'What Happened to Occult Qualities in the Scientific Revolution?', *Isis* 78 (1982) 233–53.

3.82 Joy, L. S. *Gassendi the Atomist: Advocate of History in an Age of Science*, Cambridge, Cambridge University Press, 1987.

3.83 Koyré, A. *Galileo Studies*, Brighton, Harvester, 1978.

3.84 Koyré, A. *Metaphysics and Measurement: Essays in Scientific Revolution*, London, Chapman and Hall, 1968.

3.85 McMullin, E. (ed.) *Galileo: Man of Science*, New York, Basic Books, 1967.

3.86 Molland, A. G. 'The Atomisation of Motion: A Facet of the Scientific Revolution', *Studies in History and Philosophy of Science* 13 (1982) 31–54.

3.87 Wallace, W. A. *Prelude to Galileo: Essays on Medieval and Seventeenth-Century Sources of Galileo's Thought*, Dordrecht, Reidel, 1981.

CHAPTER 4

Francis Bacon and man's two-faced kingdom

Antonio Pérez-Ramos

Two closely related but distinct tenets about Bacon's philosophy have been all but rejected by contemporary historiography. The first is Bacon's attachment to the so-called British empiricist school, that is, the perception of him as the forerunner or inspirer of thinkers such as Locke, Berkeley or Hume. This putative lineage has been chiefly the result of nineteenth-century German scholarship, beginning with Hegel's own *Vorlesungen über die Geschichte der Philosophie* and his trail of imitators and disciples.[1] The glaring fact that Bacon's name is hardly (if at all) mentioned by his progeny of would-be co-religionists, or the serious questioning of the existence of any such entity as the 'British empiricist school', has added further weight to this radical work of revision of the Lord Chancellor's significance.[2] The canon of great philosophers is, to a great extent, a matter of flux, and nationalistic attachments or polarizations should always pale beside the historically recorded use of the same idiolect in philosophical matters, as is largely the case with Descartes or Malebranche – those French 'rationalists' – and Locke, Berkeley or Hume – those 'British empiricists'.

The second tenet that awaits clarification is the exact nature of Bacon's own philosophical achievement as regards the emergence of the new scientific movement – a movement usually associated with the names of Copernicus, Galileo, Kepler, Descartes or Newton. This point is extremely difficult to assess, for it is almost demonstrably true that no such stance or category as our 'science' (any more than our 'scientist') existed in Bacon's day and for a long time thereafter,[3] and hence the web of interpretations must make generous allowances for an inevitable although self-aware anachronism. Bacon was systematically deified by the English Royal Society, by eighteenth-century French *philosophes* and by eminent Victorian figures such as Herschel or

Whewell. Research has shown, however, that the tenor of such deifi-
cations was different in each case; for example, the last-named
Baconsbild was largely prompted by criticism of supposedly Baconian
doctrines coming from David Brewster and other Scottish scientists
and philosophers, as well as from Romantic notions about the role of
'genius' in science, hardly compatible with the allegedly egalitarian
character of Bacon's methodology.[4] Be that as it may, as an example
of the sort of cultural consensus which transcends the limits of what
can be reasonably termed 'philosophy' and adopts the sweeping pathos
of an all-embracing ideology, we can profitably read this anonymous
passage[5] from the *Quarterly Review* – a sample of Bacon's cult in
Victorian England:

> The Baconian philosophy, having for its object the increase of
> human pleasures and the decrease of human pains, has on this
> principle made all its brilliant discoveries in the physical world,
> and having thereby effected our vast progress in the mechanical
> arts, has proved itself to be the all-sufficient philosophy.

This evaluation has radically changed in our century. Bacon's philosophy has been solemnly declared a fraud, bearing, as a methodology,
no relation whatsoever to the heritage of the true founding fathers of
modern science – all of them representatives of mathematically inspired
patterns of thought, that is, men such as Copernicus, Galileo, Kepler,
Descartes or Mersenne. Thus, any talk about Bacon's methodology has
been dismissed as 'provincial and illiterate'.[6] Now and then, however,
Baconian *apologiae* have appeared, for example Paolo Rossi's book
Francesco Bacone. Dalla Magia alla Scienza (Italian original published
in 1957),[7] but it is a most telling sign of the ostensibly difficult position
that would-be apologists have to defend that nowadays the terms of
the debate are most of the time centred around the 'arts of communication and rhetoric', the general history of ideas, politics and literature,
rather than dealing with philosophy proper.[8] Reminders such as Paolo
Rossi's have been all too rare, and scant attention has been paid to
Bacon's philosophical credentials:

> One very obvious thing must not be forgotten: the science of
> the 17th and 18th centuries was at once Galilean *and* Baconian
> *and* Cartesian.[9]

Yet, the sense in which a branch at least of the new science was
Baconian remains opaque if a precise answer is not given to this precise
historical query: *what exactly makes a science Baconian?*

Now, it is the great merit of T. S. Kuhn to have solved (partly
at least) this scholarly enigma by providing a highly plausible profile
of that new entity in Western culture: the Baconian sciences which,

both as regards their objects of knowledge and their methodology, entered the sanctioned canon of secular research about half a century after the death of their inspirer. Contrary to his mathematically tutored counterpart, the Baconian natural philosopher aspired to isolate some humble pieces of knowledge by drawing copious histories or inventories of the phenomena under investigation – sometimes viewing them for the first time as worthy objects of study – and then cautiously and provisionally theorizing on his findings.[10] In brief, the Baconian natural philosopher *created* or partook of a novel 'style of scientific thinking'.[11] The contention that experimenting in certain new fields of research – e.g. magnetism, electricity, living matter and so forth – in the way we observe in men like Boyle or Hooke and a host of minor virtuosi is a legitimate goal of the inquiring mind bypasses the blunt question as to Bacon's direct influence on Western science. Those thinkers and their changing relation with their mathematical counterparts established the rise of a solid experimental tradition whose ultimate source we find in the then prevalent interpretation of the Lord Chancellor's writings.[12] The fusion of the mathematical tradition with the Baconian was to become a fascinating and decisive chapter in the history of Western thought, but it took place with different rhythms and priorities in each science as well as in each country. To date, however, this is the best answer that we possess as regards the significance of Baconian ideas amongst methodologically minded scientists. As to philosophy proper and the intrinsic merits of, say, Bacon's seminal insights on method or induction (questions intriguingly absent from the concerns of the early Baconians), the only significant exception to the chorus of universal denigration seems to be the study systematically undertaken by L. Jonathan Cohen. From his interpretations there emerges, amongst other findings, the unexpected notion of a Baconian as against a Pascalian conception of probability, and the general and radical revision of Bacon's ideas in the context of scientific methodology. In fine, a new philosophical setting for re-evaluation and study is beginning to take shape.[13]

Bacon's main starting-point is expressly announced in the very title of his overambitious *Instauratio Magna* and of its second (and only completed) part: the *Novum Organum*.[14] That is, Bacon places himself, as a thinker, under the aegis of beneficent and radical innovation. Now, it would be utterly naive to presuppose that categories of innovation and novelty have been coextensive throughout history. On the contrary, men have devised different techniques when dealing with new ideas or objects whenever it was felt that the accepted fabric of meanings was unable to account for or assimilate a challenging *novum*. In Bacon's case most scholars agree that a particular kind of utopianism was the driving force that acted behind his philosophical endeavours. Nevertheless, there are many brands of utopianism and Bacon's cognitive project of a new *instauratio* blends together some of the most recondite meanings of early modern utopian thought. First of all, that thought does *not* recognize or think itself as revolutionary in our sense of the term, and therefore it does not inscribe itself in a linear conception of history, contrary to what Bacon's most vocal admirers were to assume in the eighteenth century.[15] The living roots of Bacon's utopianism, as manifested by his frequent use of the concept of *instauratio*, are simultaneously religious, ritual, civil and 'technological'. *Instaurare* is nothing less than 'restoring' man's power over Nature as he wielded it before the Fall; *instaurare*, furthermore, means to channel the pathos of novelty towards epistemic and political goals that bear the traces of spiritual edification and societal initiation (as in the phrase *instauratio imperii* to be found in the tract *Temporis Partus Masculus*, drafted *c.* 1603); and, lastly, *instaurare* strikes a technological chord because Bacon makes his own the architectural topos which the term had come to express in most Western languages.[16] Thus, Bacon explicitly refers to God as 'Deus universi, conditor, conservator, instaurator'(II, 15). Or, as he puts it in the celebrated lines of *Novum Organum* II, 52:

> Man by the Fall fell at the same time from his state of innocency and from his dominion over Creation. Both of these losses, however, can even in this life be in some part repaired, the former by religion and faith, the latter by arts and sciences.
>
> (IV, 247f.; I, 365f.)

Further yet, when Bacon expresses himself in a more sober manner, what he seems to present as his own golden age of thought turns out to be the pre-Socratic period, as though the tradition of 'yet former ages' had an unexplored potential that modern thought, however innovative, could perhaps restore but hardly surpass or emulate.

> Bacon's *instauratio ab imis fundamentis* ('a new beginning from the very foundations', IV, 53) in fact leads from past-oriented humanism and Christian ideas of innovation to the early modern concept of revolution, *for which antecedents become irrelevant.* Instauratio is a flexible vehicle that helps Bacon to leap that distance.[17]

There is a second starting-point in Bacon's speculations which is not, historically speaking, so tied to the particular kind of culture to which Bacon belonged and against which he reacted. Like Plato's Myth of the Cave or Kant's Dove of Reason, Bacon's typology of human error can be understood and appreciated (and in fact it usually is) outside the specific province of Bacon's philosophy. So his theory of the Idols or canonical forms of error imprinted on the human mind (*Nov. Org.* I, 39–41) is one of the most brilliant precedents of later attempts at systematically building up a catalogue or anthropological classification of ideologies.[18] Mankind, according to Bacon, is fatally prone to err for a variety of reasons. As a species, it has its own limitations which make error inescapable; such intellectual and sensory constraints are called *Idola Tribus* or Idols of the Tribe, and there is no hint of an optimistic note as to whether they can be overcome or cured (*Nov. Org.* I, 399–41). Moreover, each man, when trying to know anything, invariably brings with him his own set of preferences and dislikes, that is, his own psychological make-up, which will colour whatever he attempts to cognize in its purity. These prejudices are the so-called *Idola Specus* or Idols of the Cave (Bacon is alluding to Plato's image in *Republic* 514A–519D), to which all of us, as individuals, are subject (*Nov. Org.* I, 42). Further yet, man is the hopeless victim of the traps and delusions of language, that is, of his own great tool of knowledge and communication, and hence he will fall prey to the *Idola Fori* or Idols of the Marketplace, which unavoidably result from his being a speaking animal (*Nov. Org.* I, 43). And, lastly, the very act of entering into intercourse with others conjures up a great panoply of illusion and imposture, where truth succumbs to the sophistries of social convention: these are the *Idola Theatri* or Idols of the Theatre. According to Bacon, there is no thinking in a vacuum: man is beset by what others thought before him, and therefore he is the appointed heir to all past sects and philosophies. The Idols of the Theatre are for ever hovering over the prospective philosopher (*Nov. Org.* I, 44). The mind of man, in sum, is by no means a *tabula abrasa*, to use the consecrated empiricist shibboleth, but rather an 'enchanted glass' or 'distorted mirror' (St Paul, I Cor. 13: 9–10, 12). The true interpreter of Nature, that is, the true philosopher, must be always on his guard against the intrusion of such *Trugbilder* or mirages into his field of cognitive interests. Bacon, however, never expressly states that man can become entirely free from such deceiving propensities. Not even the last of them, that is, the *Idola Theatri* or unlawful children of philosophy, disappear from the menacing potential of Bacon's own speculations.

Let us go back to the technocratic component that the concept of *instauratio* encapsulated. Bacon, seemingly innocently, defines philosophy as 'the Inquiry of Causes and the Production of Effects' (*De Augmentis* III, 4: I, 550; IV, 346). Likewise, the High Priest in the *Nova Atlantis* instructs the admiring visitor by telling him that 'the end of our Foundation [that is, Salomon's House] is the knowledge of causes, and secret motions of things; and the enlarging of the bounds of human empire to the effecting of all things possible' (III, 156). Now, the decisively striking point in these and similar definitions is their second part, for traditional philosophical discourse did not contemplate the *physical* production of anything. Surely, the 'effects' (*opera*) to be achieved are dictated by the general philanthropic tenor of Bacon's philosophy, but it would be a gross mistake to confuse it, as is often done, with any form of utilitarianism.[19] First of all, we have to identify the ideological trend that Bacon is recapturing when proffering such pithy definitions. Now, this trend leads us back to a tradition which, though prior to humanistic thought, inspired a great deal of philosophical writing in the sixteenth and seventeenth centuries. In fact, the first great representative of this current in the modern epoch is Nicholas of Cusa (1401–64), who systematically reflected on the much-discussed relationship between God's and man's intellect and their *opera*. Heir to Neoplatonic traditions, Cusa establishes that man, that fallen creature, is not wholly devoid of that all-important and defining attribute of the Christian Godhead: the power to create.[20] Even as God created the world, man is empowered to create another world (that of mathematicals and abstract notions) in so far as he is not eternally condemned to copying or imitating Nature but is able to surpass her by making items (e.g. a spoon) for which Nature has no exemplar or prototype.[21] Of course, Cusa's main interests were theological and hence he did not develop a line of thought which we could easily link with 'the question of technology', as it came to be formulated much later. But it is surprising how tantalizingly close he came to giving a systematic response to many of the sporadic pronouncements – sometimes articulated in interrogative form – which abound in the perhaps better known reflections of the humanists. Let us quickly review some of them.

Juan Luis Vives (1492–1540) pithily writes that 'man knows as far as he can make',[22] posing thereby a pragmatic criterion for knowledge and certainty which others were to exploit in various forms. Cardanus (1501–76) establishes that only in mathematics is there certainty, because the intellect itself *produces* or *brings forth* the entities it operates with.[23] Leonardo (1452–1519) states that human science is a second creation.[24] The sceptic Francisco Sanches (1552–1623), in *Quod Nihil Scitur* (1581), uses this topos to castigate human reason, since only God can know what he has made.[25] Bruno (1548–1600) rejects the primacy of contemplation and argues that, where there is the power to make and to produce something, there is also the certainty of that something being known.[26] Paracelsus (1493–1541) clearly argues that Nature has to be artificially brought to the point where she discloses herself to man's enquiring gaze.[27] Even less known figures are eager to stress that it is *homo faber* only who wields the sole and true weapons enabling him to enter into Nature's mysteries. For example, the sixteenth-century Italian engineer Giuseppe Ceredi expresses the notion that modelling 'Nature as if it become mechanical in the construction of the world and of all the forms of things' would enable the natural philosopher, by proper and voluntary manipulation, to attain 'to the perfection of art and to the stable production of the effects that is expected'.[28] Now, this tradition of thought goes back to classical Antiquity, and identifies objects of knowledge and objects of construction in various fields and degrees. For example, this is done in mathematics, craftsmanship, theology, astronomy and other disciplines, and later on this topos helped people to rethink the essence and role of human art, which, in view of the fertility of man's inventiveness, could no longer be perceived as a simple mimesis or imitation of Nature.[29] Several labels can be aptly applied to this particular cast of the human mind when reflecting on the problem of knowledge: the 'ergetic ideal' is a very accurate appellation;[30] the *verum ipsum factum* principle echoes a historically consecrated formula (by Giambattista Vico in the eighteenth century); and the name 'maker's knowledge' reminds us that images of science, ideals of thought and abstract speculations on the cognitive powers of man are grounded on and ultimately lead to a handful of historically and socially given archetypes: man as beholder, man as user, man as maker.[31] For these reasons, Bacon's definition of philosophy and its 'productive' appendix turns out to be slightly less original than it appeared at first sight (or rather, at second sight, for at first sight it could well be taken for a trivial utilitarian tag). True, it must have seemed so to Bacon's contemporaries, accustomed as they were to a 'verbal' kind of culture which Bacon so directly attacks. Likewise, the famous dictum 'Knowledge is power' appears in a different light now: knowledge is that manipulatory power (*potentia*) which serves as its own guarantee.[32]

Thus far what we might term Bacon's implicit or tacit starting-point in epistemological matters. He is the (unexpected?) representative of an established but almost hidden gnoseological tradition. His driving force seems to be the vindication of a prototype or paradigm of knowledge and of a criterion to gauge it that he (unlike other thinkers) nowhere appears to have fully articulated in an abstract and systematic manner. Yet, Bacon's starting-point, as revealed by the rhetorical devices he employs in order to commend his cognitive project and by the religious mould in which he chooses to cast his programme, is as transparent as it could be. Most significantly, Bacon contrasts the progress and perfectiveness of human art, as portrayed in technical innovation, with the stagnation and backwardness of philosophy (*Parasceve* I, 399; IV, 257; *De Augmentis* II, ch. 2: I, 399f.; IV, 297f.). The printing press, the mariner's compass and the use of gunpowder are not only the indelible marks of modernity but the living proof of the fertility of the human mind when correctly applied to those things it is legitimately fit to know or invent. Yet, one should stress here the tremendous axiological shift that Bacon is silently proposing as his rock-bottom option for, on purely logical grounds, *nothing* is intrinsically more 'useful' than anything else, except with respect to a scale of values which, in itself, ought to remain beyond the very scope of discussion about fertility or sterility.[33]

The specific contents of a given philosophical discourse may originally correspond to or be the basis of an ideal of science which, for a variety of reasons, is subsequently forgotten or overshadowed by a competing one. That Bacon's insights into the nature of human knowledge constitute a coherent type of operativist or constructivist epistemology in the sense enunciated above by no means implies that the *ingredients* of Bacon's scientific ideal could not have been extracted from the original context and taken over by other cognitive programmes or proposals. Ideas about induction, experiment, matter-theory and the like belong to this class of ingredients, as do in other domains techniques of measurement or the register of natural constants. The latter build up the specific 'grammar' of a discourse (i.e. its syntactic rules, its vocabulary and so on), whilst the former are akin to the general semantics which the text ultimately appeals to or reveals. Thus, the elementary propositions of geometrical optics (e.g. the laws of refraction or reflection) can serve the purposes of and be incorporated into both a corpuscularian and an undulatory theory of light. Likewise, Bacon's seminal insights about induction or experiment may be studied, to a large extent at least, independently of any discussion about the maker's knowledge ideal.

Contrary to a widespread opinion, Francis Bacon was not the first philosopher who tried to elaborate something akin to a logic of induction, and the wealth of remarks left by Aristotle on *epagōgē* well deserve exposition and comment.[34] The scholastic tradition, by contrast, was more bent on the predominantly deductive cast of Aristotle's mind, and hence the Schoolmen's references to induction are both repetitive and shallow.[35] In brief, they distinguished between a so-called *inductio perfecta*, which enumerated all the particulars under consideration, and an *inductio imperfecta*, which omitted some of them and therefore was liable to be overthrown by any contradictory instance. In neither case, however, did the scholastics or rhetoricians consider induction as a logical process for gaining knowledge. Francis Bacon was well aware of this tradition, and so he calls 'puerile' (*Nov. Org.* I, 105: I, 205; IV, 97; cf. also I, 137; IV, 24) the imperfect induction of the Schoolmen. That he did not care to mention the *inductio perfecta* may mean that, like other theoreticians afterwards, he did not consider it induction at all.[36] Be that as it may, a cursory perusal of Bacon's description of his own form of induction, and, above all, of the illustrations he gives of its deployment and use in *Novum Organum* II, 11–12, 36, builds up a strong case for deciding that Bacon's employment of the term (even as of the term 'form', as we shall see) is but a mark of his self-confessed terminological conservatism (*Nov. Org.* II, 2), rather than a direct reference to a lexically well-established notion.

The starting-point for the deployment of Bacon's *inductio* is roughly similar to that of previous *inductiones* (as described in contemporaneous textbooks of philosophy and rhetoric).[37] Nevertheless, it covers a register of logical procedures and is directed towards an aim – i.e. the discovery of Forms – that separates it off from traditional acceptations of that term. As a matter of fact, Bacon's *inductio* belongs to the new-born movement of the *ars inveniendi*, and perhaps we should understand the term *inductio* as an umbrella word of sorts covering different steps and procedures.[38] For brevity, I shall call them (1) the inductive, (2) the deductive and (3) the analogical steps.

Bacon never tired of stressing that before his great logical machine could be put into use a vast collection or inventory of particulars should be made, building up a 'natural history' (*historia naturalis et experimentalis*) on which the investigator could firmly base himself before proceeding further. This notion of a 'natural history' found its finest hour with the members of the Royal Society, and even Descartes wrote to Mersenne most approvingly about this Baconian project.[39] The notion, however, is somewhat circular in Bacon's mind, for natural histories worth their salt should contain a record of artificial things or of 'effects' (*opera*) wrought by man, that is, 'Nature in chains' (I, 496ff.; III, 33ff.; IV, 253), and also of what we would term today 'theory-laden experiments' or, in Bacon's colourful phrase, information resulting from 'twisting the lion's tail': these are called upon to show how Nature behaves under unforeseen or 'unnatural' circumstances. The artificialist twist that Bacon gave to his original notion was not always well understood, and the full meaning of his concept of 'experience' became duly simplified as time went on and Bacon's insight simply came to mean 'compilation'.[40]

If, as L. Jonathan Cohen argues, all inductions can be divided into ampliative and summative,[41] then Bacon's concept is clearly a case of ampliative induction by way of elimination. It is not the sheer number of instances that counts in Baconian induction, but what we can term their 'quality'. This is clearly expressed by Bacon in the *Novum Organum* by isolating twenty-seven privileged or ostensibly telling manifestations of the phenomenon under study (i.e. a *natura* in Bacon's terminology) which carry a special, sometimes decisive, weight in the unfolding of the whole inquiry: *unde terminatur questio* (I, 294; IV, 150). Amongst other things, such privileged or *prerogative* instances (like main witnesses in a judicial hearing) are to help the investigator to establish the three canonical tables of Baconian *inductio*, that is, of Absence, Presence, and Degree of the *natura* in question, according as to whether a given phenomenon or *natura* appears always on its own, always accompanied by another, concomitant phenomenon, or sometimes varies in its conjunction according to circumstances that the investigator has to determine *or* manipulate (IV, 149–55; I, 261–8). Now, it is self-evident that the result of all these procedures is to isolate the phenomenon X, with whose manifestation we started, in order to find a kind of explanation (*forma*) of its essence or innermost being, as Bacon profusely illustrated with the cases of heat and motion in *Novum Organum* II, 20. In his own worked-out example, heat turns out to be, after all due rejections have been made, a species or particular class of motion, duly qualified and distinct. But here something exceptionally important happens. It is not the inductive work, that is, the summative or accumulative operation consisting of tabulating the different types of heat and their concomitant *naturae*, that seems to be functioning now, but a calculated series of deductive procedures aiming for the most part at eliminating redundant material in the form of a battery of deductive tests, that is, prerogative instances whose 'inductive' role is to serve as a deductive canon. These instances are sometimes falsification procedures of sorts, sometimes verificationist or probative attempts. For clarity, let us dwell on the following example. Bacon is here discussing the *natura* and *forma* of weight, that is, the best explanation which could answer this particular query: is weight, as a *natura*, a quality inherent in all bodies (something akin to form and extension) or is the weight of a particular body a variable depending on that body's distance from the Earth? The following reasoning belongs to Bacon's induction, but its deductive credentials are impeccable when he casts his argumentation into the scheme of an *instantia crucis*, or Instance of the Fingerpost in Victorian English:

> Let the nature in question be Weight or Heaviness. Here the road will branch into two, thus. It must needs be that heavy and weighty bodies either tend of their own nature to the centre of the Earth by reason of their proper configuration [*per proprium schematismum*]; or else that they are attracted by the mass or body of the Earth itself [*a massa corporea ipsius Terrae*] as by the congregation of kindred substances, and move to it by sympathy [*per consensum*]. If the latter be the case, it follows that, the nearer heavy bodies approach the Earth, the more rapid and violent is their motion; and that the further they are from the Earth, the feeble and more tardy is their motion (as in the case of magnetical attraction); and that this

action is confined to certain limits [*intra spatium certum*], so that if they were removed to such a distance from the Earth that the Earth's virtue could not act upon them, they would remain suspended like the Earth itself, and not fall at all.

(IV, 184f.; I, 298f.)

It is obvious from this presentation of the dilemma that Bacon is stressing the importance of a falsificationist procedure of the *modus tollens* kind: the end result expresses, logically speaking, the rejection of one hypothesis rather than the confirmation of its rival. The tacit presupposition that they exhaust the field of possible hypotheses is irrelevant at this stage; for Bacon *inductio* is an open-ended process and a third hypothesis may be suggested afterwards.

Now in order to decide between the two theories Bacon goes on to propose an experiment which reproduces a pattern of reasoning already deployed in the Table of Rejections and Exclusions. The following *instantia crucis*[42] bears the mark both of Bacon's artificialist approach to natural inquiries (the whole point now is to *create* new data) and of the eminently deductive character of the whole procedure:

> Take a clock moved by leaden weights, and another moved by the compression of an iron spring; let them be exactly adjusted, that one go no faster than the other; then place the clock moving by weights onto the top of a very high steeple, keeping the other down below; and observe carefully whether the clock on the steeple goes more slowly than it did on account of the diminished virtue of its weights [*propter diminutam virtutem ponderum*]. Repeat the experiment [*experimentum*] in the bottom of a mine, sunk to a great depth below the ground; that is, observe whether the clock so placed does not go faster than it did, on account of the increased virtue of its weights [*per auctam virtutem ponderum*]. If the virtue of the weights is found to be diminished on the steeple and increased in the mine, we may take the attraction of the mass of the Earth as the cause of weight.

(IV, 185; I, 299)

Thus, we may extract at least five deductive procedures embedded in the fabric of Bacon's so-called induction, all of them leading to an educated guess (*opinabile*) as to the Form or explanation of the phenomenon under scrutiny.[43] This of course reinforces our claim that Bacon was using the term *inductio* in an extremely loose sense, meaning perhaps what a modern would call 'a logic of scientific discovery', rather than trying to 'ameliorate' the procedure called by that name as understood by contemporary rhetoricians and philosophers.

Nor is this all. If we go back to the famous Baconian inquiry as to the Form of heat, we shall find that the (provisional) end result or *vindemiatio prima* (literally, 'first vintage') runs as follows:

> Heat is a motion, expansive, restrained and acting in its strife upon the smaller particles of bodies. But the expansion is thus modified; while it expands all ways, it has at the same time an inclination upwards. And the struggle in the particles is modified also; it is not sluggish, but hurried [*incitatus*] and with violence [*cum impetu nonnullo*].
>
> (*Nov. Org.* II, 20; iv, 153; i, 266)

This is, in Bacon's phrase, the 'first vintage' or *permissio intellectus*, which is obviously a way of saying his first *hypothesis* after the exclusions and rejections resulting from the Tables. Now, it would be utterly useless to seek the relevant adjectives (*incitatus, expansivus . . .*) in the foregoing Tables – those indeed that make possible the exercise of 'inductive' reason – nor in the main thesis itself, namely that heat is a species of motion of such and such a kind. Bacon's reasoning now is neither deductive nor inductive but *analogical*, that is, it seems to leap beyond what logic proper would allow. If Bacon calls these highly speculative jumps *permissiones intellectus*, and the moment the mind is allowed to make them *vindemiatio* or vintage, then one has to stress that in such stages negative instances are the most valuable and trustworthy of all: *major est vis instantiae negativae* (*Nov. Org.* I, 46). This, of course, no verificationist would adopt as a guideline. But when, how and why is it 'permissible' for the human intellect to proceed to such flights of creative imagination is something Bacon leaves embarrassingly in the dark: his approach is, so to speak, phenomenological as regards the inquiring mind, rather than, as with Descartes and others, foundationist or legitimatizing. Thus, that heat is a motion of such and such characteristics is the result of our 'first vintage' in the investigation of that phenomenon or *natura*, but as a theoretical statement it only possesses a certain degree of certainty: the method of inference is gradual (*Nov. Org.* II, 18), and hypothetical (*Nov. Org.* II, 18, 20). All this notwithstanding, a crucial qualification should be made here, and this sends us back to our chief thesis about Bacon's being a proponent of the ergetic ideal or of a maker's knowledge type of epistemology. In a nutshell, although the statements resulting from the first vintage are not in themselves theoretically definitive or binding and, in Bacon's gradualist epistemology, they are subject to further revisions and refinements, all of them should be true in one all-important aspect, that is, as *rules of action or as recipes for the successful manipulation of Nature*. That is why the above aphorism continues in one breath:

Viewed with reference to operation, it is the same thing [*res eadem*]. For the direction is this: If in any natural body you can excite a dilating or expanding motion, and can so repress this motion and turn it back upon itself, that the dilatation shall not proceed equably, but have its way in one part and be counteracted in another, you will undoubtedly [*proculdubio*] generate heat.

(IV, 155; I, 266)

That Bacon's 'rule of action' has rather a conative character should not detain us here. The essential point to grasp is that, though the process of investigating natural phenomena is theoretically open-ended, the investigator has to attain some kind of collateral security (*quasi fidejussione quadam: Nov. Org.* I, 206) which results from the 'production of effects' (I, 550; IV, 346) appearing in Bacon's very definition of philosophy. Such manipulation (ideally, 'production') shall shed further light on the object under investigation, in so far as by actively engaging in Nature's processes those statements may disclose new and unexpected phenomena. To put it graphically, the cognitive process which Bacon seems to have in mind would look something like Figure 4.1.[44]

As we can see, the net of theoretical pronouncements (remember, 'rules of action') does not stand on a level, but goes up the scale according as it covers more and more phenomena: sometimes an *axioma*

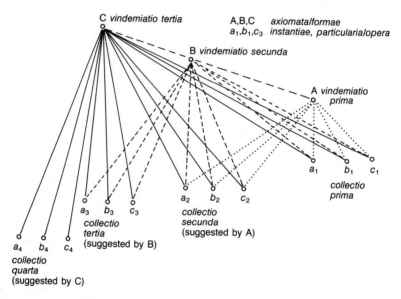

Figure 4.1 Articulation between *particularia/opera* and *axiomata/formae* in Bacon's method: ascent and descent of axioms (*Nov. Org.* I. 19, 24, 103, 106)

is 'derived' from a collection of phenomena or *naturae*; sometimes it points the way ('downwards') to unexpected and 'artificial' evidence. The leapfrogging articulation of the whole does justice, I think, to the several kinds of support that theory has to receive in Bacon's conception. The term by which an axiom or theoretical statement of a given generality is declared to be a rule of action (*ad operativam*), as well as being capable of receiving support from unforeseeable quarters, is *fidejussio*, as pointed out above, and it is a proof of Bacon's extraordinary acumen that he hit on one of the very characteristics that later theoreticians were to develop, namely that the worth of a scientific conjecture or hypothesis (an *opinabile*) is most vividly shown by evidence that it originally was *not* designed to explain.[45]

The vexed question of the Baconian Form is inextricably linked to the doctrine of induction, since the aim of Bacon's *scientia* is to discover the 'Forms of Things'. Scholars are to this day divided as to what exactly Bacon meant by this term. There are two main opposing groups: those for whom the Baconian Form was an inchoate and clumsy equivalent of our conception of natural law, and those who stress the most archaic elements of the notion and hence regard it as a remnant of a misunderstood Aristotelianism.[46] I have already mentioned Bacon's self-confessed lexical conservatism, and recent research tends to regard the Baconian Form as a highly idiosyncratic response to the then prevalent theory of 'substantial forms' which most thinkers of the modern age had to combat.[47] The doctrine of substantial forms was an elaborate attempt on the part of a renewed Aristotelianism to defend itself against the ongoing attack of particulate theories of matter such as atomism. In the words of one of its most conspicuous representatives, Francisco Suarez (1548–1617),[48]

> the most true opinion is that according to which in each composite substance there is only a substantial formal cause, and in each natural compound a substantial form.

That is, within the matter and form dichotomy, the substantial forms are presumed to penetrate into the ultimate reality of things by imparting to each lump of matter those attributes and qualities that we can perceive. Fire, for example, has a substantial form whose nature is to burn, shine and so forth; an apple tree and a pine tree are different because the substantial form which configures their timber is different. The Baconian Form, on the other hand, tried to blend traditional elements coming from Aristotelian matter theory with proto-corpuscularian doctrines close to his own, and wavering, response to atomism:[49]

> For since the Form of a thing is the very thing itself [*ipsissima res*] and the thing differs from the Form no otherwise than as

the apparent differs from the real, or the external from the internal, or the thing in reference to man from the thing in reference to the Universe; it necessarily follows that no nature can be taken as the true Form unless it always decreases when the nature in question decreases, and in like manner always increases when the nature in question increases. This Table I call the Table of Degrees [*Tabula Graduum*] or the Table of Comparisons.

(*Nov. Org.* II, 13: I, 248; IV, 137; cf. also *Nov. Org.* II, 17: I, 257f.; IV, 146)

As we see, then, there is no qualitative gulf between Forms and natures, and some of the latter can be promoted to the rank of Forms. This is so, as we saw in *Novum Organum* II, 20, whenever we find the constructivist stance built in within the Baconian formula. The notion it purports to portray in both aphorisms (II, 13, 20) is not that scientific truth may be utilized or deployed in, say, technological achievements, but that truth itself, understood now as a process inseparable from manipulation, necessarily conveys that very constructivist component: the Form is *real, internal* and *with reference to the Universe* as any genuine rule of action should be. No wonder, then, that 'in this sense truth and utility are the very same things' (*in hoc genere ipsissimae res sunt veritas et utilitas: Nov. Org.* I, 124). This is a far cry from any utilitarian and, *qua* utilitarian, reductionist credo, for truth, in Bacon's ideal, may be 'useful' but is always conceived as a result or spring of an axiologically neutral manipulation (*uti, utilitas*). Thus, it does not convey the evaluative tenor associated with utilitarianism in its historical forms.[50] It goes without saying that the reception of all these doctrines was entirely biased in favour of utilitarian and pragmatic considerations, so that, paradoxically, the ferocious satire of Jonathan Swift against the inventors of Lagado was not the brainchild of the writer's deranged imagination: the promises of real 'usefulness', both by the Royal Society and by its sister association, the Académie des Sciences, were soon sorely disappointed.[51] In sum, Bacon's notion of truth detaches itself from the theoretically inclined spirit of the greatest part of Western philosophical discourse and recaptures that subterranean current of thought to which allusion was made at the outset: maker's knowledge versus beholder's or user's. To engage actively in the processes of Nature mirrors the systematically held conviction not only that such an engagement is legitimate – a conviction which in its turn corresponds to a certain image of Nature *qua* object of human construction or fabrication[52] – but also that only from such an active engagement can truth emerge. Theoretically speaking, Bacon's epistemology is impeccably gradualist, as L. Jonathan Cohen remarks,[53] but it ceases to be so from the moment we reflect that each pronouncement, each general statement, each *axioma* has to be truth-producing *at any level* if we are genuinely after manipulative success. It hardly needs to be pointed out that all this remains an ideal, for Bacon does not even attempt to teach us how precisely we can manipulate those corpuscles he postulates as existing in each body in order to achieve this or that 'effect'. His recipes in *Novum Organum* or in other places (e.g. in III, 240) seem the imaginative or fantastic projection of a magus' mentality. But this would be, I think, a rather jejune line of criticism for a philosophically minded hermeneutic to take. Knowledge, we saw, operates with ideas as much as with ideals. If indeed Bacon failed on that particular account, the crucial point to remember is that the tradition he bequeathed to Western philosophy, in the hands of other philosophers and scientists less prone to such visionary flights of fancy, succeeded where he only sowed the seeds of its desiderata. That is, after all, a tradition that, for better or worse, our world appears to have made its own in its utilitarian, scientistic and technocratic versions.

In his indictment against the philosophers of the past, Bacon wrote in the Preface to *De Interpretatione Naturae* that they did not even teach man 'what to wish'. This criticism backfires dangerously when we consider that the realm of desires, that is, of values and priorities, is by no means dependent on nor results from any theoretically informed epistemology, no matter how brilliant its merits or how eloquent its proponents. Bacon's world, if we judge by the scattered remarks left in the unfinished *Nova Atlantis*, does not show its credentials of desirability in the apodictic manner that the Lord Chancellor expected. 'To assuage human suffering and miseries' is one thing; to maintain that the technocratic control over Nature – a control secretly wielded by a handful of men – provides the sole manner of fulfilment of the above desire is quite another. Bacon failed to work out the notion that all that wonderful machinery, that is, the realm of human art, could, however well administered, control its own controller some fateful day. It could, that is, engender a logic of its own and, as in Samuel Butler's nightmare,[54] become a parallel or second nature, as formidable to master as the first *fallen* Nature was. Bacon's man seems therefore condemned to live in a menacing two-faced kingdom: the ship sailing beyond the pillars of Hercules that the philosopher chose as the frontispiece of his *Novum Organum* is not bound for a peaceful or uneventful voyage. To be both the master and the slave at her helm is not amongst the lesser premonitions of the Lord Chancellor's dream.

❧❧ NOTES ❧❧

I cite Bacon from the standard edition of J. Spedding, R. L. Ellis and D. D. Heath, *The Works of Francis Bacon*, 14 vols (London, 1857–74; Stuttgart-Bad Cannstatt, Friedrich Frommann, 1963). Bacon's *Philosophical Works* are in vols 1–5 (Latin and English) and *De Sapientia Veterum*, misleadingly included in vol. 6 (pp. 605–764). References are to volume and page (as a rule both to the English and Latin), except when quoting from *Novum Organum*, where I have usually indicated Book and Aphorism.

1 *Vorlesungen über die Geschichte der Philosophie*, in *Werke*, ed. E. Moldenhauer and K. M. Michel (Frankfurt-am-Main, 1971), pp. xviii–xx, xx, 76ff. Hegel repeatedly calls Bacon 'der Heerführer der Erfahrungsphilosophen' ('the army-leader of the philosophers of experience') and links his name to Locke and the so-called empiricists. Kuno Fischer, *Franz Baco von Verulam: die Realphilosophie und ihr Zeitalter* (Leipzig, 1856; 2nd edn, 1875), and Wilhelm Windeband and H. Heimsoeth, *Lehrbuch der Geschichte der Philosophie* (Tübingen, 1930), pp. 328ff.), do not depart substantially from Hegel's views. Compare also H. E. Grimm, *Zür Geschichte des Erkenntnisproblems. Von Baco zu Hume* (Leipzig, 1890), and W. Frost, *Bacon und die Naturphilosophie* (München, 1927). Two very notable exceptions to the then prevalent approach are to be found in French authors: Charles de Rémusat, *Bacon, sa vie, son temps, sa philosophie jusqu'à nos jours* (Paris, 1857), and Charles Adam, *Philosophie de François Bacon* (Paris, 1890), esp. pp. 328ff.

2 cf. D. F. Norton, 'The Myth of British Empiricism', *History of European Ideas* 1 (1981) 331–4; Shapiro [4. 75]; H. G. van Leeuwen, *The Problem of Certainty in English Thought (1630–1690)* (The Hague, Nijhoff, 1963).

3 cf. Nicholas Jardine, 'Epistemology of the Sciences', in C. B. Schmitt and Q. Skinner (eds), *The Cambridge History of Renaissance Philosophy* (Cambridge, Cambridge University Press, 1988), pp. 685–712, at p. 685. Compare also M. N. Morris, 'Science as *Scientia*', *Physis* 23 (1981) 171–96, and S. Ross, ' "Scientist": the Story of a Word', *Annals of Science* 18 (1964) 65–85.

4 cf. R. Yeo, 'An Idol of the Market Place: Baconianism in 19th-century England', *History of Science* 23 (1985) 251–98; Pérez-Ramos [4.62], 7–30.

5 *Apud* R. C. Cochrane, 'Francis Bacon and the Rise of the Mechanical Arts in 18th-century England', *Annals of Science* 11 (1956) 137–56, at p. 156. Compare also A. Finch, *On the Inductive Philosophy: Including a Parallel between Lord Bacon and A. Comte as Philosophers* (London, 1872).

6 I. Lakatos, 'Changes in the Problem of Inductive Logic', in his *The Problem of Inductive Logic* (Amsterdam, 1968), pp. 315–427, at p. 318; A. Koyré, *Etudes d'histoire de la pensée scientifique* (Paris, Presses Universitaires de France, 1966). To speak of Bacon as one of the founding fathers of modern science, Koyré argues on p. 7, would be a *mauvaise plaisanterie*.

7 *Francis Bacon. From Magic to Science* [4.70]. This book is a turning point as regards the revival of Baconian studies in our century.

8 For an example of this kind of literature, cf. Farrington [4.35]; Christopher Hill, *The Intellectual Origins of the English Revolution* (Oxford, 1965); Frances

Yates, *The Rosicrucian Enlightenment* (London, Routledge, 1972); Lisa Jardine [4.45].

9 *Dictionary of the History of Ideas*, 4 vols, chief ed. P. Wiener (New York, 1968–73), s.v. Baconianism, i, pp. 172–9, at p. 172.

10 'Mathematical versus Experimental Tradition in Western Science', *The Essential Tension* (Chicago, University of Chicago Press, 1977), pp. 31–66, esp. pp. 41–52.

11 On the notion of 'scientific style', cf. Crombie [4.25].

12 cf. T. S. Kuhn, note 10; Pérez-Ramos [4.62], 33ff.

13 L. Jonathan Cohen, *The Implications of Induction* (London, Methuen, 1970); *The Probable and the Provable* (Oxford, 1977); [4.22], 219–31; 'What has Inductive Logic to Do with Causality', in L. J. Cohen and M. B. Hesse (eds) *Applications of Inductive Logic* (Oxford, Clarendon, 1980); *An Introduction to the Philosophy of Induction and Probability* (Oxford, 1988). Some of Cohen's ideas about Bacon's 'inductive' gradualism seem to have been foreshadowed by J. M. Keynes in *A Treatise on Probability* (first published London, Macmillan, 1929), ed. R. B. Braithwaite (London, Macmillan, 1973), esp. pp. 299ff.

14 A brief and accurate description of Bacon's gnoseological plan is given by M. B. Hesse in 'Francis Bacon's Philosophy of Science', in Vickers [4.14], 114–39, esp. p. 114. This plan should proceed as follows:

> (1) The classification of the sciences. (2) Directions concerning the Interpretation of Nature; i.e. the new inductive logic. (3) The Phenomena Universi, or natural history. (4) The Ladder of the Intellect, that is, examples of the application of the method in climbing from Phenomena on the ladder of axioms to the 'Summary Law of Nature'. (5) Anticipations of the New Philosophy, that is, tentative generalizations which Bacon considers of insufficient interest and importance to justify him in leaping ahead of the inductive method. (6) The New Philosophy or Active Science, which will exhibit the whole result of induction in an ordered system of axioms. If men will apply themselves to this method, Bacon thinks that the system will be the result of a few years' work, but for himself, he confesses, 'the completion of this last part is a thing both above my strength and beyond my hopes' (iv, 22, 32, 102, 252).

(*apud* Hesse [4.14], 115f.) Compare also Ducasse [4.33], 50–74. W. Schmidt-Biggeman places this and other epistemic projects in a wider context: *Topica Universalis. Eine Modellgeschichte humanistischer und baroker Wissenschaft* (Hamburg, 1983), esp. pp. 212ff.

15 Pérez-Ramos [4.62], 18ff.; M. Malherbe, 'Bacon, L'Encyclopédie et la Révolution', *Etudes Philosophiques* (1985) 387–404, esp. pp. 392ff.

16 cf. Charles Whitney, *Francis Bacon and Modernity* (New Haven, Yale University Press, 1986), *passim*; 'Francis Bacon's Instauratio: Dominion of and over Humanity', *Journal of the History of Ideas* 48 (1989), esp. pp. 377ff.

17 Whitney, 'Francis Bacon's Instauratio . . .' op. cit., p. 386.

18 cf. Karl Mannheim, *Ideologie und Utopie* (Bonn, F. Cohen, 2nd edn, 1930), pp. 14f. Hans Barth, *Truth and Ideology* (1945, 1961), trans. F. Lilge (Los Angeles, Calif., University of California Press, 1976), disputes Mannheim's

claim. Compare in general R. Boudon, *L'Idéologie. L'origine des idées reçues* (Paris, 1980), esp. pp. 53ff.

19 cf. B. Vickers, 'Bacon's So-called "Utilitarianism": Sources and Influence', in Fattori [4.12], 281–314.

20 cf. Vinzenz Rüfner, 'Homo secundus deus. Eine geistesgeschichtliche Etüde zum menschlichen Schöpfertum', *Philosophisches Jahrbuch* 63 (1955) 248–91; Hans Blumenberg, ' "Nachahmung der Natur": zur Vorgeschichte des schöpferischen Menschen', *Studium Generale* 10 (1957) 266–83.

21 *Philosophisch-Theologische Schriften*, ed. L. Gabriel, 3 vols (Vienna, 1967), iii, *De Beryllo*, pp. 8f., 68ff., *De Possest*, pp. 318f. Compare Charles H. Lohr, 'Metaphysics', *The Cambridge History of Renaissance Philosophy*, op. cit., pp. 548–56. Compare also Blumenberg, op. cit., *passim*; and, especially, *Aspekte der Epochenschwelle. Cusanus und Nolanus* (Frankfurt-am-Main, 2nd edn, 1968), pp. 34–108. The example of the spoon appears in *Idiota de mente*.

22 *Tantum scis quam operabis*, in *Satellitum Mentis, Opera Omnia*, ed. G. Mayans, 8 vols (Valencia, 1782–90), iv, 63. On the influence of Vives's views on Bacon's conception of logic, cf. Maurice B. McNamie, 'Bacon's Inductive Method and Humanist Grammar', *Studies in the Literary Imagination* 4 (1971) 81–106.

23 Gerolamus Cardanus (Cardano), *Opera Omnia*, ed. C. Spon, 10 vols (Lugduni, 1663), introduction to the facsimile edition by A. Beck; cf. *De Arcanis Aeternitatis*, cap. iv; also i, 597, and iii, 21ff.

24 cf. Rodolfo Mondolfo, *Il verum factum prima di Vico* (Naples, Guida, 1969), ch. 3.

25 *Tratados Filosóficos* (Latin/Portuguese), introduction and notes by A. M. de Sa; Portuguese translation by B. de Vasconcelos and M. P. de Meneses (Lisbon, 1955), pp. 4–157; cf. also Pérez-Ramos [4.62], 58, and Part III, *passim*, for the sceptical understanding of that ideal in (early) modern philosophy.

26 'Where there has always been the power to make, there has always been, too, the power of being made, produced and created [*onde se è sempre stata la potenza di fare, di produrre, sempre è stata la potenza di esser fatto, produto (sic) e creato*]' (*Della Causa, principio ed uno*, III, in *Dialoghi Metafisici*, ed. Giovanni Gentile, 2 vols (Florence, 1985), i, 280ff. Compare especially this passage from *Lo Spaccio della Bestia Trionfante*, vol. i:

> The gods have given [man] intellect and hands and have made him similar to them, giving him power over other animals. This consists in his being able not only to operate according to Nature and to what is usual, but also to operate outside the normal course of Nature [*poter operare secondo la Natura ed ordinario ma ed oltre, fuor le leggi di quella*], in order that by forming new or being able to form other natures, other paths and other categories with his intelligence [*ingegno*] by means of that liberty . . . he would succeed in preserving himself as god of the Earth. . . . And for that reason Providence has determined that he will be occupied in action by means of his hands and in contemplation by means of his intellect, so that he will not contemplate without act and will not act without contemplation.
>
> (*The Expulsion of the Triumphant Beast*, trans. A. D. Imerti (New York, 1964), p. 205)

I have slightly modified the translation.

27 'Die Natur dahin gebracht werden [muss], daß Sie selbst erweist', *Opus Parami-rum* (c. 1530), *apud* Werner Kutscher, *Der Wissenschaftler und sein Körper* (Frankfurt-am-Main, 1986), p. 111.

28 Giuseppe Ceredi, *Tre discorsi sopra il modo d'alzar acque da luoghi bassi* (Parma, 1567), pp. 5–7, *apud* A. C. Crombie, 'Expectation, Modelling and Assent in the History of Optics: Part I. Alhazen and the Medieval Tradition', *Studies in the History and Philosophy of Science* 21 (1990) 605–33, at p. 605.

29 Hans Blumenberg, work cited in note 20, *ad finem*, and, more generally, *Die Legitimität der Neuzeit* (Frankfurt-am-Main, 1983; English translation, Cambridge, Mass., MIT Press, 1986), Part 3, and Robert Lenoble, *Histoire de l'idée de Nature* (Paris, A. Michel, 1969), esp. pp. 311ff. As Lenoble stresses, in the perception of Nature one should never ignore or undervalue the pathos that usually presupposes and/or conveys a 'scientific style'. In the words of F. Anderson, for Bacon

> all statements of observation and experiment are to be written in truth and with religious care, as if the writer were under oath and devoid of reservation of doubt and question. The record is the book of God's works and – so far as there may be an analogy between the majesty of divine things and the humbleness of earthly things – is a kind of second Scripture.
>
> (Anderson [4.17], 264)

30 A. Funkenstein, *Theology and the Scientific Imagination* (Princeton, N.J., Princeton University Press, 1986), esp. pp. 290ff.; and my essay on this book 'And Justify the Ways of God to Men', *Studies in the History and Philosophy of Science* 21 (1990) 323–39.

31 For such archetypes, see Plato, *Cratylus* 390 A, *Euthydemus* 289 A–D, *Republic* 601 E–602 A; and Aristotle, *Politica* 128 a 17ff. J. Hintikka has studied this question in *Knowledge and the Known* (Dordrecht and Boston, Reidel, 1974), *passim*, and has been criticized by J. L. Mackie in 'A Reply to Hintikka's Article "Practical versus Theoretical Reason"', in S. Körner (ed.) *Practical Reason* (New Haven, Conn., Yale University Press, 1974), pp. 103–13. For a profound anthropological insight into that archetype (the maker is the knower *par excellence*), cf. Mircea Eliade, *Forgerons et Alchimistes* (Paris, Flammarion, 1956), ch. x: *homo faber* and *homo sapiens* coincide for the faber knows in the most obvious and convincing way, i.e. by doing, making or producing things.

32 cf. W. Krohn, 'Social Change and Epistemic Thought (Reflections on the Origins of the Experimental Method)', in I. Hronsky, M. Fehér and B. Dajka (eds) *Scientific Knowledge Socialized* (Dordrecht, 1988), pp. 165–78:

> 'The goal of the new science is a knowledge by which "one will be capable of all manner of works" (*omnis operum potentia*) in contrast with the "felicitous contemplation" (*felicitas contemplativa*) of classical philosophy (I, 144; IV, 32). For Bacon, causes are related to knowledge just as rules are to action. The equivalence between the knowledge of causes and the ability to produce something can be regarded in both directions: not only are our actions more manageable as a result of the

knowledge of the laws of Nature, but the laws of Nature can be understood better when our point of departure is not the *observation* of Nature, but the *vexationes artis*, Nature under constraint and vexed (I, 140; IV, 29). . . . This makes his [i.e. Bacon's] turning from Aristotle that much more noticeable, as his claim that a condition for the understanding of Nature is our interfering with it is irreconcilable with the Aristotelian concept of knowledge. . . . According to Bacon, laws have to be investigated with a view to the type of *praeceptum* (doctrine), *directio* (direction), *deductio* (guidance) one needs to produce something'

(I, 229; IV, 124, pp. 171f.) Paolo Rossi had already stressed this point ([4.71], esp. Appendix ii, 'Truth and Utility in Bacon', pp. 148–73). For an exegesis of the crucial term *opus/work*, cf. Pérez-Ramos [4.62], 135–49.

33 cf. Karl-Otto Apel, 'Das Problem einer philosophischen Theorie der Rationalitätstypen', in G. H. Schnädelbach (ed.), *Rationalität* (Frankfurt-am-Main, 1984) pp. 15–31.

34 cf. G. Buchdahl, *Induction and Necessity in the Philosophy of Aristotle* (London, 1963); 'Die ἐπαγωγή bei Aristoteles', *Sitzungsberichte der Bayerischen Akademie der Wissenschaften* (Phil.-hist. Klasse) (1964); W. Schmidt, *Theorie der Induktion: Die prinzipielle Bedeutung der epagōgē bei Aristoteles* (Munich, 1974); Nelly Tsouyopoulos, 'Die Induktive Methode und das Induktionsproblem in der griechischen Philosophie', *Zeitschrift für allgemeine Wissenschaftstheorie* 5 (1974) 94–122; J. R. Milton, 'Induction before Hume', *British Journal for the Philosophy of Science* 38 (1987) 49–74, esp. pp. 58ff.; C. C. W. Taylor, 'Aristotle's Epistemology', in Stephen Everson (ed.), *Epistemology* (Cambridge, Cambridge University Press, 1990), pp. 116–42.

35 See Pérez-Ramos [4.62], 72–82, for examples taken from Petrus Hispanus to Albert the Great and Aquinas.

36 Most notably, J. S. Mill, 'Of Inductions Improperly So-called', *A System of Logic, Ratiocinative and Inductive* (first published 1843; London, 1884), III, 2, pp. 188–99.

37 cf. Wilhelm Risse, *Logik der Neuzeit*, 2 vols (Stuttgart, Frommann, 1964), I, *passim*.

38 cf. W. Schmidt-Biggeman, *op. cit.*; M. B. Hesse, 'Francis Bacon's Philosophy of Science', in Vickers [4.14], esp. pp. 212–31.

39 'Nous nous complétons, Vérulamius et moi. Mes conseils serviront à étayer dans ses grandes lignes l'explication de l'univers; ceux de Vérulamius permettront de préciser les détails pour les expériences nécessaires', *Oeuvres de Descartes*, ed. G. Adam and P. Tannery, 12 vols (Paris, 1897–1910), i, 318; cf. also ii, 597f., and iii, 307. For other references amongst continental philosophers and the Cartesian perception of Bacon, cf. A. I. Sabba, *Theories of Light from Descartes to Newton* (Cambridge, Cambridge University Press, 2nd edn, 1982), pp. 33ff., esp. pp. 170–80. For a different approach, cf. Malherbe, 'L'induction baconienne: de l'échec métaphysique à l'échec logique', in Fattori [4.12], 179–200.

40 F. Kambartel, *Erfharung und Struktur. Bausteine zu einer Kritik des Empirismus und Formalismus* (Frankfurt-am-Main, 2nd edn, 1976), pp. 81ff., on the notion of *historia* and the various senses of *experientia* (*vaga*, *literata*, . . .); cf.

Malherbe, 'L'expérience et l'induction chez Bacon', Malherbe and Pousseur [4.13], 113–34.

41 Cohen, *An Introduction . . .* (cited in note 13), p. 195.

42 The felicitous phrase *experimentum crucis* is not Bacon's but Boyle's. He first used it in *Defence of the Doctrine touching the Spring and Weight of the Air* (1662). Others attribute its (independent) coinage to Robert Hooke in *Micrographia* (1665).

43 For these procedures, cf. Horton [4.43], 241–78, and Pérez-Ramos [4.62], 243–54.

44 Pérez-Ramos [4.62], 257. Reproduced by kind permission of Oxford University Press.

45 This principle (as against the sole principle of instantiation) appears as much in inductivist epistemologies as the *modus tollens* procedures; cf. J. S. Mill, *A System of Logic*, III, 10, 10, and Adolf Grünbaum, 'Is Falsifiability the Touchstone of Scientific Rationality? Karl Popper versus Inductivism', *Boston Studies in the Philosophy of Science* 39 (1976) 213–52. For a detailed account, stressing this aspect of Bacon's *ars inveniendi*, cf. Peter Urbach [4.77], where Bacon is presented as a proto-Popperian. See my criticism of this book: 'Francis Bacon and the Disputations of the Learned', *British Journal for the Philosophy of Science* 42 (1991) in press.

46 cf. Emerton [4.32], 76–105. A comprehensive summary of the whole learned dispute is to be found in Pérez-Ramos [4.62], 116f., nn. 4 and 6.

47 Peter Alexander admirably sums up the whole issue in *Ideas, Qualities and Corpuscles. Locke and Boyle on the External World* (Cambridge, Cambridge University Press, 1985). For the doctrines contained in university manuals, cf. P. Reif, 'The Textbook Tradition in Natural Philosophy', *Journal of the History of Ideas* 30 (1968) 17–32.

48 Sometimes this view was expressly linked to the Aristotelian doctrine of the four elements: cf. Alexander on Daniel Sennert, op. cit, p. 36.

49 cf. R. Macciò, 'A proposito dell'atomismo di Francesco Bacone', *Rivista Critica di Storia della Filosofia* 17 (1962) 188–96; Kargon [4.47]; and especially the erudite researches of J. Rees, 'Francis Bacon's Semiparacelsian Cosmology and the Great Instoration', *Ambix* 22 (1975) 161–73; 'Atomism and Subtlety in Francis Bacon's Philosophy', *Ambix* 37 (1981) 27–37. Compare my nuanced criticism of Rees's approach in 'Bacon in the Right Spirit', *Annals of Science* 42 (1985) 603–11.

50 Vickers, in Fattori [4.12], 281–314.

51 Jonathan Swift, *Gulliver's Travels* (first published 1726; London, Dent, 1970), Part III, ch. V, pp. 190–205. On the sources of the Academy of Lagado, cf. A. E. Case, 'Personal and Political: Satire in *Gulliver's Travels*' (1945), in *Jonathan Swift*, ed. D. Donoghue (Harmondsworth, Penguin, 1971), pp. 335ff. On contemporary charges of sterility against the new science, cf. M. Hunter, *Science and Society in Restoration England* (Cambridge, Cambridge University Press, 1981), esp. pp. 188–93.

52 cf. Lenoble (cited in note 29), pp. 217–77.

53 See, amongst other places, Cohen, *An Introduction . . .* (cited in note 13), pp. 4–12, 145–75.

54 *Erewhon* (first published 1872; London, 1951) 'The Book of the Machines', ch.

XXIIII, pp. 142ff. The literature concerning the political and social implications of the Baconian project is immense; cf. W. Leiss, *The Domination of Nature* (New York, Braziller, 1972), pp. 45–71; J. R. Ravetz, 'Francis Bacon and the Reform of Philosophy' (1972), in *The Merger of Knowledge with Power. Essays in Critical Science* (London, 1990), pp. 116–36; Timothy Paterson, 'Bacon's Myth of Orpheus. Power as a Goal of Science in *Of the Wisdom of the Ancients*', *Interpretation* 16 (1989) 429–44. For a different philosophical idiolect, cf. T. W. Adorno and M. Horkheimer, *Dialectic of Enlightenment*, trans. J. Cumming (first published 1944; New York, Herder and Herder, 1972).

❧ BIBLIOGRAPHY ❧

Standard editions

4.1 *The Works of Francis Bacon*: Latin and English, ed. with introduction and commentaries by J. Spedding, R. L. Ellis and D. D. Heath (first published London, 1857–74; reprinted Stuttgart-Bad Cannstatt, Friedrich Frommann, 1961–3). The philosophical works are in vols 1–5; *De Sapientia Veterum*, mistakenly considered as a literary work, is in vol. 6 with the *Essays*. The remaining volumes (7–14) are devoted to the literary and professional works, letters and life. This is the standard edition and, although there is an American counterpart (Boston, 1860–4), its pagination is generally used.

Selections and separate works

4.2 *Francis Bacon: Selections with Essays*, by M. and S. R. Gardiner, ed. P. E. and E. F. Matheson, Oxford, Clarendon, 1964.

4.3 *Francis Bacon: A Selection of his Works*, ed. S. Warhaft, New York, Odyssey, 1970.

4.4 *Francis Bacon: Selected Writings*, introduction and notes by H. G. Dick, New York, Modern Library, 1955.

4.5 *The Advancement of Learning and New Atlantis*, ed. Arthur Johnson, Oxford, Oxford University Press, 1974; reprinted, 1980, 1986.

4.6 *Novum Organum*, ed. with introduction and notes by Thomas Fowler, Oxford, 1878. This gives the Latin text only, but is surely the best edition.

4.7 *The New Organon and Related Writings*, ed. F. Anderson, Indianapolis, Ind., Bobbs-Merrill, 1960.

Bibliographies and concordances

Bibliographies

4.8 Gibson, G. W. *Francis Bacon: A Bibliography of his Works and of Baconiana to the year 1750*, Oxford, Scrivener Press, 1950; Supplement 1959.

4.9 Rossi, P. 'Per una bibliografia degli scritti su Francesco Bacone', *Rivista Critica di Storia di Filosofia* 12 (1957) 75–89; Appendix, *Rivista Critica di Storia di Filosofia* 29 (1974) 44–51.

4.10 Totok, W. *Handbuch der Geschichte der Philosophie*, Frankfurt-am-Main, Klostermann, 1964–81, vol. 2, pp. 473–85. This is perhaps the best bibliographical essay as regards the distribution of works on Bacon according to specific headings and books.

Concordances

4.11 Fattori, M. *Lessico del Novum Organum di Francesco Bacone*, Rome, Ateneo e Bizarri, 2 vols, 1980.

Books and articles dealing with Bacon's philosophy and influence

Collective works

4.12 Fattori, M. (ed.) *Francis Bacon. Terminologia e fortuna nel xvii secolo*, Rome, 1984.

4.13 Malherbe, M. and Pousseur, J.-M. (eds) *Francis Bacon. Science et méthode*, Paris, Vrin, 1985.

4.14 Vickers, B. (ed.) *Essential Articles for the Study of Francis Bacon*, London, Sidgwick & Jackson, 1972. With further bibliography.

4.15 *Les Etudes Philosophiques*, 1985 (monograph on Bacon).

4.16 *Revue Internationale de Philosophie*, 40 (1986) (monograph on Bacon).

Individual authors

4.17 Anderson, F. *The Philosophy of Francis Bacon*, Chicago, Ill., University of Chicago Press, 1948.

4.18 Berns, L. 'Francis Bacon and the Conquest of Nature', *Interpretation* 7 (1978) 36–48.

4.19 Bierman, J. 'Science and Society in the New Atlantis and other Renaissance Utopias', *Publications of the Modern Language Association of America* 78 (1963) 492–500.

4.20 Broad, C. D. 'The Philosophy of Francis Bacon' (1926), *Ethics and the History of Philosophy*, London, Routledge, 1952, 117–43.

4.21 Buchdahl, G. 'The Natural Philosophie', in R. Hall (ed.) *The Making of Modern Science*, Leicester, Leicester University Press, 1960, 9–16.

4.22 Cohen, L. J. 'Some Historical Remarks on the Baconian Conception of Probability', *Journal of the History of Ideas* 41 (1980) 219–31.

4.23 Cohen, M. R. 'Bacon and the Inductive Method', *Studies in Philosophy and Science*, New York, Holt, 1949, 99–106.

4.24 Crescini, A. *Il problema metodologico alle origine della scienza moderna*, Rome, Edizioni dell'Atenco, 1972.

4.25 Crombie, A. C. *Styles of Scientific Thinking in the European Tradition*, London, 1991.

4.26 Dangelmayr, S. *Methode und System: Wissenschaftsklassifikation bei Bacon, Hobbes und Locke*, Meisenheim-am-Glan, Anton Hain, 1974.

4.27 DeMas, E. *Francis Bacon*, Florence, La Nuova Italia, 1978.

4.28 Dickie, W. M. 'A Comparison of the Scientific Method and Achievement of Aristotle and Bacon', *Philosophical Review* 31 (1922) 471–94.

4.29 Dickie, W. M. ' "Form" and "Simple Nature" in Bacon's Philosophy', *The Monist* 33 (1923) 428–37.

4.30 Dieckmann, H. 'The Influence of Francis Bacon on Diderot's *L'Interprétation de la Nature*', *Romanic Review* 34 (1943) 305–30.

4.31 Dieckmann, H. 'La storia naturale da Bacone a Diderot', *Rivista di Filosofia* 67 (1976) 217–43.

4.32 Dijksterhuis, E. J. *The Mechanisation of the World Picture*, trans. C. Dikshoorn, Oxford, Oxford University Press, 1961.

4.33 Ducasse, C. J. 'Francis Bacon's Philosophy of Science', in E. H. Madden (ed.) *Theories of Scientific Method from the Renaissance through the Nineteenth Century*, Seattle, Wash., University of Washington Press, 1966, 50–74.

4.34 Emerton, N. E. *The Scientific Reinterpretation of Form*, Ithaca, N. Y., Cornell University Press, 1984.

4.35 Farrington, B. *Francis Bacon: Philosopher of Industrial Science*, London, Lawrence & Wishart, 1951.

4.36 Farrington, B. *The Philosophy of Francis Bacon: An Essay on its Development from 1603 to 1609*, Liverpool, Liverpool University Press, 1964.

4.37 Fattori, M. 'Des natures simples chez Francis Bacon', *Recherches sur le XVIIe siècle* 5 (1982) 67–75.

4.38 Fisch, H. and Jones, H. W. 'Bacon's Influence on Sprat's History of the Royal Society', *Modern Language Quarterly* 12 (1951) 399–406.

4.39 Gilbert, N. W. *Renaissance Concepts of Method*, New York, Columbia University Press, 1960.

4.40 Harrison, C. T. 'Bacon, Hobbes, Boyle and the Ancient Atomists', *Harvard Studies and Notes on Literature* 15 (1933) 191–218.

4.41 Hattaway, M. 'Bacon and "Knowledge Broken": Limits for Scientific Method', *Journal of the History of Ideas* 40 (1979) 183–97.

4.42 Hill, C. *The Intellectual Origins of the English Revolution*, Oxford, Oxford University Press, 1965.

4.43 Horton, M. 'In Defence of Francis Bacon: A Criticism of the Critics of the Inductive Method', *Studies in the History and the Philosophy of Science* 4 (1973) 241–78.

4.44 Hossfeld, P. 'Francis Bacon und die Entwicklung der naturwissenschaftlichen Methode', *Philosophia Naturalis* 4 (1957) 140–50.

4.45 Jardine, L. *Francis Bacon: Discovery and the Art of Discourse*, Cambridge, Cambridge University Press, 1974.

4.46 Jones, R. S. *Ancients and Moderns*, St Louis, Mo., Washington University Press, 1961.

4.47 Kargon, R. *Atomism in England from Hariot to Newton*, Oxford, Clarendon, 1966.

4.48 Kotarbiński, T. 'The Development of the Main Problem in the Methodology of Francis Bacon', *Studia Philosophica (Lodz)* 1 (1935) 107–37.

4.49 Lamacchia, A. 'Una questione dibattuta: probabili fonti dell' enciclopedia baconiana', *Rivista Critica di Storia della Filosofia* 39 (1984) 725–40.

4.50 Larsen, R. E. 'The Aristotelianism of Bacon's *Novum Organum*', *Journal of the History of Ideas* 23 (1962) 435–50.

4.51 Lemni, C. W. *Classical Deities in Bacon: A Study in Mythological Symbolism*, Baltimore, Md., Johns Hopkins University Press, 1933.

4.52 Levi, A. *Il Pensiero de Francesco Bacone*, Turin, Paravia, 1925.

4.53 Linguiti, G. I. 'Induzione e deduzione: riesame del Bacone popperiano', *Rivista di Filosofia* 69 (1978) 499–515.

4.54 Luxembourg, L. K. *Francis Bacon and Denis Diderot: Philosophers of Science*, Copenhagen, Munksgaard, 1967.

4.55 Maccio, R. 'A proposito dell' atomismo nel *Novum Organum* di Bacone', *Rivista Critica di Storia della Filosofia* 17 (1962) 188–96.

4.56 McRae, R. *The Problem of the Unity of the Sciences from Bacon to Kant*, Toronto, University of Toronto Press, 1961.

4.57 Merton, R. K. *Science, Technology and Society in 17th-century England* (first published in 1938 as Part 2 of vol. 4 of *Osiris*; new edn, New York, Fertig, 1970).

4.58 Milton, J. R. 'Induction before Hume', *British Journal for the Philosophy of Science* 38 (1987) 49–74.

4.59 Morrison, J. C. 'Philosophy and History in Bacon', *Journal of the History of Ideas* 38 (1977) 585–606.

4.60 Park, K., Danston, L. J. and Galison, P. L. 'Bacon, Galileo and Descartes on Imagination and Analogy', *Isis* 75 (1984) 287–326.

4.61 Penrose, S. B. L. *The Reputation and Influence of Francis Bacon in the Seventeenth Century*, New York, Columbia University Press, 1934.

4.62 Pérez-Ramos, A. *Francis Bacon's Idea of Science and the Maker's Knowledge Tradition*, Oxford, Clarendon, 1988.

4.63 Popkin, R. *The History of Scepticism from Erasmus to Spinoza*, Berkeley, Calif., University of California Press, revised edn., 1979.

4.64 Primack, M. 'Outline of a Reinterpretation of Francis Bacon's Philosophy', *Journal of the History of Philosophy* 5 (1965) 122–33.

4.65 Quinton, A. *Francis Bacon*, Oxford, Oxford University Press, 1980.

4.66 Rattansi, P. M. 'The Intellectual Origins of the Royal Society', *Notes and Records of the Royal Society* 23 (1968) 129–43.

4.67 Rees, G. 'Francis Bacon's Semi-Paracelsian Cosmology and the Great Instauration', *Ambix* 22 (1975) 161–73.

4.68 Rees, G. 'Atomism and Subtlety in Francis Bacon's Philosophy', *Annals of Science* 37 (1980) 549–71.

4.69 Righini-Bonelli, M. L. 'Trends of Interpretation of Seventeenth-Century Science', in M. L. Righini-Bonelli and W. R. Shea (eds) *Reason, Experiment and Mysticism in the Scientific Revolution*, New York, 1975, 1–15.

4.70 Rossi, P. *Francis Bacon: from Magic to Science* (1st edn (in Italian), 1957), trans. S. Rabinovitch, London, Routledge, 1968.

4.71 Rossi, P. *Philosophy, Technology and the Arts in the Modern Era* (first published as *I filosofi e le macchine*, 1962), trans. S. Attanasio, New York, Harper & Row, 1970.

4.72 Sargent, R. M. 'Robert Boyle's Baconian Inheritance: A Response to Laudan's Cartesian Thesis', *Studies in the History and Philosophy of Science* 17 (1986) 469–86.

4.73 Schmidt, G. 'Ist Wissen Macht? Uber die Aktualität von Bacons *Instauratio Magna*', *Kantstudien* 58 (1967) 481–98.

4.74 Schuhl, P. M. *Machinisme et Philosophie*, Paris, Presses Universitaires de France, 2nd edn, 1947.

4.75 Shapiro, B. *Probability and Certainty in 17th-Century England; A Study of the Relationships between Natural Science, Religion, History, Law and Literature*, Princeton, N.J., Princeton University Press, 1983.

4.76 Thorndike, L. *History of Magic and Experimental Science*, New York, Macmillan, 8 vols, 1923–58.

4.77 Urbach, P. *Francis Bacon's Philosophy of Science*, La Salle, Ill., Open Court, 1987.

4.78 Vasoli, C. *L'enciclopedismo del Seicento*, Naples, 1978.

4.79 Viano, C. 'Esperienza e Natura nella filosofia di Francesco Bacone', *Rivista di Filosofia* 45 (1954) 291–313.

4.80 Wallace, K. *Francis Bacon on the Nature of Man*, Urbana, Ill., University of Illinois Press, 1967.

4.81 Walton, C. 'Ramus and Bacon on Method', *Journal of the History of Philosophy* 9 (1971) 289–302.

4.82 Webster, C. *The Great Instauration: Science, Medicine and Reform (1626–1660)*, London, Holmes & Meier, 1975.

4.83 Weinberger, J. 'Science and Rule in Bacon's Utopia: An Introduction to the Reading of the *New Atlantis*', *American Political Science Review* 70 (1976) 865–85.

4.84 White, H. B. 'The Influence of Francis Bacon on the *philosophes*', *Studies on Voltaire and the 18th Century* 27 (1963) 1849–69.

4.85 White, H. B. *Peace among the Willows: the Political Philosophy of Francis Bacon*, The Hague, Nijhoff, 1968.

4.86 Wolff, E. *Francis Bacon und seine Quellen*, 2 vols, Berlin, 1913; Liechtenstein, Nendeln, 1977.

4.87 Wood, N. 'The Baconian Character of Locke's Essay', *Studies in the History and Philosophy of Science* 6 (1970) 43–84.

4.88 Wood, P. B. 'Methodology and Apologetics: Thomas Sprat's History of the Royal Society', *British Journal of the History of Science* 13 (1980) 1926.

N.B. This bibliography does not include all the books and articles to which allusion has been made in this chapter, since many of them did not deal specifically with Bacon's philosophy or, if they did, their reference has already been given.

CHAPTER 5

Descartes: methodology

Stephen Gaukroger

➤➤ INTRODUCTION ➤➤

The seventeenth century is often referred to as the century of the Scientific Revolution, a time of fundamental scientific change in which traditional theories were either replaced by new ones or radically transformed. Descartes made contributions to virtually every scientific area of his day. He was one of the founders of algebra, he discovered fundamental laws in geometrical optics, his natural philosophy was *the* natural philosophy in the seventeenth century before the appearance of Newton's *Principia* (Newton himself was a Cartesian before he developed his own natural philosophy) and his work in biology and physiology resulted, amongst other things, in the discovery of reflex action.[1] Descartes's earliest interests were scientific, and he seems to have thought his scientific work of greater importance than his metaphysical writings throughout his career. In a conversation with Burman, recorded in 1648, he remarked:

> A point to note is that you should not devote so much effort to the *Meditations* and to metaphysical questions, or give them elaborate treatment in commentaries and the like. Still less should one do what some try to do, and dig more deeply into these questions than the author did: he has dealt with them all quite deeply enough. It is sufficient to have grasped them once in a general way, and then to remember the conclusion. Otherwise they draw the mind too far away from physical and observable things, and make it unfit to study them. Yet it is just these physical studies that it is most desirable for men to pursue, since they would yield abundant benefits for life.[2]

Despite this, Descartes has often been considered a metaphysician in natural philosophy, deriving physical truths from metaphysical first principles. Indeed, there is still a widespread view that the 'method' Descartes espoused is the *a priori* one of deduction from first principles, where these first principles are truths of reason. This view has two principal sources: an image of Descartes as the *de facto* founder of a philosophical school – 'rationalism' – in which deduction from truths of reason is, almost by definition, constitutive of epistemology, and a reading of a number of passages in Descartes in which he discusses his project in highly schematic terms as accounts of his method of discovery. The reading of Descartes as founder of a school is largely a nineteenth-century doctrine first set out in detail in Kuno Fischer's *Geschichte der neueren Philosophie* in the 1870s. There is a hidden agenda in Fischer which underlies this: he is a Kantian and is keen to show Kant's philosophy as solving the major problems of modern thought. He sets the background for this by resolving modern pre-Kantian philosophy into two schools, rationalism and empiricism, the first basing everything on truths of reason, the second basing everything on experiential truths. This demarcation displaces the older Platonist/ Aristotelian dichotomy (which Kant himself effectively worked with), marking out the seventeenth century as the beginning of a new era in philosophy, one dominated by epistemological (as opposed to moral or theological) concerns.[3]

This reading of Descartes is not wholly fanciful, and it has been widely accepted in the twentieth century by philosophers who do not share Fischer's Kantianism. On the face of it, it has considerable textual support. Article 64 of Part II of Descartes's *Principles of Philosophy* is entitled:

> That I do not accept or desire in physics any principles other than those accepted in geometry or abstract mathematics; because all the phenomena of nature are explained thereby, and demonstrations concerning them which are certain can be given.

In elucidation, he writes:

> For I frankly admit that I know of no material substance other than that which is divisible, has shape, and can move in every possible way, and this the geometers call quantity and take as the object of their demonstrations. Moreover, our concern is exclusively with the division, shape and motions of this substance, and nothing concerning these can be accepted as true unless it be deduced from indubitably true common notions with such certainty that it can be regarded as a mathematical demonstration. And because all natural phenomena can be explained in this way, as one can judge from what follows, I

believe that no other physical principles should be accepted or even desired.[4]

This seems to be as clear a statement as one could wish for of a method which starts from first principles and builds up knowledge deductively. Observation, experiment, hypotheses, induction, the development and use of scientific instruments, all seem to be irrelevant to science as described here. Empirical or factual truths seem to have been transcended, and all science seems to be in the realm of truths of reason. One gains a similar impression from a number of other passages in Descartes, and in the *Sixth Meditation*, for example, we are presented with a picture of the corporeal world in which – because we are only allowed to ask about the existence of those things of which we have a clear and distinct idea, and because these are effectively restricted to mathematical concepts – it is little more than materialized geometry. The deduction of the features of such a world from first principles is not too hard to envisage.

Nevertheless, there are serious problems with the idea that Descartes is advocating an *a priori*, deductivist method of discovery, and I want to draw attention to four such problems briefly. First, there is the sheer implausibility of the idea that deduction from first principles could generate substantive and specific truths about the physical world. The first principles that Descartes starts from are the *cogito* and the existence of a good God. These figure in the *Meditations* and in the *Principles of Philosophy* as explicit first principles. Now by the end of the *Principles of Philosophy* he has offered accounts of such phenomena as the distances of the planets from the Sun, the material constitution of the Sun, the motion of comets, the colours of the rainbow, sunspots, solidity and fluidity, why the Moon moves faster than the Earth, the nature of transparency, the rarefaction and condensation of matter, why air and water flow from east to west, the nature of the Earth's interior, the nature of quicksilver, the nature of bitumen and sulphur, why the water in certain wells is brackish, the nature of glass, magnetism, and static electricity, to name but a few. Could it seriously be advocated that the *cogito* and the existence of a good God would be sufficient to provide an account of these phenomena? Philosophers, like everyone else, are occasionally subject to delusions, and great claims have been made for various philosophically conceived scientific methods. But it is worth remembering in this connection that Descartes is of a generation where method is not a reflection on the successful work of other scientists but a very practical affair designed to guide one's own scientific practice. It is also worth remembering that Descartes achieved some lasting results in his scientific work. In the light of this, there is surely something wrong in ascribing an unworkable methodology to him.

Second, Descartes's own contemporaries did not view his work as being apriorist and deductivist, but rather as being committed to a hypothetical mode of reasoning, and, in the wake of Newton's famous rejection of the use of hypotheses in science, Descartes was criticized for offering mere hypotheses where Newtonian physics offered certainty.[5] A picture of Descartes prevailed in his own era exactly contrary to that which has prevailed in ours, and, it might be noted, on the basis of the same texts, that is, above all the *Discourse on Method*, the *Meditations* and *The Principles of Philosophy*. The possibility must therefore be raised that we have misread these texts.

Third, if one looks at Descartes's very sizeable correspondence, the vast bulk (about 90 per cent) of which is on scientific matters, one is left in no doubt as to the amount of empirical and experimental work in which he engaged. For example, in 1626 Descartes began seeking the shape of the 'anaclastic', that is, that shape of a refracting surface which would collect parallel rays into one focus. He knew that the standard lens of the time, the biconvex lens, could not do this, and that the refracting telescope constructed with such a lens was subject to serious problems as a result. He was convinced on geometrical grounds that the requisite shape must be a hyperbola but he spent several years pondering the practical problems of grinding aspherical lenses. In two detailed letters to Jean Ferrier (a manufacturer of scientific instruments whom Descartes was trying to attract to Holland to work for him grinding lenses) of October and November 1629, he describes an extremely ingenious grinding machine, with details as to the materials different parts must be constructed of, exact sizes of components, instructions for fixing the machine to rafters and joists to minimize vibration, how to cut the contours of blades, differences between rough-forming and finishing-off, and so on. These letters leave one in no doubt that their author is an extremely practical man, able to devise very large-scale machines with many components, and with an extensive knowledge of materials, grinding and cutting techniques, not to mention a good practical grasp of problems of friction and vibration. The rest of his large correspondence, whether it be on navigation, acoustics, hydrostatics, the theory of machines, the construction of telescopes, anatomy, chemistry or whatever, confirm Descartes's ability to devise and construct scientific instruments and experiments. Is it really possible that Descartes's methodological prescriptions should be so far removed from his actual scientific practice?

Fourth, Descartes has an extremely low view of deduction. He rejects Aristotelian syllogistic, the only logical formalization of deductive inference he would have been familiar with, as being incapable of producing any new truths, on the grounds that the conclusion can never go beyond the premises:

> We must note that the dialecticians are unable to devise by their rules any syllogism which has a true conclusion, unless they already have the whole syllogism, i.e. unless they have already ascertained in advance the very truth which is deduced in that syllogism.[6]

Much more surprisingly, for syllogistic was generally reviled in the seventeenth century, he also rejects the mode of deductive inference used by the classical geometers, synthetic proof. In Rule 4 of the *Rules for the Direction of Our Native Intelligence*, he complains that Pappus and Diophantus, 'with a kind of low cunning', kept their method of discovery secret, presenting us with 'sterile truths' which they 'demonstrated deductively'.[7] This is especially problematic for the reading of Descartes which holds that his method comprises deduction from first principles, since this is exactly what he is rejecting in the case of Pappus and Diophantus, who proceed like Euclid, working out deductively from indubitable geometrical first principles. Indeed, such a procedure would be the obvious model for his own method if this were as the quotations above from the *Principles* suggest it is.

These considerations are certainly not the only ones, but they are enough to make us question the received view. Before we can provide an alternative reading, however, it will be helpful if we can get a better idea of what exactly Descartes is rejecting in traditional accounts of method, and what kind of thing he is seeking to achieve in his scientific writings.

☙ THE REJECTION OF ARISTOTELIAN ❧ METHOD

Aristotelian syllogistic was widely criticized from the mid-sixteenth century onwards, and by the middle of the seventeenth century had been completely discredited as a method of discovery. This was due more to a misunderstanding of the nature and role of the syllogism, however, than to any compelling criticism of syllogistic.

Aristotle had presented scientific demonstrations syllogistically, and he had argued that some forms of demonstration provide explanations or causes whereas others do not. This may occur even where the syllogisms are formally identical. Consider, for example, the following two syllogisms:

The planets do not twinkle
That which does not twinkle is near
The planets are near

The planets are near
That which is near does not twinkle
The planets do not twinkle

In Aristotle's discussion of these syllogisms in his *Posterior Analytics* (*A*17), he argues that the first is only a demonstration 'of fact', whereas the second is a demonstration of 'why' or a scientific explanation. In the latter we are provided with a reason or cause or explanation of the conclusion: the reason why the planets do not twinkle is that they are near. In the former, we have a valid but not a demonstrative argument, since the planets' not twinkling is hardly a cause or explanation of their being near. So the first syllogism is in some way uninformative compared with the second: the latter produces understanding, the former does not. Now Aristotle had great difficulty in providing a convincing account of what exactly it is that distinguishes the first from the second syllogism, but what he was trying to achieve is clear enough. He was seeking some way of identifying those forms of deductive inference that resulted in epistemic advance, that advanced one's understanding. Realizing that no purely logical criterion would suffice, he attempted to show that epistemic advance depended on some non-logical but nevertheless internal or structural feature which some deductive inferences possess. This question of the epistemic value of deductive inferences is one we shall return to, as it underlies the whole problem of method.

For Aristotle, the epistemic and the consequential directions in demonstrative syllogisms run in opposite directions. That is, it is knowing the premises from which the conclusion is to be deduced that is the important thing as far as providing a deeper scientific understanding is concerned, not discovering what conclusions follow from given premises. The seventeenth-century misunderstanding of the syllogism results largely from a failure to appreciate this. It was assumed that, for Aristotle, the demonstrative syllogism was a method of discovery, a means of deducing novel conclusions from accepted premises. In fact, it was simply a means of presentation of results in a systematic way, one suitable for conveying these to students.[8] The conclusions of the syllogisms were known in advance, and what the syllogism provided was a means of relating those conclusions to premises which would explain them. Two features of syllogistic are worth noting in this respect.

First, the syllogism is what might be termed a 'discursive' device. Consider the case of the demonstrative syllogism. This is effectively a

pedagogic device, involving a teacher and a pupil. If it is to be successful, the pupil must accept the conclusion: the conclusion having been
accepted, the syllogism shows how it can be generated from premises
which are more fundamental, thereby connecting what the pupil accepts
as knowledge to basic principles which can act as an explanation for
it. This reflects a basic feature of the syllogism, whether demonstrative
or not. Generally speaking, syllogistic works by inducing conviction
on the basis of shared assumptions or shared knowledge. For this, one
needs someone who is convinced and someone who does the convincing. Moreover, the conviction occurs on the basis of shared assumptions, and these assumptions may in fact be false. The kind of process
that Descartes and his contemporaries see as occurring in an argument
is different from this. Descartes, in particular, requires that arguments
be 'internal' things: their purpose is to lead one to the truth, not to
convince anyone. Correlatively, one can make no appeal to what is
generally accepted: one's premises must simply be true, whether generally accepted or not.[9] The discursive conception of argument that Aristotelian syllogistic relies upon requires common ground between oneself and one's opponents, and in seventeenth-century natural
philosophy this would not have been forthcoming. In other words, the
case against conceiving of inference in a discursive way links up
strongly with the case against appealing in one's enquiries to what is
generally accepted rather than to what is the case. It is from this that
the immense polemical strength of Descartes's attack on syllogistic
derives.

Second, conceived as a tool of discovery, the demonstrative syllogism does indeed look trivial, but this was never its purpose for Aristotle. Discovery was something to be guided by the 'topics', which were
procedures for classifying or characterizing problems so that they could
be solved using set techniques. More specifically, they were designed
to provide the distinctions needed if one was to be able to formulate
problems properly, as well as supplying devices enabling one to determine what has to be shown if the conclusion one desires is to be
reached. Now the topics were not confined to scientific enquiry, but
had an application in ethics, political argument, rhetoric and so on,
and indeed they were meant to apply to any area of enquiry. The
problem was that, during the Middle Ages, the topics came to be
associated very closely and exclusively with rhetoric, and their relevance
to scientific discovery became at first obscured and then completely
lost. The upshot of this was that, for all intents and purposes, the
results of Aristotelian science lost all contact with the procedures of
discovery which produced them. While these results remained unchal-
lenged, the problem was not particularly apparent. But when they came
to be challenged in a serious and systematic way, as they were from

the sixteenth century onwards, they began to take on the appearance of mere dogmas, backed up by circular reasoning. It is this strong connection between Aristotle's supposed method of discovery and the unsatisfactoriness not only of his scientific results but also of his overall natural philosophy that provoked the intense concern with method in the seventeenth century.[10]

➤➤ DESCARTES'S NATURAL PHILOSOPHY ➤➤

Descartes's account of method is intimately tied to two features of his natural philosophy: his commitment to mechanism, and his commitment to the idea of a mathematical physics. In these respects, his project differs markedly from that of Aristotle, to the extent that what he expects out of a physical explanation is rather different from what Aristotle expects. This shapes his approach to methodological issues to a significant extent, and we must pay some attention to both questions.

Mechanism is not an easy doctrine to characterize, but it does have some core theses. Amongst these are the postulates that nature is to be conceived on a mechanical model, that 'occult qualities' cannot be accepted as having any explanatory value, that contact action is the only means by which change can be effected, and that matter and motion are the ultimate ingredients in nature.[11] Mechanism arose in the first instance not so much as a reaction to scholasticism but as a reaction to a philosophy which was itself largely a reaction to scholasticism, namely Renaissance naturalism.[12] Renaissance naturalism undermined the sharp and careful lines that medieval philosophy and theology had drawn between the natural and the supernatural, and it offered a conception of the cosmos as a living organism, as a holistic system whose parts were interconnected by various forces and powers. Such a conception presented a picture of nature as an essentially active realm, containing many 'occult' powers which, while they were not manifest, could nevertheless be tapped and exploited if only one could discover them. It was characteristic of such powers that they acted at a distance – magnetic attraction was a favourite example – rather than through contact, and indeed on a biological model of the cosmos such a mode of action is a characteristic one, since parts of a biological system may affect one another whether in physical contact or not. The other side of the coin was a conception of God as part of nature, as infused in nature, and not as something separate from his creation. This encouraged highly unorthodox doctrines such as pantheism, the modelling of divine powers on natural ones, and so on, and, worst of all, it opened up the very delicate question of whether apparently supernatural phenomena, such as miracles, or phenomena which offered communion with God, such as the sacraments and prayer, could receive purely naturalistic explanations.[13] It is important that the conception of nature as essentially active and the attempts to subsume the supernatural within the natural be recognized as part of the same problem. Mechanists such as Mersenne[14] saw this clearly, and opposed naturalism so vehemently because they saw its threat to established religion. Mersenne himself also saw that a return to the Aristotelian conception of nature that had served medieval theologians and natural philosophers so well was not going to be successful, for many of the later Renaissance naturalists had based their views on a naturalistic reading of Aristotle which, as an interpretation of Aristotle, was at least as cogent as that offered by Christian apologists like Aquinas. The situation was exacerbated by a correlative naturalistic thesis about the nature of human beings, whereby the soul is not a separate substance but simply the organizing principle of the body. Whether this form of naturalism was advocated in its Averroistic version, where there is only one intellect in the universe because mind or soul, lacking any principle of individuation in its own right, cannot be divided up with the number of bodies, or whether it was advocated in its Alexandrian version, where the soul is conceived in purely functional terms, personal immortality is denied, and its source in both versions is Aristotle himself.[15] Such threats to the immortality of the soul were noted by the Fifth Lateran Council, which in 1513 instructed Christian philosophers and theologians to find arguments to defend the orthodox view of personal immortality.

Something was needed which was unambiguous in its rejection of nature as an active realm, and which thereby secured a guaranteed role for the supernatural. Moreover, whatever was chosen should also be able to offer a conception of the human body and its functions which left room for something essentially different from the body which distinguished it from those animals who did not share in immortality. Mechanism appeared to Mersenne to answer both these problems, and in a series of books in the 1620s he opposes naturalism in detail and outlines the mechanist response.[16]

Descartes's response is effectively the same, but much more radical in its execution. Like Mersenne, he is concerned to defend mechanism, and the idea of a completely inert nature provides the basis for dualism. Dualism in turn is what he considers to be the successful way of meeting the decree of the Lateran Council, as he explains to us in the Dedicatory Letter at the beginning of the *Meditations*. What he offers is a picture of the corporeal world as completely inert, a separation of mind and body as radical as it could be, and an image of a God who is so supernatural, so transcendent, that there is almost nothing we can say about him.

In accord with the mechanist programme, the supernatural and the natural are such polar opposites in Descartes that there is no question of the latter having any degree of activity once activity has been ascribed to the former. His contemporaries were especially concerned to restrict all causal efficacy to the transfer of motion from one body to another in impact but Descartes goes further. While he recognizes the need for such a description at the phenomenal level, at the metaphysical level he does not allow any causation at all in the natural realm.[17] Motion is conceived as a mode of a body just as shape is, and strictly speaking it is not something that can be transferred at all, any more than shape can be. The power that causes bodies to be in some determinate state of rest or motion is a power that derives exclusively from God, and not from impact with other bodies. Moreover, this power is simply the power by which God conserves the same amount of motion that he put in the corporeal world at the first instant.[18] On Descartes's account of the persistence of the corporeal world, God is required to recreate it at every instant, because it is so lacking in any power that it does not even have the power to conserve itself in existence. As he puts it in the replies to the first set of objections to the *Meditations*, we can find in our own bodies, and by implication in other corporeal things as well, no power or force by which they could produce or conserve themselves. Why, one may ask, is such a force or power required? The answer is that causes and their effects must be simultaneous: 'the concept of cause is, strictly speaking, applicable only for as long as it is producing its effect, and so is not prior to it.'[19] My existence at the present instant cannot be due to my existence at the last instant any more than it can itself bring about my existence at the next instant. In sum, there can be no causal connections between instants, so the reason for everything must be sought within the instant:[20] and since no such powers are evident in bodies, they must be located in God. Such an inert corporeal world certainly contains none of the powers that naturalists saw as being immanent in nature, it is not a world in which God could be immanent, and it is, for Descartes and virtually all of his contemporaries (Hobbes and Gassendi being possible exceptions), a world quite distinct from what reflection on ourselves tells us is constitutive of our natures, which are essentially spiritual. And it also has another important feature: a world without forces, activities, potentialities and even causation is one which is easily quantifiable.

This brings us to the second ingredient in Descartes's natural philosophy: his commitment to quantitative explanations. This is often seen as if it were a necessary concomitant of mechanism, but in fact mechanism is neither sufficient nor necessary for a mathematical physics. Most mechanists in the early to mid-seventeenth century offered mechanist explanations which were almost exclusively qualitative: Hobbes and Gassendi are good cases in point. Moreover, Kepler's thoroughly Neoplatonic conception of the universe as being ultimately a mathematical harmony underlying surface appearances could not have been further from mechanism, yet it enabled him to develop a mathematical account in areas such as astronomy and optics which was well in advance of anything else at his time. But it cannot be denied that the combination of mechanism with a commitment to a mathematical physics was an extremely potent one, and Descartes was the first to offer such a combination to any significant extent.

This question must be seen in a broad context. The theoretical justification for the use of mathematical theorems and techniques in the treatment of problems in physical theory is not obvious. To many natural philosophers it was far from clear that such an approach was necessary, justified, or even possible. Aristotle had provided a highly elaborate conception of physical explanation which absolutely precluded the use of mathematics in physical enquiry and it was this conception that dominated physical enquiry until the seventeenth century. Briefly, Aristotle defines physics and mathematics in terms of their subject genera: physics is concerned with those things that change and have an independent existence, mathematics with those things that do not change and have dependent existence (i.e. they are mere abstractions). The aim of scientific enquiry is to determine what kind of thing the subject matter of the science is by establishing its general properties. To explain something is to demonstrate it syllogistically starting from first principles which are expressions of essences, and what one is seeking in a physical explanation is a statement of the essential characteristics of a physical phenomenon – those characteristics which it must possess if it is to be the kind of thing it is. Such a statement can only be derived from principles that are appropriate to the subject genus of the science; in the case of physics, this means principles appropriate to explaining what is changing and has an independent existence. Mathematical principles are not of this kind. They are appropriate to a completely different kind of subject matter, and because of this mathematics is inappropriate to syllogistic demonstrations of physical phenomena, and it is alien to physical explanation. This approach benefited from a well-developed metaphysical account of the different natures of physical and mathematical entities, and it resulted in a physical theory that was not only in close agreement with observation and common sense, but which formed part of a large-scale theory of change which covered organic and inorganic phenomena alike.

By the beginning of the seventeenth century, the Aristotelian approach was being challenged on a number of fronts, and Archimedean statics, in particular, was seen by many as the model for a physical theory, with its rigorously geometrical demonstrations of novel and fundamental physical theorems. But there was no straightforward way of extending this approach in statics (where it was often possible to translate the problem into mathematical terms in an intuitive and unproblematic way), to kinematics (where one had to deal with motion, i.e. continuous change of place) and in dynamics (where one had somehow to quantify the forces responsible for changes in motion). Moreover, statics involved a number of simplifying assumptions, such as the Earth's surface being a true geometrical plane and its being a parallel force field. These simplifying assumptions generate all kinds of problems once one leaves the domain of statics, and the kinds of conceptual problems faced by natural philosophers wishing to provide a mathematical physics in the seventeenth century were immense.[21]

In the *Rules for the Direction of Our Native Intelligence*, Descartes outlined a number of methodological and epistemological proposals for a mathematical physics. The *Rules*, the writing of which was abandoned in 1628, is now thought to be a composite text, some parts deriving from 1619–20 (Rules 1–3, part of Rule 4, Rules 5–7, part of Rule 8, possibly Rules 9–11) and some dating from 1626–8 (part of Rule 4, part of Rule 8, and Rules 12–21).[22] The earlier parts describe a rather grandiose reductionist programme in which mathematics is simply 'applied' to the natural world:

> When I considered the matter more closely, I came to see that
> the exclusive concern of mathematics is with questions of order
> or measure and that it is irrelevant whether the measure in
> question involves numbers, shapes, stars, sounds, or any object
> whatever. This made me realize that there must be a general
> science which explains all the points that can be raised
> concerning order and measure irrespective of the subject-matter,
> and that this science should be termed *mathesis universalis*.[23]

This project for a 'universal mathematics' is not mentioned again in Descartes's writings and, although the question is a disputed one,[24] there is a strong case to be made that he abandoned this kind of attempt to provide a basis for a mathematical physics. The later Rules set out an account of how our comprehension of the corporeal world is essentially mathematical in nature, but it is one which centres on a theory about how perceptual cognition occurs. Throughout the *Rules*, Descartes insists that knowledge must begin with 'simple natures', that is, with those things which are not further analysable and can be grasped by a direct 'intuition' (*intuitus*). These simple natures can only be grasped by the intellect – pure mind, for all intents and purposes – although in the case of perceptual cognition the corporeal faculties of sense perception, memory and imagination are also called upon. The imagination is located in the pineal gland (chosen because it was believed to be at the geometrical focus of the brain and its only non-duplicated organ), it is the point to which all perceptual information is transmitted, and it acts as a kind of meeting place between mind and body, although Descartes is understandably coy about this last point. In Rule 14, Descartes argues that the proper objects of the intellect are completely abstract entities, which are free of images or 'bodily representations', and this is why, when the intellect turns into itself it beholds those things which are purely intellectual such as thought and doubt, as well as those 'simple natures' which are common to both mind and body, such as existence, unity and duration. However, the intellect requires the imagination if there is to be any knowledge of the external world, for the imagination is its point of contact with the external world. The imagination functions, in fact, like a meeting place between the corporeal world and the mind. The corporeal world is represented in the intellect in terms of spatially extended magnitudes. Since, Descartes argues, the corporeal world is nothing but spatially extended body, with the experience of secondary qualities resulting from the mind's interaction with matter moving in various distinctive ways, the representation of the world geometrically in the imagination is an entirely natural and appropriate mode of representation. But the contents of the mind must also be represented in the imagination and, in so far as the mind is engaged in a quantitative understanding, the imagination is needed in order that the mathematical entities on which the intellect works can be rendered determinate. For example, the intellect understands 'fiveness' as something distinct from five objects (or line segments, or points or whatever), and hence the imagination is required if this 'fiveness' is to correspond to something in the world. In fact, 'fiveness' is represented as a line comprising five equal segments which is then mapped onto the geometrical representations of the corporeal world.

In this way, our understanding of the corporeal world, an understanding that necessarily involves sense perception, is thoroughly mathematical. It should be noted that the intellect or mind, working by itself, could never even represent the corporeal world to itself, and *a fortiori* could never understand it.

❦ DESCARTES'S METHOD OF DISCOVERY ❦

In the *Discourse on Method*, Descartes describes the procedure by which he has proceeded in the *Dioptrics* and the *Meteors* in the following terms:

The order which I have followed in this regard is as follows. First, I have attempted generally to discover the principles or first causes of everything which is or could be in the world, without in this connection considering anything but God alone, who has created the world, and without drawing them from any source except certain seeds of truth which are naturally in our minds. Next I considered what were the first and most common effects that could be deduced from these causes, and it seems to me that in this way I found the heavens, the stars, an earth, and even on the earth, water, air, fire, the minerals and a few other such things which are the most common and simple of all that exist, and consequently the easiest to understand. Then, when I wished to descend to those that were more particular, there were so many objects of various kinds that I did not believe it possible for the human mind to distinguish the forms or species of body which are on the earth from the infinity of others which might have been, had it been God's will to put them there, or consequently to make them of use to us, if it were not that one arrives at the causes through the effects and avails oneself of many specific experiments. In subsequently passing over in my mind all the objects which have been presented to my senses, I dare to say that I have not noticed anything that I could not easily explain in terms of the principles that I have discovered. But I must also admit that the power of nature is so great and so extensive, and these principles so simple and general, that I hardly observed any effect that I did not immediately realize could be deduced from the principles in many different ways. The greatest difficulty is usually to discover in which of these ways the effect depends on them. In this situation, so far as I know the only thing that can be done is to try and find experiments which are such that their result varies depending upon which of them provides the correct explanation.[25]

But what exactly is Descartes describing here? We cannot simply assume it is a method of discovery. In a letter to Antoine Vatier of 22 February 1638, Descartes writes:

I must say first that my purpose was not to teach the whole of my Method in the Discourse in which I propound it, but only to say enough to show that the new views in the *Dioptrics* and the *Meteors* were not random notions, and were perhaps worth the trouble of examining. I could not demonstrate the use of this Method in the three treatises which I gave, because it prescribes an order of research which is quite different from the one I thought proper for exposition. I have however given a brief sample of it in my account of the rainbow, and if you take the trouble to re-read it, I hope it will satisfy you more than it did the first time; the matter is, after all, quite difficult in itself. I attached these three treatises [the *Geometry*, the *Dioptrics* and the *Meteors*] to the discourse which precedes them because I am convinced that if people examine them carefully and compare them with what has previously been written on the same topics, they will have grounds for judging that the Method I adopt is no ordinary one and is perhaps better than some others.[26]

What is more, in the *Meteors* itself, Descartes tells us that his account of the rainbow is the most appropriate example 'to show how, by means of the method which I use, one can attain knowledge which was not available to those whose writings we possess'.[27] This account is, then, clearly worth looking at.

The *Meteors* does not start from first principles but from problems to be solved, and Descartes then uses the solution of the problem to exemplify his method. The central problem in the *Meteors*, to which Book 8 is devoted, is that of explaining the angle at which the bows of the rainbow appear in the sky. He begins by noting that rainbows are not only formed in the sky, but also in fountains and showers in the presence of sunlight. This leads him to formulate the hypothesis that the phenomenon is caused by light reacting on drops of water. To test this hypothesis, he constructs a glass model of the raindrop, comprising a large glass sphere filled with water and, standing with his back to the Sun, he holds up the sphere in the Sun's light, moving it up and down so that colours are produced. Then, if we let the light from the Sun come

from the part of the sky marked AFZ, and my eye be at point E, then when I put this globe at the place BCD, the part of it at D seems to me wholly red and incomparably more brilliant than the rest. And whether I move towards it or step back from it, or move it to the right or to the left, or even turn it in a circle around my head, then provided the line DE always marks an angle of around 42° with the line EM, which one must imagine to extend from the centre of the eye to the centre of the sun, D always appears equally red. But as soon as I made this angle DEM the slightest bit smaller it did not disappear completely in the one stroke but first divided as into two less brilliant parts in which could be seen yellow, blue, and other colours. Then, looking towards the place marked K on the globe,

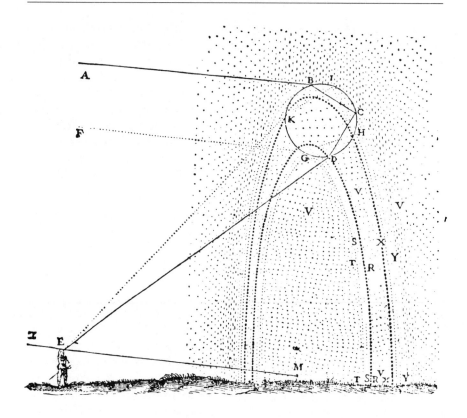

I perceived that, making the angle KEM around 52°, K also seemed to be coloured red, but not so brilliant . . . [28]

Descartes then describes how he covered the globe at all points except B and D. The ray still emerged, showing that the primary and secondary bows are caused by two refractions and one or two internal reflections of the incident ray. He next describes how the same effect can be produced with a prism, and this indicates that neither a curved surface nor reflection are necessary for colour dispersion. Moreover, the prism experiment shows that the effect does not depend on the angle of incidence and that one refraction is sufficient for its production. Finally, Descartes calculates from the refractive index of rainwater what an observer would see when light strikes a drop of water at varying angles of incidence, and finds that the optimum difference for visibility between incident and refracted rays is for the former to be viewed at an angle of 41°–42° and the latter at an angle of 51°–52°,[29] which is exactly what the hypothesis predicts.

This procedure is similar to that followed in the *Dioptrics*, and in some respects to that followed in the *Geometry*. It is above all an exercise in problem-solving, and the precedent for such an exercise seems to have been developed in Descartes's work in mathematics. Indeed, the later parts of the *Rules* turn towards specifically mathematical considerations, and Rules 16–21 have such close parallels with the *Geometry* that one can only conclude that they contain the early parts of that work in an embryonic form. Rule 16 advises us to use 'the briefest possible symbols' in dealing with problems, and one of the first things the *Geometry* does is to provide us with the algebraic signs necessary for dealing with geometrical problems. Rule 17 tells us that, in dealing with a new problem, we must ignore the fact that some terms are known and some unknown; and again one of the first directives in the *Geometry* is that we label all lines necessary for the geometrical construction, whether these be known or unknown. Finally, Rules 18–21 are formulated in almost identical terms in the *Geometry*.[30]

There is something ironic in this, for one would normally associate a mathematical model with a method which was axiomatic and deductive. Certainly, if one looks at the great mathematical texts of Antiquity – Euclid's *Elements* or Archimedes's *On the Sphere and the Cylinder* or Apollonius's *On Conic Sections*, for example – one finds lists of definitions and postulates and deductive proofs of theorems relying solely on these. If one now turns to Descartes's *Geometry*, one finds something completely different. After a few pages of introduction, mainly on the geometrical representation of the arithmetical operations of multiplication, division and finding roots, we are thrown into one of the great unsolved problems bequeathed by Antiquity – Pappus's locus problem for four or more lines, which Descartes then proceeds to provide us with a method of solving.

Descartes's solution to the Pappus problem is an 'analytic' one. In ancient mathematics, a sharp distinction was made between analysis and synthesis. Pappus, one of the greatest of the Alexandrian mathematicians, had distinguished between two kinds of analysis: 'theoretical' analysis, in which one attempts to discover the truth of a theorem, and 'problematical analysis', in which one attempts to discover something unknown. If, in the case of theoretical analysis, one finds that the theorem is false or if, in the case of problematical analysis, the proposed procedure fails to yield what one is seeking, or one can show the problem to be insoluble, then synthesis is not needed, and analysis is complete in its own right. In the case of positive results, however, synthesis is needed, albeit for different reasons. Synthesis is a difficult notion to specify, and it appears to have been used with slightly different meanings by different writers, but it is basically that part of the mathematical process in which one proves deductively, perhaps from first principles, what one has discovered or shown the truth of by analysis. In the case of theoretical analysis, one needs synthesis, because in the analysis what we have done is to show that a true theorem follows from a theorem whose truth we wish to establish, and what we must now do is to show that the converse is also the case, that the theorem whose truth we wish to establish follows from the theorem we know to be true. The latter demonstration, whose most obvious form is demonstration from first principles, is synthesis. A synthetic proof is, in fact, the 'natural order' for Greek and Alexandrian mathematicians, the analysis being only a 'solution backwards'. So what we are invariably presented with are the 'naturally ordered' synthetic demonstrations: there is no need to present the analysis as well. Descartes objects to such procedures. He accuses the Alexandrian mathematicians Pappus and Diophantus of presenting only the synthesis from ulterior motives:

> I have come to think that these writers themselves, with a kind of pernicious cunning, later suppressed this mathematics as, notoriously, many inventors are known to have done where their own discoveries were concerned. They may have feared that their method, just because it was so easy and simple, would be depreciated if it were divulged; so to gain our admiration, they may have shown us, as the fruits of their method, some barren truths proved by clever arguments, instead of teaching us the method itself, which might have dispelled our admiration.[31]

In other words, analysis is a method of discovery, whereas synthesis is merely a method of presentation of one's results by deriving them from first principles. Now it is true that in many cases the synthetic demonstration will be very straightforward once one has the analytic demonstration, and indeed in many cases the latter is simply a reversal of the former. Moreover, all equations have valid converses by definition, so if one is dealing with equations, as Descartes is for example, then there is no special problem about converses holding. But the synthetic demonstration, unlike the analytic one, is a deductively valid proof, and this, for the ancients and for the vast majority of mathematicians since then, is the only real form of proof. Descartes does not accept this, because he does not accept that deduction can have any value in its own right. We shall return to this issue below.

The case of problematical analysis with a positive outcome is more complicated, for here there was traditionally considered to be an extra reason why synthesis was needed, namely the production of a 'determinate' solution. In rejecting synthesis in this context, Descartes is on far stronger ground. Indeed, one of the most crucial stages in the development of algebra consists precisely in going beyond the call for determinate solutions. In the case of geometry, analysis provides one with a general procedure, but it does not in itself produce a particular geometrical figure or construction as the solution to a problem and, until this is done, the ancients considered that the problem had not been solved. Parallel constraints applied in arithmetic. Arithmetical analysis yields only an indeterminate solution, and we need a final synthetic stage corresponding to the geometrical solution; this is the numerical exploitation of the indeterminate solution, where we compute determinate numbers. Now in traditional terms the *Geometry* is an exercise in problematical analysis, but Descartes completely rejects the traditional requirement that, following such an analysis, synthesis is needed to construct or compute a determinate figure or number. For the mathematicians of Antiquity this was the point of the exercise, and it was only if such a determinate figure or number could be constructed or computed that one could be said to have solved the problem. Towards the end of the Alexandrian era, most notably in Diophantus's *Arithmetica*, we do begin to find the search for problems and solutions concerned with general magnitudes, but these are never considered an end in themselves, and they are regarded as auxiliary techniques allowing the computation of a determinate number, which is the ultimate point of the exercise. Descartes's approach is completely and explicitly at odds with this. As early as Rule 16 of the *Rules* he spells out the contrast between his procedure and the traditional one:

> It must be pointed out that while arithmeticians have usually designated each magnitude by several units, i.e. by a number, we on the contrary abstract from numbers themselves just as we did above [Rule 14] from geometrical figures, or from anything else. Our reason for doing this is partly to avoid the tedium of a long and unnecessary calculation, but mainly to see that those parts of the problem which are the essential ones always remain distinct and are not obscured by useless numbers. If for example we are trying to find the hypotenuse of a right-angled triangle whose given sides are 9 and 12, the arithmeticians will say that it is $\sqrt{(225)}$, i.e. 15. We, on the other hand, will write a and b for 9 and 12, and find that the hypotenuse is $\sqrt{(a^2 + b^2)}$, leaving the two parts of the expression, a^2 and b^2, distinct, whereas in the number they are run together. . . . We who seek to develop a clear and distinct knowledge of these things insist on these distinctions. Arithmeticians, on the other hand, are satisfied if the required result turns up, even if they do not see how it depends on what has been given, but in fact it is in knowledge of this kind alone that science consists.[32]

In sum, for Descartes, concern with general magnitudes is constitutive of the mathematical enterprise.

Descartes's algebra transcends the need to establish converses, because he is dealing with equations, whose converses always hold, and it transcends the traditional view that one solves a problem only when one has constructed a determinate figure or computed a determinate number. But Descartes goes further than this, rejecting the need for deductive proof altogether. The reason why he does this lies ultimately not so much in his rejection of synthetic demonstrations in mathematics but in his conception of the nature of inference. Before we look at this question, however, it is worth looking briefly at what role deduction does play in Descartes's overall account.

❦ METHODS OF DISCOVERY AND ❦ PRESENTATION

In Article 64 of Part II of *The Principles of Philosophy*, Descartes writes:

> I know of no material substance other than that which is divisible, has shape, and can move in every possible way, and this the geometers call quantity and take as the object of their demonstrations. Moreover, our concern is exclusively with the divisions, shape and motions of this substance, and nothing concerning these can be accepted as true unless it be deduced (*deducatur*) from indubitably true common notions with such certainty that it can be regarded as a mathematical demonstration. And because all natural phenomena can be explained in this way, as one can judge from what follows, I believe that no other physical principles should be accepted or even desired.

Like the passage from the *Discourse on Method* that I quoted above, there is a suggestion here that deduction from first principles is Descartes's method of discovery. Can we reconcile these and many passages similar to them with Descartes's rejection of deductive forms of inference, such as synthesis in mathematics and syllogistic in logic? I believe we can.

Descartes's procedure in natural philosophy is to start from problem-solving, and his 'method' is designed to facilitate such problem-solving. The problems have to be posed in quantitative terms and there are a number of constraints on what form an acceptable solution takes: one cannot posit 'occult qualities', one must seek 'simple natures', and so on. The solution is then tested experimentally to determine how well it holds up compared with other possible explanations meeting the same constraints which also appear to account for the facts. Finally, the solution is incorporated into a system of natural philosophy, and the principal aim of a work like the *Principles of Philosophy* is to set out this natural philosophy in detail. The *Principles* is a textbook, best compared not with works like the *Optics* and the *Meteors*, which purport to show one how the empirical results were arrived at, but with the many scholastic textbooks on natural philosophy which were around in Descartes's time, and from which he himself learnt whilst a student.[33] Such a textbook gives one a systematic overview of the subject, presenting its ultimate foundations, and showing how the parts of the subject are connected. Ultimately, the empirically verified results have to be fitted into this system, which in Descartes's case is a rigorously mechanist system presented with metaphysical foundations. But the empirical results themselves are not justified by their incorporation within this system: they are justified purely in observational and experimental terms. It is important to realize this, because it is fundamental to Descartes's whole approach that deduction cannot *justify* anything. What it can do is display the systematic structure of knowledge to us, and this is its role in the *Principles*.

Again, there is something of an irony here, for the kind of misunderstanding of Descartes's methodological concerns which has resulted in the view that he makes deduction from first principles the source of all knowledge is rather similar to the kind of misunderstanding that Descartes himself fosters in the case of Aristotle on the one hand and the Alexandrian mathematicians on the other. In the case of Aristotle, he takes a method of presentation of results which have already been established to be a method of discovery. In the case of Pappus and Diophantus, he maintains that a method of presentation is passed off as a method of discovery. Yet both followers and critics of Descartes have said exactly the same of him; taking his method of presentation as if it were a method of discovery, they have often then complained that there is a discrepancy between what he claims his method is and the procedure he actually follows in his scientific work.[34]

This suggests that there may be something inherently problematic in the idea of a 'method of discovery'. If one compares the kind of presentation one finds in the *Geometry* with what one finds in the *Principles of Philosophy*, there is, on the face of it, much less evidence of anything one would call 'method' in the former than in the latter. Certain basic maxims are adhered to, and basic techniques developed, in the first few pages of the *Geometry*, but the former are really too rudimentary to be graced with the name of 'method', and the latter are specifically mathematical. In the very early days (from around 1619 to the early 1620s), when Descartes was contemplating his grand scheme of a 'universal mathematics', there was some prospect of a really general method of discovery, for universal mathematics was a programme in which, ultimately, everything was reduced to mathematics. But once this was (wisely) abandoned, and the mathematical rules were made specifically mathematical, the general content of the 'method' becomes rather empty. Here, for example, are the rules of method as they are set out in the *Discourse on Method:*

> The first was never to accept anything as true if I did not have evident knowledge of its truth: that is, carefully to avoid precipitate conclusions and preconceptions, and to include nothing more in my judgements than what presented itself to my mind so clearly and so distinctly that I had no occasion to doubt it. The second, to divide each of the difficulties I examined into as many parts as possible and as may be required in order to resolve them better. The third, to direct my thoughts in an orderly manner, by beginning with the simplest and most easily known objects in order to ascend little by little, step by step, to knowledge of the most complex, and by supposing some order even among objects that have no natural order of precedence.[35]

There is surely little that is radical or even novel here, and the list is more in the nature of common-sense hints rather than something offering deep enlightenment (unless it is specifically interpreted as a somewhat cryptic statement of an algebraic approach to mathematics, in which case it is novel, but it then becomes very restricted in scope and can no longer have any claim to be a general statement of 'method'). The same could be said of Aristotle's 'topics': they too offer no systematic method of discovery, and certainly nothing that would guarantee success in a scientific enterprise, but rather general and open-ended guidance. But 'methods of discovery' do not perform even this modest role unaided.

It is interesting in this respect that, in this passage as in others, Descartes finds it so difficult to present his 'method of discovery' without at the same time mentioning features appropriate to his method of presentation. The reason for this lies in the deep connections between the two enterprises, connections which Descartes seems reluctant to investigate. While it is legitimate to present the deductive structure of the *Principles of Philosophy* as a method of presentation as opposed to a method of discovery, it must be appreciated that the structure exhibited in, or perhaps revealed by, the method of presentation is a structure that will inevitably guide one in one's research. It will not enable one to solve specific problems, but it will indicate where the problems lie, so to speak, and which are the important ones to solve: which are the fundamental ones and which the peripheral ones. Leibniz was to realize this much more clearly than Descartes ever did, arguing that we use deductive structure to impose order on information, and by using the order discerned we are able to identify gaps and problematic areas in a systematic and thorough way.[36] Failure to appreciate this crucial feature of deductive structure will inevitably result in a misleading picture in which the empirical results are established first and then, when this is done, incorporated into a system whose only role is the ordering of these results. But such a procedure would result in problem-solving of a completely unsystematic and aimless kind, and this is certainly not what Descartes is advocating. The method of presentation does, then, have a role in discovery: it complements discovery procedures by guiding their application. The extent to which Descartes explicitly recognizes this role is problematic, but there can be no doubt that his account of method presupposes it.

THE FUNDAMENTAL PROBLEM OF METHOD: EPISTEMIC ADVANCE

The heart of the philosophical problem of method in Descartes lies not in reconciling his general statements on method with his more specific recommendations on how to proceed in scientific investigation, or in clarifying the relation between his 'method of discovery' and his 'method of presentation', but in an altogether deeper and more intractable question about how inference can be informative. Inference is necessarily involved in every kind of scientific enterprise, from logic and mathematics to natural philosophy, and the whole point of these enterprises is to produce new knowledge, but the canonical form of inference, for Descartes and all his predecessors, is deductive inference, and it is a highly problematic question whether deductive inference can advance knowledge.

The question became highlighted in the sixteenth century when there was intense discussion of the Aristotelian distinction between knowledge how and knowledge why, and the ways in which the latter could be achieved. Turnebus,[37] writing in 1565, tells us that the (Aristotelian) question of method was the most discussed philosophical topic of the day. These debates were conducted in the context of the theory of the syllogism, and although, with the demise of syllogistic, the explicitly logical context is missing from seventeenth-century discussions of method, there is always an undercurrent of logical questions. Descartes raises the question of method in the context of considerations about the nature of inference in the following way in Rule 4 of the *Rules*:

> But if our method rightly explains how intellectual intuition should be used, so as not to fall into error contrary to truth, and how one must find deductive paths so that we might arrive at knowledge of all things, I cannot see anything else is needed to make it complete; for I have already said that the only way science is to be acquired is by intellectual intuition or deduction.[38]

Intellectual intuition is simply the grasp of a clear and distinct idea. But what is deduction? In Rule 7 it is described in a way which makes one suspect that it is not necessary in its own right:

> Thus, if, for example, I have found out, by distinct mental operations, what relation exists between magnitudes *A* and *B*, then what between *B* and *C*, between *C* and *D*, and finally between *D* and *E*, that does not entail that I will see what the relation is between *A* and *E*, nor can the truths previously learned give me a precise idea of it unless I recall them all. To remedy this I would run over them many times, by a continuous movement of the imagination, in such a way that it has an intuition of each term at the same time that it passes on to the others, and this I would do until I have learned to pass from the first relation to the last so quickly that there was almost no role left for memory and I seemed to have the whole before me at the same time.[39]

This suspicion is confirmed in Rule 14:

> In every train of reasoning it is merely by comparison that we attain to a precise knowledge of the truth. Here is an example: all *A* is *B*, all *B* is *C*, therefore all *A* is *C*. Here we compare with one another what we are searching for and what we are given, viz. *A* and *C*, in respect of the fact that each is *B*, and so on. But, as we have pointed out on a number of occasions, because the forms of the syllogism are of no aid in perceiving the truth about things, it will be better for the reader to reject them altogether and to conceive that all knowledge whatsoever, other than that which consists in the simple and pure intuition of single independent objects, is a matter of the comparison of two things or more with each other. In fact practically the whole task set the human reason consists in preparing for this operation; for when it is open and simple, we need no aid

from art, but are bound to rely upon the light of nature alone, in beholding the truth which comparison gives us.[40]

The difference between intuition and deduction lies in the fact that whereas the latter consists in grasping the relations between a number of propositions, intuition consists in grasping a necessary connection between two propositions. But in the limiting case, deduction reduces to intuition: we run through the deduction so quickly that we no longer have to rely on memory, with the result that we grasp the whole in a single intuition at a single time. The core of Descartes's position is that by compacting inferential steps until we come to a direct comparison between premises and conclusion we put ourselves in a position where we are able to have a clear and distinct idea of the connection, and this provides us with a guarantee of certainty.

What is at issue here is the question of the justification of deduction, but we must be careful to separate out two different kinds of demand for justification. The first is a demand that deductive inference show itself to be productive of new knowledge, that it result in epistemic advance. The second is a question about whether deductive inference can be further analysed or explained: it is a question about the justification of deduction, but not one which refers us to its epistemic worth for, as Dummett has rightly pointed out, our aim 'is not to persuade anyone, not even ourselves, to employ deductive arguments: it is to find a satisfactory explanation for the role of such arguments in our use of language.'[41] Now these two kinds of question were not always clearly distinguished in Descartes's time, and it was a prevalent assumption in the seventeenth century that syllogistic, in both its logical and its heuristic aspects, could be justified if and only if it could show its epistemic worth. But the basis for the distinction was certainly there, and while the questions are related in Descartes, we can find sets of considerations much more relevant to the one than the other.

The first question, that of epistemic informativeness, concerns the use of formalized deductive arguments, especially the syllogism, in the discovery of new results in natural philosophy. Earlier, we looked very briefly at how Aristotle tried to deal with this question, by distinguishing two different forms of syllogism, one scientific because it provided us with knowledge why something was the case, the other non-scientific because it only provided us with knowledge that something was the case. The logicians of antiquity were crucially concerned with the epistemic informativeness of various kinds of deductive argument, and both Aristotle and the Stoics (founders of the two logical systems of Antiquity) realized that there may be no logical or formal difference between an informative and an uninformative argument, so they tried to capture the difference in non-logical terms, but in a way which still relied on structural features of arguments, for example the way in which the premises were arranged. All these attempts failed, and the question of whether deductive arguments can be informative, and if so what makes them informative, remained unresolved.

The prevalent seventeenth-century response to this failure was to argue that deductive arguments can never be epistemically informative. Many critics of logic right up to the nineteenth century criticized syllogistic arguments for failing to yield anything new, where what is meant by 'new' effectively amounts to 'logically independent of the premises'. But of course a deductive argument is precisely designed to show the logical dependence of the conclusion on premises, and so the demand is simply misguided. Descartes's response is rather different. It consists in the idea that the deduction of scientific results, whether in mathematics or in natural philosophy, does not genuinely produce those results. Deduction is merely a mode of presentation of results which have already been reached by analytic, problem-solving means. This is hard to reconcile, however, with, say, our learning of some geometrical theorem by following through the proof from first principles in a textbook. Even if Descartes could show that one can never come to know new theorems in the sense of inventing them by going through some deductive process, this does not mean that one could not come to know them, in the sense of learning something one did not previously know, by deductive means. Indeed, it is hard to understand what the point of the *Principles* could be if Descartes denied the latter. But in that case his argument against deduction as a means of discovery is a much more restricted one than he appears to think. Moreover, I have already indicated that deduction seems to play a guiding role in discovery, in the sense of invention or 'genuine' discovery, in Descartes, because his procedures for problem-solving are quite blind as far as the ultimate point of the exercise is concerned. Finally, the way in which he sets up the argument in the first place is somewhat question-begging. We are presented with two alternatives: using his 'method', or deduction from first principles. But someone who has a commitment to the value of deductive inference in discovery, as Leibniz was to have, will not necessarily want to tie this to demonstration purely from first principles: Leibniz's view was that deduction only comes into use as a means of discovery once one has a very substantial body of information (discovered by non-deductive means). This is a possibility that Descartes simply does not account for.

On the second question, Descartes's view is expressed admirably in Rule 4 of the *Rules for the Direction of Our Native Intelligence*, when he says that 'nothing can be added to the pure light of reason which does not in some way obscure it.' Intuition, and the deductive inference that must ultimately reduce to a form of intuition, is unanalysable, simple and primitive. Like the *cogito*, which is the canonical example of an intuition, no further question can be raised about it, whether in justification or explanation. This raises distinctive problems for any treatment of the nature of deduction. It is interesting to note here the wide gulf between Aristotle's classic account of the justification of deductive principles and Descartes's approach. In the *Metaphysics*, Aristotle points out that proofs must come to an end somewhere, for otherwise we would be involved in an infinite regress. Hence there must be something that we can rely on without proof, and he takes as his example the law of non-contradiction. The law is justified by showing that an opponent who denies it must, in denying it, actually assume its truth, and by showing that arguments that apparently tell against it, such as relativist arguments purporting to show that a thing may both have and not have a particular property depending on who is perceiving the thing, cannot be sustained. Descartes can offer nothing so compelling. It is something ambiguously psychological – the 'light of reason' or the 'light of nature' – that stops the regress on Descartes's conception. Whereas Aristotle was concerned, in his justification, to find a form of argument which was irresistible to an opponent, all Descartes can do is postulate some form of psychological clarity experienced by the knowing subject. Nevertheless, it was Descartes's conception that held sway, being adopted in two extremely influential works of the later seventeenth century: Arnauld and Nicole's *Port-Royal Logic*, and Locke's *Essay Concerning Human Understanding*.[42] The reason for this is not hard to find. The Aristotelian procedure relies upon a discursive conception of inference, whereby one induces an opponent to accept what one is arguing on the basis of accepting certain shared premises: such a mode of argument works both at the ordinary level of convincing someone of some factual matter, and at the metalevel of justifying the deductive principles used to take one from premises to conclusion. But as I indicated earlier, the discursive conception was generally discredited in the seventeenth century. It requires common ground between oneself and one's opponents, and Descartes and others saw such common ground as the root of the problem of lack of scientific progress within the scholastic-Aristotelian tradition. It was seen to rest on an appeal to what is generally accepted rather than to what is the case. The 'natural light of reason', on the other hand, provided internal resources by which to begin afresh and reject tradition.

The acceptance of this view had disastrous consequences for the study of deductive logic. Descartes's algebra contained the key to a new understanding of logic. Just as Descartes had insisted that, in mathematics, one must abstract from particular numbers and focus on the structural features of equations, so analogously one could argue that one should abstract from particular truths and explore the relation between them in abstract terms. Such a move would have been tantamount to the algebraic construal of logic, something which is constitutive of modern logic. But Descartes did not even contemplate such a move, not because of the level of abstraction involved, which would not have worried him if his work in mathematics is any guide, but because he was unable to see any point in deductive inference.

❧ CONCLUSION ❧

Descartes's approach to philosophical questions of method was extremely influential from the seventeenth to the nineteenth centuries, and it replaced Aristotelianism very quickly. It was part of a general anti-deductivist movement, whether this took the form of a defence of hypotheses (in the seventeenth century) or of induction (in the eighteenth and nineteenth centuries). This influence was transmitted indirectly through Locke, however, and with the interpretation of seventeenth- and eighteenth-century philosophy in terms of two opposed schools of thought, rationalism and empiricism, this aspect of Descartes's thought tended to become forgotten, and his more programmatic statements about his system were taken out of context and an apriorist and deductivist methodology ascribed to him. The irony in this is that Descartes not only vehemently rejected such an approach, but his rejection goes too far. It effectively rules out deduction having any epistemic value, and this is something he not only could not establish but which, if true, would have completely undermined his own *Principles of Philosophy*. But this is not a simple oversight on Descartes's part. It reflects a serious and especially intractable problem, or rather set of problems, about how deductive inference can be informative, which Descartes was never able to resolve and which had deep ramifications for his account of method.

❧ NOTES ❧

1 This is, at least, the usual view. For a dissenting view see G. Canguilhem, *La formation du concept de réflexe au XVIIe et XVIIIe siècles* (Paris, Presses Universitaires de France, 1955), pp. 27–57.

2 Cottingham [5.10], 30.

3 On the issue of rationalism versus empiricism see Louis E. Loeb, *From Descartes to Hume: Continental Metaphysics and the Development of Modern Philosophy* (Ithaca, N.Y., Cornell University Press, 1981), ch. 1.

4 [5.1], vol. 8 (1), 78–9.

5 See L. Laudan, *Science and Hypothesis* (Dordrecht, Reidel, 1981), ch. 4.

6 Rule 10, [5.1], vol. 10, 406.

7 [5.1], vol. 10, 376–7.

8 See Jonathan Barnes, 'Aristotle's Theory of Demonstration', in J. Barnes, M. Schofield, and R. Sorabji (eds) *Articles on Aristotle*, vol. 1, *Science* (London, Duckworth, 1975), pp. 65–87.

9 There is one occasion on which Descartes does in fact make use of a form of argument with a distinctively discursive structure: in his treatment of scepticism. Sceptical arguments have a distinctive non-logical but nevertheless structural feature. They rely upon the interlocutor of the sceptic to provide both the knowledge claims and the definition of knowledge (i.e. the premises of the argument). The sceptic then attempts to show a discrepancy between these two. Were the sceptic to provide the definition of knowledge, or to provide knowledge claims or denials that certain things are known, the ingenious dialectical structure of sceptical arguments would be undermined. This is a very traditional feature of sceptical arguments, and it is a sign of Descartes's ability to handle it that he not only uses it to undermine knowledge claims in the *First Meditation*, but he also uses it to destroy scepticism in making the sceptic provide the premise of the *cogito*, by putting it in the form 'I doubt, therefore I exist'. In other words he is able to turn the tables on the sceptic by using the same form of argument that makes scepticism so successful. But, of course, once he has arrived at his foundation, he shuns this form of argument, for now he has premises he can be certain of and so he no longer has any need to use forms of argument which demand shared (but possibly false) premises.

10 It should be noted that 'method' was a central topic in the sixteenth century, but the focus of the sixteenth-century discussion is different, and it derives from Aristotle's distinction between scientific and non-scientific demonstration. On the sixteenth-century disputes, see Neal W. Gilbert, *Renaissance Concepts of Method* (New York, Columbia University Press, 1960).

11 For more detail on the problems of defining mechanism, see J. E. McGuire, 'Boyle's Conception of Nature', *Journal of the History of Ideas* 33 (1972) 523–42; and Alan Gabbey, 'The Mechanical Philosophy and its Problems: Mechanical Explanations, Impenetrability, and Perpetual Motion', in J. C. Pitt (ed.) *Change and Progress in Modern Science* (Dordrecht, Reidel, 1985), pp. 9–84.

12 See K. Hutchison, 'Supernaturalism and the Mechanical Philosophy', *History of Science* 21 (1983) 297–333.

13 See D. P. Walker, *Spiritual and Demonic Magic from Ficino to Campanella* (London, the Warburg Institute, 1958).

14 Marin Mersenne (1588–1648) was one of the foremost advocates of mechanism, and as well as writing extensively on a number of topics in natural philosophy and theology he played a major role in co-ordinating and making known current work in natural philosophy from the mid–1620s onwards. He attended the same school as Descartes but their friendship, which was to be a lifelong one, began only in the mid–1620s, during Descartes's stay in Paris.

15 Averroes (c. 1126–c. 1198), the greatest of the medieval Islamic philosophers, developed what was to become the principal form of naturalism in the later Middle Ages and Renaissance. The naturalism of Alexander of Aphrodisias (fl.

AD 200), the greatest of the Greek commentators on Aristotle, does not seem to have been taken seriously until the Paduan philosopher Pietro Pomponazzi (1462–1525) took it up, and even then it was never explicitly advocated as a doctrine that presents the whole truth. On the Paduan debates over the nature of the soul see Harold Skulsky, 'Paduan Epistemology and the Doctrine of One Mind', *Journal of the History of Philosophy* 6 (1968) 341–61.

16 See Robert Lenoble, *Mersenne ou la naissance de mécanisme* (Paris, Vrin, 2nd edn, 1971).

17 On this question see M. Gueroult, 'The Metaphysics and Physics of Force in Descartes', and A. Gabbey, 'Force and Inertia in the Seventeenth Century: Descartes and Newton', both in [5.27], 196–229 and 230–320 respectively.

18 See, for example, his reply to Henry More's objection that modes are not alienable in [5.1], vol. 5, 403–4.

19 [5.1], vol. 7, 108; [5.5], vol. 2, 78.

20 See Wahl [5.73].

21 For details of this issue see Stephen Gaukroger, *Explanatory Structures: Concepts of Explanation in Early Physics and Philosophy* (Brighton, Harvester, 1978), ch. 6.

22 For details see Jean-Paul Weber, *La Constitution du texte des Regulae* (Paris, 1964).

23 [5.1], vol. 10, 377–8; [5.5], vol. 1, 19.

24 See John Schuster, 'Descartes' *Mathesis Universalis* 1619–28', in [5.27], 41–96.

25 [5.1], vol. 6, 63–5.

26 [5.1], vol. 1, 559–60.

27 [5.1], vol. 5, 325.

28 [5.1], vol. 6, 326–7.

29 [5.1], vol. 6, 336.

30 See the discussion in Beck [5.39], 176ff.

31 Rule 4, [5.1], vol. 10, 276–7; [5.1], vol. 5, 19.

32 [5.1], vol. 10, 455–6, 458.

33 On the authors whom Descartes would have studied at his college, La Flèche, see Gilson [5.20]. On the textbook tradition more generally, see Patricia Reif, 'The Textbook Tradition in Natural Philosophy, 1600–1650', *Journal of the History of Ideas* 30 (1969) 17–32.

34 It is rare to find anyone who not only takes the deductive approach at face value and also believes it is viable, but there is at least one notable example of such an interpretation, namely Spinoza's *Principles of the Philosophy of René Descartes* (1663).

35 [5.1], vol. 6, 18–19; [5.5], vol. 1, 120.

36 See, for example, Leibniz's letter to Gabriel Wagner of 1696, in C. I. Gerhardt (ed.) *Die philosophischen Schriften von Gottfried Wilhelm Leibniz* (Berlin, Weidman, 1875–90), vol. 7, 514–27, especially Comment 3 on p. 523. The letter is translated in L. E. Loemker, *Gottfried Wilhelm Leibniz: Philosophical Papers and Letters* (Dordrecht, Reidel, 1969), pp. 462–71, with Comment 3 on p. 468.

37 Adrianus Turnebus (1512–65) was Royal Reader in Greek at the Collège de France. He was one of the leading humanist translators of his day, and had an extensive knowledge of Greek philosophy.

38 [5.1], vol. 10, 372; [5.5], vol. 1, 16.

39 [5.1], vol. 10, 387–8; [5.5], vol. 1, 25.

40 [5.1], vol. 10, 439–40; [5.5], vol. 1, 57.

41 M. Dummett, 'The Justification of Deduction', in his *Truth and Other Enigmas* (London, Duckworth, 1978), p. 296.

42 On this influence see, specifically in the case of Locke, J. Passmore, 'Descartes, the British Empiricists and Formal Logic', *Philosophical Review* 62 (1953), 545–53; and more generally, W. S. Howell, *Eighteenth-Century British Logic and Rhetoric* (Princeton, N.J., Princeton University Press, 1971).

❧ BIBLIOGRAPHY ❧

Original language editions

5.1 Adam, C. and Tannery, P. (eds) *Oeuvres de Descartes*, Paris, Vrin, 12 vols, 1974–86.

5.2 Alquié, F. *Oeuvres Philosophiques*, Paris, Garnier, 3 vols, 1963–73.

5.3 Crapulli, G. (ed.) *Descartes: Regulae ad directionem ingenii, Texte critique établi par Giovanni Crapulli, avec la version hollandaise du XVIIème siècle*, The Hague, Nijhoff, 1966.

5.4 Gilson, E. *Descartes: Discours de la méthode, texte et commentaire*, Paris, Vrin, 2nd edn, 1930.

English translations

Selected works

5.5 *The Philosophical Writings of Descartes*, trans. J. Cottingham, R. Stoothoff and D. Murdoch, Cambridge, Cambridge University Press, 2 vols, 1984–5.

Separate works (not included in full in 5.5)

5.6 *René Descartes: Le Monde ou Traité de la lumière*, trans. M. S. Mahoney, New York, Abaris Books, 1979.

5.7 *Descartes: Treatise on Man*, trans. T. S. Hall, Cambridge, Mass., Harvard University Press, 1972.

5.8 *Descartes: Discourse on Method, Optics, Geometry and Meteorology*, trans. P. J. Olscamp, Indianapolis, Ind., Bobbs-Merrill, 1965.

5.9 *René Descartes: Principles of Philosophy*, trans. with explanatory notes by V. R. Miller and R. P. Miller, Dordrecht, Reidel, 1983.

5.10 *Descartes' Conversation with Burman*, trans. with introduction and commentary by J. Cottingham, Oxford, Clarendon, 1976.

5.11 *Descartes: Philosophical Letters*, ed. and trans. A. Kenny, Oxford, Blackwell, 1981.

5.12 *Descartes: His Moral Philosophy and Psychology*, trans. and introduction by J. J. Blom, Brighton, Harvester, 1978.

In general, the translations of passages from Descartes are my own, although in a few cases I have followed the standard English versions.

Bibliographies

5.13 Chappell, V. and Doney, W. *Twenty-five Years of Descartes Scholarship, 1960–1984*, New York, Garland, 1987.

5.14 Sebba, G. *Bibliographia cartesiana: A Critical Guide to the Descartes Literature, 1800–1960*, The Hague, Nijhoff, 1964.

Biographies

5.15 Adam, C. *Vie et oeuvres de Descartes: Étude historique*, Paris, Léopold Cerf, 1910.

5.16 Baillet, A. *La vie de Monsieur Des-Cartes*, Paris, Daniel Horthemels, 2 vols, 1691; reprinted in 1 vol., Geneva, Slatkine Reprints, 1970.

5.17 Vrooman, J. R. *René Descartes: A Biography*, New York, G. P. Putnam's Sons, 1970.

Influences on Descartes

5.18 Gilson, E. *Etudes sur le rôle de la pensée médiévale dans la formation du système cartésien*, Paris, Vrin, 2nd edn, 1930.

5.19 Gilson, E. *Index scolastico-cartésien*, Paris, Alcan, 1913.

5.20 Gilson, E. *La liberté chez Descartes et la théologie*, Paris, Alcan, 1913.

5.21 Marion, J.-L. *Sur la théologie blanche de Descartes*, Paris, Presses Universitaires de France, 1981.

5.22 Popkin, R. H. *The History of Scepticism from Erasmus to Spinoza*, Berkeley, Calif., University of California Press, 1979.

5.23 Risse, W. 'Zur Vorgeschichte der cartesischen Methodenlehre', *Archiv für Geschichte der Philosophie* 45 (1963) 270–91.

The philosophy of Descartes: general surveys and collections

5.24 Caton, H. *The Origin of Subjectivity: An Essay on Descartes*, New Haven, Conn., Yale University Press, 1973.

5.25 Cottingham, J. *Descartes*, Oxford, Blackwell, 1986.

5.26 Doney, W. (ed.) *Descartes: A Collection of Critical Essays*, London, Macmillan, 1967.

5.27 Gaukroger, S. (ed.) *Descartes: Philosophy, Mathematics and Physics*, Brighton, Harvester, and New Jersey, Barnes & Noble, 1980.

5.28 Grene, M. *Descartes*, Brighton, Harvester, 1985.

5.29 Grimaldi, N. and Marion, J.-L. (eds) *Le Discours et sa méthode*, Paris, Presses Universitaires de France, 1987.

5.30 Hooker, M. (ed.) *Descartes: Critical and Interpretive Essays*, Baltimore, Md., Johns Hopkins University Press, 1978.

5.31 Laport, J. *Le rationalisme de Descartes*, Paris, Presses Universitaires de France, 1945.

5.32 Röd, W. *Descartes: Die innere Genesis des cartesianischen Systems*, Munich, Reinhardt, 1964.

5.33 Rodis-Lewis, G. *L'Oeuvre de Descartes*, Paris, Vrin, 2 vols, 1971.

5.34 Rorty, A. O. (ed.) *Essays on Descartes' Meditations*, Berkeley, Calif., University of California Press, 1986.

5.35 Smith, N. K. *Studies in Cartesian Philosophy*, London, Macmillan, 1902.

5.36 Smith, N. K. *New Studies in the Philosophy of Descartes*, London, Macmillan, 1952.

5.37 Williams, B. *Descartes*, Brighton, Harvester, 1978.

5.38 Wilson, M. D. *Descartes*, London, Routledge, 1978.

Methodology

5.39 Beck, L. J. *The Method of Descartes: A study of the* Regulae, Oxford: Clarendon, 1952.

5.40 Blake, R. M. 'The Role of Experience in Descartes' Theory of Method', in R. M. Blake, C. J. Ducasse and E. H. Madden (eds) *Theories of Scientific Method*, Seattle, Wash., University of Washington Press, 1960, 75–103.

5.41 Buchdahl, G. *Metaphysics and the Philosophy of Science: The Classical Origins, Descartes to Kant*, Oxford, Blackwell, 1969, ch. 3.

5.42 Clarke, D. M. *Descartes' Philosophy of Science*, Manchester, Manchester University Press, 1982.

5.43 Crombie, A. C. 'Some Aspects of Descartes' Attitude to Hypothesis and Experiment', *Collection des travaux de l'Académie internationale d'histoire des sciences*, Florence, Bruschi, 1960, 192–201.

5.44 Denissoff, E. *Descartes, premier théoricien de la physique mathématique*, Louvain, Bibliothèque de Louvain, 1970.

5.45 Gaukroger, S. *Cartesian Logic: An Essay on Descartes's Conception of Inference*, Oxford, Clarendon, 1989.

5.46 Lachterman, D. R. 'Objectum Purae Matheseos: Mathematical Construction and the Passage from Essence to Existence', in A. K. Rorty (ed.) *Essays on Descartes' Meditations*, Berkeley, Calif., University of California Press, 1986, 435–58.

5.47 Marion, J.-L. *Sur l'ontologie grise de Descartes*, Paris, Vrin, 2nd edn, 1981.

5.48 Schouls, P. A. *The Imposition of Method: A Study of Descartes and Locke*, Oxford, Clarendon, 1980.

5.49 Schuster, J. A. 'Descartes' *Mathesis Universalis*, 1619–28', in S. Gaukroger (ed.) *Descartes: Philosophy, Mathematics and Physics*, Brighton, Harvester, and New Jersey, Barnes & Noble, 1980, 41–96.

5.50 Tournadre, G. *L'Orientation de la Science Cartésienne*, Paris, Vrin, 1982.

Scientific writings

5.51 Aiton, E. J. *The Vortex Theory of Planetary Motions*, London, MacDonald, 1972, ch. 3.

5.52 Blackwell, R. J. 'Descartes' Laws of Motion', *Isis* 57 (1966) 220–34.

5.53 Boutroux, P. *L'Imagination et les mathématiques selon Descartes*, Paris, Alcan, 1900.

5.54 Burke, J. S. 'Descartes on the Refraction and the Velocity of Light', *American Journal of Physics* 34 (1966) 390–400.

5.55 Burtt, E. A. *The Metaphysical Foundations of Modern Physical Science*, London, Routledge & Kegan Paul, 2nd edn, 1932, ch. 4.

5.56 Carter, R. B. *Descartes' Medical Philosophy: The Organic Solution to the Mind-Body Problem*, Baltimore, Md., Johns Hopkins University Press, 1983.

5.57 Clarke, D. 'The Impact Rules of Descartes' Physics', *Isis* 68 (1977) 55–66.

5.58 Costabel, P. *Démarches originales de Descartes savant*, Paris, Vrin, 1982.

5.59 Dijksterhuis, E. J. *The Mechanization of the World Picture*, Oxford, Clarendon, 1961, Part IIIE.

5.60 Gabbey, A. 'Force and Inertia in the Seventeenth Century: Descartes and Newton', in S. Gaukroger (ed.) *Descartes: Philosophy, Mathematics and Physics*, Brighton, Harvester, and New Jersey, Barnes & Noble, 1980, 230–320.

5.61 Graves, J. C. *The Conceptual Foundations of Contemporary Relativity Theory*, Cambridge, Mass., MIT Press, 1971, ch. 6.

5.62 Gueroult, M. 'The Metaphysics and Physics of Force in Descartes', in S. Gaukroger (ed.) *Descartes, Philosophy, Mathematics and Physics*, Brighton, Harvester, and New Jersey, Barnes & Noble, 1980, 196–230.

5.63 Hall, T. S. 'Descartes' Physiological Method', *Journal of the History of Biology* 3 (1970) 53–79.

5.64 Hoenen, P. H. J. 'Descartes' Mechanism', in W. Doney (ed.) *Descartes: A Collection of Critical Essays*, London, Macmillan, 1967, 353–68.

5.65 Koyré, A. *Galileo Studies*, trans. J. Mepham, Brighton, Harvester, 1978, Part II.

5.66 Koyré, A. 'Newton and Descartes', in his *Newtonian Studies*, London, Chapman and Hall, 1965, 53–114.

5.67 Milhaud, G. *Descartes Savant*, Paris, Alcan, 1921.

5.68 Sabra, A. I. *Theories of Light from Descartes to Newton*, Cambridge, Cambridge University Press, 2nd edn, 1981, chs 1–4.

5.69 Scott, J. F. *The Scientific Work of René Descartes (1596–1650)*, London, Taylor & Francis, 1976.

5.70 Suppes, P. 'Descartes and the Problem of Action at a Distance', *Journal of the History of Ideas* 15 (1954) 146–52.

5.71 Taliaferro, T. C. *The Concept of Matter in Descartes and Leibniz*, Notre Dame Mathematical Lectures no. 9, Notre Dame, Ind., Notre Dame University Press, 1964.

5.72 Vuillemin, J. *Mathématiques et métaphysique chez Descartes*, Paris, Presses Universitaires de France, 1960.

5.73 Wahl, J. *Du rôle de l'idée de l'instant dans la philosophie de Descartes*, Paris, Vrin, 1953.

CHAPTER 6

Descartes: metaphysics and the philosophy of mind
John Cottingham

❦

THE CARTESIAN PROJECT

Descartes is rightly regarded as one of the inaugurators of the modern age, and there is no doubt that his thought profoundly altered the course of Western philosophy. In no area has this influence been more pervasive than in metaphysics and the philosophy of mind. But Descartes himself would perhaps have been surprised to learn that these aspects of his work were to be singled out by subsequent generations for special attention. For his own conception of philosophy, and of the philosophical enterprise he was engaged on, was enormously wide ranging; so far from being confined to 'philosophy' in the modern academic sense of that term, it had to do principally with what we should now call 'science'. Descartes attempted, in his writings on cosmology, astronomy and physics, to develop a general theory of the origins and structure of the universe and the nature of matter, and he also did a considerable amount of detailed work in more specialized areas such as optics, meteorology, physiology, anatomy and medicine. In all these fields, Descartes aimed for explanatory economy; his goal was to derive all his results from a small number of principles of great simplicity and clarity, and he took mathematics as a model for the precise and unified structure of knowledge which he was seeking.

Descartes's ambition, however, was not just to produce a clear, precise and unified system of scientific explanations. He insisted that nothing could count as genuine *scientia*, as true knowledge, if it contained any hidden assumptions or presuppositions which had not been thoroughly scrutinized. As a schoolboy, he received a thorough training in philosophy and theology from the Jesuits at the College of La Flèche, but he later observed wryly that although the school had the reputation of being 'one of the best in Europe' he found that the philosophy he was taught, 'despite being cultivated for many centuries by the most excellent minds', contained not a single point that was not 'disputed and hence doubtful'.[1] Although Descartes clearly believed that the scientific work he pursued as a young man was free from this sort of uncertainty,[2] there remained the possibility that some unexamined premise – some 'preconceived opinion'[3] – was infecting the whole system. Complete certainty could be attained only by 'demolishing everything completely and starting again right from the foundations'.[4] It is this 'foundational' project that forms the core of Cartesian metaphysics.

In addition to his celebrated architectural metaphor of demolishing and rebuilding, Descartes also made use of an organic simile to explain the importance of metaphysics: 'The whole of philosophy is like a tree: the roots are metaphysics, the trunk is physics and the branches emerging from the trunk are all the other sciences.'[5] The simile is sometimes interpreted to mean that metaphysics is, for Descartes, the most important part of philosophy; but this is in some respects misleading. Descartes himself goes on to observe that 'it is not the roots or the trunk of a tree from which one gathers fruit, but only the branches', and he evidently saw the principal goal of his system as that of yielding practical benefits for mankind: in place of the 'speculative philosophy taught in the schools' he aimed to develop a 'practical philosophy' which would be 'useful in life' and ultimately make us 'lords and masters of nature'.[6] Metaphysics was in this sense a means to an end, for Descartes, rather than an end in itself; he had no patience with abstract speculation for its own sake, and frequently told questioners and correspondents not to become bogged down in metaphysical inquiries.[7] Nevertheless, Descartes believed that at least once in a lifetime (*semel in vita*)[8] anyone pretending to construct a reliable system of knowledge would have to engage in metaphysical inquiries: without such inquiries, there could be no guarantee of the stability of the rest of the system. Indeed (and the tree simile is again illuminating here), Descartes regarded the whole of human knowledge as a quasi-organic unity: in place of the scholastic conception of knowledge (ultimately derived from Aristotle) as an amalgam of separate disciplines, each with its own standards of precision and methods of inquiry, Descartes (reverting to an older Platonic idea) saw all truths as essentially interconnected. We need to grasp, he wrote in an early notebook, that all the sciences are 'linked together' like a series of numbers;[9] later he developed the idea further: 'those long chains of very simple and easy reasonings which geometers customarily use to arrive at their most difficult demonstrations gave me occasion to suppose that all the items which fall within the scope of human knowledge are interconnected in the same way.'[10] Cartesian metaphysics attempts to start from scratch and establish, once and for all, the philosophical basis for these inter-connections, aiming thereby to provide a kind of validation for the system as a whole.

❧ THE SIMPLE NATURES ❧

From some standard accounts of Descartes's life one might get the impression that as a young man he was predominantly concerned with mathematical and scientific issues, and that his metaphysical interests came later. It is certainly true that mathematics was a major preoccu-pation of the young Descartes. Many of the results later incorporated in his *Geometry*[11] were worked out during the 1620s, and we know from his letters that a great inspiration during his early years was the Dutch mathematician Isaac Beeckman, whom he met in Holland in 1618. Beeckman seems to have played for Descartes something of the role which Hume was later to play for Kant – waking him from his dogmatic slumbers: 'you alone roused me from my state of indolence' wrote Descartes to Beeckman on 23 April 1619 'and reawakened the learning that by then had almost disappeared from my mind'.[12] One of the chief points to strike Descartes was that mathematics could attain complete clarity and precision in its arguments, and that the demonstrations it employed were completely certain: no room was allowed for merely probabilistic reasoning.[13] The mathematical model continued to influence his scientific work throughout the following decade,[14] leading up to the composition of his treatise on physics and cosmology, *Le Monde*, which announced, at any rate in outline, a comprehensive programme for the elimination of qualitative descrip-tions from science in favour of exact quantitative analysis.[15]

Even in this early period, however, Descartes's interests were never *purely* scientific (in the restricted modern sense): right from the start he seems to have been concerned with how the results achieved in mathematics and physics were to be related to more fundamental issues about the nature and basis of human knowledge. In his *Regulae ad directionem ingenii* ('Rules for the Direction of our Native Intelli-gence', written in Latin in the late 1620s but not published during his lifetime), Descartes makes it clear that his interest in subjects like geometry and arithmetic derives in large part from the fact that they are merely examples of a more general procedure of potentially universal application:

I came to see that the exclusive concern of mathematics is with questions of order or measure, and that it is irrelevant whether the measure in question involves numbers, shapes, stars, sounds or any other object whatever. This made me realize that there must be a general science which explains all the points that can be raised concerning order and measure, irrespective of the subject-matter, and that this science deserves to be called *mathesis universalis*.[16]

It is important to note that the 'universal discipline' described here does not merely encompass quantitative subject matter. Descartes believes that there is a formal structure which all valid systems of knowledge manifest, and that this structure consists essentially in a hierarchical ordering: the objects of knowledge are to be arranged in such a way that we can concentrate to begin with on the items which are 'simplest and easiest to know', only afterwards proceeding to the more complex truths which are derived from these basic starting-points.[17] The human intellect, Descartes goes on to explain, has the power to 'intuit' these 'simple natures' or fundamental starting-points for human knowledge: it simply 'sees' them with a simple and direct mental perception which allows for no possibility of error, since the simple natures are 'all self-evident and never contain any falsity'.[18]

Some of the simple natures are 'purely material'; these include shape extension and motion (and will be the building-blocks of Cartesian quantitative science). But others, Descartes asserts, are 'purely intellectual', and are 'recognized by the intellect by a sort of natural light, without the aid of any corporeal image'; it is the intellectual simple natures which enable us, for example, to recognize 'what knowledge or doubt or ignorance is'.[19] Further, in addition to the intellectual simple natures, there are what Descartes calls the 'common' simple natures, which include the fundamental laws of logic (principles 'whose self-evidence is the basis for all the rational inferences we make').[20] Using the basic rules of inference, we can make necessary connections and so link the simple natures together to build up a body of reliable conclusions. Descartes, though in the *Regulae* he goes into no details of how such reasonings are conducted, provides some striking examples: 'if Socrates says that he doubts everything, it necessarily follows that he understands at least that he is doubting'; or again, 'I understand, therefore I have a mind distinct from a body'; or again (most striking of all), '*sum, ergo Deus est*' – 'I am, therefore God exists'.[21] These examples have an unmistakable resonance for anyone familiar with Descartes's mature metaphysics. The mind's awareness of its own activity and of its incorporeal nature, and the route from knowledge of self to knowledge of God, were to be the central themes of Descartes's metaphysical masterpiece – the *Meditations on First Philosophy* (1641). But already in the *Regulae* we find a recognition that these issues are an inescapable part of any well-ordered system of knowledge. The intellectual simple natures, together with the corporeal simple natures, comprise the two fundamental sets of building-blocks for human knowledge (and, to preserve the metaphor, the common simple natures, or logical rules of inference, are the cement which binds them together in the appropriate relations). 'The whole of human knowledge', Descartes resoundingly declares in Rule 12, 'consists uniquely in our achieving a distinct perception of how all these simple natures contribute to the composition of other things'.[22] The materials, then, are ready to hand, Descartes seems to be telling us in his early writings. The task of putting them together, of constructing a reliable edifice of knowledge, remains to be undertaken. But it is already clear that this will have to involve not just our mathematical intuitions about number and measure, but our introspective reflections on our own nature as conscious beings. Descartes claimed in his intellectual auto-biography in the *Discourse on the Method* (1637) that the task was one whose importance he realized in his early twenties. Although he postponed its implementation, he knew that sooner or later a metaphys-ical journey of self-scrutiny would have to be undertaken: *je pris un jour résolution d'étudier aussi en moi-même* – 'I resolved one day to pursue my studies within myself'.[23]

❧ FIRST PHILOSOPHY ❧

In using the term 'first philosophy' to describe his fundamental meta-physical inquiries Descartes meant to draw attention to the fact that he proposed to deal 'not just with questions about God and the soul but in general with all the first things to be discovered by philosophizing in an orderly manner'.[24] The discovery of reliable first principles is effected by a characteristic technique which has come to be known as the 'method of doubt'. Descartes (though he was accused of being one[25]) is certainly no sceptic; he uses doubt purely as a means to an end, to demolish unreliable 'preconceived opinions' and clear away the result-ing rubble in order to establish a bedrock of certainty. The strategy is sketched out in Part Four of the *Discourse on the Method*, and developed fully in the First Meditation; its point is neatly summarized in the Synopsis which Descartes had printed with the first edition of the *Meditations*:

> Reasons are provided which give us possible grounds for doubt about all things, especially material things, so long as we have no foundations for the sciences other than those which we have had up till now. Although the usefulness of such extensive

doubt is not apparent at first sight, its greatest benefit lies in freeing us from all our preconceived opinions, and providing the easiest route by which the mind may be led away from the senses. The eventual result of this doubt is to make it impossible for us to have any further doubts about what we subsequently discover to be true.[26]

Although commentators often present Descartes as a revolutionary philosopher, the technique of 'leading the mind away from the senses' had a long ancestry. Augustine had compared the senses to a ship bobbing around on the ocean; to achieve reliable knowledge (e.g. of mathematics), we have to leave the ship and learn to walk on dry land.[27] The general theme goes back ultimately to Plato, who insisted that the first step to true philosophical understanding is to move away from the shifting world of sense-based beliefs.[28] Descartes begins his metaphysics, then, with a traditional softening-up process. Drawing on classical arguments for doubt (whose revival had been a major feature of renaissance philosophy[29]), he undermines our confidence in the senses as a source of knowledge by pointing out that they sometimes deceive, and 'it is prudent never to trust wholly those who have deceived us even once'.[30] He goes on to deploy the celebrated 'dreaming argument' ('there are no sure signs by means of which being awake can be distinguished from being asleep') to cast a general doubt on the reliability of the inference from sensory experiences to the existence of their supposed external causes. In the first phase of this argument, particular judgements like 'I am sitting by the fire' are impugned: any particular experience may be a dream. In the second, more radical, phase, doubt is cast on whole classes of objects: perhaps things like 'heads, eyes and hands' are all imaginary – part of some pervasive dream.[31] The conclusion reached is that any science (such as physics) whose truth depends on the actual existence of objects is potentially doubtful; and that we may rely with certainty only on subjects like arithmetic and geometry, which deal 'with the simplest and most general things, regardless of whether they exist in nature or not'.[32]

At this stage in the First Meditation Descartes launches into a far more disturbing and extreme doubt, which takes us into the heart of his metaphysics – the possibility of error even concerning the simplest and apparently most self-evident truths of mathematics. This possibility is initially introduced by invoking an idea which was much misunderstood by Descartes's contemporaries, that of divine deception. Some found the suggestion impious; others saw the thrust of the argument as leading to atheism.[33] But in fact the project of the First Meditation, which is essentially one of suspension of belief, does not permit any assumptions to be made, one way or another, about the existence of

God. Instead, we are presented with a simple dilemma: if there is an all-powerful creator, then he could 'bring it about that I go wrong every time I add two and three or count the sides of a square'; if, on the other hand, there is no God, then I owe my existence not to a divine creator but to chance, or some other chain of imperfect causes, and in this case there is even less reason to believe that my intuitions about mathematics are reliable.[34] What the argument appears to do, in effect, is to cast doubt on the most basic perceptions of our intellect – on what Descartes had earlier, in the *Regulae*, called our intuition of the 'simple natures'. But if the basic building-blocks of our knowledge are called into question, if the very framework of human cognition is suspect, then how could any cognitive process conceivably be validated?

Descartes's strategy in dealing with the dilemma he has raised is to show that even the most extreme doubt is self-defeating. 'I immediately noticed', he writes in the *Discourse*, 'that while I was trying in this way to think everything false, it was necessary that I, who was thinking this, was something'.[35] In the *Meditations*, essentially the same point is made, but in a rather more vivid way: having dramatized the extreme level of doubt by deliberately imagining a 'malicious demon of the utmost power and cunning who employs all his energies in order to deceive me', Descartes triumphantly exclaims:

> In that case I too undoubtedly exist, if he is deceiving me; and let him deceive me as much as he can, he will never bring it about that I am nothing so long as I think that I am something. So . . . I must finally conclude that this proposition, *I am, I exist*, is necessarily true whenever it is put forward by me or conceived in my mind.[36]

Elsewhere expressed in the famous dictum *Cogito ergo sum* ('I am thinking, therefore I exist'), this is the 'Archimedean point' – the first indubitable certainty which the meditator encounters; it is, says Descartes, 'so firm and sure that all the most extravagant suppositions of the sceptics are incapable of shaking it', and hence he can 'accept it without scruple as the first principle of the philosophy [he is] seeking'.[37]

The precise logical status of Descartes's *cogito* argument has called forth an unending stream of commentary and analysis. But Descartes himself regarded it as an extremely simple piece of reasoning: 'when someone says *I am thinking, therefore I exist*, he does not have to deduce existence from thought by means of any syllogism, but recognizes it as something self-evident, by a simple intuition of the mind.'[38] There is, of course, nothing necessary about either one's thought or one's existence: I might not have existed; I could cease to think, or to exist, at any time. But what is necessary is that while I am actually engaged in thinking, I must exist. The validity of the *cogito* is thus not to be analysed simply in terms of the static inference patterns of formal logic; rather, it is something to be grasped by each individual meditator as he follows the Cartesian path and becomes aware of the unavoidable fact of his own existence as a subject of conscious awareness.[39] What is more, the fact of my thinking is self-confirming, in a way which is not the case with the other simple and self-evident truths (such as 'two plus three makes five') which Descartes has hitherto been considering. For the very act of doubting that I am thinking entails that I am thinking (since doubt is a species of thought).[40] In this sense, the *cogito* has a privileged status; it enjoys a primacy in the Cartesian quest for knowledge, since it alone is validated by the very fact of being doubted.

There is, however, another, philosophically more problematic, aspect to the 'primacy' of the *cogito*. Descartes frequently described it as the 'first principle' of his philosophy; but astute contemporary critics challenged him on just this point. In order even to get as far as realizing his own existence, does not the meditator already have to have a considerable amount of knowledge – for example of what is meant by the very terms 'thought' and 'existence'.[41] In reply, Descartes conceded, and indeed insisted, that such prior conceptual knowledge was indeed required; the *cogito* was 'primary' only in the sense that it is the first existential truth which the meditator arrives at.[42] But this reply in turn raises two fascinating difficulties. The first may be termed the problem of 'Cartesian privacy', and is one whose full implications have only become apparent in the twentieth century, chiefly as a result of the work of Ludwig Wittgenstein. What Wittgenstein showed, in his famous 'private language argument' was that for a term in any language to have meaning, there must be public criteria determining its correct application.[43] Yet this result, if we apply it to the Cartesian meditator, seems to undermine his entire project. For the project requires the meditator to doubt the existence of everything and everyone apart from himself, in order to reach subjective awareness of his own existence. Yet if the very understanding of terms like 'thought' and 'existence' presupposes a public realm of criteria determining their application, there is something inherently unstable about the private, autocentric perspective of the Cartesian quest for knowledge. If, as the Wittgensteinian argument seems to show, our grasp of concepts is an inescapably public, socially mediated, phenomenon, then the very ability of the meditator to employ concepts presupposes from the outset the existence of that extra-mental world which he is supposed to be doubting. From a modern perspective, in short, the very idea of the primacy of the subjective dissolves away, and yields to the primacy of the social.

The second problematic feature about the primacy of the *cogito* arises even within the seventeenth-century context. Descartes's concession that the *cogito* is not entirely self-standing, but presupposes the meditator's grasp of the concepts involved, allows the following question to be raised. The extreme doubts of the First Meditation left open the possibility that the meditator might go astray 'every time he adds two and three or counts the sides of a square, *or in some even simpler matter, if that is imaginable*'.[44] But if a deceiving God could pervert my intuitions regarding the simplest concepts of mathematics, why could he not also pervert my grasp of the fundamental concepts I need in order to reach the *cogito*? How, in short, can I trust my basic intuitions of the 'intellectual simple natures' like the concepts of thought and of doubt, not to mention the 'common simple natures', which include the concept of existence and also the fundamental rules of logic which seem necessary for any thought process at all to get off the ground?

The correct answer to this conundrum, at least as far as Descartes's own strategy is concerned, seems to be that the doubts of the First Meditation are not intended to be as radical as is often supposed. Doubts about our grasp of mathematics are raised by the deceiving God argument, but a careful reading of the First Meditation confirms that doubts about our intuitions of the intellectual simple natures are never entertained. Despite his talk of 'demolishing everything', Descartes is chiefly concerned, as he says in the Synopsis,[45] to challenge our preconceived opinions concerning the nature and existence of the material world around us. He wants to direct the mind away from physical things, so that it can turn in upon itself and let the 'natural light' within each of us reveal the truths that cannot be doubted. The Cartesian project is not to 'validate reason',[46] for such a project would be doomed to incoherence by the very attempt to undertake it by using the tools of reason. Descartes cannot, and does not propose to, generate a system of knowledge *ex nihilo*. What he does propose to do is to demolish commonly accepted foundations for knowledge, based largely on sensory experience and preconceived opinion, and utilize instead more stable foundations derived from the inner resources which have been implanted in each soul. The project is aptly summarized in Descartes's dramatic dialogue, the *Search for Truth*, which was perhaps composed around the same time as the *Meditations*:

> I shall bring to light the true riches of our souls, opening up to each of us the means whereby we can find within ourselves, without any help from anyone else, all the knowledge we may need . . . in order to acquire the most abstruse items of knowledge that human reason is capable of possessing.[47]

❧ THE ROLE OF GOD ❧

It is scarcely possible to underestimate the role played by God in the development of Descartes's foundational project. The meditator's awareness of his own existence is a curiously transitory insight: I can be sure I exist only so long as I am thinking.[48] Admittedly, my awareness of myself as a thinking thing is quite indubitable and transparent: it surely could not turn out, Descartes observes, that 'something I perceived with such clarity and distinctness was false'; and yet the earlier suggestion that an all-powerful God might make me go wrong 'even in those matters which I think I see utterly clearly with the mind's eye' gives me pause for doubt. Although I have found one unshakeable truth, no general progress towards a systematic structure of knowledge will be possible unless I remove this residual doubt and establish 'whether God exists and, if so, whether he can be a deceiver'.[49]

Deprived, at this stage of his inquiries, of any certain knowledge of the outside world, the Cartesian meditator has to establish the existence of God drawing purely on the resources of his own consciousness. This is done by making an inventory of the ideas found within the mind. We cannot know at this stage whether our ideas correspond to anything real, but it is clear that they are 'like images of things': that is, they have a certain representational content.[50] Descartes now reasons that the content of each idea must have a cause; for nothing can come from nothing, yet 'if we suppose that an idea contains something which was not in its cause, it must have got this from nothing'. In most cases, the content of an idea presents no great explanatory problem: the content of many of my ideas, observes Descartes, could easily have been drawn from my own nature; other ideas (like those of unicorns) are simply fictitious, or made up – put together by my own imagination. But the idea that gives me my understanding of 'a supreme God, eternal, infinite, immutable, omniscient, omnipotent and the creator of all things' is different: 'all these attributes are such that the more carefully I concentrate on them, the less possible it seems that they could have originated from me alone.' So the idea of God must have, as its cause, a real being who truly possesses the attributes in question. In creating me, God must have 'placed this idea within me to be, as it were, the mark of the craftsman stamped on the work'.[51]

Of the many problematic features of this argument, the most striking is the extent to which it relies on what are (to the modern ear at least) highly questionable assumptions about causation. A swift reading might suggest that all Descartes needs is the (relatively uncontroversial) deterministic principle that everything has a cause (which Descartes expresses as the maxim that 'Nothing comes from nothing'). But in fact the argument requires much more than this: it is not just that my idea of God needs *a* cause, but that its cause must actually contain all the perfection represented in the idea. It is 'manifest by the natural light' claims Descartes, that 'there must be at least as much reality in the cause as in the effect', and hence 'that what is more perfect cannot arise from what is less perfect'.[52] What Descartes is in effect presupposing here is a theory of causation that is deeply indebted to the scholastic philosophical apparatus which it is his official aim to supplant. According to the scholastic conception, causality is generally understood in terms of some kind of property transmission: causes pass on or transmit properties to effects, which are then said to derive their features from the causes.[53] And this in turn presupposes that certain kinds of similarity relations hold between causes and effects – in the words of the traditional maxim which Descartes is reported to have quoted approvingly, 'the effect is like the cause'.[54] This allegiance to traditional models of causality casts a shadow on Descartes's bold professions of novelty – his claim to be 'starting afresh' in metaphysics. That might not matter in itself, had not the explicit goal of the whole enterprise been to build on solid foundations by demolishing unscrutinized preconceptions. Yet to read through the proof of God's existence in the Third Meditation is to be confronted with a positive barrage of traditional technical terms ('substance' and 'mode', and terms denoting various grades of reality – 'formal', 'objective', 'eminent' and the like), whose application the reader is asked to take as self-evident. The scrupulous caution and methodological rigour which were employed earlier to establish the *cogito* argument seem to dissolve away here. In short, when endeavouring to establish the metaphysical foundations for his new science, Descartes seems unable to free himself from the explanatory framework of his scholastic predecessors.[55]

But even if the details of Descartes's proofs of God are taken on trust, deeper structural problems remain. The most serious is what has come to be known as the problem of the 'Cartesian circle' which was first raised by Descartes's own contemporaries, notably Marin Mersenne and Antoine Arnauld.[56] The function of Descartes's proof of God is supposed to be to establish the possibility of systematic knowledge. If a perfect God exists, then the intellectual apparatus which he bestowed on me cannot be intrinsically inaccurate. Of course, I may make mistakes from time to time, but this is due (Descartes argues in the Fourth Meditation) to incorrect use of free will: I often rashly jump in and give my assent to a proposition when I do not have a clear and distinct perception of it. But if I confine myself to what I clearly and distinctly perceive, I can be sure of avoiding error: 'I shall unquestionably reach the truth if only I give sufficient attention to all the things which I perfectly understand, and separate these from all the cases where my apprehension is more confused and obscure'.[57] Provided I keep to this rule, I can achieve knowledge of countless things, including, most importantly, the structure of the physical universe – the 'whole of that corporeal nature which is the subject of pure mathematics'.[58] Now the problem, in a nutshell, is this: if existence of a non-deceiving God has to be established in order for me to have confidence in the clear and distinct perceptions of my intellect, then how, without circularity, can I rely on the intellectual perceptions needed to construct the proof of God's existence in the first place? Descartes's answer to this challenge appears to be that the divine guarantee enables us to construct long chains of scientific reasoning but is not needed to establish the premises needed to prove God exists, since it is impossible to doubt these so long as we are actually attending to them.[59] Unfortunately, however, the premises of Descartes's proofs for God seem to rely (suggested above) on a host of complex presuppositions which have to be taken on trust: the transparent, self-confirming quality which Descartes relied on to reach awareness of his own existence is simply not available in the elaborate causal reasoning needed to establish the existence of a perfect non-deceiving God. If this is right, then Descartes's metaphysical project must be counted a failure: the journey from indubitable subjective self-awareness to systematic objective knowledge cannot be completed. The challenge which Descartes puts into the mouth of an imaginary objector in his dialogue *The Search for Truth* seems both apt and unanswerable:

> You seem to me to be like an acrobat who always lands on his feet, so constantly do you go back to your 'first principle'. But if you go on in this way, your progress will be slow and limited. How are we always to find truths such that we can be as firmly convinced of them as we are of our own existence?[60]

❧ THE ETERNAL VERITIES ❧

The central place of God in Cartesian metaphysics should by now be more than clear. But no account of this relationship would be complete without some attention to one of Descartes's most perplexing doctrines – that of the divine creation of the eternal truths. This is a doctrine which does not emerge explicitly in the *Meditations*, but it surfaces in the *Replies* to the *Objections*, and Descartes appears to have held it consistently throughout his life. He is reported to have insisted on it in an interview held two years before his death,[61] and he explicitly asserted it, in his correspondence, as early as 1630:

> The mathematical truths which you call eternal have been laid down by God and depend on him no less than the rest of his

creatures. . . . They are all inborn in our minds just as a king would imprint his laws on the hearts of all his subjects if he had enough power to do so.[62]

Traditional theology maintained that divine omnipotence does not entail the power to do absolutely anything, if 'anything' is taken to include even what is logically impossible. God cannot, on pain of absurdity, do what is self-contradictory (e.g. make something which is both three-sided and a square); his supreme power operates, as it were, only within the sphere of the logically possible.[63] One might suppose that it is hardly an objectionable limitation on the power of God that he cannot do nonsensical and incoherent things like creating three-sided squares; but Descartes's conception of the deity is of a being of absolutely infinite power – a being who is immune to any limitation which the human mind can conceive. Thus, not only is he the creator of all actually existing things, but he is the author of necessity and possibility; he was 'just as free to make it not true that the radii of a circle were equal as he was free not to create the world'.[64] Some of Descartes's critics objected that this was incoherent, but Descartes replied that just because we humans cannot grasp something is no reason to conclude that it is beyond the power of God. God thus turns out, on Descartes's conception, to be in a real sense *incomprehensible*: our soul, being finite, cannot fully grasp (French, *comprendre*; Latin *comprehendere*) or conceive him.[65]

From Descartes's insistence on the 'incomprehensibility' of God, two profoundly disturbing problems arise for Cartesian philosophy. The first relates to Descartes's attempt to found his scientific system on secure metaphysical foundations. In the First Meditation, the possibility had been raised that the human intellect might go astray 'even in those matters which it seemed to perceive most evidently'. And the doubt so generated extended, on Descartes's own insistence, even to our fundamental intuitions about the mathematical simple natures. But what of the intellectual simple natures – the fundamental conceptual apparatus needed for the meditator to arrive at knowledge of his own existence? We suggested earlier that if the doubt was allowed to go this far, then the very possibility of the meditator's achieving any coherent reflection on his own existence as a conscious being would be foreclosed at the outset. But the doctrine of the divine creation of the eternal verities seems to entail that even our grasp of these basic concepts could be unreliable, in the sense that what is necessary for us may not be necessary for God. A gap is thus opened up between the basic processes of the human mind, and the true nature of things. And if we have no reliable hold on the true logical implications of our concepts, if there is no sure route from what is 'true for us' to what is 'true for God', the entire Cartesian journey from indubitable subjective awareness to reliable objective knowledge seems threatened at the outset.

From this nightmare of opacity, an even more disturbing threat to the Cartesian project seems to follow. If the structure of the fundamental principles of logic is not ultimately accessible to human reason, but depends on the inscrutable will of God, then the very notion of ultimate truth, of something's being 'true for God', turns out to be beyond our grasp.[66] In his programme for science, Descartes needs to insist constantly on the immutability and coherence of the fundamental laws which govern the universe. By appealing to these laws, we are able, asserts Descartes, to derive a whole structure of necessary connections which operate in the world, and unravel a complex series of results which describe the behaviour of matter in motion in accordance with the laws of mathematics.[67] But now, given that the rationale behind these necessities is ultimately opaque to us, it seems to follow that the rationally ordered universe which Cartesian science had hoped to reveal becomes in the end merely a series of arbitrary divine fiats; and against this background it is hard to see how the laws of nature could ultimately be construed as anything more than brute regularities. In short, the doctrine of the divine creation of the eternal truths generates, from our perspective at least, an ineradicable element of contingency in the system. The project of Cartesian rationalism, of uncovering a universe whose structure is supposed to be in principle transparent to the human intellect, now seems radically unstable. At the heart of the system is a worm of doubt, an element of arbitrariness which prefigures, if only faintly and in outline, the post-Humean world in which the working of the universe is in the end opaque to human reason.[68]

❧ SCIENCE AND THE HUMAN MIND ❧

The problems touched on in the previous sections have to do with the role of God in Descartes's conception of knowledge, and the status of scientific truth in the Cartesian system. But there are certain features of the Cartesian programme which remain largely unaffected by these foundational issues. Whatever the metaphysical status of the ultimate laws governing the universe, Descartes could, and did, claim that his scientific approach was, in explanatory terms, both economical and comprehensive. These two features of Cartesian science are in fact two sides of the same coin. The system could claim to be economical because it subsumed a wide variety of phenomena under a very few simple principles specifying the behaviour of matter in motion;[69] and it could claim to be comprehensive because it included hitherto separated categories of events – terrestrial and celestial, organic and inorganic, natural and artificial – under a single explanatory apparatus.[70]

In his early work, *Le Monde*, Descartes aimed to describe the evolution of a complete universe, starting from a chaotic initial configuration of matter in motion and using simple mechanical principles to explain the subsequent formation of stars and planets, the Earth and the Moon, light and heat, the ebb and flow of the tides, and much else besides. And he explicitly went on to include the human body as something which could be explained mechanically on the self-same principles. The fact that living creatures are 'automata' – that is, initiate their own movements without requiring any external impulse – was, Descartes claimed, no obstacle whatever to his explanatory programme:

> We see clocks, artificial fountains, mills and other such machines, which, although only man-made, have the power to move of their own accord in many different ways. But I am supposing this machine [of the human body] to be made by the hand of God, and so I think you may reasonably believe it capable of a greater variety of movements than I could possibly imagine in it, and of exhibiting a greater mastery than I could possibly ascribe to it.[71]

Descartes's investigations into animal physiology (he performed frequent experimental dissections during his long residence in Holland[72]) led him to the conclusion that many of the workings of the body could be explained by reference to the minute particles of matter which he called 'animal spirits', transmitted to and from the brain via the nervous system. Such 'animal spirits' were purely physical in character, operating in a way very analogous to that in which gases or fluids are transmitted along systems of pipes and conduits. There was no need to posit any internal principle such as a 'nutritive' or 'sensitive' soul in order to explain biological processes like digestion and growth; indeed, the ordinary laws of matter in motion were quite sufficient to account even for complex animal behaviour like pursuit and flight.[73] The ways in which the beasts operate can be explained by means of mechanics, without invoking any 'sensation, life or soul';[74] and even in the case of humans,

> we have no more reason to believe that it is our soul which produces the movements which we know by experience are not controlled by our will than we have reason to think that there is a soul in a clock which makes it tell the time.[75]

Reflection led Descartes to conclude, however, that there were severe limits on the power of mechanical explanations when it came to accounting for the characteristically human processes of thought and language. In the *Discourse*, he argues that one could in principle construct an artificial automaton which was indistinguishable from a dog or a monkey. But any such attempt to mimic human capacities would be doomed to failure. A mechanical android, however complex, would betray its purely physical origins in two crucial respects: first, it could never possess genuine language, and second, it could never respond intelligently to the manifold contingencies of life in the way in which humans do. The first of these arguments, the argument from language, is a crucial weapon in Descartes's strategy of showing that human capacities are not just different in degree from those of non-human animals, but are radically different in kind:

> We can certainly conceive of a machine so constructed that it
> utters words, and even utters words which correspond to
> bodily actions causing a change in its organs (e.g. if you touch
> it in one spot it asks what you want of it, and if you touch it
> in another it cries out that you are hurting it, and so on). But
> it is not conceivable that such a machine should produce
> different arrangements of words so as to give an appropriately
> meaningful answer to whatever is said in its presence, as even
> the dullest of men can do.[76]

The vital point here is that a mechanical system produces responses in accordance with a fixed schedule: there is a finite number of possible responses, each triggered by a specified stimulus. But genuine language is 'stimulus-free': it involves the ability to respond innovatively to an indefinite range of situations.[77] Hence it is 'for all practical purposes impossible for a machine to have enough different organs to make it act in all the contingencies of life in the way in which our reason makes us act'.[78]

The power of reason in human beings was thus, Descartes concluded, incapable of being explained by reference to the workings of a mechanical system; a material structure, however complex its organization, could never approach the human capacity for thought and language. And hence, even in his earliest scientific work, Descartes acknowledged a limit in principle to the scope of physical explanation. The properties of stars and planets, rainbows and vapours, minerals, plants and animals could all be reduced to complex interactions of matter in motion. But if God wanted to create a thinking human being, he would have to create, in addition to all the physiological mechanisms of the brain and nervous system, a separate entity, a 'rational soul'.[79] The nature of this soul, and its relation to the physical world, was to become one of Descartes's principal preoccupations, when he came to develop his mature metaphysics.

❧ THE INCORPOREALITY THESIS ❧

The *Discourse on the Method* contains, in outline, Descartes's central doctrines on the nature of the human soul. The central claim, which he introduces at the end of a summary of his previous work on physiology, is that 'the rational soul, unlike any other things previously dealt with, cannot be derived in any way from the potentiality of matter, but must be specially created'.[80] Anti-reductionism about the human mind – the insistence that the phenomena of cognition and rationality are not reducible to physical events – is a thesis that still finds a good deal of support among present-day philosophers. But nowadays this thesis is generally advanced as a thesis about mental *properties* or *events*: statements about such properties or events, asserts the anti-reductionist, cannot be replaced without remainder by statements about purely physical properties or events (e.g. statements about brain workings). But many modern anti-reductionists are still in some sense *physicalists*; that is, they hold that mental processes and events must be realized or instantiated in the workings of physical systems, so that, if all such systems were destroyed, no mental happenings could occur. Descartes, however, takes a far more radical line. The Cartesian view is that the distinction between mind and matter is a matter of ontology: the mind is a distinct entity in its own right, which operates, or can in principle operate, entirely independently of the material universe. This is the claim which has come to be known as Cartesian (or substantival) dualism: the mind is 'really distinct' from the body, a separate and independent substance.

Descartes's initial argument for the incorporeality of the mind or soul (he makes no distinction between the two terms[81]) arises from the meditative process which leads to the *cogito*. In becoming aware of his own existence, the meditator is able to separate or bracket off all his beliefs about the existence of an external material world:

> Next I examined attentively what I was. I saw that while I could pretend that I had no body, and that there was no world and no place for me to be in, I could not for all that pretend that I did not exist. . . . From this I knew I was a substance whose whole essence or nature is solely to think, and which does not require any place, or depend on any material thing, in order to exist. Accordingly this 'I', that is the soul by which I am what I am, [*ce Moi, c'est à dire l'Ame par laquelle je suis ce que je suis*] is entirely distinct from the body . . . and would not fail to be whatever it is even if the body did not exist.[82]

It could be (and indeed was in Descartes's own day[83]) objected that merely because I can think of 'myself' without thinking of my body, it does not follow that I could really exist if my body were destroyed. After all, I may (if I am ignorant of the real nature of gold) be able to think of gold without thinking of its atomic structure, but it does not follow that something could still exist as gold without that structure. Descartes's position, however, is that if an object (in this case the thinking thing that is 'me') can be clearly conceived of as lacking a given property (in this case having a body), then that property cannot be essential to the object in question.

The phrase 'whose whole essence or nature is solely to think' is the key to Descartes's reasoning here. Drawing on the traditional terminology of substance and attribute, Descartes maintains that each substance has a nature or essence – that is, a property or set of properties which makes it what it is. The standard scholastic view (derived from Aristotle) held that there is a large plurality of substances, but Descartes reduces created substances to just two categories: mind and matter. The principal attribute of matter is extension (the possession of length, breadth and height), and all the features of matter are reducible to 'modes' or modifications of this essential characteristic; thus a piece of wax, for example, may take on a variety of shapes, but all these are simply mathematically determinable modifications of *res extensa*, or 'extended substance'.[84] But now, just as all the properties of physical things are modifications of extension, so all the properties of a mind (thinking, willing, doubting, desiring and so on) are all modifications of *res cogitans* or thinking substance. And Descartes took it as self-evident that the properties of thought and extension were not just different but utterly distinct and incompatible. 'On the one hand,' he later wrote in the Sixth Meditation,

> I have a clear and distinct perception of myself, in so far as I
> am simply a thinking, non-extended thing; and on the other hand
> I have a distinct idea of body, in so far as this is simply an
> extended, non-thinking thing. And accordingly it is certain that
> I [that is the soul by which I am what I am] is really distinct
> from the body and can exist without it.[85]

By the time this full-blown argument is deployed in the Sixth Meditation, Descartes has more resources at his disposal than he had in the *Discourse* when he blandly observed that he could pretend he did not have a body without thereby pretending that the 'I by which I am what I am' did not exist. In the Sixth Meditation, God (whose existence is taken to have been proved at this stage) is invoked as the guarantor of the clear and distinct perceptions of the human mind. Hence, if we can clearly and distinctly conceive of X without Y, it follows that Y cannot be essential to X. The modern reader may feel uncomfortable here: surely all the argument proves is that mind and body could conceivably exist separately, not that they are in fact separate entities. But it is precisely the conceivability of mind separate from body which Descartes relies on in order to establish his dualistic thesis: 'the mere fact that I can clearly and distinctly understand one thing apart from another is enough to make me certain that the two things are distinct, since they are capable of being separated, at least by God.'[86] Whether *in fact* the mind will exist after the death of the body is something that Descartes is content to leave undetermined by reason: it is a matter of religious faith.[87] It is enough that it is, as we should say nowadays, *logically possible* that it should exist without physical matter. That possibility, which Descartes takes himself to have demonstrated, is enough to guarantee the incorporeality thesis – that what makes me *me*, the conscious awareness of myself as a *res cogitans*, cannot depend on the existence of any physical object.

What the above analysis suggests is that Descartes's version of dualism stands or falls with the claim that the existence of mind without matter is at least a logical possibility. And a good many modern philosophers, however adamantly they may be disposed to insist that mental properties are structural or functional properties of a physical or biological system (the brain, the nervous system), often concede that disembodied consciousness is at least *logically* conceivable. But what does the alleged logical possibility of mind without matter amount to? It must presumably boil down to some such claim as that there is no logical contradiction in conjoining (as Descartes does in the *Discourse*) the two statements (a) 'I exist as a conscious being at time *t*' and (b) 'my body (including my brain and nervous system) does not exist at time *t*'. But this seems a very weak argument. As Leibniz was later to observe (in a rather different context), it is not enough, to establish the coherence of a set of propositions, that one cannot immediately detect any obvious inconsistency in them. For it is quite possible that a set of propositions which seems consistent on the face of it might turn out on further analysis to contain hitherto undetected incoherence.[88] Borrowing the terminology of Karl Popper from our own time (and transferring it from the realm of philosophy of science to that of logic), we may say that claims of logical possibility are falsifiable (by producing a contradiction) but not conclusively verifiable. Now admittedly, when we are dealing with very simple and transparent truths (those of elementary arithmetic or geometry, for example), we may be entitled to be sure that there could be no hidden inconsistency which would undermine the logical coherence of a group of propositions. But when we are dealing with a phenomenon as complex and difficult as consciousness, it seems far from clear that we are entitled to declare, just by simple reflection, that its occurrence in the absence of any physical substrate is a coherent possibility. Moreover, when we start to ponder on many of the key elements that make up our conscious life – 'internal' sensations of pain and pleasure, and 'external' sensations such as those of vision, touch, hearing, taste and smell – then it becomes difficult to see how, if at all, these could be attributed to a disembodied entity.[89] Such sensory events do not of course exhaust our conscious experience: there remain what Descartes called the 'pure' cogitations of the intellect – thoughts about triangles or numbers, for example. But it is by no means clear that such 'pure' forms of abstract thought would be enough to constitute an individual conscious existence.[90] In short, the logical possibility of the continued independent existence of the *Moi* – the 'soul by which I am what I am' – is by no means as clear and straightforward a matter as Descartes invites us to suppose.

❧❧ THE RELATION BETWEEN MIND AND ❧❧ BODY

Despite his insistence on the incorporeality of the mind, Descartes both acknowledged, and made serious attempts to explain, the intimate relationship between mind and body. That relationship, as he frequently pointed out, is manifested in the facts of everyday experience:

> nature teaches me by these sensations of pain, hunger, thirst and so on, that I am not merely present in my body as a sailor is present in a ship, but that I am very closely conjoined and as it were intermingled with it, so that I and the body form a unit.[91]

Contemporaries of Descartes were puzzled by this admission: during an interview which he conducted with the philosopher in the Spring of 1648, the young Dutchman Frans Burman asked him how the soul could be affected by the body, and vice versa, given the supposed radical difference in their natures. Descartes answered that the point was 'difficult to explain', but that our own inner experience was 'so clear' that it could not be gainsaid.[92]

Reflections on the phenomenology of sensory experience help to identify what Descartes is pointing to here. When we are thirsty, to take one of his examples, we do not merely have an intellectual *understanding* that our body needs water; we experience a characteristic and intrusive sensation of a distinctive kind – the mouth and the throat 'feel dry'. What kind of event is this 'feeling'? According to the standard expositions of 'dualism' found in modern textbooks on the philosophy of mind, to have a sensation like thirst is to be in a certain kind of *conscious* state; and hence, feeling thirsty is, for the dualist, assignable to the category of mind rather than body, since all consciousness belongs on the 'mental' side of the dualist's mind–body divide. So familiar has this approach to the phenomena of 'consciousness' become that it takes some effort to realize that Descartes's own views about sensory experience are in fact rather different. Descartes does *not* say that sensations are mental events simpliciter; on the contrary, he explicitly says that 'I could clearly and distinctly understand the complete "me" without the faculty of sensation'.[93] Sensation, though it is an inescapable part of my daily experience, does not form an essential part of the *res cogitans* that is 'me'. Rather, Descartes explains, it is a 'confused' mode of awareness which 'arises from the union and as it were intermingling of the mind with the body'.[94]

It emerges from this that Descartes's universe is not quite as neat and tidy as the label 'Cartesian dualism' tends to suggest. It is true that there exist, for Descartes, examples of pure thinking things – angels are his standard example – whose existence consists essentially and entirely in modifications of intellection and volition; such beings are examples of a *res cogitans* in the strict sense. On the other side of the divide, there is pure *res extensa*, mere extended matter whose every feature can be analysed as some kind of modification of the geometrically defined properties of size and shape;[95] the human body is an example of a structure, or assemblage of structures, composed entirely of extended matter. But *human beings* fit into neither of the two categories so far described. For a human being consists of a mind or soul 'united' or 'intermingled' with a body; and when such intermingling occurs, there 'arise' further events, such as sensations, which could not be found in minds alone or in bodies alone.

Although the 'union' between body and soul is explicitly mentioned in the *Meditations*, the concept is left somewhat obscure, and it was not until he was questioned in detail by Princess Elizabeth of Bohemia that Descartes came to examine in more detail exactly what it implied. We have, he wrote in a letter to the Princess of 21 May 1643, various 'primitive notions' which are 'models on which all our other knowledge is patterned'. He proceeds to list some of the categories which he had much earlier labelled as 'simple natures': first, there are 'common' notions, such as being, number and duration, 'which apply to everything we can conceive'; second, there is the corporeal notion of extension, 'which entails the notions of shape and motion'; and third, there is the 'notion of thought, which includes the conceptions of the intellect and the inclinations of the will'. All this is straightforward Cartesian doctrine. But now Descartes adds a fourth category: 'as regards soul and body together, we have the notion of their union, on which depends our notion of the soul's power to move the body, and the body's power to act on the soul and cause sensations and passions'.[96] He later made it clear that the notion of a 'union' was meant to be taken literally:

> to conceive the union between two things is to conceive them as one single thing. . . . Everyone invariably experiences the union within himself without philosophizing. Everyone feels that he is a single person [*une seule personne*] with thought and body so related by nature that the thought can move the body and feel the things that happen to it.[97]

The notion that two different substances can unite to form a single thing is not, in itself, obscure or problematic. We are familiar nowadays, for example, with the idea that hydrogen and oxygen can unite to form water; furthermore, this 'substantial union' generates 'emergent' properties – water has properties such as that of being drinkable which were not present in its constituent elements – and this (though it is not of course Descartes's own example) might be thought to give some grip on the Cartesian notion that events like sensations emerge or 'arise' when mind and body are united, even though they are not part of the essence of either *res cogitans* or *res extensa*. Nevertheless, Descartes himself clearly felt that his notion of the 'substantial union' of mind and body presented problems. For mind and body, as defined throughout his writings, are not just different, but utterly incompatible substances: in terms of their essential characteristics, they mutually exclude one another, since mind is defined as non-extended and indivisible, whereas matter is by its nature extended and divisible. And it is not easy to see how incompatible items can be, in any intelligible sense, 'united'. As Descartes rather ruefully put it:

> it does not seem to me that the human mind is capable of conceiving at the same time the distinction and the union between body and soul, because for this it is necessary to conceive them as a single thing and at the same time to conceive them as two things, and this is absurd.[98]

❧ CAUSAL INTERACTION AND ❧ OCCASIONALISM

The idea of the union of utterly heterogeneous items is not the only problematic feature of Descartes's theory of the mind and its relation to the body. Descartes frequently talks in a way which suggests both that the mind has causal powers *vis-à-vis* the body (e.g. it can cause the body to move), and that the body has causal powers with respect to the soul (e.g. passions and feelings are 'excited' by corporeal events in the blood and nervous system). A great deal of Descartes's last work, the *Passions of the Soul*, is devoted to examining the workings of this two-way causal flow between body and mind. The following is his account of memory:

> When the soul wants to remember something, this volition makes the [pineal] gland lean first to one side and then to another, thus driving the animal spirits [the tiny, fast moving particles which travel through the nervous system] towards different regions of the brain until they come upon the one containing traces left by the object we want to remember. These traces consist simply in the fact that the pores of the brain through which the spirits previously made their way owing to the presence of this object have thereby become more apt than the others to be opened in the same way when the spirits again flow towards them. The spirits thus enter these pores more easily when they come upon them, thereby producing in the gland that special movement which represents the same object to the soul, and makes it recognize the object as the one it wanted to remember.[99]

What strikes the reader here is not so much the wealth of obsolete physiological detail (modern readers will readily be able to substitute electrochemical events in the cerebral cortex for Descartes's movements of the pineal gland and 'animal spirits') as the way in which that physiological detail is expected to 'mesh' with events in the non-physical realm of the soul. Descartes has managed to supply a host of mechanisms whereby movements, once initiated in the pineal gland, can be transferred to other parts of the brain and body; but he does not seem to have tackled the central issue of how an incorporeal soul can initiate such movements in the first place. And the same problem will apply when the causal flow is in the other direction. Descartes devotes a lot of attention to the physiological mechanisms whereby bodily stimuli of various kinds cause changes in the nervous system and brain which 'dispose' the soul to feel emotions like anger or fear.[100] But he does not explain how mere brain events, however complex their physiological genesis, could have the power to arouse or excite events in the mental realm.

Why exactly is the *causal* aspect of the mind-body relation problematic for Descartes? The answer, in brief, is that throughout the rest of his metaphysics and physics he seems to presuppose that causal transactions should be in some sense transparent to the human intellect. 'The effect is like the cause' was a standard maxim of the scholastics which (as noted earlier in this chapter) Descartes readily accepts.[101] In his causal proofs of God's existence he relies on the principle that the cause of an object possessing a given degree of perfection must itself possess as much or more perfection: whatever is found in the effect must be present in the cause. In physics, too, Descartes often seems inclined to require explanations that reveal transparent connections between causes and effects (in the unfolding of the laws of motion, for example, a simple transmission model is invoked – a cause transmits or passes on a determinate quantity of motion to its effect).[102] In all these cases, Descartes apparently wants to be able to appeal to something very simple and self-evident: if we could not 'see' how effects inherited features from their causes, we would have a case of something arising 'from nothing', which would be absurd. But now it is immediately clear that no such transparency could be available in the mind-body interactions which Descartes describes in such detail in the *Passions of the Soul*. Transparent connections can be unfolded so long as we remain within the realm of physiology and trace how the stimulation of a sense organ generates changes in the 'animal spirits' which in turn cause modifications in the movements of the pineal gland. But at the end of the story, there will be a mental event which simply 'arises' in the soul: the smooth progression of causal explanations abruptly jolts to a halt. Whatever it is that bridges the gulf between the bodily and the mental realms, it seems that it must remain opaque to causal explanation, in the sense in which that notion is normally understood by Descartes.[103]

Descartes's way round this impasse is to invoke an innate, divinely ordained, power of the human mind. In creating the human soul, God structured it in such a way that various sensory experiences will 'arise' in it whenever the body to which it is united is stimulated in a certain way. Thus, the mind has the innate capacity of 'representing colours to itself *on the occasion* of certain corporeal motions [in the brain]'. There is, in effect, no genuine causal transmission between mind and body; 'nothing reaches the mind from external objects except corporeal motions'; we make judgements about external things 'not because these things transmit ideas to our mind through the sense organs, but because they transmit something which, at exactly the right moment, gives the mind *the occasion to form these ideas by means of the faculty innate to it*.'[104] What we have here is something powerfully reminiscent of developments later in the seventeenth century – the occasionalism of Malebranche, and the Leibnizian theory of 'pre-established harmony'. And the lesson to be learned from this is that the ideas of Malebranche and Leibniz were not, as is sometimes suggested, bizarre attempts to cobble together an *ad hoc* solution to the problem of mind–body interaction which Descartes had bequeathed to Western philosophy; rather, they take their cue from Descartes's own terminology, and his insistence that the relationship between physical events and mental phenomena must be explained on the model of divinely decreed correlations rather than transparent causal transactions. The heterogeneous worlds of mind and matter cannot, properly speaking, interact; only the decrees of God can ensure that they work harmoniously together.

To conclude from this that Descartes's theory of the mind is a failure would be easy enough; but any sense of superiority that the modern commentator may feel should be tempered by the thought that, even today, the relationship between brain occurrences and conscious experience is very far from having been elucidated in a coherent and philosophically satisfying way. What may be a more fruitful theme for reflection is Descartes's own implicit recognition of the limits of human knowledge. The Cartesian project for a unified system of knowledge, founded on transparently clear first principles, faltered, as we saw in the first half of this chapter, when the human mind came to confront the incomprehensible greatness of God. And in a different way, the project faltered when it came to integrating into science that most basic fact of human awareness – our everyday experience, through our external and internal senses, of the world around us and the condition of our bodies. To 'explain' that awareness, Descartes was constrained to admit that only the decrees of God, ultimately opaque to human reason, will suffice. Causal transparency gives way to mere regular conjunction. If this, once again, seems to prefigure the thought of Hume, that should perhaps be no surprise. For however much commentators may wish to present it as a contest between opposing teams of 'rationalists' and 'empiricists', the history of the early modern period is a continuous unfolding tapestry in which the threads endlessly cross and re-cross. The picture that has come down to us is the work of many hands, but however we view it, there can be no disputing Descartes's role as one of its principal designers.

❧❧ NOTES ❧❧

1 AT VI 8: CSM I 115. 'AT' refers, by volume and page number, to the standard Franco-Latin edition of Descartes: *Oeuvres de Descartes*, ed. C. Adam and P. Tannery [6.1]. 'CSM' refers by volume and page number to the standard English translation: *The Philosophical Writings of Descartes*, vols I and II, ed. J. Cottingham, R. Stoothoff and D. Murdoch, and 'CSMK' refers to vol. III (*The Correspondence*) by the same translators and A. Kenny [6.2]. 'CB' refers to *Descartes' Conversation with Burman*, ed. and trans. J. Cottingham [6.5].
2 Compare Descartes's remarks on his early work, *Le Monde*, in Part Five of the *Discourse* (AT VI 41f.; CSM I 131).
3 For the significance of this term (Latin *praejudicium*), see *Principles of Philosophy*, Book I, arts 1 and 71.
4 First Meditation: AT VII 17; CSM II 12.
5 From the introduction to the 1647 French edition of the *Principles of Philosophy* (first published in Latin in 1644): AT VIIIA 14; CSM I 186. The simile

is also found in other writers of the period, notably Francis Bacon (*De augmentis scientiarum*, 3, i).

6 *Discourse on the Method* (1637), Part Six: AT VI 62; CSM I 142.

7 cf. *Conversation with Burman* (AT V 156; CB 30) and letter to Elizabeth of 28 June 1643 (AT III 695; CSMK 228).

8 First Meditation: AT VII 17; CSM II 12.

9 AT X 215; CSM I 3.

10 AT VI 19; CSM I 120.

11 First published in French in 1637 as one of the three 'specimen essays' (the other two were the *Optics* and the *Meteorology*) illustrating Descartes's method.

12 AT X 163; CSMK 4. Descartes dedicated to Beeckman his first work, the *Compendium Musicae*, a study of the application of mathematical methods to the understanding of harmony and dissonance.

13 cf. *Discourse*, Part Two (AT VI 19; CSM I 120) and Part One (AT VI 8; CSM I 115).

14 Descartes began work on his *Optics* and *Meteorology* prior to 1630; cf. CSM I 109f.

15 See especially AT XI 26; CSM I 89. Descartes never published *The World*. Although it was complete and ready to go to press in 1633, he suppressed the work on hearing of the condemnation of Galileo by the Inquisition for advocating the heliocentric hypothesis.

16 *Regulae*, Rule 4: AT X 378; CSM I 19.

17 See the end of Rule 4: 'I have resolved in my search for knowledge of things to adhere unswervingly to a definite order, always starting from the simplest and easiest things and never going beyond them till there seems to be nothing further to be achieved where they are concerned' (AT X 379; CSM I 20). See also Rule 5, which insists on the importance of 'ordering and arranging the objects on which we must concentrate our mind's eye if we are to discover some truth' (ibid.), and Rule 6, which asserts that the 'main secret of the method is to distinguish the simplest things from those that are complicated' (AT X 381; CSM I 21).

18 Rule 12: AT X 420; CSM I 45.

19 ibid.

20 AT X 419; CSM I 45. In addition, the common simple natures include fundamental concepts like 'unity, existence and duration' which may be applied either to the material or to the intellectual simple natures.

21 AT X 421; CSM I 46.

22 AT X 427; CSM I 49.

23 *Discourse*, Part One, AT VI 10; CSM I 116. Descartes implies that his resolution was made during his visit to Germany as a young man of 23, when he had his famous series of dreams in the 'stove heated room' near Ulm on the Danube. These early reflections are described in Part Two of the *Discourse*; see also the early notebooks (AT X 217; CSM I 4). In *Discourse*, Part Three, Descartes suggests that after postponing these metaphysical inquiries he took them up again soon after arriving in Holland (i.e. after 1629). We know from a letter to Mersenne that about this time he actually began to compose a 'little treatise on metaphysics' whose principal themes were 'to prove the existence

of God and that of our souls when they are separated from our bodies': *je ne dis pas que quelque jour je n'achevasse un petit traité de Métaphysique lequel j'ai commencé étant en Frise, et dont les principaux points sont de prouver l'existence de Dieu et celle de nos âmes, lorsqu'elles sont séparées du corps* (23 November 1630, AT I 182; CSMK 29).

24 Discussing what title to give his *écrit de métaphysique* (what we now know as the *Meditations*), Descartes wrote: *Je crois qu'on le pourra nommer ...* Meditationes de Prima Philosophia; *car je n'y traité pas seulement de Dieu et de l'âme, mais en général de toutes les premières choses qu'on peut connaître en philosophant par ordre* (letter to Mersenne of 11 November 1640, AT III 329; CSMK 158). The terms 'metaphysics' and 'first philosophy' were of course not invented by Descartes; the latter comes from Aristotle who used it to describe fundamental philosophical inquiries about substance and being, and the former from the name given by early editors to Aristotle's treatise on 'first philosophy' (the name 'metaphysics' coming originally from the fact that in collected editions of Aristotle this work was traditionally placed after (Greek *meta*) his physics). Descartes's conception of metaphysics was significantly different from the Aristotelian one, however, not least (as will appear) because of its radically subjective orientation. For a discussion of crucial disparities between Aristotelian essences and Cartesian simple natures, see J.-L. Marion, 'Cartesian metaphysics and the role of the simple natures', in J. Cottingham (ed.) *Cambridge Companions: Descartes* [6.32].

25 In particular by the Jesuit Pierre Bourdin; cf. Seventh Replies, AT VII 549; CSM II 375.

26 AT VII 12; CSM II 9.

27 *Soliloquies*, Book I, ch. 4; cf. AT VII 205; CSM II 144.

28 cf. *Republic*, 525. The abstract reasoning of mathematics is, for Plato, as it was later to be for Augustine and Descartes, a paradigm of stable and reliable cognition of the kind which sense-based beliefs could never attain. The term 'rationalism' is an over-used and problematic one in the history of philosophy, but it can serve to indicate interesting similarities between groups of philosophers: one such indisputable similarity is the mistrust of the senses which runs like a clear thread from Plato down to Descartes (and beyond). For further discussion of the label 'rationalist', see J. Cottingham, *The Rationalists* [6.12], ch. 1.

29 Compare, for example, Francisco Sanches, *Quod Nihil Scitur* (1581), ed. and trans. E. Limbrick and D. F. S. Thomson (Cambridge, Cambridge University Press, 1988). See also R. Popkin, *The History of Scepticism from Erasmus to Descartes* [6.23].

30 AT VII 18; CSM II 12. Elsewhere Descartes discusses such standard examples as that of the straight stick which looks bent in water: AT VII 438; CSM II 295.

31 AT VII 20; CSM II 14. The dreaming argument in fact has a number of complex twists and turns, but the two main phases, particular and general, are as indicated. The argument appears in much more compressed form in Descartes's summary of his metaphysical views in Part Four of the *Discourse*: *considérant que toutes les mêmes pensées que nous avons étant éveillés nous peuvent aussi venir quand nous dormons, sans qu'il y en ait aucune pour lors*

qui soit vraie, je me résolus de feindre que toutes les choses qui m'étaient jamais entrées en l'esprit n'étaient non plus vraies que les illusions de mes songes.

32 ibid.

33 cf. AT VIIIB 175; CSMK 223.

34 For more on this argument, see R. Stoothoff, 'Descartes' dilemmatic argument' [6.52].

35 AT VI 32; CSM I 127.

36 *Haud dubio igitur sum, si me fallit; & fallat quantum potest, nunquam tamen efficiet, ut nihil sim quamdiu me aliquid esse cogitabo. Adeo ut . . . denique statuendum sit hoc pronuntiatum,* Ego sum, ego existo *quoties a me profertur, vel mente concipitur, necessario esse verum* (AT VII 25; CSM II 17).

37 The phrasing here is from the *Discourse*, Part Four (AT VI 32; CSM I 127). The notion of the Archimedean point appears in the Second Meditation: 'Archimedes used to demand just one firm and immovable point in order to shift the entire earth; so I too can hope for great things if I manage to find just one thing, however slight, that is certain and unshakeable' (AT VII 24; CSM II 16). The actual phrase *cogito ergo sum* appears in the *Principles of Philosophy*, Part I, article 7; its French equivalent, *je pense, donc je suis*, in the *Discourse*, op. cit.

38 AT VII 140; CSM II 100. For discussion of the *cogito* argument, see A. Kenny, *Descartes* [6.20], ch. 3; B. Williams, *Descartes* [6.28], ch. 3; M. Wilson, *Descartes* [6.29], ch. 2.

39 Compare Descartes's comment in the Preface to the *Meditations*: 'I would not urge anyone to read this book except those who are able and willing to meditate seriously with me' (AT VII 9; CSM II 8). For the importance of the meditator's *activity*, see Wilson, op. cit., and compare J. Hintikka, 'Cogito ergo sum: Inference or Performance?' [6.46], reprinted in W. Doney, *Descartes* [6.33].

40 For more on this, see J. Cottingham, *Descartes* [6.11], 38ff.

41 cf. Sixth Objections: AT VII 413; CSM II 278.

42 See *Principles of Philosophy*, Part I, art. 10 (AT VIIIA 8; CSM I 196).

43 See L. Wittgenstein, *Philosophical Investigations*, trans. G. E. M. Anscombe (Oxford, Blackwell, 1953), I, p. 243.

44 AT VII 21; CSM II 14.

45 *In prima [Meditatione] causae exponuntur propter quas de rebus omnibus, prasertim materialibus, possumus dubitare* (AT VII 13; CSM II 9).

46 cf. H. Frankfurt, *Demons, Dreamers and Madmen. The Defence of Reason in Descartes' Meditations* [6.14].

47 AT X 496; CSM II 400. For the work's date of composition, see CSM II 399.

48 'I am, I exist – that is certain. But for how long? For as long as I am thinking . . .' (AT VII 27; CSM II 18).

49 All quotations in this paragraph are from the opening of the Third Meditation: AT VII 35–6; CSM 24–5.

50 Or what Descartes calls (using scholastic terminology) 'objective reality' (*realitas objectiva*). The more helpful reference to the 'representational' aspect of ideas is supplied in the 1647 French translation of the *Meditations* (by the Duc de Luynes) which was issued with Descartes's approval.

51 Third Meditation: AT VII 40, 45, 51; CSM II 28, 31, 35.

52 *Lumine naturali manifestum est tantundem ad minimum esse debere in causa ... quantum in ejusdem causae effectu ... Hinc autem sequitur [non] posse ... fieri ... id quod magis perfectum est ... ab eo quod minus* (AT VII 40; CSM II 28).

53 It is interesting to note that Cartesian physics, in so far as it offers explanations purely in terms of mathematical covering laws, offers the possibility of dispensing with traditional models of causality; the opportunity, however, was not fully seized by Descartes (see pp. 222–5). For more on Descartes's conception of causality, and its influence on the philosophical history of the seventeenth and eighteenth centuries, see N. Jolley, *The Light of the Soul* [6.19], ch. 3.

54 *Conversation with Burman*, AT V 156; CB 17. For more on the scholastic background to Descartes's causal proof for God's existence, see J. Cottingham, 'A New Start? Cartesian Metaphysics and the Emergence of Modern Philosophy', in T. Sorell (ed.) *The Rise of Modern Philosophy* [6.37].

55 In the Fifth Meditation, Descartes offers a further proof of God's existence, namely that since God is defined as the supremely perfect being, all perfections, including that of existence, must necessarily be part of his essential nature:

> it is quite evident that existence can no more be separated from the essence of God than the fact that its three angles equal two right angles can be separated from the essence of a triangle, or than the idea of a mountain can be separated from the idea of a valley. Hence it is no less of a contradiction to think of God (that is a supremely perfect being) lacking existence (that is, lacking a perfection) than it is to think of a mountain without a valley.

(AT VII 66; CSM II 46) A version of this argument (known since Kant as the 'ontological argument') had originally been put forward by St Anselm of Canterbury in the eleventh century, but it had been strongly criticized by Aquinas, and its revival by Descartes was a source of considerable surprise to his contemporaries. For some of the objections raised by contemporary critics, see the First Set of Objections to the Meditations, AT VII 98; CSM II 70. For a discussion of some of the problematic aspects of the argument, see further J. Cottingham, *Descartes* [6.11], 57ff.

56 Second and Fourth Objections respectively: AT VII 125; CSM II 89 and AT VII 214; CSM II 150.

57 AT VII 62; CSM II 43.

58 Fifth Meditation: AT VII 71; CSM II 49.

59 cf. Second Replies, AT VII 140ff.; CSM II 100ff.; Fourth Replies, AT VII 246; CSM II 171; *Conversation with Burman*, AT V 148; CB 6. For more on the circle objection and Descartes's reply to it, see especially A. Gewirth, 'The Cartesian Circle' [6.45] and L. Loeb, 'The Cartesian Circle', in J. Cottingham (ed.) *Cambridge Companions: Descartes* [6.32].

60 AT VII 526; CSM II 419.

61 *Conversation with Burman* (1648): AT V 160; CSMK 343.

62 Letter to Mersenne of 15 April 1630, AT I 145; CSMK 23; cf. Sixth Replies: 'God did not will that the three angles of a triangle should be equal to two right angles because he recognized that it could not be otherwise; ... it is

because he wills that the three angles of a triangle should necessarily equal two right angles that this is true and cannot be otherwise' (AT VII 432; CSM II 291).

63 See, for example, Aquinas, *Summa Theologiae*, Ia, 25, 3. See further A. Kenny, *Descartes* [6.20], 37f.

64 Letter to Mersenne of 27 May 1630; AT I 152; CSMK 25.

65 *Notre âme, étant finie, ne le puisse comprendre ni concevoir* (ibid.). For further discussion of this theme, cf. J.-M. Beyssade, 'The Idea of God' [6.38].

66 For an interesting development of this point, see S. Gaukroger, *Cartesian Logic* [6.15], ch. 2.

67 See *Principles*, Book II, art. 64.

68 I use the term 'post-Humean' in accordance with what may be called the traditional interpretation of Hume as a philosopher who undermined the idea of science as the discovery of necessary connections in the world. For an alternative interpretation, see J. Wright, *The Sceptical Realism of David Hume* (Cambridge, Cambridge University Press, 1983).

69 For the simplicity and economy claimed by Descartes for his system see the letter to Huygens of 10 October 1642 (AT II 797; CSMK 216) and *Principles*, Part IV, arts 199 and 206.

70 For the breaking down of the barriers between terrestrial and celestial, see *Principles*, Part IV, *passim*; for the barrier between organic and inorganic, see *Description of the Human Body* (AT XI 226; CSM I 315); for that between natural and artificial, see *Treatise on Man* (AT XI 120f., CSM I 99f.).

71 *Treatise on Man*: AT XI 120; CSM I 99. Though published (after Descartes's death) as a separate work, the *Treatise on Man* was originally conceived by Descartes as part of *Le Monde*. See further CSM I 79.

72 He lived for a time in Kalverstraat in Amsterdam, where he obtained carcasses for dissection from the butcher; some of his later experiments in vivisection are described in the *Description of the Human Body* (AT XI 242f.; CSM I 317f.).

73 AT VII 230; CSM II 161.

74 AT VII 426; CSM I 288.

75 *Description of the Human Body*: AT XI 226; CSM I 315.

76 *Discourse*, Part Five, AT VI 56f.; CSM I 140.

77 This feature of language has been highlighted in our own day by Noam Chomsky: for his account of language as essentially 'stimulus-free', see N. Chomsky, *Language and Mind* (New York, Harcourt, Brace & World, 1968).

78 *Discourse*, Part Five, op. cit. For more on the strengths and weaknesses of Descartes's language argument, see J. Cottingham, 'Cartesian Dualism: Theology, Metaphysics and Science', in *Cambridge Companions: Descartes* [6.32].

79 In the *Treatise on Man*, Descartes compares the nervous system to the complex set of pipes and reservoirs found in a park with fountains and moving statues:

> Visitors who enter the grottos of these fountains ... cannot enter without stepping on certain tiles which are so arranged that if, for example, they approach a Diana who is bathing they will cause her to

hide in the reeds, and if they move forward to pursue her they will cause a Neptune to advance and threaten them with his trident.

All these events happen purely mechanically, according to the 'whim of the engineers who made the fountains'. But a human being is more than a physiological system of pipes and levers:

> when a rational soul is present in the machine, it will have its principal seat in the brain and reside there like the fountain keeper who must be stationed at the tanks to which the fountain's pipes return if he wants to produce or prevent or change their movements in some way.
>
> (AT XI 131; CSM I 101)

80 *Discourse*, Part Five: AT VI 59; CSM I 141.
81 cf. Synopsis to *Meditations*: '... *l'esprit ou l'âme de l'homme (ce que je ne distingue point)* ...' (AT IX 11; CSM II 10).
82 *Discourse*, Part Four: AT VI 32f.; CSM I 127.
83 cf. AT VII 8; CSM II 7.
84 Meditation Two: AT VII 30–1; CSM II 20–1.
85 AT VII 78; CSM II 54. The gloss in square brackets does not appear in the original Latin text of 1641, but is inserted in the later French translation. See above, note 50.
86 Sixth Meditation, op. cit.
87 See AT VII 49; CSM II 33: 'I do not take it upon myself to try to use the power of human reason to settle any of those matters which depend on the free will of God.'
88 Compare Leibniz's critique of the ontological argument: *Discourse on Metaphysics*, §23. See further J. Cottingham, *The Rationalists* [6.12], 100.
89 See further T. Penelhum, *Survival and Disembodied Existence* (London, Routledge, 1968).
90 This line of thought was the basis of the 'Averroist heresy' (condemned by the Lateran council in 1513) which denied personal immortality. See further AT VII 3; CSM II 4; and Cottingham, cited in note 78.
91 Sixth Meditation: AT VII 81; CSM II 56.
92 *Conversation with Burman*, AT V 163; CB 28.
93 Imagination and sensation are faculties '*sine quibus totum me possum clare & distincte intelligere*' (AT VII 78; CSM II 54). The 'hybrid' faculties of sensation and imagination are often singled out for special treatment by Descartes. Compare a passage earlier in the same Meditation, which asserts that imagination is not a necessary constituent of my essence as a thinking thing: *vim imaginandi, prout differt a vi intelligendi, ad mei ipsius, hoc est ad mentis meae essentiam non requiri* (AT VII 73; CSM II 51). For more on the 'hybrid' faculties, see J. Cottingham, *Descartes* [6.11], 122ff.
94 Sixth Meditation: AT VII 81; CSM II 56.
95 To this should be added motion, which Descartes sometimes describes as a straightforward mode of extension (AT II 650; CSMK 217), but which, in the *Principles*, is said to be specially imparted to matter by divine action (see *Principles*, Part II, arts 36ff.
96 AT III 665; CSMK 218.

97 Letter of 28 June 1643, AT III 692 and 694; CSMK 227 and 228.
98 ibid.
99 *Passions of the Soul*, Part I, art. 42 (AT XI 360; CSM I 344). Descartes regarded the pineal gland (or *conarion*) as the 'principal seat of the soul' and the locus of psycho-physical interactions; cf. *Passions*, Part I, arts 31 and 32.
100 See for example *Passions*, Part I, art. 39.
101 See p. 211.
102 See *Principles*, II, 36 and 40.
103 It should be noted that some recent commentators have argued that Descartes did not in fact regard interaction between heterogeneous substances as problematic. See R. C. Richardson, 'The Scandal of Cartesian Interactionism' [6.51]. For criticism of this view, see J. Cottingham, *The Rationalists* [6.12], 212f. and 202.
104 *Comments on a Certain Broadsheet*: AT VIIIB 359; CSM I 304. Compare also *Optics*, Section Six: AT VI 130; CSM I 167. For more on the 'occasionalist' elements in Descartes's account of mind and body, see J. Cottingham, 'Descartes on Colour', *Proceedings of the Aristotelian Society* 90 (1989–90) Part 3, 231–46.

❧ BIBLIOGRAPHY ❧

Original language edition

6.1 Adam, C. and Tannery, P. (eds) *Œuvres de Descartes*, 1877–1913; Paris, Vrin/ CNRS, revised edn, 12 vols, 1964–76.

English translation

6.2 Cottingham, J., Stoothoff, R. and Murdoch, D. (eds) *The Philosophical Writings of Descartes*, Cambridge, Cambridge University Press, 2 vols, 1985. Volume III (*The Correspondence*) by the same translators and Anthony Kenny, Cambridge University Press, 1991.

Other editions

6.3 Alquié, F. (ed.) *Descartes, Œuvres philosophiques*, Paris, Presses Universitaires de France, 3 vols, 1936–63.
6.4 Beyssade, M. (ed.) *Descartes, Méditations métaphysiques. Texte latin et traduction du duc de Luynes, avec traduction nouvelle*, Paris, Livre de Poche, 1990.
6.5 Cottingham, J. (ed.) *Descartes' Conversation with Burman*, Oxford, Clarendon, 1976.
6.6 Gilson, E. *Descartes, Discours de la Méthode, texte et commentaire*, Paris, Vrin, 1925; 4th edn, 1967.

6.7 Marion, J.-L. (ed.) *Règles utiles et claires pour la direction de l'esprit*, The Hague, Nijhoff, 1977.

General works on Descartes, and studies of his metaphysics and philosophy of mind

6.8 Alquié, F. *La découverte métaphysique de l'homme chez Descartes*, Paris, Presses Universitaires de France, 1950; 2nd edn, 1987.

6.9 Beck, L. J. *The Metaphysics of Descartes: A Study of the Meditations*, Oxford, Clarendon, 1965.

6.10 Beyssade, J.-M. *La première philosophie de Descartes*, Paris, Presses Universitaires de France, 1979.

6.11 Cottingham, J. *Descartes*, Oxford, Blackwell, 1986.

6.12 Cottingham, J. *The Rationalists*, Oxford, Oxford University Press, 1988.

6.13 Curley, E. *Descartes against the Skeptics*, Oxford, Blackwell, 1978.

6.14 Frankfurt, H. G. *Demons, Dreamers and Madmen: The Validation of Reason in Descartes' Meditations*, Indianapolis, Ind., Bobbs-Merrill, 1970.

6.15 Gaukroger, S. *Cartesian Logic*, Oxford, Clarendon, 1989.

6.16 Guéroult, M. *Descartes selon l'ordre des raisons*, Paris, Montaigne, 1953. English translation by R. Ariew, *Descartes' Philosophy interpreted according to the Order of Reason*, Minneapolis, Minn., University of Minnesota Press, 1984.

6.17 Gouhier, H. *La pensée métaphysique de Descartes*, Paris, Vrin, 1962.

6.18 Greene, M. *Descartes*, Brighton, Harvester, 1985.

6.19 Jolley, N. *The Light of the Soul*, Oxford, Clarendon, 1990.

6.20 Kenny, A. *Descartes, A Study of his Philosophy*, New York, Random House, 1968.

6.21 Marion, J.-L. *Sur le prisme métaphysique de Descartes*, Paris, Presses Universitaires de France, 1986.

6.22 Markie, P. *Descartes' Gambit*, Ithaca, N.Y., Cornell University Press, 1986.

6.23 Popkin, R. *The History of Scepticism from Erasmus to Descartes*, New York, Harper, 1964.

6.24 Rodis-Lewis, G. *Descartes*, Paris, Librairie Générale Française, 1984.

6.25 Sorell, T. *Descartes*, Oxford, Oxford University Press, 1987.

6.26 Swinburne, R. *The Evolution of the Soul*, Oxford, Clarendon, 1986.

6.27 Watson, R. *The Breakdown of Cartesian Metaphysics*, Atlantic Highlands, N.J., Humanities Press, 1987.

6.28 Williams, B. *Descartes: The Project of Pure Inquiry*, Harmondsworth, Penguin, 1978.

6.29 Wilson, M. D. *Descartes*, London, Routledge, 1978.

Collections of critical essays

6.30 Ayers, M. and Garber, D. *Cambridge History of Seventeenth Century Philosophy*, Cambridge, Cambridge University Press, 1992.

6.31 Butler, R. J. (ed.) *Cartesian Studies*, Oxford, Blackwell, 1972.

6.32 Cottingham, J. (ed.) *Cambridge Companions: Descartes*, Cambridge, Cambridge University Press, 1992.

6.33 Doney, W. (ed.) *Descartes: A Collection of Critical Essays*, New York, Doubleday, 1967.

6.34 Hooker, M. (ed.) *Descartes, Critical and Interpretive Essays*, Baltimore, Md., Johns Hopkins University Press, 1978.

6.35 Lennon, T. M., Nicholas, J. M. and Davis, J. W. (eds) *Problems of Cartesianism*, Montreal and Kingston, McGill-Queens University Press, 1982.

6.36 Rorty, A. *Essays on Descartes' Meditations*, Berkeley, Calif., University of California Press, 1986.

6.37 Sorell, T. (ed.) *The Rise of Modern Philosophy*, Oxford, Oxford University Press, 1992.

Articles

6.38 Beyssade, J.-M. 'The Idea of God and the Proofs of His Existence', in J. Cottingham (ed.) *Cambridge Companions: Descartes*, Cambridge, Cambridge University Press, 1992.

6.39 Bousma, O. K. 'Descartes' Evil Genius', *Philosophical Review* 58 (1949) 141ff.

6.40 Cottingham, J. 'Cartesian Trialism', *Mind* 94 (1985) 226ff.

6.41 Doney, W. 'The Cartesian Circle', *Journal of the History of Philosophy* 8 (1970) 387ff.

6.42 Frankfurt, H. 'Descartes' Discussion of his Existence in the Second Meditation', *Philosophical Review* 75 (1966) 329–56.

6.43 Garber, D. 'Mind, Body and the Laws of Nature in Descartes and Leibniz', *Midwest Studies in Philosophy* 8 (1983) 105ff.

6.44 Gewirth, A. 'Clearness and Distinctness in Descartes', *Philosophy* 18 (1943); reprinted in W. Doney (ed.) *Descartes: A Collection of Critical Essays*, New York, Doubleday, 1967.

6.45 Gewirth, A. 'The Cartesian Circle', *Philosophical Review* 50 (1941) 368–95.

6.46 Hintikka, J. 'Cogito ergo sum: Inference or Performance', *Philosophical Review* 71 (1962); reprinted in W. Doney (ed.) *Descartes: A Collection of Critical Essays*, New York, Doubleday, 1967.

6.47 Kenny, A. 'The Cartesian Circle and the Eternal Truths', *Journal of Philosophy* 67 (1970) 685–700.

6.48 Loeb, L. 'The Priority of Reason in Descartes', *Philosophical Review* 99 (1990) 243ff.

6.49 Loeb, L. 'The Cartesian Circle', in J. Cottingham (ed.) *Cambridge Companions: Descartes*, Cambridge, Cambridge University Press, 1992.

6.50 Malcolm, N. 'Descartes' Proof that his Essence is Thinking', *Philosophical Review* 74 (1965) 315ff.

6.51 Richardson, R. C. 'The Scandal of Cartesian Interactionism', *Mind* 91 (1982) 20–37.

6.52 Stoothoff, R. 'Descartes' Dilemmatic Argument', *Philosophical Quarterly* 29 (1989) 294–307.

CHAPTER 7

Seventeenth-century materialism: Gassendi and Hobbes

T. Sorell

In the English-speaking world Pierre Gassendi is probably best known as the author of a set of Objections to Descartes's *Meditations*. These Objections, the fifth of seven sets collected by Mersenne, are relatively long and full, and suggestive of a number of distinctively Gassendist doctrines – for example his nominalism, his insistence on distinguishing mathematical objects from physical ones, and his doubt whether we can know the natures of things, even our selves. Perhaps more prominent than these doctrines, however, is a kind of materialism. Gassendi adopts the ironic form of address 'O Mind' in challenging Descartes's claim that one's nature has nothing to do with body. He insists that all ideas have their source in the senses, and he sketches an account of perception that dispenses with a role for a pure intellect but emphasizes the contribution of the brain. In physics he was partial to explanation in terms of the motions of matter, ultimately the motions of material atoms. These points suggest that Gassendi was a mechanistic materialist of some kind, and they link him in intellectual history with Hobbes, who proposed that physical as well as psychological phenomena were nothing more than motions in different kinds of body.

The grounds for associating Gassendi and Hobbes are contextual as well as textual. They both lived in Paris in the 1640s. They were close friends and active in the circle of scientists, mathematicians and theologians round Mersenne. They were both at odds, intellectually and personally, with Descartes. They read one another's manuscripts, apparently with approval. There are even supposed to be important similarities of phrasing in their writings about morals and politics. Gassendi wrote a tribute to Hobbes's first published work, *De Cive*, and Hobbes was reported in a letter as saying that Gassendi's system was as big as Aristotle's but much truer.

Whatever the extent of the mutual admiration and influence, it did not produce a particularly marked similarity of outlook except in psychology, where each developed strongly materialistic lines of thought, and even in psychology the match between their views is not perfect. Unlike Hobbes's materialism, Gassendi's cannot be said to be wholehearted. He held that there was an incorporeal as well as a corporeal or vegetative part of the soul, and he ascribed to the incorporeal part cognitive operations that in some respects duplicated, and in other respects surpassed, those of the corporeal part. Hobbes denied that there were such things as incorporeal souls, and he would have doubted the conceivability of an incorporeal part of the soul. His theory of knowledge invoked no purely psychological capacities and he recognized no purely spiritual entities. The different materialisms of Hobbes and Gassendi also fit into rather different systems of philosophy. Both systems were motivated by a repudiation of Aristotle and a desire to provide philosophical grounding for the new science of the seventeenth century, but Gassendi's provides that grounding in the form of a theory attributed to, or at least inspired by, an ancient authority, while Hobbes's does not. The ancient authority in question was Epicurus. Probably Gassendi revised Epicurean thought to a greater degree than he revived it; nevertheless, he took himself to be engaged in a humanist enterprise of bringing back to life a badly understood, unfairly maligned and long-discredited way of thinking. Hobbes's system was in no sense intended to rehabilitate traditional thought. It was supposed to lay out the new elements of a new natural philosophy and an even newer and largely Hobbesian civil philosophy.

❧ INTRODUCTION ❧

The different intellectual development of the two writers makes it surprising that the philosophies of Gassendi and Hobbes converge as much as they do. Gassendi was the younger of the two by about four years, born in Provence in 1592. At Digne, Ruez and Aix he received a thorough scholastic education in mathematics, philosophy and theology during which, at the age of 12, he began to train for the priesthood. He was a very talented pupil, even something of a child prodigy. At the age of 16 he was a teacher of rhetoric at Digne. He received the doctorate in theology from Avignon six years later, and in 1616, when he was 24, he won competitions for two chairs at the university of Aix, one in theology and one in philosophy. He chose the chair in philosophy. Though his career as a teacher was cut short when the university was transferred to the control of the Jesuits in 1622, Gassendi was occupied for virtually the whole of his working life with theological, philosophical, historical and scientific studies. He conducted these to begin with as a member of the chapter, and eventually as provost, of the cathedral at Digne, and at intervals under the patronage of wealthy and powerful friends in Provence and Paris. By the time he came into regular contact with Hobbes in the early 1640s he had already lectured and written extensively about the whole of Aristotle's philosophy, had carried out a number of astronomical observations, as well as investigations in biology and mechanics, had corresponded with and travelled to meet some eminent Copernicans, had read widely in natural philosophy and had engaged in numerous erudite researches concerning the lives and thought of Epicurus and other ancient authorities. He had also worked on reconciling the scientific theories that he admired with his Catholicism.

Hobbes did not have a comparable grounding in the sciences or philosophy. Prior to 1629 or 1630 he is supposed to have been completely innocent of Euclid. When he took up residence in Paris in 1640 he had a respectable grounding in the classics but a still not very deep knowledge of the elements of geometry, or the new astronomy or mechanics. He was over 40 before he took a serious interest in natural science or its methods, and he was probably over 50 before he began to articulate a considered general philosophy of his own. He had published a translation of Thucydides' *History of the Peloponnesian Wars* in 1628. He had completed a treatise on psychology, morals and politics shortly before leaving England for Paris in 1640. He may have composed a fairly substantial optical work in the late 1630s, and a so-called 'short tract' on first principles in natural philosophy as early as 1630: the date of the one and the authorship of the other are not entirely certain. But it was apparently after arriving in Paris rather than before that Hobbes engaged in any concentrated scientific research.

That he developed an interest in natural philosophy at all was probably a kind of accident. For most of his life he was attached to the households of successive Earls of Devonshire as tutor, travelling companion, secretary, confidant, political adviser, keeper of accounts and, finally, elderly retainer. From 1608, when he first entered the service of the Devonshires, to 1629, when he temporarily took employment elsewhere, he seems not to have had scientific interests. At Oxford he had received an arts degree. As tutor he gave instruction in rhetoric, logic and morals. In his spare time he studied classical poetry and history. It was not until he left the Devonshires and was employed for two years as the travelling companion of a baronet's son on the European Grand Tour that he happened to come upon an open copy of Euclid in a gentleman's study. From then on, according to Aubrey's biography, Hobbes was in love with geometry. On this journey to the Continent also he is supposed to have stopped for some months in Paris in 1629. It was then that he met Mersenne, according to the latter's correspondence, probably becoming acquainted with some of the scientific researches of Mersenne's circle.[1] Another episode at about this time is supposed to have made him curious about natural science. Either during the Grand Tour or shortly afterwards Hobbes was present at a discussion of sense perception in which it emerged that no one present was able to say what sense perception was. His best scientific work – in optics – probably had its origins in thinking that was prompted by this discussion.

After the Grand Tour Hobbes's interest in science found outlets in England. When he returned to the service of the Devonshires in 1631, he started to come into frequent contact with a branch of his master's family who lived at Welbeck, near the Devonshire family home of Hardwick Hall. For the Welbeck Cavendishes, who were headed by the Earl of Newcastle, he performed some of the duties that he had been discharging for the Earls of Devonshire. He became their adviser and agent and did other odd jobs. These Cavendishes had scientific interests. The Earl of Newcastle is known to have sent Hobbes to London in the early 1630s to find a copy of a book of Galileo's. The Earl's younger brother, Charles, had an even greater interest in science, and acted as a kind of patron and distributor of scientific writing, notably the writings of a scientist called Walter Warner. Hobbes was one of those who gave his opinion of the writings that Charles Cavendish circulated. Cavendish also had contacts with many Continental scientists, including Mersenne and Descartes.

Hobbes accompanied the third Earl of Devonshire on another Grand Tour from 1634 to 1636. He probably met Galileo in Italy and once again saw Mersenne when he passed through Paris. His activities in the 1630s, however, did not provide him with a real scientific education, and it may seem surprising that when he renewed his contact with Mersenne in the 1640s he should have been treated as the equal of people whose knowledge of natural philosophy and mathematics was far greater than his own. Perhaps his knowledge mattered less than his enthusiasm. Hobbes shared with the intellectuals that he met in Paris a profound admiration for Galileo, and a belief that deductive methods could be applied to fields outside natural science. He was applying them himself in psychology, ethics and politics, subjects that Mersenne especially was keen to see placed on a scientific footing. Then, apart from what he had in common intellectually with members of Mersenne's circle, many of them found him an agreeable personality.

It was one thing for Hobbes to be accepted as a full member of Mersenne's circle, however, and another for his views to be endorsed.

His extreme materialism could not be reconciled with orthodox theology; his views about the necessity of subordinating the ecclesiastical to the secular power could not have been accepted by members of the circle who were subject to the Catholic authorities. Mersenne and Gassendi, who were both Catholic churchmen, needed to keep their distance in matters of doctrine. Mersenne managed to do this while at the same time acting as a publicist for Hobbes's hypotheses in natural philosophy and a promoter of his political treatise, *De Cive*. His method was to be vague in identifying the author of the hypotheses, and discreet in his praise for Hobbes's civil philosophy. When Mersenne published any of Hobbes's work or reported it to correspondents, Hobbes was usually referred to merely as 'l'Anglais'. At other times Mersenne exercised an influence from behind the scenes. He encouraged the publication in 1647 of a second edition of Hobbes's political treatise, *De Cive*: the first, limited and anonymous printing had been a success in Paris five years earlier. However, Sorbière, who saw the work through the press, was instructed by Mersenne not to publish his own or Gassendi's letters praising the book. In Gassendi's case, the need to keep Hobbes at arm's length was made urgent by the parallels between his and Hobbes's responses to the *Meditations*. It is also possible that during the 1640s Gassendi saw in Hobbes's writing precisely the combination of atheistic materialism and determinism that a too sympathetic treatment of Epicurus might have committed Gassendi himself to, and that, in order to avoid this, he strengthened the theological 'corrections' to the doctrine.[2]

Though they were friends, then, and though their views coincided up to a point, Hobbes and Gassendi also had some unsurprising doctrinal differences. We shall see more of the differences to do with theology and materialism later. But there were also others. They differed in important ways in their attitudes toward the ancients. Gassendi was a critic of Aristotle throughout his intellectual life and a critic also of the neo-Aristotelian doctrines of the scholastic curriculum. In the preface to his first published work, *Exercitationes Paradoxicae Adversus Aristoteleos*, he says that he was disappointed that the philosophy that he was taught brought him none of the freedom from vexation that writers such as Cicero promised the subject could provide. Still, Gassendi did not believe that a better overall philosophy was to be found in his own age, and those of his contemporaries whom he did admire, such as Pierre Charron, made use of ancient rather than modern doctrine to criticize Aristotle. In Charron's case the ancient doctrine employed was pyrrhonism. Gassendi followed Charron's lead in his lecture courses in the university of Aix. Pyrrhonist arguments were used in criticism of the whole range of Aristotle's philosophy, and the material for these lectures was the basis in turn for the first volume of the *Exercitationes*, which appeared in 1624. Book II of this work contained arguments suggesting that science in Aristotle's sense, that is, demonstrative knowledge of the necessity of observed effects based on knowledge of the natures or essences of substances, was beyond human capacities, while a more modest science, presupposing no essences of substances and no knowledge of essences and ending up only in probabilistic conclusions about effects, *was* possible. Books III–V were devoted to would-be refutations, inspired by pyrrhonism, of Aristotelian doctrines in physics, astronomy and biology. Book VI was an attack on Aristotle's metaphysics. Finally, Book VII expounded the non-Aristotelian moral philosophy of Epicurus.

A second volume of the *Exercitationes* was planned, but it was suppressed by Gassendi for reasons that still are not well understood. He may have become dissatisfied with sceptical arguments, believing that they fuelled a potentially endless controversy about Aristotelian science without putting anything in its place. He may have come to the conclusion that others, such as Patrizi, had already criticized Aristotle so thoroughly as to make more of the *Exercitationes* redundant. He may have found in Mersenne's writings a more sophisticated and satisfactory approach to the questioning of Aristotle.[3] Or again, he may have taken his cue from the increasingly severe reaction of the educational establishment in Paris to challengers of the learned authorities: in 1624 the Sorbonne managed to prevent the public defence in Paris of a number of theses against Aristotle. Whatever his reasons for holding back the second volume, Gassendi did not cease to make use of the ancients in working out an anti-Aristotelian philosophy of science. Within a few years of the publication of the first volume, and perhaps on the advice of Mersenne, he was already studying Epicurus and contemplating the rehabilitation of his philosophy as a rival to Aristotle's. He was confirmed in this plan by a journey he made in December 1628. He travelled to Holland to meet, among others, scientists sympathetic to the Copernican approach to astronomy. The one who most impressed him was the physician and savant Isaac Beeckman, who ten years earlier had been Descartes's mentor. Beeckman discussed the physical problem of free fall with Gassendi and spoke with approval of Epicurus. It was apparently after this meeting[4] that Gassendi began to think of publishing a treatise favourable to Epicurus. That this work on Epicurus was supposed to take further the anti-Aristotelianism of what he had already published is suggested by the fact that at first Gassendi planned to bring out a demythologized life of Epicurus and an apology for Epicureanism as an appendix to the *Exercitationes*. As early as 1630, however, this modest project had given way to the much more ambitious one of writing a perfectly comprehensive exposition and defence of Epicurus, something that could articulate a positive philosophy to rival Aristotle's but without its pretensions to demonstrativeness or to acquaintance with essences that transcended appearance.

Now a little later than Gassendi Hobbes also began to plan a large-scale work: an exposition of the 'elements' of a non-Aristotelian philosophy. Perhaps by the late 1630s he had completed an outline that divided the elements into three sections, on body, man and citizen. None of these, however, was derived from traditional philosophy. Indeed, when it came to the elements expounded in the first section, Hobbes claimed that they could be collected together by reflection on the mind's contents in the abstract. In the Epistle Dedicatory of *De Corpore*, the book that opened the trilogy, Hobbes likened the process of deriving the concepts of first philosophy to the creation described in Genesis. From the inchoate and undifferentiated material of sense, distinction and order would be created in the form of a list of definitions of the most general concepts for understanding body. In arriving at the foundations of his philosophy *de novo*, Hobbes was closer to Descartes than to Gassendi. As in Descartes, an entirely ahistorical and abstract starting point is adopted and this proclaims the novelty of the philosophy subsequently developed, and its independence of the approved learned authors, Aristotle, Ptolemy and Galen.

The intention of breaking with such authorities was underlined in Hobbes's writings in his account of correct teaching or demonstration. 'The infallible sign of teaching exactly, and without error' Hobbes writes in *The Elements of Law*, 'is this: that no man hath ever taught the contrary . . .' (Pt 1, ch. 13, iii, 65). Or, as he goes on to put it, 'the sign of [teaching] is no controversy' (ibid., 66). Hobbes goes on to explain what it is about the content and format of exact teaching or demonstration that keeps controversy from breaking out. He considers the practice of successful teachers and observes that they

> proceed from most low and humble principles, evident even to
> the meanest capacity; going on slowly, and with most
> scrupulous ratiocination (viz.) from the imposition of names
> they infer the truth of their first proposition; and from two of
> the first, a third, and from two of the three a fourth, and so on.
> (ibid.)

Practitioners of this method are called 'the *mathematici*', and of the two sorts of men commonly called learned, they alone really are learned. The other sort are

> they that take up maxims from their education, and from the
> authority of men, or of authors, and take the habitual discourse

of the tongue for ratiocination; and these are called the
dogmatici.

(EL, Pt 1, ch. 13, iv, 67)

These men are the breeders of controversy, according to Hobbes, breeders of controversy precisely because they take their opinions undigested from authorities and act as mouthpieces for views they have not worked out from 'low, humble and evident' principles. He seems to be referring to the same class of men at the beginning of *De Corpore* when he speaks of people 'who, from opinions, though not vulgar, yet full of uncertainty and carelessly received, do nothing but dispute and wrangle, like men that are not well in their wits' (ch. 1, i, E I 2). And in the same spirit there is the remark in *Leviathan* that 'he that takes up conclusions on the trust of authors, and doth not fetch them up from the first item in every reckoning, which are the significations of names settled by definitions, loses his labour, and does not know anything but merely believeth' (ch. 5, E III 32).

Hobbes blames the *dogmatici* for the backward state of moral and civil philosophy before *De Cive*, and he traces the then modest development of natural philosophy to a misconception that had prevailed for a long time about how far the methods of the *mathematici* could be applied. The misconception was due to the Romans and Greeks (cf. *De corp.* ch. 6, xvi, E I 86), who wrongly believed that demonstration or ratiocination was only applicable to geometrical figures, as if it were the figures that made the conclusions of geometrical demonstrations evident. What in fact made the geometrical conclusions of writers like Euclid so compelling was not the use of figures but the use of true principles as the starting-points of geometrical demonstrations. Were other doctrines to start from similar principles, they too would enjoy conclusiveness and truth. As Hobbes writes in *De Corpore*, 'there is no reason but that if true definitions were premissed in all sorts of doctrines, the demonstrations also would be true' (ibid., E I 87). The idea that 'all sorts' of doctrine might be true, that is, that doctrines on all sorts of topics might be true, if they were to begin from true principles, has an epistemological counterpart: demonstrative *knowledge* of all sorts of truth might be acquired, were the knowledge to be the result of reasoning from definitions known to be true.

❧ GASSENDI ❧

When Hobbes warns against relying on authors and insists on reaching conclusions from evident first principles, he may seem to reflect the intellectual style of early modern philosophy better than Gassendi does by his use of Epicurus. But this impression may have more to do with a certain kind of historiography than with the facts of intellectual life in the 1600s. The usual histories of this period of philosophy emphasize novelty, revolution and methodological principles that seem to prepare the way for nineteenth- and twentieth-century science. Bacon's, Galileo's and Descartes's writings lend themselves particularly well to this conception of a time of decisive intellectual change, a time that ushered in modernity and saw out tradition, and these writings tend to be discussed to the exclusion of works of other seventeenth-century figures – even figures whom the canonical moderns respected and took for allies, such as Gassendi. The standard histories may not only be criticized for overlooking the celebrity and influence that Gassendi enjoyed in his own day; they may not only be criticized for making this celebrity hard to understand once it is pointed out; they may also be criticized for missing the strengths of the traditional form of presentation used by Gassendi in the context of the early seventeenth century.

Many of those who promoted the new science and attacked the old philosophy did so in books that they knew would meet hostility from the church and the schoolmen. By choosing for some of his works the literary form of the erudite rehabilitation of an ancient authority like Epicurus, Gassendi was employing the methods that the doctors of the church had used to appropriate Aristotle. Again, by being comprehensive in his treatment of Epicurus's critics Gassendi gave the impression of being an even-handed exponent of his chosen author, in contrast with sycophantic followers of Aristotle. He discussed the views of Epicurus in the context of the antagonisms between the ancient Greek schools of philosophy, including the Peripatetics, and so he was able to revive a sense of Aristotle and his school as representing just one way of thinking among others during a period in which Greek philosophy was sectarian, and when no one sect had any special authority. Again, by showing that the genuine Epicurus had been completely lost in the lore about Epicurus, Gassendi was able to introduce to intellectual life a virtually new figure, not just a relatively familiar one who deserved a second hearing. Apart from the novelty of the Epicurus that Gassendi revived, there was the relevance of his views to the topical issues of the anomalies in Aristotle's physics, and the significance of scepticism. In relation to scepticism, Epicureanism seemed to claim less, and so to be less vulnerable to sceptical criticism, than Aristotelianism. This was the lesson of Gassendi's exposition of Epicurean canonics as a preferred logic. In relation to seventeenth-century physics, Epicurean explanations avoided some of the anomalies that Aristotelian explanations were increasingly embarrassed by.[5] At the same time, it could be regarded as a comprehensive natural philosophy.

Finally, Gassendi was able to give special prominence to views, for example about whether the world was eternal, that showed Epicurus in a better theological light than Aristotle. Of course Epicurus needed theological correction; but so did Aristotle.

That it made sense for Gassendi to present ideas favourable to the new science in the form of erudite commentary does not mean that he hit on the most satisfactory form for such a commentary, or even one that was adequate in his own eyes. His principal work on Epicurus, *Animadversiones in Decimum Librum Diogenis Laertii* (1649), was disorderly and ran to three volumes. Gassendi allowed it to appear with great reluctance. The posthumously edited *Syntagma Philosophicum* (1658), which is generally taken to be the culmination of his work on Epicurus, is a commentary in part and contains material from redactions intended to result in a commentary, but it is also and primarily a statement of the philosophy Gassendi himself arrived at from a starting point in Epicurus. It is known that he revised the manuscripts incorporated into the *Syntagma* many times over a period of decades and that he tried out many different ways of putting together his material, never finding one that was satisfactory.[6] The point is that it was reasonable, even shrewd, to choose *some* form of erudite commentary as a medium for his ideas, given the hostile elements in the audience he was addressing. Descartes, who in the *Discourse* and the *Meditations* experimented with quite different and innovative literary styles for the presentation of his ideas, and who was either misunderstood or criticized for not being explicit enough as a result, himself turned to something like a scholastic presentation in the *Principles of Philosophy*, which was much more widely cited by his followers and critics in the second half of the seventeenth century than the other two works. And he toyed with the idea of writing an *abrégé* of a *summa philosophiae* by Eustachius a Sancto Paulo as a vehicle for some of his thought.

What were the main Epicurean ideas that Gassendi expounded? In logic, the idea that 'canons' or precepts for conceiving the real and finding the true were an antidote to the complexities of Aristotelian dialectic, and the idea that we might have, through signs, some access to what otherwise are relatively unknowable things beyond sensory experience; in physics, the idea that the universe is composed of atoms of matter in the void, and that the substances composed of these atoms do not realize purposes intrinsic to those substances; in ethics, the idea that well-being is an unperturbed state, in particular a state of freedom from pain or of elevated pleasure. To see how these ideas were adapted to the requirements of a 'modern' philosophy, it is necessary to turn to *Syntagma Philosophicum*.

Logic

Logic occupies the First Part of the *Syntagma*, and Epicurus is mentioned in different connections in each of the two introductory books. In the first of the two, *De origine et varietate logica*, Epicurus's canons for cognitive and practical judgement are listed as part of a survey of existing logical systems. The second book, *De logicae fine*, on the goal of logic, makes clear the significance of Epicurus's canons for cognitive judgement. Gassendi says (ch. 4) that the canons reveal Epicurus to be one of those who held, contrary to the sceptics, that criteria of truth and falsity exist, and that they are provided by both sense and intellect. Chapter 5 of *De logicae fine* defends the anti-sceptical claim that, with the help of signs determined by the criteria of truth and falsehood, some knowledge is possible. Among the things that are supposed to be knowable by sense are the shapes of closely observed things, that is, things observed with allowances made for the distorting effects of media like water or the failings of sight at long distances. As for things knowable by signs determined by reason – indicative signs – Gassendi explains what he means with the help of examples:

> The indicative sign pertains to things naturally hidden, not
> because it indicates a thing in such a way that the thing can
> ever be perceived and the sign can be visibly linked to the thing
> itself, so that it could be argued that where the sign is the thing
> is too, but on the contrary, because it is of such a nature that
> it could not exist unless the thing exists, and therefore whenever
> it exists, the thing also exists. An illustration of this is sweat as
> it indicates the existence of pores in the skin, for pores cannot be
> seen; still sweat is of such a nature that it would not appear
> upon the skin unless pores existed through which it could pass
> from inside to outside. Such also is vital action as it indicates
> the existence of the soul, and motion as it indicates the existence
> of the void . . . .

(Brush, 323)

These signs, when properly made use of in reasoning, are supposed to make possible a kind of science, though not one with the pretensions of the science described by Aristotelian dogmatists. That this anti-sceptical view is seen by Gassendi as Epicurean is shown by the attribution to Epicurus of a virtually identical position in an earlier manuscript commentary (IL, 256–7).

Though Gassendi seems to follow Epicurus in his views about the availability of criteria of truth, there are aspects of Epicurean logic that he finds unappealing. In Chapter 6 of *De logicae fine* he criticizes Epicurus for failing to state rules of deduction, and then blames some of Epicurus's mistaken conjectures in natural philosophy on this omission. He also complains that 'the rules for organizing thought clearly are ... lacking' (Brush, 360), and he seems to suggest that Epicurus was wrong to suppose that ethics had to make use of criteria other than those of sense and reason (ibid.). Sense has a bearing on ethical questions, he says, because pleasure and pain are among its objects (ibid.).

Gassendi's disagreements with Epicurus are reflected in the logic that he himself puts forward. He borrows only selectively from Epicurus, just as he picks and chooses from the other logics he has surveyed, logics ranging from Aristotle's to, in his own day, those of Ramus, Bacon and Descartes. Gassendi's positive logical doctrine is set out in the *Institutio Logica*, the part of the *Syntagma* that follows *De logicae fine* and that serves as transition from logic to physics. The *Institutio* is in four parts, corresponding to the four ways in which good thinking brings one closer to the truth and so to achieving the goal of logic. There are canons for (1) forming clear ideas, (2) forming propositions, (3) making sound inferences and (4) ordering or organizing correctly, by which Gassendi means methods of discovery and of instruction. Of the four sets of canons, it is the first and last that have the most philosophical interest. The third set consists almost entirely of rules for simplifying Aristotelian syllogistic. Gassendi has moved from the extreme hostility to syllogistic that he expressed in the *Exercitationes* to a guarded acceptance of its value in the last chapter of *De logicae fine*, and in the canons he suggests ways of improving Aristotelian logic rather than arguing that it should be scrapped altogether. The tedium of the rules for simplifying syllogistic is relieved by canon 16, which has some deflationary remarks about the strength and source of knowledge conferred by so-called 'scientific syllogisms'. These remarks are in keeping with Gassendi's adoption in *De logicae fine* of a *via media* between dogmatism and scepticism. The second set of canons – concerned with forming propositions – is once again mainly on Aristotelian lines.

The remaining two sets of canons, on forming clear ideas and on method respectively, have closer connections with Gassendi's physics than the other two sets, and also reflect more clearly the influence of Epicurean canons that Gassendi has discussed earlier in the logical books of the *Syntagma*. The first set is to do with ideas or images of things in abstraction from the operations of affirming or denying propositions about those things. Canons 1, 7, 8 and 18 tell us what we are to aim at in our ideas. Accuracy and vividness are desirable (canons 1 and 10); the greater the number of things of which we have ideas the better (canon 18); and, above all, ideas should be 'complete' (ibid.). Completeness in singular ideas or ideas of individuals is a matter of the comprehensiveness of parts and attributes registered:

> Since a particular thing . . . is also some kind of whole made up of its own parts, just as a man is made up of a head, trunk, arms, legs and the other smaller parts from which these are made, and is also some kind of subject endowed with its own attributes, adjuncts, properties or qualities, just as the same man is endowed with size, shape, colour, strength, wit, memory, virtue, wisdom and so on, it is quite clear that the idea of this man will be the more complete the more parts and attributes of him it represents.
>
> (IL, 91)

Gassendi recommends 'anatomy, chemistry and the other sciences' as means of acquiring more perfect singular ideas. More perfect general ideas are acquired the more particulars are known to be covered by a given genus. An idea of mankind that is at first confined to Europeans, Africans and Asians becomes more perfect if it comes to extend to Americans. In the ideal case an idea of a kind of thing can serve as its definition (canon 15). Completeness in ideas can be achieved only within the limits allowed by our ways of forming ideas, which Gassendi stipulates in the first few canons of the logic. All our ideas come from the senses and are in the first place ideas of individual things. Mental operations rather than the external world are responsible for our general, analogical and chimerical ideas (canon 3). Finally, our ideas can only aspire to perfection or completeness if we are aware of the way in which the senses deceive us and keep in mind these sources of deception as we form ideas (canons 11–14).

The fourth set of canons in Gassendi's logic have a different relation to the physics. Instead of speaking of operations of the mind that physics illuminates, they prescribe methods of ordering thought that regulate physics and other sciences. Only the first four canons govern investigation in science; the remaining ten are to do with teaching what one learns. Canon 4 reintroduces the Epicurean criteria of truth: judgements are to be submitted to sense *and* reason (IL, 160). Canon 1 recommends the use of signs as a way of finding the key or middle term in the solution of questions. Canon 3 introduces the distinction between analysis or resolution and synthesis or composition, suggesting that whichever has been used to arrive at an answer, the other should be used to check it.

When he comes to the precepts governing the presentation of one's findings for the purposes of instruction Gassendi produces by way of illustration a description of how to teach physics that is hard not to take as a blueprint for the next major part of the *Syntagma*. He is making the point that in the sciences, as in the productive arts, it pays to teach as if you were explaining how something was made; in the case of natural science, how the universe is made up from its parts:

> Thus a physicist who is giving instruction in the natural sciences places as a model before our eyes, like the larger and smaller parts of a building, only on an extended scale, the structure of nature or the machine of the world, the sky, the earth, all that they contain, and analysing them into their smallest possible components takes these as the primary units which go to make up the whole. His next step is to inquire into the precise nature and pattern of the various combinations responsible for the formation of the sun, the moon and the other heavenly bodies, and in the same way the earth and all the many inanimate, animate and sentient beings . . . until he has unfolded the entire panoply of the world like a man who has explored and thoroughly inspected a house which someone else has built.
>
> (IL, 162–3)

An order very similar to the one prescribed is apparent in the sections on physics in the *Syntagma*.

Physics

Gassendi's physics begins with questions about the number of worlds, the existence of the world-soul and the known locations of the known parts of the world. This helps to define in a preliminary way the scheme of nature that physics is concerned with. He goes on to consider the metaphysical status of place and time. From Galileo's results concerning falling bodies he knew that physical effects could be a function of elapsed time or space traversed, and yet none of the traditional categories for real things – substance, attribute, corporeal or incorporeal – seemed to classify place and time adequately: Gassendi opens his physics with reasons why the traditional categories are unsuitable and reasons why place and space and duration are real and similar in their incorporeal natures. He then tries to play down his evident departure from Aristotelian physics by saying that what he calls space is just the same as 'that space which is generally called imaginary and which the majority of sacred doctors admit exists beyond the universe' (Book II, ch. 1, Brush, 389). By 'imaginary' he does not mean fictional. Rather, as he explains, he means something that it takes imagination, and in particular the power the imagination has of constructing analogues of the space it senses, to conceive. The power of making analogues is mentioned in Part One of *Institutio Logica* (canon 3) and consists of forming a likeness to something borne in by the senses.

Section One of the physics continues with the exposition of a number of competing theories of the nature of the matter of the universe, culminating in the acceptance of a revised Epicurean atomism in Book III, ch. 8. The chapter starts with a list of departures from Epicurus. Although Gassendi agrees that 'the matter of the world and of all the things in it is made up of atoms' (Brush, 398), he denies all of the following: that the atoms are eternal; that they are uncreated; that they are infinite in number, capable of being any shape, and self-moving (ibid., 399). He claims instead that 'atoms are the primary form of matter, which God created finite from the beginning, which he formed into this visible world, which, finally, he ordained and permitted to undergo transformations out of which, in short, all the bodies which exist in the universe are composed' (ibid., 399).

He conceives matter not in Cartesian fashion as extension in three dimensions simply, but as solid or offering resistance. Atoms are indivisible particles of matter. To the question of whether a physical indivisible is conceivable, given that whatever is physical would seem to have parts, Gassendi generally replies by drawing an analogy between a physical minimum and minimum sensible. Something so small as to be at the limit of what the human eye can register – Gassendi's example is the itch mite – can nevertheless be conceived to have a surface made up of indefinitely many physical parts – atoms, say. This does not take away its claim to be the smallest visible thing; similarly, the fact that it is possible to think of the atom's extremities matched one to one with indefinitely many geometrical points does not take away its status as the smallest physical thing: though there is a way of dividing it into parts in thought, the atom cannot actually exist in parts (cf. Op. Omn. VI, 160; I, 268).

Matter coexists with the void. The existence of motion is supposed to be a sign of this, as Gassendi has already been quoted as saying in a passage on the indicative sign. The existence of relatively soft bodies is another sign of the existence of a void, or, more specifically, of the existence of a void enclosed by compound bodies. In the void there are no privileged directions and positions, and in particular no central point toward which a body like a stone might move if it were put into the void. A stone would move in any direction it is propelled or attracted to move, in a straight line with uniform velocity. The Aristotelian doctrine that there are natural positions for different substances is rejected. So is the Epicurean idea that atoms naturally move 'down' in straight lines unless deflected by an arbitrary swerve.

Gassendi has arrived at 'the primary units' of the material world. He thinks that the primary units are a very large number of atoms with a large number of different shapes. In Book IV of the *Syntagma*, on causation, he insists on viewing the primary units as active, rather in the way that the troops in an army are, once the general has given his orders (ch. 8, Brush, 418). All motion of matter is local (Op. Omn. I, 338), even gravitation, which is effected by a kind of hooking together of particles between bodies. Different atoms are endowed with different kinds of mobility, as well as different shapes, and these are capable of producing everything else observed in the physical world. Motion is at the root of effects rather than form; causation in nature is efficient rather than formal (Op. Omn. I, 283). Gassendi takes qualitative differences to be the joint effect of the primary qualities of atoms and their effects on our senses (Book 5, ch. 7). The variety in biological creation he traces to God's production in the beginning of 'the seeds, so to speak, of all things capable of generation, in other words, that from selected atoms he fashioned the first seeds of all things, from which later the propagation of species would occur by generation' (Book 3, ch. 8, Brush, 401).

Having discussed the nature of atoms and indicated in a general way how their possibilities of combination can explain the existence of big classes of substances, his next task, if we are to go by the passage about teaching physics that we quoted earlier from Part Four of *Institutio Logica*, is to 'inquire into the precise nature and pattern of the various combinations responsible for the formation of the sun, the moon and the other heavenly bodies, and in the same way the earth and all the many inanimate, animate and sentient beings . . .'. This is indeed how he proceeds in the subsequent sections of the *Syntagma*. We can pass over the astronomy and his treatment of terrestrial inanimate objects and come at once to the area where the atomistic explanation is extended to psychology, only to be curtailed in the interest of theological orthodoxy.

This occurs toward the beginning of Section III, Part 2, of the *Syntagma*, in the book *De anima*. Gassendi discusses the animating principle in non-human as well as human creatures. He thinks it is a highly mobile corporeal substance, a flame-like tissue of very subtle atoms (Op. Omn. II, 250) spread throughout the animal body. It accounts for body heat and provides the heat for digestion and nutrition; it is sustained by the circulation of the blood. This animating principle is present in humans as well as animals, but in humans it is present together with a rational soul. The rational soul is infused by God in each human being individually, presumably at the moment of conception; the non-rational soul is transmitted by the processes of biological generation themselves. A letter of 1629[7] suggests that it was only to reconcile his position with Scripture, not with biological evidence, that Gassendi departed from the simple hypothesis that a single soul was derived by each person from its parents (Op. Omn. VI, 19). Finally, in the *Syntagma* the relation of the rational soul to the human being in whom it is infused is said to be rather like that of a substantial form to the matter it informs, Gassendi suggests (Op. Omn. II, 466), lifting what is otherwise a total ban on the invocation of substantial forms in the rest of the physics.

Gassendi's account of the soul (Op. Omn. II, 237–59), and of its faculties of phantasy (II, 398–424) and intellect (II, 425–68), is for the most part an account of the biologically generated soul, not the divinely instilled one. It is the biological soul that is the seat of the faculty of imagination or phantasy, and most cognitive operations are varieties of operations on ideas in the imagination. This is true in particular of the operations regulated by the canons of Gassendi's logic: forming ideas, reasoning, correcting for the deceptions of sense and so on. The logic says that all our ideas come from the senses and are in the first place ideas of individual things. The physics explains that corpuscles constituting the sensible species enter channels in the eye, ear and so on, and make impacts on tensed membranes, the vibrations from which are communicated to the brain by nerves filled with animal spirits. The brain then interprets the vibrations and they occur to the mind as conscious sensations. Episodes of the sensation leave traces or vestiges in the brain, and these are the physical substrate of ideas. As for operations on ideas, the physics relates each of these to vestiges of sense understood as brainfolds (Op. Omn. II, 405). Habits of mind also have a material basis. Finally, various forms of deception of the senses are possible because it is possible for the same pattern of vibration reaching the brain to be produced in different ways, or for it to be interpreted in different ways.

So much for the biological soul. A rational soul is needed to account for capacities that surpass those of the imagination, such as the capacity of the soul to know itself, to know the universal independently of abstracting from particulars, and to know God. Not that it is incapable of forming, composing, analysing and ratiocination: it can do what the non-rational soul can do: but it can do more as well. On the other hand, it is dependent on the material of the imagination: when it apprehends things it apprehends the same sort of ideas that the imagination does, not intelligible species. In this sense intellection and imagination are not really distinct (as for example Descartes had claimed in *Meditation* VI). Apart from cognitive operations, the rational soul is called upon to make sense of some practical capacities, specifically the ability to will the Good rather than aim for pleasure.

Ethics and politics

In his physics Gassendi departs considerably from Epicurus but retains a version of atomism and a largely materialistic account of the biological soul.[8] The effect of the departures is to make the Epicurean doctrine cohere with Christianity. God is brought in not only as creator but as a maintainer of order in material causation: the combination of atoms by chance is outlawed. God is also brought in as immediate source of a higher immaterial soul. Epicurean physics is corrected by theology, and it is the same with Epicurean ethics, which Gassendi takes up in the third and concluding part of the *Syntagma*.[9]

Epicurus is upheld in claiming that pleasure is to be pursued and pain avoided, but the pleasure of certain types of action is interpreted by Gassendi as a divinely appointed sign of the individual or communal preservation that such actions promote, while the pain of other types of action must be seen as a sign of their interfering with conservation (Op. Omn., 701). There are pleasures of motion and pleasures of rest, and Epicurus was right, according to Gassendi, to associate happiness with enjoyment of the pleasures of rest. He was right, in other words, to prefer the quiet pleasures of the mind to the pleasures of eating, drinking and sex. The fact that it does not come naturally to us to give the quiet pleasures their due; the fact that we are inclined to pursue the earthier pleasures to the exclusion of the others; these facts do not show that happiness is beyond us. They only show that happiness is not automatically attained. Fortunately, however, we are blessed by God with a freedom that, if properly used, enables us to judge that the earthier pleasures are not superior and are even at times merely apparent rather than real pleasures. This power of correcting valuations through judgement does not deprive the lower pleasures of their attraction, or bring it about that there is nothing to disturb us once we have chosen the higher goods. In other words, our freedom cannot bring about happiness in the form of perfect freedom from perturbation; on the other hand, it does make choices of the higher pleasures into genuine choices. Someone whose valuations of pleasure were completely correct morally speaking and who was incapable of making the wrong choices would in a certain sense resemble creatures who acted badly under the influence of impulse, for they, like the unfailingly right-acting, act in the absence of spontaneity (Op. Omn. II, 822–3).

Going by the theological corrections one finds elsewhere in his system, one might expect Gassendi to make Epicurean tranquillity consist of the quiet contemplation of God in a place away from the distracting pressures of social life. This would fit in not only with the demands of piety but with Epicurus's endorsement of the life in retirement. But in fact the pleasant life appears to be both more active and more social than this (Op. Omn. II, 717, 720). For Gassendi, the preferred sort of tranquillity appears to be that of the man who quietly and calmly gets on with large undertakings (ibid., 717), rather than someone who withdraws into serene and solitary meditation. Of course, it is possible to get on quietly and calmly with purely self-interested projects, such as that of making oneself as wealthy as one can or as famous as one can, but Gassendi advocates stillness of mind in the pursuit of not just any personal project, still less any self-interested project. One is supposed to confine one's desires to those that are natural and necessary (Op. Omn. II, 694): a dedication to wealth or luxury or fame is out of keeping with the pleasant life; and so is much else – even a strong desire to stay alive may be criticized as the product of a misplaced fear of death.

Quiet determination in someone of modest desires, someone who has the pleasures of motion in proportion and under control – this comes close to the principle of a pleasant life. But it takes wisdom to aim at the right pleasures; and prudence to know how to get what one aims at. And the pleasant life calls for the exercise of other virtues, including justice. Justice is giving to each what is his right: it is the virtue that answers to the status of humans as social beings, and it is what keeps people from suffering the excesses of a natural struggle for human survival.

Justice manifests itself in the existence of mutual agreements that limit the steps anyone can take to preserve himself. It is prudent to enter such agreements, since otherwise people have a natural right to do whatever they like and go to whatever extremes they like to improve their chances of staying alive. They can take anything or do anything, and they must be prepared to see others take the same liberties (Op. Omn. II, 751). The extreme unpleasantness of a situation in which no holds are barred and no one is secure in whatever he has motivates people who are rational to lay down the natural right. Or, instead of speaking of the way the unpleasantness of pre-social existence rationally motivates people to lay down rights, Gassendi is willing to speak of a 'law of nature' (ibid., 800), or universally acknowledged rational precept, that men will come together to live in society (ibid., 802). This they do by making pacts with one another. At first they make a pact laying down their unlimited right to do and take what they like. The effect of this pact is to leave each in rightful possession of whatever the pact does not say should be given up. The pact also leaves each protected by the combined forces of the other parties to the pact. A second pact creates laws specifying rights, and so creates conditions for justice, that is, conditions for recognizing infringements of rights and determining what belongs to each by right (Op. Omn. II, 786, 795).

The two pacts already described are not by themselves sufficient for the smooth running of society, for it is impractical to have all the parties to the social contract involved in making and declaring laws. The authority to do these things must be delegated by the many to a single person or to a group of men (ibid., 755), and according to Gassendi this delegation of authority may be understood to originate in a third pact. It is by this third pact that people become subject to government. Is this third pact in their interest? It may seem not to be: the authority that the many vest in government may, Gassendi admits, be misused, as when a monarch or assembly makes too many laws or makes what laws there are too exacting. Nevertheless the interest of rulers themselves in a certain kind of pleasant life gives them a reason to refrain from making laws that overburden their subjects, while the predictable excess of pain over pleasure in rebellion or civil disobedience provides a reason for law-abidingness on the part of subjects. In Gassendi's theory of politics the pleasure principle promotes the stability of states.

⚬⚬ HOBBS ⚬⚬

How far does Gassendi's Epicurean system agree with Hobbes's philosophy? Their politics appear to provide at least one point of agreement, for the respective treatments of the state of nature and the right of nature are similar. They diverge strikingly, however, in their theories of the social contract, the laws of nature, and the relations of subjects to rulers. Not three pacts but one take people from the Hobbesian state of nature into society. Hobbes's laws of nature provide a more detailed analysis than Gassendi's of what it is to come into society, and they rest on an account that implies that people's personal judgements about the relative pleasantness of life within the state and out of it are unreliable. Accordingly, in the act by which a Hobbesian subject simultaneously contracts for protection and makes himself subject to a sovereign, he also gives up the right to let his own judgements about pleasure and pain rule his impression of his well-being. He delegates the judgements to someone – a sovereign – who has a wider and more detached view than he does.

The disagreements between Hobbes and Gassendi do not stop there. It is crucial to Hobbes's morals and politics that death be an evil and that it be rationally compulsory to avoid premature death (De cive, ch. 1, vii, E II, 8), while Gassendi's account tends to minimize the disvalue of death and the importance of staving it off. Another disagreement, this time on the borderline between ethics and politics, is over whether man is by nature sociable. Gassendi, inclining uncharacteristically toward Aristotle, thinks that man *is* naturally sociable; Hobbes, in a political treatise that Gassendi admired, argues vigorously to the contrary. The divergences extend to other sectors of philosophy. In logic Gassendi puts forward precepts that reflect his sensitivity to scepticism; Hobbes does not. In metaphysics and physics Gassendi makes much of God's activity; in comparable parts of Hobbes's philosophy, on the other hand, a discussion of God's nature and attributes is either omitted or is highly curtailed. In physics proper Hobbes doubts the existence of the vacuum (*De corp.*, ch. 26, vi-xi, E I 426–44) and probably also, though not so explicitly, the divisibility of anything material (*De corp.*, ch. 7, xiii). He is thus at odds twice over with Gassendi's belief in the existence of atoms in the void.

Where the theories of Hobbes and Gassendi do resemble one another is in the reductive and materialistic bent of their psychologies. After examining Hobbes's doctrine in this connection I shall consider the relation of his materialism to the rest of his philosophy. Then I shall ask whether there is a way of comparing Hobbes and Gassendi that takes account of their shared materialism while accommodating other points of contact.

Matter and motion

Perhaps no passage in Hobbes's writings declares his materialism with greater directness than the following one from Chapter 46 of *Leviathan*:

> The world, (I mean not the earth only, that denominates the lovers of it *worldly men*, but the *universe*, that is, the whole mass of things that are), is corporeal, that is to say, body; and hath the dimensions of magnitude, namely length, breadth, and depth: also every part of body, is likewise body, and hath the like dimensions; and consequently every part of the universe, is body, and that which is not body, is no part of the universe: and because the universe is all, that which is no part of it, is *nothing*; and consequently *nowhere*. Nor does it follow from hence, that spirits are *nothing*: for they have dimensions, and are therefore really bodies.
>
> (E III 381)

Hobbes is claiming that to exist is to exist as a material thing. Even spirits are bodies. If spirits seem not to be bodies, he goes on to suggest, that is only because in common usage 'body' is a term for things that are palpable and visible as well as extended in three spatial dimensions (ibid.).

Forthright as the passage just quoted is, Hobbes's materialism is more often implied than asserted in his writings. The reason is not that Hobbes was particularly prudent or cautious outside *Leviathan*, but that he thought that motion rather than matter was the key concept for the explanation of natural difference and change. It is true that, as he defines it, cause is motion, and motion is the displacement of body, so that his frequent references to the varieties of motion, and his frequent attempts to reduce phenomena to motion, are at the same time expressions of materialism. Still, it is through a commitment to mechanical explanation in physics, rather than as a result of some argument or requirement in an entirely prior and independent metaphysics, that Hobbes is materialistic.

An early example in Hobbes's writings of the inclination to mechanistic, rather than materialistic, reduction comes from *The Elements of Law* (1640). Just as 'conceptions or apparitions are nothing really, but motion in some internal substance of the head' he says, so '... contentment or pleasure ... is nothing really but motion about the heart ...' (Pt I, ch. 7, i, 28). In the same vein, but from the Introduction to *Leviathan*, written about eleven years later, there is the remark that 'life is but a motion of the limbs'. And that there is a principled basis for the stress on motion can be seen from the chapter on the methodology of philosophy or science in *De Corpore*, the first volume of Hobbes's three-part statement of the elements of philosophy. In that chapter, method in philosophy or science is related to the definition of philosophy as the working out of causes from effects or effects from causes. Method prescribes, as a stage in the search for causes, the identification of universal things in particulars, that is, the most general properties that can be inferred from the analysis of descriptions of specific phenomena. But to find the relevant universals is not yet to know the ultimate cause of the phenomena, for the universals themselves have a universal cause, which is motion.

Finding causes is a matter of finding one of the many varieties of motion that is capable of generating a given effect. The varieties of motion that each of the main branches of science are concerned with are described in article 6 of Chapter 6 of *De Corpore*. Geometry studies motion in general – motion in the abstract – in body in general (E I 71). The rest of the sciences deal with differentiated motions in differentiated bodies. Thus pure mechanics deals with motions in bodies considered only as numerically distinct, and as having parts. It deals with the effects of motions of the parts of bodies on whole bodies, and also with the transmission of motion in collisions involving different numbers of bodies (E I 71–2). Physics deals with the sensory effects in animate bodies of motions transmitted by inanimate bodies. It deals also with the after-effects of sensory episodes and images compounded in imagination (E I 71; ch. 25, vii, E I 396–7; cf. L, ch. 1, E III 6). Moral philosophy, or, perhaps more accurately, moral psychology, deals with further after-effects of sensation in the form of passions. In this branch of science 'we are to consider the emotions of the mind, namely, appetite, aversion, love, benevolence, hope, fear, anger, emulation, envy etc.' (De corp. ch. 1, vi, E I 72).

It should now be clear that for Hobbes physics and moral psychology are sciences of motion, and therefore branches of mechanics. Both sciences are supposed to be concerned with the motions of the mind, physics because it considers the nature of sensation, and moral psychology because it studies some of the psychological effects of sensation. It is clear also that the psychological parts of physics and moral psychology are at the same time, but secondarily, sciences of matter, and support the classification of Hobbes as a materialist.

It is time to look at these sciences in more detail. The theory of sensation is not only a part of Hobbes's physics, but the part that Hobbes thinks has to be expounded first. The reason is that the data explained by physics are appearances, and these appearances could not exist if there were no sensation to produce them. Sense being what provides the data of physics, how does it work? Hobbes's answer is that it works by reaction, reaction to motion propagated through the parts of the sense organs. The process that culminates in sense experience affects the whole living creature, but it starts with pressure on some external and sensitive part of the living creature. This is the 'uttermost' part of the sense organ. When

> it is pressed, it no sooner yields, but the part next within it is pressed also; and, in this manner, the pressure or motion is propagated through all the parts of the sense organ to the innermost.
>
> (De corp. ch. 25, ii, E I 390)

'Press' and 'pressure' are terms from the theory of pure mechanics. Hobbes defines them in Part Three of De Corpore. One body presses another when 'with its endeavour' the first body displaces the other or displaces part of the other (De corp. ch. 15, ii, E I 211). In the case of sensation, the pressure on the outermost part of the sense organ is exerted either by the body sensed, what Hobbes calls 'the object of sense', or by some part of the medium, like air, which is itself set in motion by the object of sense. The pressure on the outermost part of the organ of sense displaces the nearest internal parts, which in turn press the next adjoining, which in turn press the next. Sensation does not result simply from this communication of pressure, but from the resistance of pressed to pressing bodies. Each pressure inwards is met with resistance outwards by the parts of the sense organ, so that there is a chain of reactions to a chain of pressures in the parts of the organ. From the last of this chain of reactions and its effect on the brain 'a phantasm or idea hath its being' (ch. 25, ii, E I 391). Only the strongest of the endeavours outward from the innermost parts of the sense organ constitutes a sensory reaction, and there can only be one sensory reaction at a time. Moreover, a given sensory reaction at a time can be experience *of* no more than one object at a time (*De corp.* ch. 25, v, E I 395), if the various sense organs are applied at a single time to a single object. So sense experience is an orderly succession of images of discrete things.

This much of the theory of sense is supposed to explain more than the existence of phantasms and their occurring in orderly sequences: it explains also some features of their content. For example, since a phantasm or idea results from the last of a chain of reactions *outwards* in the parts of the sense organ, to have a phantasm of a thing is to have an experience as of something *outside* the organ of sense (ibid.). Again, the theory as so far sketched makes some sense of the fact that 'things when they are not the same seem not to be the same but changed' (cf. *De corp.* ch. 6, vi, E I 72). Hobbes gives the example of things that appear to sight to be different sizes at different times. This is the effect of variations in the angle at which motion from the innermost part of the organ of sight is propagated outwards (*De corp.* ch. 25, xi, E I 405). Another phenomenon is variation in the number of stars visible in the heavens. This is the effect not of generation or destruction of stars, but of the state of the medium through which the motion of the stars is propagated. Cold air facilitates, and hot air hinders, stellar action on the eyes; so more stars appear on cold, calm nights, than on warm, windy ones (cf. *De corp.* ch. 25, xi, E I 406).

Hobbes's theory of sense is an account not only of the objects and causes of phantasms but also of the cognitive operations performed with them. To be endowed with sense, Hobbes believes, is not merely to be the momentary site of phantasms; it is to be able to recall ideas to mind, and to be able to compare and distinguish them. Indeed, judgement, which is the capacity to keep track of differences between objects presented to the senses (*De corp.* ch. 25, viii, E I 399; L, ch. 8, E III 57), is not really a capacity distinct from sense (*De corp.* ch. 25, viii, E I 399). Neither, apparently, is memory or imagination. Even the distinction between imagination and dreaming is not very firmly drawn (cf. EL, Pt 1, ch. 3, viii, 12; L, ch. 2, E III6f.; *De corp.* ch. 25, ix, E I 399f.). The reason is that Hobbes tries to mark differences between these psychological capacities with the same apparatus he has applied in the account of sense proper. To explain the variety of sense experience he appeals to the variety of the sense organs, the different ways in which the sense organs are linked up with the nervous and arterial systems, differences in the objects of sense, and differences in the motions they impart to the sense organs. But when it comes to accommodating the variety of ways in which sense information can be operated upon after transactions between the sense organ and external objects are completed, he no longer has available to him a wide enough array of distinct causes for the distinct operations. He must make the retention of motion in the sentient suffice as a basis for memory, imagination and many other apparently quite distinct mental capacities. Unsurprisingly, this basis proves too slight for explaining the range of effects proper to the individual capacities. By memory, for example, we are not only supposed to be able to compare and distinguish the individuals we observe; we are also supposed to be able to hit upon regularities involving them so as to be able to form expectations (EL, Pt 1, ch. 4, vii, 15). Can all of this be managed by short-lived reflection on qualitative similarity and difference in objects we have fleeting contact with? Can even qualitative comparison and discernment be accomplished by memory if it is no more than a device for storing and scanning the colours, shapes, smells etc. of unsorted bodies? Hobbes offers a sophisticated reconstruction of the mechanisms that make it possible for us to be affected with phantasms, but he lacks the resources for a substantial account of the various operations – memory is only one – that cognition involves.

Hobbes's account of the motions of the mind extends beyond sensation and cognition. There is also a theory of the passions. Passions are understood as after-effects of sense. For example, when someone sees something, the thing imparts motion to the innermost part of the organ of sight. One effect of the motion is to set up an outward reaction to the brain that produces visual experience. But there can be an additional effect. The 'motion and agitation of the brain which we call conception' can be 'continued to the heart, and there be called passion' (EL, Pt 1, ch. 8, i, 31). The heart governs 'vital motion' in the body, that is, the circulation of the blood. In general, when motion derived from an act of sense encourages vital motion, the sentient creature experiences pleasure at the sight, smell or taste of the object of sense, and is disposed to move his body in such a way as to prolong or intensify the pleasure (De corp. ch. 25, xii, E I 407). If the object of sense is at some distance from the sentient creature, the creature will typically move toward it (ibid.). In De Corpore Hobbes describes the physiological processes that underlie the approach. Animal spirits impulse into the nerves and retract again, causing muscular swelling and relaxation and eventually full-scale movements (E I 408). The 'first beginnings' of this process, the small movements in the body below the threshold of consciousness that start the process off, constitute what Hobbes calls 'appetite' (E I 407). With appropriate adjustments aversion is treated in the same way. Aversion is connected with retreat from an object of sense whose effect on a creature is to retard vital motion.

In roughly the way that he tries to conjure imagination, memory and other cognitive operations out of the basic capacity for sense, Hobbes tries to relate a long list of passions to the basic affections of appetite and aversion. There are many complexities, but the idea that the passions are kinds of motion involving the heart is never abandoned. The heart and its motion are also appealed to in Hobbes's conception of biological life, and his conception of biological life is brought into deflationary interpretations of the ideas of spirit, soul, eternal life and resurrection. In a famous passage in Chapter 44 of *Leviathan* he says:

> The *soul* in Scripture signifieth always, either the life, or the living creature; and the body and soul jointly, the body alive.
>
> (E III 615)

As for life itself, 'it is but motion' (L, ch. 6, E III 51). When God is said in *Genesis* to have *'inspired* into man the breath of life, no more is meant than that God gave him vital motion' (L, ch. 34, E III 394). Death consists of the ceasing of this motion, but the ceasing of this motion at a time does not preclude an after-life. If God created human life out of dust and clay, it is certainly not beyond Him to revive a carcass (E III 614–15). For the same reason, it is unnecessary to hold that a soul leaves the body at death in order to make sense of resurrection. One can say that life stops and then starts again at the resurrection, with no intervening incorporeal existence.

Hobbes's materialism and Hobbes's system

Hobbes identifies the ensouled human body with the living body, and he thinks that the living body is a body with vital motion, that is, a body with a heart pumping blood through the circulatory system. He identifies the passions with different effects of vital motion, and he identifies thought or cognitive operations with various effects on the sense organs, nerves and brain of impacts of external bodies. It is a thoroughgoing materialistic psychology, and it is in keeping with the method and first philosophy that Hobbes prescribes for natural philosophy in *De Corpore* and other writings. Effects or phenomena of all kinds are referred to bodily motion, the specific kinds of motion depending on the analysis of the descriptions of the phenomena as well as relevant experiments. This is the approach Hobbes follows for geometrical effects, pure mechanical effects, physical and psychological effects. In the teaching of the elements of philosophy as a whole, the assignment of causes to these effects is supposed to be preliminary to stating the rules of morality and polity. Are the rules of morality and politics supposed to be materialistic or mechanistic or based on a mechanical conception of nature?

In some formulations Hobbes's theory of politics does indeed draw on mechanistic psychology. But in others, notably that of the official statement of his politics in De Cive, the third volume of his trilogy, no properly scientific claims about the passions or about psychology are employed at all. The Preface to De Cive indeed insists on the independence of the principles of morals and politics from those of the sciences of body and man treated earlier in the trilogy (E II xx). And similar comments are made in Leviathan (ch. 31, E III 357) and De Corpore (De corp. ch. 6, vi, E I 74). Hobbes's insistence on the autonomy of his morals and politics seems to go against the claim that his morals and politics are derived from, or a case of, mechanistic materialism. It is better to say that the morals and politics are consistent with, and sometimes worked out against the background of, mechanistic materialism, but not strictly deduced from mechanistic materialism.

Let us consider how Hobbes's mechanistic psychology contributes to Hobbes's morals and politics when he does choose to make use of it, as in Leviathan. A crucial passage in this connection, which incidentally shows Hobbes in disagreement with Gassendi, concerns the sort of happiness that man can aspire to while he is alive.

> Continual success in obtaining those things which a man from time to time desireth, that is to say, continual prospering, is that men call FELICITY; I mean the felicity of this life. For there is no such thing as perpetual tranquillity of mind, while we live here, because life itself is but motion, and we can never be without desire, nor without fear, no more than without sense.
>
> (E III 51)

He is claiming that desire, fear and sense are permanent facts of life, and that life being motion, it cannot be tranquil. Desire is a fact of life because it is an inescapable effect of the vital functions of sense and vital motion; fear is a fact of life because it is a probable effect of sense and vital motion. We learn through trial and error what to avoid and pursue, and trial and error reveals that some things we might otherwise try and get can harm us. So long as our environment is not wholly hospitable there are bound to be fearful things. As for life being but motion, this is an assertion of Hobbes's identification of life with vital motion.

The claim that human life can never be without fear and desire has a natural scientific grounding, and it in turn helps to support a central thesis of Hobbes's moral philosophy: that the prospects of felicity in human life in its natural condition are not very good. For one thing, the pursuit of felicity is unending, there always being a next desire to satisfy, and risky, there being things to fear. The unendingness of desire and the constant presence of fearful things both diminish the prospect of continual success in getting what one wants unless one has tremendous resources to put into the pursuit of felicity. The unendingness of desire and the permanence of fear are among the harsh natural conditions of life that the construction of a body politic is supposed to alleviate. So Hobbes's mechanistic psychology does some of the stage-setting for Hobbes's civil philosophy.

It would be a mistake, however, to suppose that it is very extensive stage-setting. A state or commonwealth or body politic is an answer to the problem of war, and it takes more than continual desire and ever-present fear in the pursuit of felicity to create conditions of war. War involves competition, insecurity of possession and, crucially, what Hobbes calls 'the right of nature', that is, the right of each person to be able to take whatever steps he thinks are appropriate for his security and well-being (cf. L, ch. 14, E III 116). These additional conditions, and especially the last, do not belong to a description of the state of nature purely in terms of matter in motion. And while there may be analogies between the way that human beings come into conflict with one another, and what happens when inanimate bodies meet on a collision course, the explanation of war and the prescriptions for avoiding it are not for Hobbes primarily mechanistic. War and peace are primarily things that can be deliberated about and chosen or rejected. They are only secondarily the effects of blind impersonal forces within human beings. That is why Hobbes presents the causes of peace in the form of precepts it is rational to follow and the causes of war as seditious beliefs or ill-conceived policies of action that it is rational to abandon.

At the heart of his case-both for following the precepts and abandoning the seditious beliefs is the fearfulness of death through war and (though less prominently) the desirability of commodious living in the commonwealth (EL, Pt 1, ch. 14; De cive ch. 1; L, ch. 13). War is what the pursuit of felicity degenerates into when each human being is the rightful judge of how to pursue felicity, that is, when no-one can be blamed by any one else for any choice of means to ends, and when it is common knowledge that this is so. In these circumstances, whatever one's character or personality, it can make sense to injure or dispossess one's neighbour. Vainglorious people will be disposed to pursue felicity ruthlessly anyway, and will not stop at fraud or theft or even, if there is nothing to stop them, killing to get what they want. Moderate people, concerned with safety before felicity, will have reason to act violently to pre-empt the attacks of the vainglorious. And in any case people will be set against one another by the mere fact of having to compete for goods everyone wants. Whether they are vicious, virtuous or morally indifferent, people who pursue felicity, and who have no common power to fear, must suffer from the general insecurity Hobbes calls 'war'.

By 'war' he does not mean only open fighting between large numbers of men. It is enough that most men show that they are *willing* to come to blows (EL, Pt 1, ch. 14, xi, 73; De cive ch. 1, xi, E II 11; L, ch. 13, E III 113). Hobbes recognizes what we would now call 'cold war', and he does not underestimate its costs. When most people show that they are willing to enter a fight that can be foreseen to be a fight to the death, most people are unlikely to channel their efforts into production. If people agree to work at all while under the threat of all-out war, then, according to Hobbes, they will tend to produce things on their own and for themselves. War, even cold war, threatens production by the division of labour, and indeed threatens to halt production of any kind (ibid.). And the effects of open as against latent war are of course much worse. Besides the loss of the good of society, open war brings the loss of reliable shelter, the loss of methods of distributing goods in general demand, the decline of learning, the good of assured survival, the probable loss of life and, what is worse, a probably painful death. The life of man is reduced to being 'solitary, poor, nasty, brutish and short' (E III 113).

The fearfulness of war is supposed to give people who are at war a reason for putting an end to it and people who are not at war a reason for continuing to live in peace. The goal of securing peace and the means of doing so are specified by the so-called laws of nature (L, chs 14 and 15), about eighteen such laws in all. The fundamental laws require one to seek peace if it is safe to do so; and to lay down rights that will enable peace to be made and kept. These two laws, as well as one requiring that one keep one's agreements, are the laws of nature that enable the state to be established and war ended. Further laws of nature call for traditionally recognized virtues: equity, gratitude, a willingness to be accommodating and so on.

Now anyone who sees that peace is good and sees that the behaviours enjoined by the laws of nature are means to peace has a reason for abiding by the laws of nature – even in the course of a war. Each person has a reason for abiding by the laws of nature, but not an utterly compelling or categorical reason. For in a state of war each person retains the right of conducting himself as he likes, and may judge that it is better to violate the laws of nature even while others obey them. Since those who obey the laws put themselves at risk by doing so, and since even the laws of nature do not have to be observed when it is unsafe to do so, the general uncertainty over how others will behave makes the laws of nature into ineffective instruments of peace.

Hobbes's solution to this problem is to make the right of private judgement one of the rights laid down for the sake of peace. He describes a covenant that transfers responsibility for the personal safety and well-being of individuals from those individuals themselves to a man or body of men who are empowered to act for the safety and well-being of them all. The covenanters become subjects of the responsible individual or assembly, and are obliged to obey his or their laws for as long as it is not life-threatening to do so. In other words, the parties to the covenant delegate the right to see to security and well-being to others, in return for more certainty about survival and well-being. The man or body of men to whom the decisions are delegated then declares, in the form of coercive civil laws, those things that must and must not be done if the peace is to be kept and security and well-being promoted. The laws can touch virtually any sphere of private or public life, though Hobbes counsels against a legal regime that is very intrusive and very exacting. The authority of the sovereign power extends in particular to declaring what forms of religious practice are lawful and who may or may not preach. This, in a nutshell, is Hobbes's solution to the problem of war: the many are to agree to subject themselves absolutely to a sovereign with undivided and absolute power.

Hobbes's system and Gassendi's

How satisfactory is it to classify Hobbes's system as a whole – the elements of natural and civil science taken together – as materialistic or mechanistic? Plainly the mechanical conception is prominent in all of Hobbes's writings in natural science. In morals and politics, on the other hand, it is far less conspicuous, and in *De Cive* it virtually disappears. Commentators sometimes claim that, however different in content they are, Hobbes's natural and civil sciences are nevertheless worked out according to the same methodological precepts, precepts calling for the resolution of bodies – either natural or artificial – into properties for which causes can be found, causes which, when put together, make the body from which one started fully intelligible.[10] Though Hobbes himself encourages the idea that there is a close parallel between the methods of civil and natural philosophy, it is very difficult to read any of the political treatises as exercises in the resolution of a state or civil society into its parts.[11] They are better seen as justifying precepts for the behaviour of subjects and sovereigns engaged in the common project of keeping the peace.

Another interpretation of Hobbes's system, which avoids the implication that Hobbes's civil philosophy is mechanistic, or that natural and civil philosophy are methodologically unified, is to the effect that each of the two principal parts of Hobbes's system are responses to the seventeenth-century pyrrhonist challenge to science: on this reading, the metaphysics and natural philosophy attempt what Descartes attempts in the *Meditations*, only without relying on doubtful proofs of God's existence, while the civil philosophy meets a sceptical challenge to a science of morals along the lines of one that Grotius tried to meet.[12] Putting these readings together, the whole system may be regarded as 'post-sceptical'. If this interpretation were correct, it would have the considerable merit of linking not only the two parts of Hobbes's system but the two systems of Hobbes and Gassendi; for it can hardly be doubted that Gassendi's system has consciously anti-sceptical motivation.

Unfortunately, the textual evidence for the claim that Hobbes directed his philosophy against pyrrhonism is very slight.[13] The main proposer of the 'post-sceptical' interpretation has mainly relied on Hobbes's association with Gassendi and Mersenne. Though the interpretation seems uncompelling, its form seems to me to be right. That is, it seems sensible to look for a way of unifying the two parts of Hobbes's philosophy and the two systems of Hobbes and Gassendi in something they were both reacting against. There is much stronger evidence for the claim that it was Aristotelianism than that it was scepticism about the possibility of science. We have already seen that Gassendi was attracted to Epicureanism partly because it could rival Aristotle's philosophy, and because Gassendi was from early on dissatisfied with Aristotelianism. In Hobbes's case equally the departures from Aristotle's theory of causation and the categories, as well as the theory that man is naturally sociable and that one exercises the duties of citizenship by judging and legislating rather than obeying, are very clear and well documented.

Hobbes does not believe, as people do who take scepticism seriously, that one can live long or well by appearances alone. He thinks that to live and live well in both nature and society one needs science, that is, some methodical way of finding the causes of appearances and the consequences of one's actions. But he also thinks, this time very much as Gassendi does, that, except with regard to the appearances of things we make, appearances of artefacts, science does not reveal the necessary causes of appearances; and though he believes that science can be acquired by human beings he does not think that they have a natural aptitude for it. Similarly, though he thinks that virtue can be acquired, and even that there can be a science of virtue in the form of the system of the laws of nature, he does not think that the virtues can be learned by simple habituation, or that there is the relation of virtue to pleasure or virtue to personal judgement and experience that Aristotle insists upon. In all of these respects he is anti-Aristotelian.

With Gassendi Hobbes is a mechanistic anti-Aristotelian in natural philosophy. He is a different kind of anti-Aristotelian in civil philosophy. In civil philosophy he is anti-Aristotelian in redrawing the distinction between natural and artificial so that politics no longer falls on the 'natural' side of the divide; aptness for the polity is not written into human nature, according to Hobbes: man has to be *made* sociable and the order with the polity is not a natural one either, but one that is artificial and expressible in the terms of a contract. Gassendi, too, is a contract theorist, but apparently not one who invests the fact that contracts are made and states manufactured with anti-Aristotelian significance. For him entering into a contract can be the expression of natural sociableness, albeit understood in an Epicurean rather than Aristotelian way.

❧ ABBREVIATIONS ❧

The following abbreviations are used in references. Gassendi: Op. Omn. – *Opera Omnia* (Lyon, 1658), 6 vols, references are by volume and page number; Brush – *The Selected Writings of Pierre Gassendi*, trans. C. Brush (New York, Johnson Reprint, 1972); IL – *Institutio Logica*, ed. and trans. Howard Jones (Assen, Van Gorcum, 1981). Hobbes: EL – *The Elements of Law Natural and Politic*, ed. F. Tönnies (London, Simpkin & Marshall, 1889), references are by part, chapter, section and Tönnies page number; L – *Leviathan, or the Matter, Form and Power of Commonwealth, Ecclesiastical and Civil*, references are by chapter and page number to the edition in vol. 3 of the *English Works* (E), ed. Sir W. Molesworth (London, 1869), 11 vols; *De corp.* – *Elementorum Philosophiae, Sectio prima de corpore*, references are by chapter, section and page number of the English translation in vol. 1 of Molesworth; *De cive* – *Elementorum Philosophiae, Sectio tertia, de cive*; I use 'De cive' to refer to the English translation, *Philosophical Rudiments concerning Government and Society*, in vol. 2 of Molesworth; DP – *Decameron physiologicum or Ten Dialogues of Natural Philosophy*, vol. 7 of Molesworth.

❧ NOTES ❧

1 For more detail, see A. Beaulieu, 'Les Relations de Hobbes et de Mersenne', in Y.-C. Zarka and J. Bernhardt, *Thomas Hobbes: Philosophie Première, Théorie de la science et politique* (Paris: Presses Universitaires de France, 1990), pp. 81–90.
2 See Sarasohn [7.32], 370–1.
3 See Joy [7.13].
4 For more detail, see Clark [7.17], 353.
5 See Brundell [7.11], ch. 2.
6 See Brundell's Introduction for more detail.
7 Quoted in Brett [7.10], 114n.
8 For a review of the textual evidence of Gassendi's materialism which adds to the details given here, see Bloch [7.9], ch. 12.
9 I am indebted in my discussion of Gassendi's ethics and politics to Sarasohn [7.31].
10 The originator of this interpretation is J. W. N. Watkins. See Watkins [7.61], 47–81.
11 See Sorell [7.50], ch. 2.
12 See Richard Tuck, 'Sceptics and Optics', in E. Leites (ed.) *Conscience and Casuistry in Early Modern Europe* (Cambridge, Cambridge University Press, 1988), pp. 235–63; 'Hobbes and Descartes', in G. A. J. Rogers and A. Ryan (eds) *Perspectives on Thomas Hobbes* (Oxford, Clarendon, 1988), pp. 11–42; Tuck [7.53].
13 See my 'Hobbes without Doubt', forthcoming in M. Bell and N. Martin (eds) *Scepticism and Modern Philosophy*.

❧ BIBLIOGRAPHY ❧

GASSENDI

Original language editions

7.1 *Opera Omnia*, Lyon, Anisson/Devenet, 6 vols, 1658; reprinted Olms, Hildesheim, 1964.
7.2 *Animadversiones in Decimum Librum Diogenis Laertii*, Lyon, Barbier, 1649.

Translations and abridgements

7.3 Bernier, F. *Abrégé de la philosophie de Gassendi*, Lyon, 8 vols, 1678.
7.4 *Dissertationes en forme de Paradoxes contre les Aristoteliciens (Exercitationes Paradoxicae adversus Aristoteleos)*, Books I and II, trans. B. Rochot, Paris, Vrin, 1959.
7.5 *Disquisitio Metaphysica, seu Dubitationes et Instantiae adversus Renati Cartesii Metaphysicam et Responsa*, trans. B. Rochot, Paris, Vrin, 1962.

7.6 *Institutio Logica*, trans. H. Jones, Assen, Van Gorcum, 1981.
7.7 *The Selected Works of Pierre Gassendi*, trans. C. Brush, New York, Johnson Reprint, 1972.

Correspondence

7.8 Rochot, B. (ed.) *Lettres familières à François Luillier pendant l'hiver 1632–1633*, Paris, Vrin, 1944.

Gassendi's philosophy: general surveys

7.9 Bloch, O. R. *La Philosophie de Gassendi: Nominalisme, Matérialisme et Métaphysique*, La Hague, Nijhoff, 1971.
7.10 Brett, G. R. *The Philosophy of Gassendi*, London, Macmillan, 1908.
7.11 Brundell, B. *Pierre Gassendi: From Aristotelianism to a New Natural Philosophy*, Dordrecht, Reidel, 1987.
7.12 Gregory, T. *Scetticismo ed empiricismo. Studio su Gassendi*, Bari, Editori Laterza, 1961.
7.13 Joy, L. *Gassendi the Atomist: Advocate of History in an Age of Science*, Cambridge, Cambridge University Press, 1987.
7.14 Rochot, B. *Les Travaux de Gassendi sur Epicure et sur l'atomisme*, Paris, Vrin, 1944.

Gassendi's metaphysics and physics

7.15 Bloch, O. R. 'Un rationaliste de 17e siècle: Gassendi', *Cahiers rationalistes* 160 (1957) 27–31.
7.16 Bloch, O. R. 'Gassendi critique de Descartes', *Revue philosophique* 156 (1966) 217–36.
7.17 Clark, J. T. 'Pierre Gassendi and the Physics of Galileo', *Isis* 54 (1963) 352–70.
7.18 Humbert, P. *L'oeuvre astronomique de Gassendi*, Paris, Hermann, 1936.
7.19 Kargon, R. H. 'Walter Charleton, Robert Boyle and the acceptance of Epicurean atomism in England', *Isis* 55 (1964) 184–92.
7.20 Kargon, R. H. *Atomism in England from Harriot to Newton*, Oxford, Oxford University Press, 1966.
7.21 Lenoble, R. *Mersenne ou la naissance du Mécanisme*, Paris, Vrin, 1943.
7.22 Pintard, R. *Le libertinage érudit dans la première moitié du XVIIe siècle*, Paris, Boivin, 2 vols, 1943.
7.23 Popkin, R. *The History of Scepticism from Erasmus to Descartes*, New York, Harper Torch, 1964.
7.24 Popkin, R. 'Scepticism and the Counter-reformation in France', *Archiv für Reformations-geschichte* 51 (1960) 58–87.

7.25 Rochot, B. 'Gassendi et la "logique" de Descartes', *Revue philosophique* 145 (1955) 300–8.

7.26 Rochot, B. 'Gassendi et l'expérience', *Mélanges Alexandre Koyré* Collection Histoire de la Pensée, Paris, Ecole Pratique des Hautes Etudes, Sorbonne, 1965.

7.27 Rochot, B. 'Gassendi et les mathématiques', *Revue d'histoire des sciences* (1957) 69–78.

7.28 Rochot, B. 'Beeckman, Gassendi et le principe d'inertie', *Archives internationales d'histoire des sciences* 5 (1952) 282–9.

Gassendi's ethics and politics

7.29 Bloch, O. R. 'Gassendi et la théorie politique de Hobbes', in Y.-C. Zarka and J. Bernhardt (eds) *Thomas Hobbes: Philosophie première, théorie de la science et politique*, Paris, Presses Universitaires de France, 1990, 339–46.

7.30 Murr, S. 'La science de l'homme chez Hobbes et Gassendi', in Y.-C. Zarka and J. Bernhardt (eds) *Thomas Hobbes: Philosophie première, théorie de la science et politique*, Paris, Presses Universitaires de France, 1990, 193–208.

7.31 Sarasohn, L. 'The Ethical and Political Philosophy of Pierre Gassendi', *Journal of the History of Philosophy* 20 (1982) 239–60.

7.32 Sarasohn, L. 'Motion and Morality: Pierre Gassendi, Thomas Hobbes, and the Mechanical World View', *Journal of the History of Ideas* 46 (1985) 370–1.

HOBBES

Original language editions

7.33 Molesworth, Sir W. (ed.) *The English Works*, London, J. Bohn, 11 vols, 1839–45; reprinted, Aalen, Scientia Verlaag, 1962.

7.34 Molesworth, Sir W. (ed.) *Thomase Hobbes Malmesburiensis Opera Philosophica quae Latine scripsit omnia*, London, J. Bohn, 5 vols, 1839–45.

7.35 Tönnies, F. (ed.) *The Elements of Law*, London, Marshall & Simpkin, 1889. New editions are being published by the Clarendon Press under the direction of Noel Malcolm, and in French by Vrin under the direction of Y.-C. Zarka.

7.36 Texts of letters from Hobbes to the Earl of Newcastle in *Manuscripts of his Grace the Duke of Portland Preserved at Welbeck Abbey*, London, Eyre & Spottiswoode, 1893.

English translations

7.37 Introduction and chapters 10–15 of *De Homine*, trans. Charles T. Wood, T. S. K. Scott-Craig and B. Gert, in *Man and Citizen*, Garden City, N.Y., Anchor-Doubleday, 1972.
7.38 *Thomas White's De Mundo Examined*, trans. H. Jones, Bradford, Bradford University Press, 1976.

Bibliographies

7.39 Hinnant, C. H. *Thomas Hobbes: A Reference Guide*, Boston, Mass., G. K. Hall, 1980.
7.40 MacDonald, H. and Hargreaves, M. *Thomas Hobbes: A Bibliography*, London, Bibliographical Society, 1952.
7.41 Sacksteder, W. *Hobbes Studies (1879–1979): A Bibliography*, Bowling Green, Ohio, Philosophy Documentation Centre, 1982.

Influences on Hobbes

7.42 Bernhardt, J. 'L'apport de l'aristotélisme à la pensée de Hobbes', in *Thomas Hobbes. De la métaphysique à la politique*, ed. M. Malherbe and M. Bertman, Paris, Vrin, 1989, 9–15.
7.43 Schuhmann, K. 'Thomas Hobbes und Francesco Patrizi', *Archiv für Geschichte der Philosophie* 68 (1986) 254–79.
7.44 Schuhmann, K. 'Hobbes and Telesio', *Hobbes Studies* 1 (1988) 109–33.

The philosophy of Hobbes: general surveys

7.45 Jessop, T. E. *Thomas Hobbes*, London, Longman, 1960.
7.46 Laird, J. *Hobbes*, London, Ernest Benn, 1934.
7.47 Peters, R. *Hobbes*, Harmondsworth, Penguin, 1956.
7.48 Reik, M. *The Golden Lands of Thomas Hobbes*, Detroit, Mich., Wayne State University Press, 1977.
7.49 Robertson, G. C. *Hobbes*, Edinburgh, Blackwood, 1886.
7.50 Sorell, T. *Hobbes*, London, Routledge, 1986.
7.51 Spragens, T. *The Politics of Motion: The World of Thomas Hobbes*, Lexington, Ky., University Press of Kentucky, 1973.
7.52 Taylor, A. E. *Hobbes*, London, Constable, 1908.
7.53 Tuck, R. *Hobbes*, Oxford, Oxford University Press, 1989.

Hobbes: physics and metaphysics

7.54 Bernhardt, J. 'Nominalisme et Mécanisme chez Hobbes', *Archives de philosophie* 48 (1985) 235–49.

7.55 Brandt, F. *Thomas Hobbes's Mechanical Conception of Nature*, London, Hachette, 1928.

7.56 Pacchi, A. *Convenzione e ipotesi nela formazione della filosofia naturale di Thomas Hobbes*, Florence, La Nuova Italia, 1964.

7.57 Panochia, D. 'La science de la nature corporelle', *Studia Spinozana* 3 (1987) 151–73.

7.58 Shapin, S. and Schaffer, S. *Leviathan and the Air-pump*, Princeton, N.J., Princeton University Press, 1985.

7.59 Shapiro, A. 'Kinematic Optics: A Study of the Wave Theory of Light in the 17th Century', *Archive for the History of the Exact Sciences* 11 (1973) 134–266.

7.60 Talaska, R. 'Analytic and Synthetic Method according to Hobbes', *Journal of the History of Philosophy* 26 (1988) 207–37.

7.61 Watkins, J. W. N. *Hobbes's System of Ideas*, London, Hutchinson, 1965.

7.62 Zarka, Y.-C. *La décision métaphysique de Hobbes. Conditions de la politique*, Paris, Vrin, 1987.

Hobbes: ethics and politics

7.63 Ashcraft, R. 'Ideology and Class in Hobbes' Political Theory', *Political Theory* 6 (1978) 27–62.

7.64 Baumgold, D. *Hobbes's Political Theory*, Cambridge, Cambridge University Press, 1988.

7.65 Botwinick, A. *Hobbes and Modernity: Five Exercises in Political Philosophical Exegesis*, Lanham: University Press of America, 1983.

7.66 Copp, D. 'Hobbes on Artificial Persons and Collective Actions', *Philosophical Review* 89 (1980) 579–606.

7.67 Gauthier, D. *The Logic of Leviathan: The Moral and Political Theory of Thomas Hobbes*, Oxford, Clarendon, 1969.

7.68 Gauthier, D. 'Taming Leviathan', *Philosophy and Public Affairs* 16 (1987) 280–98.

7.69 Gert, B. 'Hobbes and Psychological Egoism', *Journal of the History of Ideas* 28 (1967) 503–20.

7.70 Goldsmith, M. *Hobbes's Science of Politics*, New York, Columbia University Press, 1966.

7.71 Goyard-Fabre, S. *Le droit et la loi dans la philosophie de Thomas Hobbes*, Paris, Klincksieck, 1975.

7.72 Hampton, J. *Hobbes and the Social Contract Tradition*, Cambridge, Cambridge University Press, 1986.

7.73 Hood, F. C. *The Divine Politics of Thomas Hobbes: An Interpretation of Leviathan*, Oxford, Clarendon, 1964.

7.74 Kavka, G. *Hobbesian Moral and Political Theory*, Princeton, N.J., Princeton University Press, 1986.

7.75 McNeilly, F. S. *The Anatomy of Leviathan*, London, Macmillan, 1968.

7.76 Mintz, S. *The Hunting of Leviathan*, Cambridge, Cambridge University Press, 1962.

7.77 Oakeshott, M. *Hobbes on Civil Association*, Oxford, Blackwell, 1975.

7.78 Polin, R. *Politique et philosophie chez Hobbes*, Paris, Presses Universitaires de France, 1953.

7.79 Raphael, D. D. *Hobbes: Morals and Politics*, London, Allen & Unwin, 1977.

7.80 Rogers, G. A. J. and Ryan, A. *Perspectives on Thomas Hobbes*, Oxford, Clarendon, 1988.

7.81 Skinner, Q. 'The Context of Hobbes's Theory of Political Obligation', *The Historical Journal* 9 (1966) 286–317.

7.82 Taylor, A. E. 'The Ethical Doctrine of Hobbes', *Philosophy* 13 (1938) 406–24.

7.83 Tuck, R. *Natural Rights Theories*, Cambridge, Cambridge University Press, 1979.

7.84 Walton, C. and Johnson, P. (eds) *Hobbes's Science of Natural Justice*, Dordrecht, Nijhoff, 1987.

7.85 Strauss, L. *The Political Philosophy of Hobbes: Its Basis and Genesis*, trans. E. Sinclair, Oxford, Clarendon, 1936.

7.86 Warrender, H. *The Political Philosophy of Hobbes: His Theory of Obligation*, Oxford, Clarendon, 1965.

CHAPTER 8

Spinoza: metaphysics and knowledge

G. H. R. Parkinson

The philosophical writings of Spinoza are notoriously obscure, and they have been interpreted in many ways. Some interpreters see Spinoza as (in the words of a contemporary)[1] 'the reformer of the new [sc. Cartesian] philosophy'. That is, they see him as someone who has been deeply influenced by Cartesianism, but who has introduced major changes in it, without rejecting it altogether (as, say, philosophers such as Hobbes and Gassendi did). Others, however, see Spinoza's philosophy as deeply imbued with medieval thought, both Jewish and Christian. In the words of one prominent exponent of this view,[2] 'his mind is crammed with traditional philosophic lore and his thought turns along the beaten logical paths of mediaeval reasoning'. Such a way of thinking would be alien to that of Descartes, who (like many seventeenth-century philosophers) spurned the philosophy of the Middle Ages. There are other disagreements between Spinoza's interpreters. For example, some see his philosophical writings as a way of expressing a kind of mystical insight, but others deny this.[3] In trying to decide between these interpretations, it will be helpful to begin by giving some account of the social and intellectual *milieu* within which Spinoza formed his ideas.

Spinoza was born in Amsterdam on 24 November 1632. His father, Michael de Spinoza, was a Jewish merchant, one of many Portuguese Jews who had taken refuge in the Netherlands to escape religious persecution. The family language would have been Portuguese, and the philosopher who later called himself by the Latin name 'Benedictus' was generally known in his youth by the Portuguese name 'Bento'. (It is worth adding that the Hebrew name 'Baruch', which is still sometimes used to refer to Spinoza, was for ritual purposes only.) The Portuguese Jews of Amsterdam had founded in 1616 a school, the

'Talmud Torah' ('The Study of the Law'), and the young Spinoza would have attended this school. Here, there were in effect two divisions, a junior and a senior. Instruction in the junior division continued until a boy's thirteenth year;[4] it was confined to the Bible and the elements of the Talmud, more advanced study being reserved for the senior division. The registers of this senior division have been preserved, and it is notable that, among the entries for the relevant years, the name of Spinoza is not to be found. It would be wrong, then, to suppose that Spinoza was deeply read in Talmudic lore in his youth, and that he was intended to be a rabbi. Rather, it seems to have been Michael de Spinoza's intention that Spinoza should concentrate on a career in business; and indeed, when Michael died in 1654 Bento and his brother Gabriel carried on the family business for a time.

The mature Spinoza displays far more knowledge of Jewish thought and history than could have been acquired by a twelve-year old, however precocious; and in fact when Spinoza left school he continued his Jewish studies as a member of a 'Yeshivah', a kind of study-circle, led by the famous rabbi Saul Levi Morteira. Spinoza, however, proved to be a rebellious pupil, and on 27 July 1656 he was formally excommunicated on account of what were called his 'wrong opinions' and 'horrible heresies'.[5] The exact nature of these heresies is not certain. It can be said with certainty that they were not the philosophical views for which Spinoza later became famous; it is very improbable that they were even Cartesian views, which at that time were being keenly discussed in the Netherlands – so keenly, indeed, that in 1656 Dutch university professors were required to take an oath that they would not propound Cartesian doctrines that were found offensive.[6] The slender evidence that is available suggests that Spinoza was already taking up a critical attitude towards the Bible, that he disbelieved in the immortality of the soul, and that his views about God were deistic in character. These doctrines suggest, not so much the ideas of Descartes, as those of the French 'libertins' or free-thinkers of the period.[7]

There is much that is obscure about the next five years of Spinoza's life, but it is certain that they were a decisive period in his philosophical development. By the time that his surviving correspondence begins (26 August 1661) Spinoza appears as a man who has a philosophy of his own, which is treated with respect by such men as Henry Oldenburg, who was to become the first secretary of the Royal Society in London. At this stage, Spinoza was already critical of Cartesianism, but this is not to say that he owed nothing to Descartes. Rather (as a friend of his remarked) 'The philosophical writings of the great and famous René Descartes were of great service to him.'[8] What is not certain is just when and in what way Spinoza obtained his knowledge of Descartes's philosophy. There is reason to believe that Spinoza may have attended philosophy lectures, on an informal basis, at the University of Leiden at some time between 1656 and 1659; if he did so – and the evidence is inconclusive[9] – he would almost certainly have studied Descartes there. It is also possible that it was a common interest in Descartes which led Spinoza to associate with members of some of the smaller Christian sects of the period, the Collegiants and the Mennonites. The Collegiants were a group of people who tried to dispense with clergy, and who met together in groups, *collegia*, for the purpose of worship. The Mennonites were followers of the Dutch Anabaptist Menno Simons (1496–1561); holding themselves aloof from politics, they did not suffer the persecution that many Anabaptists did.

It was in about 1661 – that is, five years after his excommunication – that Spinoza wrote his first philosophical works. These were the *Tractatus de Intellectus Emendatione (Treatise on the Correction of the Intellect)* and the *Korte Verhandeling van God, de Mensch en deszelfs Welstand (Short Treatise on God, Man and his Well-being)*. The first-named of these was a treatise on method, which was meant to be the first part of a two-part work, the second part of which was to have dealt with metaphysics.[10] Spinoza did not complete the work, which was first published in 1677 as part of his posthumous works. The *Short Treatise* may be a first draft of the work on metaphysics which was to have followed. Confused and obscure, it was clearly not intended for publication in the form in which it stands.[11]

In both these works Spinoza's distinctive philosophy is already present, though in a form that is still immature. The works are also interesting in that they afford a clear view of some of the influences on Spinoza. The *Short Treatise* is particularly instructive in this respect. Not surprisingly, Spinoza makes use of Descartes; for example, arguments for the existence of God contained in the eleventh chapter of Part I of the work are clearly derived from Descartes's *Meditations*, Numbers 3 and 5. Equally interesting are the Dutch sources – more specifically, the Leiden sources – that Spinoza uses. In his account of God as cause[12] he uses a classification of causes introduced by Franco Burgersdijck (d. 1636), who had been a professor of philosophy at Leiden; his *Institutionum Logicarum Libri Duo* (Leiden, 1626) and his *Synopsis Burgersdiciana* (published posthumously at Leiden in 1645), a manual of scholastic logic, were popular textbooks. It is not certain, however, that Spinoza read Burgersdijck's works; he may have known them only through the works of Burgersdijck's successor at Leiden, Adrian Heereboord (d. 1651). Heereboord produced a revised version of the *Synopsis*, entitled *Hermeneia Logica* (Leiden, 1650), which includes an exposition of Burgersdijck's classification of causes; he also commented on this doctrine in his *Meletemata Philosophica* (Leiden,

1654), a work actually quoted by Spinoza.[13] Spinoza could also have found in the *Meletemata* the antithesis between *natura naturans* and *natura naturata*, used in the *Short Treatise*, and later in the *Ethics*.[14] Heereboord is of particular interest in that he sympathized both with Descartes and with the scholastics, and in particular with Suarez. One should not assume, therefore, that whenever Spinoza uses scholastic terms this indicates a study of the original texts; he may well be using the scholastic Cartesian Heereboord.[15]

Spinoza wrote the *Tractatus de Intellectus Emendatione* and the *Short Treatise* at Rijnsburg, a village near Leiden, to which he had moved in about 1660. It was at Rijnsburg also that he began work on his first published book, a geometrical version of the first two parts of Descartes's *Principia Philosophiae*, together with an appendix of 'Metaphysical Thoughts' (*Cogitata Metaphysica*), published in Amsterdam in 1663. Spinoza's version of Descartes's *Principia* is purely expository, and the *Cogitata Metaphysica* is as it were a Cartesian exercise, dealing with traditional problems of metaphysics in a Cartesian way (G i, 131). By the time that he wrote this book, Spinoza was already severely critical of Descartes, and it is not surprising that he should have said, 'I do not acknowledge as my own everything that is contained in this treatise'.[16] However, this does not mean that he rejected everything that the work contains. The author of the preface to the book (Spinoza's friend Lodewijk Meyer) stated that 'He judges some of it to be true' (G i, 131), and indeed several passages in Spinoza's mature works refer to his geometrical version of Descartes or to the *Cogitata Metaphysica* as expressing his own views.[17] All this is consistent with the view of Spinoza stated at the beginning of this chapter: namely, that he is the reformer of the Cartesian philosophy, not its destroyer.

Spinoza left Rijnsburg in April 1663 and moved to Voorburg, a village near the Hague. In 1670 he moved to the Hague itself, where he continued to live until his death from consumption on 21 February 1677. Between 1663 and 1677 Spinoza wrote the works for which he is most famous. He seems to have begun work on his masterpiece, the *Ethics*, whilst still at Rijnsburg; certainly, he sent the first propositions of what appears to be a draft of the book to his friends in Amsterdam in February 1663 (Ep 8). By June 1665 a draft of the work was near completion. At that stage, incidentally, the work consisted of three parts; the third of these was later expanded into what became Parts Three, Four and Five of the final version. However, Spinoza suspended work on the *Ethics* in the latter half of 1665 (Ep 30; to Oldenburg, September/October 1665), so that he could concentrate on a book which was to be published in 1670 as the *Tractatus Theologico-Politicus*. In this book, Spinoza aimed to show (contrary to the views of the Dutch Calvinists) that the Scriptures are compatible with freedom of thought. In pursuit of this end he offered one of the first critical accounts of the Bible, presenting it as a historical document. The book was published anonymously and under a false imprint, but its authorship was widely known and Spinoza was attacked in print by numerous defenders of religious orthodoxy. After 1670 Spinoza returned to work on the *Ethics*, and by July 1675 it was complete (Ep 68). However, Spinoza thought it advisable to delay publication, and the work did not appear until after his death, as part of his posthumous works. These appeared in December 1677 (G ii, 313–4) in both the Latin original and a Dutch translation.[18] They contained, besides the *Ethics*, the *Tractatus de Intellectus Emendatione*, an unfinished *Tractatus Politicus* on which Spinoza was working during his last years, an incomplete *Compendium of Hebrew Grammar*, and those items of Spinoza's correspondence which his editors believed to be of philosophical importance.

The correspondence of Spinoza is valuable, not only for the philosophical arguments that it contains, but also for the light that it throws on his interests, and so indirectly on his philosophy as a whole. I have argued that Spinoza owed much to Descartes; now, Descartes's philosophy was closely connected with the science of his time, and it is therefore not surprising that Spinoza's letters should display an interest in science. Of the eighty-seven letters to or from Spinoza that have survived,[19] nineteen touch on scientific or mathematical issues.[20] That some of these – Ep 36, 39, 40, 46 – should deal with problems of optics, and more specifically with problems concerning lenses, is not surprising; it is well known that Spinoza, after his expulsion from the synagogue, supported himself by grinding and polishing lenses. But other letters display an interest in science that is not purely professional. Spinoza corresponds with Robert Boyle about nitre, fluidity and firmness (Ep 6, 11, 13, 16); he discusses with the secretary of the Royal Society, Henry Oldenburg, recent work on comets (Ep 29–32) and Descartes's theories about the planets (Ep 26); he comments on Descartes's laws of motion and Huygens's criticism of these, and asks for news of an experiment carried out in the Royal Society to test a hypothesis of Huygens (Ep 32, 33); he discusses the calculation of chances (Ep 38) and reports on an experiment of his own about pressure (Ep 41). This interest in the sciences is confirmed by a list of books from his library that were put up for sale after his death.[21] Of the 161 books listed, roughly a quarter are mathematical or scientific works.[22]

To sum up, my aim has been to determine the intellectual context within which Spinoza's thought is to be placed. I have argued that there is no reason to believe that Spinoza was deeply imbued with the Jewish or Christian philosophy of the Middle Ages. He may occasionally quote the medievals in order to make a point, but they are not the well-spring of his philosophy. His interest is not in old philosophical ideas, but in modern ones, in particular the philosophy of Descartes, which he 'reforms', and the new science of his time.

I have spoken of Spinoza's interest in contemporary science; before going further into his philosophy, something must be said in general terms about the way in which he saw the relations between science and his philosophy. It is a commonplace that, whereas Descartes was chiefly concerned with the answer to the question, 'What do I know, and how do I know it?', Spinoza is chiefly concerned with the question, 'What is a good life for a human being?' It may be that had Spinoza lived longer the *Ethics* would not have had the dominant position in his output that it now has; it might have been accompanied, not only by a completed *Tractatus Politicus*, but by a revised and completed version of his treatise on method, a book on physics, and an introduction to algebra.[23] Notwithstanding all this, there is no doubt that Spinoza's initial and chief motive for philosophizing was a moral one. In the famous autobiographical opening of his *Tractatus de Intellectus Emendatione*, he writes:[24]

> After experience had taught me that all the things which occur frequently in ordinary life are vain and futile; when I saw that all the things on account of which I was afraid, and which I feared, had nothing of good or bad in them except in so far as the mind was moved by them, I resolved at last to inquire if there was some good which was genuine and capable of communicating itself, and by which the mind would be affected even if all the others were rejected.

Since the time of Hume,[25] many philosophers have taken the view that there is a gap between questions of fact and questions of value, between 'is' and 'ought'. Philosophers who take a contrary view, and argue that human nature is relevant to questions about the nature of what is morally good, are termed 'naturalists'. Spinoza is such a naturalist. He argued that if we are to discover the kind of life that is good for a human being, we must discover the true nature of human beings, and that this implies seeing ourselves in the context of nature as a whole. Human beings, he says,[26] follow the universal laws of nature; the position of man in nature is not that of a kingdom within a kingdom. One could summarize his view by saying (adapting a phrase used by A. J. Ayer)[27] that man is a subject for science. More will be said of Spinoza's views about science and philosophy in the course of this chapter, which is concerned with Spinoza's metaphysics and theory of knowledge (see especially pp. 287–9); his views about ethics and politics will be discussed by Dr Blom in the next chapter.

In discussing Spinoza, I shall take as my primary source his *Ethics*. This is his acknowledged masterpiece; a work of great range, covering not only moral philosophy but also metaphysics and theory of knowledge, besides containing the outlines of a system of physics and a theory of politics. The full title of the book is *Ethics, demonstrated in geometrical order*, and indeed the most immediately striking feature of the book is the geometrical order in which it is presented. It is worth noting that, in presenting his philosophy in this form, Spinoza is following a lead given by Descartes. The relevant topic here is Descartes's distinction between 'analysis' and 'synthesis', and although this has already been discussed in a previous chapter,[28] it will not be superfluous to return to it here. In Part II of his *Discourse on Method*, Descartes had written (CSM i, 120) that 'Those long chains composed of very simple and easy reasonings, which geometers customarily use to arrive at their most difficult demonstrations, had given me occasion to suppose that all the things which can fall under human knowledge are interconnected in the same way.' This might lead one to expect that Descartes would present his philosophy in geometrical form, and indeed in the Second Set of Objections to Descartes's *Meditations* Mersenne suggested that this would be a worthwhile undertaking (CSM ii, 92). Descartes's reply turns on that distinction between analysis and synthesis which has just been mentioned. The distinction goes back to classical Greek mathematics, and there is a famous account of it in the writings of Pappus (fourth century AD), which Descartes is known to have studied. Pappus states[29] that

> In analysis, we assume as a fact that which we seek [to prove] and we consider what arises out of this assumption; then we consider what *that* follows from, and so on until, proceeding in this way, we come upon something which is already known, or is one of our principles.

In short, in analysis we proceed back from what has to be proved to first principles (Descartes calls them 'primary notions': *Reply to Second Objections*, CSM ii, 111). Synthesis, on the other hand, is the reverse of this; as Descartes explains (ibid.) one starts with first principles and demonstrates conclusions from them, employing 'a long series of definitions, postulates, axioms, theorems and problems'. Descartes stated a preference for the analytic method, which was, he said, the method that he had used throughout the *Meditations* (CSM ii, 111). However, in response to Mersenne's suggestion he concluded his reply to the *Second Objections* by arguing 'in synthetic style' for some of the propositions argued for in the *Meditations*. But he insisted (CSM ii, 113) that these proofs were not a substitute for the *Meditations*, and said indeed that the analytic reasoning used in that work was superior.

Spinoza, on the other hand, clearly thought that the best way in which to discuss ethics was by means of the synthetic method. One naturally asks what Spinoza hoped to achieve by the use of this method; that is, what he thought he would gain by presenting his philosophy in the form of theorems, derived from definitions and axioms. The answer may seem to be obvious. Spinoza does not explain how he viewed axioms, but there can be no doubt that he would have agreed with the remarks made by his friend Lodewijk Meyer, in the Preface that Meyer wrote to Spinoza's geometrical version of Descartes's *Principles*. In that Preface, Meyer said (G i, 127) that axioms are 'statements so clear and evident that all who simply understand correctly the words that they contain can in no way refuse their assent to them'. Axioms, in short, are self-evident truths, and Spinoza's aim in the *Ethics* is to derive from these, by deductive means, other propositions whose truth is not self-evident. In this way, he will demonstrate the truth of these propositions.[30]

I said just now that this explanation of Spinoza's use of the geometrical method may seem to be obvious. By this I did not mean that the explanation is wrong; I meant only that there is more to be said. Spinoza has a deeper reason for using the geometrical method, as can be seen from the Preface to Part III of the *Ethics*. Here (G ii, 138) Spinoza discusses his application of a geometrical method to human emotions, and contrasts his approach with that of those who 'prefer rather to abuse and ridicule the emotions and actions of men than to understand them'. Such people, he says, will find it extraordinary that he should want to demonstrate with sure reasoning (*certa ratione*) what they merely condemn rhetorically. But, he continues, human emotions follow from the same necessity and power of nature as other things do, and 'acknowledge certain causes through which they are understood, and have certain properties equally worthy of our knowledge as the properties of any other thing, the contemplation alone of which delights us'. This shows that Spinoza thinks that the geometrical method, although it is certainly a means of establishing truths, is more than that. The person who has grasped the reasoning of the *Ethics*, Spinoza claims, will not just know the truth of a number of propositions, but will *understand* why things are as they are. In short, Spinoza is concerned not just to establish truths but to offer explanations.

That this is Spinoza's view of the geometrical method is confirmed by his use of definitions in the *Ethics*.[31] These definitions are usually stated in the form, 'By . . . I understand . . .'; and this raises a problem. Spinoza is in effect saying that he proposes to take a term in such and such a way. Such definitions seem to be of the kind that is commonly called 'stipulative', and it is now usually held that (in the words of a modern textbook of logic) 'a stipulative definition is neither true nor false, but should be regarded as a proposal or resolution to use the definiendum to mean what is meant by the definiens, or as a request or command'.[32] Given that that is so, one may ask why one should accept Spinoza's definitions. Why should we use words in the way that he tacitly requests or commands? Why play one particular language game, rather than another?

To answer this question, it will be useful to consider first what Spinoza is excluding when he states his definitions. The terms that he defines are not words that he has invented; he uses terms that others had used, but he often uses them in a new way. So when he says something of the form 'By . . . I understand . . .', he is often excluding what some, and perhaps most, philosophers understood by the term defined. His reason for rejecting such definitions, and for defining terms in the way that he does, is made clear in the course of the definitions of the emotions in Part III of the *Ethics*. Here, Spinoza says that 'It is my purpose to explain, not the meanings of words, but the nature of things.'[33] What he is doing when he defines terms has a parallel in the practice of scientists, who sometimes coin completely new terms and sometimes use old terms in a new way – as when a scientist uses the word 'velocity' to mean, not just speed, but speed in a certain direction.[34]

Definitions form an integral part of the geometrical method, so what has just been said confirms the view suggested earlier: namely, that Spinoza uses the geometrical method not just to establish truths, but also to *explain*, to achieve *understanding*. This point will meet us again when we consider the distinctive way in which Spinoza uses the terms 'true' and 'false' (see pp. 296–7). At present, however, there is a further question to be raised. The idea that deductive reasoning can be used to provide explanations was by no means new with Spinoza, or indeed in the seventeenth century in general; on the contrary, it can be traced back as far as Aristotle. In the *Posterior Analytics* (I 13, 78 a38-b3) Aristotle explains the fact that all planets shine steadily by presenting it as the conclusion of a deductive, or more precisely a syllogistic, argument.[35] This raises the question why Spinoza should have chosen to present his explanatory system in geometrical, rather than in syllogistic, form. The answer must surely be that he was influenced by the new science of his time. For this science, mathematics was the key to the understanding of nature. So, for example, Descartes had declared in his *Principles of Philosophy* (Pt II, 64; CSM i, 247) that the only principles that he required in physics were those of geometry and pure mathematics; to this one may add Spinoza's observation, made in the Appendix to Part I of the *Ethics* (G i, 79), that truth might have lain hidden from the human race through all eternity had it not been for mathematics. As to the possibility of an explanatory system cast in syllogistic form, Spinoza would probably have agreed with Descartes that the syllogism is useful only as a means of instruction, which enables others to understand what their teachers already know, and that its proper place is in rhetoric, not in philosophy.[36]

From a discussion of Spinoza's reasons for putting his philosophy in the form of a deductive system we turn now to an account of the system itself. I said earlier (p. 278) that Spinoza takes the view that, if one is to discover what is the genuine good for human beings, one must get to know their true nature; and further, that this implies seeing human beings within the context of nature as a whole. In the *Ethics*, Spinoza (following the synthetic method) starts from certain definitions and axioms which enable him to derive conclusions about the universe in general, and from these, with the help of further definitions and axioms, he derives a number of conclusions about the nature of human beings in particular, and about what is good for us.

The first part of the *Ethics* is concerned with what Spinoza calls 'God'. His first definition, however, is not of God, but of a 'cause of itself' – though it later emerges that to speak of God and of a cause of itself is to speak of one and the same being. Spinoza explains that by 'cause of itself' he understands 'that whose essence involves existence; or, that whose nature cannot be conceived except as existing'. The term 'essence' plays an important part in the *Ethics*, though it does not receive a formal definition until Part II. In the first definition of Part I, Spinoza is implying that the predicate P (here, existence) belongs to the essence of S if one *has to think* of the nature of S as involving the predicate P.[37] Some observations made by Descartes in his *Notae in Programma quoddam* ('Comments on a certain Broadsheet', Amsterdam 1648; CSM i, 297) are helpful here. The nature of contingent things, Descartes says, leaves open the possibility that they may be in either one state or another state, for example he himself may at present be either writing or not writing.

> But when it is a question of the essence of something, it would
> be quite foolish and self-contradictory to say that the nature
> of things leaves open the possibility that the essence of something
> may have a different character from the one it actually has.

So it belongs to the essence of a mountain that it exists with a valley; or, as Spinoza would say, the nature of a mountain cannot be conceived except as existing with a valley.

Let us now return to Spinoza's definition of a cause of itself as that whose essence involves existence. This is reminiscent of what is commonly called the 'ontological argument' for the existence of God; and indeed, the definition of a cause of itself plays an important part (by way of Proposition 7 of Part I) in the first of Spinoza's arguments for the existence of God in Proposition 11 of Part I. It is worth noting, however, that the term 'ontological argument' is used of two different arguments, which have in common the fact that they move from a definition of something to an assertion of the existence of what is defined. In the version which is familiar from Descartes's fifth *Meditation* (CSM ii, 44–9) the argument is based on the definition of God as a most perfect being, together with the thesis that existence is a perfection. This is basically the same as the argument put forward by Anselm, in the eleventh century AD, in his *Proslogion*, although there the argument proceeds from the definition of God as 'that than which nothing greater can be thought'.[38] Spinoza, on the other hand, is arguing from the concept of a *necessary* being. His argument is that a necessary being is a being which has to be thought of as existing; and that which has to be thought of as existing, necessarily exists. It may be added that another seventeenth-century rationalist, Leibniz, put forward both versions of the argument, though he declared his preference for the second version.[39]

The concept of a cause of itself is interesting, not only for the relation that it has to Spinoza's version of the ontological argument, but also because it illustrates his distinctive views about causality. Someone who (like Hume or Kant[40]) takes the view that a cause must precede its effect in time will find the concept of a cause of itself self-contradictory; for how can something first exist, and then cause its own existence? Spinoza, however, does not view causality in this way; his view is a version of what it is usual to call the rationalist theory of causality. According to this theory, to state the cause of X is to give a reason for X's existence or nature. So much might be generally agreed, if this is taken to mean that to give a reason is to answer the question 'Why?', and that in stating the cause of something one is answering such a question. What is distinctive about the rationalist theory of causality is the view that, in giving such a reason, one is doing what geometers do when they state the reason for the truth of some geometrical proposition – as when, for example, it is said that the reason why the base angles of a certain triangle are equal is the fact that the triangle in question is isosceles. In such a case, the relation between the triangle's being isosceles, on the one hand, and having base angles which are equal, on the other, is a *timeless* relation; and Spinoza takes the view that such a relation holds in every case of a cause-effect relation. This is what he means when, in the second proof of the existence of God in Proposition 11 of Part I of the *Ethics*, he uses the phrase 'cause, or reason' (*causa seu ratio*; G ii, 52–3), where 'reason' is used in the non-temporal sense that has just been described.[41] This being so, to speak of a cause of itself is not to speak of that which exists before it produces itself; rather, it is to speak of that whose existence is self-explanatory.

Why Spinoza should have taken this view of the nature of causality can only be conjectured, but it does not seem fanciful to relate his view to the science of his time. I have said already that this science was mathematical in character (p. 281); now, many causal propositions belong to the sciences, and it would have been tempting to see the causal propositions asserted by physicists as not different in kind from the propositions asserted by geometers, and from this to argue that absolutely all causal propositions are to be viewed in this way. It may be added that the influence of the rationalist theory of causality was still felt in the eighteenth century; certainly, Hume thought it worthwhile to refute the view that inferences from cause to effect are 'demonstrative', that is, that when one thing causes another, 'the contrary is impossible, and implies a contradiction'.[42] But there is no reason to believe that he was attacking Spinoza in particular.[43]

The 'God' whose existence is argued for in Proposition 11 of Part I of the *Ethics* is defined by Spinoza in a distinctive way. By 'God', he says (*Ethics*, Pt I, Definition 6), he understands a being which is absolutely infinite, that is, 'a substance consisting of infinite attributes, each of which expresses eternal and infinite essence'. Superficially, there is nothing here to which any of Spinoza's contemporaries might object (though the absence of any reference to God as creator might have caused some surprise). But from what is said about substance and its attributes in Part I of the *Ethics*, it becomes clear that the God defined by Spinoza is very different from the God of theism. This section will be concerned with Spinoza's views about substance and attribute.

There is no one philosophical problem of substance; rather, there are two main problems.[44] These are: 'What is it that really exists?' and 'What is it that remains the same when some change occurs?' Spinoza's theory of substance is concerned only with the first of these.[45] In the third definition of Part I of the *Ethics*, Spinoza says of substance that it is 'that which is in itself'. A seventeenth-century reader would have seen this as involving concepts which go back to Aristotle. In Chapter 5 of the *Categories* Aristotle says that a substance is that which is 'neither said of a subject nor in a subject' (2 a11–13, trans. J. L. Ackrill). The first part of the definition is not important here (although it does matter in the case of the philosophy of Leibniz); what matters is the idea that a substance is not 'in' a subject. Aristotle explains (*Categories*, ch. 2, 1 a24–5) that, in this context, to say that something is in a subject is to say that it cannot exist apart from the subject. A substance, then, is something which has an independent existence. Spinoza means much the same when he says that a substance is 'in itself', with the difference that he maintains that a substance, though not dependent on anything other than itself, has to be regarded as self-dependent, by which he presumably means that its existence depends solely on its own nature. Spinoza adds (going beyond the account of substance in Aristotle's *Categories*) that a substance is also *conceived through* itself. Once again, the idea of not being dependent on anything external is present. Spinoza is asserting that, in thinking of a substance, we do not have to think of anything else; that is, a substance is *logically* independent of anything else. The notion of something which is conceived through itself will re-emerge in the context of Spinoza's theory of attributes.

So far, Spinoza's account of substance may seem to travel along a well-worn path.[46] However, Spinoza forsakes this for a much less-used path when he considers the question, 'What satisfies the criteria of a substance?' For the Aristotle of the *Categories* there are many substances: this man, this horse and so on (2 a11–13). For Spinoza, on the other hand, there is and can be only one substance, and that substance is God. The argument for this conclusion that is contained in Proposition 14 of Part I of the *Ethics* is obscurely expressed, but it is clear that it rests on the concept of God as an *infinite* substance.[47] The thrust of the argument is that God's infinity as it were crowds out all other possible substances, God remaining as the one and only substance. Descartes, too, understood by 'substance' that which depends on no other thing for its existence, and said that there is a sense in which the only substance is God (*Principles of Philosophy*, Pt I, 51; CSM i, 210). However, he said that there is another sense of 'substance', in which we may call by the name of 'substance' that which depends for its existence only on God; in this sense, we may speak of corporeal substance and of created thinking substance.[48] Spinoza will not allow this second sense of the word 'substance'; indeed he would argue (as will be seen shortly) that, by using it, Descartes had rendered insoluble the problem of the relations between mind and matter. In place of corporeal and thinking substances, Spinoza refers to 'extension' and 'thought', and says that these are not substances but are attributes of the one substance.

Spinoza defines an attribute in the fourth definition of Part I of the *Ethics* as 'that which the intellect perceives of substance as constituting its essence'; he also speaks of the attributes as 'expressing' the essence of substance.[49] In mentioning the intellect in his formal definition of an attribute, Spinoza has seemed to some scholars to make the relation between substance and attribute a subjective one; the intellect has been thought to impose attributes on a substance which is in reality without them. This, however, is surely wrong. From the mass of evidence that has been brought against the subjectivist interpretation,[50] it will be sufficient to cite a remark contained in the proof of Proposition 44 of Part II. Here, Spinoza says that 'It is of the nature of reason to perceive things truly . . . namely, . . . as they are in themselves.' If, as is reasonable, one equates the 'reason' that is mentioned here with the 'intellect' mentioned in the definition of an attribute, then Spinoza is saying that, if the intellect perceives X as constituting the essence of substance, then X does indeed constitute the essence of substance.

In the first part of the *Ethics*, Spinoza's discussion of the attributes is carried on in quite general terms; nothing is said expressly that enables the reader to say that this or that is an example of an attribute.[51] Only in the first two propositions of Part II are we told that, of the infinite attributes that God has, two are extension and thought.[52] Two points must be noted here. First, it must be realized that the attributes of extension are not abstractions, even though Spinoza uses abstract nouns to refer to them. Spinoza makes it clear that to speak, for example, of the attribute of extension is to speak of God as extended, God as an 'extended thing' (*Ethics*, Proposition 2 of Part II). Second, each attribute (by Definition 6 of Part I) is infinite; so to talk about extension is to talk about an extended reality that is infinite.

In saying that extension and thought express the essence of substance, Spinoza obviously means that each is of fundamental importance to our understanding of reality. What is perhaps not so obvious is that his views about attributes are not entirely at variance with those of Descartes. When Descartes spoke of corporeal and thinking substance, he implied that each has many attributes (*Principles of Philosophy*, Pt I, 53; CSM i, 210), understanding by an attribute (ibid., Pt I, 56) that which always remains unmodified, such as existence and duration in the case of created things. Each substance, however, has one 'principal attribute', and these are extension in the case of corporeal substance and thought in the case of thinking substance. Spinoza and Descartes, then, agree in holding that one must explain physical nature in terms of extension and mental states and events in terms of thought. They also agree to some extent (though here there are also important differences) that we must explain the former in terms of extension alone and the latter in terms of thought alone. Descartes expresses this by saying (*Meditation* VI, CSM ii, 54) that corporeal and thinking substance are 'really distinct'.[53] Spinoza would say that Descartes was right in holding that we cannot mix mental terms with physical terms when we try to explain either mind or matter – still less can we reduce mental terms to physical terms (as in the case of materialism) or physical terms to mental terms. But, he would say, the metaphysics in terms of which Descartes made this point was seriously at fault. Contrary to Descartes, there is only one substance, and what Descartes says in terms of two substances must be translated into terms of the attributes of thought and extension, each of which is 'conceived through itself'.[54]

Spinoza would also argue that by regarding thought and extension in this way – as self-enclosed attributes, which are attributes of *one* substance – he can solve a problem which had faced Descartes: that of the relation between mind and body. Descartes wanted to maintain two theses: first, that corporeal and mental substance are really distinct, but second, that mind and body act on each other, and indeed that the human being is a unity of mind and body. The problem for Descartes was to explain how these propositions can both be true, and Spinoza thought (as many others have thought) that he failed to do so. To grasp Spinoza's solution, however, it is necessary to go further into his system. This is because the problem is one which concerns particular minds and particular bodies, and this means that one has to see how Spinoza accommodates these within his system. That is, it is necessary to consider his theory of 'modes'.

Spinoza argues, not only that the infinite substance must be unique, but that it must also be indivisible, and that the same can be said of any of its attributes.[55] This raises the question of how the indivisible substance, or its indivisible attributes, is to be related to the particular things that we meet in our experience. That is, it raises the question: what is the place of the concept of a particular thing in Spinoza's system? The answer is that it enters by way of the concept of a 'mode'. Particular things, Spinoza says, are simply 'modes by which attributes of God are expressed in a certain and determinate manner'.[56] Spinoza has already defined a mode in the fifth of the definitions of Part I of the *Ethics*, saying that it is 'that which is in something else, through which it is also conceived'. This definition can be illuminated by relating it to what Descartes has to say about real and modal distinctions. For Descartes, a real distinction holds between two or more substances, and is recognized by the fact that one can be clearly and distinctly understood without the other (*Principles of Philosophy*, Pt I, 60; CSM i, 213). A mode, on the other hand, cannot be understood apart from the substance of which it is a mode. 'Thus there is a modal distinction between shape or motion and the corporeal substance in which they inhere; and similarly, there is a modal distinction between affirmation or recollection and the mind' (ibid., Pt I, 61; CSM i, 213). Although Spinoza rejects the idea that there can be a real distinction between substances, he accepts the distinction between a mode and that of which it is a mode, the only difference from Descartes being that Spinoza's modes are modes of the one substance, or of its attributes. He is saying in effect that when we talk about particular things, then (even though there is in a sense only one being, God) we are not indulging in mere fantasy. What would be a mistake, and a serious one, would be to regard as independent substances what are in fact modes of the one substance.

What makes Spinoza's concept of a mode more than just a terminological exercise is the use to which he puts it. It will be convenient to begin by considering his views about the modes of the attribute of extension, where the line of thought is easier to follow. In the first definition of Part II of the *Ethics*, Spinoza explains that by a 'body' he understands a mode of the attribute of extension. (This, incidentally, is a good example of his use of definitions. By calling a body a 'mode', he claims, we understand what a body really is.) A body, then, is distinct from another body in that they are different modes of one and the same attribute. To explain the precise way in which they differ, Spinoza inserts in the *Ethics*, between the Scholium to Proposition 13 of Part II and the next proposition (G ii, 97–102), a sketch of a theory of physics. He takes it as axiomatic that all bodies either move or are at rest, and that each body moves now more slowly and now more quickly. What differentiate bodies (Lemma 1) are differences in respect of motion and rest, speed and slowness; and these are *modal* differences. Spinoza singles out motion and rest for special mention, saying that they follow from the absolute nature of the attribute of extension, and exist for ever and infinitely.[57] This means in effect that motion and rest (which scholars call an 'immediate infinite mode' of extension) are universally present in matter, and are of fundamental importance for the physicist.

Spinoza goes on to say that those bodies which are differentiated *only* by motion or rest, speed or slowness, may be called 'most simple bodies' (Axiom 2 after Lemma 3). These corpuscles are the basic building-blocks of Spinoza's system of physics; they correspond roughly to atoms,[58] with the difference that Spinoza's 'most simple bodies' are modes, not independent substances. The most simple bodies combine to form groups (Definition after Lemma 3), and each such group is called by Spinoza *one* body, or an 'individual'. An individual has a certain structure, and as long as that structure is preserved, we say that the individual is the same. (This, incidentally, has a bearing on one of the two problems of substance mentioned on p. 284 – namely, the problem of what it is that remains the same when change occurs). Individuals are of varying complexity, culminating in an individual of infinite complexity – that is, the whole of nature, 'whose parts, that is, all bodies, vary in infinite ways without any change of the individual as a whole' (Scholium to Lemma 7). In *Epistolae* 64 Spinoza calls this individual the 'aspect of the whole universe' (*facies totius universi*). Scholars refer to it as a 'mediate infinite mode' – mediate, because it depends on motion and rest. Spinoza seems here to be thinking of the whole physical universe as manifesting some general law – perhaps that of the overall preservation of the same ratio of motion to rest.[59]

All this throws light on the way in which Spinoza saw the relations between science and philosophy. I have mentioned (p. 277) Spinoza's deep interest in the science of his day; but this does not mean that he accepted without question the propositions of contemporary science, and tried to generalize from them.[60] I have indeed suggested (p. 281) that his preference for a geometrical order in philosophy was influenced by the mathematical physics of his time. But this merely explains his preference for one sort of explanatory deductive system – one cast in the form of a work of geometry – over another kind, cast in the form of syllogisms. It does not imply that he thought it impossible to provide a rational justification of the truths of science. In his view, such justification would on the whole proceed in the way that metaphysical truths are justified – namely, by deduction from self-evident truths. In sum, science for Spinoza is not something on whose conclusions philosophers merely reflect; rather, philosophy is needed in order to justify the propositions of science.

I said just now that Spinoza thought that scientific propositions could 'on the whole' be justified by deducing them from self-evident truths. The type of corporeal 'individual' which is of most interest to him, as a moral philosopher, is of course the human body. Now, Spinoza's account of the human body is based on a number of 'postulates' (indeed, the assertion that the human body is a highly complex individual is itself a postulate: see Postulate 1 after Lemma 7). By a 'postulate' Spinoza means a proposition which is assumed to be true, but which does not have the self-evidence that belongs to axioms. The question is why a postulate should be assumed to be true. Spinoza's answer is contained in an assertion made later (Scholium to Proposition 17 of Part II) that his postulates contain hardly anything that is not borne out by experience. This raises the question of the place that Spinoza gives to experience in his system; but before this can be discussed (pp. 297–9 below) it is necessary to consider his account of the modes of thought.

When Spinoza says that a body is a mode of the attribute of extension he can be regarded as adapting, to his own theory of substance, Descartes's views about corporeal substance. For there are indications that Descartes held that there is just one corporeal substance, whose parts are distinguished only modally.[61] But where the human mind is concerned, the situation is very different. Descartes believes that every human mind is a substance – more specifically, a thinking substance – and such a plurality of substances is something that Spinoza cannot allow. For him, the human mind has to be viewed in terms of the concept of mode. To talk of the human mind is to talk of something complex (Proposition 15 of Part II of the *Ethics*), just as to talk of the human body is to talk of something complex. In the case of the mind, the basic units are again modes, but modes of the attribute of thought. Spinoza calls these modes 'ideas'.[62]

In what he says about 'ideas', Spinoza is opposing Descartes. Descartes had introduced his sense of the term in the third of the *Meditations*, in which he said (CSM ii, 25) that ideas are those thoughts which are 'as it were the images of things . . . for example when I think of a man, or a chimera, or the sky, or an angel, or God'. The force of the phrase 'as it were' is that one cannot have a genuine mental picture of an angel or of God; however, it does seem that for Descartes an idea is at any rate picture-like, and that it is an entity which the mind perceives, as distinct from the activity of perceiving. So, for example, in his reply to the third *Objections*, Descartes explains (CSM ii, 127) that the word 'idea' means 'whatever is immediately perceived by the mind'. Spinoza, on the other hand, insists that an idea is an activity. In his definition of an idea in Definition 3 of Part II of the *Ethics*, he says that an idea is a 'conception' (*conceptus*) of the mind, and adds that he prefers the term 'conception' to 'perception' because the former term 'seems to express an action of the mind'. It emerges later[63] that, when Spinoza speaks of an action of the mind here, he means that to have an idea of X is to think of X, in the sense of making a judgement about it, that is, affirming or denying something of it. It may be added that in using the term 'idea' in this way Spinoza is not being innovative, but is taking up a suggestion which Descartes had put aside. In the Preface to the *Meditations* (CSM ii, 7) Descartes had said that the term 'idea' could be taken to mean an operation of the intellect, but went on to say that this was not how he proposed to use the word.

It emerges from what is said later in the *Ethics* that Spinoza has two chief reasons for preferring his definition of the word 'idea'. Briefly, these are as follows: (i) Descartes's sense of the term forms part of a mistaken theory of judgement. Descartes believed that two faculties are involved, namely the intellect and the will (*Meditation* IV; CSM ii, 39). Spinoza, on the other hand, argues[64] that the two are the same. To think of something (i.e. to have an idea of something) is to make a judgement about it; for example, to think of a winged horse is to affirm wings of a horse. (ii) Descartes is unable to explain our knowledge of the truth; for how can we know that a true idea agrees with that of which it is the idea?[65]

All this is intelligible as a criticism of Descartes, but Spinoza's own views raise a problem: namely, that of the way in which an idea, as a mode of thought, is related to the attribute of thought. The problem springs from the infinity of the attribute of thought. In what sense, one asks, can an idea which a particular person has be called a mode of this infinite attribute? One might perhaps suggest that (by analogy with the attribute of extension and its modes) Spinoza views the attribute of thought as some kind of infinite mind-stuff; but it is not at all clear what might be meant by such a stuff. It may be that some light is thrown on the problem by Spinoza's theory of truth, which is discussed on pp. 296–7. To anticipate, Spinoza holds that a true idea fits, and a false idea does not fit, into an explanatory system, and it may be that the relation between an idea and its attribute has to be conceived along such lines. However, perhaps enough has been said here about Spinoza's theory of ideas to enable one to grasp his answer to the problem posed on p. 287 – the problem of mind-matter relations.

It will be recalled that the problem arose for Descartes because he wanted to maintain two propositions. On the one hand, he wanted to say that mind and body are 'really distinct'; on the other hand, he felt compelled to grant that, despite this, mind and body act on one another, and indeed that the human being is a unity of mind and matter. Spinoza's answer to the problem is given in terms of his theory of attributes and modes. In effect, he holds that Descartes was right in saying (Reply to *First Objections*, CSM ii, 86) that one has a complete understanding of what a body is without ascribing to it anything that belongs to the nature of a mind, and conversely in the case of a mind. Descartes's error, Spinoza would say, lay in his supposition that there must exist substances of basically different kinds, namely mental and corporeal substances. Really, there exists just one substance with different attributes, each of which (and here Spinoza expresses a qualified agreement with Descartes) must be 'conceived through itself'.

It is because the attributes are conceived through themselves that we must explain physical states and events in physical terms only, and mental states and events in mental terms only. Yet the human mind and body are not wholly unrelated; for any state of or event in the one there is a corresponding state of or event in the other. This is because thought and extension are different attributes of one and the same substance. As Spinoza puts it in an important note to Proposition 7 of Part II of the *Ethics*,

A mode of extension and the idea of that mode are one and the same thing, but expressed in two ways. . . . For example, a circle existing in nature and the idea of an existing circle . . . is one and the same thing, though explained through different attributes.

In Proposition 2 of Part III of the *Ethics*, Spinoza observes that it follows from what he has said about the nature of the attributes that 'The body cannot determine the mind to think, nor the mind the body to motion, nor to rest.' As he recognizes, this may seem paradoxical. Suppose, for example,[66] that some craftsman is building a temple; surely the craftsman's mind must guide the movements of his hands? Spinoza replies that this cannot be so, and that people only suppose that it must be so because 'they know not what a body can do, or what can be deduced from mere contemplation of its nature'. He goes on to hint that, when people think of the capabilities of the human body, they tend to think in terms of the machines they can construct. But 'the construction of the human body (*corporis humani fabrica*[67]) . . . far surpasses any piece of work made by human art'. So (Spinoza implies) there is no reason to think that the movements of the craftsman's hands cannot be explained in purely physical terms.

Spinoza's theory of the relations between mind and body is often, and with some justice, said to be a form of 'psycho-physical parallel-ism'. By this is meant the view that body does not act on mind, nor mind on body, but that the states of mind and body are such that for each bodily state there is a corresponding mental state and conversely; and similarly for bodily and mental events. However, to describe Spino-za's theory of mind-body relations in this way does not identify it completely. This is because to talk of psycho-physical parallelism is to talk, not of one theory, but of a group of theories. One could say, for example, that Leibniz's theory of pre-established harmony,[68] as applied to the relations between mind and body, is a form of psycho-physical parallelism; but Leibniz's theory of mind-body relations is very differ-ent from Spinoza's. To categorize Spinoza's theory more precisely, we have to consider his answer to the question why the parallelism should hold. The answer, as we have seen, is that each attribute is not only 'conceived through itself' but is also an attribute of *one and the same substance*. Seen in this way, Spinoza's theory of the relations between mind and body is a classical form of what is often called the 'double-aspect theory'.[69] This theory is clearly defined in Baldwin's *Dictionary of Philosophy and Psychology* (London, 1901) as the theory which states that 'mental and bodily facts are parallel manifestations of a single underlying reality'. The theory

profeses to overcome the onesidedness of materialism and idealism by regarding both series as only different aspects of the same reality, like the convex and the concave views of a curve; or, according to another favourite metaphor, the bodily and the mental facts are really the same facts expressed in different language.

Spinoza never calls an attribute an 'aspect' of substance; however, he often describes the relation between substance and attribute in terms of expression (cf. pp. 285–6), and it has just been noted (p. 292) that he says expressly that a mode of extension and the corresponding mode of thought are 'one and the same thing, but expressed in two ways'.

What Spinoza has to say about the relation between God and his modes is intimately connected with what he has to say about God as a cause. It has already been seen that God is self-caused, *causa sui* (p. 282); but Spinoza also says that God is the efficient cause of all modes. His reason for saying this[70] is that an infinity of modes follows from the necessity of the divine nature. Now, by virtue of Spinoza's thesis that the causal relation is a logical relation (p. 283), this is the same as saying that God is the cause of an infinity of modes.

In calling God an 'efficient cause', Spinoza is using traditional terminology, which goes back to Aristotle. Such a cause, according to Aristotle, is a source of change or coming to rest (*Physics* II, 3, 194 b29–32). So, for example, a man who gave advice is a cause in this sense, and a father is the efficient cause of his child. In these cases, the cause is outside the effect, and of course Spinoza's substance, God, is not outside the modes. However, this does not prevent Spinoza from calling God the efficient cause of what is in him; God, as he explains in a letter (Ep 60, G iv, 271) is an internal efficient cause, or, as he says in Proposition 18 of Part I of the *Ethics*, God is the 'immanent' cause of things. This means that Spinoza has to reject the idea of a creative deity, as understood by theistic philosophers.[71]

Efficient causality was traditionally distinguished from 'final' causality. A 'final' cause, for Aristotle, is the end or purpose for the sake of which something is done – as, for example, health is the cause of taking a walk (*Physics* II, 3, 194 b32–195 a3). Spinoza insists that, although we can and indeed must think of God as an efficient cause, we cannot ascribe final causality to God. In this respect he is in partial agreement with Descartes. In the *Principles of Philosophy*, Descartes had declared that 'It is not the final but the efficient causes of created things that we must inquire into' (Pt I, 28; CSM i, 202). So far, Spinoza would have agreed; but he would not have agreed with Descartes's reason for the assertion. Descartes does not deny that God has purposes, but is content to say that we cannot know God's purposes (ibid.; cf. op. cit., Pt III, 2; CSM i, 248). For Spinoza, on the other hand, the notion of a purposive God has no sense. Such a concept, he says, would be inconsistent with the perfection of God;[72] for if God were to act on account of an end, he would necessarily be seeking something that he lacks (Appendix to Part I of the *Ethics*, G ii, 80). But, as an absolutely infinite being, God can lack nothing.

Not only does Spinoza think that the concept of final causality cannot be applied to God, but he also thinks that it cannot be applied to finite beings such as ourselves. This thesis is not only of intrinsic interest, but also leads to a deeper understanding of Spinoza's views about God's causality. Spinoza would concede that finite beings, unlike God, can in a sense be said to have purposes; but, he would say, such purposive activity has to be explained in terms of efficient causation. In order to understand Spinoza's position, it is necessary to consider what he says about the ways in which things follow from God as a cause. He says that some modes follow from the absolute nature of God; these are the so-called 'infinite modes' (cf. pp. 288–9). Finite modes, on the other hand, cannot follow from the absolute nature of God (for that would make them infinite); instead, they must be determined by God, in so far as God is conceived as modified by some mode (*Ethics*, Pt I, Proposition 28). The upshot of this is (ibid.) that each particular thing is determined by some other particular thing, and that by another, and so on to infinity. This may seem to make each finite mode the helpless plaything of external forces – something which is merely pushed about. But in an important note to Proposition 45 of Part II, Spinoza indicates that this is not so. This note shows that there is a dual causality in God, or that there are two distinct ways in which a thing's existence and nature follows necessarily from something else. What Spinoza says is that although each particular thing is determined by another to exist in a certain way, yet 'the force wherewith each of them persists in existing follows from the eternal necessity of the nature of God'.

This force or power [73] is something which is usually referred to as 'conatus' (literally, 'endeavour'). Spinoza is here anticipating the important sixth proposition of Part III of the *Ethics*, which states that 'Each thing, in so far as it is in itself (*quantum in se est*) endeavours to persist in its own being.' The phrase 'is in itself' echoes Spinoza's definition of substance in Definition 3 of Part I (cf. p. 284), and serves to connect Proposition 6 of Part III with the Scholium to Proposition 45 of Part II, which was discussed in the last paragraph. For since there is only one substance, Proposition 6 of Part III must be taken to mean that each thing endeavours to persist in its own being in so far as it is God – or (to use the language of the Scholium to Proposition 45 of Part II) in so far as it 'follows from the eternal necessity of the nature of God'. This concept of *conatus* is central to Spinoza's moral philosophy, and a detailed discussion of it belongs to the next chapter. But it is worth noting here that, for Spinoza, *each* particular thing – and not just the very complex things that we call living beings – endeavours, in so far as it is 'in itself', to persist in its own being. So when Spinoza says, in the Corollary to Lemma 3 of Part II of the *Ethics*, that 'a moving body continues in motion until determined to rest by another body', this may be regarded as an example of *conatus* – namely, the kind that is displayed by a 'most simple body'.

What is most striking about Spinoza's views concerning the causality of God is the extreme form of determinism that they display. We have already seen several respects in which Spinoza's God differs from the God of the theist: how God, although an efficient cause, does not create the universe from nothing, and how God cannot act for an end. But there is another major difference. The God of the theist creates *freely*: that is, God chooses to create, and could have chosen differently. God's freedom of choice was something on which Descartes laid great stress; Spinoza, on the other hand, says[74] that God does not act out of free will, but that things could not have been produced by God in any other way or order from that in which they were produced. This means that there is no objective justification for calling things contingent. Just what Spinoza is claiming here can be seen from the way in which he argues for his conclusion. We know that, if B is caused by A, then B follows necessarily from A. Now, everything is, in the last analysis, caused by God, that is, follows necessarily from him; but God (by Proposition 11 of Part I of the *Ethics*) exists necessarily. Therefore everything that exists *cannot but* exist, and in the way that it does; or to put this in another way, strictly speaking no other world order is conceivable. More than this, Spinoza argues that whatever we conceive to be in God's power (i.e. whatever is logically possible) necessarily exists (*Ethics*, Pt I, Proposition 35). From this it follows that, if something does not exist, then it is impossible that it should have existed. In calling this an extreme form of determinism, I meant that Spinoza is not content to say that *given* a certain set of laws, and *given* an initial state of the universe, then absolutely all states of the universe can in principle be inferred from these. Such a position is consistent with the supposition that there could have been other laws, or that the initial state of the universe could have been different. For Spinoza, on the other hand, both the laws and the initial state are necessary, in the sense that no others are strictly speaking thinkable.

Spinoza's chief concern in the *Ethics* is with the human being, and more specifically with the human mind. It has already been seen that

Spinoza, contrary to Descartes, argues that the human mind is not a substance; on the positive side he argues that, just as the human body is something highly complex, so also is the human mind. More precisely, the human mind is an idea which is composed of many ideas (*Ethics*, Pt II, Proposition 15). Spinoza's account of the human mind is much more elaborate than his account of the human body, and falls into two main sections. The first of these, which occupies much of Part II of the *Ethics*, concerns topics which belong to the theory of knowledge – namely, the nature of a true idea, and of the kinds of knowledge. The second section, which begins in the course of Part III, concerns the human mind as something which is appetitive and has emotions. Our primary concern in this chapter is with the topics that belong to the theory of knowledge.

Spinoza speaks both of 'true ideas' and 'adequate ideas'; these are closely related. He says of a true idea that it must 'agree with' its object; an adequate idea is a true idea which is as it were abstracted from its relation to its object and considered only in respect of its internal properties.[75] In speaking of truth as 'agreement', Spinoza might seem to have in mind some version of the correspondence theory of truth. It will be recalled that, for Spinoza, to have an idea involves making a judgement (p. 290); so one might suppose him to mean that my idea of (say) an existent Peter is true when my judgement that Peter exists corresponds to a certain fact, namely, Peter's existence. In fact, however, this is not so; when Spinoza speaks of a true idea he is speaking not so much of truth as of knowledge.

Perhaps the first hint of this is given in Proposition 43 of Part II of the *Ethics*, where Spinoza says that 'He who has a true idea, knows at the same time that he has a true idea.' This may seem to be a glaring error; Plato, one may object, was obviously right when he said (*Meno*, 97a) that to have a true belief that this is the road to Larissa is not the same as *knowing* that this is the road to Larissa. However, the appearance of paradox vanishes when it is realized that Spinoza is using the term 'true' in a special sense. A passage from the early *Tractatus de Intellectus Emendatione* is relevant here. Spinoza says (G ii, 26) that

> If anyone says that Peter, e.g., exists, but does not *know* that Peter exists, his thought is, as far as he is concerned, false – or, if you prefer, is not true – even though Peter really does exist. The assertion 'Peter exists' is true only with respect to a person who knows for certain that Peter exists.[76]

That this was also Spinoza's view in the *Ethics* is indicated by the note to Proposition 43 of Part II, which states that to have a true idea is to 'know something perfectly or in the best way'. When Spinoza says in the *Ethics*, therefore, that a person who has a true idea knows that he has a true idea, he is not saying something that is inconsistent with what Plato had said about knowledge and true belief; what he is saying is that the person who knows, knows that he knows.

There is more to be said about Spinoza's views concerning knowledge and truth. In the note to Proposition 43 of Part II of the *Ethics* that has just been cited, Spinoza says, not just that to have a true idea is to know, but that it is to know something 'perfectly or in the best way' (*perfecte sive optime*). Here, he is referring to a point already made in Part II of the *Ethics* (Note 2 to Proposition 40) – namely, that there are various kinds of knowledge.[77] Now, from what he says about these kinds of knowledge it emerges that it is possible to have knowledge of a sort – knowledge which is not perfect – without having a true idea, in that the idea that one has is only inadequate. The suggestion that one can know that p, even though the proposition that p is not true, may seem to be yet another paradox. However, a consideration of what Spinoza has to say about the kinds of knowledge shows that the paradox is only apparent.

In the note just mentioned, Spinoza says that there are three kinds of knowledge, which he calls respectively 'imagination', 'reason' and 'intuitive knowledge'. The first of these is the one that is relevant to the topic now at issue, and will concern us in the rest of this section. 'Imagination' includes particular propositions that are based on sense experience and general propositions which are derived by induction from particular instances.[78] Spinoza says that such knowledge is knowledge from what one may render as 'uncertain' or 'inconstant' (*vaga*) experience. By this he means (ibid.) that the ideas involved are fragmentary and without rational order; he also says that they are 'inadequate and confused' (Proposition 41 of Part II). This means, then, that there is a kind of knowledge – namely, imagination – which involves inadequate or false ideas. Light is thrown on this by Spinoza's remark (*Ethics*, Pt II, Proposition 28) that confused ideas are 'like consequences without premises'. What Spinoza means may be explained as follows. Suppose that I see a certain pen in front of me; suppose, too, that there really is a pen there – i.e. no sense illusion is involved. Now, my seeing this pen is the result of a complex set of causes; but in so far as I merely see the pen, I am unable to trace these causes. That is, I am unable to *give an explanation* of what it is for me to see this pen. So although I know that there is a pen there (more of this later) I have only an inadequate idea of the pen. If I am to have an adequate idea of it, I must make use of knowledge which does not rest on sense experience alone. For example, I must make use of physics, to explain the relation between the pen and my sense organs and brain, and I must also make use of metaphysics, to explain the relation between a corporeal state and the corresponding idea.

Another sort of imagination recognized by Spinoza is knowledge based on induction. His account of this is very brief but appears to proceed along lines that are similar to his account of sense experience. Just as there is knowledge that rests on sense experience, so there is knowledge that rests on induction; indeed, in the *Tractatus de Intellectus Emendatione* Spinoza says that such knowledge is of great importance in everyday life (G ii, 11). One may infer that Spinoza regards such knowledge as defective in that it does not give us any satisfactory explanation of *why* the inductive generalization holds. It tells us (say) that oil feeds a fire, but does not tell us why it does so.

It is clear from all this why Spinoza should regard sense experience and induction as involving inadequate ideas; what is not so clear is why he regards them as providing us with *knowledge*. Some indication of an answer is provided by the note to Proposition 17 of Part II of the *Ethics*, already quoted on pp. 291–2. In this, Spinoza defends his postulates on the grounds that they contain scarcely anything that is not borne out by experience. This itself may seem to stand in need of justification, in view of the attacks on the reliability of sense experience contained in the first and sixth of Descartes's *Meditations*, and in fact Spinoza attempts to provide this. What he says is that we may not doubt of experience 'after having shown that the human body as we sense it exists'. Spinoza is in effect saying that sense experience may not be doubted once it has been backed up by sound science and sound metaphysics, that is, once we realize that sense experience is the expression in the attribute of thought of that which, in the attribute of extension, consists of causal processes involving the percipient's body and the external world.[79]

What Spinoza says about imagination, and in particular what he says about sense experience, is important in that it serves to correct the impression that he believes that human beings, in their search for knowledge, could in principle proceed in a purely *a priori* way, in the sense that all they have to do is to deduce consequences from definitions and axioms. The passage just quoted, in which Spinoza supports his postulates by an appeal to sense experience, shows that this is not so, and this is confirmed by an early letter (Ep 10, *c.* March 1663). In this, Spinoza says that we need experience in the case of those things 'which cannot be inferred from the definition of a thing, as e.g. the existence of modes'. What he seems to mean is that (say) the true proposition that there is a pen in front of me is something that cannot be established by deductive means; if its truth is to be known, it can only be by means of sense experience. Spinoza, then, is not advocating arm-chair science; for him, experience has an important part to play in the acquisition of knowledge. At the same time, however, he would insist that, if we are to obtain the explanations that we seek, we must be able to place the data of experience within the context of a deductive system, whose axioms are self-evident.

The second and third kinds of knowledge – 'reason' and 'intuitive knowledge' – are said to involve adequate ideas (*Ethics*, Pt II, Proposition 41). This means that (unlike imagination) they do not present us with conclusions that are cut off from their premises. In the case of 'reason', Spinoza says that it is the kind of knowledge that we have when we possess 'common notions and adequate ideas of the properties of things', and derive valid conclusions from them.[80] The term 'common notions' was in general use in Spinoza's time to refer to axioms;[81] for example, in the deductive arguments that conclude his replies to the *Second Objections*, Descartes lists a number of 'axioms or common notions' (CSM ii, 116; see also *Principles of Philosophy*, Pt I, 49; CSM i, 209). Spinoza also requires for his system certain undefined concepts, which he uses in his definitions, and it may be assumed that these also are included in the 'common notions'. In speaking of the 'properties of things', Spinoza appears to be following traditional usage, according to which a property of X is something that belongs necessarily to X but is not part of its essence.[82] More exactly, he seems to have in mind that which follows from the definition of X (and therefore belongs necessarily to X) but is not a part of that definition. So, for example, in Proposition 31 of Part II of the *Ethics* Spinoza demonstrates that it is a property of any particular thing that it is caused by another, and that by another, and so on *ad infinitum*.

Unlike the imagination, reason grasps the necessary relations between things (*Ethics*, Pt II, Proposition 44). A corollary of this is that reason perceives things 'under a certain species of eternity' (*sub quadam aeternitatis specie*). What this means can be understood by referring to Definition 8 of Part I of the *Ethics*, in which Spinoza defines 'eternity' as a certain kind of existence – namely, that which follows from the definition of God. The existence in question 'is conceived as an eternal truth . . . and therefore cannot be explained by duration or time, even though the duration is conceived as wanting beginning and end' (ibid.). Eternity, then, has no relation to time; 'in eternity there is no *when, before* and *after*'.[83] As applied to reason, this means that to know things by the second kind of knowledge is not simply to say 'This happened, then that happened'; the relations that are grasped are timeless, logical relations.

Reason has another important feature. The bases of reason, Spinoza says, 'explain the essence of no particular thing' (Corollary 2 of Proposition 44 of *Ethics*, Pt II). This must mean that common notions and adequate ideas of the properties of things do not enable us to explain (say) the essence of this particular angry man, but only of anger in general. The same point is made later in the *Ethics* when Spinoza says (Pt V, Scholium to Proposition 36) that knowledge of the second kind is 'universal'. On the basis of this one can say that when Spinoza, in the *Ethics*, provides us with general propositions which are deduced from definitions and self-evident truths, he is providing us with examples of the second kind of knowledge, reason.

The universality of the second kind of knowledge is important in that it is this which distinguishes the second from the third kind of knowledge, which (ibid.) is a 'knowledge of particular things'. With the third kind of knowledge, 'intuitive knowledge', we enter upon one of the most obscure and controversial regions of Spinoza's philosophy. Some interpreters see this kind of knowledge as a kind of mystical vision of the whole; others think that a more prosaic account is called for. Here, I will state a number of features of intuitive knowledge which are not controversial, and which any interpretation must take into account; I will then suggest an interpretation which relates this kind of knowledge both to Descartes's views about knowledge and to Spinoza's moral philosophy.

Four features can safely be ascribed to intuitive knowledge.

1   Like reason, it is necessarily true;[84] that is, the truths known by such knowledge are necessary truths.
2   Like reason, intuitive knowledge conceives and understands things 'under a species of eternity'.[85]
3   Unlike reason, intuitive knowledge is (as has just been pointed out) knowledge of particular things.[86]
4   Unlike reason, again, intuitive knowledge is, as its name suggests, 'intuitive'.

It is this last feature of intuitive knowledge which causes most difficulty. The difficulty arises out of a passage in the second Scholium to Proposition 40 of Part II of the *Ethics*, in which Spinoza illustrates all three kinds of knowledge by a single mathematical example.[87] He takes the problem of finding a fourth proportional. One is given three numbers, and one is required to find a fourth number which is to the third as the first is to the second. Spinoza points out that, in this case, there is a well-known rule: multiply the second number by the third and divide the product by the first. The use of this rule, however, raises two questions. First, on what grounds is the rule accepted? And second, is the use of such a rule always requisite if the problem is to be solved? With regard to the first question, Spinoza points out that some people may have found the rule to work for small numbers, and generalize it to cover all numbers. This would be a case of inductive reasoning, and belongs to the first kind of knowledge, imagination. Others may accept the rule because they know the proof given in Euclid VII, 19. This is based on what Spinoza calls a 'common property' of proportionals, and belongs to the second kind of knowledge, reason. But when the numbers involved are small numbers – say, 1, 2 and 3 – there is no need to make use of a rule. In such a case, Spinoza says, everyone sees that the fourth proportional is 6; this is because 'we infer the fourth number from the very ratio which, with one intuition, we see the first bears to the second'. Or, as Spinoza says in the *Tractatus de Intellectus Emendatione* (G ii, 12), we see the 'adequate proportionality' of the numbers 'intuitively, without performing any operation'. To see things in this way is to make use of the third kind of knowledge, 'intuitive knowledge'.

The problem is that what Spinoza says about the third kind of knowledge appears to be self-contradictory. On the one hand, he seems to hold the view that intuitive knowledge is immediate, in the sense that no process of inference, no application of a general rule to a particular instance, is involved. Yet when he describes intuitive knowledge in the *Ethics* he speaks of *inferring* a fourth number. However, it may be that one can get some help here from Descartes. Although Spinoza does not refer to Descartes in the context of the third kind of knowledge, what he says about such knowledge can be illuminated by comparing it with what Descartes says about his famous utterance, *Cogito, ergo sum*. It is well known that Descartes denied that, in saying 'I am thinking, therefore I exist', he was deriving existence from thought by a kind of syllogism. ('Everything that thinks, exists; I am a being that thinks; therefore . . . etc.') (Reply to *Second Objections*, CSM ii, 100). Rather, he said that he recognized his existence 'as something self-evident by a simple intuition of the mind' (ibid.). This may seem to involve him in a difficulty which is similar to Spinoza's: namely, that Descartes expresses this 'simple intuition' in what appears to be the form of an inference, in that it involves the term 'therefore'. What is of great interest here is the solution that Descartes offered in his conversation of 1648 with the young Dutch scholar Frans Burman.[88] Burman had asked about the nature of *Cogito, ergo sum*; in his reply, Descartes said that the universal proposition 'Everything that thinks, exists' is logically prior to 'I am thinking, therefore I exist', but that I do not need to know the former proposition before I can recognize the truth of the latter. He went on to say, 'We do not separate out these general propositions from the particular instances; rather, it is *in* the particular instances that we think them'. Now, it is not suggested here that Spinoza knew of Descartes's conversation with Burman,[89] or indeed that he would have regarded *Cogito, ergo sum* as an instance of the third kind of knowledge. The point is simply that we can make sense of what he says about intuitive knowledge by supposing him to be thinking along lines similar to those followed by Descartes. That is, when Spinoza says that, in order to discover a fourth proportional, we do not have to appeal to a universal rule but can make use of intuitive knowledge, what he means can be put in Descartes's terms by saying that we think of the general rule in the particular instance.

The question now arises whether the *Ethics* contains any substantive examples of the third kind of knowledge, or whether it, at best, only points the way towards such knowledge. There is of course the case of the discovery of a fourth proportional; but this is merely illustrative, and does not play an essential part in the structure of the work. However, there does seem to be an important use of intuitive knowledge in the *Ethics*. This is to be found in Proposition 36 of Part V, together with its Corollary and Scholium. In the Scholium, Spinoza remarks that, from what he has said elsewhere in the work, 'It is quite clear to us how and in what way our mind follows with regard to essence and existence from the divine nature and continually depends on God', and he continues by saying that this is an example of the third kind of knowledge. The Scholium does more than give an example of the third kind of knowledge; it also shows precisely how this kind of knowledge differs from the second, and why Spinoza ascribes such importance to it. Spinoza says (ibid.) that, in the first part of the *Ethics*, he has already shown[90] that 'all things (and consequently the human mind) depend on God with regard to essence and existence'. This, he says, is an example of the second kind of knowledge; what is more, the proof of this proposition is 'perfectly legitimate and placed beyond the reach of doubt'. We have, then, no reason to suppose that Spinoza thinks that propositions known by the second kind of knowledge are in any respect less true than those known by the third kind. Rather, the superiority of intuitive knowledge lies in the fact that (ibid.) it is 'more powerful' than reason, affecting the mind in a different way. And it is more powerful precisely because it is not universal knowledge, but is the knowledge of particular things.

Spinoza's explanation of the way in which intuitive knowledge is more powerful involves the difficult propositions (beginning in Proposition 32 of Part V of the *Ethics*) in which he expounds his doctrine of the intellectual love of God. This cannot be discussed here;[91] however, one can perhaps get some idea of what is meant by the greater power of intuitive knowledge by considering a hypothetical case. Consider a man who is convinced by Spinoza's proof (in Proposition 45 of Part IV of the *Ethics*) of the universal proposition that hatred can never be good. Despite his acceptance of the truth of this universal proposition, such a man may still hate some particular individual who has injured him. Now contrast such a man with another who has intuitive knowledge of the proposition in question, that is, who grasps it in the particular instance of a person who has offended him. The latter kind of knowledge may be called more powerful in that (as Spinoza would say) it affects his mind in a different way, taking away his urge to hurt the offender in question. This, it must be stressed, is only a hypothetical case, offered as a means of throwing light on what Spinoza says. But what can be said without hesitation is that Spinoza's theory of knowledge was not intended to be purely a contribution to epistemology, but has to be seen in an ethical context.

❧ ABBREVIATIONS ❧

The following abbreviations are used in Chapters 8 and 9.

Spinoza's works

DPP *Renati des Cartes Principiorum Philosophiae*, Parts I and II
E   *Ethica, ordine geometrico demonstrata*. In referring to the contents of the *Ethics*, 'P' is used for 'Proposition' and 'S' for 'Scholium'. So, for example, E II P40S2 refers to *Ethics*, Part II, Proposition 40, Scholium 2. 'Ax' is used for 'Axiom', 'C' for 'Corollary', 'D' for 'Definition' and 'L' for 'Lemma'
Ep   *Epistolae*
G   C. Gebhardt (ed.), *Spinoza, Opera* (cf. [8.1]); references are to volume and page
KV   *Korte Verhandeling van God, de Mensch en deszelfs Welstand*
TDIE *Tractatus de Intellectus Emendatione*
TP   *Tractatus Politicus*
TTP *Tractatus Theologico-Politicus*

Other works

CSM J. Cottingham, R. Stoothoff and D. Murdoch (eds.) *The Philosophical Writings of Descartes* (Cambridge, Cambridge University Press, 3 vols, 1985, 1991).

❧ NOTES ❧

1 Nicolaus Steno (the Danish scientist Niels Stensen). The phrase occurs in an open letter published by Stensen in 1675; the original letter had been written four years previously. (See M. Walther (ed.) *Baruch de Spinoza: Briefwechsel* (Hamburg, Meiner, 1977), p. 410.) The text is published as No. 67a of Spinoza's correspondence (G iv, 292–8).

2 Wolfson [8.43], vol. I, p. vii.

3 For a brief survey of the dispute, see H. G. Hubbeling, *Spinoza* (Freiburg/ Münich, Alber, 1978), pp. 81–2.

4 For this and other valuable information about Spinoza's youth, see A. M. Vaz Dias and W. G. van der Tak, *Spinoza, Mercator et Autodidactus* (The Hague, Nijhoff, 1932), pp. 56ff.

5 For the circumstances of this excommunication, and in particular the relation between Spinoza and Dr Juan de Prado, see C. Gebhardt, 'Juan de Prado', *Chronicon Spinozanum* 3 (1923) 269–91; Révah [8.23]; Révah [8.24]; Yirmiyahu Yovel, *Spinoza and other Heretics* (Princeton, N.J., Princeton University Press, 1989), vol. I, *The Marrano of Reason*, pp. 57–83.

6 Thijssen-Schoute [8.27], 210.

7 Révah [8.23], 43. On the *libertins*, see A. Adam, *Les libertins au 17e siècle* (Paris, Buchet/Chastel, 1964: a selection of texts), and Popkin [8.22], 87–109.

8 Jarig Jelles, Preface to Spinoza's *Posthumous Works*. See C. Gebhardt, *Spinoza: Lebensbeschreibungen und Gespräche* (Leipzig, Meiner, 1914), p. 3. On the Mennonite Jelles, cf. Siebrand [8.26], 25, 35–49.

9 Révah [8.23], 31–2, 36.

10 See Ep 6 (G iv, 36); also Joachim [8.45], 5–7, 14–15.

11 A useful summary of scholarly discussions of this work may be found in Curley [8.4], 46–53.

12 KV I, 3.

13 *Cogitata Metaphysica*, II, 12 (G i, 279); cf. Gueroult [8.55], 245n.

14 KV I, 8–9; E I P29S; cf. Gueroult [8.55], 564, and note 71 below.

15 It is hardly necessary to add that Descartes, too, sometimes used scholastic terminology. On Spinoza's use of the works of Heereboord, see H. de Dijn, 'Historical Remarks on Spinoza's Theory of Definition', in J. G. van der Bend (ed.) *Spinoza on Knowing, Being and Freedom* (Assen, Van Gorcum, 1974), pp. 41–50.

16 Ep 13 (G iv, 63).

17 For details, see Parkinson [8.47], 6 n3.

18 *B.d.S. Opera Posthuma* and *De Nagelate Schriften van B.d.S.* Both must be based on manuscript sources, and so the Dutch version can be used as a check on the Latin text. It has been argued by Gebhardt (G ii, 341–3) that the Dutch version of the first two parts of the *Ethics* was based on an early text which Spinoza abandoned in 1665 when he turned aside to work on the *Tractatus Theologico-Politicus*, but this view has been called in question (F. Akkerman, 'L'édition de Gebhardt de l'Ethique et ses sources', *Raison présente* 43 (1977) 43).

19 This includes a recently discovered letter to Meyer of 26 July 1663. For this letter, see S. Hessing (ed.) *Speculum Spinozanum* (London, Routledge, 1977), pp. 426–35.

20 Ep 6, 7, 11, 13, 14, 16, 25–6, 29–33, 36, 38–41, 46.

21 See J. Freudenthal, *Die Lebensgeschichte Spinozas* (Leipzig, Veit, 1899), pp. 160–4. The list is perhaps more readily accessible in Préposiet [8.16], 339–43.

22 The mathematical works include books by Euclid, Diophantus, Descartes and Viète. Works on astronomy include 'The Sphere' (*Sphaera*) by Johannes de Sacrobosco (John of Holywood), a thirteenth-century writer whose account of

the heavens was still widely used in the sixteenth and seventeenth centuries, and a book by Christian Longomontanus, a Danish astronomer who had been Tycho Brahe's assistant. The works on physics in Spinoza's library included books by Descartes, Huygens, James Gregory, Robert Boyle and Niels Stensen. Spinoza also owned a number of books on anatomy, including Descartes's *De Homine* and works by Stensen and by the Dutch physician Nicolaes Tulp.

23 See the Preface to the *Opera Posthuma* (Gebhardt, *Spinoza: Lebensbeschreibungen und Gespräche*, p. 7); also Ep 60, January 1675, and Ep 83, 15 July 1676.

24 All translations from Spinoza in this chapter are my own, with the exception of the translation of the *Ethics*, where Boyle [8.9] is used.

25 *A Treatise of Human Nature*, Book III, Pt 1, sec. 1.

26 E III Pref. (G ii, 137).

27 'Man as a Subject for Science', in Ayer, *Metaphysics and Common Sense* (London, Macmillan, 1969), p. 219.

28 See Chapter 5, pp. 183–6. The distinction was known to Spinoza; it is mentioned by Meyer, in his Preface to Spinoza's geometrical version of Descartes's *Principles of Philosophy* (G i, 129).

29 *Collection*, beginning of Book VII. I translate from the Latin version by the Renaissance mathematician Federico Commendino (Venice, 1589), which Descartes used. (cf. E. Gilson, *René Descartes, Discours de la Méthode* (Paris, Vrin, 1947), p. 188.) On the concept of analysis in Pappus, see also H.-J. Engfer, *Philosophie als Analysis* (Stuttgart, Frommann-Holzboog, 1982), pp. 78–89.

30 In the case of Spinoza's geometrical version of the *Principles* of Descartes, where not all the derived propositions are held by Spinoza to be true (cf. p. 276 above), it may be assumed that Spinoza would say that some of the axioms are false.

31 I have discussed this topic at greater length in my paper 'Definition, Essence and Understanding in Spinoza', in J. A. Cover and Mark Kulstad (eds) *Central Themes in Early Modern Philosophy: Essays presented to Jonathan Bennett* (Indianapolis, Ind., Hackett, 1990), pp. 49–67.

32 I. M. Copi, *Introduction to Logic* (New York, Macmillan, 3rd edn, 1968), p. 98.

33 E III, Definitions of the Emotions, No. 20 (G ii, 195); cf. Parkinson, in Cover and Kulstad, op. cit., pp. 52–4.

34 In his *Introduction to Logic*, p. 101, Copi calls such definitions 'theoretical definitions' and points out how, in the course of the history of science, 'one definition is replaced by another as our knowledge and theoretical understanding increase'.

35 The major premise is 'All bodies near the earth are bodies that shine steadily', the minor premise is 'All planets are bodies near the earth', giving the conclusion 'All planets are bodies that shine steadily'.

36 Descartes, *Discourse on Method*, Part II (CSM i, 119); *Regulae*, No. 10 (CSM i, 37).

37 Spinoza's formal definition of the essence of a thing in E II D2 is much more complex. I have discussed it in Cover and Kulstad, op. cit., pp. 58–62.

38 See, for example, John Marenbon, *Early Medieval Philosophy* (London, Routledge, 1983), pp. 98–101.

39 For Leibniz's views about the ontological argument, cf. G. H. R. Parkinson,

Logic and Reality in Leibniz's Metaphysics (Oxford, Clarendon, 1965; reprinted, New York, Garland, 1985), pp. 77–85.

40 Hume, *Treatise of Human Nature*, Book I, Pt 3, sec. 2; Kant, *Critique of Pure Reason*, B 247–8.

41 The rationalist theory of causality is also implicit in E I P16 and its three corollaries, where Spinoza begins (E I P16) by speaking of certain things as 'necessarily following from' the divine nature, and then goes on to describe the various ways in which God is a cause.

42 *An Abstract of a Treatise of Human Nature*: see Hume, *An Enquiry concerning Human Understanding*, ed. A. G. N. Flew (La Salle, Ill., Open Court, 1988), p. 34; cf. *A Treatise of Human Nature*, Book I, Pt 3, sec. 3.

43 There is indeed no evidence that Hume had read Spinoza at all; his views about Spinoza appear to be derived from a well-known article in Bayle's *Dictionary* (cf. *A Treatise of Human Nature*, Book I, Pt 4, sec. 5). Of this dictionary, Flew says (op. cit., p. 186, n. 121) that it was, in some version or other, 'in every gentleman's library throughout the eighteenth century'.

44 cf. Nicholas Jolley, Chapter 11 of this volume, pp. 385–6.

45 This is not to say that Spinoza ignores the second problem, but his answer to it involves, not his concept of substance, but his concept of an 'individual'. See p. 288.

46 Though Spinoza's assertion that a substance must be conceived through itself could hardly be accepted by Aristotle. For Aristotle (though not for Spinoza) Socrates would be a substance; but Aristotle would say that Socrates is not 'conceived through himself', in that Socrates has to be conceived through various genera and species.

47 The argument appears to rest on E I P8 and E I P11. E I P8 says in effect that, if there is a substance, then it is infinite; E I P11 asserts that there is such a substance – namely, God.

48 The reference to 'created' thinking substance serves to distinguish minds such as ours from the mind of God, the uncreated substance.

49 E I P10S, P11, P16, P19, P29S.

50 For a very thorough survey of the issue, see F. S. Haserot, 'Spinoza's definition of attribute', in Kashap [8.36], 28–42.

51 Though there is a hint of this in E I P14C2.

52 Spinoza regards these as two out of an infinity of attributes, the rest of which are, and indeed must be, unknown to us. Some scholars have argued that he regarded thought and extension as the only attributes, and that in calling them 'infinite' he meant that they are all the attributes that exist. (See A. Wolf, 'Spinoza's Conception of the Attributes of Substance', in Kashap [8.36], 24–7.) But this is hard to reconcile with the textual evidence: see especially E II P7S and Ep 64.

53 *Principles of Philosophy*, I, 60 (CSM i, 213).

54 E I P10.

55 E I P13 and C3; cf. E I P15S.

56 E I P25C.

57 E I P21. This is explained in Ep 64.

58 Incidentally, Spinoza had the greatest respect for the atomists among the classical Greek philosophers (Ep 56).

59 Ep 32 (G iv, 173); cf. DPP II P13.

60 For a contrary view, see Donagan [8.31], 68.

61 See especially the synopsis of *Meditation* II, CSM ii, 110: 'secondly we need . . .'.

62 E.g. E II P9.

63 See especially E II P49 and S.

64 E II P49C and S. For a discussion of Spinoza's criticism of Descartes's theory of judgement, see J. G. Cottingham, 'The Intellect, the Will and the Passions: Spinoza's Critique of Descartes', *Journal of the History of Philosophy* 26 (1988) 239–57.

65 E II P43S: 'And again how can anyone . . .'.

66 E III P2S (G ii, 142–3).

67 Perhaps an echo of the title of Vesalius's famous treatise on anatomy, *De Humani Corporis Fabrica* (1543).

68 On which see Chapter 11 (pp. 404–7).

69 cf. G. N. A. Vesey, 'Agent and Spectator', in G. N. A. Vesey (ed.), *The Human Agent*, Royal Institute of Philosophy Lectures, vol. 1 (1966–7) (London, Macmillan, 1968), pp. 139–40. Spinoza's theory could also be regarded as belonging to what D. M. Armstrong calls 'attribute' or 'dual-attribute' theories of the mind-body relationship. See Armstrong, 'Mind-Body Problem: Philosophical Theories', in R. L. Gregory (ed.), *The Oxford Companion to the Mind* (Oxford, Oxford University Press, 1987), p. 491.

70 E I P16 and C1.

71 In explaining the immanent causality of God, Spinoza makes use of a distinction that has since achieved some fame. This is the distinction (E I P29S) between 'natura naturans' and 'natura naturata', which may be rendered as 'active nature' and 'passive nature'. By 'active nature' Spinoza means substance or its attributes, that is, God conceived as the ultimate explanation of everything; by 'passive nature' he means the totality of modes, conceived not as so many isolated entities, but as following from, that is, as the effects of, God. By calling both God and his effects types of 'nature', Spinoza makes the point that God is not outside his effects.

72 In E I P11S, Spinoza hints that by 'perfection' he means 'reality'; this is confirmed by the formal definition of perfection in E II D6. In traditional language, Spinoza's God is the *ens realissimum*, that whose being is the most rich. (cf. E I P9: the more reality a thing has, the more attributes belong to it.)

73 cf., for example, E III P7.

74 E I P32C1, E I P33 and 33S1.

75 E I A6, E II D4.

76 cf. J. J. McIntosh, 'Spinoza's Epistemological Views', in G. N. A. Vesey (ed.) *Reason and Reality*, Royal Institute of Philosophy Lectures, vol. 5 (1970–1) (London, Macmillan, 1972), p. 38; also G. H. R. Parkinson, ' "Truth is its Own Standard". Aspects of Spinoza's Theory of Truth', in Shahan and Biro [8.40], 42–5.

77 In the *Tractatus de Intellectus Emendatione* (G ii, 10–12), Spinoza recognizes four kinds of knowledge, the first two of which correspond to the first of the

three kinds recognized in the *Ethics*. The *Short Treatise* recognizes three kinds only, but the account that it offers of these is sketchy.

78 Spinoza also counts as an example of the first kind of knowledge what he calls 'knowledge from signs' (E II P40S2; cf. E II P18S). This raises interesting questions concerning Spinoza's views about language, which I have discussed in my 'Language and Knowledge in Spinoza', reprinted in Grene [8.33], 73–100.

79 It is not clear how Spinoza would have attempted to justify his view that induction is a kind of knowledge.

80 E II P38–9, P40 and S2; cf. E V P36S.

81 This is in fact a literal translation of the Greek term 'koinai ennoai', used by Euclid to refer to the axioms of his system.

82 cf. Aristotle, *Topics*, I 5, 102 a18–19. On 'essence' in Spinoza, cf. p. 282.

83 E I P33S2.

84 E II P41.

85 E V P31 and S.

86 E V P36S.

87 See also TDIE, G ii, 12, and KV II.1, G i, 54–5.

88 For this conversation, see *Descartes' Conversation with Burman*, ed. and trans. J. G. Cottingham (Oxford, Clarendon, 1976), esp. p. 4 (also CSM iii, 333).

89 Burman's record of the conversation remained in manuscript until 1896. In principle, Spinoza could have had access to the manuscript, but there is no evidence that he had any contact with Burman, or with the Cartesian philosopher Clauberg, who also contributed to the manuscript.

90 The reference is probably to E I P15, mentioned in E V P36S. It could perhaps be to E I P25, but this itself involves a reference to E I P15.

91 This doctrine, and the related doctrine of the eternity of the human mind, has been severely criticized. See, for example, Bennett [8.28], 357–63, 369–75; Delahunty [8.30], 279–305; Martha Kneale, 'Eternity and Sempiternity', in Grene [8.33], 227–40. A more sympathetic account is given by Joachim [8.35], 230–3, 298–309.

❧ BIBLIOGRAPHY ❧

Original language editions

8.1 Gebhardt, C. (ed.) *Spinoza, Opera*, Heidelberg, Winter, 4 vols, 1924–8.

8.2 van Vloten, J. and Land, J. P. N. (eds) *Benedicti de Spinoza Opera quotquot reperta sunt*, The Hague, Nijhoff, 1st edn, 2 vols, 1882–3; 2nd edn, 3 vols, 1895; 3rd edn, 4 vols, 1914.

English translations
Complete and selected works

8.3   *The Chief Works of Benedict de Spinoza*, trans. R. H. M. Elwes, London, Bell, 2 vols, 1883–4; reprinted, New York, Dover Publications, 1955.

8.4   *The Collected Works of Spinoza*, trans. E. Curley, Princeton, N.J., Princeton University Press, vol. 1, 1985.

8.5   *The Ethics and Selected Letters*, trans. S. Shirley, Indianapolis, Ind., Hackett, 1982.

8.6   *Spinoza, the Political Works. The Tractatus theologico-politicus in part and the Tractatus politicus in full*, trans. A. G. Wernham, Oxford, Clarendon, 1958.

Separate works

8.7   *The Correspondence of Spinoza*, trans. A. Wolf, London, Allen & Unwin, 1928.

8.8   *Ethic: from the Latin of Benedict de Spinoza*, trans. W. Hale White and Amelia Stirling, London, Fisher Unwin, 1894.

8.9   *Ethics*, trans. A. Boyle, revised G. H. R. Parkinson, London, Dent, 1989.

8.10 *On the Improvement of the Understanding*, trans. J. Katz, New York, Liberal Arts Press, 1958.

8.11 *The Principles of Descartes' Philosophy*, trans. H. H. Britan, La Salle, Ill., Open Court, 1905.

8.12 *Spinoza's Short Treatise on God, Man and his Well-being*, trans. A. Wolf, London, Black, 1910.

8.13 *Tractatus Theologico-Politicus*, trans. S. Shirley, Leiden, Brill, 1989.

Bibliographies and concordances
Bibliographies

8.14 Boucher, W. I. *Spinoza in English: A Bibliography from the Seventeenth Century to the Present*, Leiden, Brill, 1991.

8.15 Oko, A. S. *The Spinoza Bibliography*, Boston, Mass., Hall, 1964. (An exhaustive bibliography of Spinoza literature up to 1940.)

8.16 Préposiet, J. *Bibliographie spinoziste*, Paris, Les Belles Lettres, 1973.

8.17 van der Werf, T. *A Spinoza Bibliography, 1971–83*, Leiden, Brill, 1984.

8.18 Wetlesen, J. *A Spinoza Bibliography, 1940–70*, Oslo, Universitetsvorlaget, 1971.

Concordances

8.19 Boscherini, E. G. *Lexicon Spinozanum*, The Hague, Nijhoff, 2 vols, 1970.

8.20 Gueret, M., Robinet, A. and Tombeur, P. *Spinoza, Ethica. Concordances, Index, Listes de fréquences, Tables comparatives*, Louvain-la-Neuve, CETEDOC, 1977.

Influences on Spinoza

8.21 Gebhardt, C. 'Spinoza und der Platonismus', *Chronicon Spinozanum* 1 (1921) 178–259. (Spinoza and Leone Ebreo.)
8.22 Popkin, R. H. 'Spinoza and La Peyrère', in R. W. Shahan and J. I. Biro (eds) *Spinoza: New Perspectives*, Norman, Okl., University of Oklahoma Press, 1978, 177–96.
8.23 Révah, I. S. *Spinoza et le Dr. Juan de Prado*, Paris, Mouton, 1959.
8.24 Révah, I. S. 'Aux origines de la rupture spinozienne', *Revue des études juives* 3 (1964) 359–431.
8.25 Roth, L. *Spinoza, Descartes and Maimonides*, Oxford, Clarendon, 1924.
8.26 Siebrand, H. J. *Spinoza and the Netherlanders*, Assen, Van Gorcum, 1988.
8.27 Thijssen-Schoute, C. L. 'Le Cartésianisme aux Pays Bas', in E. J. Dijksterhuis (ed.) *Descartes et le Cartésianisme hollandais*, Paris, Presses Universitaires de France, 1950.

The philosophy of Spinoza: general surveys

8.28 Bennett, J. *A Study of Spinoza's Ethics*, Cambridge, Cambridge University Press, 1984.
8.29 Brunschvicg, L. *Spinoza et ses contemporains*, Paris, Presses Universitaires de France, 1923.
8.30 Delahunty, R. J. *Spinoza*, London, Routledge & Kegan Paul, 1985.
8.31 Donagan, A. *Spinoza*, London, Harvester, 1988.
8.32 Freeman, E. and Mandelbaum, M. (eds) *Spinoza: Essays in Interpretation*, La Salle, Ill., Open Court, 1975.
8.33 Grene, M. (ed.) *Spinoza: A Collection of Critical Essays*, New York, Doubleday, 1973.
8.34 Hampshire, S. N. *Spinoza*, Harmondsworth, Penguin, 1951.
8.35 Joachim, H. H. *A Study of the Ethics of Spinoza*, Oxford, Clarendon, 1901.
8.36 Kashap, S. P. (ed.) *Studies in Spinoza*, Berkeley, Calif., University of California Press, 1972.
8.37 Kennington, R. (ed.) *The Philosophy of Baruch Spinoza*, Washington, D.C., Catholic University of America, 1980.
8.38 Pollock, F. *Spinoza, His Life and Philosophy*, London, Kegan Paul, 1880.
8.39 Scruton, R. *Spinoza*, Oxford, Oxford University Press, 1986.
8.40 Shahan, R. W. and Biro, J. I. (eds) *Spinoza: New Perspectives*, Norman, Okl., University of Oklahoma Press, 1978.
8.41 van der Bend, J. G. (ed.) *Spinoza on Knowing, Being and Freedom*, Assen, Van Gorcum, 1974.
8.42 Walther, M. *Metaphysik als anti-Theologie. Die Philosophie Spinozas im Zusammenhang der religionsphilosophischen Problematik*, Hamburg, Meiner, 1971.
8.43 Wolfson, H. A. *The Philosophy of Spinoza*, Cambridge, Mass., Harvard University Press, 2 vols, 1934.

Methodology and theory of knowledge

8.44 Hubbeling, H. G. *Spinoza's Methodology*, Assen, Van Gorcum, 1964.

8.45 Joachim, H. H. *Spinoza's Tractatus de Intellectus Emendatione*, Oxford, Clarendon, 1940.

8.46 Mark, T. C. *Spinoza's Theory of Truth*, New York, Columbia University Press, 1972.

8.47 Parkinson, G. H. R. *Spinoza's Theory of Knowledge*, Oxford, Clarendon, 1954.

8.48 Parkinson, G. H. R. 'Language and Knowledge in Spinoza', *Inquiry* 12 (1969) 15–40. Also in M. Grene (ed.) *Spinoza: A Collection of Critical Essays*, New York, Doubleday, 1973, 73–100.

8.49 Savan, D. 'Spinoza and Language', *Philosophical Review* 67 (1958) 212–25. Also in S. P. Kashap (ed.) *Studies in Spinoza*, Berkeley, Calif., University of California Press, 1972, 236–48.

8.50 Walker, R. C. S. 'Spinoza and the Coherence Theory of Truth', *Mind* 94 (1985) 1–18.

Metaphysics and philosophy of mind

8.51 Barker, H. 'Notes on the Second Part of Spinoza's Ethics', *Mind* 47 (1938) 159–79, 281–302, 417–39. Also in S. P. Kashap (ed.) *Studies in Spinoza*, Berkeley, Calif., University of California Press, 1972, 101–67.

8.52 Curley, E. *Spinoza's Metaphysics*, Cambridge, Mass., Harvard University Press, 1969.

8.53 Deleuze, G. *Spinoza et le problème de l'expression*, Paris, Editions de Minuit, 1968.

8.54 Donagan, A. 'Essence and the Distinction of Attributes in Spinoza's Metaphysics', in M. Grene (ed.) *Spinoza: A Collection of Critical Essays*, New York, Doubleday, 1973, 164–81.

8.55 Gueroult, M. *Spinoza: Dieu (Ethique, 1)*, Paris, Aubier, 1968.

8.56 Gueroult, M. *Spinoza: L'Ame (Ethique, 2)*, Paris, Aubier, 1974.

8.57 Haserot, F. S. 'Spinoza's Definition of Attribute', *Philosophical Review* 62 (1953) 499–513. Also in S. P. Kashap (ed.) *Studies in Spinoza*, Berkeley, Calif., University of California Press, 1972, 28–42.

8.58 Kneale, M. 'Eternity and Sempiternity', *Proceedings of the Aristotelian Society* 69 (1968–9) 223–38. Also in M. Grene (ed.) *Spinoza: A Collection of Critical Essays*, New York, Doubleday, 1973, 227–40.

8.59 Parkinson, G. H. R. 'Spinoza on Miracles and Natural Law', *Revue internationale de philosophie* 31 (1977) 145–57.

8.60 Parkinson, G. H. R. 'Spinoza's Philosophy of Mind', in G. Fløistad (ed.) *Contemporary Philosophy: A New Survey*, The Hague, Nijhoff, 1983, vol. 4, 105–31.

8.61 Robinson, L. *Kommentar zu Spinozas Ethik*, vol. 1, Leipzig, Meiner, 1928. (Covers the first two parts of the *Ethics*.)

8.62 Sprigge, T. L. S. 'Spinoza's Identity Theory', *Inquiry* 20 (1977) 419–45.

8.63 Wolf, A. 'Spinoza's Conception of the Attributes of Substance', *Proceedings of the Aristotelian Society* 27 (1927) 177–92. Also in S. P. Kashap (ed.) *Studies in Spinoza*, Berkeley, Calif., University of California Press, 1972, 16–27.

CHAPTER 9

The moral and political philosophy of Spinoza

Hans W. Blom

Spinoza as a moral and political philosopher was the proponent of a radical and extremely consistent version of seventeenth-century Dutch naturalism. As a consequence of the burgeoning bourgeois self-confidence during the heyday of their Golden Age, Dutch philosophers, attracted by Ciceronian republican moral ideas prepared the way for a philosophy of man and society in which natural processes and mechanisms had an important role to perform. Although they understood themselves as partisans of widely divergent philosophers like Aristotle or Descartes, they shared the conviction that man's moral predicament should be analysed from a naturalistic point of view, by advocating an almost autonomous position for philosophy separate from religion. They were sure that sufficient attention paid to the natural capabilities of mankind would show the way to overcome human weakness. This philosophical programme, propagated by otherwise conventional Calvinists, was constructed on the basis of a theological notion of means–end relations, but its proponents were unaware that in the end it would turn out to secularize human teleology completely. The most outstanding outcome was to be Adam Smith's theory of the invisible hand, in which individual and societal teleology are interrelated by means of the laws of human nature. In this perspective, Spinoza's philosophy of man and society presents itself as an early and thorough attempt to realize the seventeenth-century Dutch naturalistic programme of secularizing the human condition. We shall follow Spinoza in this attempt and develop his moral and political philosophy against its Dutch background, eventually indicating why the response he met with was so critical and hostile.

So after the introduction there will follow an overview of political philosophy in the Dutch Republic, next the presentation of Spinoza's reaction to the key issues involved therein, especially as far as his moral philosophy is concerned, and then his political philosophy proper. After the conclusion there follows a select bibliography.

❧ INTRODUCTION ❧

Political philosophy may well be seen as one of the most important topics in Spinoza's philosophical system, as far as modern Spinoza research is concerned. This is also evident from Spinoza's own principles as a philosopher. I remind the reader of some of these central convictions. First of all, he proferred the view – in his writings, the *Treatise on the Emendation of the Intellect* and the *Short Treatise on God, Man, and His Well-Being* – that the realization of philosophy's goal is a social activity (TDIE 14; KV XXVI, 10) (for the abbreviated form of titles etc. see the list of abbreviations at the end of Chapter 8). Not only do people need each other in their quest for truth, but also specific conditions have to be fulfilled for this quest to be pursued in a successful way: peace, security and toleration. Not by accident, then, did Spinoza postpone the writing of his *Ethics* in the mid–1660s to complete the *Tractatus Theologico-Politicus*, published in 1670. In this, his first publication on politics, Spinoza opens with a forceful attack on superstition and the belief in signs and all kinds of insincerity that put prejudices ahead of rational analysis. He seems to be confident that the causes of these dogmatic hindrances of philosophical enquiry should be looked for in the political order. As is well known, the *Tractatus Theologico-Politicus* concludes with a dramatic plea for tolerance. But before reaching this peroration, the social and political reality is discussed and central conceptions like 'power', 'right', 'reason', 'belief' and 'passion' have their intermingled relations disentangled and are employed to a further understanding of the meaning and limits of sovereign power.

The central contentions of Spinoza's political philosophy itself point to its relevance in the overall philosophical system. Freedom, being the core concept of the *Ethics*, refers as by logical necessity to the social and political conditions of its realization. How far is the individual's freedom hindered or enhanced by power relations between men? Can man be free in a society that is not free? Can a society be arranged in the interest of the promotion of freedom of its members? The answer to these and related questions necessitates a perspective on individual self-determination and social determination, as well as on their interaction. How do we understand the bonds that tie and relate men? What about laws, ordinances, rights and power? What is their origin, what their legitimacy, what their effect?

These interests led Spinoza to write a second treatise on politics, the *Tractatus Politicus*. In this posthumously published work, he discusses the several forms of government, their principles and most rational practical application. In this book is evident again Spinoza's conviction that philosophy is inherently a social affair. As in his involvement in religion, tolerance and the state in the *Tractatus Theologico-Politicus*, here again Spinoza takes issue with contemporary opinions and debate as he found it in the Dutch Republic. He comes forward as an 'interventionist' who wants to change not only philosophy but political practice as well. One of our further interests will be to define Spinoza's role as an interventionist in the political debate and strife of his own times.

From a systematic point of view also, political philosophy presents itself as an unavoidable sequel to the *Ethics*. Quite a few propositions of the latter must have invited or even challenged the author to check the consistency of their interhuman consequences. Principles like the parallelism of the attributes of substance, the identity of right and might, and the conception of the individual as a persisting arrangement of individuals of a different order, all seem to have a meaning for groups and organizations of men as well. Spinoza will even argue for his political philosophy by presenting it as a deduction from the *Ethics*. In doing so, he takes issue with rival conceptions of politics in his time, coming forward as a theoretical interventionist as well.

In terms of Hannah Arendt's distinction between political philosophers (Plato, Hobbes, Marx, for example) and political thinkers (Machiavelli, Rousseau), Spinoza must be classified as belonging to both categories. Like the former, he formulates his political conceptions within a philosophical system, and like the latter he engages in verbal political action. His practical and his theoretical interests went hand in hand. His practical involvement in politics is partly evidence here. Possibly connected to his alleged acquaintance with the pensionary Johan de Witt, Spinoza's strong reaction to the murder of the de Witt brothers in 1672 is well documented. It was only the intervention of his landlord that prevented him from nailing a placard saying *ultimi barbarorum* (outrage of barbarism) at the location of the murder. In the *Tractatus Politicus* he alludes to this episode by censuring the Dutch 'regenten' for using the pensionary as a scapegoat for their own shortcomings. His visit to the headquarters of the French occupation army in Utrecht in 1673, for all its possibly purely intellectual purposes, was regarded by the man in the street as an act bordering on treason. His practical involvement in politics is also evident from his appreciation of Machiavelli and Pieter de la Court.

In presenting Spinoza's moral and political philosophy, therefore, we could scarcely pass over the contextual element. We may well draw attention to the anomaly that this context as a matter of fact was. When Spinoza was born, the seven Provinces were still (since 1568) at war with Spain. Only in 1648 did a peace treaty materialize; only then was the Dutch Republic *de jure* accepted in the European system of states. But being a republic, and a very powerful one, it was a double anomaly. The relatively egalitarian society of shopkeepers and traders, governed by brewers and merchants, stood out for a relatively free intellectual climate. This anomaly stood in need of self-definition, as old conceptions had run out of relevance and new ones were yet to be invented. Philosophers and theologians, lawyers and politicians, lay and professional alike, all had their share in this redefinition of their political situation. Spinoza may be depicted by some modern commentators as a savage anomaly in relation to the main traditions of philosophy, but more importantly he was engaged in surmounting the double anomaly the Dutch confronted. It can be no surprise that the Dutch were keen on new developments in philosophy and reacted to thinkers like Thomas Hobbes and René Descartes. But their main motivation came from what we might call by hindsight their bourgeois understanding of their own society. We shall turn first to some of its elements as a background relevant to Spinoza's moral and political philosophy.

❧ ASPECTS OF MORAL AND POLITICAL ❧ CONCERN IN THE DUTCH REPUBLIC

To provide some context to Spinoza's moral and political philosophy we shall present three distinct contributions. In the first place the Stoic–Aristotelian approach of Justus Lipsius (1547–1606) and Franco Burgersdijk (1590–1635) will be discussed. Here we find not only the basic arguments of Orangist political theory, but also the beginnings of naturalistic tendencies. In the second place, we will deal with the innovative contribution of Lambertus van Velthuysen (1622–85). Velthuysen attempted, on the basis of a rather general Cartesian methodology, to define the implications of the new individualism of Grotian–Hobbesian natural law in his peculiarly Aristotelian teleological scheme. In the third place, we must pay attention to the intense, rhetorical intervention in mid-seventeenth-century political debate of Johan and Pieter de la Court.

Stoic–Aristotelian dimensions

When Justus Lipsius published his *Six Books on Politics* in 1589, the Dutch Revolt was raging. Although the Low Countries had proved to be a difficult target for the far superior Spanish forces, there was no expectation of a conclusion of the war being at hand. Lipsius, for whom philosophy was most of all ethics and politics, tried to cope with the turbulence of his times. Taking politics to be the 'order of governing and obeying', he set out to give a highly practical answer, shunning the abstract categories of scholasticism, harking back to Tacitus, Machiavelli, Seneca and Cicero. This Neostoic practical philosophy provided him with a realistic morality: we have to live according to Nature, accepting what is inevitable, but working hard upon what is within our power. Morality of rulers and ruled alike consists in practical morality, of which the central instruments and targets are virtue and prudence. Lipsius preferred to see his philosophical task as different from theology. He did not abstain from using metaphysical concepts of the theological repertoire, especially that of primary and secondary causes, but put them to use in his analysis of human nature as a secular concept. The stability of the state, as far as that can be realized, was the central point of reference for him. The subjects have to accept their hardship if it must be, the rulers have to care for unity and concord. The *conservatio sui*, self-preservation, is an important principle. The influence of Cicero is evident, as when it is stated that nothing preserves a republic better than *fides*, (good) faith. As for religion, Lipsius believed that the power of the state depends on religious peace, to be had only if there is but one religion and only if that religion is subjected to the jurisdiction of the prince. Nevertheless, he was convinced that consciences could not be forced, only persuaded. He was forcefully attacked by Dirk Coornhert, who believed that Lipsius betrayed their common cause of tolerance. But Lipsius kept to his opinion that the unity and concord of the country should not be placed in jeopardy. As Tacitus said, as a state is a single body, it should be ruled by a single mind. Lipsius concluded from this that monarchy is the superior form of government. A virtuous and prudent prince will further the *potentia*, the power of the state, which he described (referring to Cicero) as 'the faculty regarding useful things to keep one's own and to acquire those of foreigners'. This Ciceronian realism was complemented by a Senecan emphasis on *sapientia*, wisdom as the ultimate goal and moral end.

Lipsius's practical intent shows in the guidelines for warfare he presented in Book V of his *Politics*. Prince Maurice, who was not known for literary interests, was an ardent reader of this text and applied it to practice with a lot of success. However important this last aspect of Lipsius's work may have been, his lasting influence proved to be the introduction of Neostoicism into Dutch intellectual life. In particular, Franco Burgersdijk, who held Lipsius's chair at Leiden, was keen to continue this programme, be it under the disguise of his own brand of Neo-Aristotelianism, much more fashionable in Calvinist circles. We may therefore speak of a Neostoic–Aristotelian programme, which is realistic, practical and, for all its pagan overtones, presented as a complement to Calvinist theology. Practical morality, that is, prudence and virtue, can be studied independently of blessedness. Practical philosophy was studied as part of the propaedeutical curriculum, in the 'lower faculty' in contradistinction to the higher faculties of theology, law and medicine. Politics and ethics are central to practical philosophy. In his *Idea politica* (1644), Burgersdijk was in complete agreement with Lipsius except for one important point. He tried to accommodate Lipsius's notion of unity and concord and his subsequent emphasis on monarchy with the by then established Dutch practice of aristocracy supplemented with the institution of the *stadhouder*, the military leadership of the Princes of Orange. Central to this accommodation was Burgersdijk's argument that the best form of government may not always concur with the preferences of the people. Indeed, for a people of shopkeepers and tradesmen, liberty is an important asset, which they unwillingly forgo. Therefore, Burgersdijk tried to formulate the principles that may promote unity and concord in a mixed constitution. In doing so, he provided for the adherents of the Orangist party, who sustained the Princes of Orange against the more specifically aristocratic preferences of the States party that consisted of the majority of the *regenten*. We shall see this Burgersdijkian concept of a mixed, Orangist constitution reappear in Spinoza's treatment of monarchy in the *Tractatus Politicus*.

In moral philosophy, too, Burgersdijk continued and improved upon the lines set out by Lipsius. Although Burgersdijk subscribes to the opinion that we aim at good things when we understand them to be good, he is not content to leave this principle unanalysed. He wants to understand how it is that we are moved to act. To this purpose he introduces the concept of '*affectus*', apparently in a rather innocent way by identifying it as *pathè*, passion pertaining to the irrational part of the soul. But, as we shall see, he makes out of this 'passion' the basic concept of action. 'Affect is a movement of the sensuous desire, when by a non-natural bodily modification directed at a good object or a bad one, suggested and judged by the imagination, this is made to be sought for or that is made to be evaded.' Affects are not natural faculties of the soul, but functions or 'movements' of a natural faculty. Indeed, the seat of the affects is the *facultas appetens*, the desiring faculty. The *principle* of movement is the faculty of knowing, and the *effect* of movement is the modification of heart and body (the faculty of acting). Affects, so to say, represent a conceptual unity between knowing, desiring and acting, thereby suggesting that the three faculties are really aspects, and not parts, of the soul. In a subsequent rebuttal of the Stoic analysis of '*affectus*', Burgersdijk exhibits his fundamental move away from Aristotle's psychology. Indeed, referring to the passage in the *Tusculanae Disputationes* where Cicero suggests the translation of *pathè* by 'disturbances' (*perturbationes*) instead of by 'illness' (*morbi*), Burgersdijk points out that the Stoic notion of '*affectus*' is wrong. That is, Burgersdijk continues one step further on the Ciceronian path of naturalizing *pathè* to a central psychological concept, by transforming it to the one motivational link between desire and action. Although being a Calvinist, Burgersdijk defends free will (*liberum arbitrium*). According to his simplified version of the history of philosophy, the Stoics reduced everything to providence, fate and the unchangeable concatenation of causes; the Peripatetics affirmed free will and denied divine providence. The Christians combine providence and free will, because they believe that 'God rules individual things by secondary causes each according to the mode of their own nature, in such a way that necessary things happen by necessity, and free things freely such that whatever has to follow from their actions is produced freely'. Will itself is defined as the faculty to follow what is good and to shun what is evil; it is a blind capability (*potentia caeca*) because it depends on the direction of the practical intellect.

We shall have ample opportunity to refer to Burgersdijk's moral philosophy when we discuss Spinoza.

Velthuysen's naturalistic programme

In 1651 the young medical doctor Lambertus van Velthuysen published an anonymous book entitled *A Dissertation written as a Letter on the Principles of the Just and the Decent* (*Epistolica dissertatio de principiis justi ac decori*). One would misunderstand this title if it did not contain the supplement: 'containing a defense of the treatise *De Cive* of the most eminent Hobbes'. But neither is it just a defence of Hobbes. In the book, Velthuysen introduces three separate topics: first a teleological conception of morality, second a description of the rules of morality on the basis of 'the fundamental law of self-preservation', and third a political philosophy. In the 1680 reprint of the book, Velthuysen repressed his youthful expressions of enthusiasm for Hobbes without, however, changing the substance or even the wording of his own views. He might not have been a Hobbesian at all, but a 'modern' in search of support.

Velthuysen's target is to formulate the principles of morality from a naturalistic point of view. His argument is on a level with Burgersdijk's use of the doctrine of secondary causes. God has created the world and man in particular to some purpose, some end. In doing so

He must have willed the means necessary to this end (here God is compared with someone who builds a house). Man's nature, especially his natural appetites and the sparks of reason, are the means he has provided mankind with. Therefore, man is totally justified in using these means, most of all since he is only slowly recovering from the dark times after the Fall, learning by experience the principles that, before the Fall, he followed from the goodness of his nature. Inevitably 'nature incites', where reason fell short. Nature does not provide man in vain (*non frustra*) with his natural inclinations. Pudency or shame is one of Velthuysen's favourite social mechanisms by which decency is inculcated in man. The natural appetites and social mechanisms explain most of the historical development of moral codes in human society. We understand from this perspective why, for example, in our 'more enlightened age' we sustain monogamy against polygamy as was the moral practice in the Old Testament, and still is among the Turks. Justice, however, should be understood from the 'fundamental law of self-preservation'. Man has a right to put things and animals to his own use, but not his fellow creatures. He has a right to defend himself against others' invasion of his goods and person, and to punish them, but not to invade others' rights in turn. This would be unjust, and injustice collides with God's purpose with the world. This Ciceronian–Grotian conception of justice is the basis for Velthuysen's political theory. A sovereign is essential to the proper functioning of the body politic. A sovereign body can perform this function even better than one person, since the accommodation of divergent interests is central to politics. The sovereign is either absolute, or party to a contract. Against an absolute ruler the people have no right at all, although even an absolute ruler has to refrain from doing certain things (i.e. neglecting justice, usurping the citizens' property, violating women or chastity in general) because that would result in the ruin of the state. In religion, Velthuysen argues that the sovereign has to respect the accepted beliefs, and should not follow up claims from religious zealots because religious matters are not decided by a majority. A tyrannical sovereign has to be admonished by the lesser magistrates.

Velthuysen's political philosophy, all in all, falls short of the naturalistic principles of his ethical theory, as the Grotian conception of justice dominates here. In this respect, we find a more radical approach in de la Court.

Political theory of the bourgeois middle classes: Johan and Pieter de la Court (1622–60/1618–85)

The brothers de la Court represent the rapidly increasing category of non-academic, bourgeois philosophers in the Republic. Both studied at Leiden University in the 1640s and made a Grand Tour to France, Italy and England; however, they eventually took over their father's business as cloth manufacturers and traders. So they practised philosophy as dilettanti, in more than one respect along the lines of the 'Rederijkers', the literary circles of the beginning of the century. Their intellectual interest was to understand their society; their practical interest was related to the promotion of the new commercial interest against monopolies of guilds and government alike. The brothers de la Court were curious and investigative. Pieter, in particular, who outlived his brother by twenty-five years, had a lively interest in the new philosophy of Descartes and Hobbes, was well versed in the classical authors of the republican tradition, like Tacitus, Machiavelli and Guicciardini, and practised the Protestant religion in a personal and independent way.

Following the death of his brother, Pieter – possibly profiting by some manuscripts of Johan – proved to be a prolific author. He published five editions of his *Considerations of State, or Political Balance* between 1660 and 1662, *Interest of Holland, or Foundations of the Well-being of Holland* (nine different editions in 1662), *History of the Regime of Counts in Holland* (four editions since 1662), *Political Discourses* (three editions, 1662–3), *Demonstration of the Beneficent Political Foundations and Maxims of the Republic of Holland and West Frisia* (two editions, 1669 and 1671), a collection of emblemata entitled *Meaningful Fables* (1685) and a manuscript on the 'Well-being of Leiden'. So de la Court's career as an amateur philosopher was a political fact of outstanding importance. One may appreciate this even better if one considers the fact that the anonymous book *De jure ecclesiasticorum* (1665) was (falsely) attributed until far into the eighteenth century both to de la Court and Spinoza. De la Court was perceived by the defenders of the House of Orange and orthodox Protestants as a defender of republicanism without a stadholder, but by the governing circle of regenten he must have been seen as a critic of their burgeoning practice of closed shop and monopolistic tendencies.

As de la Court is, next to Machiavelli and Hobbes, one of the political writers that Spinoza refers to explicitly, we briefly sketch the outlines of his ideas. The power and charm of de la Court have to be found in his many figures of speech and his florid way of expressing himself. Here he brings the bourgeois understanding of himself and his group to the fore. We may distinguish two patterns. On the one hand he wants to make clear that man is always striving for independence and self-reliance: 'home, sweet home', 'better a minor lord, than a mayor servant', or the Spanish expression 'en mi hambre mando yo' (for all my hunger I command), and a host of other, similar ones. On the other hand, he expresses the dominant (and praiseworthy) principle of self-interest: 'nobody suffers from another's pain', 'he who eats the porridge, cooks it the best', 'own always takes precedence', or somewhat more malicious, 'set another's house to fire, to warm oneself by its coals', 'don't trust, so you won't be betrayed'. These figures of speech are more than rhetoric, they are the substrate of the ideas. Their abundant use of Tacitus follows similar lines. Tacitus is used as a common-place book, to provide support for the de la Courts' own ideology.

On a theoretical level, however, de la Court is rather more shallow. He presents us with a scarcely elaborated compilation of Cartesian psychology and Hobbesian politics. His interpretation of Hobbes can prove the point. He starts with the state of nature and men's strife for as many goods as possible to promote their uncertain conservation. But then he argues that, in the state of nature, man is subject to the laws of nature, the principal of which is, 'don't do unto another, that which you don't want to suffer yourself': Grotian moralism instead of Hobbesian rationalism. Remarkable is the statement that 'homo homini lupus in statu naturae' (man is man a wolf in the state of nature), but 'homo homini Deus in statu politico' (man is man a God in the political state). The reference to Hobbes's *De Cive* is maladroit, since it shows that he must have misread its introduction, where Hobbes says that 'homo homini Deus' refers to paradise. It is clearly not a Hobbesian notion to see the state as paradise. That is more in accordance with Machiavelli's Renaissance conception of the state as work of art.

The Machiavellian element is more prominent and more genuine. Man may be born subject to passions, but reasoning and experience permit him to suppress and regulate these in the perspective of enlightened self-interest. The state is necessary to promote order and law, because laws make men morally good. But since everybody is aiming at his self-interest political order should be arranged in such a way that it is in the interest of all to promote the common interest. 'The best government is where the fortune and misfortune of the rulers is connected to the fortune and misfortune of the subjects', a formula Spinoza will repeat in *Tractatus Politicus* VII, 31. De la Court's political theory can be seen as a compendious elaboration of this notion. In the first place, it is central to his attack on absolute monarchy. Princes are driven by their self-interest to promote the misfortune of their subjects.

They surround themselves with flatterers, they have an interest in not educating their children for fear of being overthrown, they are war-prone and exacting of the economy. It is quite likely that Algernon Sidney in his 'Court Maxims' was elaborating on de la Court in this respect. In any case, Spinoza did so in his construction of a constitutional monarchy. A republic can more easily be arranged according to the self-interest principle. Rotation of office, open access to offices, measures to prevent (religious) cabals and factions (all of which was *not* the standing Dutch practice), would bring the rulers' self-interest into accordance with that of the citizens.

De la Court's double target is evident. Although he wrote in the preface to the *Considerations* that he 'had no intent to harm any person in the world, let alone an innocent child', the most evident practical implication was that the 'child of State', the then minor William III, should never become a stadholder in the Republic. But also he was convinced that the regenten were too keen on 'warming themselves at the coals' of the burning houses of others.

❧ SPINOZA'S POSITION ❧

Spinoza elaborates his conception of morality and politics against the background of his predecessors, using their arguments, examples and concepts. The result of this elaboration is both recognizable and totally different. Spinoza aims at conceptual integration and reformulates the convictions of spirits kindred to his own so as to adapt them to his own principles. Notwithstanding the evident ideological preoccupations of these authors, Spinoza believed that in all judgements there is some element of truth. We do not correct false statements by pointing out their falsity, but by improving on their truth, as Spinoza already explained in his *Short Treatise* and postulated in E II P35.

Teleology

We have seen how on the foundations of the Leiden Neostoic–Aristotelian tradition, Velthuysen gave teleology a central place in his moral and political thought. Spinoza reacts at length to this notion. In E I App, he explains that the teleological conception of nature is a projection of man, who takes his own goal-oriented behaviour as a paradigm, unconscious of the fact that in reality everything happens according to causality. This projection leads to awkward consequences: 'But while they sought to show that nature does nothing in vain (i.e. nothing which is not of use to men), they seem to have shown only that nature and the Gods are as mad as men.' Indeed, nature has also provided many inconveniences (storms, earthquakes, diseases etc.) and they are imputed to the Gods being angry with men. Man may see himself as the maker of things (e.g. a house) and even form universal ideas or models to which these things have to conform, but this does not apply to nature.

> The reason, therefore, or cause, why God, or Nature, acts, and the reason why he exists, are one and the same. As he exists for the sake of no end, he also acts for the sake of no end. Rather, as he has no principle or end of existing, so he has also none of acting. What is called a final cause is nothing but a human appetite insofar as it is considered as a principal, or primary cause, of some thing.
>
> (E IV Praef)

This is typically Spinozistic argumentation. An opinion or imagination is reinterpreted in terms of a more general theory. The opinion is not denied, but restricted in its applicability. These opinions cannot be taken as knowledge of nature, because they are a consequence or part of nature.

But this cannot be all there is to teleology. However much we might realize that causality is behind our conviction of goal-oriented behaviour, this does not provide us as such with a better understanding of our own behaviour. Why do we strive to realize certain things, and try to escape others? What should we strive for, and why? To answer these questions we need a more precise understanding of what a causal explanation of human behaviour amounts to. Burgersdijk and his school regarded affects as modifications of sensitive appetite caused by non-natural causes. Affects are in a way the movement of this sensitive appetite, implying that affects are the prerequisite of any actual appetite, as appetite is the prerequisite of actual behaviour. This position entailed furthermore that each affect, being a motivation of behaviour, necessarily contains both bodily and rational elements. And lastly, they asserted affects to be passions, as far as they did not concur with the judgement of practical reason, and to be actions as far as they did concur. The ultimate end of ethics is then to let the affects be in concurrence with practical reason, and thereby directed at beatitude, that is, the good life. Ethics is for them the desire for the good life, or eudaimonia.

With this Neostoic, naturalistic 'theory of behaviour', Spinoza seems to have less difficulty than with teleology. Indeed, we find in Spinoza a theory of affects, of appetite and desire. The Neostoic principle of self-preservation surfaces in the *conatus*, the conscious striving of each thing to persevere in its being (E III P9). We cannot overlook the role of the active–passive distinction in Spinoza, nor the importance of the body for the conception of action. 'A great many things happen from the laws of nature alone', that is, from the nature of the body, Spinoza emphasizes in E III P2S where he explains the relative autonomy of body and mind. Furthermore, Spinoza's conception of the evolution of passion to action shares a conviction with Neostoicism: passive affects are not to be suppressed, but can proceed by natural force to become active. That education should not be practised by force or punishment, but by admonition and example, is a point of view that is a complement to this notion of passion.

But it is precisely against this background of shared ideas that in Spinoza's philosophical system no function is left for teleology. In this, he is drawing the naturalism of his predecessors to its full conclusion. The projection onto Nature of man's self-experienced goal-directedness is not a sign of action but of passion. Activity is living according to one's own nature, i.e. according to one's being as a particle in Nature, instead of (passion driven) believing oneself to be Nature's master.

What was at issue in the debate on teleology was (and is) the formulation of practical rules for actual behaviour in the perspective of an ultimate goal. As it is presumably God's end for mankind to realize X, man has a duty to act so as to further X. Velthuysen amends this: God's end is X, man is provided with means M, so employing M will by God's provident ordering of Nature to further X. In this version M provides in a derivative fashion the criteria for our practical behaviour. One of Velthuysen's main criteria is the 'fundamental law of self-preservation'. However, Velthuysen had to accept that M is necessary but not sufficient, as where he has to fall back on X in arguing that men cannot use each other as means to their own goal. Spinoza is the more radical thinker of the two. We can know God only in so far as we adequately understand ourselves as part of Nature, or God. Our being a part of Nature is essentially our being caused by Nature to exist and to act in a certain determined way. This excludes teleology. Second, in analysing our being part of Nature in more detail, we should not 'prefer to curse and laugh at the Affects and actions of men, rather than understand them', but to 'consider human actions and appetites just as if they were a question of lines, planes, and bodies' (E III Praef). Indeed, Spinoza wants to judge human actions according to their correspondence with reason, but here we should take 'reason' to be Spinoza's theory of human nature. So by really naturalizing M, Spinoza is driven to eliminate X as irrelevant to his problem. Or, in a slightly different light, if morality is to live according to one's own nature, X is internalized.

We might sum up by saying that those who live by their passions believe or imagine they are free and their own master, whereas one who lives according to reason knows he is determined (by his own nature) and is therefore really free. Isn't thus our imagination of freedom a passion that may lead us in the end to real freedom?

Affects, passions, freedom: censuring the theory of the faculties

Spinoza presents his moral philosophy in the three last parts of the *Ethics*, dealing respectively with the affects, with the passions, and with human freedom. Fundamental propositions of the first two books are applied, such as the thesis of the parallelism of mind and body, and the doctrine of ideas. In this context we should first discuss Spinoza's rebuttal of the doctrine of the three faculties as he found it defended by his Neostoic–Aristotelian predecessors. One step in his argument is formulated at the end of Book II, where it is argued that will and intellect are one and the same (E II P49C). A further step is the integration of both will and intellect with acting, by means of the appetite.

First, Spinoza argues that 'there is in the Mind no absolute faculty of understanding, desiring, loving, etc. From this it follows that these and similar faculties are either complete fictions or nothing but Metaphysical beings, or universals, which we are used to forming from particulars' (E II P48S). From thinking oneself to be free, as we have already seen, we may be apt to conclude that freedom exists, but only wrongly so. Universals are not to be formed by way of generalization. Our so-called faculties are to be investigated as singulars. Spinoza is interested in particular volitions, not in the obscure faculty of willing, and he defines a volition as the affirming or denying of something true or false. Volition is a mental category, and therefore it is to be seen in relation to ideas. Having an idea, and affirming it, or conversely having the idea that something is not the case, and denying it, cannot be different from each other. Spinoza is focusing here exclusively on the affirming/denying part of volition, thereby permitting himself to repeat his criticism of criteriology in E II P43. Therefore, he can conclude in II P49: 'In the Mind there is no volition, or affirmation and negation, except that which the idea involves insofar as it is an idea.' This proposition is then defended against the Cartesian conception of infinite will and finite knowledge, and against the notion of the indifference of the will. In a way, Spinoza's dealing with volition is rather abstract here, only to become understandable when he moves on to discuss appetite.

Minds and bodies being but modes of attributes and not substances, the activating principle of human behaviour no longer simply to be identified with volition, Spinoza argues for the equivalence of mind and body. 'The very structure of the human Body, which, in the ingenuity of its construction, far surpasses anything made by human skill' (E III P2S) is not to be regarded as an instrument for use of the mind, nor as its temple, but as much part of nature as the mind is. The body could not act if it were not determined to act *qua body*. However, for Spinoza the notion of 'thing' indicates existing objects without special reference to the attributes. Since he is convinced that all things can be analysed according to the two attributes we are acquainted with, and that the order and concatenation of matter is the same as that of ideas, he holds that we can explain things both ways. For sure, Spinoza does not follow up this principle in all details. In particular, since we lack precise knowledge about the workings of the human body, we had better concentrate on human psychology. This is what happens when Spinoza has introduced his central notion of *conatus* in E III P6–P9.

> P6: Each thing, as far as it can by its own power, strives to persevere in its being.
> P7: The striving by which each thing strives to persevere in its being is nothing but the actual essence of the thing.
> P9: Both insofar as the Mind has clear and distinct ideas, and insofar as it has confused ideas, it strives, for an indefinite duration, to persevere in its being and it is conscious of this striving it has.

The two attributes are introduced in P9S as follows:

> When this striving is related only to the Mind, it is called Will; but when it is related to the Mind and the Body together, it is called Appetite. This Appetite, therefore, is nothing but the very essence of man, from whose nature necessary follow those things that promote his preservation.

Spinoza adds that '*desire* can be defined as *appetite together with consciousness of the appetite*' (emphasis in the original). This is somewhat problematic, since here Spinoza affirms a quality of things that precedes the thing's explanation in terms of the attributes (i.e. conatus or appetite), but at the same time connects it in a rather complicated way to the attributal explanations. With this introduction of 'will' we have no quarrel, nor with appetite as synonymous with conatus; but can Spinoza consistently introduce the notion of 'consciousness of the appetite'? That is, can ideas, which are ideas of the body, be also of something that is common to mind and body? We may argue that Spinoza has no other option but to introduce a concept (desire) that expresses the fact that man is a mind–body, instead of being a mind related to a body. Man forms ideas of his *own* body, that is, his consciousness of personal identity is precisely the consciousness of being a striving mind–body.

The remainder of Spinoza's moral philosophy is an elaboration of 'desire', in which he shows that being active is living according to the laws of one's own nature, instead of passively behaving from external causes. Central in this is the analysis of the affects or emotions, that is of *laetitia* (joy, pleasure), *tristitia* (sadness, pain) and *cupiditas* (desire), and their numerous derivatives like love, hate, hope or fear. Joy is the emotion that furthers one's capability (potentia) – it is so to say an active emotion; sadness hampers one's capability to act. We should therefore prefer joy and its derivatives to sadness. Here we find the Stoic conception of living according to nature transformed into an active moral principle, without however neglecting contemplation. The intellectual love of God is Spinoza's ultimate joy, since to understand ourselves as particles of Nature is equivalent to being active. To strive for this ultimate goal is what morality is about. But we cannot go along this path unless the mind–body goes this way. An active mind necessarily corresponds to an active body. The emotions as habits of the mind–body have to evolve from merely passive to predominantly active. Only the emotions can do the trick; it is not our will, but our checking emotions by emotions. The final apex of Spinoza's ethics is contained in the programme that man be active or free:

> All our strivings, or Desires, follow from the necessity of our
> nature in such a way that they can be understood either
> through it alone, as through their proximate cause, or insofar as
> we are a part of nature, which cannot be conceived adequately
> through itself without other individuals. The Desires which
> follow from our nature in such a way that they can be
> understood through it alone are those that are related to the
> Mind insofar as it is conceived to consist of adequate ideas.
> The remaining Desires are not related to the Mind except insofar
> as it conceives things inadequately, and their force and growth
> must be defined not by human power, but by the power of
> things that are outside us. The former, therefore, are rightly
> called actions, while the latter are rightly called passions. For
> the former always indicate our power, whereas the latter
> indicate our lack of power and mutilated knowledge.
>
> (E IV App)

Thus reason and the power of nature are identified and will lead Spinoza in the fifth part of the *Ethics* to a series of intricate and exciting conclusions concerning, among other things, the immortality of the soul. Here Spinoza is dealing with what full rationality might mean for man. But man is mostly driven by passions, and thereby dependent on things outside. We shall explore this interdependence in the next section on Spinoza's political theory.

❧ MORAL PHILOSOPHY AND POLITICS ❧

In the same way that man is not his own creator, social institutions are not the result of human creation. Adam Ferguson was to express this towards the end of the eighteenth century by saying that men stumble 'upon establishments, which are indeed the result of human action, but not the execution of any human design'. How radical was Spinoza in this respect? Some commentators have recognized two different answers to this question. They judge that Spinoza provided a contractarian answer in his first book on politics, but an evolutionary one in the second. This has disconcerted others, since the problem of 'design' versus 'action' seems to them to be solved, as far as individual man is concerned, in favour of 'action'. A divergent position in the political realm would smack of inconsistency, a type of judgement on Spinoza most are reluctant to uphold. More specifically, this argument is triggered by statements by Spinoza that indeed do seem to be inconsistent. In the *Tractatus Theologico-Politicus* the founding of the state is described as a decision of a multitude of men to unite and to live guided as it were by one mind. The state seems to be created in a constitutional act. In the *Tractatus Politicus*, however, these contractarian notions are completely absent, and evolutionary explanations are proffered. Here we are instructed to regard the formation of political institutions as the outcome of socio-psychological mechanisms. In presenting Spinoza's political philosophy in this section, we shall deal with this central problem in a somewhat roundabout way. We shall see that, by presenting the complexity of both books, the problem will solve itself. Spinoza is indeed as radical in his political philosophy as he is in his ethics. But political theory has special problems of its own, among them being predominant the question of the audience it is addressed to.

So what was the reason for writing the *Tractatus Theologico-Politicus*? In fact there was more than one. Working at the *Ethics*, Spinoza must have deepened the theoretical foundation of his criticism of Bible scholarship that had provoked the scorn and indignation of the Jewish authorities, leading to his expulsion from the Jewish community in 1656. Indeed, more than half of the text is about Bible interpretation. Furthermore, the kind of problems he had met with in Jewish circles were far from being restricted to these alone. However tolerant the Dutch Republic may have been in comparison with surrounding nations, a continuing debate was going on about its real nature and limits, possibly even because of this relatively large degree of tolerance. De la Court pointed to the ambition of the ministers of the church who, not satisfied with their duty of spiritual care, were keen to profit from any opportunity to meddle with political affairs that came their way. So quite a few ministers tried to give support to the Orangist faction by giving William III pride of place in their weekly prayer for God's help for the magistrate, although William was still in his minority. Attempts to suppress this kind of weekly prayer provoked a lot of unrest and even protest. Evidently, this political meddling was contrary to an important ideological tradition, going back to Erasmus and defended heatedly in the seventeenth century by Hugo Grotius and others. According to this Arminian set of beliefs, the church should restrict itself to its purely spiritual duties, and the government was granted the sole authority in mundane matters. Tolerance, according to this view, was founded in the individual's conscientious responsibility to God alone. This so-called 'internal religion' could be a subject for 'brotherly admonition', but the 'external religion' including the church order had to be regarded as a subject of public order and therefore a matter of civil government alone. This party regarded the Dutch Revolt to have been *libertatis ergo*, for the sake of liberty.

But these opinions were far from uncontested. Puritan theologians, for example Paulus Voetius from Utrecht, referred to the Revolt as *religionis causa*, for reason of (true) religion. As they were convinced that each act of a Christian should be under the aegis of faith, they evidently felt compelled to impose religious limits on the civil magistrates. Moreover, they found an interested ear on the part of the Princes of Orange for their claims against the regenten aristocracy. They did have substantial support among the people at large, but found opposition from latitudinarian groups like the Arminians. The authorities, for their part, were keen to present the case as a conflict of doctrines among theologians, and to emphasize their own responsibility for public peace and order. The issue of tolerance was therefore a very complicated matter, used partly by the regenten to argue their indifference in doctrine, partly by the conflicting religious groups and partly by the Orangist faction in its quest for a power base. A whole list of practical topics became related to the concept: apart from traditional ones like freedom of conscience and the persecution of heretics, there were such topics as public peace, sovereignty and lese-majesty, the freedom of the academic and popular press. The dominant policy of the authorities was to balance and mitigate, in all its diverse dealings with (purportedly) religious matters. This resulted in *de facto* toleration, although not without setbacks. The publication of books that aroused public indignation could still be forbidden, although that was not always enforced in a strict way. But in exceptional cases the authorities felt the necessity to persecute authors of 'heretical' works by putting them in jail, and by a prolonged preparation of the trial they waited for better weather. The conditions in jail, however, were often so bad that the indicted authors did not survive.

The situation was strained by developments in the field of academic philosophy. Cartesianism and Hobbism were among the targets in Voetius's circle. The separation of philosophy from theology was much scorned. The situation was aggravated when dilettanti like Lodewijk Meyer started to use the new philosophy in theological debate. His *Philosophy, expounder of the Holy Writ* (1666) produced much unrest, even among latitudinarians who were worried lest the fragile balance of toleration might be disturbed.

To this complicated situation Spinoza wanted to address himself in the *Tractatus Theologico-Politicus*. His stated purpose was to show 'that freedom to philosophise can not only be granted without injury to Piety and the Peace of the Commonwealth, but that the Peace of the Commonwealth and Piety are endangered by the suppression of this freedom', as the title page ran. His argument proceeded in the following manner.

1 In the Preface and the first six chapters, the character and function of religion in the Jewish state is discussed. Although Spinoza sets out to vehemently criticize superstition, and the slavery of totalitarian theocracies like that of the Turkish empire, the positive effects of religion in the Jewish state of the Old Testament are emphasized. It provided for the legitimacy of the political order, and taught the basic principles of morality. Spinoza explains that the Pentateuch imprinted on the Jewish people the natural light and the natural divine law, by appealing to the imagination of the people. The civil laws and religious ceremonies were strengthened by the special relationship that Moses, the lawgiver, was understood to have to God. The teachings of the Bible concern obedience, but not philosophy.

2 In the next seven chapters, the method of Bible interpretation is discussed. Theologians tend to read their own prejudices into the Holy Writ, by taking it as contrary to reason and nature. This is incorrect. The study of the Bible should be undertaken like the study of nature, that is, only from the Bible itself can one come to the correct interpretation. This interpretation is to be found by means of (a) a study of its language, (b) a careful classification of the text and (c) accounting for the historical circumstances. By applying this new method, Spinoza goes on to prove that the Bible teaches nothing but simple rules of behaviour, that is, obedience. About God's nature he finds only simple statements, relevant to morality alone. God's word is promulgated by testimony, by fraternal admonition and, in argumentation, is free from philosophical speculation. Spinoza is shocked to

see the theologians of his time bring abstruse matters into religion, introduce philosophy, and practise theology as a science and as fit for debate.

3 The last seven chapters are devoted to the relationship between theology, philosophy and the state. Theology has to do with *pietas*, morality, philosophy with truth; the former is subject only to moral certainty, the latter to demonstrative certainty. Reason and belief are of a different order: we can never prove that simple obedience is the way to salvation. The concept of civil laws developed along philosophical lines, from the notions of natural right and sovereignty. Spinoza elaborates on this by discussing the interdependence of legitimacy and sovereignty, and the limits of power, by historical and actual examples. In the last chapter, in the context of a eulogy of the Republic, Spinoza puts forward and defends his central tenets.

> 1. That it is impossible to deprive men of the freedom to say what they think.
> 2. That this freedom can be granted to everyone without infringing the right and authority of the sovereign, and that the individual citizen can preserve this freedom without infringing that right, provided that he does not presume therefrom to make any innovation in the constitution or to do anything that contravenes the established laws.
> 3. That every man can possess this freedom without endangering public peace, and any troubles that may arise from this freedom can be easily held in check.
> 4. Finally, that this freedom can be granted without detriment to the public peace, to piety, and to the right of the sovereign, and indeed it must be granted if these are to be preserved.
>
> (TTP XX)

The *Tractatus Theologico-Politicus*, therefore, really contains three distinctive arguments: one on the role of religion in the state, one on the interpretation of the Bible, and one on the role of reason in the state. In comparison with the doctrines of toleration of his compatriots, Spinoza clearly separates the distinct positions of faith and reason. His attempt at freeing philosophy from theological tutelage is founded in secularizing the state by referring theology to its proper constraints, without falling into the trap of absolutism. Not the absolute rule of the state, but the absolute rule of nature is the point of reference. Let us therefore follow more closely Spinoza's conception of the rule of nature in politics. We do so under three headings: the nature of political order; the constitution of political order; and the development of political order.

The nature of political order

The formation of a society is advantageous, even absolutely essential, not merely for security against enemies but for the efficient organisation of an economy. If men did not afford one another mutual aid, they would lack both the skill and the time to support and preserve themselves to the greatest possible extent. All men are not equally suited to all activities, and no single person would be capable of supplying all his own needs. Each would find strength and time fail him if he alone had to plough, sow, reap, grind, cook, weave, stitch, and perform all the other numerous tasks to support life, not to mention the arts and sciences which are also indispensable for the perfection of human nature and its blessedness. We see that those who live in a barbarous way with no civilising influences lead a wretched and almost brutish existence, and even so their few poor and crude resources are not acquired without some degree of mutual help.

(TTP V)

Spinoza is arguing here from 'universally valid principles', and one is tempted to refer to E IV 18S: 'To man, then, nothing is more useful than man'. But if we look into Spinoza's arguments for this notion of mutual utility, we find two statements explained. First, referring back to E II Post4, he states that men can never do without external things in their striving for the preservation of their being. Second, he deduces that no external things are 'more excellent than those that agree entirely with our nature'. Men who agree in all things will therefore seek the common good of all. They will want nothing for themselves that they do not desire for other men. As often in Spinoza, we have here the choice between a minimal and a maximal interpretation. If we take 'agree' in a maximal sense, it seems to indicate the agreement of all living equally according to the dictates of reason, but then we would have difficulty in understanding how, for example, a farmer and a philosopher can completely agree with each other. We would not want this agreement to consist in a shared certainty about the necessity of mutual help, since that is what we are trying to understand. On the minimal interpretation, agreement refers to those things about which persons in fact agree, as, for example, in an exchange of external goods. That is, to man nothing is more useful than man because people find their exchanges profitable as soon as they come to an agreement. On this minimalist interpretation only, agreement(s) explain mutual help. We may understand Spinoza to allude to this last interpretation when he concludes E IV 18S by justifying his argument so as 'to win, if possible, the attention of those who believe that this principle – that everyone is bound to seek his own advantage – is the foundation, not of virtue and morality, but of immorality'. Reading this last remark against the background of de la Court, we easily see Spinoza here defending the morality of mutual aid on the basis of the diversity of human capabilities and preferences and the subsequent possibility of mutual advantage in agreed-upon exchange.

There is one type of agreement, however, that stands out as a prerequisite for mutual aid, that is, good faith, the determination 'to keep appetite in check in so far as it tends to another's hurt, to do to no one what they would not want done to themselves, and to uphold another's right as they would their own' (TTP XVI), or, in the expression of E IV 18S, that men 'want nothing for themselves that they do not desire for other men. Hence, they are just, honest (faithful), and honourable.' Men can only provide each other external goods if they recognize each other as equals in a fundamental respect. That was also the opinion of Velthuysen. He, however, formulated it as a normative principle, whereas Spinoza confines himself to a prerequisite. If men do not keep their agreements, mutual aid is impossible. For Spinoza, unlike in Grotian natural law, for example, it is no self-evident rule that men should keep their promises. It is a fact about human life, however, that even a 'few poor and crude resources are not acquired without some degree of mutual help'.

A somewhat different argument for human co-operation that surfaces now and again (e.g. TTP XVI, TP II, 13, and E IV 18S) is that the capability power of a group of men is the sum of the capabilities of each of them. This may seem an echo of Burgersdijk's emphasis on concord and unity. However, Spinoza does not really make much use of this principle in explaining the nature of the state. On the one hand, he seems uncertain about the exact law of aggregation involved. If, for example, a hundred chess players unite to play against another player, no one would be willing to regard their combined chance of winning as the sum of the individual chances of each of them. In general, the effect of combining forces will depend on the principles of co-operation that apply. On the other hand, Spinoza uses the notion to emphasize the central function of agreement in a state. As a sovereign is instituted by agreement, and agreement is based on utility, a sovereign loses his power to enforce his rulings as soon as a relevant proportion of the people unite in opposition against him. That is, it is the combining of forces that creates political power, not the legal title to such power. Sometimes Spinoza expresses this by his notorious remark that men's right is co-extensive with their capability power. Social power, we may now say, is the result of combining forces. But combining forces is mutual help, so agreement and good faith. Power and right both express the level of social co-operation. A strong state is strong because it is legitimate, that is, because it expresses the principles of actual co-operation. But by being the form of powerful co-operation it is, it is legitimate.

Now, by way of introducing a limiting case, Spinoza states that, if everyone lived according to reason, a state would be superfluous, because men would be just, faithful and honourable on their own accord. This not being the actual situation, political order is an institutionalized form of power, a pattern of external causes that brings about human co-operation, where reason as internal cause fails. This institutionalized power can also be referred to as law, that is, human law. A human law is 'an enactment from which good or ill consequences would ensue not from the intrinsic nature of the deed performed but only from the will and absolute power of some ruler'. Moreover, a law is ordained by men 'for themselves and for others with a view to making life more secure and more convenient, or for other reasons' (TTP IV). In particular, since the true purpose of the law is usually apparent only to the few and is generally incomprehensible to the great majority in whose lives reason plays little part, laws are enforced by sanctions. We have seen that the capability of man is greater according to the extent to which man is more active, that is, less dependent on external power. As the capability of a society of men is in some way a function of their individual capabilities, ways of enforcing a law that promote the activity of men are more useful than others. In particular, if a ruler can make people comply without the use of sanctions, but by influencing their behaviour by other means, he enhances the capability of the society. Most effective in this respect is making 'the motive of self-interest' depend on the state or, in other words, 'no more effective means can be devised to influence men's minds . . '. as joy springing from devotion, that is love mingled with awe' (TTP XVII). Although it is not the motive for obedience, but the fact of obedience, that constitutes a subject, the means that contribute to men's willingness to obey are crucial. Convincing others means referring to their conception of things, for example by taking seriously their conviction of free will. This brings Spinoza to his version of the theory of political contract.

The origins of the state

We are now in a position to present Spinoza's 'contractual' explanation of the origins of the state. In TTP XVI Spinoza points out that 'in order to secure a secure and good life, men *had* necessarily to unite in one body', and 'therefore *arranged* that the unrestricted right naturally possessed by each individual should be put into common ownership, and that this right should no longer be determined by the strength and appetite of the individual, but by the power and will of all together' (emphasis added). The argument about mutual assistance is rephrased here in terms of unity, and in this specific political form as well social co-operation is contingent on the existence of a *de facto* willingness in good faith 'to be guided in all matters by the dictates of reason'. But this willingness is far from being a principle of nature. Against Hobbes, however, Spinoza points out that it is just as absurd to demand that a man should live according to reason as to say that a cat has the duty to live according to the laws of a lion's nature. In particular, contracts bind by their utility alone. So the unity that is presupposed by political order should be founded in utility. To show how this is possible is the aim of Spinoza's sixteenth chapter. How do men succeed in living according to the 'will and power of all together'? Had they been guided by appetite alone they would have failed, he writes. Therefore they bound themselves by the most stringent pledges to live according to the dictates of reason. These pledges are effective since 'nobody ventures openly to oppose [these], lest he should appear to be without the capacity to reason': Ulysses is bound to the mast of reason by his appetites. In more detail, we find the same principle reappearing when political obligation and legitimacy are discussed. Since contracts are kept only as long as they are profitable, solemn pledges help people to stick to their contracts for fear of public disrespect. Note that contracts as such were only introduced as a symbolism or ideology to keep the disruptive effects of appetite in check. We may therefore very well say that Spinoza explains the origins of the state by the desire for unity, that is, according to the *Ethics*, the appetite for it together with the consciousness of it. These appetites are founded in utility, and like good faith in co-operation, solemn pledges in politics have the function of enforcing the desire for unity by putting additional utility in the outcome. In a highly significant argument, Spinoza explains why rulers are not bound by international contracts or treaties, 'except through hope of some good or apprehension of some evil': 'For he [the ruler] cannot keep whatever promise he sees likely to be detrimental to his country without violating his pledge to his subjects, a pledge by which he is most firmly bound, and whose fulfilment usually involves the most solemn promises'! In other words, disrespect among his subjects is more detrimental to a ruler than the possible consequences of breaking a treaty. The well-being of the country is guaranteed by the ruler's care for his own interest, and not by contracts in themselves. We easily recognize de la Court's principle of public interest, cared for by the rulers because it is connected to their own interest. This connection is furthered by conceiving it as a contractual bond, since that threatens disrespect to anyone who would break it. Spinoza's naturalistic theory of the state thus explains the state as an effect of the laws of nature, as well as showing the utility of an ideological conception of the state in terms of contract.

In this respect we can understand why Spinoza believes that a state would be unnecessary if everybody lived according to the dictates of reason. Here Spinoza is more like Proudhon or Kropotkin than like Hobbes. But men being what they are, Spinoza is far from being an anarchist. Men who do not live according to reason are not '*sui iuris*', and therefore are by definition subject to other powers. A stable system of powers is a state, and such a stable pattern is expressed by civil laws. Imagination plays the role that reason cannot perform. This imagination is the more effective the more men believe, or imagine, that they have instituted it by free will, that is, have contracted to abide by the civil laws. As a consequence, Spinoza is anxious to demonstrate that this set of imaginations is a consistent one. Formulating his position on a topic that appears in Hobbes and Locke as well, he says:

> We therefore recognize a great difference between a slave, a son, and a subject, who accordingly may be defined as follows. A slave is one who has to obey his master's commands which look only to the interest of him who commands; a son is one who by his father's commands does what is to his own good; a subject is one who, by command of the sovereign power, acts for the common good, and therefore for his own good also.

Imagination is a consistent and effective mechanism that provides men with what we may call a provisional political morality (cf. E II P49S). Its consistency is explained in the language of imagination itself, since this is of concern to those who live according to the imagination. Its effectiveness can only be explained in terms of the laws of nature. In reading the *Tractatus Theologico-Politicus*, these two different languages should be distinguished carefully, especially where they are implied in one and the same argument. We can illustrate this best in relation to Spinoza's often distorted contention that right is might.

'By the right and established order of Nature I mean simply the rules governing the nature of every individual thing, according to which we conceive it as naturally determined to exist and to act in a definitive way', that is, right equals *potentia*: 'the right of the individual is co-extensive with its determinate power'. This appears to be a stipulative definition, since the concept of right surfaces here for the first time. 'Right', or 'ius', is evidently presented as an explication of the freedom that is permitted individuals by the rules that apply to them, be they natural or civil rules. Inevitably then, civil right equals civil power, whereby an individual is free to do whatever is in his power. Spinoza is aware, however, that men have all kinds of explanations for rights differing from his. They explain rights by divine origins, or as originating from a wise lawgiver, or from contract. So he preferred to explain them from 'proximate causes', that is, from the human will. But in this Chapter XVI, where the effectiveness of civic contracts has to be discussed, he can no longer refrain from giving a full explanation. So let us ask therefore: can one expect that an individual's power increases or decreases according to his redefining his rights? Surely not. In this we might compare Spinoza with Hume, who was to demolish the theory of contract by arguing that people do not obey a sovereign because they have contracted to do so, but embellish their obedience by the fiction of a contract. On the other hand we have seen that a man's power or capability can increase or decrease, that is, man can become more active or more passive. Hope and fear are Spinoza's main examples. Freedom from fear and hope for advantages are indications of increasing capabilities. The imagination that obedience will bring in its wake the promotion of one's own good is the expression of such a hope. So we reach the somewhat paradoxical conclusion that, by granting the sovereign a right to dictate one's actions, man is promoting his capability. By enlarging one's capability, man is enlarging his right (by definition). So Spinoza can only maintain that might equals right by granting that in a political order the powers of both individuals and the collectivity are increased. This increase goes with co-operation. If men were completely rational they would not need the imagery of the transference of rights to sustain such co-operation. Affection-driven man, however, cannot co-operate in this way unless forced by a supposedly self-imposed additional argument to do so. These arguments take the form of rights: rules that are enforced by sanctions some way or other. Each political organization has therefore the system of laws it deserves, be it a contract with God as in the Jewish state or a contract between men as in the Dutch Republic.

The developing state

In the beginning of the next chapter, TTP XVII, Spinoza points out that the authority of rulers in previous ages used to be strengthened by clothing it in the garments of divinity. The Persians looked to their kings as Gods. Indeed, men do not want to be ruled by their equals, but only by outstanding leaders. Moses was attributed this quality, and rightly so. He gave the Jewish people a very wise constitution. Spinoza emphasizes the determination of Moses to put all laws and thereby obedience under the aegis of religion. The Hebrews' love for their country was not a mere case of patriotism but of piety and religious duty. And next to that, the political institutions were arranged according to the *ratio utilitatis*, the principle of utility. As Lipsius had seen, most patriotism is self-interest in disguise, and so it was highly efficient that in the Jewish state it was made useful to men not to desert their country. These two wise principles that Moses put at the foundation of the Jewish state were a clear promise of the stability and continuity of the Jewish state. But this was not going to be the case.

The worship of the golden calf, this undeniable expression of superstition, made for a change that produced the downfall of the Jewish state in the end. As Spinoza expresses it, God punished his people by giving it laws that were more a kind of vengeance than a contribution to their well-being. He decided that from then on only the Levites, who did not join in the worship of the golden calf, should have care of the law. This was the germ of decay. The ambitions of the successors of Moses as well as the zeal of the scribes resulted in the introduction of kingship and in sectarianism and Pharisaism. From this came civil war and the downfall of the state in the end. From this Spinoza concludes (a) that the original constitution of a state should be kept intact, and especially that if a people does not have a king kingship should not be introduced, (b) that religion should be separated from politics and (c) that in a state where ambition is permitted both (a) and (b) will be difficult to follow. Spinoza points to the history of England where monarchy was supposedly abrogated in 1642, only to be reintroduced under a different name under Cromwell, and reinstituted in its original form in 1660. The Dutch Republic proves the same. There never was a king, and the short experiment with Queen Elizabeth's lieutenant Leicester was bound to fail.

A political system is an intricate mechanism that cannot be changed overnight. The predominant suggestion from the *Tractatus Theologico-Politicus* is that there is a grand secular trend according to which superstition is gradually overcome, and that more rational political systems are more free and more powerful. Spinoza seems more interested to suggest the superiority of the Dutch Republic by rhetorical comparison than to provide his readers with a full theory. Indeed, in the *Tractatus Theologico-Politicus* his aim must have been to make an intervention in Dutch political life. He points out that ambition leads to war for honour's sake (as de la Court had seen) and to curtailing the people's freedom, to the downfall of the state if one makes the same mistakes as the Jewish people, that is, elects kings and admits the zeal of the scribes. Indeed, this was exactly what was threatening to happen around the Synod of Dordt (1618–19), and would have happened if the death of Prince Maurice had not curtailed the process.

Along what lines did the philosopher Spinoza expect his intervention to be effective? What constituted the force of his argument?

Was he hoping to contribute to the collective imagery of the state? Or to its explanation? We have seen that intervention was Spinoza's most central concern. He adapted his mode of explanation to his audience, although in Chapters XVI and XVII he could not circumvent references to the order and concatenation of things that is the real explanation. However, his decision to explain in terms of the will was indeed an adaptation to his audience. Spinoza's final chapter of the *Tractatus Theologico-Politicus* brings the intervention to its final conclusion. Here he shows what the implications are of the Dutch self-understanding of their republic along Spinozan lines. These implications have been presented on pp. 333–5. They do not differ much from run of the mill arguments about the relationship of church and state, except for one point: tolerance is defended as a virtue of a republic, especially as far as philosophy is concerned. This intervention was barely successful among those who were not convinced by the argument in the first place. Even Remonstrant theologians, who had always defended the same position, were made rather uncomfortable about this 'support' from a philosopher who presented God as Nature, and in his determinism denied human freedom, and hence sin and morality. Velthuysen, in his later writings, criticized Spinoza heavily. The Amsterdam Remonstrant and later friend of Locke, Philip van Limborch, scorned Spinoza for his fatalism. Spinoza's influence was in other quarters. Among autodidacts, like himself, among idiosyncratic intellectuals, like the author of the Spinozistic novel *The Life and Times of Philopater*, his appeal was remarkable. But Spinoza must have been disappointed that the *Tractatus Theologico-Politicus* produced so few of the effects he had hoped for. In the *Tractatus Politicus* he came forward with a different style, and with different targets. In that book, he no longer aims at the imagination, but wants to present a political philosophy that is deduced from the *Ethics*, and formulated as a scientific theory.

The theory of the Tractatus Politicus

I have resolved to demonstrate by a certain and undoubted course of argument, or to deduce from the very condition of human nature, not what is new and unheard of, but only such things as agree best with practice. And that I might investigate the subject-matter of this science with the same freedom of spirit as we generally use in mathematics, I have laboured carefully, not to mock, lament, or execrate, but to understand human actions; and to this end I have looked upon passions such as love, hatred, anger, envy, ambition, pity, and the other perturbations of the mind, not in the light of vices of human nature, but as properties, just as pertinent to it, as are heat, cold, storm, thunder, and the like to the nature of the atmosphere, which phenomena, though inconvenient, are yet necessary, and have fixed causes, by means of which we endeavour to understand their nature, and the mind has just as much pleasure in viewing them aright, as in knowing such things as flatter the senses.

(TP I, 4)

This scientific, naturalist approach is put forward against the utopianism of the philosophers. We can learn more from practical politicians for whom experience is the teacher. This does not imply, however, that Spinoza opts for an empiricist approach to politics. He intends to formulate in a systematic and theoretical way, and to explain what politicians know from practical experience. He is the abstruse thinker of David Hume's essay 'On Commerce', who fits the insights of the shallow thinkers of practical competence within an explanatory whole. And in this programme, he is as critical as Adam Smith of the 'men of systems' who suppose they can adapt human life to their schemes. In the *Tractatus Politicus* the human will as proximate cause has lost the prime position it enjoyed in the *Tractatus Theologico-Politicus*. In doing so, Spinoza elaborates more fully on the concept of *potestas*, or coercive power, as distinct from *potentia*, or capability power. Second, the explanation of the origins of the state is more fully developed. Third, the various forms of government are distinguished and analysed as to their principles and to the organization that best accords with these principles. We shall see Spinoza argue for constitutional monarchy as the only reasonable form of monarchy, and for two types of aristocracy in a reflection of the differences between city-states like Venice and federative republics like the Dutch. Democracy is not discussed fully, since Spinoza died before completing the last chapters of the *Tractatus Politicus*.

We may describe *potentia* as a power *per se*, as the capability that is in a thing, and *potestas* as a power *ad aliud*, as the power over other things. This has several consequences. First, in the case of states, one might expect that the capability of a state relates to its power in relation to other states. A state that acts according to its own nature is less dependent on external causes, that is, on other states. Whether it effectively is more powerful than other states is a different matter, because to answer this question we have to look into the capabilities of these other states. But *ceteris paribus* we must understand the more capable state as more powerful.

In a general sense, a state arranged according to reason is more capable. We can understand this to say that a state that is ordered so as to promote the common good, and thereby the well-being or the capability of its citizens makes for a greater aggregated capability. It is in this sense that we can understand Spinoza's saying that a democracy is the strongest state (TTP XVI; TP XI, 1) since it unites the capabilities of its citizens most fully or most absolutely. This absolute unity requires, however, a rational organization, and therefore citizens are most free when they abide by the laws of a rational political system.

The relationship between citizens and the superior powers (*summae potestates*; in Dutch, Hoogmogende Heren, i.e. Sovereign Lords) is bi-directional, *and* has an aggregative aspect. The rule or dominion (*imperium*) of the sovereign powers is their capability, determined by the capability of the multitude that is guided as by one mind (TP II, 15; III, 2). We may well compare this with Spinoza's analysis of the individual man: just as in that case, he does not want to separate the body (politic) from its director (or ruler). The capability of the sovereign is the organization of the state (in which the sovereign naturally is an element). So, when Spinoza continues in TP III, 2, by remarking that the right of a subject is the lesser the greater the capability of the collectivity, we understand this in the same way: in a well-organized state neither sovereign nor subject can live according to their appetites alone, but are directed towards the common good, and thereby to their own.

Spinoza distinguished four ways in which this societal direction can take place. By taking away one's arms and means of defence, or by preventing one's escape, the state constrains one in a bodily way. By inspiring someone with fear, or by obliging one by favours, the state rules body and mind alike. These four ways of directing someone's behaviour are forms of power over an individual, and are the ways in which the state is present as an external cause. This presence is inherently dynamic. It can only operate via the emotions of its target, and may lead to such diverse reactions as anger, hatred or hope, and devotion (i.e. love together with awe). These emotions may have an aggregative effect, as when, for example, some policy leads to collective indignation because of a wrong done to a subject. The collectivity may then become directed as by a different mind and endanger the rule of the sovereign, and thereby the stability or even continuity of the state. Naturally, indignation is likely to result when the interests of subjects are infringed upon, or when one who earns praise is declared unjust.

In this respect, Spinoza tries to come to grips with the barbarous and slavish Turkish empire, which he deems despicable although very stable. 'Yet if slavery, barbarism, and desolation are to be called peace, men can have no worse misfortune' (TP VI, 4). His argument is a dissection of the true nature of absolute monarchies, where in fact more often the whims of concubines and minions decide. Repeating the analysis of de la Court, Spinoza demonstrates that in an absolute monarchy the king is always afraid of his subjects, and even of his own children, and 'will look more for his own safety, and not try to consult his subjects' interests, but try to plot against them, especially against those who are renowned for learning, or have influence through wealth' (TP VI, 6). It is clear that Spinoza measures states not according to their stability, but according to their rationality.

In this perspective Spinoza again investigates the origins of the state. Unlike the emphasis on the will and the ensuing contract in the *Tractatus Theologico-Politicus*, now he tries to explain by causal mechanisms.

> Inasmuch as men are led, as we have said, more by passion than reason, it follows, that a multitude comes together, and wishes to be guided, as it were, by one mind, not at the suggestion of reason, but by some common passion – that is (Ch. III, 3), common hope, or fear, or the desire of avenging some common hurt. But since fear of solitude exists in all men, because no one in solitude is strong enough to defend himself, and procure the necessaries of life, it follows that men naturally aspire to the civil state; nor can it happen that men should ever utterly dissolve it.
>
> (TP VI, 1)

In the Latin of Spinoza we find that the multitude 'ex communi aliquo affectu naturaliter convenire', that is, 'from some shared emotion agree by nature'. 'Agreement' being a somewhat more precise translation than Elwes's 'coming together', we find here the principle of co-operation explained that we had been looking for in the *Tractatus Theologico-Politicus*. In the shared or common emotion we see the civil state arise. What kind of emotion is Spinoza thinking of? In TP III, 6, he points to the removal of general fear and the prevention of general sufferings as a natural cause of the state. These 'communes miserias' seem to refer to the emotion of *misericordia*, compassion. We find it again in TP I, 5, together with jealousy or envy, vengeance, and ambition and glory. These passions predominate in an ordinary man, especially since men are led more by passion than by reason. Anyone who thinks otherwise believes in a chimera or in a utopia, or in the golden age of the poets (TP I, 1). It is clear, however, that we need something more than just these passions. Thomas Hobbes would explain the war of all men against all men from these passions. How can Spinoza come to the explanation of the state? We have to take a close look at the term '*convenire*', agree.

We will then be dealing with the pre-political state, that is, as long as the condition is not realized 'that all, governing and governed alike, whether they will or no, shall do what makes for the general welfare: that is, that all, whether of their own impulse, or by force or necessity, shall be compelled to live according to the dictate of reason' (TP VI, 3). As long as this condition is not realized, any order that may arise is not stable. People may agree for a moment, but disintegrate in the next. How can such an unstable agreement develop into a stable one? This may happen if such a temporary agreement induces people to agree on further points, leading to patterns of behaviour, habits and preferences that can be redefined as a political order. Spinoza seems to suggest this much when he says that compassion can induce men to alleviate the misery of others, from ambition or love of glory. Such ambitious men may want to continue to attract the praise of others, because they see it as a consequence of their help. Others may want the same, and thereby ambition becomes a motive for political leadership. Now, jealousy could follow if there is not room enough for all ambitious men, and fear and hate might follow as well. In that case, the evolution is thwarted. But if the surrounding world poses enough challenges, the effects may well be positive. Then, 'love of liberty, desire to increase their property, and hope of gaining the honours of dominion' (TP X, 8) will be the sure emotions leading to a stable political order. Interdependence of emotions makes for political order, but this process may equally well degenerate according to the circumstances.

This dual character of emotive interdependence provides a good explanation of Spinoza's use of positive and negative examples of political order. Positive examples (the kingdom of Aragon, the Dutch Republic) are indicative of the necessary conditions for their respective forms of government; negative examples (the Jewish state, Rome, France, Venice) show disturbing factors. On this reading, Spinoza's statement that states are not to be invented, but do exist, explains to us that the historical process of growth and decline is central in his political theory. By being actual existences, they can be explained.

We may point out that Spinoza in the *Tractatus Politicus* again is intervening in Dutch political debate. Taking issue with the major ideological positions of Orangism, republicanism and radicalism, he aims at objectifying the problems at hand. Orangists used to enforce their position by pointing out the heroic past of the Princes of Orange, but from Spinoza's deduction of a feasible monarchy we learn that not the person of the prince but the quality of the institutions is the decisive factor: 'And so, that a monarchical dominion may be stable, it must be ordered, so that everything be done by the king's decree only, that is, so that every law be an explicit will of the king, but not every will of the king a law' (TP VII, 1). These decrees have to be prepared by councils that embody a form of collective rationality. In the same vein,

Spinoza reconstructs the republican argument. Here also passions have to be kept in check by institutional arrangements, linking the citizens' private interest to that of the commonwealth. The radical position of dissenting religious groups is reconstructed in Spinoza's analysis of democracy. Although this was unfinished, it is evident that democracy cannot imply license, but the broadening of the category of citizens to the whole male, adult, economically self-supporting population. That is, only those who have an articulated interest can be institutionally integrated into the pursuit of the common interest. However detached and objective this analysis may be, it is evident that Spinoza takes republicanism (or aristocracy) to correspond most closely to the Dutch situation. He may be saying: here are the feasible possibilities, pick your choice, but the institutional and economic arrangements of the Dutch Republic are closest to that of his model of federalist aristocracy. The Orangists, and William III in particular, who stated that he had rather be a Doge of Venice than a king in the Dutch Republic, would scarcely feel comfortable in Spinoza's monarchy. But the events of the eighteenth century showed that Spinoza had foreseen the weaknesses of the Dutch stadholderate. But even in that century of Christian enlightenment, an atheist like Spinoza was not going to be heard. Spinoza's principled political philosophy was going to inspire philosophers elsewhere, who like him understood the birthpangs of modernity. In France Rousseau and in Great Britain Adam Smith continued the project, just as in our day libertarians, marxists and even postmodern philosophers follow his lead. This radical naturalist of the seventeenth century is a present-day companion in our quest for understanding man and society.

❧ BIBLIOGRAPHY ❧

Citations in the text are from *The Collected Works of Spinoza*, ed. and trans. E. Curley, vol. I, Princeton, N.J., Princeton University Press, 1985 (*Ethics*); *Tractatus Theologico-Politicus*, trans. Samuel Shirley with introduction by Brad S. Gregory, Leiden, Brill, 1989; *A Theologico-Political Treatise* and *A Political Treatise*, trans. with an introduction by R. H. M. Elwes, London, Routledge, 1883 (*Tractatus Politicus* citations only).

For an explanation of abbreviations used in the text, see Chapter 8, p. 303.

Editions

Full editions of the *Tractatus Theologico-Politicus*

9.1   *Tractatus Theologico-Politicus [. . .]*, from the Latin, with an introduction and notes by the editor, London, Trübner, 1862.

9.2   *A Theologico-Political Treatise* and *A Political Treatise*, trans. with an introduction by R. H. M. Elwes, London, Routledge, 1883; revised edition London, Routledge, 1895; reprinted, New York, Dover, 1951.

9.3   *Tractatus Theologico-Politicus*, trans. Samuel Shirley with introduction by Brad S. Gregory, Leiden, Brill, 1989.

9.4   *Writings on Political Philosophy*, ed. with an introduction by Albert G. A. Balz, New York, Appleton-Century, 1937.

Partial editions of the *Tractatus Theologico-Politicus*

9.5   *The Political Works: The Tractatus Theologico-Politicus in Part and the Tractatus Politicus in Full*, ed. and trans. with an introduction and notes by A. G. Wernham, Oxford, Clarendon, 1958.

9.6   *Spinoza on Freedom of Thought: Selections from Tractatus Theologico-Politicus and Tractatus Politicus*, ed. and trans. T. E. Jessop, Montreal, Mario Casalini, 1962.

Editions of the *Tractatus Politicus*

9.7   *A Treatise on Politics*, trans. William Maccall, London, Holyoake, 1854. *See also above*: [9.2], [9.4], [9.5], [9.6].

Studies on Spinoza

Studies of Spinoza's moral and political philosophy

9.8   Bennett, J. *A Study of Spinoza's 'Ethics'*. Cambridge, Cambridge University Press, 1984.

9.9   Bidney, D. *The Psychology and Ethics of Spinoza*, New York, Russell and Russell, 1940; 2nd edn, 1962.

9.10 Caird, J. *Spinoza*, Edinburgh, Blackwood, 1888.

9.11 Curley, E. *Behind the Geometrical Method: A Reading of Spinoza's Ethics*, Princeton, N.J., Princeton University Press, 1988.

9.12 De Deugd, C. (ed.) *Spinoza's Political and Theological Thought*, Amsterdam, North-Holland, 1984.

9.13 Delahunty, R. J. *Spinoza*, London, Routledge & Kegan Paul, 1985.

9.14 Den Uyl, D. J. *Power, State and Freedom. An Interpretation of Spinoza's Political Philosophy*, Assen, Van Gorcum, 1983.

9.15 Duff, R. A. *Spinoza's Political and Ethical Philosophy*, Glasgow, Maclehose, 1903; reprinted New York, A. M. Kelley, 1970.

9.16 Feuer, L. S. *Spinoza and the Rise of Liberalism*, Boston, Mass., Beacon Press, 1958; 2nd edn, New Brunswick, N.J., Transaction Books, 1987.

9.17 Grene, M. (ed.) *Spinoza: A Collection of Critical Essays*, Notre Dame, Ind., University of Notre Dame Press, 1973.

9.18 Gunn, J. A. *Benedict Spinoza*, Melbourne, Macmillan, 1925.

9.19 Hampshire, S. *Spinoza*, Harmondsworth, Penguin, 1951; 2nd edn, 1987.

9.20 Joachim, H. H. *A Study of the Ethics of Spinoza*, Oxford, Clarendon, 1901.

9.21 Kashap, S. P. *Spinoza and Moral Freedom*, Albany, N.Y., State University of New York Press, 1987.

9.22 Mandelbaum, M. and Freeman, E. (eds) *Spinoza: Essays in Interpretation*, La Salle, Ill., Open Court, 1975.

9.23 Martineau, J. *A Study of Spinoza*, London, Macmillan, 1882.

9.24 McShea, R. J. *The Political Philosophy of Spinoza*, New York, Columbia University Press, 1968.

9.25 Negri, A. *The Savage Anomaly: the Power of Spinoza's Metaphysics and Politics*, trans. M. Hardt, Minneapolis, Minn., University of Minneapolis Press, 1991.

9.26 Neu, J. *Emotion, Thought and Therapy*, Berkeley, Calif., University of California Press, 1977.

9.27 Parkinson, G. H. R. 'Spinoza on the Freedom of Man and the Freedom of the Citizen', in Z. Pelczynski and John Gray (eds) *Conceptions of Liberty in Political Philosophy*, London, Athlone Press, 1984, 39–56.

9.28 Pollock, F. *Spinoza: His Life and Philosophy*, London, Kegan Paul, 1880; 2nd edn, London, Duckworth, 1899; 3rd edn, 1912; reprinted New York, American Scholar Publications, 1966.

9.29 Strauss, L. *Spinoza's Critique of Religion*, New York, Schocken Books, 1965.

9.30 *Studia Spinozana* (yearbook), Munich, Walther Verlag, vol. 1 (1985): *Spinoza's Philosophy of Society*; vol. 3 (1987): *Hobbes and Spinoza*.

9.31 Wetlesen, J. (ed.) *Spinoza's Philosophy of Man*, Oslo, Universitetsforlaget, 1978.

9.32 Wolfson, H. A. *The Philosophy of Spinoza*, 2 vols, Cambridge, Mass., Harvard University Press, 1934; reprinted, 1948; Cleveland, Ohio, World Publishing, 1958; New York, Schocken Books, 1969; New York, Meridian Books, 1978.

Spinoza and the 'Dutch connection'

9.33 de la Court, P. *The True Interest and Political Maxims of the Republic of Holland*, London, 1746.

9.34 Gregory, B. S. 'Introduction', in *Tractatus Theologico-Politicus*, trans. Samuel Shirley with introduction by Brad S. Gregory, Leiden, Brill, 1989, 1–45.

9.35 Haitsma Mulier, E. O. G. *The Myth of Venice and Dutch Republican Thought in the Seventeenth Century*, Assen, Van Gorcum, 1980.

9.36 Kossmann, E. H. 'The Development of Dutch Political Theory in the Seventeenth Century', in J. S. Bromley and E. H. Kossmann (eds) *Britain and the Netherlands*, vol. 1, London, Chatto, 1960, 91–110.

9.37 Lipsius, J. *Six Bookes of Politickes or Civil Doctrine*, London, 1594.

9.38 Oestreich, G. *Neostoicism and the Early-modern State*, Cambridge, Cambridge University Press, 1982.

9.39 Rowen, H. H. *The Low Countries in Early Modern Times*, New York, Harper, 1972.

9.40 Van Bunge, L. 'On the Early Dutch Reception of the *Tractatus Theologico-Politicus*', *Studia Spinozana* 5 (1989) 225–51.

9.41 van Gelderen, M. 'The Political Thought of the Dutch Revolt (1555–1590)' Ph.D. thesis, European University, Florence, 1988 (forthcoming at the Cambridge University Press).

CHAPTER 10

Occasionalism

Daisie Radner

The seventeenth-century doctrine known as occasionalism arose in response to a perceived problem. Cartesian philosophy generated the problem and provided the context for the answer. In the Cartesian ontology, mind and matter are substances totally different in nature. Souls or minds have modes of thought but not modes of extension; bodies have modes of extension but not of thought. Modes are properties that affect or modify substances. A substance with a particular mode can be conceived as not having this mode, but the mode cannot be conceived apart from the particular substance of which it is the mode. The modes of each substance belong to that substance alone and cannot belong to any other substance.[1] Each mind has its own thoughts, that is, its own perceptions and volitions, and they are numerically distinct from the thoughts of every other mind. Likewise, each body has its own figure, and each moving body has its own motion. Even when two bodies are said to have the same shape, the mode which is the figure of one body is numerically distinct from the mode which is the figure of the other.

In the 1640s, the following question was put to Descartes by Pierre Gassendi and again by Princess Elizabeth of Bohemia: how can the human mind act on the human body, and the body on the mind, if they are two substances totally different in nature? Descartes responds to Gassendi by dismissing the question:

> The whole problem contained in such questions arises simply from a supposition that is false and cannot in any way be proved, namely that, if the soul and the body are two substances whose nature is different, this prevents them from being able to act on each other.[2]

To Elizabeth, he acknowledges that the question is a fair one. He appeals to the notion of the union of soul and body, 'on which depends our notion of the soul's power to move the body, and the body's power to act on the soul and cause sensations and passions'.[3] He considers the notion of the union of soul and body to be a primitive notion and does not attempt to analyse it.

> What belongs to the union of the soul and the body can be known only obscurely by pure intellect or by intellect aided by imagination, but it can be known very clearly by the senses. That is why people who never philosophize and use only their senses have no doubt that the soul moves the body and that the body acts on the soul.[4]

The problem of mind–body interaction stems not from the Cartesian dualism *per se*, but from the dualism together with a certain view of efficient causation. Statements of this view are found in Descartes's *Third Meditation* and *Second Replies*. 'There is nothing in the effect which was not previously present in the cause, either in a similar or in a higher form.'[5] The reason why what is in the effect must preexist in the cause is that the cause communicates reality to the effect. 'For where, I ask, could the effect get its reality from, if not from the cause? And how could the cause give it to the effect unless it possessed it?'[6] How can the body cause sensations and passions in the soul, when it contains no such modes either in a similar or in a higher form? How can the soul move the body? Even if the soul is considered to contain motion in a higher form in so far as it has the idea of motion, how does the soul give reality to the body's motion?

The causation of motion is no less problematic in the action of one body upon another. Consider the instance in which a moving body B comes into contact with a smaller body C, which is at rest. According to Descartes's fifth rule of impact, body B 'transfers' part of its motion to C, as much of it as would permit the two bodies to move at the same speed.[7] In a letter to Henry More, Descartes admits that 'motion, being a mode of a body, cannot pass from one body to another'.[8] If no literal transference of motion occurs, then how does the moving body produce motion in the body moved?

Descartes never explicated the concept of communication of reality. To the philosophers we are about to consider, there seemed to be only two ways in which a cause could give to an effect something that it possessed in itself: either the cause transfers something from itself to the effect, or else it creates something in the effect comparable with what it has in itself. A created substance cannot transfer anything from itself to another substance, since everything in it is a mode of it, and the modes of one substance cannot be modes of another. The only way in which one substance can cause a change in another is by creating a new mode in the other substance. If a mode comes into existence and no created substance has the power to create it, then it must have been produced by God.

Occasionalism may be characterized in general as the view that causal efficacy belongs to God instead of to creatures. A being with causal efficacy is one having the power to produce a substance or a mode of substance. Occasionalism may be either partial or complete in the extent to which causal efficacy is denied to creatures. In partial occasionalism, at least some created substances have the power to modify themselves or other things. Some modes are produced by creatures; the rest are produced directly by God on the occasion of certain creatures being in certain states. A complete occasionalist denies that created substances have any causal efficacy whatever. In complete occasionalism, no creature has the power to bring any mode into existence, either in itself or in another thing. All modes are produced directly by God on the occasion of certain creatures being in certain states.

Who was the first Cartesian philosopher to advocate occasionalism? Descartes himself sometimes uses the word 'occasion' to describe the body's action on the soul. For example, he writes in the *Treatise on Man* that, when the nerve fibres are pulled with a force great enough to separate them from the parts to which they are attached, they 'cause a movement in the brain which gives occasion for the soul . . . to have the sensation of *pain*'.[9] Descartes ought not on this account to be taken for an occasionalist, however. He does not assert that God produces the sensation on the occasion of the body's motion, but only that the motion gives occasion for the soul to have the sensation. There is no textual evidence that he tied the notion of giving occasion to a denial of causal efficacy. As Gouhier observes, for Descartes 'occasion' is a word of ordinary language rather than a substitute for the word 'cause'.[10]

There are hints of occasionalism in the work of the German Cartesian philosopher Johannes Clauberg (1622–65). In *De corporis et animae in homine conjunctione*, published in 1664, Clauberg argues that since the effect cannot be nobler than the cause the movements of the body are only *procatarctic* causes, which give occasion to the mind as principal cause to elicit ideas that are potentially in it. He also claims that the soul does not produce movement in the body but only directs it as a coachman directs a carriage. Nevertheless, the key element of occasionalism, the assignment of causal efficacy to God in specific instances, is missing in his writings.[11]

Occasionalism has three originators: Louis de La Forge (1632–66); Géraud de Cordemoy (1626–84); and Arnold Geulincx (1624–69). La Forge was the first Cartesian to use the term 'occasional cause'.[12] His *Traitté de l'esprit de l'homme* appeared at the end of 1665, although it carries the publication date of 1666. According to a contemporary, Jacques Gousset, La Forge disclosed his occasionalist opinion about 1658.[13] Cordemoy's *Discernement du corps et de l'âme* was published in 1666. At the beginning of the Fifth Discourse, on the union of the mind and the body and how they act on each other, he remarks that he told some friends about his ideas seven or eight years earlier. Battail takes this as evidence that Cordemoy's occasionalism was already mature in 1658 or 1659.[14] Thus La Forge and Cordemoy developed and published their occasionalist views at the same time. It is possible that there was communication between these two philosophers.[15] But there is no evidence of any actual meeting.[16] Neither author refers to the other. According to the editor of Clauberg's *Opera*, Clauberg corresponded with La Forge.[17] La Forge refers to Clauberg in the *Traitté*, but not in reference to occasionalism.

Geulincx's occasionalism is in the *Ethica*, the first part of which was published in 1665, and in the *Metaphysica vera*, published posthumously in 1691. There is no evidence of influence in either direction between Geulincx on the one hand and La Forge and Cordemoy on the other. According to Vleeschauwer, occasionalism was present in Geulincx's work in 1652, and his system was fixed by 1664. Although it is possible that Clauberg could have influenced him in the consolidation of his system, Geulincx could not have known about the ideas of La Forge and Cordemoy before he published his own.[18] Influence in the other direction, from Geulincx to La Forge and Cordemoy, is equally untenable: there is no evidence that either of them was familiar with his work.[19]

While there is some question about the influence of the early occasionalists on one another, it is undeniable that at least some of them were sources for the occasionalist system of Nicolas Malebranche (1638–1715). Malebranche cites Cordemoy's *Discernement* in his own *Search after Truth*.[20] He had a copy of La Forge's *Traitté* in his library.[21] Although his occasionalism has affinities to that of Geulincx, there is no evidence that Malebranche read Geulincx's *Ethica* or *Metaphysica vera*. He never refers to Geulincx, and these books were not in his library, although he did have a copy of Geulincx's *Saturnalia seu questiones quodlibeticae*.

When Malebranche devised his theory of causation, he was very much in tune with the times. His achievement is best understood when viewed against a historical background. Thus, before I turn to Malebranche's occasionalism, I shall sketch the occasionalist positions of La Forge, Cordemoy and Geulincx.

❧ LA FORGE ❧

Louis de La Forge was born in La Flèche and lived in Saumur, where he practised medicine. He collaborated with Clerselier on the 1664 edition of Descartes's *Treatise on Man*, adding his own *Remarques*. He has been called the physiologist of Cartesianism.[22] The full title of his treatise reveals his main concern: *Traitté de l'esprit de l'homme, de ses facultez et fonctions, et de son union avec le corps, suivant les principes de René Descartes*. La Forge saw himself as a disciple of Descartes, but he was dissatisfied with Descartes's cursory treatment of the mind–body problem. He sought to complete Descartes's system by providing an account of the nature of the mind–body union. A union, he says, is a relation by which two things are considered as constituting one in a certain manner. The union of mind and body is a relation of mutual dependence between the actions and passions of one substance and the actions and passions of the other. Motions in the body make the mind perceive, and the mind's volitions make the body move.[23]

How do the passions of the mind depend on the actions of the body and vice versa? La Forge says that it is 'as equivocal cause that the mind by its thought constrains the body to move, and that the body in moving gives occasion to the mind to produce some thought'.[24] The term 'equivocal cause' is not a synonym for 'occasional cause'. Equivocal causes are contrasted with univocal causes: a cause is univocal when its effect resembles it, equivocal when its effect does not resemble it. Unlike the term 'occasional cause', the term 'equivocal cause' is applicable to God as well as to creatures. 'For God is no less the creator of all things, and artisans creators of their works, though all these things are only the equivocal causes of these effects.'[25]

Occasional causes are contrasted with real (i.e. efficacious) causes. La Forge uses the term 'occasional cause' in discussing the causation of ideas. There are, he says, two causes of ideas, 'the one principal and real, the other remote and merely occasional'.[26] He goes on to say that bodies

> can be at most only the remote and occasional cause of them, which by means of the union of mind and body constrains the faculty we have of thinking, and determines it to the production of those ideas of which it is the principal and real cause.[27]

An occasional cause, then, is something that determines the real cause to produce the effect. From the passage just quoted, it is evident that La Forge is not a complete occasionalist, for he grants that the mind has causal efficacy with respect to its own ideas. A few pages later, he identifies the mind's causal power with its will: 'Thus we must not doubt that there exists in the mind an active power that produces and forms ideas which it perceives voluntarily, and we must be certain that this power is its will.'[28]

The problem of causation extends beyond the interaction of mind and body. It also includes the action of one body upon another.

> If I said that it is no more difficult to conceive how the mind of man, without being extended, can move the body, and how the body, without being a spiritual thing, can act on the mind, than to conceive how a body has the power to move itself and to communicate its motion to another body, I do not think I would find credence in the minds of many people; yet there is nothing more true.[29]

It is evident that bodies communicate motion to one another, but not so evident how this is accomplished.

> Do our senses teach us how motion can pass from one body into another? Why does only part of it pass, and why cannot a body communicate its motion in the same way as a master communicates his knowledge, without losing anything of what he gives?[30]

For his causal analysis of the communication of motion, La Forge follows Descartes in distinguishing motion, or the transport of a body from one vicinity to another, from the force that transports the body. Motion is 'a mode, which is not distinct from the body to which it belongs, and which can no more pass from one subject into another than the other modes of matter, nor befit a spiritual substance'.[31] Moving force is not in moving bodies. 'If a body cannot move itself, then in my opinion it is evident that it cannot move another. And thus every body in motion must be impelled by a thing entirely distinct from it, which is not body.'[32] Moving force is not in bodies, because the idea of extension is not involved in its concept. 'Thus we have reason to believe that the force which moves is no less really distinct from matter than thought is, and that it pertains as well as it to an incorporeal substance.'[33]

Human minds lack the force to move matter, not because minds are incorporeal, but because matter is already moved by its creator. In creating bodies, God produces them at rest or in motion. No creature, whether spiritual or corporeal, can make a body change its place 'if the creator does not do it himself, for it is he who produces this part of matter in place A'.[34] Not only must God continue to create a body if it is to persevere in being; he must also 'put it himself in place B if he wills that it should be there; for if he put it anywhere else, no force would be capable of dislodging it'.[35]

God is thus 'the first, universal, and total cause' of all motions in the world.[36] Bodies and minds function as 'particular causes of these same motions . . . by determining and obliging the first cause to apply his moving force upon bodies upon which he would not have exercised it without them'.[37] God's moving force is determined by bodies in accordance with the laws of motion, and by minds according to the extent to which bodily movement is subject to the will; 'the force that bodies and minds have of moving consists in that alone.'[38]

Some commentators claim that La Forge was reluctant to embrace occasionalism.[39] Their main textual evidence is the following statement: 'Nevertheless, you ought not to say that God does everything, and that the body and the mind do not really act upon each other.'[40] This statement need not be taken to mean that the mind and the body are causally efficacious with regard to each other, however. La Forge goes on to explain why it is incorrect to say these things: 'For if the body had not had such a motion, the mind would never have had such a thought, and if the mind had not had such a thought, perhaps also the body would never have had such a motion.'[41] This reason is quite compatible with an occasionalist account of the mind–body relation. In occasionalism, God's productive activity is determined by certain creatures being in certain states. The mind would not have a certain thought if the body did not have a certain motion, because God would not have produced that thought were it not for the body's motion. Likewise, the body would not move in a certain way if the mind lacked a certain thought, because God does not give the body that motion unless the mind has that thought. The mind and the body 'really act upon each other' in the sense that each plays a decisive role in what happens to the other.

CORDEMOY

Géraud de Cordemoy was born in Paris in 1626. Originally a lawyer, he served as *lecteur* to the Grand Dauphin. His philosophical works include *Le Discernement du corps et de l'âme* (1666); *Lettre écrite à un sçavant religieux de la Compagnie de Jésus*, dated 5 November 1667 and published in 1668; *Discours physique de la parole* (1668); and two small *Traités de métaphysique*, published in 1691, seven years after his death.

Cordemoy had close ties with the Cartesian school. His *Discours de l'action des corps*, which appears as the second discourse in the *Discernement*, was first published in the 1664 edition of Descartes's *Le Monde*. Cordemoy explicitly defends Descartes in the *Lettre écrite à un sçavant religieux*, the aim of which is 'to show that all that Monsieur

Descartes has written concerning the system of the world, and concerning the soul of beasts, seems to be drawn from the first chapter of Genesis'.[42]

Although he is generally in agreement with Cartesian principles, Cordemoy diverges from Descartes's teaching on atoms and the void. According to Cordemoy, matter is an aggregate of indivisible extended substances. He bases his atomism on the metaphysical principle that substances, as unities, are indivisible. 'I say that each body is an extended substance, and consequently indivisible; and that matter is an assemblage of bodies, and consequently divisible into as many parts as there are bodies.'[43] By his terms, the human body is not really a body but matter. Nevertheless, he follows common usage in referring to it. We call it a *body*, he explains, because the arrangement of its parts leads us to regard it as a single thing.[44]

Like La Forge, Cordemoy sees the problem of mind–body interaction as part of a larger problem of causation, which also includes the action of one body upon another. The following statement in the *Discernement* echoes La Forge's in the *Traitté*: 'Unquestionably, it is no more difficult to conceive the action of minds upon bodies, or that of bodies upon minds, than to conceive the action of bodies upon bodies.'[45] A moving body collides with a body at rest. The first body stops moving; the second one starts. That, says Cordemoy, is all we see. The belief that the first body gives motion to the second is a prejudice, which comes from judging things solely by what we see. A moving body cannot communicate its motion to another body, 'for the state of one body does not pass into another'.[46] 'It is evident that the motion of each is only a manner of being of it, which, not being separable from it, cannot in any way whatsoever pass into the other.'[47]

To cause motion is an action. An action can be continued only by the agent that began it. Thus the cause of motion in bodies is the agent that began to move them. This first mover of bodies is not a body; for if it were, it would have motion of itself. But no body has motion of itself, because a body would still be a body if it lost all its motion, and a thing does not have of itself what it can lose without ceasing to be what it is. Since there are just two sorts of substances, mind and body, and the first mover of bodies is not a body, it must be a mind. This mind continues to move bodies.[48] Thus, when body B, in motion, collides with body C, which is at rest, C is moved after the collision by the same cause that moved B before, namely, by the mind that first set bodies in motion. The collision is 'an occasion for the mind that moved the first to move the second'.[49] The true cause of motion is insensible, and we are often content to stop at what we see. In such cases, we say that the motion of bodies is explained by the fact that other bodies collided with them, 'thus alleging the occasion for the cause'.[50]

The human body is moved by the same mind that moves all other bodies. We observe that when we will to move our body in a certain way, it moves accordingly. But we also know that motions occur in our body in the absence of volitions, and that motions sometimes fail to occur even though we will them. Hence our will is neither necessary nor sufficient for bodily movement. Our weakness shows us that we do not cause motion simply by willing it. This impotence of our will is due to our being dependent on something else for our existence.

> But if we consider that this permanent defect of our mind comes only from its not being through itself, and that if it were through itself, it would lack nothing, so that all that it willed would exist; we would readily apprehend that there is a first Mind, who, being through himself, needs only his will in order to do everything; and that, nothing being lacking to him, as soon as he wills that what is capable of being moved should be in motion, that must necessarily happen.[51]

God exercises his power according to laws he has laid down: laws of collision between bodies; and, between minds and bodies, laws by which certain motions in the body are followed by certain perceptions in the mind, and volitions of the mind are followed by bodily movements.[52] Although bodies do not really cause motion, one body can be said to act upon another, 'when on its occasion, this other body begins to be arranged or moved otherwise than it was previously'.[53] A body can be said to act upon a mind if this body, or a mode of it, is perceived by the mind, 'so that on its occasion, this mind has thoughts that it did not have previously'.[54] A mind can be said to act on a body if, as soon as the mind wills that the body should be moved in a certain direction, the body is so moved. One can say that our mind acts on our body, even though

> it is not really our mind that causes the movement . . . . And, as one is obliged to acknowledge that the collision of two bodies is an occasion for the power that moves the first to move the second, one should have no difficulty in conceiving that our will is an occasion for the power that already moves a body to direct its movement in a certain direction corresponding to this thought.[55]

In the *Discernement*, Cordemoy deprives bodies of all causal efficacy, and human minds of the power to move bodies. In the *Discours physique de la parole*, he adds that minds do not cause any of their own perceptions: 'It is as impossible for our souls to have new perceptions without God, as it is impossible for bodies to have new motions without him.'[56] Thus Cordemoy is a more complete occasionalist than La Forge, who allowed the mind the power to produce its own ideas.

Does the mind have any causal efficacy with respect to its volitions? Cordemoy takes up this question in the second *Traité de métaphysique*, 'That God does everything real in our actions, without depriving us of our liberty'. Bodies, he says, are capable of being acted upon, but not of acting. Minds are capable of both passions and actions. Their perceptions are their passions; their volitions are their actions. God causes the actions of minds, just as he causes their passions.

> And, as it cannot be said that the passions of minds are his passions, but only that they are the passions of minds, it cannot be said that the actions of minds are his actions, but only that they are the actions of minds.[57]

When the mind wills, God causes the volition, but it is still the mind that wills.

God has made all things for himself. Bodies do not know this end, but minds do and thus need action to pursue it. God gives minds an unceasing desire for this end, and an inclination to choose a means to it. When presented with several alternatives, minds can resolve not to choose, or they can deliberate and then decide on one. This resolution or this decision 'is an action, which in truth would not be in them without God, but which is their action, and not God's'.[58] Because it is theirs, they can be held responsible for it. God produces all that is real in the willing situation, but 'if the minds have chosen badly, it is a fault of which they alone are guilty. God has made . . . what suffices to act well, and the minds have not used the power that he put into them.'[59]

❧ GEULINCX ❧

Arnold Geulincx was born in Antwerp. He was a professor of philosophy at the University of Louvain from 1646 until 1658, when he was dismissed for unspecified reasons.[60] He moved from Belgium to the Netherlands and converted to Calvinism. With some difficulty, he obtained a position at the university in Leyden, first as reader, then as *professor extraordinarius*. He died of the plague in 1669, at the age of 45. The first complete edition of the *Ethica* appeared in 1675. Geulincx's occasionalist views are found in this work, as well as in the *Metaphysica vera*, published in 1691.

Geulincx's philosophy is a synthesis of Cartesianism and Jansenism. Cartesian elements include the *cogito*, the dualism and the inertness of matter. From Jansenism comes the theme of human impotence. Occasionalism provides an analysis of human impotence in terms compatible with Cartesian metaphysics. Geulincx's treatment of occasionalism is less systematic than that of either La Forge or Cordemoy. In particular, he pays little attention to the problem of interaction between bodies. As a moral philosopher, he is concerned more with the ethical implications of occasionalism than with the elaboration of it as a causal theory.

Geulincx argues against the causal efficacy of created things, using a principle which he says is evident in itself: *Quod nescis quomodo fiat, id non facis* – if you do not know how it is done, you do not do it. He applies this principle to bodies as well as to minds. Material objects cannot cause sentiments in minds, because they are *res brutae*, brute things, with no thought of any kind. Lacking knowledge, they cannot know how sentiments are produced. Minds do not cause sentiments in themselves, since they, too, are ignorant of how it is done. Sentiments are produced in the mind by a thinking being, one that has the knowledge needed to make them. This being acts through the mediation of the human body, giving the mind a diversity of sentiments as the body is diversely affected.[61]

The mind cannot cause movement in the body, not even so-called voluntary movement, for the mind does not know how it is accomplished. Most people are entirely ignorant of the nerves and pathways through which motions are communicated from the brain to the limbs. Those who learn anatomy and physiology were able to move their limbs before they gained such knowledge, and they move them no better afterwards. This shows that it is not by one's own knowledge that one's limbs are moved. The author of my bodily movement, then, is a being other than myself.[62] I want my body to move in a certain manner, as in talking or walking; 'thereupon certain parts of my body are moved, not in fact by me, but by the mover'.[63] 'Certainly, it is never done, strictly speaking, because I will, but because the mover wills.'[64]

In the Annotations to the *Ethica*, Geulincx compares the mind and the body to two clocks:

> My will does not move the mover to move my limbs; but the one who has imparted motion to matter and has laid down the laws to it, the same one has formed my will and thus has closely united these very dissimilar things (the motion of matter and the determination of my will), so that, when my will wishes, motion of the desired kind is present, and, on the contrary, when the motion is present, the will has willed it, without any causality or influx from one to the other. Just as with two

clocks that agree with each other and with the daily course of the sun: when one sounds and indicates the hours to us, the other sounds in the same way and indicates the same number of hours to us; not because there is any causality from one to the other, but because of the mere dependence, in which both are constructed by the same art and by similar activity.[65]

The analogy of two clocks has an obvious affinity to the analogy later used by Leibniz.[66] Leibniz uses the analogy to differentiate three systems: interactionism, occasionalism and his own system of pre-established harmony. Geulincx, by contrast, has only two alternatives in mind: interactionism and occasionalism. In Leibniz's version of occasionalism, the craftsman continually adjusts the clocks to keep them in agreement. In Geulincx's version, the clockmaker ensures agreement by the way in which he constructs the clocks. In this respect, the occasionalism of Geulincx is like the pre-established harmony of Leibniz.

Geulincx's occasionalism is unlike Leibniz's system in that God acts directly on the mind and the body, producing changes in one corresponding to the changes he produces in the other. This aspect is not brought out in the analogy of the two clocks. It is illustrated by another analogy, which Geulincx presents just before his clock analogy. A baby in a cradle wants to be rocked. If the cradle rocks, it does so not because the baby wills it, but because his mother or nurse rocks it. Just as the cradle rocks in accordance with the baby's wish, though it is rocked by someone else, so, too, our limbs move in accordance with our will, but the movement is caused by a will other than our own.

Having made the point that God is the one who produces voluntary motion, Geulincx introduces the analogy of the clocks to illustrate a further aspect of occasionalism, namely, the regularity of God's action. The two clocks stay in agreement, even though there is no causal connection between them, because their maker acts according to general laws. Geulincx says in the *Ethica* that God produces his effects 'according to laws most freely established by him and depending solely on his decision'.[67] He adds that if my tongue moves at the command of my will, but the earth does not tremble at my command, the sole difference is that God decided that the first movement should occur when I will it, but not the second. In the annotation to this passage, he evokes the clock metaphor: God has willed and arranged that when the clock of my will sounds, the clock of my tongue sounds also, whereas he has not arranged a similar agreement between the clock of my will and the clock of the earth.[68]

The human condition consists in being an embodied mind, that is, a mind united to a body in such a way that it seems to act on and to be acted on by it.[69] Nevertheless, we have no more causal efficacy with respect to our own bodily movements than we have with respect to the rising and setting of the stars or the ebb and flow of the sea. 'Thus, I am a mere spectator of this machinery. I make nothing in it, I amend nothing in it; I neither construct nor destroy anything. All that is the work of a certain other.'[70] 'I can, in this world, do nothing outside myself. . . . I merely look on this world.'[71] I am not, however, a mere spectator of my own volitions. To will or not to will is my deed. I have the power to conform my will to Reason or to refuse to do so. The greatest freedom is achieved by willing what Reason prescribes and not willing what it prohibits.[72]

❧❧ MALEBRANCHE ❧❧

The occasionalist movement culminates in the work of Nicolas Malebranche, a priest of the congregation of the Oratory. Although he accepted the Cartesian ontology of substance and mode, mind and matter, Malebranche did not hesitate to depart from Descartes's teaching when reason or experience demanded it. His disagreement with Descartes is most explicit on the questions of the nature of ideas and the laws of motion.

Like La Forge, Malebranche was dissatisfied with Descartes's refusal to explicate the union of mind and body. One cannot dismiss the question simply by saying that experience plainly shows that the body and the mind act on each other. Experience teaches that the mind feels pain when the body is injured, but not that the body has any power to act upon the mind.[73] It is not enough to say that the body and the mind interact by virtue of their union. 'The word "union" explains nothing. It is itself in need of explanation.'[74] Moreover, it cannot be part of the explanation that the mind and the body become capable of the same sorts of modifications.

> Each substance remains what it is, and as the soul is incapable
> of extension and movement, so the body is incapable of
> sensation and inclinations. The only alliance of mind and body
> known to us consists in a natural and mutual correspondence
> of the soul's thoughts with the brain traces, and of the soul's
> emotions with the movements of the animal spirits.[75]

Malebranche's arguments for occasionalism are found in a number of his writings, especially *The Search after Truth*, first published in 1674–5 (the Elucidations were added in the third edition of 1677–8); *Méditations chrétiennes et métaphysiques* (1683); and *Dialogues on*

Metaphysics and on Religion (1688). He considers all cases of alleged causal action by created things: bodies acting on bodies; bodies acting on minds; minds acting on bodies; minds acting on themselves to produce sentiments, ideas and volitions. He rejects each of them in turn.

Malebranche gives two types of argument against the causal efficacy of bodies. The first proceeds from the premise that material substance is passive by nature. The only kinds of properties that pertain to extension are figure and motion. As extended things, bodies have the passive faculty of receiving such modes, but they lack the active faculty of producing them. 'A mountain, a house, a rock, a grain of sand, in short, the tiniest or largest body conceivable does not have the power to move itself.'[76] Moreover, no body has the power to produce ideas or sentiments in a mind. 'Do you think that a figure can produce an idea, and a local movement an agreeable or disagreeable sentiment?'[77]

The second type of argument has the form of *reductio ad absurdum*. Suppose that bodies had a power to act or to bring about change. The exercise of this power would involve some state of affairs that is incompatible with the Cartesian ontology. Malebranche uses this form of argument against the human body as cause of sensations in the mind, and also against one body as cause of another body's motion. Suppose that the human body acquired a power to act on the mind by virtue of its union with the mind. This power would have to be either a substance or a mode. If it is a substance, then the mind is acted on by this substance and not by the body. If the power is a mode, then there is a mode of extension which is neither figure nor motion. But this is impossible. Consequently, the body can have no power of acting on the mind.[78] Similarly, suppose that bodies in motion have moving force in themselves and that they communicate this force to bodies they encounter. This would involve the transference of a mode from one substance to another, which is impossible. 'If the moving force belonged to the bodies in motion, it would be a *mode* of their substance; and it is a contradiction that *modes* go from substance to substance.'[79] 'If it is a mode, it is a contradiction that it passes from one body into another, since the mode is only the substance in such and such a manner.'[80]

Malebranche gives a further reason why bodies could not communicate moving force even if they had it: 'For the bodies that collide communicate their motion with a regularity, a promptitude, a proportion worthy of an infinite wisdom.'[81] In some passages, he suggests that bodies would need knowledge in order to exercise their alleged power in a manner appropriate to the circumstances:

For it is evident that a wisdom, and an infinite wisdom, is necessary in order to regulate the communication of motions with the precision, the proportion, and the uniformity that we see. Since a body cannot know the infinite bodies that it meets at every turn, it is obvious that even if one supposes some knowledge in it, it could not itself have brought about, in the instant of collision, the distribution of the moving force that transports it.[82]

But suppose that this body really had the force to move itself. In what direction will it go? At what degree of speed will it move itself? . . . I even grant that this body has enough freedom and knowledge to determine its movement and the degree of its speed: I grant that it is master of itself. But take care, . . . for, supposing that this body finds itself surrounded by an infinity of others, what will become of it when it encounters one of which it knows neither the solidity nor the size?[83]

Any similarity here between Malebranche and Geulincx is only superficial. For Geulincx, the mere fact that bodies lack knowledge is sufficient to deprive them of causal efficacy. Malebranche's point is not that bodies need knowledge in order to produce motion *per se*, but that they need it in order to produce motion with the regularity that it actually exhibits. No explanation of this regularity can be found in the nature of bodies, even if one supposes them to have moving force.

Moving force, the power to move bodies, lies not in bodies but in their creator. Like La Forge, Malebranche defends this position by appeal to the Cartesian doctrine of continuous creation and the principle that to create a body is to create it at rest or in motion.

Creation does not pass: the conservation of creatures is on the part of God simply a continued creation, simply the same volition which subsists and operates unceasingly. Now, God cannot conceive, nor consequently will, that a body be nowhere or that it not have certain relations of distance with other bodies. Hence, God cannot will that this chair exist and, by his volition, create or conserve it without His placing it here or there or elsewhere. Hence, it is a contradiction that one body be able to move another.[84]

When God creates individual substances, he wills that they exist in certain manners, that is, he wills that they have certain modes. Rest consists in an unchanging relation of distance to other bodies; motion, in a changing relation of distance. A body must have one or the other of these modes. So long as God creates a body in motion, nothing can bring that body to rest; so long as he creates it at rest, nothing can set it in motion.

> No power can transport it where God does not transport it, nor fix or stop it where God does not stop it, unless it is because God accommodates the efficacy of His action to the inefficacious action of his creatures.[85]

Finite minds do not have the power to move bodies. Like Cordemoy, Malebranche denies causal efficacy to created minds on the ground that there is no necessary connection between their volitions and the occurrence of what is willed. A true (i.e. efficacious) cause is 'one such that the mind perceives a necessary connection between it and its effect'.[86] There is such a relation between God's will and its effects, for it follows from the idea of God as an omnipotent being that whatever he wills necessarily takes place. It is a contradiction that God wills my arm to be moved and it remains motionless. There is no necessary connection, however, between my will and the movement of my arm; no contradiction is involved in the statement that I will to move my arm but it does not move. Thus I am not the true cause of the movement.[87]

Minds are equally impotent with regard to their own sentiments, and for the same reason: there is no necessary connection between the mind's volition to have a certain sentiment and its having that sentiment. This is shown by the fact that we often feel otherwise than we wish to feel. 'But it is not my soul either that produces in itself the sensation of pain that afflicts it, for it feels the pain in spite of itself.'[88]

Malebranche also denies causal efficacy to minds on the ground that they lack the knowledge required to produce their alleged effects. He argues in this way against the mind as cause of ideas and of bodily movements. In both contexts, the argument is based on the Cartesian principle that the mind can will only what it knows, or, as Descartes puts it, 'we cannot will anything without understanding what we will'.[89] The structure of the argument is as follows. If the mind produces X, then it does so by willing that X exist. In order to will that X exist, the mind must know what X is. But the mind does not know what X is. Hence the mind cannot produce X. With regard to ideas, Malebranche writes: 'I deny that my will produces my ideas in me, for I do not see even how it could produce them, because my will, which is unable to act or will without knowledge, presupposes my ideas and does not produce them.'[90] This argument figures in the case for the vision in God. When we wish to think of some object, the idea of that object becomes present to the mind. The mind cannot have produced the idea, for in order to form the idea of an object, one must already have an idea of it, an idea which does not depend on the will.[91]

When the knowledge argument is applied against the mind as cause of bodily movement, the premise needs more elaboration. I will to move my arm and my arm moves. I know what I will in the sense that I have the idea of my arm moving. But this idea does not contain sufficient information to enable me to will the movement into existence. My arm moves by a complex physiological process. Animal spirits pass through certain nerve ducts toward muscles in the arm, distending and contracting them, thereby moving the arm in a particular way. In order to produce the motion by an act of will, it is not enough for me to will that the end result occur. I must will the physiological process in all its detail. And in order to will the process, I must know what it is. Yet people who do not know that they have animal spirits, nerves and muscles move their limbs perfectly well, often better than those most learned in anatomy. This observation appears in *The Search after Truth* and in the *Méditations chrétiennes et métaphysiques*. In the latter, the Word goes on to ask: 'Can one do, can one even will, what one does not know how to do?'[92] In the *Search*, Malebranche goes on to conclude:

> Therefore, men will to move their arms, and only God is able and knows how to move them. If a man cannot turn a tower upside down, at least he knows what must be done to do so; but there is no man who knows what must be done to move one of his fingers by means of animal spirits.[93]

Here Malebranche is close to Geulincx. Geulincx's axiom was: 'If you do not know how it is done, you do not do it.' Malebranche, too, speaks of knowing how something is done, and he equates this with knowing how to do it. In Malebranche, however, the principle clearly hinges on the Cartesian principle that knowing is a necessary condition of willing, and as such it applies exclusively to beings having a faculty of will. To be sure, Malebranche applies the principle to bodies, as we saw earlier; but he does so only on the supposition that bodies are endowed with something akin to will.

Does the mind have causal efficacy with respect to its volitions? Like Cordemoy, Malebranche insists that God produces all that is real in the willing situation. Will is the natural impression that carries us toward the good in general.[94] Malebranche compares the mind's inclinations to the motions of bodies. Like corporeal motion, an inclination of the mind requires a force to produce it; and like the moving force of bodies, the 'willing force' of souls is the action of God's will.[95] God creates us with an inclination toward whatever appears good to us, or with an invincible desire to be happy. He also gives us all our agreeable and disagreeable perceptions. When we perceive a real or apparent good, we have a natural inclination toward it, and God produces this particular inclination in us. As the creator of minds, God is the true cause of all their modes, both perceptions and inclinations. The mind's only power is that of giving or suspending consent to its inclinations. In doing so, it produces no new mode in itself. 'I have always maintained that the soul was active; but that its acts produce nothing material, or bring about by themselves, by their own efficacy, no new modalities, no material change, either in the body or in itself.'[96] In suspending consent, we judge that a particular good will not make us truly happy. Herein lies our freedom.

> The principle of our freedom is that as we are made for God and are joined to Him, we can always think of the true good or of goods other than those of which we are actually thinking – we can always withhold our consent and seriously examine whether the good we are enjoying is or is not the true good.[97]

ᨆ GENERAL LAWS ᨆ

Occasionalism has both a positive and a negative side. The negative side is the denial of causal efficacy to created things. The positive side is the attribution of causal efficacy to God. It is tempting to dismiss the positive side as philosophically uninteresting. As true cause, God produces effects by willing them into existence, a process that is at bottom incomprehensible, as Malebranche himself admits:

> The saints, who see the divine essence, apparently know this relation, the efficacious omnipotence of the creator's volitions. For our part, although we believe it by faith, although we are persuaded of it by reason, the necessary connection of the act with its effect is beyond our comprehension; and in this sense we have no clear idea of his power.[98]

The positive side of occasionalism has more to it, however. God produces effects, but he does so according to general laws, on the occasion of certain creatures being in certain states. All of the occasionalists refer to general laws of divine causation, but Malebranche's exposition of the lawlike manner of God's action is by far the most thorough.

God is a general cause as well as a true cause. He is a true cause, in that his will is efficacious by itself: there is a necessary connection between a divine volition and its object. God is a general cause, in that he produces effects by general volitions rather than by particular volitions. Malebranche distinguishes between general and particular volitions as follows:

> I say that God acts by general volitions, when he acts according

to the general laws that he has established. . . . I say, on the contrary, that God acts by particular volitions, when the efficacy of his will is not determined by some general law to produce some effect.[99]

A general volition is a volition that effects of type E occur whenever conditions of type C are present. Examples of general volitions are the volition that minds feel pain whenever the bodies to which they are joined are disturbed in certain ways, and the volition that whenever bodies collide, motion is distributed in certain proportions according to their mass, speed and direction. A particular volition, by contrast, is simply a volition that a particular effect occur, for instance that a certain mind feel pain, or that a body move in a certain way, irrespective of the circumstances.

A true cause can act either by general volitions or by particular volitions. That God is a true cause follows from his omnipotence. That he is a general cause follows from his wisdom and immutability. It shows more wisdom to achieve a variety of effects by following a set of laws selected in advance than to achieve the same variety by introducing a separate volition for each effect. Moreover, the former way of acting bears the character of immutability, since it is uniform and constant, whereas the latter requires changes of conduct at every turn.[100] Aside from the initial creation of the world, God acts by particular volitions only when such conduct expresses his goodness or justice better than action by general volitions expresses his wisdom and immutability. This happens 'only on certain occasions that are entirely unknown to us'.[101]

God's general laws are in principle discoverable, at least in rough outline. They fall into two main categories: laws of nature and laws of grace. The laws of nature are known through reason and experience. They include (1) laws of the communication of motion, according to which motions are produced in animate and inanimate bodies; (2) laws of the union of soul and body, for the production of voluntary movements in human bodies and of sentiments in human minds; and (3) laws of the union of soul with God or universal Reason, by which we perceive ideas in God. The laws of grace are learned from Scripture. They include (4) laws giving angels power over bodies, for the distribution of temporal goods and ills; and (5) laws giving Jesus Christ power over minds and bodies, for the distribution of temporal and eternal goods.[102]

Each of the five sets of laws has a specific type of occasional cause associated with it. An occasional cause is a state of affairs that determines what particular effect will be brought about in a given case. The desires of Jesus and the angels are occasional causes in the realm of grace: God moves bodies as the angels wish, and he gives sentiments of grace to people as Jesus wishes. In the realm of nature, occasional causes are discoverable by examining the circumstances under which the effects take place and noting the regularities.

> God never moves bodies unless they are struck; and when they are struck, he always moves them. The soul never feels the pain of a prick unless the body is pricked, or unless there occurs in the brain the same disturbance as if the body were pricked; and God always makes the soul feel the pain of a prick when the body is pricked, or when there occurs in the brain the same disturbance as if the body were pricked. God never moves my arm, except when I have the volition to move it; and God never fails to move it, when I have the volition that it move.[103]

The impact of bodies is the occasional cause that determines the efficacy of the laws of motion. Motions in the human body and volitions in the mind are the occasional causes determining the efficacy of the laws of the union of soul and body. As for the laws of the union of soul with God, the occasional cause is the soul's desire or attention. 'The soul's desire is a natural prayer that is always fulfilled, for it is a natural law that ideas are all the more present to the mind as the will more fervently desires them.'[104]

There is some overlap in the scope of application of the three sets of natural laws. The mind has both pure and sensible perceptions of ideas in God. It has pure perceptions on the occasion of its attention, according to the laws of the union of soul with God. It has sensible perceptions on the occasion of brain traces of sensible objects, according to the laws of soul–body union.[105] In some situations one set of laws takes precedence; in other situations, another set. For example, when we are distracted from our study of geometry by a loud noise, our minds are modified according to the laws of soul–body union. Were the distraction not present, the desired perceptions would be given to us according to the laws of the union of soul with universal Reason.

Similarly, our bodies have both voluntary and involuntary motions. The former are produced according to the laws of soul–body union; the latter, according to the laws of the communication of motion. God moves my arm when and only when I wish it to move, provided that there is not some countervailing circumstance that determines him to act otherwise according to the laws of motion. For instance, the sight of an impending fall may set off a chain of physiological events leading to the involuntary raising of an arm. Such mechanical actions often cannot be prevented by an act of will, but sometimes they can. Indeed, for Malebranche, one of the strongest indications of the absence of soul in animals is their inability to halt the mechanical operations of their bodies. Dogs cry out when they are injured. This shows, Malebranche says, not that they have souls but that they lack them;

> for a cry is a necessary effect of their machine's construction. When a man in full health fails to cry out when he is injured, it is a sign that his soul is resisting the operation of its machine. If he had no soul and if his body were in the right state, certainly he would always cry when injured. When our arm is to be bled, we all feel it withdraw mechanically when it is pricked – unless the soul is there to resist.[106]

Malebranche admits, then, that sometimes my arm moves without my willing it to move. Yet elsewhere he says that God moves my arm whenever I will it, and only when I will it. There is no contradiction between these two claims. One is a statement of observation; the other is a simplified description of a general volition of God. We do not actually observe that our arms move when and only when we will them to move. We do, however, observe that there is an association between our volitions and the movement of our limbs; and on the basis of this association, we infer that this is one of the laws according to which motion is produced in human beings. The fact that my arm sometimes moves in the absence of any volition on my part shows that this law is not the only one by which such motion is produced. Sometimes another type of occasional cause determines the efficacy of another of God's general volitions to produce the same sort of effect.

In addition to the laws of nature, God must also have higher-order general volitions for determining which set of laws is operative when two sets overlap in scope. Malebranche does not explicitly assert that God has such higher-order volitions, but it is implicit in his discussion of the interrelations among the different sets of natural laws. 'Thus,' he writes in the Second Elucidation of the *Search*,

> provided that our capacity for thought or our understanding is not taken up by the confused sensations we receive upon occasion of some bodily event, whenever we desire to think about some object the idea of that object is present to us; and as experience teaches us, this idea is clearer and more immediate as our desire is stronger or our attention more vivid and as the confused sensations we receive through the body are weaker and less perceptible.[107]

When attention and bodily sensations compete as occasions for the production of perceptions in the mind, the winner is the one with greater relative strength. If attention is strong and sensation is weak, then the perceptions are produced according to the laws of the union of soul with universal Reason. If attention is weak and sensation is strong, then God gives the mind perceptions according to the laws of the union of soul and body.

One of the laws of soul–body union is 'that all the soul's inclinations, even those it has for goods that are unrelated to the body, are accompanied by disturbances in the animal spirits that make these inclinations sensible'.[108] The soul can alter the operation of the body 'only when it has the power of vividly imagining another object whose open traces in the brain make the animal spirits take another course'.[109] Thus, when there is competition between physiological conditions and the soul's inclinations as possible occasional causes of certain classes of bodily motions, the strength of the soul's sentiment of the desired good determines whether the effect happens according to the laws of motion or according to those of soul–body union.

Does occasionalism have any merit as a philosophy of science? So long as one focuses exclusively on the assignment of causal power to God, it seems that occasionalism cuts off any serious attempt at causal explanation. For any particular effect E, the answer to the question 'What produced E?' is always the same, namely God. But there is more to causal explanation than citing the productive cause – even for an occasionalist. A causal explanation of a particular effect must show why this effect occurred rather than some other. Such an explanation has not been provided if the explanans works equally well for anything else that might have happened instead. Suppose one wants to know why linen dries when it is placed near the fire.

> I shall not be a philosopher [Malebranche says] if I answer that God wills it; for one knows well enough that all that happens, happens because God wills it. One does not ask for the general cause, but for the particular cause of a particular effect. I ought therefore to say that the small parts of the fire or of the agitated wood, hitting against the linen, communicate their motion to the parts of water on it, and detach them from the linen; and then I shall have given the particular cause of a particular effect.[110]

Instead of closing the door to scientific investigation of the causes of natural events, occasionalism clarifies the topic of inquiry; one is looking not for causal powers, but for conditions that determine the efficacy of natural laws.

Since all natural effects are produced by general volitions of God, and since the general volitions that constitute the laws of nature are discoverable by reason and experience, every part of the natural world is in principle amenable to scientific inquiry. Malebranche offers little hope for a science of mind; for he insists that we know our own minds only through our inner feeling of what takes place in us, and other minds only by analogy with our own.[111] He does, however, lay the foundation for an empirical science of human behaviour. According to Cartesian doctrine, animal behaviour is ultimately explainable by the laws of motion alone, whereas human behaviour is not. For Malebranche, human behaviour is explainable by a judicious combination of the laws of motion with those of soul–body union.

There are affinities between the mechanisms of animal and human behaviour. In both animals and humans, there is a natural connection between brain traces and the motion of the animal spirits. Different patterns of behaviour are associated with different brain traces. There are two kinds of brain traces: natural and acquired. Natural traces are common to all members of a species and can never be completely destroyed. Acquired traces are gradually lost unless they are reinforced by continual application of the conditions that originally gave rise to them. When acquired traces incline an individual toward behaviour contrary to that which is characteristic of its species, the individual tends to revert to its natural behaviour. The natural traces

> have, so to speak, secret alliances with other parts of the body, for all the organs of our machine help maintain themselves in their natural state. All parts of our bodies mutually contribute to all the things necessary for this conservation, or for the restoration of natural traces. And so they cannot be completely erased, and they begin to revive just when one believes they have been destroyed.[112]

In addition to the natural connection between brain traces and motions of animal spirits, there are also, in human beings, natural connections between these bodily occurrences and mental states. Malebranche gives the following example. When we see a wounded person, animal spirits flow into the part of our body corresponding to the injured part in the other person. This bodily sympathy is the occasional cause of a feeling of compassion, which excites us to help the other person. The same sort of process gives rise to feelings of compassion towards animals.[113] Although Malebranche wholeheartedly accepts the Cartesian beast–machine doctrine, he considers the human tendency to socialize with animals as part of the institution of nature, and he seeks to explain it in terms of the same laws as other human behaviours. Brain traces in the master, when he sees his dog wagging its tail, lead him to feel that his dog knows and loves him. On the occasion of these traces, animal spirits take their course into his arm to pat his dog and to share food with it.

Man would not be precisely as he is, the doleful looks and

pleasing movements of the dog would not naturally produce any sentiment in the soul of man, or any motion in the course of his animal spirits, if God had not willed to establish a liaison between man and dog.[114]

According to Malebranche, all human behaviour is motivated by pleasure.

One can love only that which pleases. . . . It is thus certain that all men, righteous or unrighteous, love pleasure taken in general, or will to be happy; and that it is the sole motive that determines them to do generally all that they do.[115]

All passions, including those springing from the perception of some evil, are accompanied by 'a certain sensation of joy, or rather of inner delight, that fixes the soul in its passion'.[116] Malebranche defines the passions of the soul as 'impressions from the Author of nature that incline us toward loving our body and all that might be of use in its preservation'.[117] They are interconnected, by the institution of nature, with bodily states. 'The passions are movements of the soul that accompany those of the spirits and the blood, and that produce in the body, by the construction of the machine, all the dispositions necessary to sustain the cause that gave birth to them.'[118] One cannot rise above one's passions simply by resolving not to be affected by the things that occasion them, as the Stoics advise. It is ridiculous to tell people not to be upset at the death of a family member or delighted at success in business, 'for we are tied to our country, our goods, our parents, and so on, by a natural union that does not now depend on our will'.[119] Given the way the mind–body union is set up, the only effective way to counter the passions is to substitute other pleasures for theirs. 'The false delight of our passions, which makes us slaves to sensible goods, must be overcome by joy of mind and the delight of grace.'[120] No love is disinterested, not even the love of God. We love God because he makes us solidly happy. Grace enables us not merely to know but to feel that God is our good. 'For the grace of Jesus Christ, by which one resists disorderly pleasures, is itself a holy pleasure; it is the hope and foretaste of supreme pleasure.'[121]

❧ LEIBNIZ'S OBJECTION ❧

Seventeenth-century works against occasionalism include *Doutes sur le système physique des causes occasionnelles* (1686) by Bernard le Bovier de Fontenelle; and Antoine Arnauld's *Dissertation sur les miracles de l'ancienne loi*, and his *Réflexions philosophiques et théologiques sur le nouveau système de la nature et de la grace*, both published in 1685. The main objections in these works are that the manner of acting ascribed to God is unworthy of him; that causal efficacy is no less intelligible in created things than in God; and that creatures need causal power in order to determine the efficacy of God's general volitions. The most well-known, though not necessarily the most devastating, objection to occasionalism is that it involves a perpetual miracle. This is Leibniz's objection. I shall pass over the objections of Fontenelle and Arnauld here and consider only Leibniz's.[122]

Leibniz agrees with the occasionalists that interactionism involves the transference of modes from one substance to another and consequently must be rejected as inconceivable. 'Speaking with metaphysical rigor, *no created substance exerts a metaphysical action or influence upon another*. For . . . it cannot be explained how anything can pass over from one thing into the substance of another.'[123] Occasionalism, too, he finds unsatisfactory.

> But problems are not solved merely by making use of a general
> cause and calling in what is called the *deus ex machina*. To do
> this without offering any other explanation drawn from the
> order of secondary causes is, properly speaking, to have
> recourse to miracle.[124]

When reminded that the God of the occasionalists produces his effects according to general laws, Leibniz responds that, even so, 'they would not cease being miracles, if we take this term, not in the popular sense of a rare and wonderful thing, but in the philosophical sense of that which exceeds the powers of created beings'.[125]

> I admit that the authors of occasional causes may be able to give
> another definition of the term, but it seems that according to
> usage a miracle differs intrinsically and through the substance of
> the act from a common action, and not by an external accident
> of frequent repetition, and that strictly speaking God performs
> a miracle whenever he does something that exceeds the forces
> which he has given to creatures and maintains in them.[126]

Leibniz presents occasionalism as though its proponents believed that miracles were rare events, and as though their only defence against the charge of invoking miracles is that the effects occur frequently. This is an oversimplification of the occasionalist position. In the *Réponse aux Réflexions philosophiques et théologiques de Mr. Arnauld sur le Traité de la nature et de la grace* (1686), Malebranche observes that the term 'miracle' is equivocal. In its most common usage, it means 'a *marvel* which surprises us, and which we admire because of its novelty'. In its precise philosophical sense, it means 'all effects which are not *natural*, or which are not results of natural laws'.[127] Natural laws are God's general volitions. 'Thus, whether an effect is common or rare, if God does not produce it according to his general laws, which are the natural laws, it is a true miracle.'[128] In other words, a miracle in the second sense is something produced by a particular rather than a general volition of God. Occasionalism does not invoke miracles in either of these senses to explain ordinary events. God could, Malebranche says, produce the most common effects by particular volitions, in which case they would be miracles in the second sense. But God does not do so. Instead, he produces them according to general laws. Even marvels are produced in this manner, according to laws giving angels power over bodies; they are miracles in the first sense but not in the second.[129]

In Malebranche's second or philosophical sense, the miraculous is opposed to the natural. The same is true of Leibniz's philosophical sense. The two philosophers disagree, however, on what counts as being natural. According to Malebranche, natural effects are those that are produced in accordance with natural laws. Leibniz finds this characterization inadequate: 'It is not enough to say that God has made a general law, for besides the decree there is also necessary a natural means of carrying it out.'[130] Malebranche could reply that there is indeed a natural means of carrying it out: the efficacy of the natural laws is determined by occasional causes. The latter can and should be cited as the natural and particular causes of the effects in question. This answer will not satisfy Leibniz. When he says that there must be a natural means of executing the decree, he means that 'all that happens must also be explained through the nature which God gives to things'.[131] For Leibniz, the natural is that which pertains to the nature of created things, and the nature of created things is identified with their power to act.[132] For Malebranche, by contrast, natural laws are simply laws according to which events are regularly produced. They can be specified without ascribing natures to individual things and without attributing metaphysical powers to them. In this respect, Malebranche's view of natural laws is closer to the modern conception than Leibniz's is.

Does Leibniz misrepresent the occasionalist hypothesis? In some passages, he characterizes God's action in occasionalism as interference or meddling in the natural course of events. In the Postscript of a Letter to Basnage de Beauval (3/13 January 1696), where he introduces the analogy of two clocks to differentiate interactionism, occasionalism and pre-established harmony, he says that the system of occasional causes is like 'making two clocks, even poor ones, agree' by turning them over to a skilled artisan 'who adjusts them and constantly sets them in agreement'.[133] Similarly, in his response to Bayle's criticisms of the New System (1698), he says that the occasionalists explain the correspondence between soul and body 'as if a man were charged with constantly synchronizing two bad clocks which are in themselves incapable of agreeing'.[134] It seems that the workman's action is needed, not to make the clocks run *per se*, but to keep them running in agreement. Without constant adjustments, the clocks would still run, albeit badly. Analogously, were it not for God's continual meddling, the mind and the body would each follow a different course. In the correspondence with Arnauld, Leibniz presents the system of occasional causes 'as though God on the occasion of occurrences in the body aroused thoughts in the soul, which might change the course that the soul would have taken of itself without that'.[135]

> For it introduces a sort of continual miracle, as though God
> were constantly changing the laws of bodies, on the occasion
> of the thoughts of minds, or changing the regular course of the
> thoughts of the soul by arousing in it other thoughts, on the
> occasion of the movements of bodies.[136]

In so far as he suggests that creatures would act on their own if God did not intervene, Leibniz misrepresents occasionalism. True, Malebranche does say that the human body would behave in certain ways – for instance, it would cry out whenever it was injured – if the soul did not resist. If the body behaves in one way when the soul resists and in another way when such resistance is absent, this is not because the body moves itself by one set of laws whereas God moves it by another set. God moves the body in both cases: in the one case, according to the laws of motion alone; in the other, by the laws of the union of soul and body.

Leibniz claims that in occasionalism God changes the laws of bodies on the occasion of the thoughts of minds. A more accurate statement of the occasionalist position is this: God acts on the body solely according to the laws of motion, except when the mind has certain kinds of thoughts, in which case he acts by the laws of soul-body union. To Leibniz, the suspension of one set of laws in favour of another set is a miracle. Thus, in addition to the perpetual miracle of God's direct action on creatures, there is a further perpetual miracle, having to do with the manner of God's action. The decision to act according to one set of laws rather than another set is not grounded in the nature of individual things; therefore, by Leibniz's definition, it is miraculous. By Malebranche's definition, however, it is not miraculous but natural, since there are laws for which set of laws applies in a given situation, and these higher-order laws are in principle discoverable, just as are the laws of motion and those of soul-body union.

❧ NOTES ❧

The following abbreviations are used in the notes:

AT   C. Adam and P. Tannery (eds) *Oeuvres de Descartes* [10.1]

CSM   J. Cottingham, R. Stoothoff and D. Murdoch (trans.) *The Philosophical Writings of Descartes* [10.2]

GP   C. I. Gerhardt (ed.) *Die philosophischen Schriften von Gottfried Wilhelm Leibniz* [10.55]

LO   T. M. Lennon and P. J. Olscamp (trans.) *The Search after Truth and Elucidations of the Search after Truth* [10.36]

OC   A. Robinet (ed.) *Oeuvres complètes de Malebranche* [10.35]

1 Descartes, *Principles of Philosophy*, Pt I, 56, 61. AT 8A: 26, 29–30; CSM 1: 211, 213–14. Descartes to ***, 1645 or 1646. AT 4: 348–9; *Philosophical Letters* [10.3], 186–7.

2 Appendix to Fifth Objections and Replies, AT 9A: 213; CSM 2: 275.

3 Descartes to Elizabeth, 21 May 1643, AT 3: 665; *Philosophical Letters* [10.3], 138.

4 Descartes to Elizabeth, 28 June 1643, AT 3: 691–2; *Philosophical Letters* [10.3], 141.

5 Second Replies, AT 7: 135; CSM 2: 97.

6 Third Meditation, AT 7: 40; CSM 2: 28.

7 *Principles*, Pt 2, 50, AT 8A: 69.

8 Descartes to More, August 1649, AT 5: 404; *Philosophical Letters* [10.3], 258.

9 AT 11: 144; CSM 1: 103. See also *The World*, AT 11: 5–6; CSM 1: 82; *Optics*, AT 6: 114; CSM 1: 166; *Notae in Programma*, AT 8B: 360.

10 Gouhier, [10.42], 83–7.

11 Hermann Müller argues for this position in Müller [10.11].

12 Gouhier [10.42], 89.

13 Quoted in Prost [10.7], 103n.

14 Battail [10.23], 8.

15 Prost [10.7], 103.

16 Battail [10.23], 145.

17 Quoted in Clair [10.15], 64. In the nineteenth century, it was conjectured that La Forge and Clauberg met during the latter's visit to Saumur (Damiron [10.6], 127; Bouillier, *Histoire de la philosophie cartésienne* [10.5], 1: 294). This conjecture was plausible only because of the uncertainty about La Forge's date of birth. Both Damiron (p. 24) and Bouillier (p. 511) put it at the beginning of the seventeenth century. Clauberg visited Saumur in 1646, when La Forge was 14 years old and living in La Flèche (Clair [10.13], 40).

18 Vleeschauwer [10.34], 396–401.

19 Battail [10.23], 143; cf. Prost [10.7], 154.

20 Malebranche, *The Search after Truth*, Book 1, ch. 10, OC 1: 123; LO, 49.

21 Item number 139 in Lelong's catalogue (OC 20: 237).

22 Damiron [10.6], 3, 23, 60; Bouillier [10.5], 1: 511.

23 La Forge, *Traitté de l'esprit de l'homme* [10.12], ch. 13; *Oeuvres philosophiques* [10.13], 212–13.

24 ibid., p. 213.
25 ibid.
26 *Traitté* [10.12], ch. 10; *Oeuvres philosophiques* [10.13], 175.
27 ibid., p. 176.
28 ibid., p. 179.
29 *Traitté* [10.12], ch. 16; *Oeuvres philosophiques* [10.13], 235.
30 ibid.
31 ibid., p. 238.
32 ibid.
33 ibid.
34 ibid., p. 240.
35 ibid.
36 ibid., p. 241.
37 ibid., p. 242.
38 ibid.
39 Damiron [10.6], 56–7; Gouhier [10.42], 101; Watson [10.18], 174.
40 *Traitté* [10.12], ch. 16; *Oeuvres philosophiques* [10.13], 245.
41 ibid.
42 Cordemoy, *Oeuvres philosophiques* [10.20], 257.
43 Cordemoy, First Discourse, *Le Discernement du corps et de l'âme*, *Oeuvres philosophiques* [10.20], 99.
44 ibid., p. 101.
45 Fifth Discourse, *Discernement*, *Oeuvres philosophiques* [10.20], 149.
46 Fourth Discourse, *Discernement*, *Oeuvres philosophiques* [10.20], 138.
47 Fifth Discourse, *Discernement*, *Oeuvres philosophiques* [10.20], 150.
48 Fourth Discourse, *Discernement*, *Oeuvres philosophiques* [10.20], 135–7.
49 ibid., p. 139.
50 ibid.; cf. p. 142.
51 ibid., p. 143.
52 ibid., p. 144.
53 Fifth Discourse, *Discernement*, *Oeuvres philosophiques* [10.20], 148.
54 ibid., p. 149.
55 ibid., p. 151.
56 Cordemoy, *Discours physique de la parole*, *Oeuvres philosophiques* [10.20], 255.
57 Cordemoy, *Traité de métaphysique II*, *Oeuvres philosophiques* [10.20], 283–4.
58 ibid., p. 284.
59 ibid., p. 285.
60 For discussion of possible reasons for the dismissal, see Land [10.30], 227–8; Lattre [10.31], 10–11; Vleeschauwer [10.34], 401.
61 Geulincx, *Metaphysica vera*, Pars 1, sc. 5 and 6, *Sämtliche Schriften* [10.24], 2: 150–2.
62 Geulincx, *Ethica*, Tract. 1, cap. 2, s. 2, *Sämtliche Schriften* [10.24], 3: 32.
63 *Metaphysica vera*, Pars 1, sc. 9, *Sämtliche Schriften* [10.24], 2: 154.
64 *Metaphysica vera*, Pars 1, sc. 11, *Sämtliche Schriften* [10.24], 2: 155.
65 *Annotata ad Ethicam*, 19, *Sämtliche Schriften* [10.24], 3: 211–12; cf. *Annotata ad Metaphysicam*, *Sämtliche Schriften* [10.24], 2: 307.
66 The analogy appears in Leibniz's 'Second Explanation of the New System' (Postscript of a Letter to Basnage de Beauval, 3/13 January 1696). The first

complete edition of Geulincx's *Ethica*, with all the Annotations, was published twenty-one years earlier. Leibniz did not necessarily get the analogy from Geulincx, however. For discussion of this issue, see Haeghen [10.28], 161–3.

67 *Ethica*, Tract. 1, cap. 2, s. 2, *Sämtliche Schriften* [10.24], 3: 36.

68 *Annotata ad Ethicam*, 48, *Sämtliche Schriften* [10.24], 3: 220.

69 *Metaphysica vera*, Pars 1, sc. 11, *Sämtliche Schriften* [10.24], 2: 155; *Annotata ad Metaphysicam*, *Sämtliche Schriften* [10.24], 2: 307.

70 *Ethica*, Tract. 1, cap. 2, s. 2, *Sämtliche Schriften* [10.24], 3: 33.

71 ibid., p. 36.

72 *Ethica*, Tract. 1, cap. 2, s. 1, *Sämtliche Schriften* [10.24], 3: 23.

73 Malebranche, *Dialogues on Metaphysics and on Religion*, Dialogue 7, sec. 2, OC 12: 151; [10.38], 149.

74 *Dialogues* 7, sec. 4; OC 12: 153; [10.38], 151. See also *The Search after Truth*, Elucidation 15, OC 3: 226; LO, 669–70.

75 *Search*, Book 2, Pt 1, ch. 5, OC 1: 215; LO, 102.

76 *Search*, Book 6, Pt 2, ch. 3, OC 2: 312–13; LO, 448.

77 *Méditations chrétiennes et métaphysiques*, Med. 1, sec. 8, OC 10: 13. See also *Dialogues* 7, sec. 2, OC 12: 150; [10.38], 147.

78 *Dialogues* 7, sec. 2, OC 12: 150–1; [10.38], 147.

79 *Réponse à une Dissertation de Mr. Arnauld*, ch. 7, OC 7: 515.

80 *Réflexions sur les Doutes sur le système des causes occasionnelles*, OC 17–1: 584.

81 *Réponse à une Dissertation*, ch. 7, OC 7: 515; *Méditations* 5, sec. 8, OC 10: 50.

82 *Search*, Elucidation 15, 1678 edition. This passage is omitted from the 1712 edition. OC 3: 209n.

83 *Méditations* 5, sec. 4, OC 10: 47–8; cf. *Dialogues* 7, sec. 5, OC 12: 155; [10.38], 151.

84 *Dialogues* 7, sec. 10, OC 12: 160; [10.38], 157.

85 ibid. See also *Méditations* 5, sec. 8, OC 10: 50.

86 *Search*, Book 6, Pt 2, ch. 3, OC 2: 316; LO, 450.

87 ibid., OC 2: 313–16; LO, 448–50. See also *Méditations* 6, sec. 12, OC 10: 64.

88 *Dialogues* 7, sec. 3, OC 12: 151–2; [10.38], 149; cf. *Search*, Elucidation 17, OC 3: 326; LO, 733.

89 Descartes to Regius, May 1641, AT 3: 372; *Philosophical Letters* [10.3], 102.

90 *Search*, Elucidation 15, OC 3: 226; LO, 669.

91 *Search*, Book 3, Pt 2, ch. 3, OC 1: 424–5; LO, 223. See also *Méditations* 1, sec. 7, OC 10: 13.

92 *Méditations* 6, sec. 11, OC 10: 62.

93 *Search*, Book 6, Pt 2, ch. 3, OC 2: 315; LO, 450; cf. Elucidation 15, OC 3: 228; LO, 670–1.

94 *Search*, Book 1, ch. 1, OC 1: 46; LO, 5. *Méditations* 6, sec. 16, OC 10: 65.

95 *Réflexions sur la prémotion physique* 12, OC 16: 46–7.

96 *Prémotion physique* 10, OC 16: 41.

97 *Search*, Elucidation 1, OC 3: 20; LO, 548–9. For critical discussion of Malebranche's notion of freedom, see Radner [10.46], 119–33.

98 *Prémotion physique* 23, OC 16: 132. See also *Entretien d'un philosophe chrétien et d'un philosophe chinois*, OC 15: 33.

99 *Traité de la nature et de la grace*, Elucidation 1, OC 5: 147–8; *Réponse au Livre des Vraies et des fausses idées*, ch. 4, OC 6: 36–7.

100 *Réponse aux VFI*, ch. 4, OC 6: 37–8; *Entretien d'un philosophe chrétien et d'un philosophe chinois*, OC 15: 28.

101 *Search*, Elucidation 15, OC 3: 219–20; LO, 666.

102 *Traité de la nature et de la grace*, Last Elucidation, OC 5: 204–5; *Réponse aux Réflexions philosophiques et théologiques de Mr. Arnauld sur le Traité de la nature et de la grace*, Letter 2, ch. 2, OC 8: 705–6; *Dialogues* 13, sec. 9, OC 12: 319–20; [10.38], 321.

103 *Réponse aux VFI*, ch. 4, OC 6: 38.

104 *Search*, Elucidation 2, OC 3: 39; LO, 559. See also *Traité de la nature et de la grace*, Second Discourse, sec. 37, OC 5: 102; *Méditations* 13, sec. 11, OC 10: 144.

105 *Réponse à la troisième lettre de M. Arnauld*, OC 9: 959.

106 *Search*, Book 5, ch. 3, OC 2: 150; LO, 352.

107 *Search*, Elucidation 2, OC 3: 39–40; LO, 559.

108 *Search*, Book 5, ch. 2, OC 2: 139; LO, 345.

109 *Search*, Book 5, ch. 3, OC 2: 150; LO, 351.

110 *Conversations chrétiennes* 3, OC 4: 77. See also *Search*, Elucidation 15, OC 3: 213–14; LO, 662.

111 *Search*, Book 3, Pt 2, ch. 7, OC 1: 451–5; LO, 237–40.

112 *Search*, Book 2, Pt 1, ch. 7, OC 1: 250; LO, 121.

113 ibid., OC 1: 236–7; LO, 114.

114 *Prémotion physique* 25, OC 16: 146. See also *Search*, Book 5, ch. 3, OC 2: 151–2; LO, 352–3.

115 *Traité de l'amour de Dieu*, OC 14: 9–10.

116 *Search*, Book 5, ch. 3, OC 2: 145; LO, 349.

117 *Search*, Book 5, ch. 1, OC 2: 128; LO, 338.

118 *Traité de morale*, Pt 1, ch. 13, sec. 3, OC 11: 147.

119 *Search*, Book 5, ch. 2, OC 2: 133–4; LO, 342.

120 *Search*, Book 5, ch. 3, OC 2: 146; LO, 349.

121 *Traité de l'amour de Dieu*, OC 14: 10.

122 For discussion of the other objections, see Radner [10.46], 36–46.

123 Leibniz, 'First Truths', *Opuscules et fragments inédits de Leibniz* [10.56], 521; *Philosophical Papers and Letters* [10.57], 269.

124 'A New System of the Nature and the Communication of Substances, as well as the Union between the Soul and the Body', *Journal des savants*, 27 June 1695, GP 4: 483; *Philosophical Papers* [10.57], 457. See also 'Discourse on Metaphysics', sec. 33, GP 4: 458; *Philosophical Papers* [10.57], 324.

125 'Clarification of the Difficulties which Mr. Bayle has found in the New System of the Union of Soul and Body', *Histoire des ouvrages des savants*, July 1698, GP 4: 520; *Philosophical Papers* [10.57], 494.

126 Leibniz to Arnauld, 30 April 1687, GP 2: 93; *The Leibniz-Arnauld Correspondence* [10.58], 116.

127 *Réponse aux Réflexions*, Letter 2, ch. 1, OC 8: 695–6. 'Natural laws' here is synonymous with 'general laws', and includes both the so-called laws of nature and those of grace.

128 ibid., OC 8: 696.

129 ibid., OC 8: 697; *Méditations* 8, sec. 25–8, OC 10: 91–3.
130 'Clarification of the Difficulties', GP 4: 520; *Philosophical Papers* [10.57], 494.
131 ibid. See also Leibniz's critique of François Lamy's *Connoissance de soy-même*, GP 4: 587.
132 'On Nature Itself, or on the Inherent Force and Actions of Created Things', sec. 5, GP 4: 506–7; *Philosophical Papers* [10.57], 500. Leibniz's Fifth Paper to Clarke, sec. 112, GP 7: 417; *Philosophical Papers* [10.57], 715.
133 Postscript of a Letter to Basnage de Beauval, 3/13 January 1696, GP 4: 498; *Philosophical Papers* [10.57], 459–60.
134 'Clarification of the Difficulties', GP 4: 520; *Philosophical Papers* [10.57], 494.
135 'Remarks upon M. Arnauld's letter', May 1686, GP 2: 47; *The Leibniz-Arnauld Correspondence* [10.58], 51–2.
136 Leibniz to Arnauld, 4/14 July 1686, GP 2: 57–8; *The Leibniz-Arnauld Correspondence* [10.58], 65.

∾ BIBLIOGRAPHY ∾

Occasionalism: background and general surveys

10.1 Adam, C. and Tannery, P. (eds) *Oeuvres de Descartes*, Paris, Léopold Cerf, 12 vols, 1897–1913; reprinted, Paris, Vrin, 1964–76.
10.2 *The Philosophical Writings of Descartes*, trans. J. Cottingham, R. Stoothoff and D. Murdoch, Cambridge, Cambridge University Press, 2 vols, 1985.
10.3 *Descartes: Philosophical Letters*, trans. A. Kenny, Oxford, Clarendon, 1970.
10.4 Balz, A. G. A. *Cartesian Studies*, New York, Columbia University Press, 1951.
10.5 Bouillier, F. *Histoire de la philosophie cartésienne*, Paris, Delagrave, 2 vols, 3rd edn, 1868.
10.6 Damiron, J.-P. *Essai sur l'histoire de la philosophie en France au XVIIe siècle*, Paris, Hachette, vol. 2, 1846; reprinted, Geneva, Slatkine Reprints, vol. 2, 1970.
10.7 Prost, J. *Essai sur l'atomisme et l'occasionalisme dans la philosophie cartésienne*, Paris, Henry Paulin, 1907.
10.8 Radner, D. 'Is There a Problem of Cartesian Interaction?', *Journal of the History of Philosophy* 23 (1985) 35–49.

Johannes Clauberg

10.9 Clauberg, J. *Opera omnia philosophica*, ed. J. T. Schalbruchii, Amsterdam, Blaev, 2 vols, 1691.
10.10 Balz, A. G. A. 'Clauberg and the Development of Occasionalism', in his *Cartesian Studies*, New York, Columbia University Press, 1951, 158–94.
10.11 Müller, H. *Johannes Clauberg und seine Stellung im Cartesianismus mit*

besonderer Berücksichtigung seines Verhältnisses zu der occasionalistischen Theorie, Jena, Hermann Pohle, 1891.

Louis de La Forge

Works

10.12 *Traitté de l'esprit de l'homme, de ses facultez et fonctions, et de son union avec le corps, suivant les principes de René Descartes*, Paris, Theodore Girard, 1666.
10.13 Clair, P. (ed.) *Oeuvres philosophiques*, Paris, Presses Universitaires de France, 1974.

Secondary works

10.14 Balz, A. G. A. 'Louis de La Forge and the Critique of Substantial Forms', in his *Cartesian Studies*, New York, Columbia University Press, 1951, 80–105.
10.15 Clair, P. 'Louis de La Forge et les origines de l'occasionalisme', in *Recherches sur le XVIIème siècle*, Paris, Centre d'Histoire des Sciences et des Doctrines, vol. 1, 1976, 63–72.
10.16 Clair, P. 'Biographie', in P. Clair (ed.) *Oeuvres philosophiques*, Paris, Presses Universitaires de France, 1974, 17–68.
10.17 Gousset, J. *Causarum primae et secundarum realis operatio rationibus confirmatur, et ab objectionibus defenditur. De his Apologia sit pro Renato des Cartes*, Leovardiae, Halma, 1716.
10.18 Watson, R. A. 'The Cartesian Theology of Louis de La Forge', in R. A. Watson, *The Breakdown of Cartesian Metaphysics*, Atlantic Highlands, N.J., Humanities Press, 1987, 171–7.

Geraud de Cordemoy

Works and English translations

10.19 *Le Discernement du corps et de l'âme en six discours pour servir à l'éclaircissement de la physique*, Paris, Florentin Lambert, 1666.
10.20 Clair, P. and Girbal, F. (eds) *Oeuvres philosophiques*, Paris, Presses Universitaires de France, 1968.
10.21 *A Philosophicall Discourse Concerning Speech and A Discourse Written to a Learned Frier*, trans. anonymous, London, John Martin, 1668, and London, Moses Pitt, 1670; reprinted, New York, AMS Press, 1974.

Secondary works

10.22 Balz, A. G. A. 'Geraud de Cordemoy, 1600–1684', in his *Cartesian Studies*, New York, Columbia University Press, 1951, 3–27.

10.23 Battail, J.-F. *L'avocat philosophe Géraud de Cordemoy (1626–1684)*, The Hague, Nijhoff, 1973.

Arnold Geulincx

Works and translations

10.24 de Vleeschauwer, H. J. (ed.) *Sämtliche Schriften in fünf Bänden*, Stuttgart, Friedrich Frommann, 3 vols, 1965–8; reprint of J. P. N. Land (ed.) *Opera Philosophica*, The Hague, Nijhoff, 3 vols, 1891–3.
10.25 *Arnold Geulincx: Présentation, choix de textes et traduction*, trans. A. de Lattre, Paris, Editions Seghers, 1970.
10.26 *Etica e Metafisica*, trans. Italo Mancini, Bologna, Zanichelli, 1965.
10.27 *Ethik oder über die Kardinaltugenden*, trans. Georg Schmitz, Hamburg, Richard Meiner, 1948.

Secondary works

10.28 van der Haeghen, V. *Geulincx. Etude sur sa vie, sa philosophie et ses ouvrages*, Ghent, A. Hoste, 1886.
10.29 Land, J. P. N. *Arnold Geulincx und seine Philosophie*, The Hague, Nijhoff, 1895.
10.30 Land, J. P. N. 'Arnold Geulincx and His Works', *Mind* 16 (1891) 223–42.
10.31 de Lattre, A. *L'occasionalisme d'Arnold Geulincx*, Paris, Editions de Minuit, 1967.
10.32 de Vleeschauwer, H. J. 'Three Centuries of Geulincx Research', *Mededelings van die Universiteit van Suid-Afrika* 1 (1957) 1–72.
10.33 de Vleeschauwer, H. J. 'Occasionalisme et conditio humana chez Arnold Geulincx', *Kant-Studien* 50 (1958) 109–24.
10.34 de Vleeschauwer, H. J. 'Les sources de la pensée d'Arnold Geulincx (1624–1669)', *Kant-Studien* 69 (1978) 378–402.

Malebranche

Works and English translations

10.35 Robinet, A. (ed.) *Oeuvres complètes de Malebranche*, Paris, Vrin, 20 vols + index, 1958–70.
10.36 *The Search after Truth and Elucidations of the Search after Truth*, trans. T. M. Lennon and P. J. Olscamp, Columbus, Ohio, Ohio State University Press, 1980.
10.37 *Dialogues on Metaphysics and on Religion*, trans. M. Ginsberg, London, Allen & Unwin, 1923.
10.38 *Dialogues on Metaphysics*, trans. W. Doney, New York, Abaris Books, 1980.

Secondary works

10.39 Alquié, F. *Le cartésianisme de Malebranche*, Paris, Vrin, 1974.
10.40 Church, R. W. *A Study in the Philosophy of Malebranche*, London, Allen & Unwin, 1931.
10.41 Dreyfus, G. *La volonté selon Malebranche*, Paris, Vrin, 1958.
10.42 Gouhier, H. *La vocation de Malebranche*, Paris, Vrin, 1926.
10.43 Gouhier, H. *La philosophie de Malebranche et son expérience religieuse*, Paris, Vrin, 2nd edn, 1948.
10.44 Gueroult, M. *Malebranche (II. Les cinq abîmes de la providence: l'ordre et l'occasionalisme)*, Paris, Aubier, 1959.
10.45 Laporte, J. 'La liberté selon Malebranche', *Revue de Métaphysique et de Morale* 45 (1938) 339–410. Also in J. Laporte, *Etudes d'histoire de la philosophie française au XVIIe siècle*, Paris, Vrin, 1951, 193–248.
10.46 Radner, D. *Malebranche*, Assen, Van Gorcum, 1978.
10.47 Robinet, A. *Système et existence dans l'oeuvre de Malebranche*, Paris, Vrin, 1965.
10.48 Rodis-Lewis, G. *Nicolas Malebranche*, Paris, Presses Universitaires de France, 1963.
10.49 Rome, B. K. *The Philosophy of Malebranche*, Chicago, Ill., Henry Regnery, 1963.
10.50 Walton, C. *De la Recherche du Bien: A Study of Malebranche's Science of Ethics*, The Hague, Nijhoff, 1972.

Critics of occasionalism

10.51 Arnauld, A. *Oeuvres de Messire Antoine Arnauld*, Paris, Sigismond d'Arnay, 43 vols, 1775–83; reprinted, Brussels, Culture et Civilisation, 1964–7.
10.52 Arnauld, A. *Dissertation sur la manière dont Dieu a fait les fréquents miracles de l'ancienne loi par la ministère des anges*, in *Oeuvres de Messire Antoine Arnauld*, Brussels, Culture et Civilisation, 1964–7, vol. 38, 673–741.
10.53 Arnauld, A. *Réflexions philosophiques et théologiques sur le nouveau système de la nature et de la grace*, in *Oeuvres de Messire Antoine Arnauld*, Brussels, Culture et Civilisation, 1964–7, vol. 39, 155–856.
10.54 le Bovier de Fontenelle, B. *Doutes sur le systême physique des causes occasionnelles*, in *Oeuvres de Fontenelle*, new edn, Paris, Jean-François Bastien, vol. 8, 1792, 19–81.
10.55 Gerhardt, C. I. (ed.) *Die philosophischen Schriften von Gottfried Wilhelm Leibniz*, Berlin, Weidmann, 7 vols, 1875–90; reprinted, Hildesheim, Olms, 1960–1.
10.56 Couturat, L. (ed.) *Opuscules et fragments inédits de Leibniz*, Paris, Félix Alcan, 1903; reprinted, Hildesheim, Olms, 1961.
10.57 *Gottfried Wilhelm Leibniz: Philosophical Papers and Letters*, trans. L. E. Loemker, Dordrecht, Reidel, 2nd edn, 1970.
10.58 *The Leibniz-Arnauld Correspondence*, trans. H. T. Mason, Manchester, Manchester University Press, 1967.

CHAPTER 11

Leibniz: truth, knowledge and metaphysics
Nicholas Jolley

Leibniz is in important respects the exception among the great philosophers of the seventeenth century. The major thinkers of the period characteristically proclaim the need to reject the philosophical tradition; in their different ways Descartes, Hobbes and Spinoza all insist that new foundations must be laid if philosophy is to achieve any sure and lasting results. Even Malebranche, who seeks to revive the teaching of Augustine, joins in the general chorus of condemnation of Aristotle and his legacy. Leibniz, by contrast, does not share in this revolutionary fervour. Although he is capable of criticizing the Aristotelian tradition, he is also careful to remark that much gold is buried in the dross.[1] Leibniz of course is as enthusiastic as any of his contemporaries about the new mechanistic science; indeed, he is one of its most distinguished advocates and exponents. But by temperament Leibniz is not a revolutionary but a synthesizer; in philosophy, as in politics and religion, he deliberately sets out to mediate between opposing camps. As he himself said, 'the majority of the sects are right in a large part of what they assert but not so much in what they deny'.[2]

The distinctive character of Leibniz's reconciling project needs to be made a little clearer. Other philosophers in the period had of course also tried to show that the new science was compatible with natural theology. Descartes, for example, sought to find a place in his philosophy for such orthodox doctrines as the existence of a personal God and the immortality of the soul. But in contrast with Descartes, Leibniz sought to retain as much as possible of the Aristotelian framework and to combine it with the emerging scientific and philosophical ideas; we shall see, for example, that Leibniz seeks to fuse Aristotelian and Cartesian conceptions of the soul. The synthesizing spirit of Leibniz's philosophy is one of its fascinations, but it is also a source of weakness; Leibniz sometimes seems to be trying to reconcile the irreconcilable.

The structure of the present chapter is as follows. The first three sections are devoted to the analysis of Leibniz's general metaphysics. In the first two sections we shall see how Leibniz formulates an Aristotelian theory of corporeal substance in his first mature work, the *Discourse on Metaphysics* (1686), and how he seemingly attempts to derive a number of metaphysical doctrines from purely logical considerations concerning truth. In the third section we shall see how in his later writings Leibniz abandons his theory of corporeal substance for a form of idealism; this is the famous doctrine of monads. In the fourth section we shall look at the anti-Newtonian theories of space and time which Leibniz formulated at the very end of his career. In the following section we shall study Leibniz's somewhat ill-conceived attempt to apply his general theory of causality to the problem of the relationship between mind and body which Descartes bequeathed to his successors. Finally, in the last two sections we shall analyse Leibniz's psychology and his theory of knowledge; here we shall see how Leibniz seeks to reinterpret some ideas deriving from Descartes and Spinoza.

❧ THE ARISTOTELIAN BACKGROUND: ❧ SUBSTANCE AND AGGREGATE

The synthesizing spirit of Leibniz's philosophy is clearly visible in Leibniz's first mature work, the *Discourse on Metaphysics*, and in the correspondence with Arnauld which it precipitated. One way of looking at these works is to see that Leibniz is trying to revive Aristotelian doctrines about substance and to show that they are in conformity with the new science; indeed, they are largely free of the conceptual difficulties which plague the more recent Cartesian ideas. It is true that Leibniz thinks that Aristotle did not say the last word about substance. But it is still possible to see Leibniz as engaged in extending, rather than replacing, the Aristotelian project.

We must begin by reminding ourselves of two very influential claims that Aristotle made about substance. First, for Aristotle, a substance is what may be termed an 'ultimate subject of predication'. Thus, by this criterion Alexander is a substance because while we can predicate properties of Alexander – we can say, for instance, that he was a Macedonian – he himself is not predicable of anything else; there is nothing of which we can say that it is an Alexander. To put the point another way, the noun 'Alexander' can appear only in the subject position in a sentence and never in the predicate position. By contrast, honesty is a subject of predication but not an ultimate one; for though we can predicate properties of honesty, honesty itself is predicable of other things – for instance, a person who possesses the virtue.[3] Second, in response to the characteristically Greek preoccupation with flux, Aristotle claims that substances are substrata of change: 'The most distinctive mark of substance appears to be that while remaining numerically one and the same, it is capable of admitting contradictory qualities.'[4] Thus, although he never instantiates both properties simultaneously, Alexander as an infant is two feet tall and as an adult, say, six feet tall. To say that Alexander is a substance is a way of drawing our attention to the fact that one and the same individual persists through the change in qualities. The relation between these two claims about substance is not entirely clear, but on the face of it, they do not seem to be equivalent; it seems that there could be items which are ultimate subjects of predication, even though they do not persist through time. A lightning flash, for example, is instantaneous, but it is a subject of predication which is not itself obviously predicable of anything else.

Although Leibnizian substances characteristically satisfy the condition, in the *Discourse on Metaphysics* Leibniz is silent, at least officially, about the idea that substances are substrata of change. But early on in this work Leibniz approvingly cites Aristotle's claim that substances are ultimate subjects of predication: 'It is of course true that when several predicates are attributed to a single subject, and this subject is not attributed to any other, it is called an individual substance.'[5] It is true that in the next breath Leibniz indicates that this definition is not fully satisfactory: 'But this is not enough, and such an explanation is merely nominal.'[6] Presumably Leibniz's point is, not that the definition fails to capture necessary and sufficient conditions, but that it is somehow shallow compared with the one which, as we shall see, he goes on to propose. But in any case, whatever the grounds for his partial dissatisfaction, Leibniz seems to make fruitful use of the Aristotelian idea that substances are ultimate subjects of predication. In the Arnauld correspondence, in particular, Leibniz deploys this idea in order to reach anti-Cartesian conclusions about the status of bodies and at least to prepare the ground for the very Aristotelian thesis that the paradigm substances are organisms.

In the correspondence with Arnauld Leibniz argues for a remarkable negative thesis; he seeks to show that most of the things which both the man in the street and the Cartesians take to be substances are not really substances at all. In general, Leibniz's thesis is that no non-organic body is a substance. The argument in outline is as follows:

1   No aggregate is an ultimate subject of predication.

2   All non-organic bodies are aggregates.

3   Therefore, no non-organic body is an ultimate subject of predication (and hence not a substance).

The basic idea behind the argument is that if the notion of an ultimate
subject of predication is thought through, we shall see that it disquali-
fies tables, chairs and the like from counting as substances.

Why does Leibniz think that an aggregate, such as an army, is not
an ultimate subject of predication? An army of course is at least a subject of predication in the sense that we can ascribe various properties to
it; we can say, for example, of a given army that it fought bravely. But
it is not an ultimate subject of predication because in Leibniz's words,
'it seems ... that what constitutes the essence of an entity through
aggregation is only a state of being of its constituent entities; for
example, what constitutes the essence of an army is only a state of being
of the constituent men'.[7] In the words of one recent commentator,

> an aggregate is a state of being of those entities that compose it
> in the sense that any truths about the aggregate can be expressed
> in propositions that ascribe modes and states to the composing
> entities without any need to refer to the aggregate itself.[8]

Thus, a proposition such as 'The army fought bravely' is reducible to
propositions which ascribe various properties to the members of the
aggregate, namely, the individual soldiers.

Perhaps more controversial is the second premise of the argument.
A non-organic body such as a block of marble does not seem to be
on a par with clear-cut examples of aggregates such as an army or a
flock of sheep. Leibniz must admit that a block of marble is more
tightly bonded than these aggregates, but he would claim that this fact
is not metaphysically significant; a block of marble is no less an entity
by aggregation than a flock of sheep.[9] But in that case what is a block
of marble an aggregate of? At first sight it seems that Leibniz would
say that a block of marble is an aggregate of physical parts which are
themselves aggregates and so on *ad infinitum*. But though he shows
some hesitancy on this issue, in the correspondence with Arnauld
Leibniz suggests that a marble slab is an aggregate of organisms no less
than a flock of sheep: 'perhaps this marble block is merely a heap of
an infinite number of living bodies, or is like a lake full of fish, although
these animals are ordinarily visible only in half-rotten bodies.'[10] This
thesis draws support from the empirical discoveries made possible by
the recent invention of the microscope.

Thus Leibniz reaches an important negative conclusion which is
in obvious conflict with Cartesian theses; no non-organic bodies are
substances.[11] But this conclusion still leaves open the question of Leibniz's positive views on the issue of what items qualify as substances.

Recent work has shown that around the time of the *Discourse on Metaphysics* Leibniz was remarkably hesitant on this issue; indeed, he flirted with a number of possible positions.[12] He was perhaps particularly uncertain as to whether anything physical counted as a substance, but as we shall see, he also had doubts about the ontological status of souls. Despite his hesitations, the view to which he seems to have been most attracted is that organisms, and perhaps souls, are the only substances; organisms are what Leibniz calls 'corporeal substances'. With regard to physical objects, then, Leibniz's teaching is that every body is either itself a corporeal substance or an aggregate of corporeal substances.

Leibniz's somewhat tentative positive thesis raises an obvious question: why are organisms better candidates for substantiality than non-organic bodies? Leibniz's short answer to this question is clear: organisms are not just aggregates but true unities, and every entity which is endowed with a true unity is a substance. For Leibniz, an organism is truly one by virtue of possessing a soul or principle of life which confers unity on it; in scholastic terminology the soul is said to inform the body. Indeed, Leibniz even goes so far as to revive the scholastic doctrine that the soul is the substantial form of the body; here he is drawing on the fact that in medieval philosophy it is the presence of a substantial form that makes a body a natural unity.[13]

The thesis that only the presence of a soul can confer unity on a body, and thus make it a genuine substance rather than an aggregate, obviously needs to be justified. Leibniz is not totally forthcoming on this subject, but he does throw out some suggestive hints which make it possible for us to see what he has in mind. In correspondence with Arnauld he explains that the unity of an aggregate is a matter of convention only.[14] The unity of a university department, for example, is conventional in the sense that it depends on certain human interests; for teaching purposes, let us say, it is convenient to group a Leibniz specialist with a philosopher of language rather than with a seventeenth-century historian. But there is no metaphysical fact of the matter which determines this classification. The unity of a human body, however, is not at all like that. The fact that my hand and foot belong together, but not my hand and the table in front of me, is determined not by convention but by nature, or rather by the metaphysical truth that my soul animates my body. I can, for example, feel pain in my hand and foot, but I cannot feel pain in the table in front of me. Thus the presence of a soul provides a wholly non-conventional basis for classifying some physical parts together.

Leibniz's doctrine that organisms are true substances was the target of two shrewd objections from Arnauld. In the first place, Arnauld objected that Leibniz seemed to be smuggling in a merely stipulative definition of substance. As Arnauld sees it, Leibniz redefines substance as that which has a true unity, and on this basis he reaches the anti-Cartesian conclusion that no bodies except organisms are substances. But in that case he has covertly abandoned the traditional definition of substance as that which is neither a mode nor state; using more Aristotelian language, we could restate Arnauld's point by saying that Leibniz has abandoned the definition of substance as an ultimate subject of predication.[15] Leibniz is of course entitled to offer a stipulative definition of substance if he chooses, but he is not entitled to switch back and forth between such a definition and a more traditional one. Leibniz's reply to this objection is important: he answers Arnauld by saying that far from abandoning Aristotle's definition of substance he is simply drawing out a consequence of it: being a true unity is implied by being an ultimate subject of predication. Indeed, the concepts of a true unity and of an ultimate subject of predication are logically equivalent. 'To be brief, I hold as axiomatic the identical proposition, which varies only in emphasis: that what is not truly *one* entity is not truly one *entity* either. It has always been thought that 'one' and 'entity' are interchangeable.'[16]

Arnauld also objected to Leibniz's reintroduction of animal souls or substantial forms. As a good Cartesian, Arnauld made the familiar points against this doctrine; it is superfluous for the purposes of explaining animal behaviour, and it raises embarrassing difficulties concerning the status of animal souls after the destruction of their bodies. Arnauld cited the case of a worm both parts of which, when cut in two, continue to move as before, and challenged Leibniz as to what he would say about it.[17] The serious philosophical point behind Arnauld's raillery is that an animal is no more a genuine unity than a non-organic body such as a table. Thus the chopping up of a worm is in principle no different from the chopping up of a table; in both cases we are simply left with parts of the original body. In reply Leibniz seeks to reconcile the facts about the case of the worm with his thesis that animals are genuine substances which possess true unity by virtue of the souls which animate them. From the fact that both parts of the worm continue to move, it does not follow that we must postulate either two souls or none. The soul may continue to animate one of the parts, and it is this part which is strictly to be identified with the worm. In this sense the worm survives the division of its body.[18]

LOGIC AND METAPHYSICS

The originally Aristotelian idea of substance as an ultimate subject of predication thus plays a major role in the *Discourse on Metaphysics* and the correspondence with Arnauld; it provides the basis for Leibniz's persistent claim that substances are genuine unities. But as we have seen, Leibniz thinks that the Aristotelian doctrine does not go far enough. In the *Discourse on Metaphysics* Leibniz seeks a deeper understanding of what is involved in being a substance, and he finds it in what we may call the 'complete concept theory': this is the famous claim that 'the nature of an individual substance or a complete being is to have a notion so complete that it is sufficient to contain and to allow us to deduce from it all the predicates of the subject to which the notion is attributed'.[19] In the following sections of the *Discourse* Leibniz develops a train of thought which led Bertrand Russell and the French scholar, Couturat, to claim that Leibniz derived his metaphysics from his logic.[20]

As a general theory about the roots of Leibniz's metaphysics, the Russell-Couturat thesis has come in for a good deal of criticism. For one thing, the thesis does not seem to apply to the writings of Leibniz's later period; there purely logical theories seem to play little or no role in generating metaphysical doctrines. Even at the time of the *Discourse*, Leibniz appeals to non-logical considerations in support of his metaphysics. Leibniz invokes his physical theory that in collisions 'bodies really recede from other bodies through the force of their own elasticity, and not through any alien force'.[21] In this way Leibniz seeks to confirm his metaphysical doctrine that there is no causal interaction between substances. Moreover, at least as formulated by Russell, the so-called 'logicist' thesis suffers from a different kind of difficulty. According to Russell, Leibniz *validly* derived his metaphysics from his logic; against this, it has been remarked that there are in fact serious problems with the purported deduction. Considerations like these have led some writers to argue that Leibniz did not so much derive his metaphysics from his logic as tailor his logic to a metaphysics to which he is attracted for independent reasons.[22] Nonetheless, there does seem to be some truth in the Russell-Couturat thesis. At least in the *Discourse* and other writings of the same period, Leibniz certainly seems to rely on logical premises in arguing for metaphysical conclusions. This is not to say that as it stands the deduction is watertight; at points Leibniz seems to be smuggling in certain unstated non-logical premises.

The claim that Leibniz derived his metaphysics from his logic is more mysterious than it need be. When Russell and Couturat put forward this thesis, they had something quite specific in mind when they spoke of Leibniz's 'logic': they were referring to his theory of truth. The theory of truth in question is explicitly stated, not in the *Discourse on Metaphysics*, but in the correspondence with Arnauld where it appears almost as an afterthought. However, the theory makes itself felt in the *Discourse*, for it seems to ground the deep analysis of the nature of substance which Leibniz offers as a supplement to Aristotle.

Leibniz's distinctive theory of truth can best be explained by way of contrast. Perhaps the most intuitive doctrine of truth is some version of the correspondence theory; in other words, truth consists in a relation of correspondence between propositions and states of affairs in the world. It is some version of the correspondence theory that Aristotle seems to have had in mind when he defined truth as saying of that which is that it is and of that which is not that it is not.[23] Although he sometimes seems to suggest that he is simply following in Aristotle's footsteps, Leibniz in fact advances a radically different theory. For Leibniz, truth consists not in a correspondence between propositions and states of affairs but in a relation between concepts. Leibniz provides a succinct summary of his theory in a letter to Arnauld: 'In every true affirmative proposition, necessary or contingent, universal or particular, the concept of the predicate is in a sense included in that of the subject: *praedicatum inest subjecto*; or else I do not know what truth is.'[24] Let us call this 'the concept-containment theory of truth'.

Leibniz's theory of truth can be seen as a generalization of a more familiar and more limited claim. Consider the proposition: 'Gold is a metal'. It is plausible to say that the proposition is true because the concept expressed by the predicate term is contained in the concept expressed by the subject term; in other words, an analysis of the concept of gold would reveal that the concept of metal is one of its constituent concepts. (Analysis is conceived of here as a matter of replacing a given term by its definitional equivalent.) As his comment to Arnauld shows, Leibniz wishes to extend this insight to all affirmative propositions, including singular ones such as 'Julius Caesar crossed the Rubicon'. Thus Leibniz holds that the proper name 'Julius Caesar' is not simply an arbitrary label; it expresses a concept no less than the term 'gold' does. The proposition 'Julius Caesar crossed the Rubicon' is true because the concept of crossing the Rubicon is contained in the concept of Julius Caesar. From this general, concept-containment theory of truth Leibniz's distinctive claim about the nature of individual substances follows as a special case; by virtue of the general theory, all the predicates which are true of an individual substance are contained in the concept of that substance.[25]

'From these considerations there follow a number of important paradoxes.'[26] This remark in the *Discourse* is key evidence for the claim that Leibniz derived his metaphysics from his logic, and it is certainly true that Leibniz goes on to present a number of remarkable doctrines about the basic structure of the world. Commentators tend to come up with slightly different lists of the doctrines that are so derived, but there are five major doctrines which are generally included.

1   The identity of indiscernibles: there cannot be two substances which are exactly alike.
2   The expression thesis: every substance expresses or mirrors the whole universe.
3   The denial of causal interaction between (created) substances.
4   Every substance is the causal source of all its states.
5   The hypothesis of concomitance (or what is later termed by Leibniz 'The pre-established harmony'): the states of substances are harmonized by God so that they give the appearance of causal interaction. (The phrase 'pre-established harmony' is also sometimes used by Leibniz and by commentators to refer to the conjunction of theses 3–5.)

The relation of these doctrines to Leibniz's logic is more problematic in some cases than in others. In the case of (at least one version of) the identity of indiscernibles, the derivation is relatively straightforward. The complete concept of an individual substance is presumably a concept under which no more than one individual can fall. Thus if there were two substances exactly alike there would be two substances with the same complete concept, which is impossible. It should be noted, however, that the complete concept theory seems to provide the basis for only a weak version of the identity of indiscernibles; for all the argument so far shows, this principle would be satisfied by two substances which differed solely in terms of their spatial relationships. However, for reasons which will become clearer, Leibniz in fact subscribes to a stronger version of the identity of indiscernibles to the effect that two substances cannot be exactly alike in terms of their intrinsic (i.e. non-relational) properties.

Leibniz's more popular statements about the identity of indiscernibles can be unhelpful. For example, Leibniz sometimes tries to provide *a posteriori* support for the principle by means of an anecdote; he tells how a courtier was challenged to find two leaves exactly alike, and how after a while he abandoned the search as fruitless.[27] Picturesque as it is, this story is doubly misleading. First, in so far as it follows from the complete concept theory, the identity of indiscernibles is a thesis about substances. Strictly speaking, for Leibniz, dead leaves are not substances but aggregates of substances. Second, and more importantly, the identity of indiscernibles is not an empirical generalization but a necessary truth. The thesis is not that as a matter of contingent fact there are no two substances exactly alike, but that there could not be two such substances.

More serious problems of derivation are presented by the other main metaphysical theses 2–5. Different commentators locate the main difficulties in different places, but they agree in the general diagnosis: Leibniz tends to slide from what is true at the level of concepts to claims about what is true at the level of substances in the world. Leibniz may have been unwittingly encouraged in this tendency by the imprecision of his terminology; as used by Leibniz, terms such as 'subject' and 'predicate' are dangerously ambiguous. The word 'subject' for example is ambiguous as between subject-concept and the substance in the world which instantiates the concept: *mutatis mutandis*, the term 'predicate' is similarly ambiguous.[28] Bearing this ambiguity in mind, in the remainder of this section we shall, then, examine the problems presented by 2–4.

Despite the unusual terminology, on one level at least the expression thesis is straightforward. Leibniz was pressed by Arnauld as to what he meant by 'expression', and in reply he made clear that it was a technical term which he explained as follows: 'one thing *expresses* another (in my terminology) when there exists a constant and fixed relation between what can be said of one and of the other.'[29] When Leibniz says that every substance expresses the whole universe, at least part of what he wants to say is that, given a complete knowledge of the concept of any individual substance, say Alexander, it is possible in principle to read off the predicates (i.e. predicate-concepts) of every other substance. We can see that Leibniz must hold this by virtue of the fact that there are relational truths linking Alexander to everything else in the universe. It is a fact about Alexander, for example, that he was born so many years before Ronald Reagan became President of the United States. It follows, then, that all such relational predicates must be contained in the complete concept of Alexander, and so on for every other substance. Thus if one really knew the complete concept of Alexander, one would *ipso facto* also know everything there was to be known about the universe.

When Leibniz says that every substance expresses the universe, he also wants to assert a more controversial and more metaphysical thesis. In the *Discourse on Metaphysics* Leibniz claims that 'there are at all times in the soul of Alexander traces of everything that has happened to him and marks of everything that will happen to him, and even traces of everything that happens in the universe, even though God alone could recognize them all'.[30] But of course it is not easy to see how from the fact that the concept of Alexander timelessly includes the predicate of dying in 323 BC, it follows that there must be marks of this event in Alexander's soul even before it happens. It has been suggested that Leibniz is thinking along the following lines.[31] Since it is a timeless fact about Alexander that he dies in 323 BC, throughout his history there must be something about Alexander himself by virtue of which this proposition is true; there must be some persistent structural modification of Alexander corresponding to the fact of his dying. This modification remains quiescent until the event when it bursts into activity; subsequently, it reverts to a state of quiescence.

Commentators have similarly stressed the difficulty of seeing how theses 3 and 4 follow from Leibniz's logic. From the fact that every individual substance has a complete concept Leibniz infers that all the states of a substance are a consequence of that concept; from this he concludes, apparently, that there is no causal interaction between created substances. But this argument seems fallacious.[32] Consider the proposition: 'Julius Caesar was killed by Brutus and Cassius.' Here a causal relational predicate 'killed by Brutus and Cassius' is truly ascribed to Julius Caesar. This causal predicate must, then, be contained in the concept of Julius Caesar. But then it clearly does not follow from the complete concept theory that there is no causal interaction between created substances. Nor does it help matters to point out that, though in the *Discourse* Leibniz derives 4 from 3, he sometimes reverses the order of the derivation. For if it is difficult to see how 3 follows from the complete concept theory, it is no less difficult to see how 4 follows from that theory.[33]

One way of dealing with these problems is to suppose that the derivation of 3 from Leibniz's logic is mediated by a doctrine that we have not so far discussed; this is the doctrine that 'there are no purely extrinsic denominations', which is itself a consequence of the 'marks and traces' version of the expression thesis.[34] The claim that there are no purely extrinsic denominations is one of Leibniz's more obscure doctrines, but is generally taken to assert the reducibility of relations; in other words, all relational truths about individual substances can be deduced from non-relational truths about those substances. For example, the relational proposition 'Smith is taller than Jones' is reducible in the sense that it can be derived from the non-relational propositions 'Smith is six feet tall', and 'Jones is five feet ten inches tall'. Thus by virtue of his thesis that there are no purely extrinsic denominations, Leibniz would claim that the proposition 'Julius Caesar was killed by Brutus and Cassius' is reducible to propositions which ascribe only non-relational predicates to those individuals.[35] But this approach does not really solve the problem. The thesis that there are no purely extrinsic denominations asserts at most that relational propositions are theoretically dispensable; it does not assert that such propositions are actually false. But it seems that it is the stronger thesis which is required if the claim that there are no purely extrinsic denominations is to provide a basis for 3; for Leibniz is committed by 3 to saying that propositions which assert causal relations between created substances are all of them, strictly speaking, false.

An alternative way of dealing with these problems is to reinterpret Leibniz's notion of a complete concept. One writer, in particular, has been impressed by those passages in which Leibniz tells Arnauld that the complete concept of an individual contains the laws of its world.[36] On this basis it has been suggested that a Leibnizian complete concept is constituted by a combination of basic (i.e. non-relational) predicates and laws – the laws of its universe. These laws are taken to include a law of succession for the states of the substance; such a law would imply that a substance's states causally depend only on itself. On this interpretation, then, there is no danger that the complete concept of Julius Caesar, say, will contain causal predicates such as being killed by Brutus or Cassius; such a predicate must be excluded because it suggests of course that a state of Julius Caesar causally depends on other created substances. We may still wonder, however, whether this interpretation can do justice to the expression thesis, given that relational predicates are excluded from complete concepts. But here again the crucial point is taken to be that laws are built into complete concepts. The idea is that the concept of an individual substance contains non-causal laws of coexistence with other substances; from this it follows, as the expression thesis requires, that the predicates of all other substances can be deduced from the concept of a given substance. It is in this sense, then, that 'every individual substance involves the whole universe in its perfect concept'.[37] This interpretation is attractive, for it frees Leibniz's argument from its otherwise obvious invalidity. But as its proponent acknowledges, it does so at a heavy price; a complete concept turns out not to be a purely logical notion, for Leibniz has packed some of his metaphysics into it. Thus the difficulty now is not that Leibniz's argument involves a *non sequitur* but that it is effectively question-begging.

Before we conclude this section, it is worth clarifying thesis 4 – that every substance is the causal source of all its states. At a minimum Leibniz holds that every state of a substance is caused by an earlier state of that substance.[38] But Leibniz seems to be committed to more than this when he claims, as he often does, that a substance gets all its states 'out of its own depths';[39] this phrase suggests something crucial about the way in which the states of a substance are caused by its earlier states. In fact, Leibniz's view of intra-substantial causality seems to draw on the 'marks and traces' version of the expression thesis. Remember that, according to that thesis, a substance bears within itself the marks of all its future states. Thus Leibniz holds that when an earlier state causes a later state, this later state was in a sense latent or dormant in the substance all along; when the state is caused, it emerges from quiescence and bursts into activity; subsequently, it reverts to a condition of quiescence. The causing of a state thus seems to be the activation of a 'mark' that was pre-existent in the substance throughout its previous history.

❧ THE DOCTRINE OF MONADS ❧

The metaphysical doctrines 1–5 which, in the *Discourse on Metaphysics*, Leibniz deduces from his logic all concern substances, and throughout his subsequent career Leibniz continues to assert these doctrines; they are some of the great constants of his philosophy. None the less, Leibniz's metaphysics underwent a major development between the *Discourse* (1686) and the *Monadology* (1714). Although Leibniz never recants any of the five doctrines, he changes his mind about what sort of items really fall under the concept of substance. In the *Discourse* Leibniz holds, despite some hesitation, that all substances are either organisms or souls; in his later philosophy he comes to hold that, strictly speaking, there are no corporeal substances; rather, all substances are either souls or at least soul-like. The later philosophy is thus a form of idealism inasmuch as it maintains that the basic furniture of the universe is mental or spiritual in nature. This is the famous doctrine of monads.[40] It may of course be questioned just how sharp this transition was, and it is true that there are times in his later writings when Leibniz speaks as if there really are corporeal substances. But the dominant character of Leibniz's later metaphysics is well represented by his remark to De Volder: 'Considering the matter carefully, it must be said that there is nothing in the world except simple substances and in them, perception and appetite.'[41] Taken strictly, this claim implies that there are no corporeal substances.

The term 'monad' derives from a Greek word for unity. The fact that Leibniz chose this term to denote the fundamental entities in his later metaphysics shows that there is continuity in his thought; as before in the *Discourse* and the correspondence with Arnauld, a substance is a genuine unity. But a monad, unlike a corporeal substance, is a unity in a quite straightforward sense; it has no parts, or, in other words, it is simple. Now the simplicity of monads is a clue to further aspects of their nature. Since they are simple, monads are immaterial – which, for Leibniz, means that they are spiritual, for everything material has parts. The simplicity of monads also entails, for Leibniz, that they are indestructible. Here the underlying idea is that destruction consists in decomposition, and that where there are no parts, there can be no decomposition. Hence, in the case of monads, 'there is no dissolution to fear'.[42]

The fact that monads are immaterial and spiritual imposes a radical restriction on the properties of which they are capable; it rules out all such physical properties as size, shape and even position. As the quotation from the letter to De Volder bears out, the basic properties of monads are perception and appetite, or appetition. The notion of perception, which Leibniz defines as 'the expression of the many in the one',[43] is central not just to Leibniz's metaphysics but also to his psychology, and it will accordingly be discussed in the penultimate section of this chapter. But something may be said here about appetition. Appetition is the dynamic principle in the monad; it is that by virtue of which a monad changes its state. Yet, as one writer has suggested, it is possible that, for Leibniz, appetitions and perceptions are not two kinds of modifications but rather the same modification viewed differently.

> From one point of view every passing state is an expression of the many in the one and as such it is a perception. From the other point of view every passing state is a tendency to a succeeding state and as such it is an appetition.[44]

A possible parallel would be Spinoza's doctrine that every finite mode of substance can be viewed under the attributes of both thought and extension.

The doctrine of monads is not merely idealistic; it is also in a sense monistic. But the term 'monism' is a little misleading and needs clarification. Monadology is certainly not monistic in the sense in which Spinoza's metaphysics is monistic; Leibniz is not asserting, as Spinoza does, that there is only one substance (*Deus seu Natura*). Rather, monadology is monistic in the sense that, according to Leibniz, there is only one *kind* of basic entities, namely souls. In this respect the contrast with Spinoza's monism is at a maximum. Far from asserting that there is just one substance, Leibniz holds that there are infinitely many simple substances and that, by virtue of the identity of indiscernibles, no two are exactly alike.

Monads are in fact hierarchically arranged. At the top of the hierarchy is God who seems to be the supreme monad;[45] at the bottom of the hierarchy are what Leibniz calls 'bare monads' which provide the metaphysical foundation for inanimate matter. The basis for this hierarchical classification is quality of perception; borrowing Cartesian terminology, Leibniz says that monads differ in terms of the clarity and distinctness of their perceptions. For example, the minds of human beings are near the top of the hierarchy by virtue of their capacity for a very high grade of perception, namely reason. A striking feature of monadology, however, is that although monads differ enormously in terms of the quality of perception, in a sense they do not differ in terms of the objects they perceive; for giving a new twist to his expression thesis Leibniz holds that every monad perceives the whole universe according to its point of view. The qualification tacked on to this thesis is to be understood in terms of the doctrine that there are qualitative differences among perceptions. To say that two monads differ in their point of view is to say that they do not enjoy exactly the same distribution of clarity and distinctness over their perceptual states. In this way Leibniz can also explain how the identity of indiscernibles applies to monads in spite of the fact that they all perceive the whole universe.

These are remarkable doctrines, and we may well wonder how Leibniz came to arrive at them. In fact, however, the basic argument for the fundamental principles of monadology is quite straightforward; it turns on two main assumptions: the infinite divisibility of matter and the thesis that there must be basic or ultimate entities. For Leibniz, it would be shocking to reason, or at least to divine wisdom, if everything in the universe were composed of compounds whose components were themselves compounds, and so on *ad infinitum*. The infinite divisibility of matter implies that these basic entities cannot be physical, for everything physical is a compound of the sort just described. Thus although physical atoms are a fiction, there can and must be 'spiritual atoms' or monads.

A natural initial reaction to monadology is to wonder at Leibniz's willingness to prefer it to the more down-to-earth metaphysics of the *Discourse*. But in response to the argument outlined above we may wonder why Leibniz was not in a position to advance it earlier. Certainly throughout his career Leibniz holds that the universe must consist of basic or ultimate entities. Moreover, in his earlier philosophy Leibniz also held a version of the thesis of the infinite divisibility of matter; matter, considered in abstraction from souls or substantial forms, is infinitely divisible 'in innumerable possible ways but not actually divided in any'.[46] So at the time of writing the *Discourse* Leibniz believed, as he continued to believe, that nothing purely material could be a basic entity. But the difference between Leibniz's earlier and later views seems to be this. In the *Discourse* Leibniz held that, though in the abstract, matter is infinitely divisible, taken concretely it is composed of organisms which are material beings endowed with souls, and that these organisms are genuinely basic entities. In his later philosophy Leibniz may have continued to hold that matter is in some sense composed of organisms, but he gave up the thesis that organisms are genuinely basic entities or intrinsic natural unities.

Why, then, did Leibniz give up the view that organisms are basic entities? A plausible answer is that he came to feel that some of the claims about substance which he had deduced from his logic did not clearly apply to organisms. According to the *Discourse* substances are indivisible but, as we saw earlier, in the correspondence with Arnauld Leibniz had difficulty defending the thesis that organisms are indivisible. Possibly Leibniz became dissatisfied with his answer to Arnauld's puzzle about the worm that is cut in two. By contrast, monadology is largely free from these difficulties: as a simple, immaterial being a monad satisfies the indivisibility criterion much more clearly than an organism. Moreover, the earlier, Aristotelian metaphysics fares less well than monadology in accommodating the thesis that there is no causal interaction between substances. In the earlier metaphysics this thesis implies that no two organisms interact, but it has no such implications for other bodies; for instance, it does not entail that no two billiard balls interact. And this may well have come to seem arbitrary to Leibniz. By contrast, monadology suffers from no such problem. For one thing, it is perhaps fairly intuitive to say that souls cannot causally interact. But in any case, by restricting the thesis to souls or soul-like entities, Leibniz is at least able to escape the charge that he is simply drawing an arbitrary line through the physical world.

An obvious problem for an idealist philosopher who holds that reality is ultimately spiritual is to determine the status of bodies. Leibniz's idealism certainly implies that bodies cannot be substances, but beyond that it leaves their status unspecified. For one thing, idealism does not discriminate between eliminativist and reductionist approaches to this issue; in other words, it does not discriminate between the thesis that bodies do not exist and the thesis that, although bodies exist, they are to be reduced to something which is ontologically more basic. Fortunately, on this issue Leibniz leaves us in no doubt about his position: in a letter to De Volder he remarks:

> I do not really eliminate body, but I reduce it to what it is. For
> I show that corporeal mass, which is thought to have something
> over and above simple substance, is not a substance, but a
> phenomenon resulting from simple substances, which alone
> have unity and absolute reality.[47]

Leibniz is thus in some sense a reductionist about bodies; what is less clear is the nature of the reduction. Some writers have claimed that Leibniz anticipated Berkeley's phenomenalism; they have thought that he came to espouse the thesis that bodies are sets of harmonized perceptions.[48] Leibniz seems to have flirted with this thesis on occasion; in a very Berkeleian passage he tells Des Bosses:

> It is true that things which happen in the soul must agree with
> those which happen outside of it. But for this it is enough for
> the things taking place in one soul to correspond with each other
> as well as with those happening in any other soul, and it is
> not necessary to assume anything outside of all souls or monads.
> According to this hypothesis, we mean nothing else when we

say that Socrates is sitting down than that what we understand by 'Socrates' and by 'sitting down' is appearing to us and to others who are concerned.[49]

Leibniz was certainly well placed to defend a version of phenomenalism. Other phenomenalists, such as Berkeley, who hold that the supply of souls or minds is finite are forced to analyse statements about the existence of physical objects in terms of statements about possible perceptions; they are forced to appeal to the perceptions which a mind would have in such and such circumstances. Leibniz, by contrast, does not have to take this line since he holds that the number of souls is infinite and that every possible point of view on the phenomena is actually occupied. Thus Leibniz can analyse all statements about the existence of physical objects in terms of other statements which are exclusively about the actual perceptions of monads.[50]

Phenomenalism, however, does not seem to be Leibniz's considered view. Most characteristically Leibniz states that a physical object is, not a set of perceptions, but an aggregate of monads or simple substances. In saying this Leibniz is careful to point out that he does not mean that monads are parts of bodies; rather, any part of a body is itself physical, and since matter is infinitely divisible, there will be no part of matter which does not have parts which are themselves smaller bodies. Leibniz sometimes explains the relationship between bodies and monads by saying that bodies are 'beings by aggregation' which result from monads or simple substances.[51] Bodies are also said to be 'well-founded phenomena';[52] they are well-founded in the sense that they are appearances which are grounded in monads.

Despite some differences in formulation, Leibniz's main view seems to be that bodies are aggregates of monads. We may well wonder how this can be so; how can an aggregate of simple, unextended substances be identified with a physical object? It would seem that a physical object must have properties which no aggregate of monads could have. Certainly a physical object must have properties which no *individual* monad can have. Perhaps Leibniz would insist on the logical point that, from the fact that individual monads are unextended, it does not follow that an aggregate of monads is unextended; to suppose otherwise is to commit the fallacy of composition. This fits in well with Leibniz's claim that 'aggregates themselves are nothing but phenomena, since things other than the monads making them up are added by perception alone by virtue of the very fact that they are perceived at the same time'.[53] In other words, to talk of aggregates is to go beyond the reality of the monads themselves and to make essential reference to the contribution of the perceiving mind. Alternatively Leibniz may hold, as he is traditionally interpreted as holding, that a body is not, strictly speaking, identical with an aggregate of monads; rather, an aggregate of monads is misperceived by us as a physical object having the properties of size, shape and position.[54]

According to Leibniz's monadology, there is really nothing in the world but simple substances; strictly speaking, there are no corporeal substances. Leibniz makes only one concession to the privileged status which he had accorded organisms in his earlier philosophy: where organisms are concerned, in the corresponding aggregate of monads there is one monad which is dominant with respect to other members of the aggregate. The dominance relation is to be spelt out in terms of superior clarity and distinctness of perceptions. For example, in the case of human beings the mind is the dominant monad with respect to the aggregate of monads that constitute the body. But towards the end of his life Leibniz seems to have become dissatisfied with this theory; he appears to have felt that the 'hypothesis of mere monads' did not do justice to the unity possessed by organic bodies. In other words, the presence of a dominant monad was not enough to fill this role. Leibniz seems to suggest that, in addition, we must postulate something substantial which unifies the monads; this is what he came to call a 'substantial bond' (*vinculum substantiale*).

Some scholars have expressed scepticism as to whether Leibniz ever committed himself to the theory of the *vinculum substantiale*.[55] The basis for such scepticism is that Leibniz first proposed the theory in correspondence with the Jesuit Des Bosses who invited him to explain how monadology could accommodate the Catholic dogma of transubstantiation: this is the dogma that in the Eucharist the whole substance of the consecrated bread and wine is changed into the substance of the body and blood of Christ. It has thus been suggested that the doctrine of substantial bonds is merely the concession of a diplomat intent on accommodating Catholic dogma. But there are grounds for doubting this interpretation. In the first place, Des Bosses was not entirely happy with the theory of substantial bonds; he raised theological scruples against it. Second, and more importantly, the philosophical fit between the theory and the dogma of transubstantiation is not a very close one.[56] The theory of substantial bonds is intended to account for the unity of organisms. The consecrated bread and wine, however, are not themselves organisms, but rather aggregates of them.[57] Indeed the indications are that Leibniz was engaged in pursuing an independent train of thought about the unity of organisms which led him to the idea of substantial bonds, and that he then adapted this idea to meet the demands of the dogma of transubstantiation.

❧ SPACE AND TIME ❧

As we have seen, Leibniz speaks of monads as having points of view, but this expression is metaphorical; it must not be taken literally as implying that monads occupy positions in space. This is clearly not Leibniz's view. Unfortunately, Leibniz never offers a detailed account of the relations between his doctrine of monads and his theory of space, but he seems to hold that spatial relations are logical constructions out of the perceptual states of monads. In other words, the claim that a certain body is in such and such a spatial position is to be ultimately analysed in terms of propositions about monads and their properties. Thus from his knowledge of the perceptual states of monads, God could read off all the facts about the spatial relations of bodies in the universe. Leibniz is committed, it seems, to the same view of time *mutatis mutandis*. Strictly speaking, monads are no more in time than they are in space, but the temporal relations of events can in principle be read off from the properties of monads. How consistently or rigorously Leibniz adhered to this view of time is unclear.

At the very end of his life the nature of space and time was the subject of a fierce controversy between Leibniz and Newton's disciple, Samuel Clarke; the exchange thus took place at a point in Leibniz's career when the doctrine of monads was securely in position. Despite this, in the controversy with Clarke Leibniz does not seek to reveal the idealist groundfloor of his metaphysics. Throughout this exchange Leibniz argues at an intermediate level of philosophical rigour;[58] for the sake of argument he assumes that the phenomenal world of bodies in space is ontologically basic. We should also note that while the nature of space and time is the dominant topic in the correspondence with Clarke, it is by no means the only issue that divides Leibniz and Newton; Newton's theory of universal gravitation is also one of Leibniz's chief targets. Indeed, in his later years, Leibniz was engaged in a full-scale assault on the foundations of Newtonian science. According to Leibniz, Newtonian science was not only philosophically inept; it was a direct threat to natural religion.[59]

In the correspondence with Clarke Leibniz puts forward two positive theories about the nature of space and time. In the first place, Leibniz argues that space and time are not substances or attributes but relations. 'Space is the order of co-existences; time is the order of successive existences.'[60] Thus Leibniz directly opposes the Newtonian absolute theory according to which space and time are entities which exist independently of bodies and events. For Leibniz, by contrast, bodies are logically prior to space and events are logically prior to time; in other words, there would be no space if there were no bodies and there would be no time if there were no events.[61] Second, Leibniz argues that space and time are ideal. This thesis follows from the relational theory in conjunction with Leibniz's oft-repeated claim that substances alone are fully real, everything else being a mere *ens rationis* or mental construct. The claim that space and time are ideal might lead one to suppose that it is intimately tied in with the doctrines of the monadology, but in fact it is not; although it is fully consistent with those doctrines, it does not depend on them. We can see that this is so by reflecting that Leibniz would still subscribe to the ideality thesis if he held, as he earlier did, that there are genuinely corporeal substances. For the ideality thesis, the crucial point is that space and time are relations and are therefore merely mental constructs.

In his letters to Clarke Leibniz offers two main arguments against the Newtonian theory. The first argument is from the principle of sufficient reason. Notoriously, this principle takes many different forms in Leibniz's philosophy, but here it can be understood to mean simply that there must be a reason for God's choice. The argument can be put in the form of a *reductio ad absurdum*. Suppose that the Newtonian theory of absolute space is true. Now the parts of this space are indiscernible, and so if God created a world he could have no reason for creating it at one point in space rather than some other. But we know both that God has created a world and that he never acts without a reason. The argument thus leads to a contradiction: God both does, and does not, act without a reason. It follows, then, that the theory of absolute space is false. *Mutatis mutandis* the argument can also be directed against the theory of absolute time.[62]

Leibniz's second argument has proved to be of greater philosophical interest in our own time. This argument depends on a version of the identity of indiscernibles which, as various writers have noted, is really tantamount to the modern verificationist principle.[63] According to Leibniz, the Newtonians are committed to saying that it makes sense to suppose that God could, for example, move the universe a few miles to the west while keeping its internal structure unchanged. Leibniz has no patience with such suppositions. If God were to do such things, no change would be observable even in principle. In a remarkable passage Leibniz then states the verificationist objection:

> Motion does not indeed depend on being observed; but it does depend on its being possible to be observed. There is no motion when there is no change that can be observed. And when there is change that can be observed, there is no change at all.[64]

The supposition in question can thus be dismissed as meaningless or, as Leibniz sometimes says, an impossible fiction.

Ever since Clarke Leibniz's readers have been bothered by a seeming inconsistency in his position. The first argument seems to assume that, though absolute space and time are contrary to the divine wisdom, they are at least logically possible; the second argument, by contrast, seeks to establish a stronger claim: the theory of absolute space and time is an impossible fiction. Relatedly, there seems to be an inconsistency in Leibniz's claims about the identity of indiscernibles. Sometimes he says that to suppose two indiscernible entities or states of affairs is to suppose two things under the same name;[65] at other times he says that, though logically possible, the existence of two indiscernible entities would be contrary to the divine wisdom.[66] The problem of interpretation, however, is not really a serious one; it can be solved by assuming that Leibniz is mounting a two-pronged attack on the Newtonian position. Leibniz's main argument turns on the claim that the identity of indiscernibles is a necessary truth: on this argument the supposition of two indiscernible entities is indeed an impossible fiction. But Leibniz is also prepared to argue in a more concessive vein: even if it is granted that two indiscernible entities are logically possible, it can still be shown that they would never obtain because they are contrary to the divine wisdom.

CAUSALITY, PRE-ESTABLISHED ➤➤ HARMONY, AND THE MIND–BODY ➤➤ PROBLEM

The seventeenth and eighteenth centuries were a period of intense interest in the nature of causality. Indeed, in this period the whole concept of causality was going through a process of transformation which was to culminate with Hume. But though early modern philosophers, such as Malebranche and Leibniz, anticipated some of Hume's insights, at least officially they tended to cling to traditional, Aristotelian ideas about the nature of causality which Hume himself was to discard; as a result they often seem to occupy half-way positions on the road to Hume. In general we can say that seventeenth-century philosophers tended to operate with a stronger concept of causality than is current today. This fact is something which needs to be borne in mind when interpreting their metaphysical doctrines about causal relations. Rationalist philosophers, in particular, often seem to be announcing surprising news about the world, but to some extent they can be read as doing something rather different; they are insisting that a certain strong concept of causality is not satisfied by certain events and processes which we might take to be causal.

Malebranche and Leibniz illustrate these points very clearly. In the case of Malebranche his occasionalism arises from his insistence that there must be a logically necessary connection between cause and effect; on this basis he concludes that no creature is a genuine cause.[67] Anticipating Hume he insists that it is not logically necessary, for instance, that the kettle should boil soon after I light a fire under it or that my arm should go up when I will to raise it.[68] Unlike Malebranche, Leibniz is not so wedded to the idea that necessary connection is a requirement for true causality; rather, he accepts the scholastic assumption that genuine causality involves a kind of contagion whereby properties are literally passed on from the cause to the effect. It is true that Leibniz's position is not free from tensions. For instance, he criticizes the scholastic Suarez's definition of 'cause' as 'what flows being into something else' on the grounds that it is barbarous and obscure.[69] Yet Leibniz famously denies that monads causally interact on the ground that they have no windows through which anything could enter or depart.[70] In other words, no properties can be literally transmitted from one simple substance to another. Yet if this is his ground for denying that substances causally interact, then Leibniz must be assuming something like the 'contagion' view of causality. And it is surely this concept of causality which Suarez was trying to capture, however clumsily, in his definition in terms of influx. Thus, rather than abandon traditional assumptions about causality, both Leibniz and Malebranche choose the heroic course of denying the existence of genuine causal relations between finite substances. In other words, they stop short of Hume's revolutionary rethinking of the nature of causality.

Leibniz's doctrine of pre-established harmony, like Malebranche's occasionalism, has been seriously misunderstood. It has been assumed that both doctrines are merely more or less *ad hoc* solutions to the mind–body problem which Descartes is supposed to have bequeathed to his successors. But this assumption is mistaken. Recall that on pp. 393–5 we saw how Leibniz tried to deduce his doctrine of the pre-established harmony (understood as the package of metaphysical theses 3–5) from purely logical considerations; in particular, he tried to deduce it from his complete concept theory. The doctrine of the pre-established harmony is thus not simply an *ad hoc* solution to the mind–body problem; it is a general theory about the relations between finite, created substances. In this respect it resembles Malebranche's occasionalism. But in another respect there is an important relevant difference between the two theories. Because of his Cartesian assumptions, Malebranche is able to offer an occasionalist solution of the mind–body problem as a special case of a more general theory; it is not clear, however, whether Leibniz is really in a position to do the same. Indeed, at points in his philosophical career it is not even clear whether the mind–body problem really arises in his philosophy. We see, then, that

Leibniz pays a price for his attempt to retain Aristotelian ideas while addressing characteristically Cartesian concerns.

To understand the force of these observations it is useful to compare the positions of Descartes and Leibniz. In Descartes's philosophy the mind–body problem is traditionally taken to arise from the fact that he holds that mind and body are both substances and that they are completely heterogeneous; the nature of mind consists wholly in thinking and the nature of body consists wholly in being extended. It has thus seemed difficult to Descartes's readers to see how there could be any union or interaction between two such different substances. By contrast, at no point in his philosophical career did Leibniz accept all the assumptions which generate the mind–body problem in its pure Cartesian form. In the first place, although in his later philosophy Leibniz insists that the soul is a substance, he is much less certain about its status around the time of writing the *Discourse on Metaphysics*. Using scholastic terminology Leibniz notes: 'the soul, properly and accurately speaking, is not a substance, but a substantial form, or the primitive form existing in substance, the first act, the first active faculty.'[71] But if the soul is only an element of substance, then it is not clear that it makes sense to speak of a mind–body problem. Second, throughout his career Leibniz holds that the human body is not a substance but an aggregate of substances. It is true that the nature of the aggregate changes as his metaphysics develops: in the *Discourse* the body is an aggregate of organisms; in the *Monadology* it is an aggregate of monads. But at no time does Leibniz regard the human body as a substance in its own right. Finally, at least in his later philosophy, mind and body, for Leibniz, are not fundamentally heterogeneous, for the body is an aggregate of entities that are themselves soul-like. Now there may well be a case for saying that monads cannot causally interact, but it clearly has nothing to do with considerations of heterogeneity. As we have seen, it has rather to do with the fact that monads have no windows. In other words, causal interaction requires the literal transmission of properties, and in the case of monads this requirement cannot be met.

In its classical form, then, the mind–body problem is a puzzle about the relations between two heterogeneous substances, and in this form the problem cannot arise in Leibniz's philosophy. At most Leibniz faces a problem concerning the relation between a substance (mind) and an aggregate of substances (body). But in that case a solution to this problem cannot be straightforwardly derived from the general doctrine of pre-established harmony. For from the fact that no two substances can interact it does not follow that a substance cannot interact with an aggregate of substances.

Despite these anomalies, Leibniz often writes as if he were in a position to solve the mind–body problem which Descartes bequeathed to his successors; he boasts, for instance, that his doctrine of pre-established harmony solves 'the great mystery of the union of the soul and the body'.[72] In passages like these Leibniz tends to downplay the extent of his Aristotelian-scholastic commitments; he suggests that he shares the dualist assumptions that generate the mind–body problem, and refuses to follow Descartes only in his commitment to interaction-ism. Leibniz then exploits his doctrine of the pre-established harmony in the following way. Although mind and body appear to interact, the metaphysical truth of the matter is that each is simply following its own laws: the body is acting in accordance with the laws of mechanism, the mind is acting in accordance with the laws of psychology. In the former case the causality involved is efficient, in the latter it is teleologi-cal.[73] Thus, for example, my mind and my body have been so pro-grammed by God that, when I form the volition to raise my hat, my arm is ready to execute the appropriate movement.

PSYCHOLOGY: EXPRESSION, ❧ PERCEPTION, AND *PETITES* ❧ *PERCEPTIONS*

Leibniz's solution to the mind–body problem struck many of his con-temporaries as remarkably similar to Malebranche's occasionalism – a comparison which Leibniz resisted.[74] In fact, however, Leibniz's posi-tion is in some ways more reminiscent of Spinoza's. Like Spinoza, Leibniz insists on the autonomy of the physical and mental realms; every physical event has a physical cause, and every mental event has a mental cause. There are of course also important differences between their views. Unlike Spinoza, Leibniz subscribes to the traditional Christian conception of a personal God and he holds, at least in his later philosophy, that the mind is a naturally immortal, immaterial substance. But these very differences suggest a way of viewing Leibniz's project, at least with regard to the mind–body problem; he is seeking to do justice to some of Spinoza's key ideas within the framework of traditional Christian theology.

There is indeed much that is Spinozistic in Leibniz's psychology. Consider, for instance, how Leibniz applies his concept of expression to the relationship between mind and body. According to Leibniz, the mind does not interact with the body, but it expresses it in the technical sense of the term which he explained for Arnauld's benefit. Indeed, Leibniz tells Arnauld that the mind expresses its own body better than it expresses anything else in the universe.[75] In response to Arnauld's query Leibniz explains that he does not mean by this that our mind has clearer thoughts of, say, the activity of its lymphatic glands than of the satellites of Jupiter; he means rather that given a complete knowledge of my mental states a supermind would find it easier to read off truths about my physical states than about the celestial bodies.[76] As Spinoza wrote, 'the ideas that we have of external bodies indicate the constitution of our own body more than the nature of external bodies'.[77] Leibniz might have stopped at this point, but in fact he goes further; he claims that the mind expresses its body by perceiving it, perception being a species of expression; indeed the mind perceives everything that happens in its body.[78] Here again Leibniz seems to be following in Spinoza's footsteps, for Spinoza had similarly written that 'whatever happens in the object [i.e. the body] of the idea constituting the human mind is bound to be perceived by the human mind'.[79] But whereas Spinoza does little to dispel the mystery surrounding this claim, Leibniz offers a body of theory which plugs the gaps in Spinoza's account. This is the famous doctrine of unconscious perceptions.

Here it is helpful to recall Leibniz's hierarchical arrangement of monads. All monads perceive, but they differ vastly in terms of the quality of their perceptions. Human minds or spirits are distinguished not only by reason but also by 'apperception' which means consciousness or perhaps even self-consciousness. But though Leibniz holds that human minds are set apart from lower monads by their capacity for (self)-conscious awareness, he further believes that they also have unconscious or little perceptions (*petites perceptions*); such perceptions are little because they are low in intensity. Not merely do large stretches of our mental life consist wholly in little perceptions, but even conscious mental states are composed of such perceptions. The doctrine of unconscious perceptions is perhaps Leibniz's principal innovation in psychology, and it is of course profoundly anti-Cartesian in its implications. For Descartes subscribes to the view that the mind is transparent to itself; he is explicit that there is nothing in the mind of which we are not conscious.[80]

In the *New Essays on Human Understanding*, his reply to Locke, Leibniz remarks that there are 'thousands of indications' in favour of unconscious perceptions.[81] Obviously there is an element of hyperbole in this claim, but even so, Leibniz certainly has a battery of arguments for his doctrine. Some of these arguments are based on *a priori* principles such as the identity of indiscernibles which requires that any two minds must be qualitatively, not just numerically, different. Although Leibniz is not quite explicit about this, another assumption of the argument seems to be that minds at or before birth have no conscious experiences; thus the individuating characteristics required by the identity of indiscernibles must occur below the threshold of consciousness.[82] Other arguments are less tied to the distinctive principles of Leibniz's metaphysics, but not all of them are more cogent. Leibniz is fond of arguing that, in order to hear the waves breaking on the shore, we must hear the noise of each individual wave.[83] This argument has been criticized as being as dubious as arguing, from the fact that we feel the weight of a stone, that we must have an unconscious perception of each of the molecules that make it up.[84]

Perhaps more interesting is what we may call Leibniz's 'attention argument' which may be illustrated by the following scenario.[85] Suppose that two people, Smith and Jones, are having a conversation and that, throughout, a drill has been operating in the background; Smith has not been conscious of the noise, but he now suddenly has his attention drawn to it by Jones. Leibniz argues that in the act of attention Smith is really remembering a past perception of the noise. But *ex hypothesi* this earlier perception was not a conscious one and must therefore have been 'little' or unconscious. This argument clearly depends on the premise that attention involves memory, and one might wonder why one should accept this. If it is supposed to be true by definition, then the definition seems merely stipulative. Nonetheless, there is something attractive about the suggestion that cases like this force us to recognize the existence of unconscious perceptions, and Leibniz can support his conclusion in other ways. For example, it was implicitly assumed in our description of the case that Smith's sense organs are equally stimulated by the drilling both before and during the act of attention. Now Leibniz cannot of course strictly ascribe any psychological effects to a physical stimulus, but by virtue of his theory of expression he can and does insist that some state of the soul must correspond to any such stimulation;[86] and by hypothesis, as we have seen, the mental state which precedes the act of attention is not a conscious awareness of the noise. Leibniz can also fall back on an appeal to the law of continuity;[87] there would be a flagrant breach of this law if the stimulus which 'produced' a conscious perception of the noise during the act of attention 'produced' no perception at all in the mind before the act.

The doctrine of unconscious perceptions is a key element in Leibniz's attack on the Cartesian view that mentality is all or nothing. For Leibniz, by contrast, mentality is a continuum which extends below the threshold of consciousness. Sometimes, as we should expect, Leibniz's rejection of Descartes's view of the mental life provides the basis for the rejection of other Cartesian doctrines. Leibniz sides with common sense against the notorious Cartesian thesis that animals are mere automata. He argues that the Cartesians were led astray by their failure to distinguish between thought and perception; in other words, the Cartesians have made the mistake of confusing a species with its corresponding genus.[88] Thus even if animals have no thought (*cogitatio*), it does not follow that they have no perceptions. Leibniz is clear, then, that animals have a mental life, but he is less clear about its precise nature. He seems to have believed that, unlike humans, animals have no capacity for self-consciousness, but whether he believed that they could consciously feel pain is less certain. Unfortunately, the issue is complicated by an obscurity in Leibniz's concept of apperception which, as we have suggested, is ambiguous between consciousness and self-consciousness.[89]

Somewhat curiously, however, at other times Leibniz uses his theory of perception to defend Cartesian theses, although often in a seriously modified form. Here too the doctrine of unconscious perceptions plays a key role. As against Locke, for example, Leibniz exploits the doctrine in order to defend, or rather re-work, the Cartesian thesis that the mind always thinks. For Leibniz, the mind always thinks, not in the sense of being always conscious, but rather in the sense of never being without some perceptions; for example, even in dreamless sleep or a coma the mind has its *petites perceptions*. It is thoroughly characteristic of Leibniz's concerns that his defence of this Cartesian thesis is in the service of a larger goal – the vindication of an immaterialist theory of mind against what he sees as Locke's subversive attack on this doctrine. For Leibniz, the immateriality of the mind entails that it is naturally immortal, and this in turn entails that it always perceives.[90]

❧ KNOWLEDGE AND IDEAS ❧

In contrast with Locke and the other British empiricists, Leibniz has traditionally been classified as a rationalist, and this classification is fundamentally an epistemological one: a rationalist philosopher is one who believes that it is possible to know substantive truths about the world *a priori*, by reason alone. We might expect, then, that in his full-length reply to Locke, the *New Essays*, Leibniz would seize the opportunity to provide a systematic defence of the rationalist position in epistemology. Yet on the whole this expectation is disappointed. On the contrary, as I have already indicated, Leibniz's main purpose in this work is not epistemological at all: it is metaphysical. Leibniz told a correspondent that in writing this work he was above all concerned to defend the immateriality of the soul.[91]

This fact about the work is remarkably suggestive of Leibniz's overall philosophical orientation. Unlike Descartes and the British empiricists, Leibniz was not greatly interested in what have since come to be regarded as the central issues in epistemology; the problem of our knowledge of the external world, for instance, was never at the forefront of his philosophical concerns. As we have seen, Leibniz some-

times toys with phenomenalism, and in the hands of Berkeley phenomenalism serves as an answer to the challenge of scepticism. Leibniz,
however, does not seem to have been primarily attracted to phenomenalism for this reason. On occasion, of course, Leibniz can make some
shrewd criticisms of the attempts of other philosophers to solve epistemological questions. Leibniz is rightly suspicious of Descartes's
appeal to clear and distinct ideas, and he ruthlessly exposes the weaknesses of Descartes's proof of the existence of the external world; he
remarks with some justice that Descartes's proof is so feeble that it
would have been better not to try.[92] But some of Leibniz's criticisms
of Descartes indicate a lack of deep engagement with the issues. Leibniz
states that *Varia a me cogitantur* ('Various things are thought by me')
has as strong a claim as the *Cogito, ergo sum* to be regarded as a first
principle of knowledge.[93] But this comment suggests a blindness to the
peculiarly self-verifying character of the *cogito*.

Perhaps Leibniz's chief interest in the theory of knowledge lies
in defending a version of the Cartesian, and ultimately Platonic, doctrine of innate ideas. Not surprisingly, Leibniz's main defence of this
doctrine is to be found in the *New Essays*; indeed, it constitutes the
single most substantive treatment of epistemological issues in that work.
But Leibniz's case for innate ideas does not stand on its own; it is an
application of a theory of ideas in general, and it is best to begin by
taking a brief look at this theory.

Leibniz's theory of ideas can be understood against the background of a famous controversy between Malebranche and Arnauld.[94]
There are a number of issues in this controversy, but for our purposes
the central problem is the ontological status of ideas. As an orthodox
Cartesian Arnauld argued that ideas or concepts – e.g. the concept of
a triangle – are mind-dependent entities; indeed, they are modifications
of the mind.[95] Malebranche, by contrast, argued that ideas are not in
human minds at all; rather, they are in God.[96] By thus locating ideas
in God, Malebranche is self-consciously reviving the Augustinian doctrine of divine illumination; in order to achieve genuine knowledge of
the world, our minds must be illuminated by the light of God's ideas.
But Malebranche's philosophical point can perhaps be explained by
removing the theological trappings; in contrast with Arnauld and orthodox Cartesians, he argues that ideas (concepts) are not psychological
but abstract entities.

Leibniz approves of Malebranche's revival of the doctrine of
divine illumination, and like Malebranche he speaks of God as the
region of ideas.[97] But despite his tendency to echo Malebranche's language, Leibniz does not really follow him in regarding ideas as irreduci-
bly abstract entities. Unlike Malebranche, Leibniz is a nominalist who
cannot countenance such entities as basic items of ontology.[98] Certainly

Leibniz's official definition of the term 'idea' is uncompromisingly psychological; ideas are 'in the mind' and they are 'faculties' – that is, dispositions to think in certain ways.[99] For Leibniz, then, since it is a psychological disposition, an idea is a persistent property of the mind. Thus, unlike Arnauld, Leibniz does not simply identify ideas with particular mental episodes. This definition of 'idea' does justice to something which Descartes recognized, if less explicitly and only intermittently: a person can have an idea of x even if at that moment he is not actually thinking of x.

On such a theory of ideas it is not hard to see what is involved in a commitment to innate ideas. For if ideas are themselves mental dispositions, then innate ideas are innate mental dispositions; they are dispositions which we have had at least since birth. This is the form of the doctrine which Leibniz has primarily in mind when he defends the innateness of mathematical and metaphysical concepts against Locke. In his polemic Locke had adopted a two-pronged strategy of attack on innate ideas. According to Locke, the thesis of innate ideas is either empirically false – it ascribes highly abstract concepts to infants – or it is condemned to triviality.[100] In reply Leibniz seeks to show that his own dispositional theory of innate ideas constitutes a third option which is not caught in the mesh of Locke's polemic. To claim that the mind has an innate idea of x is not just to say, as Locke supposes, that it is capable of thinking of x; a distinction must be drawn between dispositions and 'bare faculties'.[101] That Leibniz is right to draw such a distinction can be shown by reference to the case of a physical disposition such as fragility. When we call an object fragile, we are not just saying that it is capable of breaking; otherwise any object which breaks is fragile. Leibniz's theory of innate ideas thus implies at least that the mind is differentially predisposed to form certain thoughts rather than others. Here Leibniz seems to be reviving Descartes's thesis that ideas are innate

> in the same sense as that in which we say that generosity is 'innate' in certain families, or that certain diseases such as gout or stones are innate in others; it is not so much that the babies of such families suffer from these diseases in their mother's womb, but simply that they are born with a certain 'faculty' or tendency to contract them.[102]

In one way, however, Leibniz's dispositional theory of innate ideas seems to differ from Descartes's. Unlike Descartes, Leibniz seems to hold that mental dispositions cannot be basic properties; they need to be grounded in fully actual, non-dispositional properties of the mind. Here Leibniz may be responding to Malebranche's criticism that the Cartesians inconsistently countenanced basic powers in psychology, while rightly banishing them from physics.[103] But while it is obvious how, say, fragility can be grounded in structural properties of the glass, it is less clear what could serve to ground mental dispositions. In order to meet this requirement, it seems that Leibniz once again appeals to his doctrine of unconscious perceptions. My innate disposition to think of a triangle, for example, would be grounded in an unconscious perception which has triangle content. It is this doctrine which Leibniz appears to have in mind when he writes in the *New Essays* that 'ideas and truths are innate in us – as inclinations, dispositions, tendencies, or natural virtualities, and not as actions; although these virtualities are always accompanied by certain actions, often insensible ones, which correspond to them.'[104]

The dispositional theory is Leibniz's main theory of innate ideas, but it is not the only one. Leibniz also advances what we may call the 'reflection account'. According to this account, the idea of substance, for example, is innate in the sense that we can acquire it by turning our mental gaze inward and reflecting on the fact that our minds are substances. Leibniz seems to have been pleased with this theory, and it inspires some of his best-known remarks about innate ideas; it underlies such claims as 'We are innate to ourselves' and 'There is nothing in the intellect which was not previously in the senses, except the intellect itself'.[105] None the less, for all Leibniz's evident pride in the doctrine, it does not seem very satisfactory. For one thing, on this account ideas turn out to be innate only in the minimal sense that they are not acquired through the senses. Moreover, the theory faces obvious difficulties in explaining our acquisition of mathematical concepts, and these are generally numbered among the *explananda* for any theory of innate ideas. We may perhaps acquire the idea of substance by reflecting on the fact that our minds are substances, but we can hardly acquire the concept of a triangle by reflecting on the fact that our minds are triangular.

So far we have been chiefly concerned with Leibniz's defence of a theory of innate ideas against the Lockean objection that it must reduce to triviality. But what positive arguments does Leibniz offer in favour of the innatist doctrine? In the *New Essays* Leibniz is much more forthcoming on this score in connection with innate propositions than with innate concepts. In part this fact reflects the emphasis of Locke's own discussion, but it also testifies to Leibniz's concern with a problem which has exercised philosophers at least since Plato: this is the problem of explaining how we can have *a priori* knowledge of necessary truths, as we do in the case of mathematics. Leibniz follows the Platonic tradition by arguing that it is impossible to explain such knowledge except on the assumption that it is innate in our minds.[106] Through the senses, for example, we may perhaps come to believe that the Pythagorean theorem is true of all observed right-angled triangles, but we would never come to believe that this theorem expresses a necessary truth about such triangles.

Leibniz's case for innate knowledge has a distinguished ancestry, but it seems to be in danger of running together two separate issues.[107] In the first place, there is a causal question: how do we acquire beliefs to the effect that necessarily p? Second, there is a question of justification: how do we justify our claim to know that necessarily p? Leibniz sometimes seems to say that both questions can be answered in terms of an appeal to innateness, but this claim is distinctly dubious. The hypothesis of innateness may be a plausible answer to the first question, but it is more difficult to see how it helps with the second, normative issue; on the face of it, it seems entirely possible that our innate beliefs should all be false. It is true that the innatist hypothesis would help to answer the second question on the further assumption of divine benevolence; a good God can be trusted not to inscribe a pack of lies on our minds. Unlike Descartes, however, Leibniz is reluctant to appeal to divine benevolence in order to solve epistemological questions.

Leibniz's philosophy, and his metaphysics in particular, is an extraordinarily ambitious work of synthesis. His system seeks, for example, to combine Aristotelian and Cartesian insights within a framework of Christian theology. Sometimes Leibniz's attempts at synthesis seem overambitious and even misguided; on occasion Leibniz seeks to address issues – such as the mind–body problem – without indicating how far he has departed from the assumptions which initially gave rise to them. Leibniz may well have been aware of such stresses in his system, and it may have been because of this awareness that he never ceased to develop as a philosopher; he continued to seek new ways of assembling the materials of his philosophy into a coherent whole. Indeed, in some ways, despite its strangeness, his later idealism is more coherent than the earlier, Aristotelian metaphysics. But though Leibniz had to struggle to achieve overall coherence, in the process he made major contributions to philosophical thought about the issues he discussed; his theories of substance, identity, causality, space and time, and innate ideas are illuminating and historically influential. For all its internal tensions and unresolved problems, his system in its various forms remains one of the most impressive examples of speculative metaphysics.

❧ ABBREVIATIONS ❧

A   German Academy of Sciences (ed.) *G. W. Leibniz: Sämtliche Schriften und Briefe* (Darmstadt, 1923-). References are to series and volume.

AG   R. Ariew and D. Garber (ed. and trans.), *Leibniz: Philosophical Essays* (Indianapolis, Ind., and Cambridge, Mass., 1989)

AT   C. Adam and P. Tannery (eds) *Oeuvres de Descartes*, 12 vols (Paris, 1897–1913; reprinted Paris, 1964–76)

CSM   J. Cottingham, R. Stoothoff and D. Murdoch (trans.), *The Philosophical Writings of Descartes*, 2 vols (Cambridge, 1985)

F de C   A. Foucher de Careil (ed.) *Nouvelles Lettres et Opuscules Inédits de Leibniz* (Paris, 1857)

G   C. I. Gerhardt (ed.) *Die Philosophischen Schriften von G. W. Leibniz* (Berlin, 1875–90)

Grua   G. Grua (ed.) *G. W. Leibniz: Textes Inédits*, 2 vols (Paris, 1948)

L   L. E. Loemker (ed.) *G. W. Leibniz: Philosophical Papers and Letters* (Dordrecht, 2nd edn, 1969)

MP   H. T. Mason (ed. and trans.) and G. H. R. Parkinson (intro.) *The Leibniz-Arnauld Correspondence* (Manchester, 1967)

NE   *New Essays on Human Understanding (Nouveaux Essais sur l'Entendement Humain)*. References are to series VI, volume 6, of the Academy edition and to the Remnant and Bennett translation. The pagination of Remnant and Bennett is identical with that of the Academy text; one page number thus serves for both

RB   P. Remnant and J. Bennett (trans. and eds) *G. W. Leibniz: New Essays on Human Understanding* (Cambridge, 1981)

I have generally followed the cited translations; any significant modifications are indicated in the notes.

❦ NOTES ❦

1 See, for example, NE IV.viii, A VI.vi, RB 431.
2 Leibniz to Remond, 10 January 1714, G III 607.
3 See J. Bennett, *A Study of Spinoza's Ethics* (Cambridge, Cambridge University Press, 1984), pp. 55–6.
4 Aristotle, *Categories*, ch. 5, 4a.
5 *Discourse on Metaphysics* 8, G IV 432, L 307.
6 ibid., G IV 433, L 307.
7 Leibniz to Arnauld, 30 April 1687, G II 96–7, MP 121.
8 Sleigh [11.27], 123.
9 cf. Bennett, op. cit., p. 58.
10 Leibniz to Arnauld, 30 April 1687, G II 100–1, MP 126.
11 Strictly speaking, for Descartes, there is only one body or extended substance: the entire physical universe.
12 See Sleigh [11.27], 98–101.
13 See Broad [11.29], 49–51.
14 Leibniz to Arnauld, 30 April 1687, G II 101, MP 126.
15 Arnauld to Leibniz, 4 March 1687, G II 86, MP 107.
16 Leibniz to Arnauld, 30 April 1687, G II 97, MP 121.
17 Arnauld to Leibniz, 4 March 1687, G II 87–8, MP 109.

18 Leibniz to Arnauld, 30 April 1687, G II 100, MP 125–6.
19 *Discourse on Metaphysics* 8, G IV 433, L 307.
20 Russell [11.38]; Couturat [11.43]; Couturat [11.44].
21 'First Truths', C 521, L 269. (Translation modified.)
22 See, for example, M. Ayers, 'Analytical Philosophy and the History of Philosophy', in J. Rée, M. Ayers and A. Westoby, *Philosophy and its Past* (Brighton, Harvester, 1978), p. 45. See also B. Brody, 'Leibniz's Metaphysical Logic', in Kulstad [11.34], 43–55.
23 Aristotle, *Metaphysics* 1011 b 27.
24 Leibniz to Arnauld, 14 July 1686, G II 56, MP 63.
25 As Arnauld noted (Arnauld to Leibniz, 13 March 1686, G II 15, MP 9), these remarkable doctrines of Leibniz's logic raise a number of puzzles concerning freedom and contingency. On these see, for example, Sleigh [11.27].
26 *Discourse on Metaphysics* 9, G IV 433, L 308.
27 Leibniz's Fourth Paper to Clarke, G VII 372, L 687.
28 See Parkinson [11.58], 6–8.
29 Leibniz to Arnauld, 9 October 1687, G II 112, MP 144.
30 *Discourse on Metaphysics* 8, G IV 433, L 308. (Translation modified.)
31 See Broad [11.29], 24–5.
32 See Loeb [11.55], 279.
33 It is worth noting here that, strictly speaking, there is a logical gap between 3 and 4 themselves. If 4 is derived from 3, then it is tacitly assumed that every state of a substance must have a cause. If, on the other hand, 3 is derived from 4, then it is tacitly assumed that there is no causal overdetermination. Both these assumptions would be congenial to Leibniz.
34 Parkinson [11.58], 147.
35 ibid., p. 151.
36 Loeb [11.55], 286.
37 'First Truths', C 521, L 269. See Loeb [11.55], 289.
38 See Sleigh [11.27], 11.
39 See, for example, *New System*, G IV 484, L 457.
40 On the development of Leibniz's philosophy, see Broad [11.29], 87; D. Garber, 'Leibniz and the Foundations of Physics: The Middle Years', in K. Okruhlik and J. R. Brown (eds) *The Natural Philosophy of Leibniz* (Dordrecht, Reidel, 1985), pp. 27–130.
41 Leibniz to De Volder, 30 June 1704, G II 270, L 537.
42 *Monadology* 4, G VII 607, L 643.
43 Revision note of 1697–1700 to 'A New Method for Learning and Teaching Jurisprudence', A VI.i p. 286, L 91n.
44 R. McRae [11.69], 60.
45 Whether God is a monad is not entirely clear. However, there are places where Leibniz seems to say that God is a monad – for example, Grua II 558.
46 See Broad [11.29], 75, for a helpful discussion of these issues.
47 Leibniz to De Volder, undated, G II 275, AG 181.
48 M. Furth, 'Monadology', in Frankfurt [11.32], 99–135, esp. p. 122; Loeb [11.55], 304–5.
49 Leibniz to Des Bosses, 16 June 1712, G II 451–2, L 605.
50 Furth, in [11.32], 118–19.

51 See, for example, Leibniz to Des Bosses, 31 July 1709, G II 379; Leibniz to Des Bosses, January 1710, G II 399.
52 See, for example, Leibniz to Arnauld, 9 October 1687, G II 118–19, MP 152.
53 Leibniz to Des Bosses, 29 May 1716, GP II 517, AG 203.
54 See, for example, Broad [11.29], 91. For criticisms of the 'misperception' interpretation, see Rutherford [11.59], 11–28.
55 'Nowhere does Leibniz himself assert that he believes it. . . . Thus the *vinculum substantiale* is rather the concession of a diplomatist than the creed of a philosopher' (Russell [11.38], 152; cf. Broad [11.29], 124–5).
56 cf. Broad [11.29], 127.
57 Leibniz to Des Bosses, 20 September 1712, G II 459, L 607.
58 C. D. Broad, 'Leibniz's Last Controversy with the Newtonians', in Woolhouse [11.62], 171.
59 Leibniz's First Paper to Clarke, G VII 352, L 675.
60 Leibniz's Third Paper to Clarke, G VII 363, L 682.
61 cf. Broad, in [11.62], 158–9.
62 Leibniz's Third Paper to Clarke, G VII 364, L 682–3.
63 Alexander [11.12], xxiii; Broad, in [11.62], 166.
64 Leibniz's Fifth Paper to Clarke, G VII 403–4, L 705.
65 Leibniz's Fourth Paper to Clarke, G VII 372, L 687.
66 Leibniz's Fifth Paper to Clarke, G VII 395, L 700.
67 N. Malebranche, *The Search After Truth*, 6.2.3.
68 ibid.
69 See the Preface to an edition of Nizolius, G IV 148. For an illuminating discussion of these issues, see H. Ishiguro, 'Pre-established Harmony versus Constant Conjunction', in A. Kenny (ed.) *Rationalism, Empiricism, and Idealism* (Oxford, Oxford University Press, 1986), pp. 61–85.
70 *Monadology* 7, G VII 607; L 643.
71 'Notes on Some Comments by Michel Angelo Fardella', AG 105; F de C 323.
72 *Discourse on Metaphysics* 33, G IV 458, L 324.
73 *Monadology* 33, G VI 620, L 651; *Principles of Nature and of Grace* 3, G VI 599, L 637.
74 See Chapter 10 for a discussion of Leibniz's attitude towards Malebranche's occasionalism. See also Sleigh [11.27], 151–70.
75 See Leibniz to Arnauld, 28 November/8 December 1686, G II 74, MP 92; cf. Leibniz to Arnauld, 30 April 1687, G II 90, MP 113.
76 See Leibniz to Arnauld, 9 October 1687, G II 112, MP 143–4.
77 *Ethics* Part 2, Proposition 16, Corollary 2.
78 Leibniz to Arnauld, 9 October 1687, G II 112, MP 144.
79 *Ethics* Part 2, Proposition 12.
80 First Set of Replies, AT VII 107, CSM II 77.
81 NE Preface, A VI.vi, RB 53. (Translation modified.)
82 ibid., p. 58.
83 ibid., p. 54.
84 J. Cottingham, *The Rationalists* (Oxford, Oxford University Press, 1988), p. 152.
85 NE Preface, A VI.vi, RB 54.
86 ibid.

87 See Leibniz's appeal to the law of continuity, ibid., p. 56.

88 Leibniz to Treuer, 21 May 1708; see Jolley [11.22], 117; cf. *Principles of Nature and of Grace* 4, G VI 600, L 637.

89 McRae argues that Leibniz's position on the issue of whether animals have sensation is contradictory. 'On the one hand what distinguishes animals from lower forms of life is sensation or feeling, but on the other hand apperception is a necessary condition of sensation, and apperception distinguishes human beings from animals' (McRae [11.69], 30). Leibniz certainly holds that self-consciousness distinguishes man from other animals, but whether he consistently equates self-consciousness with apperception is less clear.

90 See Jolley [11.22], 104.

91 Leibniz to Jaquelot, 28 April 1704, G III 473.

92 'Critical Thoughts on the General Part of Descartes's *Principles*', G IV 360, L 391.

93 ibid., G IV 357, L 385.

94 This controversy was initiated by Arnauld's *On True and False Ideas* (1683) which attacked Malebranche's theory of ideas. On this controversy see S. Nadler, *Arnauld and the Cartesian Philosophy of Ideas* (Princeton, N.J., Princeton University Press, 1989); Jolley [11.65].

95 *On True and False Ideas*, ch. 5, Definition 3.

96 *Search After Truth* 3.2.6.

97 'On the Radical Origination of Things', G VII 305, L 488.

98 The case for Leibniz's nominalism is well argued in Mates [11.57], ch. 10.

99 'What is an Idea?', G VII 263, L 207.

100 J. Locke, *Essay Concerning Human Understanding* I.ii.

101 NE I.i., A VI.vi, RB 79–80.

102 *Comments on a Certain Broadsheet*, AT VIII-B 358, CSM I 304.

103 Elucidation Ten, *Search After Truth*.

104 NE Preface, A VI.vi, RB 52.

105 NE Preface, A VI.vi, RB 51; ibid., II.i, 111. Strictly speaking, even the reflection account involves a dispositional component, since it is a theory of how we acquire ideas, and ideas are mental dispositions.

106 ibid., Preface, p. 49.

107 For this line of criticism see S. Stich (ed.) *Innate Ideas* (Berkeley and Los Angeles, Calif., University of California Press, 1975), Introduction, pp. 17–18.

~ BIBLIOGRAPHY ~

Original language editions

11.1 G. W. *Leibniz: Sämtliche Schriften und Briefe*, ed. German Academy of Sciences, Berlin and Darmstadt, Akademie Verlag, 6 series, 1923–.

11.2 *Die Philosophischen Schriften von G. W. Leibniz*, ed. C. I. Gerhardt, Berlin, Weidmann, 7 vols, 1875–90.

11.3 *Opuscules et fragments inédits de Leibniz*, ed. L. Couturat, Paris, Alcan, 1903.

11.4   G. W. *Leibniz: Textes Inédits*, ed. G. Grua, Paris, Presses Universitaires de France, 2 vols, 1948.

English translations

Collections and selected works

11.5   G. W. *Leibniz: Philosophical Essays*, trans. R. Ariew and D. Garber, Indianapolis, Ind., Hackett, 1989.
11.6   G. W. *Leibniz: Philosophical Papers and Letters*, trans. L. E. Loemker, Dordrecht, Reidel, 2nd edn, 1969.
11.7   *Leibniz: Philosophical Writings*, trans. M. Morris and G. H. R. Parkinson, London, Dent, 1973.
11.8   G. W. *Leibniz: Logical Papers: A Selection*, trans. G. H. R. Parkinson, Oxford, Clarendon, 1966.
11.9   *Leibniz: Political Writings*, trans. P. Riley, Cambridge, Cambridge University Press, 2nd edn, 1988.

Separate works

11.10 *Leibniz: Discourse on Metaphysics*, trans. P. G. Lucas and L. Grint, Manchester, Manchester University Press, 1953.
11.11 *The Leibniz–Arnauld Correspondence*, trans. H. T. Mason with an introduction by G. H. R. Parkinson, Manchester, Manchester University Press, 1967.
11.12 *The Leibniz–Clarke Correspondence*, ed. H. G. Alexander, Manchester, Manchester University Press, 1956.
11.13 G. W. *Leibniz: Theodicy*, trans. E. M. Huggard, London, Routledge & Kegan Paul, 1952.

Bibliographies and concordances

Bibliographies

11.14 Ravier, E. *Bibliographie des Oeuvres de Leibniz*, Paris, Alcan, 1937.
11.15 Schrecker, P. 'Une Bibliographie de Leibniz', *Revue philosophique de la France et de l'étranger* 63 (1938) 324–46.
11.16 Heinekamp, A. (ed.) *Leibniz Bibliographie: die Literatur über Leibniz bis 1980*, Frankfurt, Klosterman, 2nd edn, 1984.
11.17 Totok, W. 'Leibniz Bibliographie', in *Handbuch der Geschichte der Philosophie*, vol. 14, Frankfurt, Klosterman, 1981, 297–374.

Each volume of *Studia Leibnitiana* – from vol. 1 (1969) onwards – contains a bibliographical survey of the year's work in Leibniz studies.

Concordances

11.18 Finster, R., Hunter, G., McRae, R. F., Miles, M. and Seager, W. E. (eds) *Leibniz Lexicon: a Dual Concordance to Leibniz's 'Philosophische Schriften'*. Concordance I: Printed Philosophical Register with Large Contexts. Concordance II: Microfiche Key-Word-in-Context Concordance. Hildesheim, Olms-Weidmann, 1988. (Concordance to *Die Philosophischen Schriften von G. W. Leibniz*, ed. C. I. Gerhardt, Berlin, Weidmann, 7 vols, 1875–90).

Leibniz's relations to other philosophers

11.19 Belaval, Y. *Leibniz, critique de Descartes*, Paris, Gallimard, 1960.

11.20 Friedmann, G. *Leibniz et Spinoza*, Paris, Gallimard, 1946.

11.21 Hall, A. R. *Philosophers at War: The Quarrel between Newton and Leibniz*, Cambridge, Cambridge University Press, 1980.

11.22 Jolley, N. *Leibniz and Locke: A Study of the* New Essays on Human Understanding, Oxford, Clarendon, 1984.

11.23 Loemker, L. E. *Struggle for Synthesis: The Seventeenth-Century Background to Leibniz's Synthesis of Order and Freedom*, Cambridge, Mass., Harvard University Press, 1972.

11.24 Mates, B. 'Leibniz and the *Phaedo*', *Studia Leibnitiana Supplementa* 12 (1973) 135–48.

11.25 Popkin, R. 'Leibniz and the French Sceptics', *Revue internationale de philosophie* 20 (1966) 228–48.

11.26 Schrecker, P. 'Leibniz and the *Timaeus*', *Review of Metaphysics* 4 (1950–1) 495–505.

11.27 Sleigh, R. C., Jr, *Leibniz and Arnauld: A Commentary on their Correspondence*, New Haven, Conn., Yale University Press, 1990.

The philosophy of Leibniz: general surveys

11.28 Belaval, Y. *Leibniz: Initiation à sa philosophie*, Paris, Vrin, 1962.

11.29 Broad, C. D. *Leibniz: An Introduction*, Cambridge, Cambridge University Press, 1975.

11.30 Brown, S. *Leibniz*, Brighton, Harvester, 1984.

11.31 Cassirer, E. *Leibniz' System in seinen wissenschaftlichen Grundlagen*, Marburg, Elwert, 1902.

11.32 Frankfurt, H. G. (ed.) *Leibniz: A Collection of Critical Essays*, New York, Doubleday, 1972.

11.33 Hooker, M. (ed.) *Leibniz: Critical and Interpretive Essays*, Minneapolis, Minn., Minnesota University Press, 1982.

11.34 Kulstad, M. (ed.) *Essays on the Philosophy of Leibniz*, Rice University Studies 63, Houston, Tex., Rice University Press, 1977.

11.35 MacDonald Ross, G. *Leibniz*, Oxford, Oxford University Press, 1984.

11.36 Rescher, N. *The Philosophy of Leibniz*, Englewood Cliffs, N.J., Prentice Hall, 1967.

11.37 Rescher, N. *Leibniz: An Introduction to his Philosophy*, Oxford, Blackwell, 1979.

11.38 Russell, B. *A Critical Exposition of the Philosophy of Leibniz*, London, Allen & Unwin, 1900.

11.39 Van Peursen, C. A. *Leibniz*, trans. H. Hoskins, London, Faber & Faber, 1969.

Logic and metaphysics

11.40 Adams, R. M. 'Phenomenalism and Corporeal Substance in Leibniz', in P. A. French, T. E. Uehling and H. K. Wettstein (eds) *Contemporary Perspectives on the History of Philosophy*, Midwest Studies in Philosophy 8, 1983, 217–57.

11.41 Broad, C. D. 'Leibniz's Last Controversy with the Newtonians', in [11.62], 157–74.

11.42 Brody, B. 'Leibniz's Metaphysical Logic', in M. Kulstad (ed.) *Essays on the Philosophy of Leibniz*, Rice University Studies 63, Houston, Tex., Rice University Press, 1977, 43–55.

11.43 Couturat, L. *La logique de Leibniz*, Paris, Alcan, 1901.

11.44 Couturat, L. 'Sur la métaphysique de Leibniz', *Revue de métaphysique et de morale* 10 (1902) 1–25; English translation by R. Ryan in H. G. Frankfurt (ed.) *Leibniz: A Collection of Critical Essays*, New York, Doubleday, 1972, 19–45.

11.45 Fleming, N. 'On Leibniz on Subject and Substance', *Philosophical Review* 96 (1987) 69–95.

11.46 Furth, M. 'Monadology', *Philosophical Review* 76 (1967) 169–200; also in H. G. Frankfurt (ed.) *Leibniz: A Collection of Critical Essays*, New York, Doubleday, 1972, 99–135.

11.47 Garber, D. 'Motion and Metaphysics in the Young Leibniz', in M. Hooker (ed.) *Leibniz: Critical and Interpretive Essays*, Minneapolis, Minn., Minnesota University Press, 1982, 160–84.

11.48 Garber, D. 'Leibniz and the Foundations of Physics: The Middle Years', in K. Okruhlik and J. R. Brown (eds) *The Natural Philosophy of Leibniz*, Dordrecht, Reidel, 1985, 27–130.

11.49 Gueroult, M. *Dynamique et métaphysique leibniziennes*, Paris, Les Belles Lettres, 1934.

11.50 Hacking, I. 'Individual Substance', in H. G. Frankfurt (ed.) *Leibniz: A Collection of Critical Essays*, New York, Doubleday, 1972, 137–53.

11.51 Hacking, I. 'A Leibnizian Theory of Truth', in M. Hooker (ed.) *Leibniz: Critical and Interpretive Essays*, Minneapolis, Minn., Minnesota University Press, 1982, 185–95.

11.52 Ishiguro, H. *Leibniz's Philosophy of Logic and Language*, London, Duckworth, 1972.

11.53 Ishiguro, H. 'Pre-established Harmony versus Constant Conjunction', in A. Kenny (ed.) *Rationalism, Empiricism, and Idealism*, British Academy

Lectures on the History of Philosophy, Oxford, Clarendon, 1986, 61–85.

11.54 Jolley, N. 'Leibniz and Phenomenalism', *Studia Leibnitiana* 18 (1986) 38–51.

11.55 Loeb, L. E. 'Leibniz's Denial of Causal Interaction between Monads', in his *From Descartes to Hume: Continental Metaphysics and the Development of Modern Philosophy*, Ithaca, N.Y., Cornell University Press, 1981, ch. 7, 269–319.

11.56 Martin, G. *Leibniz: Logic and Metaphysics*, trans. K. Northcott and P. Lucas, Manchester, Manchester University Press, 1964.

11.57 Mates, B. *The Philosophy of Leibniz: Metaphysics and Language*, New York and Oxford, Oxford University Press, 1986.

11.58 Parkinson, G. H. R. *Logic and Reality in Leibniz's Metaphysics*, Oxford, Clarendon, 1965.

11.59 Rutherford, D. 'Phenomenalism and the Reality of Body in Leibniz's Later Philosophy', *Studia Leibnitiana* 22 (1990) 11–28.

11.60 Sleigh, R. C. 'Truth and Sufficient Reason in the Philosophy of Leibniz', in M. Hooker (ed.) *Leibniz: Critical and Interpretive Essays*, Minneapolis, Minn., Minnesota University Press, 1982, 209–42.

11.61 Wilson, C. *Leibniz's Metaphysics: A Historical and Comparative Study*, Manchester, Manchester University Press, 1989.

11.62 Woolhouse, R. S. (ed.) *Leibniz: Metaphysics and the Philosophy of Science*, Oxford, Oxford University Press, 1982.

Philosophy of mind and theory of knowledge

11.63 Bolton, M. 'Leibniz and Locke on the Knowledge of Necessary Truths', in J. A. Cover and M. Kulstad (eds) *Central Themes in Early Modern Philosophy*, Indianapolis, Ind., Hackett, 1990, 195–226.

11.64 Brandom, R. 'Leibniz and Degrees of Perception', *Journal of the History of Philosophy* 19 (1981) 447–79.

11.65 Jolley, N. *The Light of the Soul: Theories of Ideas in Leibniz, Malebranche, and Descartes*, Oxford, Clarendon, 1990.

11.66 Kulstad, M. 'Two Arguments on *Petites* Perceptions', in M. Kulstad (ed.) *Essays on the Philosophy of Leibniz*, Rice University Studies 63, Houston, Tex., Rice University Press, 1977, 57–68.

11.67 Kulstad, M. 'Some Difficulties in Leibniz's Theory of Perception', in M. Hooker (ed.) *Leibniz: Critical and Interpretive Essays*, Minneapolis, Minn., Minnesota University Press, 1982, 65–78.

11.68 Kulstad, M. *Leibniz on Apperception, Consciousness and Reflection*, Munich, Philosophia, 1991.

11.69 McRae, R. *Leibniz: Perception, Apperception, and Thought*, Toronto, University of Toronto Press, 1976.

11.70 Parkinson, G. H. R. 'The Intellectualization of Appearances: Aspects of Leibniz's Theory of Sensation and Thought', in M. Hooker (ed.) *Leibniz: Critical and Interpretive Essays*, Minneapolis, Minn., Minnesota University Press, 1982, 3–20.

11.71 Savile, A. 'Leibniz's Contribution to the Theory of Innate Ideas', *Philosophy* 47 (1972) 113–24.

11.72 Wilson, M. D. 'Leibniz and Materialism', *Canadian Journal of Philosophy* 3 (1974) 495–513.

11.73 Wilson, M. D. 'Leibniz: Self-Consciousness and Immortality: in the Paris Notes and After', *Archiv für Geschichte der Philosophie* 58 (1976) 335–52.

11.74 Wilson, M. D. 'Confused Ideas', in M. Kulstad (ed.) *Essays on the Philosophy of Leibniz*, Rice University Studies 63, Houston, Tex., Rice University Press, 1977, 123–37.

Glossary

affect: a term that renders the Latin noun 'affectus'. Some seventeenth-century Dutch philosophers used the term to mean 'passion': Spinoza, however, took the term in a wider sense, recognizing both active and passive 'affects', in the sense of active and passive emotions and desires.

analysis and synthesis: terms used by sixteenth- and seventeenth-century philosophers in the senses in which they were used in classical Greek mathematics. Analysis is a type of proof in which one starts from the proposition to be proved and works back to the first principles on which the proposition logically depends. Descartes declared that he used the method in his *Meditations*. 'Synthesis' refers to the derivation of theorems from first principles, as in Euclid's geometry, and in Spinoza's *Ethics*.

a posteriori: see '*a priori*'.

a priori: an *a priori* proposition is a proposition such that, in getting to know its truth, one does not have to appeal to sense experience. Kant pointed out in the *Critique of Pure Reason* (1781) that the distinguishing marks of such a proposition are necessity and strict universality, that is, universality such that no exceptions to it are allowed (e.g. 'All bachelors are unmarried' – understanding 'bachelor' to mean 'unmarried male'). Propositions which are not *a priori*, in that knowledge of their truth does rest on sense experience, are termed *a posteriori*.

Arminianism: the Arminians (also known as 'Remonstrants') were members of a religious sect founded by the Dutch Protestant theologian Jacobus Arminius (Hermans or Harmens: 1560–1609). The Arminians opposed the determinism (q.v.) of the Calvinists (see 'Calvinism'). Their views were condemned at the Synod of Dort (1618–19).

ars inveniendi: the 'art of discovery'. In the seventeenth century, philosophers looked for such an art or technique, which would establish rules for inquiry and do away with the need for individual genius or flair on the part of the inquirer. This 'art' was traditionally distinguished from the '*ars judicandi*', the 'art of judgement'; this was used to test the truth of propositions that were proposed to one, and involved syllogistic (q.v.).

attribute: in its basic sense, an 'attribute' is that which is attributed to, or predicated of, something. Descartes held that each substance (q.v.) has a *principal* attribute – extension in the case of corporeal substance, thought in the case of mental substance – which constitutes the substance's essence (q.v.). This view is related to (though by no means the same as) Spinoza's theory that thought and extension are two attributes of the one substance.

Averroism: the theories of the Islamic philosopher Ibn Rushd (Averroes: 1126–98). A much-cited commentator on Aristotle, Averroes was probably best known for his interpretation of what Aristotle said about the 'active intellect' in *De Anima*, III, 5. Averroes argued that the active intellect is divine, and as such is one. The human being does not enjoy personal immortality; human beings are immortal only in so far as the divine intellect is present in them. Not surprisingly, this view was condemned by many medieval Catholic theologians; however, it survived until the Renaissance.

Calvinism: the theology of the French Protestant theologian John Calvin (1509–64). From a philosophical point of view, Calvinism is interesting as a deterministic system (see 'determinism'), based on the absolute predestination of God, whose eternal decree has predestined some of his creatures to salvation and some to eternal damnation. Calvin also declared that the state was subordinate to the Church, as opposed to Luther (1483–1546) who argued that the state is supreme over religion.

causality, rationalist theory of: a theory about the nature of causal necessity. It is commonly held that if E is the cause of F, then given E, F *must* occur. The rationalist theory of causality argues that causal necessity is *logical* necessity; that is, that to say that E causes F is to say that F is the logical consequence of E. The most famous exponent of this theory was Spinoza.

cause, efficient: a translation of 'causa efficiens', a term which was used by medieval philosophers and which was still in use in the seventeenth century. The term goes back to Aristotle, who stated that an 'efficient' cause is a source of change or of coming to rest (*Physics*, II, 3). So, for example, a man who gives advice is an efficient cause, and a father is the efficient cause of his child.

cause, final: a term that renders the Latin 'causa finalis'. 'Final' does not mean here last or ultimate, as when one speaks of a 'final curtain'. Rather, a final cause is that *for the sake of which* something is done. The term goes back to Aristotle, who said that a final cause is an *end*: e.g. health is the final cause of taking a walk (*Physics*, II, 3). See also 'teleology'.

cause, primary and secondary: as explained in a seventeenth-century textbook of logic, a 'primary cause' is one which produces an effect by its own power; a 'secondary cause' is one which, in various ways, assists in the production of the effect (Heereboord, *Hermeneia Logica* (1650), pp. 106–9).

cause, procatarctic: a term derived from the Greek 'prokatarktikos', 'antecedent'. A procatarctic cause was regarded as one kind of secondary cause (q.v.); it is external to a primary cause, and excites it to action.

cause, proximate and remote: a proximate cause is one which is immediately prior to the effect. Thus, if a billiard ball B moves because it is struck by billiard ball A, the impact of A on B is the proximate cause of the movement of B. The movement of A is itself the effect of some other cause or causes, say the movement of the cue which strikes A. In such a case, the movement of the cue will be the proximate cause of the movement of A, and the remote cause of the movement of B.

common notions: a translation of the Latin term 'notiones communes', which is in turn a translation of the Greek 'koinai ennoai', by which Euclid referred to the axioms of his geometry. The term is used by both Descartes and Spinoza, who also employ the term 'axioma', a Latin version of a Greek word whose use in mathematics is mentioned by Aristotle (*Metaphysics*, Book Gamma, ch. 3).

compositio: a Latin version of the Greek term 'synthesis'. See 'analysis and synthesis'.

concept: philosophers now regard a concept as the meaning of a word or phrase; so, for example, to speak of 'the concept of mind' is to speak of the meaning of the word 'mind'. In the seventeenth century and before, philosophers (whilst agreeing that a meaningful word must stand for a concept) would not have said that to have a concept is necessarily to be a word-user. A philosopher such as Leibniz would say that God has concepts, but would have denied that God uses words.

constructivism: a theory about the meaning and truth of mathematical propositions. For the constructivist, to understand the meaning of a mathematical proposition is to be able to recognize a proof of it when such a proof is presented to one, and to say that a mathematical proposition is true is to say that we have a proof of it. In effect, the constructivist regards mathematical entities as creations of the human mind, and not as abstract objects with an independent existence.

continuity, law of: regarded by Leibniz as one of the laws of philosophy. Put non-technically, the law states that nature makes no leaps. So, for example, there is no absolute distinction between motion and rest; rest is motion which is of infinite slowness.

contradiction, law of: a law of classical logic (defended by Aristotle in *Metaphysics*, Book Gamma, chs 3–6) which states that a proposition cannot be both true and false. Some philosophers prefer to call this law 'the law of non-contradiction'.

correspondence theory of truth: see 'truth, correspondence theory of'.

creation *ex nihilo*: the idea that God created the universe *ex nihilo*, from nothing, appears to have entered Western philosophy by way of the Judaeo-Christian tradition. For the ancient Greeks the question was not 'Why is there anything at all?', but rather, 'Why is what there is a cosmos – that is, why does it display order?'

deduction: a deductive argument is one in which one cannot without self-contradiction assert the premises (q.v.) and deny the conclusion. Some standard dictionaries say that deduction is reasoning from the general to the particular. This is often, but by no means always, the case: e.g. 'if p, then q; therefore if not q, then not p' is a deductive argument.

deductivism: the thesis that the methods of science are deductive, not inductive (see 'induction').

definition, stipulative: to be contrasted with a 'descriptive' definition, which states how a term is actually used, and as such can be true or false. Such definitions are to be found in dictionaries; hence the alternative term 'lexical definitions'. A stipulative (or 'prescriptive') definition, on the other hand, declares the utterer's intention to use words in a certain way, as when Humpty Dumpty, in Lewis Carroll's *Through the Looking Glass*, uses the word 'glory' to mean 'a nice knock-down argument'. Although a stipulative definition cannot be true or false, it can be assessed in other ways: e.g. it can be enlightening, or merely perverse.

deism: the deist, unlike the atheist, believes in the existence of one supreme being, creator of the world. So, too, does the theist; but the deist differs from the theist in that the theist accepts the idea of revelation. Many deists also rejected the idea that God intervenes in the workings of the created universe by means of miracles.

denomination, extrinsic: a term of medieval logic used by Leibniz. Roughly speaking, an extrinsic denomination is a relational property of a thing, as opposed to an intrinsic denomination which is a non-relational property. So, for example, to say that Aristotle is learned is to state an intrinsic denomination of Aristotle; to say that he is more learned than Alexander the Great is to state an extrinsic denomination of Aristotle.

determinism: a term covering a wide variety of views, which have in common the thesis that every event or every state of affairs belonging to a certain class is determined by certain factors, in the sense that given these factors the event must occur or the state of affairs must hold. In the past (and particularly in the seventeenth century) philosophers readily accepted the idea that determinism held in the natural world; but many of them were reluctant to believe that it also held in the sphere of human actions. They believed that (whatever might be the case in the natural world) the will was free, in the sense that, whenever a human agent chooses to do something, that agent could always have chosen to do otherwise. However, there were also those who argued that human actions are determined, and that the will is not free. Their reasons for this fell into two groups. One group involved theological propositions, such as the assertion that God is omniscient, or that all events are predestined, in that they figure in God's eternal and irresistible plan. The other reason for denying human free will lay in the idea that absolutely all events have a cause, and that a cause necessitates its effect.

disposition: in contemporary philosophy, to speak of a 'disposition' of X is to say what X will do, if . . . , or of what X would have done, if. . . . So, for example, brittleness is a disposition, in that to call something brittle is to say what it will do if, or would have done if, something strikes or had struck it.

double aspect theory: a theory of the relations between mind and body. According to it, mind and body are different aspects of, or expressions of, an underlying reality. The most celebrated exposition of a double aspect theory in the seventeenth century is to be found in the writings of Spinoza.

dualism: this term has two senses. (a) 'Substance dualism': this is a theory of the nature of the mind and of the body, and asserts that minds and bodies are substances of radically different kinds. (b) Some modern philosophers also recognize what they call 'property dualism', according to which the properties of things can be sharply differentiated into two groups, mental and physical. Descartes was an upholder of substance dualism; Spinoza rejected this, but accepted property dualism.

emergent properties: it has been argued that, in the course of evolution, there come into existence 'emergent properties', that is, properties which could not have been predicted on the basis of a knowledge of previous properties. This is also put by saying that there come into existence properties which cannot be 'reduced' (see 'reductionism') to other properties. It has been argued that life and reflective thought are emergent properties in this sense.

epistemology: the theory of knowledge (from the Greek word 'epistēmē'). Strictly, this is the branch of philosophy which considers the nature and criteria of knowledge, together with its sources, kinds and extent. However, books and articles on epistemology often discuss also the relevant topics of meaning and truth.

ergetic: having to do with work (Greek, 'ergon').

essence: the term 'essence' (Latin, 'essentia') goes back to Aristotle's account of 'ousia'. Broadly, if something is of the essence of X, then it belongs *necessarily* to X. But not everything of this sort is of the essence of X: e.g. to be capable of learning grammar is something that belongs necessarily to human beings, but does not, according to Aristotle, belong to their essence. (Traditionally, it would be called a 'property', from the Latin 'proprium'.) What is of the essence of X is more than this: it is also something that is of fundamental importance if we are to understand what X is.

falsificationalism: now usually taken to be the view that any meaningful utterance must be one which can be falsified. (Contrast 'verification, principle of'.) However, Karl Popper, who drew attention to the importance of falsification, regarded falsifiability as a criterion by which one could distinguish a genuinely scientific utterance from one which is pseudo-scientific.

fatalism: a form of determinism (q.v.) according to which what will happen, will happen, and there is nothing that humans can do to alter the course of events. Although all fatalists are determinists, not all determinists are fatalists.

first philosophy: a term which translates the Latin 'philosophia prima'. This in turn translates the Greek 'prōtē philosophia', a term which Aristotle used to refer to what was later to be called 'metaphysics'.

form, substantial: a term derived from the philosophy of the scholastics (see 'scholasticism') and ultimately from Aristotle. A substantial form is that which explains changes which arise from a substance's own nature, as opposed to changes which are brought about in it from outside. The substantial form is the fully developed state of the substance, which the substance tries to achieve.

foundationalism: the thesis that everything that is known has an unshakeable foundation, in the sense that every known truth is either one that cannot rationally be denied, or one that can be derived from such a truth or truths. The task of the philosopher, foundationalists argue, is to discover such foundations; only then can our claims to knowledge be justified. Descartes and Spinoza were foundationalists, but not all foundationalists are rationalists. For example, a philosopher who says that all our knowledge is based on indubitable propositions about the content of our sense experience is a foundationalist.

gnoseology: another term for epistemology (q.v.).

habitus: a Latin translation of Aristotle's term 'hexis' (cf. *Categories*, ch. 8), translated into English as either 'habit' or 'state'. A *habitus* is a stable and long-lasting quality of something: e.g. the various kinds of knowledge and virtue, as opposed to (say) sickness and health, or feelings of warmth and coldness.

Hermeticism: doctrines derived from the so-called 'Hermetic books', a collection of Greek and Latin works on a medley of subjects – magic, astrology, theology and philosophy. They were supposed to have been written in the remote past by Hermes Trismegistus ('Hermes the thrice-greatest'), a Greek name for Thoth, the Egyptian god of learning. In fact, the works are not of great antiquity – they were written between the first and third centuries AD – and contain little that is distinctively Egyptian.

humanism: in the sense used in this book, the ideas and attitudes that distinguished the 'humanists' of the Renaissance. These were students and teachers of the *studia humanitatis* – 'the humanities'. Their work involved the correct establishment and close study of classical texts that concerned the main five subjects – grammar, rhetoric, poetics, moral philosophy and history.

idea: a term which was introduced into philosophy by Plato. For him, an 'idea' (a term related to the Greek word for 'to see') was related to understanding; e.g. the idea of justice is what one sees with the mind's eye when one understands the true nature of justice. Plato insisted that such ideas (or 'forms': eidē) are not in the human mind but have an existence that is independent of us. Later Platonic philosophers, the so-called 'neo-Platonists' (see 'neo-Platonism') agreed with him about this, but said that ideas existed in the mind of God. It was this neo-Platonic usage to which Descartes appealed when he gave the word 'idea' a new sense, referring to certain types of thoughts which human beings have and which 'are, as it were, the images of things' (*Meditations*, III). Spinoza and Leibniz agreed with Descartes that human beings have ideas, but offered different views about their nature; Malebranche's view was reminiscent of neo-Platonism.

idea, innate: for Descartes, Leibniz and others, not all ideas come to us through the senses; some are innate, such as the idea of God, or of geometrical figures. In effect, innate idea theorists were drawing attention to the special status of *a priori* (q.v.) concepts and truths.

idealism: there are three main types of philosophical idealism, all of which have in common the thesis that the external world – the world of physical things – is in some way a product of mind. (a) The first historically was Berkeleian idealism. Bishop Berkeley (1685–1753) argued that a material object consists of nothing but ideas, either in the mind of God, or in the mind of conscious beings such as ourselves. (b) 'Transcendental idealism' was a term used by Kant (1724–1804) to refer to his view that the spatial and temporal properties of things have no existence apart from our minds. (c) 'Objective' or 'absolute' idealism, first propounded by Hegel (1770–1831) is distinguished by the fact that it is a kind of monism (q.v.), asserting that everything that exists is a form of the one 'absolute mind'.

indiscernibles, identity of: a term employed by Leibniz, and still used, to refer to the thesis that if x has every property that y has, and y has every property that x has, then x and y are identical.

induction: an inductive argument is an argument in which, from the proposition that all observed members of a certain class have a certain property, one proceeds to the conclusion that all members of the class have this property. Philosophers recognize various types of induction (see below).

induction, ampliative: here, the conclusion as it were amplifies or goes beyond the evidence, in that from the proposition that all observed members of a class C have the property f, one infers that absolutely all members of the class – unobserved as well as observed – have this property. Contrast 'induction, summative'.

induction, eliminative: in this, one is looking for what Bacon (*Novum Organum*, I, 105) called 'the contradictory instance'. That is, one is looking for a member of the class C which does *not* have the property f.

induction by simple enumeration: here (in contrast with eliminative induction) one tries to establish the truth of the proposition that all members of the class C have the property f by looking for cases in which members of this class have the property f. Notoriously, this procedure is liable to be upset by the discovery of a contradictory instance.

induction, summative: unlike ampliative induction (q.v.), this form of induction merely summarizes the evidence. An example would be: 'Mary is tall, and Joan is tall, and Sally is tall; Mary, Joan and Sally are all the women in this room; therefore all the women in this room are tall.'

instrumentalism: in the philosophy of science, the view that scientific theories are not descriptions of the real world but are simply devices which enable scientists to make successful predictions on the basis of the data they have.

intelligences, planetary: in Aristotle's astronomical theory, the movements of the Sun, Moon, planets and stars involve the rotation of spheres to which they are fixed. Medieval philosophers asserted that each of these spheres is governed by an 'intelligence'.

Jansenism: a system based on the writings of the Dutch theologian Cornelius Otto Jansen (1585–1638). Jansenism is a deterministic system (see 'determinism'), denying human freedom. The reasons for this denial are distinctive, in that they are based on a view about the grace of God – that is, about the assistance that God gives to human beings, with a view to their salvation. The Jansenists argued that, without the grace of God, human beings could not obey his commandments, and that this grace was not something that they could freely accept or reject but was irresistible. Probably the most famous followers of Jansen were the mathematician Blaise Pascal (1623–62) and the philosopher Antoine Arnauld (1612–94).

knowledge, theory of: see 'epistemology'.

logica modernorum: the medievals regarded their logic as having three main periods. The first was the period of the *logica vetus*, the 'old logic', when the only logical works of Aristotle known to the West were the *Categories* and the *De Interpretatione*. When the rest of Aristotle's logical works became accessible in about 1150 there began the period of the *logica nova*, the 'new logic'. Both the 'old' and the 'new' logic were concerned primarily to comment; but in about 1250 there began a new period of logic, that of the *logica moderna* or *logica modernorum*, the 'logic of the moderns'. This was directed towards problems rather than towards commentary, and discussed problems not handled by Aristotle. The 'modern logicians' referred to both the *logica vetus* and the *logica nova* as *logica antiqua* – 'ancient logic'.

magic: for the Renaissance, magic was a practical technique that was based on theory. In his *De occulta philosophia* (1510; enlarged edition, 1533) Agrippa von Nettesheim divided the universe into three worlds – elemental, celestial and intellectual. The first of these was the province of natural magic; the second, of celestial magic (involving astrology); and the third, of ceremonial magic, which was directed towards the world of angelic spirits. Agrippa was careful to distinguish magic of this sort from demonic magic, which involved the use of evil spirits.

metaphysics: (a) as the term is used in this book, a metaphysical theory is a theory about that which, in the last analysis, really exists; or (and this may come to the same) about that which provides the ultimate explanation of everything. (b) There is another sense of the term 'metaphysics', in which it refers to accounts of the general conceptual schemes which structure our experience. Metaphysics of this kind is called 'descriptive', and may stand in opposition to metaphysics of type (a), which is often called 'revisionary', in that it calls on us to revise some of our commonly held ideas.

mode: a translation of 'modus', a term taken by Descartes from medieval philosophy. For Descartes, a modal distinction holds between a mode and the substance of which it is a mode: e.g. between shape and the corporeal substance which has a shape, or between affirming and the mind which affirms. Spinoza adapted the modal terminology to his monistic (see 'monism') metaphysics.

modus tollens: 'the mood that denies'. An inference of the form 'If p, then q; but not q; therefore not p'. This is contrasted with 'modus ponens' ('the mood that affirms'), which has the form 'If p, then q; but p; therefore q'.

monad: in classical Greek, 'monas' meant a unit. Leibniz used the term to refer to his simple, non-extended substances, each of which is genuinely one.

monism: a term which usually refers to the doctrine that there is one and only one substance, and that particular things are not substances but are forms of the one substance. However, during the twentieth century the term has been used in such a way as to be compatible with the existence of several substances, provided that these are of the same kind. For example, 'neutral monism' is the theory that minds and bodies are not substances of fundamentally different kinds; to talk of minds and bodies is to group in different ways certain basic entities which are all of the same kind and of which no one is either mental or physical.

naturalism: as a view about what exists and how it is known, naturalism is the thesis that everything that exists or happens is that which is studied by the sciences, whether natural or human; there is no place for supernatural beings such as God. The term is also used in place of 'ethical naturalism' (q.v.).

naturalism, ethical: the thesis that ethical concepts can be defined in terms of statements of fact, such as 'That is morally good which produces the greatest happiness of the greatest number'.

necessity, hypothetical: an Aristotelian concept (see *Physics*, II, 9), used by Leibniz in his attempt to reconcile the freedom of the human will with his thesis that everything has a cause. Something has hypothetical necessity if it is necessary, *given that* such and such is the case. Thus, the present state of the world is hypothetically necessary in that it follows, in accordance with the laws of nature, from any given preceding state. Hypothetical necessity is opposed by Leibniz to 'logical' or 'metaphysical' necessity, which is the necessity possessed by a truth whose denial would involve a contradiction.

neo-Platonism: a philosophy developed in the late classical world, from roughly the middle of the third to the middle of the sixth century AD. The neo-Platonists, of whom the most important was Plotinus (205–c. 270 AD), claimed to preserve the philosophy of Plato, but were ready to incorporate the doctrines of other Greek philosophical schools provided that these could be reconciled with what they saw as Platonism. Neo-Platonism is a form of pantheism (q.v.); everything is regarded as flowing timelessly from a supreme principle, 'the One', which is such that it cannot be grasped by mere rational thought.

nominalism: see 'universals'.

non-contradiction, law of: see 'contradiction, law of'.

occasionalism: the thesis that causal activity belongs to God, and to God alone. According to the occasionalist, to say that the movement of a billiard ball is the effect of its being struck by a cue is inaccurate; strictly, one should say that God causes the ball to move *on the occasion of* the cue's making contact with the ball.

occult quality: a concept of the scholastics, traceable back to the medical writings of Galen (129–c. 199 AD) and severely criticized in the seventeenth century by rationalist philosophers and others, such as Newton. To explain something by means of an occult quality was to explain the observed behaviour B of a thing by saying that there exists some hidden B-producing quality.

ontological argument: a term used to describe a group of related arguments for the existence of God, which have in common a move from a definition of God to the conclusion that the being defined must exist. The argument was first stated by St Anselm (1033–1109), who defined God as a being than which a greater cannot be thought. Descartes argued along similar lines, defining God as a most perfect being and saying that existence is a perfection. Spinoza's definition of God involved the thesis that God is a necessary being, that is, a being such that it must be thought of as existing.

ontology: (a) a branch of metaphysics (q.v.) which is concerned with the study of pure being, that is, being in its most abstract aspects. (b) The assumptions about what exists that underlie any conceptual scheme. So if we refer to a certain person's 'ontology' we refer to the views that that person holds about what there is.

Organon: literally, 'instrument' (Greek). A collective name for Aristotle's logical works, as the 'instrument' of all reasoning.

pantheism: the theory that God and the universe are identical, encapsulated by Spinoza in the phrase, *'Deus, seu Natura'* – 'God, or in other words, nature'. Pantheism is to be distinguished from 'panentheism', which asserts that God includes the whole universe but is not identical with it.

paradigm: a term given a technical sense by Thomas Kuhn, and used in the philosophy of science. In this sense, a paradigm may be either (a) a whole set of beliefs or methods shared by a group of scientists or (b) concrete solutions of problems which are used as examples, and as such can serve as a basis for the solution of other scientific problems. Kuhn is much concerned with changes of paradigm, or 'paradigm shifts'; these are due to the discovery of an ever-increasing set of anomalies within a reigning paradigm, which lead to the production of a new paradigm.

parallelism, psycho-physical: a theory of the relations between mind and body.

It asserts that mental and physical events are quite independent of each other, but that for any mental event there is a corresponding physical event, and conversely.

peripatetic: a term meaning 'Aristotelian'. The 'Peripatetic school' was the Aristotelian school of philosophy in Athens. The term comes from a 'peripatos', or covered walk, in the buildings which the school occupied. The story that the term originated from Aristotle's habit of walking about (peripatein) whilst lecturing is now regarded as a legend.

phenomenalism: when used of the philosophies discussed in this volume, the term refers to the thesis that material things are simply classes of the ideas (q.v.) possessed by conscious beings such as ourselves. In this century, a different sort of phenomenalism has been put forward: this speaks, not of the nature of material things as such and of the entities of which they are composed, but of the nature of propositions about them.

premiss (premise): (plural, 'premisses' or 'premises'). The proposition or propositions from which the conclusion of an argument follows.

procatarctic: see 'cause, procatarctic'.

pyrrhonism: a form of ancient scepticism (q.v.), revived in the Renaissance when the writings of the Pyrrhonist philosopher Sextus Empiricus (fl. *c.* 200 AD) were published in the 1560s. Unlike some sceptics, the Pyrrhonists did not say that nothing can be known; in their view, such an assertion was as dogmatic as the assertion that something can be known. Rather, they proposed that we should suspend judgement about all claims to knowledge when these go beyond appearances.

qualities, primary and secondary: these terms express a distinction drawn by some philosophers between (a) the qualities which a physical object really has (its 'primary' qualities: e.g. extension and solidity) and (b) the qualities which it does not really have, but is perceived as having, and which can be explained in terms of the primary qualities. These are its 'secondary qualities': e.g. colour and sound.

rationalism: (a) in one sense of the term, rationalism has a relation to religious belief. A rationalist in this sense is someone who tries to eliminate from such beliefs everything that does not satisfy rational standards. This may lead to a total rejection of religion; however, rationalism is compatible with religious belief of a sort, as in the case of deism (q.v.). For example, Voltaire was a deist, but would normally be regarded as a rationalist in sense (a) of the term. (b) The philosophical sense of the term 'rationalism' is different. In this sense, rationalism is the thesis that it is possible to obtain, simply by reasoning from propositions which cannot rationally be denied, the knowledge of necessary truths about what exists. Spinoza combined both sorts of rationalism, but by no means all rationalists in sense (a) are rationalists in the second sense.

reductio ad absurdum: a means of proving a proposition by showing that the assumption of its falsity leads to an absurdity, in the sense of a logical contradiction.

reductionism: a reductionist tries to minimize the number of basic entities that are recognized in our conceptual schemes. For example, a philosopher might argue that propositions about societies can be 'reduced' to propositions about the individuals who constitute them; that, in other words, a society is *nothing but* a collection of individuals.

Remonstrants: see 'Arminianism'.

resolutio: a Latin term for the Greek word 'analysis'. See 'analysis and synthesis'.

scepticism: if one says of a man that he is sceptical about (say) the existence of Robin Hood, one means that he does not go so far as to assert that there was no such person, but rather that he holds that the evidence brought to support the assertion that Robin Hood existed does not satisfy the required standards. Philosophical scepticism is distinguished by the fact that the philosophical sceptic casts doubt on a whole range of assertions. For example, a philosophical sceptic might say that the evidence brought to support *any* assertion about the past can never be adequate.

scholasticism: a term sometimes used to mean Western medieval Christian philosophy as a whole. In a more precise sense, however, 'scholasticism' refers to only a part of such philosophy, namely the philosophical movement that began in cathedral schools in the eleventh century AD and reached its peak in the universities of Paris and Oxford in the thirteenth and fourteenth centuries. Such philosophy relied heavily on ancient thought, and especially (though by no means exclusively) on the philosophy of Aristotle.

semantics: the study of meaning, often regarded as one part of 'semiotics', the general theory of signs. Other parts of semiotics are syntactics, namely the study of the grammar and syntax of language, and pragmatics, the study of the purposes and effects of language.

sublunary: the Aristotelian universe was a system of concentric spheres, with a spherical earth at rest in the centre. Around the earth there rotated invisible spheres, carrying the Sun, Moon, planets and stars. The region within the sphere of the Moon was known as the 'sublunary' world. It consisted of the four elements (earth, air, water and fire), which constantly pass into each other. It was distinguished from the 'superlunary' world of the heavens, the matter of which is of a distinct type, the so-called 'quintessence' ('fifth essence'), which is free from generation and destruction.

substance: when Renaissance philosophers and the seventeenth-century rationalists discussed problems of substance, they were dealing with concepts which go back to Chapter 2 of Aristotle's *Categories*. A substance, Aristotle said, is (a) that which is not 'in' a subject, that is, it has an independent existence. (b) It is that which is not 'said of' a subject, that is, it is an ultimate subject of predication. (c) It is that which remains the same through qualitative change. Much of the controversy about the nature of substance among the seventeenth-century rationalists was about the correct answer to the question of what satisfied one or other of these criteria.

Summa: literally, a 'summary', this was a literary form which was characteristic of scholasticism (q.v.). The *Summa* was a systematic and comprehensive treatise, and it contained both a statement of relevant authorities and rational arguments for the conclusions presented. The greatest of the *Summae* were the *Summa contra Gentiles* and the *Summa Theologiae* of St Thomas Aquinas (*c.* 1225–74).

syllogistic: the theory of the syllogism, which was first stated systematically by Aristotle and which forms a large part of what is termed 'traditional logic'.

A syllogism is a form of deductive argument (see 'deduction') in which there are three and only three terms, and in which one proposition, the 'conclusion', is inferred from two other propositions, the 'premises' (q.v.). For example: 'All Greeks are rational, all Athenians are Greeks, therefore all Athenians are rational.'

synthesis: see 'analysis and synthesis'.

teleology: having to do with an end or purpose (Greek, 'telos'). See also 'cause, final'.

third world: more exactly, 'world 3'. A term introduced into philosophy by Karl Popper in *Objective Knowledge* (1972). World 1 is the physical world; world 2 is the world of our conscious experience, also termed 'subjective knowledge'; world 3 is objective knowledge, e.g. theories published in journals or books.

truth, correspondence theory of: a theory of the nature of truth, which states that truth consists in the agreement of a proposition with a fact. There has been much debate about the meaning of the terms 'agreement' and 'fact' in this context.

truth, double: the thesis, associated with Averroism (q.v.) and rejected by many Catholic theologians, that a proposition can be true in philosophy and false in religion, and conversely. The thesis was prompted by the fact that some propositions (e.g. that the world is eternal) drawn from Aristotle conflicted with propositions based on the Bible or the Koran.

truth, necessary: see '*a priori*'.

universals: it has been argued that universal terms, such as 'triangle', can have meaning only if there exist in some way entities which are called 'universals', e.g. the triangle as such, or triangularity. 'Conceptualism' is the thesis that such entities exist only in the way that concepts exist; 'realism' is the thesis that universals have a real existence. 'Nominalism' is the thesis that universal terms are just words which are applied to a number of things.

verification, principle of: also called the 'principle of verifiability'. This term has two senses. (a) It can refer to a criterion of meaning; according to this, a proposition is factually significant if, and only if, it can be verified in principle. (b) The term can also be applied to a theory of the nature of meaning; this states that the meaning of a proposition *is* the method of verifying it.

Index of names

Acciaiuoli, Donato 22
Agricola, Georgius 106
Agricola, Rodolphus 80
Agrippa von Nettesheim, Heinrich
  Cornelius 71, 77–8, 85–6, 88
Albertus Magnus 22–3, 25
Aldus *see* Manutius, Aldus
Alexander of Aphrodisias 21–2, 26, 29,
  37, 38, 41, 175, 195–6
Ampère, André Marie 117
Anaxagoras 131
Anselm, St 229, 283
Apelles *see* Scheiner, Christopher
Apollonius 183
Aquinas, St Thomas 18, 23, 25, 31, 34,
  36, 38, 39, 41, 45, 77, 81, 82, 83, 175,
  229
Archimedes 107, 183
Arendt, Hannah 315
Argyropulos, Johannes 21–2, 28, 40
Aristippus, Henricus 26
Aristotle 5, 7, 20, 30, 32, 39, 40, 41, 42,
  44, 47, 48, 71, 73, 77, 79, 80, 111,
  125–6, 147, 171–5, 177, 187, 188, 191,
  193, 202, 218, 239, 240, 241, 243,
  255, 265, 281, 284–5, 293, 313, 319,
  384, 385–6, 391
Arnauld, Antoine 193, 211, 372, 375,
  385, 386, 388–9, 391, 407, 411–12
Arriaga, Roderigo de 82
Aubrey, John 10, 237
Augustine, St 19, 26, 28, 206, 384, 411
Averroes 18, 21–2, 24, 25, 29, 32, 34,
  37, 38, 41, 43, 175, 195

Avicenna 34
Ayer, A.J. 278

Bacon, Francis 1, 5–6, 48, 109–10,
  140–55, 246
Bacon, Roger 34
Baldwin, J.M. 292
Barbaro, Ermolao 24–5, 40, 45, 79
Baronius, Cardinal Cesare 121
Basnage de Beauval, Henri 374
Battail, J.-F. 352
Bayle, Pierre 85, 87, 374–5
Beeckman, Isaac 203, 240
Bellarmine, Cardinal Robert 122
Berkeley, Bishop 6, 87, 399, 411
Bessarion, Cardinal 22, 29, 30, 31–3, 34,
  37, 41
Boderie, Guy Lefèvre de la 75
Boderie, Nicolas Lefèvre de la 75
Boehme, Jakob 73, 78
Boethius 9, 115
Boulliau, Ismael 118
Boyle, Robert 142, 277
Brahe, Tycho 113–14, 116, 117
Brewster, David 141
Bruni, Leonardo 19–21, 22, 23, 26–7,
  33, 34, 36, 41
Bruno, Giordano 49–50, 145, 158
Burckhardt, Jakob 3–4
Burgersdijck, Franco 275, 317–19, 324,
  334
Burley, Walter 22
Burman, Frans 167, 220, 301
Butler, Samuel 155

Cajetan, Thomas de Vio 81
Cardano, Girolamo 145
Cavalli, Francesco 25
Ceredi, Giuseppe 146
Cesalpino, Andrea 42
Chalcidius 26
Champier, Symphorien 75
Charron, Pierre 84, 87, 239
Chomsky, N. 230
Chrysoloras, Manuel 19–20, 27
Cicero 20, 28, 43, 85, 239, 317
Clarke, Samuel 13, 402–3
Clauberg, Johannes 351, 380
Clerselier, Claude 353
Cohen, L.J. 142, 154
Colet, John 76
Coornhert, Dirk 317
Copernicus, Nicolaus 110–13
Cordemoy, Géraud de 351–2, 355–8, 364, 365, 381–2
Court, Johan de la 316, 321
Court, Pieter de la 315, 316, 321–3, 330, 334, 336, 339, 343
Couturat, Louis 390
Cremonini, Cesare 1, 42
Crombie, A.C. 109
Cromwell, Oliver 339
Cusanus 28, 49, 71, 145

Decembrio, Pier Candido 27
Decembrio, Uberto 27
Des Bosses, Bartholomaeus 399, 401
Descartes, René 5, 6, 7–8, 14, 81, 82, 86–7, 107, 108–9, 124, 129–32, 148, 167–234, 235, 239, 240, 241, 244, 246, 251, 264, 273, 274–5, 276, 277, 278, 279, 281–2, 283, 285, 286–91, 298, 300–2, 313, 321, 349–51, 353, 355–6, 361, 384, 385, 406–7, 408, 409, 410, 412, 414
Devonshire, Third Earl of 238
Diacceto, Francesco da 46–7
Diogenes Laertius 85
Diophantus 108, 171, 184, 185, 187
Donato, Girolamo 25
Dondi, Giovanni 105
Duns Scotus 38, 45
Du Vair, Guillaume 84, 87

Ebreo, Leone see Hebreo, Leon
Eckhart 72
Elizabeth, Princess of Bohemia 221, 349
Empedocles 131
Epictetus 84
Epicurus 10, 236, 240, 243–9, 251–2, 265–6
Erasmus, Desiderius 4, 40, 75–6, 77, 330
Euclid 171, 183, 237
Eustachius a Sancto Paulo 244

Ferguson, Adam 329
Ferrier, Jean 170
Ficino, Marsilio 33–7, 46, 72, 76, 79
Filelfo, Francesco 28
Fischer, Kuno 168
Fludd, Robert 79
Fonseca, Pedro da 83
Fontenelle, Bernard le Bovier de 372
Foscarini, Paolo 122
Foucher, Simon 87, 91

Galen 241
Galileo 41, 42, 114, 118–24, 238, 248
Gassendi, Pierre 1, 10, 48, 70, 79, 84, 86, 88, 132, 176, 177, 235–7, 239–40, 242–55, 261, 265–9, 273, 349
Gaza, Theodore 22–3, 29, 31–2, 40
George of Trebizond 22–3, 28–9, 30–1, 36, 41
Geulincx, Arnold 6, 7, 10, 351–2, 358–61, 363, 365, 382
Gilbert, William 117
Giorgi, Francesco 45–6, 74
Giunta, Tommaso 41
Gouhier, H. 351
Gousset, Jacques 352
Grassi, Horatio 122
Gregory XIV, Pope 47
Grotius, Hugo 82, 87, 264, 322, 330, 334
Guicciardini, Francesco 321

Harriot, Thomas 119
Harvey, William 109
Hebreo, Leon 74
Heereboord, Adrian 275–6
Hegel, G.W.F. 7, 140

Helmont, Francis Mercury van 74, 77
Helmont, John Baptiste van 78–9
Henry III, King of France 76
Henry IV, King of France 77
Hermes Trismegistus 36, 46, 47
Herschel, William 140
Hobbes, Thomas 1, 10–11, 132, 176,
   177, 235–9, 241–2, 254–66, 269–72,
   273, 319, 321, 322, 336, 337, 343, 384
Hooke, Robert 142
Hume, David 6, 85, 87, 214, 225, 278,
   283, 284, 338, 341, 404, 405
Huygens, Christiaan 277

Iamblichus 34
Ignatius of Loyola 80
Innocent VII, Pope 27

Jacquier, François 124
Jaeger, Werner 41
John XXIII, Pope 27

Kant, Immanuel 168, 229, 283
Kepler, Johannes 111, 114–18, 177
Knowles, David 3
Koyré, A. 105, 126
Kropotkin, Prince Peter 337
Kuhn, T.S. 121, 141

La Forge, Louis de 351–5, 356, 361,
   363, 381
La Mothe le Vayer, François 85
Landino, Cristoforo 34
Lefèvre d'Étaples, Jacques 80
Leibniz, Gottfried Wilhelm 6, 7, 8, 9,
   10, 14, 44, 70, 72, 73, 74, 81, 82,
   89–90, 91–2, 189, 192, 219, 224, 231,
   283, 284, 360, 373–5, 384–423
Leicester, Earl of 339
Leonardo da Vinci 106, 145
Leonico Tomeo, Niccolò 40–1
Le Seur, Thomas 124
Lessius, Leonard 82–3
Limborch, Philip van 340
Lippershey, Hans 119
Lipsius, Justus 83–4, 316–18, 339
Locke, John 6, 86, 193, 194, 337, 408,
   410, 413

Lucretius 49
Luther, Martin 75, 79, 112–13

Machiavelli, Niccolò 315, 321, 332
Maestlin, Michael 114
Malebranche, Nicolas 6, 7, 10, 87, 224,
   352, 361–75, 382–3, 384, 404–5, 407,
   411–12
Manutius, Aldus 25
Mariana, Juan de 76, 82
Maurice, Prince of Orange 119, 317,
   339
Maxwell, James Clerk 117
Medici, Cosimo de' 120
Mehmed II, Sultan 31
Melanchthon, Philipp 79
Mersenne, Marin 129, 148, 175, 195,
   211, 235, 238, 239, 240, 265, 279
Meyer, Lodewijk 276, 280, 331
Molina, Luis de 83
Montaigne, Michel de 82, 84, 85–6, 87
More, Henry 74, 350
More, Thomas 76
Morteira, Saul Levi 274
Moses 338

Newcastle, Earl of 238
Newton, Isaac 108, 117, 118, 124, 131,
   167, 170, 402–4
Nicholas V, Pope 22, 28
Nicholas of Cusa see Cusanus
Nicole, Pierre 193
Nizolio, Mario 43–4, 47
Numenius 36

Ockham, William of 18, 82
Oldenburg, Henry 274, 276
Osiander, Andreas 113

Pappus 107–8, 171, 183–4, 187, 279
Paracelsus 73, 78, 145
Patrizi, Francesco da Cherso 47–8, 49,
   240
Paul of Venice 26, 34, 37
Peter Lombard 81
Petrarch 4, 17–19, 21, 23, 24, 26, 29, 36,
   37, 47, 105
Philoponus 41

Pico della Mirandola, Gianfrancesco 44–5, 47
Pico della Mirandola, Giovanni 24, 35, 45–6, 74, 79
Plato 6, 20, 29, 30, 32, 33, 34, 36, 37, 206, 296–7, 413
Playfair, J. 104
Plethon, Georgios Gemistos 29–30, 31
Plotinus 33, 34–5, 47, 72
Plutarch 107
Poliziano, Angelo 23–4, 34, 35, 40, 45
Pomponazzi, Pietro 1, 38–40, 46
Popper, K. 106, 219
Porphyry 34
Proclus 26, 33, 34, 35, 72
Proudhon, P.J. 337
Pseudo-Dionysius 72
Ptolemy 73, 110, 241

Quintilian 43

Ramus, Petrus 5, 80–1, 88, 246, 251
Randall, J.H. 109
Reuchlin, Johannes 74
Rheticus, Georg Joachim 115
Rosenroth, Christian Knorr von 74
Rossi, Paolo 141
Rousseau, Jean-Jacques 345
Russell, Bertrand 390
Ryle, Gilbert 5

Sanches, Francisco 76, 86, 88, 145
Savonarola, Girolamo 44
Scheiner, Christopher 120
Schelling, F.W.J. 73, 74
Scioppius 84
Seneca 84, 317
Sextus Empiricus 44, 85
Sidney, Algernon 323
Simons, Menno 275
Simplicius 41
Smith, Adam 313, 341, 345
Sorbière, Samuel 239
Spinoza, Benedictus de 6, 7, 8, 9, 10, 14, 49, 273–348, 384, 385, 397, 407–8
Spinoza, Gabriel de 274
Spinoza, Michael de 273–4

Steuco, Agostino 46–7
Suarez, Francisco 81–3, 87, 90, 153, 276, 405
Swift, Jonathan 154
Synesius 34

Tacitus 317, 321, 322
Telesio, Bernardino 48–9
Themistius 25, 26, 36, 41
Thucydides 237
Turnebus, Adrianus 189, 196

Urban VIII, Pope 122

Valla, Lorenzo 9, 43, 79
Vatier, Antoine 180
Velthuysen, Lambertus van 319–20, 323, 325, 334, 340
Vergil 34
Vernia, Nicoletto 25–6, 37, 38
Vesalius, Andreas 110, 307
Vico, Giambattista 146
Viète, François 108
Vitoria, Francisco de 81
Vives, Juan Luis 76, 88, 145
Vleeschauwer, H.J. de 352
Voetius, Paulus 330–1
Volder, Burchard de 396–7, 399

Wallace, W.A. 109
Ward, Seth 118
Warner, Walter 238
Weigel, Valentin 73
Welser, Mark 120
Westman, R.S. 113
Whewell, W. 104, 141
William III, Prince of Orange 323, 330, 345
William of Moerbeke 26
Wilson, Curtis 118
Witt, Johan de 315
Wittgenstein, Ludwig 208
Wolff, Christian 7

Zabarella, Jacopo 41–2
Zilsel, E. 105

Index of subjects

activity 325, 328, 335
affects 318–19, 324–5, 328
aggregates 386–8, 392, 400–1, 406
anaclastic 170
analysis 107–8, 183–5, 247, 279–80
animals: behaviour of 215, 368–9,
    371–2, 389, 409–10
apperception 408, 410
appetite 259, 327, 334, 336
appetition 397
Aristotelianism: Renaissance attitude to
    19–26, 29–30, 35, 37–42, 79–80
Arminianism 330
ars inveniendi 148
astrology 34, 40
astronomy: Aristotelian 111
atomism 130–1, 153, 244, 248–50, 255,
    288, 356
attribute 285–7, 291–2, 327
automata 215–16, 230–1
aversion 260
axioms 280

Bible, interpretation of 329, 331–2
body: action on other bodies 350, 354,
    356, 362–4, 368; most simple 288;
    relations with mind; *see* mind

Cabbala 45–6, 74
Calvinism, Dutch 276, 313, 318–19
canons: Epicurean 244–6; Gassendi's
    246–7, 251
Cartesian circle 211–12
causality: Descartes' views on 176, 211;
    Leibniz's views on 405; rationalist

theory of 283–4, 293, 306; Spinoza's
    views on 283–4, 293, 306;
    transparent to intellect 223–5
cause: efficient 125, 250, 293–4, 350;
    equivocal 353; final 125, 293–4, 324;
    general 366; immanent 293;
    occasional 351, 353–4, 367–8, 374,
    375; of itself 282–3; primary 317;
    procatarctic 351; proximate 338;
    remote 353; secondary 317, 319, 373;
    true 364, 366–7; univocal 353
celestial region 125
certainty 202, 205
change: substratum of 386
Christianity: Renaissance philosophy
    and 4
clocks 105; analogy of 359–60, 374–5
cogito ergo sum 169, 193, 207–9, 210,
    217, 301, 358, 411
cognition 258–9, 260
Collegiants 275
compassion 343–4, 371
compatibilism 9
composition 42, 109, 247
conatus 294–5, 324, 327
concept: complete 390–5, 405
consciousness 219, 220–1, 225
constructivism 147, 154
continuity, law of 409
contract: political 266, 329, 335–8, 343
contradiction: principle of 72, 193
co-operation: human 333–5, 336, 338
Copernican theory 49, 110–13, 118,
    120, 126

covenant 263–4
creation 19, 27, 29, 30, 31, 32, 36, 37,
    46, 72, 293, 295, 367; continuous
    176, 354, 363
culture: laicization of 4

deception: divine 206–7, 209
deduction 170–1, 184, 186, 187, 190–4;
    justification of 191
deductivism 169–71
definitions 242; Spinoza's use of 280–1,
    288; stipulative 280–1, 337, 389, 409
deism 9, 13, 274
demonstration 242
denominations: extrinsic 394
desire 261–2, 327–8
determinism 30, 295
discovery: method of 172, 179–89; see
    also ars inveniendi
disposition 412–13
dogmatici 241–2
Dort, Synod of 339
double aspect theory 10, 292–3
doubt, method of 8, 205
dreams 206
dualism: Cartesian 217, 219, 220–1, 350

effect: like the cause 211, 223
ego: Cartesian 218, 220
elasticity 390
empiricism: British 140
ens realissimum 307
Epicureanism 75, 76, 84
epochē 85
ergetic ideal 146, 151
essence 240, 282, 285–6
eternity 299; species of 299–300
existence 208, 255
experience 289, 297–8
experiment 109, 142, 148, 150, 180, 186,
    260
experimentum crucis 161
explanation: deductive 172, 177, 281–2;
    quantitative 176–9
expression: Leibniz's concept of 393,
    395, 397, 407–8; Spinoza's concept
    of 285–6, 292–3
extension 218, 221, 286–7, 291

fact: value and 278
faculties: mental 326
falsification 149, 150, 219
fear 261–2
fideism 77, 85, 86
force: moving 354, 363
form: Baconian 149, 153–4; substantial
    10, 34, 153, 250, 388–9, 398, 406
foundations: search for 7–8, 202, 205,
    210, 384
freedom 326, 328, 366; political 314;
    positive 14

geometrical method: Spinoza's 280–1,
    289
geometry: analytical 108
God: causal efficacy of 366–70; idea of
    210; incomprehensibility of 213–14;
    infinity of 49, 285; intellectual love
    of 302, 328; nature of 8–9, 284;
    omnipotence of 213; Spinoza's
    concept of 284; vision in 364
good: true 366
government 254
grace 367–8, 372
gravitation 249, 402

harmony: pre-established 224, 292, 392,
    405–7
history: natural 148
humanism 3, 11, 17, 75, 77, 81, 87
hypotheses 109, 113, 132, 151, 153, 170,
    181–2

idea: adequate 296; clear and distinct
    14; complete 246–7; confused 297;
    Descartes' concept of 210, 290; innate
    411–14; Leibniz's concept of 412;
    Malebranche's concept of 411;
    Spinoza's concept of 290–1, 326
idealism 5, 7, 87, 396, 399
idols: Baconian 144
ignorance: learned 72
illumination: divine 411
imagination 179, 231, 248, 251, 258,
    297–9, 300, 337; Spinoza's concept
    of 297–9

indiscernibles: identity of 392, 397,
    403–4, 408
individual: Spinoza's concept of 288
induction 5–6, 42, 109, 132, 147–50,
    298, 300; ampliative 148; imperfect
    147; perfect 147; summative 148
inference: discursive conception of
    172–3, 193
instance: negative 151
instantia crucis 150
instauratio 143
instrumentalism 113
intellect: unity of 21–2, 25, 26, 32, 38,
    41, 175
intuition: intellectual 178, 190, 191,
    192–3, 207, 301
ius gentium 82

justification: demand for 191

knowledge: *a priori* 8, 413; intuitive
    300–3; kinds recognized by Spinoza
    297–303; maker's 6, 146, 151, 154,
    159; unity of 202

language: human beings and 216
Lateran Council, Fifth 37, 39, 175, 231
law: civil 264, 335; international 81;
    natural *see* nature: law of *libertins*
    274, 304
life 256, 260, 261
logic: Leibniz's metaphysics and
    389–96

macrocosm 73
magic 5, 34, 86
materialism 10, 235–6, 239, 255–64, 286
mathematici 241–2
mathematics: Aristotle's conception of
    177; universal 178, 188, 204
matter 218, 249; infinite divisibility of
    398
mechanics: Galileo's 125–9, 215–16
mechanism 174, 175, 255–6, 261, 262
memory 258–9
Mennonites 275
Merton rule 128

method 88, 106–7, 169; Cartesian
    174–9; hypothetico-deductive 132
microcosm 73, 78
mind: always thinks 410; incorporeal
    217–20, 410; interaction with body
    9–10, 217, 222–5, 286–7, 291–3, 327,
    349–50, 353–5, 357, 359–62, 364–5,
    405–8; relations with ideas 353, 359,
    364; relations with sentiments 364;
    relations with volitions 358, 365–6;
    union with body 221–2, 349–50, 353,
    361, 368, 370, 371, 372, 375, 407
miracles 40, 45, 174, 373–5
mode 287–9, 291, 298, 349–50, 362, 363,
    366; finite 294; immediate infinite
    288, 294; mediate infinite 289, 294
monad 74, 396–401; dominant 401;
    point of view of 398; quality of
    perceptions of 397, 408; spirituality
    of 396; windowless 405–6
monism 397
motion 255–7, 259, 260, 261, 354, 363;
    causation of 350, 354, 356;
    conservation of 176; Descartes' laws
    of 131; Hobbes' theory of 255–6,
    260; voluntary and involuntary 368–9

natura naturans 276, 307
natura naturata 276, 307
naturalism 278
nature: concept of 374, 375; law of 82,
    253–4, 263, 265, 334, 367–71, 374
necessity: hypothetical 14
Neoplatonism 33–4, 46, 48, 72–3, 77
nominalism 44, 79, 82, 235, 411
nothing comes from nothing 210, 224
notion: common 221, 299

occasionalism 224–5, 349–83, 404–5,
    407; merits of 370
ontological argument 8, 229, 231, 283
order: political 333–5

pacts 253
pantheism 174
parallelism: psycho-physical 292
passion 259, 261, 318, 325, 328, 343,
    345, 358, 372

peace 263–4

perception: clear and distinct 211, 218–19; Leibniz's concept of 397, 408; unconscious 408–10, 413

phantasm 257–8, 259

phenomena: saving the 112; well-founded 400

phenomenalism 399–400, 411

philosophy: first 205, 227; nature of 2; occult 77–8; Renaissance 2–3, 70–1, 88

physics: Aristotle's concept of 177; see also motion

pineal gland 179, 223, 224, 232

Platonism: Renaissance attitude to 19, 26–37, 45

pleasure 252, 256, 259, 372

plenum 130

point: Archimedean 207, 228

postulate 289

potentia 328, 337, 341

potestas 341

power: occult 174

predication: ultimate subject of 385–7, 389

presentation: method of 172, 184, 187–9, 192

pressure 257

printing 105–6

privacy: Cartesian 208

private language argument 208

property 299, 301; emergent 222

pyrrhonism 85, 86, 239–40, 264–5

qualities: occult 186; primary and secondary 87, 179, 250

rainbow: nature of 181–3

rationalism: nature of 6–7, 168, 227, 410

reality: objective 228

reason: Spinoza's concept of 299–300

reflection 413

Renaissance: nature of 2–4

resolution 42, 109, 247

right: civil 337; natural 82, 253, 262, 337–8

scepticism 4–5, 12, 44, 84, 85–7, 88, 195, 205, 243, 245, 254

scholasticism 2–3, 7, 10, 16–18, 71, 80–3, 87, 147, 174

science: middle 83; modern 7, 140, 167, 281, 385

self-interest 322–3, 335

self-preservation: law of 317, 319–20, 324–5

sensation 220–2, 251, 257–8

simple natures 178, 203–5, 207, 209, 213, 221

slavery 82

soul: biological 250–1; corporeal 236; immortality of 27, 29, 32, 36–7, 38–9, 46, 175; incorporeal 236, 251; rational 250–1

sovereign 254, 264, 320, 334, 338, 342

space: imaginary 248; nature of 402–4

spirits: animal 215, 223, 224, 259, 361, 365, 370, 371

state: nature of 262–4, 334–5, 343–5

statics: Archimedean 177–8

Stoicism 30–1, 83–4, 91, 191, 316–17, 319, 324, 325, 328, 372

subject: of a proposition 393

sublunary region 125

substance 217, 218, 284–5, 385–6; causal relations with others 394–5, 399, 405; Descartes' theory of 285, 289–90; indivisible 287, 356, 389, 399; Leibniz's theory of 385–401; organic nature of 386–9, 398, 401; simple see monad; soul and 388; source of all its states 392, 395; Spinoza's theory of 284–8, 292–3; uniqueness of 285, 297; unity of 356, 388–9, 396

sufficient reason: principle of 403

syllogistic 170–4, 177, 189, 191, 246, 282

synthesis 107–8, 183–5, 247, 279–80, 282

technology 105, 106, 143, 145

teleology 319, 323–6; see also cause: final

telescope 119

theology: negative 72
third world 106
thought 208, 218, 221, 286–7, 291
time: nature of 402–4
tolerance 317, 330, 332, 340
topics 173, 188
tranquillity 252
transubstantiation 401
Trent: Council of 75, 76
truth: and concept containment 391;
    correspondence theory of 296, 391;
    double 17, 18, 22, 25, 35, 38, 45, 49;
    eternal 212–14; Leibniz's theory of
    390–1; necessary 413–14; Spinoza's
    theory of 291, 296–7

universals 38, 39, 44, 251, 256, 326
universe: aspect of the whole 289;
    infinity of 49, 73

utilitarianism 145, 154
utopianism 142–3

verificationism 151, 403
vinculum substantiale 401
vintage: Baconian 151
void 41, 48, 249, 254–5
volition 326, 358; general 366–7,
    369, 370, 374; particular 366–7,
    374
vortices 130–1

war 263; just 81
will 327, 354, 357, 359–61, 364–5;
    freedom of 9, 14, 75, 83, 211, 252,
    319, 326

Zohar 74